PERSONNEL ADMINISTRATION

an experiential skill-building approach

PERSONNEL ADMINISTRATION

an experiential skill-building approach

SECOND EDITION

Richard W. Beatty

Graduate School of Business Administration
University of Colorado

Craig Eric Schneier

College of Business and Management
University of Maryland

ADDISON-WESLEY PUBLISHING COMPANY
Reading, Massachusetts • Menlo Park, California • London
Amsterdam • Don Mills, Ontario • Sydney

Library of Congress Cataloging in Publication Data

Beatty, Richard W
  Personnel administration.

  Includes bibliographies and index.
  1. Personnel management.   I. Schneier, Craig Eric,
II. Title.
HF5549.B328   1981   658.3   80-28815
ISBN 0-201-00172-1

Reprinted with corrections, May 1982

ISBN: 0-201-00172-1
  MNOP-MU-89

To:
Dena
Nancy
Otis Lipstreu

PREFACE TO THE SECOND EDITION

In the four years since this book was first published, significant changes have continued to occur in Personnel Administration, both as an academic discipline and as a profession. The accreditation system, developed and administered through the auspices of the American Society for Personnel Administration (ASPA), has enhanced the professional status of Personnel. This book was used by both test developers and test takers.

Personnel administrators continue to increase their impact on organizations, as predicted in the *Introduction* of the first edition. The 1980s will see an ever-advancing interest in human resource management, with personnel specialists being looked to for their skills, guidance, and knowledge. We feel the second edition of *Personnel Administration: An Experiential Skill-Building Approach* will continue to provide professionals with a realistic, current body of knowledge and with practical exercises to use as they perfect their skills.

Regarding the academic discipline of personnel administration, or human resource-management, continued popularity at both the undergraduate and graduate levels will be seen. Curricula in these areas are being refined, and courses are being added in both conceptual and applied areas. We feel the first edition of this experiential book made an impact on curricula and texts, if imitation is any measure. We are flattered by the emphasis on experiential learning in personnel since the first edition was published and are proud to have helped people to learn what those in personnel actually *do*.

We have taken the comments, positive and negative, of the many adopters and reviewers very seriously as we prepared this edition. It is an extensive revision, not just an update. We have added three entirely new exercises: Career Development and Career Management (Exercise 12), Costing Human Resources (Exercise 19), and Personnel Research (Exercise 20). These reflect important new areas of concern in the field, and in the case of Exercises 19 and 20, an emphasis on the economic, or cost/benefit, aspects of human-resource management programs—on the importance of demonstrating how more effective human-resource management impacts the organization's "bottom line."

The exercises of the first edition were revised thoroughly with updated references and many additions to the *Introductions* which reflect recent work in each area. For example, Exercise 2 contains a discussion of the utility of simulation in human-resource planning and forecasting, Exercise 3 discusses quantitative job-analysis techniques, and Exercise 6 now has a detailed discussion and examples of weighted application blanks. The Testing exercise (Exercise 9) and the Equal Employment Opportunity exercise (Exercise 17) have been revised to incorporate new sets of federal guidelines as well as recent court decisions. Further, a few exercises in the first edition have been combined into a single exercise, all have been streamlined to remove redundant requirements, and ambiguities in forms have been addressed. The *Implementor's Manual* has also undergone extensive revision to make it more concise and useful.

We have, of course, retained the salient features of the original edition. These include the experiential approach, the presentation of a conceptual overview to each exercise, and the inclusion of a large number of exercises, as well as parts within each exercise, from which Implementors can choose assignments according to students' interests and level. We have left intact the numerous activities themselves (augmenting their realism where possible) which made the first edition "come alive" for students.

Because the revision is so extensive, we used a very thorough review process. First, we gathered feedback from adopters throughout the four years the book was used in classes and took advantage of others' experiences with the book, as well as our own. Next, we sent a detailed questionnaire to adopters, soliciting their comments on a wide variety of issues, both general and specific. The return rate was high and the results were tabulated and studied carefully. We then asked noted experts to thoroughly review the exercise in his or her specialty. These very busy people were extremely helpful in providing specific comments in the exercises. The reviewers of specific exercises were: George Milkovich (Cornell University), John Fossum (University of Michigan), John Bernardin (Virginia Polytechnic Institute), Wayne Cascio (Florida International University), Mariann Jelinek (Dartmouth College), William Owens (University of Georgia), Joel Moses (AT&T), James Beatty (San Diego State), Edwin Locke (University of Maryland), Lloyd Baird (Boston University), Judi Komaki (Georgia Institute of Technology), Marc Wallace (University of Kentucky), William Bigoness (University of North Carolina), James Sharf (Richardson, Bellows, and Henry), and Milton Hakel (Ohio State University). We owe these reviewers a great debt for their thoughtful and useful comments, and we are honored to have such a distinguished and highly respected group of people review our book.

Our Colleagues in Organizational Behavior and Industrial Relations at the University of Maryland and in Management and Organization at the University of Colorado provided the professional, stimulating, supportive environment which is a large part of the success of any such effort. The enormous typing, retyping, correcting, filing, mailing, and other administrative tasks associated with this revision were handled admirably and in more good humor than we had a right to expect by Gloria and Georgianne at the University of Colorado, as well as Mariam and Armondo Gringas and the Faculty Services unit in the College of Business and Management at the University of Maryland. The staff at Addison-Wesley again performed their usual wizardry on our "manuscript." We, of course, remain solely responsible for any errors, omissions, or inadequacies in this work.

College Park, Maryland   *CES*
Boulder, Colorado   *RWB*
March 1981

CONTENTS

PERSONNEL ADMINISTRATION
an experiential skill-building approach

i

INTRODUCTION

PERSONNEL ADMINISTRATION: THE PROCUREMENT, DEVELOPMENT, AND UTILIZATION OF HUMAN RESOURCES

Personnel administration refers broadly to the procurement, development, and utilization of an organization's human resources. Regardless of what product or service an organization provides and no matter what its size, age, or location, it must procure human resources in order to remain viable. Further, if the organization is to survive, it must design programs to develop its human resources to their fullest capacities and to maintain ongoing worker commitment.

Obviously, organizations differ in their degree of reliance on the three above-mentioned processes. The relative importance of any one process may also vary both within an organization and over time. For example, a prestigious accounting firm with branches in several cities may not have problems procuring or attracting human resources, but may exhaust a great deal of time, effort, and expense in developing these resources. A voluntary organization, on the other hand, may see procurement as a problem, but due to the nature of most tasks, may expend only minimal effort in human resource development. A new university may initially experience a faculty procurement problem in some academic departments; however, after a few decades in which academic prestige builds, this aspect of personnel administration may become less problematic than utilizing its faculty efficiently and/or maintaining a high level of instructor performance.

Personnel administration, as opposed to personnel management, refers more to the design, implementation, evaluation, and administration of human-resource programs. While the personnel manager's job may typically be one of supervising and directing his or her staff, the personnel administrator's job routinely consists of problem identification through program design, implementation, and evaluation. Clearly, these two titles are quite similar and duties often may overlap, but the approach taken here emphasizes the administration of human resource programs.

Personnel is a rapidly changing profession. This is due in part to the changing external environment in which organizations operate. Labor legislation, rising expectations of workers, unionization, and foreign competition are but a few examples of environmental forces shaping the personnel profession. Internal environmental conditions are also creating challenges for those in personnel. These include organizations' size, complexity, and interdependence, as well as coordination problems between various subunits or functional areas, such as production, marketing, finance, and research and development.

In one sense, personnel must be all things to all people in an organization. As a staff or advisory function, it supports other line (or producing) areas, such as manufacturing. It also services other staff areas, such as the legal or public-relations departments. "Service" in this context refers to record keeping, data gathering, advising, auditing, evaluating, and other support functions. In addition, the personnel department is often given responsibility for helping to solve the organization's most difficult problems: absenteeism, poor performance, turnover, inadequate incentive systems, lack of coordination and planning, and forecasting future needs.

Thus, personnel faces three general demands. First, it must help the organization to cope with a changing environment—with constraints and opportunities developed externally, such as those stemming from government legislation and labor unions. Second, it must cooperate with other line and staff areas to achieve the organization's goals. It must secure the respect, trust, and confidence of the members of these units in order to effectively implement its programs—in short, to do its own job. Third, it is required to respond to certain serious human resource management problems organizations face.

These demands involve complex human behavior, as well as complex laws, technologies, and interrelationships between groups. To succeed in personnel administration one must possess substantial knowledge and skill in the areas of human behavior, interpersonal relations, organizational structure and process, labor relations, general administration and supervision, and in such technical areas as psychological testing, learning theory, employment legislation, statistics, and human motivation and performance. In other words, personnel work has become more and more demanding and, accordingly, those in the field are granted increased prestige, respect, and compensation, as well as a powerful central position in many organizations.

TOWARD A RATIONAL AND INTEGRATED PERSONNEL SYSTEM

All of the many different personnel programs are related in that their ultimate goal is the improvement of organizational effectiveness through the use of human resources. Organizational effectiveness refers to the results or outcomes of activity in an organizational setting. These results can be defined in terms of profit, cost, services provided, sales volume, interest earned, money raised, patients discharged, test score improvements, etc. Each type of organization (e.g., educational, industrial, voluntary, military, governmental, professional) would measure its results differently, and each may use several measures.

How do personnel programs impact on organizational effectiveness? Such impacts are many and complex. Personnel programs that are able to select successful performers, increase skills and abilities through training, secure commitment through wage and salary administration, measure human performance, and identify desired behaviors obviously will improve a system's efficacy. The ultimate link between these pro-

grams and organizational effectiveness is, of course, also determined by such additional factors as organizational policies, individual preferences and desires, and general economic conditions. Nevertheless, the personnel department does help to control a major determinant of organizational effectiveness—an organization's human resources.

The personnel system explained here must be discussed in its proper context. As Fig. 1 shows, a personnel system does not operate in isolation. It is influenced by and influences its environment significantly. On the one hand, the personnel system of programs to procure, develop, and utilize human resources lies within an environmental *external* to the organization and affected by general economic, sociocultural, and political conditions (e.g., a period of high unemployment). Two aspects of this environment, Equal Employment Opportunity (EEO) laws and guidelines and labor unions, have had such a pervasive effect on personnel that they are noted explicitly in Fig. 1. On the other hand, the personnel system is actually one of a number of other coexisting *internal* organizational systems that determine organizational effectiveness and are served by the personnel department. The interface between the personnel system and these other organizational systems ultimately determines the effectiveness of the programs the personnel department implements.

Working with line managers is sometimes the most difficult task in personnel, as personnel's staff position typically precludes complete authority and autonomy for its programs. Certainly those in personnel must be able to work very well with others, present their ideas clearly and concisely, and realize that the success of their programs often ultimately rests on their relationship with line managers. More will be said about interfaces between line managers and personnel staffs throughout the exercises in this book. The other systems with which personnel works may include functional areas such as marketing, finance, manufacturing, research and development, etc.

The uppermost box in Fig. 1 depicts the internal and external environmental influences on the personnel system and is directly connected to each of the core personnel programs (shown in the boxes). The five core personnel programs form the base of the personnel system. They are typically sequentially developed, although they certainly interact with each other and are dependent on each other. Each core program corresponds to a section in this book, and specific exercises in each section are indicated by their numbers in Fig. 1.

A first task in personnel is planning. Personnel planning involves forecasting for future human resource needs in light of a changing environment and

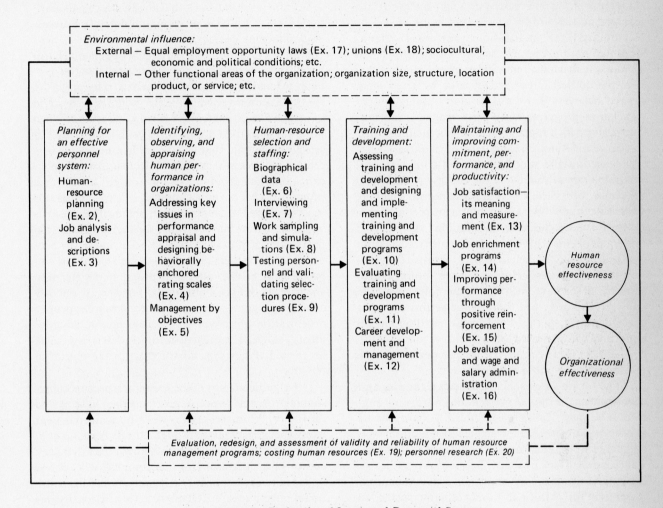

Fig. 1. Toward a Rational and Integrated Personnel System

long- and short-run organizational objectives. Planning also consists of analyses of jobs in the organization in order to determine their tasks and convert them into human requirements and characteristics. Such planning enables the personnel staff to gather the data required to make subsequent personnel decisions and forms the foundation for all personnel programs. It enables us to answer such questions as, "How many managers are needed to produce the new product line?" and "What are the responsibilities given to a person holding that job?"

The second core personnel program is that of identifying, observing, and appraising human performance. In a way, this program, like the previous one, is a preliminary step before human resources can be procured, developed, or utilized effectively. However, it is an extremely vital process. Desired performance must be defined before people are selected in order to establish a standard for appraising their on-the-job effectiveness. Further, setting standards and developing performance appraisal scales or formats to help in the observation and evaluation of performance redirects attention to job behavior—what people are expected to do on the job. While job analyses may identify job tasks (e.g., operating a machine), the performance identification and appraisal process can identify actual standards or desired behaviors (e.g., operating the machine at a rate of fifty pieces per hour).

Both types of information are required—that is, we would not only want to select someone who could operate the machine, but someone who could operate it at the desired rate. Further, once we know what desired behavior is, we can develop training and/or motivation programs when performance is too low. The performance appraisal system thus facilitates performance measurement and improvement.

Selection and staffing, the third core personnel program, refers broadly to the process of matching people to jobs. Selection is actually decision making under uncertainty. We are attempting to predict future job performance based on information from past and present performance. Obviously, as much information as is practical is gathered in order to improve this decision-making process. However, once future human resource needs have been forecasted, jobs have been analyzed and described, and desired performance has been identified, the information gathered about job applicants can be related to a standard or to a set of job and human requirements. Hence personnel decision making becomes more rational.

The fourth core personnel process is training and development. Certainly, we cannot improve or augment skill, ability, or knowledge unless we have selected persons and observed and evaluated their performance, compared it to standards, and concluded that any deviance is due to lack of ability. Training, actually learning in the organizational context, is aimed at improving present job performance and preparing persons to assume higher-level positions in the future. Due to the dynamic nature of the job environment, it is important for the organization to maintain a pool of potential replacements for key jobs and to help individuals manage successful careers.

Personnel staffs are given the responsibility, in coordination with managers and supervisors in other functional areas, of maintaining and improving commitment, performance, and productivity. This fifth core personnel system can really become effective only after commitment or performance problems have been noted and inadequate training has been eliminated as a cause. Numerous types of specific motivational, incentive, or wage and salary programs are in use, often in combination. Although their assumptions may differ, their common objective is to insure that the level of performance and commitment required is maintained

and, if possible, improved. This core personnel program recognizes that individuals require certain inducements, by no means limited to financial, to insure their contributions to organizational effectiveness.

Fig. 1 also indicates that the five core personnel programs, as well as those programs developed to meet environmental constraints and opportunities, need continual evaluation and redesign. All personnel programs must be subjected to a rigorous evaluation, perhaps through a cost/benefit analysis. The provision for evaluation must be built into program design, and costs must be estimated and benefits measured. When program objectives are not met, as in, for example, a selection program that fails to predict the desired percentage of successful performers from a group of applicants, or when program costs are judged to outweigh economic and/or noneconomic benefits, programs must be altered. Accurate data is obtained by conducting research on the programs themselves. Personnel professionals must also be able to estimate the economic costs of their programs, as well as the costs of problems (e.g., turnover) their programs are meant to alleviate. Redesign is also called for when previously effective programs become outmoded as jobs, people, organization objectives, and organizational environments change. The most detailed job description must be revised if new machinery changes the nature of the job.

A significant part of the evaluation process of personnel programs concerns assessing their validity and reliability. While these terms will be explained in their many specific contexts throughout this book,[1] a brief definition can be given here. Validity refers to the accuracy of a program: Did it accomplish what it was intended to accomplish? Did it contribute to organizational effectiveness? Reliability refers to consistency and repeatability: Were similar, predictable, accurate results obtained over time?

Both validity and reliability relate to the evaluation of a program's effectiveness, but they are very difficult to measure. As noted above, many variables influence organizational effectiveness, and often it is defined itself by several different measures. Reliability and validity are also related, and a program that is not valid will in many cases not be reliable.

Because of the great difficulty in ascertaining reliability and validity, it is tempting to settle for "soft" criteria in evaluating success. For example, a training program may be termed valid because people reacted favorably to it. But did the program achieve its real purpose? Were objectives for the program ever set and

---

[1] See Exercise 9.

later met? Are people's reactions accurate? These are tough questions. So many factors can account for the outcome of any personnel program that they are difficult to sort out.

For some programs, such as testing, detailed validity and reliability studies may sometimes be required by law. A valid test for leadership ability would be able to predict, on the basis of its results, successful and unsuccessful future job performance of test takers. Validity would also be inferred if scores attained by a group of people correlated with scores the same people received on another test also designed to measure leadership ability and if their scores did not correlate highly with scores from a test measuring an opposite characteristic, such as "need for followership." A reliable test would be one on which individuals achieved similar scores from one administration of the test to another. That is, if they scored high initially on the test, they would also score high on the second administration.

But how do we validate a human-resource forecasting effort or plan or a wage and salary system? Clearly, ascertaining whether the effort accomplished what it set out to do would be difficult unless we were sure of the original objectives. But this standard may be too unrealistic or subjective.

Thus, the evaluation and reliability of entire personnel programs are a difficult problem, and the problem becomes even more acute if programs are closely related. This is because the validity or reliability of one is often difficult to separate from the others. Attempts at assessing validity and reliability are necessary, however, for several reasons: they facilitate the effective evaluation of personnel programs' impact on organizational effectiveness; their demonstration is often required by law; and their determination pinpoints weaknesses in programs, which helps to facilitate program redesign.

PERSONNEL ADMINISTRATION FROM AN EXPERIENTIAL/SKILL-BUILDING PERSPECTIVE

In writing this book, we took a different approach than do most textbook authors. Typically, a book's content is decided by answering the question: What should people *know* at the end of this course? We asked that question too. But we also asked another question: What should people be able to *do* at the end of the course? In answering this second question, we developed a set of exercises designed to build participants' skill, as well as their knowledge, in the field of personnel administration. These exercises all require participants to take an active part in the learning process— to learn by doing.

While many textbooks contain much of the information required in personnel administration, they have no provision for *skill acquisition*. This set of exercises will hopefully provide you with the experiences necessary to begin to build skills in the areas of, for example, training, selection, and performance appraisal. You can thus move from the learning environment into the organizational environment with not only some knowledge of what to do but also with some expertise on *how* to do it.

Experiential Learning. Experiential learning differs from more traditional classroom learning in several ways. First, the learner is active. You must participate in the learning situation, rather than merely sitting back and absorbing material. Second, the implementor acts more as a coach, director, or resource person than as an evaluator or transmitter of information. The instructor is thus a manager of the learning environment. Third, learning takes place not only while you participate directly, but also while you observe others participate. They can act as your models for both ineffective and effective behavior. Fourth, experiential learning involves your behavior and your emotions or attitudes, as well as your thought processes. You must act as well as think, and your actions and those of others may affect you in a positive or negative way. But if you are perceptive, you may learn much about yourself, about the way you behave in groups, about your preferences for certain tasks or for amounts of authority, in addition to course content. Finally, once you have experienced something, have actually done it, your learning has a much higher probability of transferring from the classroom environment to the environment in which you will be required to use the skill and knowledge.

The Role of the Participant in Experiential Learning. In order to maximize the learning from these exercises, a few hints are offered. Participate seriously. Try to place yourself in the situation described and act accordingly. Use the information given in the exercises as a jumping-off point for your own extrapolation and improvisation. Make assumptions you think are necessary according to your own perception of the situation, recognizing that these assumptions may differ from those of others (as is often the case in actual situations).

Try to incorporate the conceptual material from the *Introductions* of the exercises, from lectures, and from other sources into your experiences. Concepts, ideas, and theories you gather will help to integrate the exercises, make them a richer experience, and allow you to predict their outcomes more accurately. After you have completed each exercise, reflect on your learning and try to pinpoint precisely what new information you possess and particularly what skills you have begun to develop. A form for this self-assessment process follows each exercise. Finally, try to be an effective group or team member. As many of the tasks require small-group effort, you must work with others closely and cooperatively in order to perform well. As noted above, you can learn much from your team members' behavior as well as from your own.

THE ORGANIZATION AND CONTENTS OF THIS TEXT

This book contains twenty exercises. Each topic and the activities in each exercise were chosen to reflect the important personnel programs currently in use in all types of modern organizations. The exercises are grouped into seven broad sections, each preceded by a statement of introduction to the topic area. Each section contains one or more exercises.

Section 1 contains one exercise designed to familiarize you with the roles and duties of people in personnel work. Sections 2 through 6 each include two or more exercises pertaining to each of the five core personnel programs explained above. As shown in Fig. 1, the five core programs are presented in order. The first two exercises in Section 7 deal with environmental impacts on personnel and the last two exercises in Section 7 relate to evaluating the costs, benefits, and overall effectiveness of human resource management programs.

USING THE TEXT

Each exercise contains all the information you will need to complete it. All forms required are also included, and the perforated pages facilitate your tearing out certain forms your implementor may ask you to hand in.

Each exercise begins with a *Preview,* to give you a glimpse of the exercise's content. Next, *Objectives* spell out the aims of the exercise in some detail and the *Premeeting Assignment* informs you of reading tasks to be completed before you begin or parts you are not to read until told to do so. The *Introduction* serves as a brief summary of the topic and will provide a set of relevant terms, concepts, and issues that can be used to facilitate your understanding of the exercise and enable you to integrate it with others. The *Procedure* explains your tasks in a step-by-step fashion. As with any other experience, having all the terms, concepts, rules, and

procedures firmly in mind *before you begin* will aid your performance, understanding, and enjoyment. Careful reading and study of the *Procedure* and your serious attempts at staying within time guidelines will facilitate learning.

For Further Reading suggests a good number of related sources of information to be used by those who want to learn about a topic in more depth or for those seeking material for term papers and other projects. The references were chosen to provide a representative sample of the many different levels and types of literature, very current ideas and classic issues, research, and practical guidelines.

The forms follow the reading list. The lettered parts of the exercise and the numbered forms correspond to those explained in the procedure. The instructions for filling out the forms are detailed in the *Procedure.* Finally, an *Assessment of Learning* form is placed at the end of each exercise. The first few questions on the form are the same for every exercise. Subsequent positions pertain to each particular exercise.

A FINAL NOTE

Now that you are familiar with the organization and content of this book, you can more readily see how we answered the question posed earlier: What should people be able to *do* at the end of this course? Simply put, they should be able to begin to *design, implement,* and *evaluate* personnel programs in order to procure, develop, and utilize human resources in organizations. This emphasis on design, implementation, and evaluation was incorporated into each exercise and, coupled with knowledge you glean from this book, the exercises facilitate skill building in personnel. Hopefully, you can thus learn not only what to do, but you can begin to learn *how* to do it.

The activities offered here cannot, of course, substitute for actual experience in organizations. Nor were they meant to incorporate every variable, consideration, problem, or complexity you may encounter in an actual organizational setting. Simply following these guidelines will not assure an effective personnel system. The activities do, however, incorporate the most important and pervasive considerations and problems you would typically encounter in an organization and, while they are simulations, they were all designed around actual organizational practices. They offer you the opportunity to gain valuable experience and to try out your ideas, thereby developing an understanding of how personnel programs are implemented and how they can impact on organizational effectiveness.

Remember that the responsibility for your learning ultimately rests with *you,* the learner, not with your implementor. Be prepared to take an active role in learning; be prepared to experience, observe, experiment, assess, and evaluate your own learning; and be prepared to have some fun, for fun and learning need not be mutually exclusive.

Section 1

THE PERSONNEL
ADMINISTRATOR

This section of the book contains one exercise, yet it serves many purposes. For participants unfamiliar with the duties and roles of people in the personnel field, Exercise 1 can provide information about the type of work expected from professionals in personnel, human resource management, or employee-relations departments. In addition, the first exercise allows participants to gain some practice in using this book. You will become familiar with the format, how various parts are arranged, and how specific assignments in exercises are made. By completing Exercise 1, you can also gain practice in analyzing cases, in role playing, and in group discussion—activities that are all required in subsequent exercises.

Therefore, Section 1 is a preview to the personnel administrator's job as well as to the experiential/skill-building method of learning used in this book. Try to reflect back on Exercise 1 as you participate in other exercises, and think about two questions. First, as you finish each exercise, ask yourself how your perception of the duties and roles of the personnel administrator has changed. Are you developing a clearer picture of what organizations do to attend to their human resource management needs? Secondly, consider your own skill development. Are you picking up new skills that would enable you to design, implement, and evaluate human resource programs?

Personnel administration, or human resource management, is a dynamic, challenging academic field of study and profession. As Exercise 1 points out, the role of the personnel administrator in an organization is becoming quite technical and increasingly important. He or she is typically responsible for making many decisions that influence people's careers and the organization significantly, for controlling information vital to the organization's functioning, and for helping to solve one of an organization's most difficult problems—how to procure, develop, and utilize its human resources most effectively.

Exercise 1
Hiring a personnel administrator: an exploration of job duties and roles

PREVIEW

In this exercise, you simulate the process of interviewing and hiring a personnel administrator for a small manufacturing company. As you participate in the exercise, you will discover the duties and responsibilities of personnel administrators, as well as their roles in an organization. Three applicants for the job of personnel administrator are interviewed by a company's board of directors and one of them is eventually chosen. As the exercise proceeds, try to identify the combination of education, experience, knowledge, and personal characteristics which would be desirable for a prospective personnel administrator job applicant and how these would change as characteristics of the organization change.

OBJECTIVES

1. To become acquainted with the job duties and roles of a personnel administrator in an organization.

2. To gain experience in the interviewing process and to begin to appreciate its strengths and weaknesses.

3. To begin thinking about job performance—how it can be described, measured, and predicted.

PREMEETING PREPARATION

Read the *Introduction* and Forms 1, 2, and 3. Do not read past Form 3 until you are assigned a role by the implementor.

INTRODUCTION

The Job Duties and Roles of the Personnel Administrator

The Traditional Role. Traditionally, the personnel administrator had responsibility for staffing the organization, for selection, for benefit administration, and for interfacing with unions on a day-to-day basis. These activities were part of the staff or advisory role of the personnel departments during the early part of the twentieth century. The personnel administrator typically had little or no direct authority over the decisions made by managers and supervisors involved in the actual production of a product or service. These "line" managers had the authority to hire, fire, or promote their workers, and the personnel staff attempted to advise them in these matters. In addition, there was

little government interference in the form of laws and guidelines as the personnel administrator carried out his or her duties. Decisions regarding selection methods, promotions, etc. were left primarily to top management, with advice from the personnel administrator. The union was the primary constraint on management decision making in the personnel area in the period before World War I.

External Environmental Influences on the Role of the Personnel Administrator. This "laissez-faire" era for management and the personnel administrator began to change, however, as several external influences emerged to affect their roles.[1] The foremost of these influences was the federal government. Due to a series of legislation enacted in the past few decades, the personnel administrator's role has permanently changed. Among these acts are the Manpower Training and Development Act (MTDA) of 1962, Title VII of the Civil Rights Act of 1964, the Occupational Safety and Health Act (OSHA) of 1970, and the Equal Employment Opportunity (EEO) Act of 1972. These laws, coupled with major labor laws and the numerous other manpower laws, set guidelines, quotas, and often strict rules for the personnel administrator and the organization in all areas of personnel.[2]

One of the most notable ramifications of these laws was the illegality of discrimination in hiring practices. This forced all concerned with the personnel function to take a hard look at, for example, their selection tests, in order to ensure their "fairness." Finding selection tests that do not discriminate against certain groups is a difficult and controversial task for the personnel administrator, but one which makes the role even more challenging. Research and new technical developments are required to meet this challenge, and many such techniques and implications of the complex laws and guidelines are discussed in later exercises.

Beside government influence, several other factors have contributed to the changing nature of the role of the personnel administrator. Among these have been shifts in the composition of the labor force toward more white-collar workers, a more highly educated labor force, and more skilled-labor and managerial positions. These trends have made it more difficult for the personnel administrator to recruit people for certain jobs. The changes in attitudes, values, and the rising expectations of many workers today also make motivation programs and wage, salary, and benefit administration more challenging and difficult. General economic conditions and unemployment rates certainly affect the personnel administrator's job by altering the supply of labor available to an organization.

Finally, the role of the personnel administrator is being influenced by changes in the internal environment of the organization itself. Not only are physical environments beginning to reflect people's needs (e.g., bright colors, recreation facilities, etc.), but organization structure and technology are also rapidly changing. More authority is given to lower-level workers, and many decisions are made by a work group or team.

Looser organizational structures and less-formal authority are becoming more pervasive. Thus, to accommodate these changes, the personnel administrator is forced to revise training methods to emphasize interpersonal and group relations. The computer and its technology are also pervasive in organizations, and the personnel administrator may be required not only to staff and train those who will work with computers, but also to use computers effectively in his or her own department.

A New Role for the Personnel Administrator. The environmental influences noted previously, both external and internal to the organization, have vastly expanded the role of the personnel administrator. The personnel administrator essentially has responsibility for obtaining, utilizing, and developing the human resources of an organization. In this role, he or she must still carry out traditional activities such as selection, training, and wage and salary administration, but even these activities must conform to the reporting and legal requirements of the government. The role of developing human resources requires the personnel administrator to take a much broader view of training, which may encompass career development and interpersonal relations in addition to skill building. The personnel administrator must now anticipate the changes in the labor force and in the human resource requirements of the organization and attempt to mesh the two with sophisticated planning and forecasting techniques. Finally, the personnel administrator is now often seen as the primary change agent or catalyst for change in the organization.[3] He or she often has responsibility for changing the structure of the organization and the people in it in order to adapt to the rapid pace of change in our society.

In fact, because of this revolution in the field of human resources the Bureau of Labor Statistics estimates that jobs in the personnel field will increase by 50 percent or more by 1985 from its estimates of 320,000 personnel workers in 1974. Table 1 shows how the personnel field is growing relative to other concerns. Perhaps this growth has also caused the American Society for Personnel Administration (ASPA) to begin an effort (now independent of ASPA) to accredit personnel professionals through a series of professional examinations. This accreditation may help to make the area more specialized and based in technical knowledge of the field.[4]

[1] T. H. Patton, "Personnel Management in the 1970's: The End of Laissez Faire," *Human Resource Management* 12, no. 3 (Fall 1973): 7–11.

[2] See Exercises 9 and 17 for discussions of laws relating to hiring practices. Major labor laws are outlined in Exercise 18.

[3] S. H. Applebaum, "Contemporary Personnel Administrators: Agents of Change," *Personnel Journal* 53, no. 11 (November 1974): 835–837.

[4] "Accreditation: The Dream Becomes Reality," *The Personnel Administrator* 21, no. 8 (1976).

These new roles for the personnel administrator have added significantly to his or her status and importance in the organization. What has traditionally been a staff function is now becoming a vital part of the central decision-making and goal-setting processes in an organization. The personnel administrator now has considerable authority based upon (a) his or her possession of vital information regarding laws, the labor force, and the current manpower inventory of the organization; and (b) his or her control over such vital organizational functions as selection, training, and wage and salary administration. In fact, personnel administrators are being chosen as chief executive officers in organizations with increasing regularity.[5]

Table 1. Careers that Are Expected to Grow by 50 Percent or More by 1985

	Minimum increase expected
Secretaries, stenographers	875,000
Local truckdrivers	400,000
Cooks and chefs	266,250
Registered nurses	240,000
Machinists	171,900
Welders	165,000
Teachers' aides	160,000
Carpenters	151,500
Construction-machinery operators	150,000
Engineering, science technicians	146,250
Retail trade-sales workers	135,000
Accountants	129,750
Police officers	125,000
Real-estate agents, brokers	112,500
Construction laborers	107,250
Auto mechanics	105,000
Lawyers	99,000
Bookkeepers	85,000
Computer-operating personnel	84,750
Personnel, labor-relations workers	83,750
Social workers	82,500
Beauticians	82,100
Drafters	80,000
Bank officers, managers	75,000
Insurance agents, brokers	69,750

Challenges for the Personnel Administrator. The changes and complexities in the role of the personnel administrator offer considerable challenge for those in

this position. The personnel administrator is now challenged to devise valid and fair selection tests, to develop relevant and job-related selection tools in addition to the interview and biographical data, to make training programs more effective and transferable to actual job situations, and to motivate people on the job by using rewards and programs rather than strictly monetary inducements. Increasingly, the challenge for the personnel administrator is to *develop* people in their jobs to their fullest potential, rather than merely *place* them in jobs.

Simultaneously fulfilling the demands of government, management, employees, and unions is the major challenge facing the personnel administrator. Merging organizational efficiency and productivity with individual and career development will require extremely creative efforts.

Background, Training, and Experience of the Personnel Administrator. What type of person is able to meet the challenges discussed above? What experience and training should they have? What specific duties will they be asked to perform? The answers to these questions are the concern of this exercise. As you prepare criteria for selection of a personnel administrator and/ or interview prospective candidates, you will be confronted with these issues.

In selecting a person for any job, several types of standards or criteria may be used to help make the decision. Based on what you now know about the role of the PA, we may group these criteria into the following four broad categories:

1. General administrative skills;
2. Interpersonal skills (e.g., communicating); and
3. Technical knowledge and skills.

Because the personnel administrator will have broad administrative and managerial duties as he or she develops and implements programs, some skill and ability in planning, organizing, controlling, and general supervision seems essential. The personnel administrator must implement specific programs in the areas of, for example, training and wage and salary administration, and thus some specific skills in these content areas is desirable. Today he or she must also be familiar with the content of the many laws that affect the job, as well as with other technical information, such as safety standards, in each industry. Finally, certain specific behaviors may be desirable for a personnel administrator—for example, facility in verbal and/or written communication.

The selection of any job applicant will depend on the candidate's current ability in each of these four

[5] D. Henning and W. French, "The Mythical Personnel Manager," *California Management Review* 3, no. 4 (Summer 1961): 33–45; H. E. Meyer, "Personnel Directors Are the New Corporate Heroes," *Fortune* 93, no. 2 (February 1976): 86–88+; "Personnel: Fast Track to the Top," *Dun's Review* 105, no. 4 (April 1975): 74–77.

areas, as well as on the competence he or she can be expected to obtain through post-selection training. In addition, the selection decision will rest on the specific nature of the job and the organization. As you develop selection criteria for the personnel administrator in this exercise, try to keep these two points in mind.

PROCEDURE

Overview. Several of you will be asked to play the role of a candidate for the job of a personnel administrator of a small firm, while others are asked to be the owners and officers of the firm who comprise its board of directors. The remaining participants form groups whose task is to devise a list of criteria for selecting the candidate and to decide on a method for weighting these criteria.

PART A

STEP 1: Everyone should read all of the information in Forms 1–3.

STEP 2: Three people are chosen to be the candidates for the job of personnel administrator. They are to prepare their personal resumes for the board of directors and to read Forms 1–3 carefully.

PART B

STEP 3: A group is chosen to be the company's board of directors and each is given one of the seven roles in Form 4. The board will discuss its interview strategy and prepare for the interview.

PART C

STEP 4: Remaining participants form small groups to determine the criteria each would use to select a personnel administrator for the company and how these criteria would be used or weighted to evaluate candidates in an interview. These groups are also to design a scale (see Form 5) to use as they observe the candidates being interviewed. As candidates are interviewed, group members will rate them in various areas using this scale. The criteria are not to be known to the interviewers or interviewees. Each of the remaining participants are to rate each interviewee 1 to 10 on a scale for each dimension its group has determined.

TIME: Each group should take about 30 minutes to prepare (Parts A, B, and C).

STEP 5: The candidates for the job of personnel administrator are interviewed by the board. Candidates should not observe another interview unless they have already been interviewed.

TIME: About 20 minutes per interview.

PART D

STEP 6: After the interviews are completed:

a) The board should select one candidate (the "best" person for the job in question) and compose letters to the person selected and to those rejected informing the candidates of their decision. These letters are then delivered to the appropriate candidates.

b) Each group that composed selection criteria and observed the interviewing process should also select a candidate and prepare a rationale for their choice.

c) The candidates decide among themselves who should be selected and discuss their strengths and weaknesses during the interview.

TIME: About 25 minutes.

STEP 7: Each of the three groups (candidates, interviewers, and groups that observed the process and developed criteria) reveal their decisions and their rationales for the decision to all other groups. Emphasis should be placed on the reasons for the choice and whether these reasons could withstand possible litigation initiated by rejected candidates who might feel they were victims of prejudice.

STEP 8: Each of the candidates is permitted to respond briefly to the letter received.

FOR FURTHER READING

Each reference is followed by either the roman numeral I or II, meant to indicate the general level of difficulty of the reference. Those followed by the numeral I are introductory references that can be read and understood by those with little or no background in the specific topic, other than what is contained in the exercise itself. These are also sources that contain information especially useful to practitioners and professionals, as they develop guidelines, suggestions, etc. They are not, however, overly simplistic or unrealistic. References followed by the numeral II are at a somewhat higher level of complexity and may require previous knowledge of the topic if the reader is to derive their full benefit. These can be very useful to those wishing more detailed information on a particular topic. References followed by an R are research articles or books containing primarily research. They of course contain data analyses and research methodology discussions and are typically also noted with the numeral II, as they may require some background in research statistics and methods. The categories of references are certainly somewhat subjective, and the codes should therefore not restrict users of these exercises from exploring any reference that seems appropriate for their needs. All references were chosen on the basis of their content, and we have attempted to provide a representative sample of the various types of literature available for each subject.

American Management Association. *The Personnel Job in a Changing World.* New York: American Management Association, 1964. (I)

"An Interview with Bob Berra." *The Personnel Administrator* 21, no. 2 (February 1976): 29–33. (I)

Applebaum, S. H. "Contemporary Personnel Administrators: Agents of Change." *Personnel Journal* 53, no. 11 (November 1974): 835–837. (I)

Appley, L. A. "Management *Is* Personnel Administration." *Personnel* 46 (March–April 1969): 8–15. (I)

Barrett, G. V. "Research Models of the Future for Industrial and Organizational Psychology." *Personnel Psychology* 25 (1972): 1–18. (II)

Bass, B. M. "Organizational Life in the 1970s and Beyond." *Personnel Psychology* 25 (1972): 19–30. (II)

Beatty, R. W. "Personnel Systems and Human Performance." *Personnel Journal* 54 (1973): 307–312. (I)

Brady, G. F. "Assessing the Personnel Manager's Power Base." *The Personnel Administrator* 25 no. 7 (1980): 57–61. (I)

Burack, E. H., and E. L. Miller. "The Personnel Function in Transition." *California Management Review* 18 (Spring 1976). (I)

Cassell, F. H. "A New Role in Corporate Management." *Personnel Administration* 34, no. 6 (November–December 1971): 33–37. (I)

Coleman, C. J. "Personnel: The Changing Function." *Public Personnel Management* 2 (May–June 1973): 186–193. (I)

Dunnette, M. D. "Research Needs of the Future in Industrial and Organizational Psychology." *Personnel Psychology* 25 (1972): 31–40. (II)

Dunnette, M. D., and B. M. Bass. "Behavioral Scientists and Personnel Management." *Industrial Relations* 2 (1963): 115–130. (I)

Edny, F. R. "The Greening of the Profession," *The Personnel Administrator* 25, no. 7 (1980): 27–30+. (I)

Fowlkes, F. K. "The Expanding Role of the Personnel Function." *Harvard Business Review* 53, no. 2 (March–April 1975): 71–84. (I)

French, W. "The Contemporary and Emerging Role of the Personnel Department." In W. French, *The Personnel Management Process,* 3d ed. Boston: Houghton Mifflin, 1974, Chap. 30. (I)

French, W., and A. D. Ebling. "Predictions for Personnel and Industrial Relations in 1985." *Personnel Journal* 40, no. 6 (1961): 249–253. (I)

Guthrie, R. R. "Personnel's Emerging Role." *Personnel Journal* 53, no. 9 (September 1974): 657–664. (I)

Henning, D., and W. French, "The Mythical Personnel Manager." *California Management Review* 3, no. 4 (Summer 1961): 33–45. (I)

Hunt, T. "Critical Issues Facing Personnel Administrators Today." *Public Personnel Management* 3, no. 6 (November–December 1974): 464–472. (I)

Johnson, R. J. "The Personnel Administrator of the 1970's." *Personnel Journal* 50, no. 4 (April 1971): 298–305. (I)

Ling, C. C. *The Management of Personnel Relations: History and Origins.* Homewood, Ill.: Irwin, 1965. (I)

Meyer, H. E. "Personnel Directors Are the New Corporate Heroes." *Fortune* 93, no. 2 (February 1976): 86–88+. (I)

Meyer, H. H. "The Future of Industrial and Organizational Psychology." *American Psychologist* 27 (1972): 608–614. (II)

Miner, J. B., and M. G. Miner. "Careers in Personnel and Industrial Relations." In J. B. Miner and M. G. Miner, *Personnel and Industrial Relations,* 2d. ed. New York: Macmillan, 1973, Chap. 23. (I)

Mitchell, J. M., and R. E. Schroeder. "Future Shock for Personnel Administration." *Public Personnel Management* 3, no. 4 (July–August 1974): 265–69. (I)

Myers, C. A. "New Frontiers for Personnel Management." *Personnel* 41, no. 3 (May–June 1964): 381–384. (I)

Nash, A. N., and J. B. Miner. *Personnel and Labor Relations, An Historical Approach.* New York: Macmillan, 1973. (I)

Patton, T. H. "Personnel Management in the 1970's: The End of Laissez Faire." *Human Resource Management* 12 (Fall 1973): 7–19. (I)

Patton, T. H. "Is Personnel Administration a Profession?" *Personnel Administration* 31, no. 2 (March–April 1968): 4 plus. (I)

"Personnel—Fast Track to the Top." *Dun's Review* 105, no. 4 (April 1975): 74–77. (I)

Ritzer, G., and H. M. Trice. *An Occupation in Conflict: A Study of the Personnel Manager*. Ithaca, New York: New York State School of Industrial and Labor Relations, Cornell University, 1969. (II–R)

Sloane, A. R. "Creative Personnel Management." *Personnel Journal* 53, no. 9 (September 1974): 662–666. (I)

PART A

Form 1 Letter to Personnel Administrator Candidates

Date_____

Dear_____

We are happy to inform you that you are one of the finalists for the position of Personnel Administrator of Acme Precision Planter Company. The Board of Directors has reviewed the resumes of many well qualified applicants. We have a few questions relative
to your education or experience, but our main concern is how well we feel you personally
mesh with our personal values and our organization's needs. Accordingly, we invite you
to meet with the Board for a final interview.

Some of the things we would like to explore are: (1) your general concept of the role
of personnel in an organization of some 650 employees (after expansion); (2) how the
personnel function fits into the general functional pattern of an organization; (3) generally what the personnel department should do and roughly the priority of activities
you would emphasize; (4) how formalizing personnel would affect the presently decentralized personnel authority; (5) examples of how a personnel function could add to the
profitability of our firm and provide relief for our operating executives without
impairing their control over personnel; (6) your attitudes relative to labor unions,
hiring the disadvantaged, including Mexican Americans, relationships with employees,
expectations of employees; and (7) your plans for avoiding litigation problems in
personnel activities.

We are looking forward to visiting with you for an hour or so on _____
at _____ in the Board Room. If you have any questions about our operations which
may facilitate our interview with you, please do not hesitate to give us a call.

Please bring copies of your latest resume with you to give to our Directors.

Sincerely,

Vice President

PART A

Form 2 The Company

The company is a relatively young organization having been founded five years ago by the current president. It is located in a city having an estimated population of 13,500, located some thirty miles due north of a major midwestern city.

The company became a reality when the president invented an exceptionally sophisticated product which could position various seedlings at optimal depths for growth and spacing, thus minimizing the need for expensive tree-thinning operations. The product chassis is of conventional design, hardly distinguishable from those of major producers. But the outstanding competitive advantage of the product is in the precision positioning mechanism. From its initial appearance on the market five years ago, it has had an amazing market performance, only limited by problems of a developing organization and "debugging" of a new invention.

The president invented the product in his machine shop when he became dissatisfied with the performance of standard products. It worked so well on his farm that he interested a local mechanic, the present general manager of the firm, in the development phase. Together with a friend, another mechanic and now the production manager, they improved the product until they were satisfied that it was marketable.

The three incorporated the organization and leased an abandoned, former assembly manufacturing building in a downtown area (see Form 3). They immediately enlarged the board of directors to include the president of the First City Bank, a wealthy local cattle feeder, and the wife of the general manager, a former commercial-science teacher in Beetland High School who also serves as secretary-treasurer-office manager of the Company.

The almost incredible initial market performance of the product indicated a fabulous success for the company. However, as so frequently occurs with a new invention, "debugging" problems occurred to dim early promise. The difficulty arose when a shipment to northern California failed to perform effectively. The succeeding six months resulted in a large expenditure for the services of experts from a nearby university, and subsequent modifications of the product. This financial setback plus the inexperience of the new managers in organizing and operating a fairly complex manufacturing enterprise very nearly resulted in economic disaster.

The president, general manager, and the production manager, recognized their inexperience and agreed to the recruitment of a vice president from a successful Cleveland, Ohio, assembly plant who had relatives in the area and usually visited the area on his vacations. He had become acquainted with the president and the bank president.

The production manager was elected to the board of directors, given stock options, and designated as vice president of the organization. This proved to be a turning point since he moved immediately to smooth out production irregularities and to upgrade the skills of the work force. However, the company still had the persisting problem of lack of financial liquidity.

To further complicate the problem, a certain type of metal alloy which had proved essential in the effective performance of the product's precision mechanism had recently been severely limited by government requisistioning for use in missle and aircraft manufacturing. This cutback in supply of the essential material resulted in a recent layoff within the past month of 100 personnel, leaving the present work force at 250.

The vice president anticipated cutback problems soon after his arrival and began negotiations with the Northwest Aircraft Manufacturing Company for a subcontract to produce a subassembly. Landing-gear subassemblies made by Northwest were similar to that of the present product. Only two special-purpose machines would be required for the new operation and both of these would enhance machining operations and reduce contract-out work on the planter. The eighteen-month contract for $5,000,000 could net as much as $300,000 profits, providing both financial liquidity as well as releasing sufficient supplies of government stores of the metal alloy for use in the present product.

Current product production would be continued on the first shift with its hours moved to a 6:00 A.M. starting time. With a thirty-minute brunch break, the second shift, landing-gear subassemblies, could begin after a thirty-minute conversion period, at 3:00 P.M., using the same assembly lines. This would enable the second shift to terminate by 11:00 P.M., including a half-hour supper break. No formal rest periods were scheduled for either shift. A small third shift of maintenance and housekeeping personnel would begin at 11:00 P.M., overlapping briefly the last thirty minutes of the second shift and the initial hour of the first shift.

In order to man the additional shifts, approximately 400 new personnel would be needed, 100 to bring the planter operation up to full scale production, and 300 for the new landing-gear assembly. Thus the company projected 650 employees. It was planned that upon completion of the government contract, the company will continue planter production on a two-shift basis, retaining the majority of the work force.

This "dream" became a reality when the company was awarded a subcontract for $5,000,000 to be initiated from the first of the ensuing month. The contract has a $2,500 a day penalty provision. The vice president anticipates that the minimum production time required to complete the contract will be sixteen months, giving a maximum of two months to develop a pilot operation and a try-out operation. Hopefully, in six weeks from the first of the coming month, both operations will be in full production.

The vice president has convinced the board of directors that a formalized personnel department is essential for satisfactorily affecting the expansion and the ultimate success of the organization. He has been authorized to hire as soon as possible, with the approval of the board of directors, a personnel administrator to assume the personnel activities presently handled by the secretary-treasurer and to develop a complete program commensurate with the needs of a plant of 650 personnel.

PART A

Form 3 The City

Altitude: 1200 feet   *Population:* (latest census estimates) 13,500

Annual mean temperature: 53° F   *Annual precipitation:* 16 inches

Location: The city is located thirty miles north of a major metropolitan area. The city is connected by four-lane highway with the metropolitan area and is near major universities and colleges.

Industry: The city is located in the center of one of the state's most productive irrigated agricultural areas. Farms are about 80 percent irrigated and 20 percent dry land and grazing. Major crops are sugar beets, corn, wheat, beans, alfalfa, etc. Cattle feeding, dairy farming, and poultry raising are important occupations. Products from industries include beet sugar, livestock feeds, frozen foods, electronic equipment, brass, aluminum and iron and steel castings, irrigation equipment, and sausage.

Educational facilities: Total school enrollment in schools is 4,500. The high school is fully accredited. A new high school under construction will be occupied soon.

Employment: Persons interested in employment should contact the State Office of Employment. Although Beetland is growing rapidly, employers do not offer employment as an inducement for people to move to this area, since there are generally more people seeking employment than there are jobs.

Housing: Generally speaking, rental housing is in short supply—depending on the time of year. Rental housing and apartments can usually be obtained within a few days to a week. Again this depends on the taste of the home seeker. New homes are available in both quantity and variety. A list of local realty firms will be forwarded on request. The local newspaper want-ad section lists both rentals and homes for sale. Subscription rate is $1.50 per month by mail.

Business opportunities: There are always a few businesses for sale in the area, as well as farm property. Please make inquiries of this nature to local real-estate firms. A list of firms is available on request.

Cost of living: No specific information available. Due to the city's close proximity to the metropolitan area, prices here must be competitive with those areas. Recent figures show the city's cost of living to be approximately 5 percent below that of the metropolitan area.

Taxes and mill levies: The overall tax rate per $1,000 of assessed valuation (1974) is 80 mills. Property is assessed at 100 percent of 1941 replacement cost, less depreciation. This would average 30 percent of today's value.

Miscellaneous: The city has council-manager type government. Municipal utilities owned include electricity, water, and sewer. Rates among lowest in area. Natural gas supplied by Public Service Company. The city has two hospitals, a community hospital (80 bed), a community osteopathic hospital (25 bed), and twenty medical doctors. There are thirty-two active churches (list available on request), including most denominations. One daily paper, *The Bugle*, and a radio station KMOO serve the area. Television reception is excellent from five stations. Three city parks provide a variety of facilities for recreation and family use. A Carnegie library with approximately 30,000 volumes and a museum provide plenty of reading and information. An excellent year-round recreation program is co-sponsored by city and schools. A nine-hole municipal golf course is rated "tops" by area golfers. Local citizens and visitors are able to avail themselves of hunting, fishing, hiking, camping, and sightseeing only thirty minutes away. Surfaced, all-weather roads lead to resorts and scenic areas.

Additional information: The company has the single largest payroll in the city. A beet-sugar mill on the city outskirts employs 150 people at the height of the season (the fall). The remainder of the year its personnel requirements fluctuate from 15–50. An electronics firm has broken ground on the outskirts of the city with an estimated employment in two years of 2,000. The firm will be in pilot operation within six months, employing by that time approximately 50, predominantly women. The population is 80 percent Anglo-American with about 12 percent Spanish-American, 7 percent Negro, and 2 percent Japanese ethnic minorities. The company has no ethnic minority employees at this time. In fact, the implied hiring policy of the company has been to hire only Anglos. It hires women only in the office. None are hired on the assembly lines or in the plant.

PART B

Form 4 The Board Members

The board of directors consists of the chairman of the board (president of the company), the treasurer (president of the First City Bank), the secretary (the secretary-treasurer of the company), a wealthy cattle feeder-rancher, the vice president, general manager, and production manager of the company. The stock is held among the members of the board, with the president of the company retaining 51 percent.

President. The president has been a successful farmer-rancher all of his adult life. He inherited one section (640 acres) of irrigated agricultural land from his parents and, through his skill and energy, has added four additional sections of agricultural and grazing land to his holdings. As previously indicated, he invented the current product. His interest in mechanics was stimulated during his two years in the nearby state agricultural and mechanical college. He did not finish his education, leaving school on the death of his father to operate the farm, since he was an only child. He is an exceptionally intelligent, alert man in his late fifties. As a manager, he is a good farmer, with little interest in organizational theory, delegation, and the like. His managerial style, if it can be so-called, is exceedingly informal, characterized by general disregard for any formal lines of communication. This has proved distressing to those managerial personnel who require more orderly and formalized structure and exercise of authority. He is happily married, has no children, and enjoys frequent Florida vacations, especially during the winter months. The president is extremely active in all activities of the enterprise. In the president's absence, the vice president is the nominal head of the firm and typically serves as executive vice president.

Vice president. The vice president joined the company three years ago. He is in his late thirties, an engineering graduate of the Case Institute of Technology. Immediately after graduation he was employed in the production-control department of a large manufacturing plant in the Cleveland area. After becoming manager of production control, he resigned to take the position of general manager of a middle-sized Cleveland assembly plant. From this position he was recruited for his present position. He is progressive, personable, technically capable, perceptive, and a student of managerial practices, having a particularly keen interest in the application of the behavioral sciences to management. He is divorced, has no children, and is devoted to the task of developing the company into a major producer. If he is successful, he stands to become quite well-to-do as a result of stock options which were a major attraction, along with the growth potential, for his joining the company.

General manager. The general manager is a former machine-shop operator and the codeveloper with the president of the current product. He is a high-school graduate and the husband of the secretary-treasurer. His knowledge of managerial practices is limited and he tends to be an intuitive manager of some skill. He is not enthusiastic about newer ideas of motivation, but relies basically on the "carrot and the stick" approach. Although tough-minded, he is considered to be a good boss, fair and consistent. Although he has the title of general manager, he tends to operate as a first-line supervisor. His ability to keep the machinery working, to innovate, and to operate efficiently on a shoe string, has earned him the admiration of his colleagues and employees. He tends to be impatient in group meetings and with what he calls "gobbledegook," red tape, and discussions that solve no problems. Next to the president, he and his wife own the largest block of stock in the company.

Secretary-treasurer. The secretary-treasurer, formerly the head of the commercial-science department in Beetland High School, is the wife of the general manager and the mother of two boys, one in junior high and the other in the agricultural and mechanical college nearby. As office manager and financial manager, she is thorough but relatively uninformed concerning more progressive and complex aspects of financial management. Although limited in her understanding of personnel management, she has performed a record-keeping function relative to personnel and is proud of her informational system. She is chairman of the personnel committee of the company, comprised of the operating executives of the board. In addition to managing the office and what centralized personnel activities are considered requisite (mainly record keeping, recruitment, rough screening, induction, and changes in employment status), she handles the wage administration function, including payroll. As secretary to the board, she plays a key role in many major decisions, and realizes it. She is not adverse to "throwing her weight around." Of the board members, she could be expected to be the least cooperative with the new personnel director.

Production manager. The production manager was formerly a mechanic in the machine shop of the general manager and assisted in the development of the planter. He is a skilled mechanic (not a machinist) who dropped out of school in the fifth grade to help support his family on the death of his father. He is without doubt the weakest link in the management team. He does not operate as a manager, but rather as a mechanical troubleshooter, leaving most of the organization and management to the general manager and vice president. He has extremely close relations with the employees, and on several occasions when union organizers appeared to be making headway in the company, he was instrumental in aborting election attempts. He is a slow-thinking, happy-go-lucky, somewhat superficial individual, often overimbibing, even on the job—an individual who has achieved status above his aspiration level. The president is extremely fond of him, having known him since he was "a little tyke." He is in his early fifties, married, and the father of seven children, varying in age from seven through thirty. None of the children has attended an institution of higher learning.

Banker. The banker member of the board is president of the First City Bank and chairman of the financial committee of the board. She is a dignified, somewhat pompous, "self-styled" financial expert. Although she never attended college, she has completed, through self-study, most of the American Institute of Banking courses. An excellent financial advisor

Form 4 (continued)

for farming and ranching operations, she has little understanding of modern financial operations in manufacturing. Her bank has loaned the company over $100,000 and she was elected to the board more to "ride herd" on the loan than to bring any financial expertise. She is extremely conservative, having been a member of the Daughters of the American Revolution in the early days of that organization's prominence. At seventy, she is a sharp, outspoken little woman.

Rancher. The last member of the board is a rancher—a local millionaire who operates one of the largest cattle-feeding operations in the West. He is an unimpressive-looking gentleman, normally wearing ranch clothing and cowboy boots. He has the third largest block of stock. Although he got his start from inherited land, he became a self-made millionaire by sheer hard work, and is an exponent of the Horatio Alger philosophy and the Protestant Ethic, using the flimsiest of excuses to expound at some length on how America is going to the devil, aided and abetted by the Democrats. He attended the state Agricultural College for one year, quitting in disgust because, as he frequently comments, "I knew more than the professors."

Name _____ Group Number _____

Date _____ Class Section _____ Hour _____ Score _____

PART C

Form 5 Criteria for Selecting a Personnel Administrator and Ratings of Job Applicants on the Criteria

Criteria: Major dimension of the personnel administrator's job (e.g., personal characteristics, knowledge, duties, skills, etc.)	Weight of the criteria	Job-applicant rating on the criteria (1–10) Applicant			Comments about applicants' performance and reasons for ratings
		1	2	3	
1.					
2.					
3.					
4.					
5.					
6.					
7.					
8.					
9.					
10.					
Total Scores					Final ordering of applicants 1st choice _____ 2nd choice _____ 3rd choice _____

Name _____ Group Number _____

Date _____ Class Section _____ Hour _____ Score _____

ASSESSMENT OF LEARNING IN PERSONNEL ADMINISTRATION

EXERCISE 1

1. Try to state the purpose of this exercise in one concise sentence.

2. Specifically what did you learn from this exercise (i.e., skills, abilities, and knowledge)?

3. How might your learning influence your role and your duties as a personnel administrator?

4. Describe the primary roles of a personnel administrator in a medium-sized manufacturing organization.

5. Additional questions given by your implementor:

Section 2 PLANNING FOR AN EFFECTIVE HUMAN RESOURCE SYSTEM

An effective system of human resource programs requires advance planning and information gathering. The specific decisions made concerning human resources, such as who should receive a promotion or how to improve performance, depend on the coordination of several types of informaiton about the organization, the environment in which it operates, its workers, and its jobs. Fig. 1 provides an overview of these processes.

MACROLEVEL:
Human Resource Planning and Forecasting

Section 2 contains two exercises which describe the major personnel planning and data-gathering processes. Planning at the organizational, or macro, level is required in order to ascertain the numbers and types of people required by an organization for various periods into the future. Organizations expand, merge, and/or change their product lines. Competent human resource forecasting is vital to determine the "gaps" between the current and desired levels and types of human resources needed to fulfill the organization's objectives, and the feasibility of alternative human resource strategies. Obviously, organizations cannot anticipate all future events, but they can put systems into place that can cope with and take advantage of changes. Worker succession (i.e., persons leaving and replaced by others) further complicates the forecasting task. As the dynamic nature of staffing an organization is considered, internal succession plans are required to point to appropriate successors. Human resource plans and forecasts, examined in Exercise 2, provide the data to facilitate organizational decision making under uncertain environmental conditions and internal worker succession.

MICROLEVEL:
Job Analysis

Planning and data gathering are also required at the job, or micro, level. Here, jobs must be analyzed in order to decide what tasks are to be performed and the worker characteristics (knowledge, skills, and abilities) required. This job information is then transformed into selection standards, performance standards, and training needs, forming the foundation for other human resource programs. Probably no single personnel activity is so fundamental and basic as job analysis. Exercise 3 describes the job-analysis process, how job descriptions are derived from such an analysis, and how job performance is thus identified.

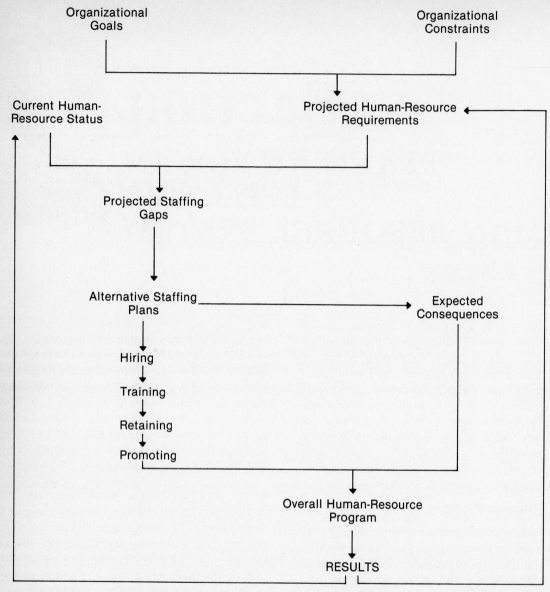

Fig. 1. An Overall View of Human-Resource Analysis and Planning (Adapted from G. T. Milkovich and T. A. Mahoney, "Human Resource Planning and PAIR Policy," in D. Yoder and H. G. Heneman, Jr., eds., *ASPA Handbook of Personnel and Industrial Relations,* vol. 4, Washington D.C., Bureau of National Affairs, Inc., 1976.)

Exercise 2
Human resource planning and forecasting

PREVIEW

In order to help assure that the future human resource needs of organizations are fulfilled with highly qualified personnel, considerable planning and analysis may be required. This type of planning is often initiated or facilitated either by the personnel administrator or by his or her own staff. To utilize the skills or present human resources most effectively, as well as to plan for future personnel needs in light of the rapidly changing external environments in which many organizations operate, all phases of personnel work must be coordinated and integrated. For example, without an accurate performance appraisal system an organization would not be able to identify its most promotable workers, those who must assume its top positions in the future. Without an effective training program, necessary skills cannot be added to workers' repertoires to enable them to assume more responsibility. Therefore, human resource planning is, in a way, an activity that utilizes and depends on the other personnel programs.

It is also, however, an activity on which the other personnel programs depend as well. Once the number and type of workers are known, their selection can be made more effectively. Once the skill levels an organization would require in the future due to product or technology changes are forecasted, training programs can be designed to impart these skills and prepare workers for future demands. Competent human-resource planning and forecasting enables the personnel specialist to achieve a broad, overall view of where his or her organization is headed in terms of human resource utilization. This overall forecast can then be related to each specific area or personnel program, beginning with job analyses. Finally, once the overall forecasts are complete, the costs of adding additional human resources (including benefits) can be estimated and evaluated for feasibility.

This exercise enables you to simulate the human resource planning process for an organization by assessing its current skills; by developing a forecast of human resource requirements and costs five years in the future after analyzing the organization's goals and environment; and finally by deciding who, from amongst the organization's current pool of workers, should assume anticipated future openings based on their present performance levels and their potential. The *Introduction* provides an overview of human resource planning, including its purposes, its importance, and the process of implementing plans.

OBJECTIVES

1. To gain an understanding of the purpose and importance of accurately forecasting future human resource requirements of organizations.

2. To analyze current personnel skill inventories and to make forecasts of future human resource needs.

3. To analyze present performance and potential of managers, using this data to decide who should fill future forecasted vacancies.

4. To estimate the human resource costs associated with human resource forecasts.

PREMEETING PREPARATION

Read the entire exercise, paying careful attention to the *Procedure.*

INTRODUCTION

Planning for Future Human Resource Requirements

Essentially, human resource planning efforts have as their goal the estimation and recognition of future human resource requirements and the development of strategies to insure that these requirements will be met by securing a supply of human resources from outside the organization and by developing the organization's present supply of human resources.

Organizations exist in environments that are dynamic to varying degrees. These environments contain elements that present uncertainties to organizations because they change—often very rapidly and unpredictably. For example, due to changing societal values and norms, consumers' tastes change, in turn causing certain products' sales to decline and others' to rise. The earth's supply of resources (such as oil and natural gas) changes, causing shifts in technology and numbers of job openings in specific industries. Organizations can never be totally accurate in predicting what effects various environmental changes will have, but to the extent that these can be anticipated and planned, organizations are better able to diminish possible adverse effects and/or turn new circumstances into opportunities.

One of the most crucial areas in which organizations must plan and anticipate changes concerns its human resources. No employee can be counted on forever. Eventually, all personnel change ("turnover") and must be replaced due to promotions, retirements, job changes, expansions, mergers, terminations, etc. In addition to employees leaving organizations to find better or different jobs, external environmental changes like those noted above, as well as planned expansion, contraction, merger, and acquisitions, all contribute to changing human resources in an organization. These changes must be anticipated. Plans to recruit, train, and place new human resources must be made in order to assure the smooth and continued functioning of an organization.

The changing composition of the United States labor force presents further uncertainties. Numbers of workers in service-oriented industries are increasing, as are demands for scientific and engineering personnel, while percentages of blue-collar workers are declining. Women are comprising an ever-larger percentage of the work force, as are younger people, and the average educational levels for workers are certainly increasing.[1] These changes are augmented by changes in job content. Computers and other technological advances have changed how many people do their jobs. Further, migrations of workers—for example, from rural to urban areas—have been observed for some time.

All of these changes are compounded by the belief of some researchers that an upcoming shortage in managerial resources is imminent. John Miner, who has studied the supply of managers and college graduates' inclinations to be managers, stated:

> It seems likely, then, that by the mid-1980s the major constraint on corporate growth will not necessarily be a shortage of monetary or material resources, but rather a shortage of managerial resources—there will not be enough good managers around. . . .[2]

The forecasting of future human resource needs is beset by uncertainty. However, this very uncertainty now makes human resource planning as important to the success of an organization as inventory, financial, or product planning have been in the past. Also, human resource planning *must* be viewed as a critical component of a larger, total business planning effort that is linked to the overall organizational mission.

Human resource plans are most often coordinated and begun at top levels of an organization—for example, the chief executive officer may "groom" a replacement. While many managers prefer a personal say in determining their replacement as they retire or are promoted, a broader set of organizational needs must be considered. Therefore, planning should be integrated across all organizational levels.

Plans are also made for various time periods. These range from immediate plans, which forecast needs in the next few months, to long-range plans, which involve forecasts ten or more years hence. Ob-

---

[1] See various annual issues of the *Manpower Report of the President* (Washington, D.C.: U.S. Government Printing Office).

[2] J. B. Miner, "The Real Crunch in Managerial Manpower," *Harvard Business Review* 51, no. 6 (November–December 1973): 147.

viously, the certainty and accuracy of the plans decline as the time interval increases, but long-range plans are still necessary in order to assure, for example, adequate staffing for tasks involving technology that is now only in its infancy but which may eventually become commonplace.

The strategies or plans actually developed to meet human resource requirements are closely related to other personnel programs, as noted earlier in the *Preview*. Job analyses and descriptions enable planners to zero in on the types of tasks in which openings will arise; performance appraisals allow for accurate identification of potential promotees to fill future vacancies; selection techniques help bring in valuable human resources from sources external to the organization; training and development programs prepare personnel for future assignments; and motivation programs help provide the incentive to workers to add skills and abilities and/or to perform well enough to be included in the lists of replacements for those now at upper levels.

The Sequential Process of Human-Resource Planning. The broad tasks required to design and implement a human resource planning system are pictured as a sequential process in Fig. 1. Each of the major steps in the process is discussed briefly below.

Inputs. In order to develop plans and forecasts of future needs, planners must identify and analyze the goals or intentions of organizations. For example: Is expansion or contraction intended? (See Fig. 2.) Are new products or services requiring new technologies

intended? In addition, various aspects of the external environment must be measured and used to make plans. These might include general economic conditions, societal norms and values, the political and legal climate, or the size and composition of the labor supply. All of this data forms the inputs into the planning system and thus is the rationale for the plans and forecasts themselves.

Analysis of current human resource skills. The second phase of the planning process would be an analysis of internal employee availability within the organization in terms of human resources. These internal labor supplies are often referred to as "stocks" of employees.

This process results in an inventory of skills, potential, age, time in current position, and salary for each employee. Figs. 2, 3, 4, and 5 provide graphic illustrations of such distributions for an organization. Such illustrations can help an organization to better understand its human resources status and more effectively plan for the future. Adequate performance appraisal systems (Exercises 4 and 5) would be required to measure current skill levels accurately, as would Assessment Centers (see Exercise 8) or other similar techniques that might be required to evaluate the potential of workers. This data is used to form a baseline or current level of human resource abilities which would be available for future requirements. Differences between the eventual forecast of numbers, types, and skill levels of future human resources and the levels represented by the current inventory must be either developed from existing personnel, based on

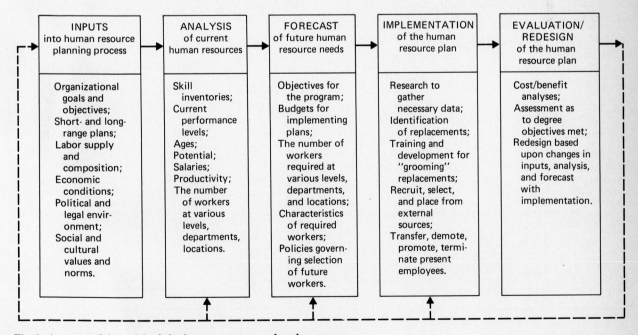

Fig. 1. A sequential model of the human-resource planning process

their potential, or secured from sources external to the organization.

Forecasts. Armed with the intended goals of the organization, other external environmental inputs, and what is currently available in terms of human resources, planners can begin to synthesize all of this data into forecasted requirements for different time periods. They extrapolate from past environmental trends and intended future goals; estimate the progression of employees in terms of skills and movement through levels of the hierarchy; account for retirement, turnover, etc.; and use any other relevant data in order to come up with a forecast of the number and type of human resources required for various future periods, such as one, two, or five years hence. An example of an actual and forecasted age distribution for an organization is provided in Fig. 5.

Planners must then develop budgets that reflect the costs of securing or developing the necessary workers. Costs might include recruiting new personnel, orientation and training programs, and retraining and developing current workers. Policies and guidelines are also necessary in order to advise decision makers regarding such matters as how future replacements will be selected, whether full- or part-time workers will be needed, or how career development should proceed. The specific data needed in order to implement plans must be identified. This might include current performance levels, age, turnover ratios, or salary levels.

Implementation. Once the forecasts of future needs for various time periods have been made, the plan must be implemented. Implementation of the plan may involve actually conducting research to gather the necessary data on which to base decisions; the recruitment of human resources to fill vacancies; the appraisal of performance to determine strengths, deficiencies, and promotability potential; training and development to prepare employees to meet future needs; and transfers, terminations, promotions, and other placement changes designed to minimize the match between job requirements and workers' abilities. Changes or movement of internal labor supplies are referred to as "flows" of employees.

Implementation of human resource plans is very difficult and must be closely coordinated with line personnel, as they help supply necessary data and make decisions. The time period of this phase, of course, depends on the time frame for which the plan was intended. For example, a plan designed to meet staffing requirements for a new plant scheduled to begin operations in twelve months must be completed before that time.

Evaluation and redesign. No plans are perfect and no forecasts are completely accurate, simply because they are based on imperfect information about the future. Of the many things that can change during the course of a human resource planning effort, changes in organizational goals, turnover of key personnel, and changes in economic conditions are but a few.

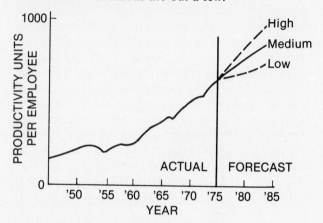

Fig. 2. Productivity per employee over time

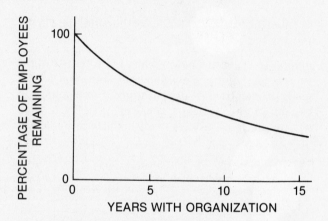

Fig. 3. Retention rates of employees with zero to fifteen years of experience with the organization

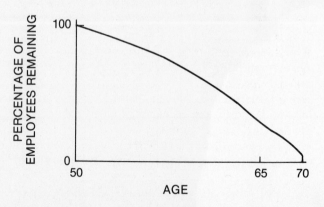

Fig. 4. Retention rates of employees age 50 to 70

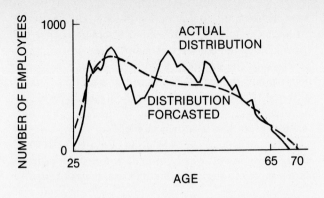

Fig. 5. Actual and forecasted age distribution of employees

Therefore, plans must be monitored, evaluated, and redesigned to assure their effectiveness by correcting errors and amending details as changes in inputs or forecasts occur. Plans should also be carefully evaluated as to their ability to attain their stated objectives. A plan designed to upgrade the skills of twenty military officers and to recruit officers to take their place would be evaluated on the basis of whether all the officers were able to successfully perform their new jobs, whether all twenty replacements were found and trained within the desired time period, and, of course, whether this was all done at the least possible cost.

Evaluation and redesign thus involve gathering data about the effectiveness of plans and amending them accordingly. The dotted feedback-loop lines in Fig. 1 represented this notion, as well as the ideas that human resource planning is a continual organizational process rather than a one-time event, responding to changes in an organization's goals and environment.

Other Issues in Human Resource Planning. This brief introduction has been quite selective. Actually, many other considerations, which can only be noted here, would be important in human resource planning.[3]

Career development is closely related to human resource planning and involves the provisions an organization (or an individual) makes in order to upgrade skills, abilities, and knowledge such that the individual can progress through several jobs in an occupation over time (see also Exercise 12). A career orientation is important for the organization, for it helps to assure loyalty and a source of experienced personnel. An opportunity for periodic promotion is also a powerful incentive to individuals. Many organizations have adopted a career orientation to certain classes of jobs

---

[3] Refer to *For Further Reading* for more information on these and other topics.

and design training and development programs which, when coupled with human resource planning, identify "paths" workers follow throughout their careers. A method of mathematically gauging the movement of employees in a path is through the use of a "transition matrix." An example of a transition matrix is shown in Fig. 6. The transition matrix depicts flows of people in an organization. For example, assume an organization had 100 Technician I's and 50 Technician II's in 1979. In 1981, they may have only 80 of the original Technician I group as Technician I's, and only 30 of the Technician II's still employed by the organization as Technician II's. This "flow" of technicians is represented as percentages in the transition matrix below:

1979	1981	
	Technician II	Technician I
Technician II	60%	
Technician I		80%

Now, suppose that 10 of the Technician I's were promoted to Technician II jobs, and that 10 of them left the organization. Also during the same period, 15 of the Technician II's left the organization and 5 were demoted to Technician I's. This flow analysis would appear in the transition matrix as:

1979	1981			
	Technician II	Technician I	Out of System	Total
Technician II	60%	10%	30%	100%
Technician I	10%	80%	10%	100%

Perhaps this will help in the interpretation of Fig. 6, which shows such a matrix for an entire organization for ten levels (positions) over a five-year time-span and also notes the percentage of total organizational hires in each of the ten positions.

In order to predict further into the future and to better anticipate the consequences of specific human resource plans, simulation is often employed. A model, representation, or abstraction of some type (e.g., mathematical or schematic) is made of a set of circumstances which describes a forecasted future state of an organization. The model defines the essential characteristics of the situation and the relationship between them. For example, a model of an intended merger might depict the relative number of workers in departments of one organization to those in similar departments of the other organization. Then different possible alternative outcomes (e.g., transfers, layoffs, etc.) are set and the model helps to predict, often with the aid of a computer, the consequences of the different outcomes.

If we wanted to determine how many workers might be required in five years in a certain department of the newly merged organization, we could put values in our model for the relationships between key variables. These might include the relative numbers of employees in the relevant departments of each separate organization before the merger, their past rates of growth, their past turnover rates, anticipated technology changes, etc. We could then, through mathematical manipulation or on a computer, arrive at an estimated number of workers. We could also put in other values for our variables and come out with an estimate of the number of workers required in other departments, in the entire merged organization, or at different time periods. A view of the strategies, critical variables, and objectives used in modeling human resource planning is shown in Fig. 7.

An example of the estimating of human resource hiring requirements which combines a transition matrix with simple estimating techniques is shown in Fig. 6:[4]

INTERNAL MANPOWER MOVEMENT*
FIVE YEAR TIME INTERVAL

Time I		A	B	C	D	E	F	G	H	I	J	Out	Total %
		Time II (5 years later)											
		Job Category											
Vice President	A											1.00	1.00
Department Head	B	1.00											1.00
Division Head	C		.11	.83								.06	1.00
District Head	D			.03	.97								1.00
Unit Head	E				.10	.87	.03						1.00
Technician II	F					.05	.90					.05	1.00
Technician I	G						.35	.65					1.00
Secretary	H								.85			.15	1.00
Clerk II	I								.10	.65	.05	.20	1.00
Clerk I	J									.10	.50	.40	1.00
% of total organizational recruitment								.18	.62		.20		1.00

*In percentages, not raw numbers.

Fig. 6. Internal manpower movement, five-year time interval

[4] Adapted from Robert H. Flast, "Taking the Guesswork Out of Affirmative Action Planning," *Personnel Journal* 56, no. 2 (February 1977): 68–71.

STRATEGIES	CRITICAL VARIABLES	OBJECTIVES

Organization
  skill mix
  task organization
  team organization		

Individual performance
  performance standards
  feedback policy		

Staffing
  recruiting efforts
  selection criteria
  promotion and transfer
    policy
	Technology
	
	Manpower and man-hours
	
	External labor force
		Sales
		
		Productivity
		
		Output

Training and development
  educational level
  skills training
  team building
  career development
  experience requirements
	Skills and job matches
	
	Effort and motivation
	
	Absenteeism and turnover
		Labor costs
		
		Legal compliance

Compensation
  wage level
  salary structure
  increase policy
	External labor supplies	

Labor relations
  bargaining scope
  negotiation strategy
  grievance process		

Fig. 7. Strategies, critical variables, and objectives in human resource planning (adapted from G. T. Milkovich and T. A. Mahoney, "Human Resources Planning and PAIR Policy," in D. Yoder and H. G. Heneman, Jr., eds., *APSA Handbook of Personnel and Industrial Relations,* vol. 4, Washington, D.C., Bureau of National Affairs, Inc., 1976.)

If we analyze Fig. 8 and now ask whether the organization will reach its hiring goals given the past flows of employees and the forecasted hiring patterns, the answer to this question is calculated as indicated in Fig. 9.

Thus the organization has fallen short of its goals for both professionals (i.e., $63 < 80$) and managers (i.e., $36 < 40$) at the end of the second year. What, then, would be the annual hiring requirements given this set of assumptions.?[5]

_____

[5] The answer is 31 professionals and 8 managers per year as determined by the following linear programming equations attempting to minimize E (the greater of the two excesses):

Minimize E
Subject to:
$$0 \leqslant (30.60 + 1.60P + 0.05M) - 80 \leqslant E$$
$$0 \leqslant (24.10 + 0.10P + 1.80M) - 40 \leqslant E$$
$$0 \leqslant P, M$$

There are, however, limitations or warnings about applying transition matrices in human resource planning. First, the time interval must be long enough for movement to occur, yet short enough not to have many multiple movements. Second, smaller sample sizes increase the standard error of estimate for each movement. Third, the state or conditions used are also limited by sample size; thus, the use of multiple options within each state (e.g., reasons for leaving as options for the turnover states) is reduced. A fourth major assumption required is the presumed stability of external conditions and organizational structure. If a major reorganization has occurred externally, this

_____

An elaboration of linear programming is beyond our scope here; it is merely noted to demonstrate how such problems can be solved. It should also be noted that there are possible methods for achieving the goals other than increasing the hiring rates, such as reducing turnover.

Annual Flows of Employees

Time II (T plus 1 yr.)

Time I (T)	Professionals	Managers	Out	Σ
Professionals	60%	10%	30%	100%
Managers	5%	80%	15%	100%

Forecasted Need in 2 Years

	Number of current employees	Number of employees 2 years hence
Professionals	80	80
Managers	20	40
Σ	100	120

Annual Planned Hiring Objectives

	Average number of hires in the past	Planned number of hires for *each* of the next 2 years
Professionals	10	20
Managers	2	5
Σ	12	25

Fig. 8. Past flows of employees and forecasted hiring patterns

Year 1

	Retained	Hired	Moved from other position	Σ
Professionals	48 (.6 × 80)	20	1 (.05 × 20)	69
Managers	16 (.8 × 20)	5	8 (.10 × 80)	29

Year 2

	Retained	Hired	Moved from other position	Σ
Professionals	41.4 (.6 × 69)	20	1.45 (.05 × 29)	62.85
Managers	23.2 (.8 × 29)	5	6.9 (.10 × 69)	35.10

Fig. 9. Calculation of required employees

confuses the real rates of career movement. Finally, the longer the forecasted period, the greater the probability of inaccuracy of the forecast.[6]

---

[6] H. G. Heneman III and M. G. Sandver, "Markov Analysis in Human Resource Administration: Applications and Limitations," *Academy of Management Review* 2 (October 1977): 535–542.

Of course, the accuracy of any estimate depends on the accuracy of the data the model used and the accuracy of the relationship between the variables. But simulation can allow us to anticipate consequences of various alternatives without actually having to manipulate employees or resources. Simulation can provide planners with important information, provided it is based on accurate data.

The final consideration in this discussion of human resource planning is its relation to the public policy goals of eliminating unemployment and of increasing and upgrading the employment situation of minority-group members. Public policy regarding human resource planning on a national level has changed considerably over the years. One of the most striking changes is the nature of vocational education in the United States as it has evolved into new uses for developing human resources at all levels in American society. Vocational education (i.e., training people for employment in trades) is no longer confined to the secondary-school level. Programs such as the Model Cities Program, the Special Impact Program, the New Careers Program, Operation Mainstream, the Concentrated Employment Program (CEP), and the Work Incentive Program (WIN) are all aspects of contemporary human resource development and planning, as well as poverty fighting, which illustrates the federal government's and other organizations' concern with these issues.

The federal government has realized that it cannot single-handedly solve all of the complicated social problems involved in human resource planning and development, and it has increasingly asked industry to intervene. Industry, in turn, has shown willingness to participate widely in administering Job Corps centers, accepting on-the-job trainees under the Manpower Training and Development Act (MTDA), and in making proposals for the expansion of vocational curricula in junior colleges and in high schools where funds from the Vocational Education Act of 1963 and 1968 amendments are being expended.

There is little doubt that the human resources "revolution" of the 1960s (i.e., all of the legislation enacted during that decade) will continue to influence education, employment, and planning. The emphasis on federal government programs in education and human resources continues to influence school administrators at state and local levels to use human resource planners in their organizations in order to reassess their own human resource plans in light of federal programs and objectives.

While there is still much work to be done in coordinating and formulating federal educational and organizational programs into a cohesive human-resources plan that incorporates the goals and needs of each, some progress has been made. However, the uncertainty and change that surround the planning process will no doubt become more prevalent in the future, thus making human resource planning not only more important but also more difficult. This area offers one of the greatest challenges to those beginning personnel careers in the near future.

PROCEDURE

Overview. You are to determine the human resource needs in the situations described and plan how these needs will be met. Human resource projections, cost estimates, and skill inventories are provided to help you develop a human resource forecast.

PART A

STEP 1: In Form 1 there are basic questions about the status of an organization as it faces growth. Essentially, the questions are about the "stock" of employees at the beginning of a three-year period and at the end of the period. The calculations required ask you to forecast future human resource requirements, the cost of additional employees, and the sales levels required to finance the expansion of the labor force. You are to calculate the costs and other projections asked in Form 1.

   TIME: About 30 minutes.

STEP 2: In Form 2 is a simple transition matrix demonstrating the annual flows of the internal labor supplies for professionals who become (promoted, demoted, etc.) managers and vice versa. Use the information provided in Form 2 to answer Questions 1–3.

   TIME: About 35 minutes.

STEP 3: In Form 3 is a transition matrix from which you are to make a decision about the "flows" as you observe them in the matrix. Please answer the questions at the bottom of the matrix.

   TIME: About 25 minutes.

PART B

STEP 4: For this part you may be assigned to groups for forecasting the entire organization or to a group for only one department of the organization. Your instructor will advise you. Several forms are necessary in order to complete Step 1. Form 4 provides information about Happy-

day Corporation, the company for which your human-resource plan is to be written. Form 5 provides an estimated annual average of job openings and an estimate of whether the openings can be filled with qualified applicants for the next ten years relative to certain job statistics for the southern United States. Forms 6 and 7 are examples of information kept on each Happyday manager's skill level and potential, which provides data for the skill inventory the personnel department maintains. A summary of the vital data for each manager is found on Form 8, the personnel department's skill inventory for the entire group of ninety-seven managers in Happyday Corporation. Complete Form 10 by answering *all* of the questions.

Develop an organizational chart for Form 10 (you may be assigned only one department on the entire organization). Then decide how many managers will be required to meet the needs of Happyday in three years and draw a new organizational chart on Form 11. Decide how many people are available to fill vacancies and who should fill them (i.e., fill in names of actual workers from Form 8). If positions can not be filled from internal organizational sources, indicate that external sources will be used. Form 11 should reflect the department's personnel and their organizational levels. For example, if you feel that the accounting department should have twenty managers in three years, twenty names (or "external hire" designations) are placed on Form 11.

In forecasting, you should consider possible retirements and persons you wish to terminate or demote. These are your decisions for the forecasted organization. You should also consider the rates at which departments should grow. For example, will marketing and manufacturing grow at the rate of roles growth? What about finance and accounting? Are there any economies of scale to be gained? At what rate will personnel grow with the additional hiring requirements?

   TIME: About 1½ hours.

STEP 5: After you have completed your future organizational chart, you are to calculate the costs of your department using the information on Form 13.

   TIME: About 1 hour.

STEP 6: If you have done only one department, you

may now be directed by your instructor to meet with other departments and negotiate over managers that have been placed by others in their departments as opposed to yours. A discussion of what the final organizational chart would look like could then be held. The *total* costs of the expansion could then be determined and compared to the forecasted sales to see if the costs exceed the 46 percent of the sales figure of $54,000,000 (see the bottom of Form 13).

TIME: About 1 hour.

FOR FURTHER READING*

Alfred T. M. "Checkers or Choice in Manpower Management." *Harvard Business Review* 45 (1967): 157–169. (I)

Batholomew, D. J., and A. F. Forbes, *Statistical Techniques for Manpower Planning.* Chichester, England: Wiley, 1979, pp. 85–164. (II)

Bright, W. E. "How One Company Manages Its Human Resources." *Harvard Business Review* 54 (January-February 1976): 81-93. (I)

Brummet, R. L., W. C. Pyle, and E. G. Flamholtz. "Human Resource Accounting in Industry." *Personnel Administration* 32 (July-August 1969): 34-46. (I)

Burack, E. H. *Manpower Planning and Programming.* Morristown, New Jersey: General Learning Press, 1971. (II)

Burack, E. H., and T. J. McNichols. *Human Resource Planning.* Kent, Ohio: Kent State University, Comparative Administration Research Institute, 1973. (II)

Burack, E. H., and J. W. Walker, eds. *Manpower Planning and Programming.* Boston: Allyn and Bacon, 1972. (II)

Cierillo, V. R., and R. B. Frantzreb. "A Human Resource Planning Model." *Human Factors* 17 (1975): 35-41. (II)

Clough, D. J. et al., eds. *Manpower Planning Models.* New York: Crane Russak, 1974. (II)

Coleman, B. "An Integrated System for Manpower Planning." *Business Horizons* 13 (October 1970): 89-95. (I)

Crites, J. O. *Vocational Psychology.* New York: McGraw-Hill, 1969. (II)

Davies, G. K. "Needed: A National Job Matching Network." *Harvard Business Review* 47 (1969): 63-72. (I)

*See also references listed in Exercise 12 pertaining to career planning and development.

Deckard, N. S., and K. W. Lessey. "A Model for Understanding Management Manpower: Forecasting and Planning." *Personnel Journal* 54 (1975): 169-173+. (I)

Dill, W. R., D. P. Gavar, and W. C. Weber. "Models and Modeling for Manpower Planning." *Management Science* 13 (1966): B142-B167. (II)

Drandell, M. "A Composite Forecasting Methodology for Manpower Planning Using Objective and Subjective Criteria." *Academy of Management Journal* 18 (1975): 510-519. (II-R)

Dukes, C. W. "EDP Personnel File Searching: A Variable Parameter Approach." *Personnel* 44 (July-August 1972): 20-26. (I)

Glickman, A. S. et al. *Top Management Development and Succession.* Supplementary paper #27, Committee for Economic Development, November 1968. (II)

Heneman, H. G., Jr., and G. Seltzer. "Employer Manpower Planning and Forecasting." *Manpower Research Monograph No. 19.* Washington, D.C.: U.S. Government Printing Office, 1970. (I)

Heneman, H. G., III, and M. G. Sandver. "Markov Analysis in Human Resource Administration: Applications and Limitations." *Academy of Management Review* 2 (October 1977): 535-542. (II-R)

Holland, J. L. "Vocational Preferences." In M. D. Dunnette, ed., *Handbook of Industrial/Organizational Psychology.* Chicago: Rand McNally, 1976. (II)

Kelley, S. C. et al. *Manpower Forecasting in the United States: An Evaluation of the State of the Art.* Columbus: Ohio State University Center for Human Resource Research, 1975. (II)

Ledvinka, J., and R. L. LaForge. "A Staffing Model for Affirmative Action Planning." *Human Resource Planning* 3 (1978): 135-150. (II-R)

Lenninger, R. A. "Personnel Management and the Computer." *Personnel Administrator* 20, no. 1 (January 1975): 54-55. (I)

Lester, R. A. *Manpower Planning in a Free Society.* Princeton, New Jersey: Princeton University Press, 1966. (I)

Levitan, S. A., and J. K. Zickler. *The Quest for a Federal Manpower Partnership.* Cambridge, Mass.: Harvard University Press, 1974. (I)

Livingston, J. S. "The Myth of the Well-Educated Manager." *Harvard Business Review,* January-February 1971. (I)

Mace, Myles L. *The Growth and Development of Executives.* Boston: Graduate School of Business Administration, Harvard University, 1950. (I)

Mahoney, T. A., and G. T. Milkovich. "Computer

Simulation: A Training Tool for Manpower Managers." *Personnel Journal* 54 (December 1975): 609–612+. (II)

Mahoney, T. A., and G. T. Milkovich. "An Empirical Investigation of Internal Labor Markets." *Proceedings of Annual Meeting of Academy of Management,* 1972, pp. 203–207. (II–R)

Mangum, G. *The Emergence of Manpower Policy.* New York: Holt, 1969. (I)

Manpower Report of the President. Washington, D.C.: U.S. Government Printing Office (annually). (II)

Martin, R. "Skills Inventories." *Personnel Journal* 48 (1967): 28–30. (I)

Milkovich, G. T., A. J. Annoni, and T. A. Mahoney, "The Use of Delphi Procedures in Manpower Forecasting." *Management Science* 19 (1972): 281–288. (II–R)

Milkovich, G. T., and T. A. Mahoney, "Human Resource Planning Models: A Perspective." *Human Resource Planning* 1 (1978): 19-30. (II)

Milkovich, G. T., and T. A. Mahoney, "Human Resource Planning and PAIR Policy." In D. Yoder and H. G. Heneman, Jr., eds., *ASPA Handbook of Personnel and Industrial Relations,* Vol. 4. Washington, D.C.: Bureau of National Affairs, Inc., 1976. (I)

Milkovich, G. T., and F. Krzystofiak. "Simulation and Affirmative Action Planning." *Human Resource Planning* 2 (1979): 65–82. (II–R)

Miner, J. B. *The Human Constraint: The Coming Shortage of Managerial Talent.* Washington, D.C.: Bureau of National Affairs, 1974. (I)

Miner, J. B. *Studies in Management Education.* New York: Springer, 1965. (I)

Patten, T. J., Jr. *Manpower Planning and the Development of Human Resources.* New York: Wiley, 1972. (II)

Pinto, P. R. et al. *Career Planning and Career Management: Perspectives of the Individual and the Organization. An Annotated Research Bibliography.* Minneapolis, Minn.: Industrial Relations Center Bulletin No. 62. University of Minnesota, 1975. (I)

"Plotting a Route to the Top." *Business Week,* Personal Business Supplement, 12 October 1974.

Singleton, W. T., and P. Spurgeon, eds. *Measurement of Human Resources.* New York: Halsted, 1975. (I)

Snyder, R. J., and G. Herman. *Manpower Planning: A Research Bibliography.* Minneapolis, Minn.: Industrial Relations Center, Bulletin No. 45, University of Minnesota, 1967. (I)

Staszak, F. J., and N. J. Mathys. "Organiztion Gap: Implications for Manpower Planning." *California Management Review* 17 (Spring 1975): 32-38. (I)

Steiner, G. A. *Top Management Planning.* New York: Macmillan, 1969. (I)

Vetter, E. W. *Manpower Planning for High Talent Personnel.* Ann Arbor, Mich.: University of Michigan, Bureau of Industrial Relations, 1967. (II)

Vroom, V. H., and K. R. MacCrimmon. "Toward a Stochastic Model of Managerial Careers." *Administrative Science Quarterly* 13 (1968): 26–46. (II–R)

Walker, J. W. "Problems in Managing Manpower Change." *Business Horizons* 13 (1970): 63–68. (I)

Walker, J. W. "Forecasting Manpower Needs." *Harvard Business Review* 47 (1969): 152–164. (I)

Wickstrom, W. S. *Manpower Planning: Evolving Systems.* New York: Conference Board, 1971. (I)

Wortman, M. "Manpower: The Management of Human Resources." *Academy of Management Journal* 13 (1970): 198-208. (I)

Yoder, D. "Manpower Management Planning." In D. Yoder, *Personnel Management and Industrial Relations.* 6th ed. Englewood Cliffs, New Jersey: Prentice-Hall, 1970, Chap. 8. (I)

Zalesnick, A. et al., eds. *Orientation and Conflict in Career.* Cambridge, Mass.: Harvard Business School, 1970. (II–R)

Name _____ Group Number _____

Date _____ Class Section _____ Hour _____ Score _____

PART A

Form 1 Forecasting Human Resources

1. An organization's sales will increase 30 percent (adjusted for inflation) at the end of the next three-year period. If its managerial labor force increased by half this percentage, how many additional managers are needed at the end of the three-year period if the organization has 60 managers presently?

   Number of additional managers needed at the end of the three-year period: _____

   Calculation:

2. If the organization's managerial salaries average $25,000 plus 35 percent in fringe benefits, what is the net additional annual cost for the added managers at the end of the three-year period? (Assume a 9 percent annual rate of inflation on both wages and fringes for each of the three years. Remember to compound the 9 percent over three years.)

   Net cost addition for adding 15 percent new managers in three years: _____

   Calculation:

3. If the organization has a span-of-control ratio of 5:1, how many nonmanagerial employees will need to be added by the end of the three-year period?

   Number of nonmanagerial persons added: _____

   Calculation:

4. If nonmanagerial employees' average wages are $11,000 plus 30 percent fringes, what is the net annual additional cost for adding nonmanagerial employees at the end of the three-year period? (Again, assume 9 percent annual inflation rate on both wages and fringes.)

   Net annual cost addition of adding nonmanagerial employees at the end of the three-year period: _____

   Calculation:

Form 1 (continued)

5. What is the annual employee cost of both the additional managerial and nonmanagerial employees?

   Net additional employee cost at the end of the three-year period: _____

   Calculation:

6. If total labor costs are 60 percent of sales, what additional sales volume must be achieved at the end of the three-year period to cover the additional employee costs?

   Sales volume increase needed to cover additional employees in years: _____

   Calculation:

7. Given the historical and projected sales growth pattern shown below, will the organization be able to afford the additional cost of expanding its number of human resources? _____

Two years ago:	Last year:	This year:	Projected at the end of three years:
20 million	22.5 million	26 million	34 million

   Calculation:

Name _____ Group Number _____

Date _____ Class Section _____ Hour _____ Score _____

PART A

Form 2 Projected Hiring Needs to Meet Human Resource Forecasts

Annual Flows of Employees

Time II (T + 1 yr.)

Time I (T)	Professionals	Managers	Out	Σ
Professionals	70%	10%	20%	100%
Managers	5%	85%	10%	100%

Forecasted Need in 2 Years

	Number of current employees	Forecasted number of employees needed in 2 years
Professionals	90	120
Managers	20	60
Σ	110	180

Annual Planned Hiring Objectives

	Average number of hires in the past	Planned number of hires for *each* of the next 2 years
Professionals	5	20
Managers	10	30
Σ	15	50

QUESTIONS TO BE ANSWERED:

1. What is the staffing level in professional and managerial jobs *one year* from now? _____

    Number of Managers: _____

    Calculation:

Form 2 (continued)

Number of Professionals: _____

Calculation:

2. What is the staffing level for both jobs *two years* from now?

Managers: _____

Professionals: _____

3. Did the organization meet its goal?   Yes ____   No ____

If it did not exactly meet its goal, what could be done by the organization in the two-year period to help it reach its goals?*

1. _____   5. _____
2. _____   6. _____
3. _____   7. _____
4. _____   8. _____

4. What would the one- and two-year staffing patterns look like if the organization doubled its *projected* hiring rates and cut in half the hiring rate for managers?

_____

*You could write a set of linear programming equations to solve this problem (i.e., determine the approximate number of hirings each year for both professional and managerial jobs to exactly meet the goal—assuming the organization wants to keep its staffing activity at about the same level each year to avoid swings in the personnel department's effort).

Name _____ Group Number _____

Date _____ Class Section _____ Hour _____ Score _____

PART A

Form 3 Internal Human Resource Allocation—Females—Five-Year Time Interval

TIME II

TIME I		A	B	C	D	E	F	G	H	I	J	Out	Total
Vice President	A												
Director	B			1.00									1.00
Prin. Scientist	C												
Assoc. Sci.	D												
Assist. Sci.	E			.25	.25	.50							1.00
Technician II	F						1.0						1.00
Technician I	G						.10	.78	.10			.02	1.00
Secretary	H							.10	.65			.25	1.00
Clerk II	I								.20	.70		.10	1.00
Clerk I	J									.40	.50	.10	1.00
	Recruited			.06	.04	.30	.30			.03	.27		1.00

1. On which job in the transition matrix is there an error?

   A—Vice president
   B—Director
   C—Principal scientist
   D—Associate scientist
   E—Assistant scientist

2. On which job in the transition matrix is there no movement of females?

   A—Vice president
   B—Principal scientist
   C—Associate scientist
   D—Technician II
   E—Clerk I

3. From what jobs listed below have women been demoted?

   A—Vice president
   B—Technician II
   C—Associate scientist
   D—Assistant scientist
   E—Director

4. What conclusions can you reach from the information found in this transition matrix?

   A. _____

   B. _____

   C. _____

PART B

Form 4 Descriptive Information for the Happyday Corporation

Happyday, located in a large southern city, is a small to medium-sized manufacturer of consumer goods relating to sports and recreation activities. It is a family-controlled organization begun about twenty-five years ago. In the late 1970s, Happyday was considering a major expansion of facilities and product lines to tap the rapidly growing and diversified recreational market.

The five-year outlook for obtaining and developing key managerial personnel was not especially bright in the light of technological changes and corporate expansion plans which would require much technical expertise and innovative ability. Basically, the production techniques, the products, and the consumers themselves had grown very sophisticated in the last decade, and in order to maintain a competitive advantage in an industry dominated by huge companies, Happyday had to be extremely creative and current regarding the technology required to produce its products. The plan for modernizing and expanding existing facilities indicated substantial redefinition of job roles, requiring innovative human-resource planning and organization design. It was predicted that future business needs would create demands for new specializations (particularly those in engineering).

Currently, Happyday has ninety-six persons in managerial positions. The managers are divided among departments as follows:

	Number of managers	Present average salary (without fringes)
Manufacturing	34	$26,065
Accounting	17	28,454
Finance	6	29,140
Marketing	13	37,900
Engineering	21	28,731
Personnel	5	26,248
	96	

However, because Happyday still plans to greatly increase its productive capacity, based on continued optimistic demand data for recreation and leisure products, they will need to add human resources in some areas and perhaps decrease them in other areas within the next five years in order to facilitate the expansion.

Specifically, Happyday is planning to begin increasing productive capacity within the next few months. Initially, contractors, architects, etc., will be needed as management has already decided the expansion is wise. Market research, new-product development, financial planning, and production planning and scheduling have each conducted independent analyses and have all agreed that expansion is feasible, desirable, and necessary at this time. Only personnel has not yet given its plan for future human-resource requirements and the feasibility of obtaining them.

The planned expansion includes additions to the engineering department for new product development and prototypes, to manufacturing for new work processes and scheduling, and to marketing for added sales capability and advertising. Of course, since new products will be designed, manufactured, and (hopefully) sold, these areas must grow. However, support areas would seem to grow also to serve the needs of the larger manufacturing organization.

Within the next three years, productive capacity is projected to increase by 50 percent. Physical facilities are already being finished to house manufacturing and administration expansion. The executive committee's estimate of sales three years from now, allowing for inflation, is $54,000,000.

Happyday has had a policy of promoting qualified personnel from within the organization before seeking outside candidates. This policy further implies consideration of the best-qualified people from all departments within the company rather than simply promoting only from within that department in which an opening occurs. This, according to the top management, fosters morale and better assures that the company promotes the best person from among all of its employees. It also affords the varied experience deemed necessary for top positions.

Typically, the personnel department provides assistance in locating qualified candidates and takes pride in its "Skill Inventory" (see Forms 7 and 8) of all personnel, an extremely current, and therefore valuable, selection and planning aid. A standard procedure in the past has been to consider at least two candidates from outside a department, as well as one or more from within, before a selection decision is made to fill a position. If no adequate applicants are found in this search, the organization turns to external labor sources, but stays within the southern United States for such recruiting efforts and usually enlists the aid of an executive search organization. The average retirement age at Happyday is 63, although the mandatory age is, of course, 70.

Each departmental vice president thus has the responsibility for seeking opportunities for promotion of qualified personnel, both in and out of his or her own department. While Happyday has always been concerned with human-resource planning and development, it has never before actually formulated an explicit human-resource

Form 4 (continued)

plan for a future three-year period. However, due to the importance and size of the planned expansion (including physical facilities, product lines, marketing capability, and technological advances), a formal plan of human-resource needs seems vital.

The financial picture of Happyday has been consistently bright and improving. The organization, witnessed by the historical balance-sheet (see Exhibit A), has a sound capital structure and relatively small debt obligations. Sales volume and net income have also increased in eight of the last ten years.

Exhibit A: Historical Abbreviated Financial Data for Happyday Company (in thousands of dollars)

Assets	Two years ago	Last year	This year
Cash	49	48	53
Marketable securities	150	165	170
Receivables, net	199	205	208
Inventories	300	310	324
Net plant and equipment	1300	1280	1273
Total assets	2000	2008	2028

Claims on Assets			
Accounts payable	60	59	63
Notes payable	100	97	106
Accruals	9	9	9
Federal income taxes accrued	131	135	140
Mortgage bonds	500	495	500
Stock	600	620	632
Retained earnings	600	593	578
Total claims on assets	1998	2008	2028

	Two years ago	Last year	This year
Net sales volume	30,000	32,500	36,000
Net income (after taxes)	921	1235	1386

Additional vital information on Happyday concerns its specific departments. These are reasonably autonomous units and their director or vice president typically has considerable authority for the departments' activities. However, due to Happyday's policy of attempting to fill a vacancy in any department with members of other departments before it resorts to external selection, the best people of various departments sometimes get "picked off" by others, thus leaving some with weak personnel at the top. Additional information about each department follows.

Manufacturing. The largest and most powerful department, it contains the two top (i.e., level 1) members of the organization. They are brothers. Directors or vice presidents are no higher than second-level officers, subordinates to the two persons at the top of the manufacturing department. The department lacks direction, as its senior people must take charge of the entire operation and their reluctance to delegate any authority in manufacturing is the reason for their failure to promote anyone to challenge their authority in the manufacturing department. Equipment is modern, but expertise in production planning and control is shallow. Ties to engineering are weak.

Accounting. Accounting is not a large group, but is very professional. It boasts graduates from very prestigious business schools and people from the "Big Eight" public accounting firms. The goals of the department are to educate managers in accounting practices and set up Happyday as an example in the industry of an organization that is able to implement the latest accounting conventions and rules correctly and efficiently.

Finance. This department is quite small, perhaps due to the family-owned nature of the company. One member of the department is a member of the family of the founders and owners of Happyday. The remainder of the department consists of managers with little power.

Marketing. This department is very viable and visible. It has a pool of creative people who have developed a very effective sales network. Their goals are to expand and begin to develop in-house advertising capability.

Form 4 (continued)

Engineering.   The engineering department is large, but contains many people who direct the maintenance system for machinery and other tangible assets. Liaison with the manufacturing department is poor, and this hinders morale in engineering. The best people hope for transfers to manufacturing where things actually happen. Engineering contains a small research and development (R-and-D) group who are given excellent physical resources and who are quite visible. However, their work is seldom advanced through manufacturing where the ideas for new products always seem to originate. R-and-D has been called a public-relations gimmick by some. The director of engineering was recently hired to develop the department into a viable force, particularly R-and-D, but is having problems retaining people. Turnover is a huge problem.

Personnel.   Personnel is the smallest department as far as number of managers, but has several clerks because of its record-keeping functions. Personnel is involved in an affirmative-action program, in union negotiations, and in contract administration almost exclusively. Selection and training are primarily decentralized (i.e., left to line managers). Performance appraisal and career development are the department's strong points. The assessment center method for spotting future managers is used very heavily.

PART B

Form 5 Current and Projected Employment Data for Selected Job Classes in the Southern United States*

Job class	Latest employment estimate	Predicted annual average job openings for next decade
ADMINISTRATION		
Accountants[†]	143,000	8,380
City managers	500	30
Credit officers	22,800	1,500
Personnel workers	48,000	4,160
Public relations workers	17,400	3,480
Total	231,700	17,550
COUNSELING		
Employment counselors[†]	1,700	160
Rehabilitation counselors[†]	3,200	340
School counselors	8,600	580
Total	13,500	1,080
OTHER SELECTED PROFESSIONS		
Architects	7,400	660
Commercial artists	8,000	600
Industrial designers	2,000	800
Landscape architects	2,500	200
Lawyers	61,000	4,000
Photographers	12,000	700
Programmers[†]	37,200	2,600
Systems analysts[†]	20,100	2,000
Total	150,200	11,560
MANAGERS		
Bank officers	45,000	4,000
Administrative officers	26,600	3,750
Office managers[†]	33,000	6,500
Supervisors (first level)	200,000	20,500
Total	304,600	34,750
ENGINEERS		
Aerospace[†]	12,400	340
Agricultural[†]	2,400	100
Ceramic	2,000	100
Chemical	9,400	300
Civil	35,400	1,700
Electrical	46,200	2,200
Industrial[†]	25,000	1,480
Mechanical	41,800	1,780
Metallurgical	2,000	100
Mining[†]	800	20
Total	177,400	8,120
PHYSICAL SCIENCES		
Chemists	26,800	1,360
Food scientists[†]	1,250	60
Physicists	9,800	300
Total	37,850	1,720

Form 5 (continued)

Job class	Latest employment estimate	Predicted annual average job openings for next decade
TECHNICIANS		
Computer servicepersons[†]	9,000	820
Draftspersons[†]	65,400	3,580
Engineering/science workers[†]	141,400	7,320
Total	215,800	11,720
SALES		
Manufacturers' salespersons[†]	106,700	5,000
Retail trade salespersons	576,000	43,000
Wholesale trade salespersons	125,600	6,200
Total	808,300	54,200

* Illustrative data.
† Jobs for which estimated number of qualified applicants will be smaller than number of openings.

PART B

Form 6 Sample Skill-Inventory Data Sheet Kept for Each Happyday Manager

Name _____ Employee No. _____ Age _____ Current position _____

Began current position _____ Evaluated by _____ Title _____ Date _____

I. **SKILLS:** Estimate current skill levels by checking the appropriate boxes below.

A. **Personal Independence:** Rate the amount of supervisory time required by individual. Consider time and assistance required in areas of problem solving, decision making, flexibility, creativity, initiative, follow-through.
[   ] 1. Seeks a great deal of supervisor's time.
[   ] 2. Occasionally requires attention beyond nature of assignments.
[   ] 3. Follows directions and instructions easily. Requires only routine checks on performance.
[   ] 4. Performs most tasks independently and requires help only in difficult situations.
[   ] 5. Can operate without direct supervision and can be left to complete assignments independently.

B. **Interpersonal Skills:** Evaluate individual's ability to work constructively with others without causing hard feelings. Measure tactfulness and human relations skills.
[   ] 1. Relations with co-workers and business associates is often poor.
[   ] 2. Gains moderate acceptance over time, but is not particularly active.
[   ] 3. Generally achieves good acceptance from co-workers and business associates.
[   ] 4. Actively establishes good interpersonal relations with associates.
[   ] 5. Is extremely successful at gaining quick and lasting acceptance from others.

C. **Oral and Written Communications:** Evaluate this individual's ability to express thoughts and ideas and have them understood by others.
[   ] 1. Fails to communicate with satisfactory clarity and organization.
[   ] 2. Occasional lack of clarity and conciseness in communications.
[   ] 3. Quite acceptable communication skills in the tasks associated with current assignment.
[   ] 4. Noticeably well organized in communication of thoughts, reports, and comments.
[   ] 5. Outstanding communicating skills, extremely well-organized reports and messages that are clear, concise, and timely.

D. **Priorities:** Does this individual recognize the most important demands of assignment, and plan and organize to meet these demands?
[   ] 1. Shows little or no recognition of priorities in accomplishing work.
[   ] 2. Shows a fair understanding of priority needs, is not consistent in actually meeting them.
[   ] 3. Generally meets priority needs of regular assignments.
[   ] 4. Consistently meets priority needs of regular assignments. Usually adjusts to changing demands as they occur.
[   ] 5. Consistently meets priority needs of regular job. Anticipates changing demands and adjusts appropriately.

E. **Thoroughness:** Indicate thoroughness with which individual performs work assignments. Are all relevant factors considered?
[   ] 1. Overlooks important details.
[   ] 2. Covers most important factors but slights some of the less-obvious or critical ones.
[   ] 3. Is usually thorough and recognizes most of the relevant factors.
[   ] 4. Is thorough in carrying out assignments. Rarely misses any factors that affect assignments.
[   ] 5. Completely covers all aspects of work assignments and overlooks no possibilities.

F. **Leadership:** Evaluate ability or potential to obtain results through others. Consider willingness to lead and acceptance by others.
[   ] 1. Does not have desire to lead, or is not accepted as a leader.
[   ] 2. Occasionally evidences leadership ability, receives some acceptance.
[   ] 3. Generally assumes a leadership role, and is accepted as a leader.
[   ] 4. Evident leader when in a group; very well accepted.
[   ] 5. Outstanding leadership skills; demands and receives everyone's attention and respect.

Form 6 (continued)

Skill Summary: Total of the six categories _____

II. **PERFORMANCE:**   This judgment should be based on how well individual met objectives, or position requirements.

[   ] 1. *Marginal or unsatisfactory.* Below standard, corrective action needed.
[   ] 2. *Adequate.* Below average, and below normally expected standards for position.
[   ] 3. *Competent.* Performance is average and meets all position requirements.
[   ] 4. *Superior.* Above average, performance is consistently above requirements.
[   ] 5. *Outstanding.* Clearly recognized and exceptional performance, much more than position requires.

Comments _____

_____

_____

_____

_____

PART B

Form 7 Sample Skill Inventory of Managerial Potential Data Sheet Kept for Each Happyday Manager

Name _____ Employee No. _____ Age _____ Current position _____

Began current position _____ Evaluated by _____ Title _____ Date _____

I. *Potential Rating:* Check one box only.

Promote now

10 [   ] Extremely promotable *NOW*. Top executive potential very high.

9 [   ] Promotable now; top executive potential.

8 [   ] Promotable now; can assume more responsibility.

Potential, needs time, training

7 [   ] Promotable; needs more time to develop (6–12 months).

6 [   ] Promotable; needs more time to develop (1–2 years).

5 [   ] Possibly promotable; requires considerable training and development.

Not promotable

4 [   ] Probably not promotable; could be effective in present job with some training and development.

3 [   ] Not promotable; possibly effective in present job with extensive retraining.

2 [   ] Definitely not promotable; effectiveness in present job not probable; consider transfer/discharge.

1 [   ] Definitely not promotable; ineffective in present job; consider discharge.

II. *Comments:* Indicate major strengths, weaknesses, training plans and needs, areas of competence, etc.

_____
_____
_____
_____
_____
_____
_____
_____
_____
_____
_____
_____
_____
_____
_____
_____
_____
_____
_____
_____
_____
_____

PART B

Form 8 Happyday Corporation Employee Listing by Department and Management Level

Name of employee	Depart-ment (1)	Current per-form-ance level (1 to 5; 5 is highest) (2)	Age (3)	Present manage-ment level (1-7) in hierarchy (1 is highest) (4)	Current mana-gerial skill level (6-30; see Form 6) (30 is highest) (5)	Educa-tion (highest degree) (6)	Assess-ment center report (rank in one of four groups of 24 each)* (7)	Poten-tial level rating (1-10; see Form 7) (10 is highest) (8)	Current salary ($/yr.) (9)	Time in present job (mos.) (10)	Minority status (minor-ity = 1) (11)	Sex (M-F) (12)
Frank R. Shanks	ACC	5	43	2	028	BA	2	10	54700.	61	0	M
Jeffrey Neal Marks**	ACC	1	52	3	009	MBA/CPA	21	4	44800.	92	0	M
Stanley F. Allen	ACC	2	38	4	010	BS	17	2	37700.	43	0	M
Michael Kennelly	ACC	5	36	4	028	MBA	4	9	39400.	83	0	M
Lance W. Weintraub	ACC	4	52	5	024	MBA	15	4	32700.	46	0	M
Sean Jones	ACC	4	54	3	027	MBA	3	9	31250.	26	0	M
Robert N. Nilsen	ACC	4	61	5	026	HS	13	5	35700.	81	0	M
Lucas Anthony	ACC	2	45	6	009	MS/CPA	19	3	24000.	28	1	M
Curtis Hack	ACC	5	42	6	030	HS	1	10	24600.	20	0	M
J. E. Larson	ACC	3	59	6	017	BS	17	4	25700.	82	0	M
Edward F. Pederson	ACC	3	52	6	020	MBA/CP	17	4	28500.	68	0	M
Oscar Kirchoffner	ACC	4	34	7	018	BS/CPA	7	7	16000.	8	0	M
Harold S. Larson	ACC	3	48	7	020	BS	20	3	16000.	18	0	M
Perry Henrich	ACC	3	36	7	012	BS	17	4	16600.	28	0	M
Pedro Robison	ACC	3	33	7	021	MBA		7	17000.	6	1	M
E. Michel Conway	ACC	3	43	7	019	BS	13	6	20600.	133	0	M
Walter C. Goodwin	ACC	5	58	7	028	HS	6	7	25700.	150	0	M
C. Beryl Anderson	ENG	3	51	2	017	BS	15	4	26500.	14	0	M
G. J. Upton	ENG	3	47	3	020	BS	14	4	41700.	3	0	M
Pamela Jil Savransky	ENG	4	54	3	023	MBA	2	10	43400.	21	1	F
Thaddeus Reitan	ENG	4	53	4	026	BS	14	5	21600.	48	0	M
Carl Hesselgrave	ENG	4	48	4	022	MS	13	6	35000.	43	0	M
Carl K. Cayou	ENG	5	33	4	027	MS	3	10	37000.	8	0	M
Donald D. Steinmetz	ENG	5	38	5	029	MBA	1	10	37700.	50	0	M
Edward B. Young	ENG	3	50	5	013	BS	12	4	39400.	21	0	M
William Fehlman	ENG	4	53	5	023	BS	11	7	38700.	89	0	M
George R. Merrill	ENG	2	46	6	011	BS	22	3	19700.	43	0	M
Edward A. Bull	ENG	3	34	6	017	BS	18	2	21900.	91	0	M
Marilyn Sass	ENG	5	37	6	029	PHD	5	7	23500.	3	1	F
Harlon Knoll	ENG	5	35	6	029	PHD	2	10	27600.	3	0	M
Bert S. Schneider	ENG	3	45	6	016	HS	23	2	27700.	93	0	M
U. W. Craig	ENG	2	34	7	010	BS	20	4	11400.	24	0	M
Andrew J. Elliott	ENG	3	23	7	016	BS	16	5	12500.	9	0	M
Dayton Caroon	ENG	5	31	7	030	MBA	1	10	14000.	2	1	M
Leslie A. N. Hanah	ENG	4	29	7	022	BS	12	5	16500.	12	0	M
Avald R. Murray	ENG	4	40	7	028	BS	9	5	17400.	3	0	M
James Chapmen	ENG	5	38	7	026	BS	4	9	18100.	11	0	M
Marvin A. Fredericks	ENG	4	45	7	026	BS	9	8	19900.	69	0	M
Herbert Walden	FIN	5	46	2	030	MBA	6	8	50700.	18	0	M
William Hernandez	FIN	2	48	3	007	BS	9	7	37500.	14	1	M
Wilbur Hall	FIN	4	36	4	021	BS	15	4	38000.	91	0	M
Pando Kiiski	FIN	4	43	5	022	MS	8	7	31500.	26	0	M
Bernard T. Benson	FIN	3	50	5	018	BS	24	3	34700.	82	0	M
Maurice Rydberg	FIN	3	55	5	020	BA	22	3	35000.	106	0	M
L. C. Lennon	MFG	4	60	2	027	MS	2		97500.	180	0	M
Walter C. Adams	MFG	3	61	3	006	BS	10	3	46700.	62	0	M
Howard Bloom	MFG	4	40	4	026	HS	11	6	33200.	72	0	M
O. W. Knapp	MFG	5	55	4	027	BS	11	8	33400.	123	0	M
Bernard A. Ortiz	MFG	5	58	5	028	MBA	7	8	36700.	3	1	M
T. R. H. Foster	MFG	4	59	5	021	HS	14	6	23400.	136	1	M
Sarah K. Vest	MFG	4	47	6	021	BS	12	3	23400.	11	1	F

Form 8 (continued)

Name of employee	Depart-ment (1)	Current per-form-ance level (1 to 5; 5 is highest) (2)	Age (3)	Present manage-ment levels (1-7) in hierarchy (1 is highest) (4)	Current mana-gerial skill level (6-30; see Form 1) (30 is highest) (5)	Educa-tion (highest (6)	Assess-ment center report (rank in one of four groups of 24 each)* (7)	Poten-tial level rating (1-10. see Form 8) (10 is highest) (8)	Current salary ($/yr.) (9)	Time in present job (mos.) (10)	Minority status (minor-ity = 1) (11)	Sex (M-F) (12)
Herman Enslow	MFG	4	29	6	025	BS	22	2	23500.	63	0	M
Roy Arneson	MFG	4	53	6	024	BS	21	4	24700.	100	0	M
Wendy Sue Nuntley	MFG	1	37	6	009	BA	22	3	24700.	21	0	F
Boyd Hill	MFG	5	61	5	029	HS	5	9	26500.	49	0	M
James Sorenson	MFG	5	41	6	027	MBA	4	9	26700.	3	0	M
Charles R. Harry	MFG	3	56	5	013	BS	20	3	27500.	183	0	M
William Spiker	MFG	4	36	7	021	MBA	18	3	11300.	3	0	M
Harry Jackson	MFG	2	33	7	012	BS	15	4	13000.	2	0	M
Diane Kay Painter	MFG	4	34	7	023	BS	24	2	14000.	71	1	F
Conrad W. Laboy	MFG	3	38	7	018	HS	19	5	14700.	37	0	M
Alec Leusick	MFG	5	48	7	028	BS	5	9	15000.	18	0	M
Ralph Hanson	MFG	4	27	7	021	MBA	7	7	15700.	11	0	M
Arthur B. Jackson	MFG	3	39	7	019	MBA	14	6	15700.	8	0	M
Dena B. Feren	MFG	5	23	7	029	MBA	12	5	16000.	3	1	F
Leo J. Petrykows	MFG	2	51	7	012	BS	20	2	16700.	4	0	M
James Bershon	MFG	5	26	7	029	MBA	8	3	17000.	19	0	M
Roy L. Muta	MFG	3	38	7	022	BS	19	3	17500.	3	0	M
Warren L. Griggs	MFG	5	63	7	029	HS	3	10	18000.	8	0	M
Nancy Kimble	MFG	3	37	7	018	BS	18	8	18500.	120	1	F
H. C. Reeves	MFG	3	41	7	013	HS	24	2	18700.	2	0	M
Clarence Schmidt	MFG	3	49	7	019	HS	18	2	18700.	36	0	M
Heath Adam	MFG	5	53	7	030	BS	11	6	19500.	53	0	M
Henry "Hank" Polmer	MFG	2	37	7	017	BA	20	6	19600.	18	0	M
Harmon E. Tower	MFG	5	29	7	025	BS	8	6	19800.	4	0	M
Harry C. Ulrey	MFG	3	63	7	018	BA	16	4	20000.	13	0	M
Elino Baus	MFG	4	46	7	023	HS	19	6	20500.	144	0	M
William Bickle	MFG	3	47	7	016	HS	23	3	23000.	102	0	M
J. C. Swartout	MKT	5	61	2	026	HS	3	9	63700.	6	0	M
Don I. Ingle	MKT	4	52	3	025	HS	5	10	39700.	34	0	M
Lester Schoeben	MKT	4	40	4	023	BS	10	5	33400.	9	0	M
Louis Miller	MKT	5	64	4	027	BA	6	7	37000.	14	1	M
Sibyl Ann Fine	MKT	4	39	6	022	BA	7	6	27000.	23	1	F
Lauren Polo Kay	MKT	3	56	5	019	MS	16	3	29700.	12	0	F
Gabriel Hill	MKT	5	51	5	029	BS	10	7	33400.	106	1	M
Julian Galpin	MKT	5	33	6	028	MBA	6	9	13800.	44	0	M
Dan Kron	MKT	4	26	7	027	MBA	13	3	15900.	14	0	M
R. Ludvig Biros	MKT	2	43	6	008	BS	16	4	18000.	1	0	M
Paul Olson	MKT	5	34	7	029	BA	4	8	18400.	36	0	M
Sande Lehrer	MKT	5	42	7	027	BA	10	5	18400.	31	0	M
Stephen Paul Streeter	MKT	4	44	7	028	MBA	10	5	21500.	62	0	M
Lester Belcheff	PER	4	50	3	021	MBA	9	6	43300.	8	0	M
Theodore W. Traudt	PER	5	48	4	029	BS	8	7	28700.	3	0	M
Allen Anderson	PER	5	33	5	028	MBA	1	10	23000.	9	0	M
Rosena Marie Manley	PER	3	31	6	014	MBA	23	2	24700.	82	1	F
Albert Ranallo	PER	1	58	7	009	MBA	21	2	26000.	91	1	M
J. E. Lennon	CEO	5	61	1	028	HS	3	10	97000.	173	0	M

*Ties were possible. N/A = not available. An assessment center is an intensive one-, two-, or three-day program whereby managers are evaluated with several types of techniques in order to arrive at an overall performance level (see also Exercise 8). A rank of 1 is the highest possible

**Brother-in-law of Lennon

Name _____   Group Number _____

Date _____ Class Section _____ Hour _____ Score _____

PART B

Form 10 Supporting Comments and Assumptions for Human Resource Forecast of Happyday Corporation

Answer these questions based on the next five-year period.

1. What basic changes do you see for Happyday?

2. What major assumptions have you made in developing your changes (e.g., what are
   the bases for estimating growth such as sales, manufacturing capacity, etc.)?

3. What specific human-resource skills are likely to be in more demand? Why?

4. What specific human-resource skills are likely to be in less demand? Why?

5. What departments will gain the most people and power? Why?

Form 10 (continued)

6. What departments will lose the most people and power (or remain static)? Why?

7. What is the average current salary in Happyday by hierarchical level and by department? The average number of months in current jobs by level and department? The average age by level and department?

8. What additional information would be useful to you as you develop your human resource plans?

Name _____ Group Number _____

Date _____ Class Section _____ Hour _____ Score _____

PART B

Form 11 Present Organizational Chart

Department _____

Insert the name(s) of the person(s) presently occupying the positions at the levels specified.

Total number of managers at each level

Level 2 _____ (   )

Level 3 _____ / _____ / _____ / _____ (   )

Level 4 _____ / _____ / _____ / _____ / _____ (   )

Level 5 _____ / _____ / _____ / _____ / _____ / _____ (   )

Level 6 _____ / _____ / _____ / _____ / _____ / _____ (   )

Level 7 _____ / _____ / _____ / _____ / _____ / _____ / _____ (   )

Total number of managers   _____

Name _____ Group Number _____

Date _____ Class Section _____ Hour _____ Score _____

PART B

Form 12 Future Organizational Chart (In 3 years)

Department _____

Insert names of persons to hold each level of job if they are from internal labor supply. If they are from an external labor supply, simply write "external" in the space provided.

Total number of managers at each level

Level 2 _____ (   )

Level 3 _____ / _____ / _____ / _____ (   )

Level 4 _____ / _____ / _____ / _____ / _____ (   )

Level 5 _____ / _____ / _____ / _____ / _____ / _____ (   )

Level 6 _____ / _____ / _____ / _____ / _____ / _____ (   )

Level 7 _____ / _____ / _____ / _____ / _____ / _____ / _____ (   )

Total number of managers   _____

Name _____ Group Number _____

Date _____ Class Section _____ Hour _____ Score _____

PART B

Form 13 Preliminary Staffing Pattern Developed by Representatives of Each of the Six Functional Departments

	Manufac- turing		Accounting		Finance		Marketing		Engineer- ing		Personnel	
	Int.	Ext.	Int.	Ext.	Int.	Ext.	Int.	Ext.	Int.	Ext.	Int.	Ext.
Net Additions												
TOTAL $\Sigma =$												
Present Levels $\Sigma =$	34		17		6		13		21		5	
Present Cost of Management Payroll												
Future Cost of Management Payroll												
Present Cost of Non- Management Payroll												
Future Cost of Non- Management Payroll												
Present Cost of Total Payroll												
Future Cost of Total Payroll												

If sales in three years are to reach $54.0 million and if the labor cost of sales is 46%, will the increased labor costs be covered by the increase in sales?   Yes _____   No _____

You are to use the following assumptions:

> 5:1 span of control per manager
> 7% annual wage and salary inflation rate
> $30,000 average annual salary per manager hired from external labor supplies, plus 35% in fringes.
> For the managers presently employed by Happyday, use current salary adjusted for inflation; however, if promoted or demoted, adjust salaries appropriately.
> $15,000 average annual salary per nonmanagerial employee, plus 30% in fringes.

Calculation:

Name _____   Group Number _____

Date _____   Class Section _____   Hour _____   Score _____

ASSESSMENT OF LEARNING IN PERSONNEL ADMINISTRATION
EXERCISE 2

1. Try to state the purpose of this exercise in one concise sentence.

2. Specifically what did you learn from this exercise (i.e., skills, abilities, and knowledge)?

3. How might your learning influence your role and your duties as a personnel administrator?

4. Why is human-resource planning an important personnel activity?

5. How would you evaluate a human-resource forecast to assess its effectiveness?

Exercise 3
Collecting job-related information for personnel decision making: analyzing jobs and writing job descriptions

PREVIEW*

This exercise enables you to actually analyze jobs using a variation of a technique used by the U.S. Office of Personnel Management (and the U.S. Training and Employment Service) as well as explaining and using alternative job analysis methodologies.

The job description, which includes a statement of duties, responsibilities, background, personal characteristics, education, etc., can then be used to develop other personnel programs, such as career paths, selection procedures, performance appraisals, and wage and salary programs. A systematic job analysis thus can be the foundation on which many programs in personnel are built.

In order to write a description of a job, a few job holders are selected and instructed to fill out a questionnaire that indicates how they spend their time on the job. People then interview the job holder in order to learn more about the job. Finally, job descriptions are written from the data obtained in the interviews.

OBJECTIVES

1. To become familiar with the different methods of job analysis and to understand the importance of and uses of job descriptions.

2. To gain experience and develop skill both in interviewing job incumbents to gather information about jobs using quantitative and nonquantitative approaches to analyze jobs, and in writing job descriptions from this information.

3. To become aware of the nature of job performance and how it differs both from behavior on the job and job effectiveness.

PREMEETING PREPARATION

Read the entire exercise.

INTRODUCTION
Job Analysis and the Identification of Job Performance

Many of the decisions made in personnel administration are based on what people *do* in an organization. When we select someone for a job, we want to know what activities this person would have to perform. Before we can train someone, we want to know what we are training them to do. How do we obtain this information?

The type of information we need in order to make "job related" decisions in personnel administration can be derived from job analysis. Decisions may be job re-

*The help of Region VIII of the U.S. Civil Service Commission, especially Steven Shikes, Evy Milstein, and George Dwyer, is gratefully acknowledged.

lated if they are based on a systematic process of collecting information about what a "job calls for in employee behaviors."[1] If we can identify the *desired behaviors* called for in a job and then design our performance appraisal, selection, training, motivation, and other personnel systems around these behaviors, we may begin to make more rational and effective decisions in these areas. Decisions should be based on what people do in their jobs, not on attitudes or personality factors unrelated to job performance.

There are two questions which must be asked of job analysis: 1) For what *purpose* do we conduct these analyses? 2) What *methods* should we use? We will attempt to answer both of these questions below. The answers to these questions dictate the type of information to be used, the format for data collection, and the agents by which the data will be collected.[2]

Job Analysis and the Law.[3] Several recent pieces of legislation concerning equal employment opportunity and discrimination in employment (e.g., the Civil Rights Act of 1964—see Exercise 17) have certain provisions that impact on job-analysis techniques. Basically, these state that an organization must show that the job behaviors or work outcomes discovered through job analysis are actually performed during a significant portion of working time or are critical to the required performance outcomes of the job. This is a major issue in personnel administration, as can be seen in the following quote from the Uniform Guidelines on Employee Selection Procedures:

> *Job analysis or review of job information.* A description of the procedure used to analyze the job or group of jobs, or to review the job information should be provided (Essential). Where a review of job information results in criteria which may be used without a full job analysis (see section 14B(3)), the basis for the selection of these criteria should be reported (Essential). Where a job analysis is required a complete description of the work behavior(s) or work outcome(s), and measures of their criticality or importance should be provided (Essential). The report should describe the basis on which the behavior(s) or outcome(s) were determined to be critical or important, such as the

proportion of time spent on the respective behaviors, their level of difficulty, their frequency of performance, the consequences of error, or other appropriate factors (Essential). Where two or more jobs are grouped for a validity study, the information called for in this subsection should be provided for each of the jobs, and the justification for the grouping (see section 14B(1)) provided (Essential).[4]

The preceding quote forces one to focus on the nature of the job itself and on the methods used to capture information.

The key point is specific information about the job itself which is sought. The types of information sought have been described by McCormick as:[5]

1. **Work-oriented activities:**
   Task-oriented activities (description of the work activities performed, expressed in "job" terms, usually indicating what is accomplished, such as galvanizing, weaving, cleaning, etc. Sometimes such activity descriptions also indicate how, why, and when a worker performs an activity; usually the activities are those involving active human participation, but in certain approaches they may characterize machine or system functions)
   —Work activities/processes
   —Procedures used
   —Activity records (films, etc.)
   —Personal accountability/responsibility

2. **Worker-oriented activities**
   A. Human behaviors (behaviors performed in work such as sensing, decision making, performing physical actions, communicating, etc.)
   B. Elemental motions (such as used in methods analysis)
   C. Personal job demands (human expenditures involved in work, such as energy expenditure, etc.)
   D. Machines, tools, equipment, and work aids used:
   E. Job-related tangibles and intangibles
   —Materials processed
   —Products made
   —Knowledge dealt with or applied (such as law or chemistry)

[1] M. D. Dunnette, *Personnel Selection* (Belmont, Cal.: Wadsworth, 1966), p. 69.

[2] J. P. Campbell et al., *Managerial Behavior, Performance, and Effectiveness* (New York: McGraw-Hill, 1970).

[3] C. E. Schneier, "Content Validity: The Necessity of a Behavioral Job Description," *The Personnel Administrator* 21, no. 2 (February 1976): 38–44.

[4] Uniform Guidelines on Employee Selection Procedures, *Federal Register,* August 25, 1978. The word "essential" means this must be accomplished as a minimum to meet EEOC validity requirements.

[5] E. J. McCormick, "Job and Task Analysis," in M. D. Dunnette, ed., *Handbook of Industrial and Organizational Psychology* (Chicago: Rand McNally, 1976.)

—Services rendered (such as laundering or repairing)

F. Work performance
—Work measurement (i.e., time taken)
—Work standards
—Error analysis
—Other aspects

G. Job context
—Physical working conditions
—Work schedule
—Organizational context
—Social context
—Incentives (financial and nonfinancial)

H. Personnel requirements
—Job-related knowledge/skills (education, training, work experience, etc., required)
—Personal attributes (aptitudes, physical characteristics, personality, interests, etc., required)

Job Analysis Terminology. Before discussing the methods of job analysis or its many uses, a brief examination of terminology may be helpful, because considerable confusion can easily occur in this area and it is important to have a consistent set of terms with which to begin. The most basic term of course is job analysis. *Job analysis* is the collection of job-related information for each unique job for organizational decision-making purposes. The process of job analysis may be looked at as what is to be done (physical and mental responses), how it is to be done (tools, equipment, methods, judgments, calculations, etc.), and why it is to be done (overall purpose and how tasks relate to one another). *Job specifications* are usually the ability, skills, background, or characteristics that are presumably required in order to successfully perform the job. These might include such items as hand-eye coordination, typing, years of experience, and stress tolerance for high levels of noise. Once all of this data is obtained it is often recorded on a document referred to as a job description. A *job description* merely indicates the nature of the job (what,

how, why, etc.), in task-related behaviors. The description may also include other information such as data indicating the job's class. A *job class,* or *job classification,* is a grouping of jobs due to their functional or task similarity. *Job evaluation* is a means of determining the worth of a job in dollars, and it is often based on the data represented in a job description, although some job evaluation plans require data to be collected which are not on the job description. Job evaluation is thus the determination of a job's or a class of job's worth relative to other jobs within the organization (see Exercise 16).

The Scope of Job Analysis and Job Descriptions. A job analysis may examine the job title, activities performed, procedures used, the physical environment of the job, the social environment of the job, and other conditions of employment. Eventually, after the job is analyzed, experience and education levels are specified and supervision, performed and received, is added to the analysis in order to make it a complete job description. Other possible factors to include in a job description are training times, physical health, and personal interests required. The job desicripton is frequently used as a basis for decisions in personnel administration. Thus, we may want to include not only what workers do on the job, but also the outputs or effectiveness indices of the job (e.g., sales volume expected). Here, we must emphasize behaviors or activities that are known to separate successful from unsuccessful performers. These characteristics can be used in job specifications, the characteristics to look for in hiring people for the job. Also, from job descriptions (comprehensive statements about the nature of the job) job classifications (the groupings of similar jobs) can be developed. Job classifications may then be used for job evaluations (i.e., the determination of the financial worth of the job classes). Thus the sequence of the development of job-related information for the purposes of the personnel system is shown in Fig. 1.

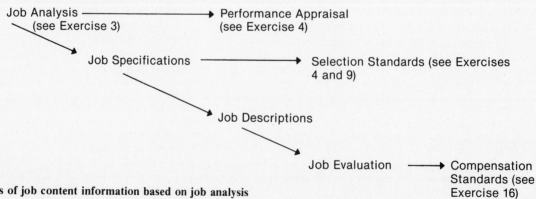

Fig. 1. The uses of job content information based on job analysis

Methods of Job Analysis.   There are several ways to gather information about jobs. We can interview people performing the job, we can observe people performing the job, we can examine the work environment and equipment used, we can study previous job descriptions and other job information, or we can use a structured (quantitative) job analysis questionnaire. All of these methods have considerable merit and can be used in combination.

There are several approaches that focus on different units of analysis for studying jobs. The task-oriented approach is used in the military[6] and in several civilian settings;[7] the worker-oriented approach is suggested by McCormick[8] and by Fleishman.[9] Other, although less widely used, models include dimensions of human motivation,[10] critical behaviors,[11]

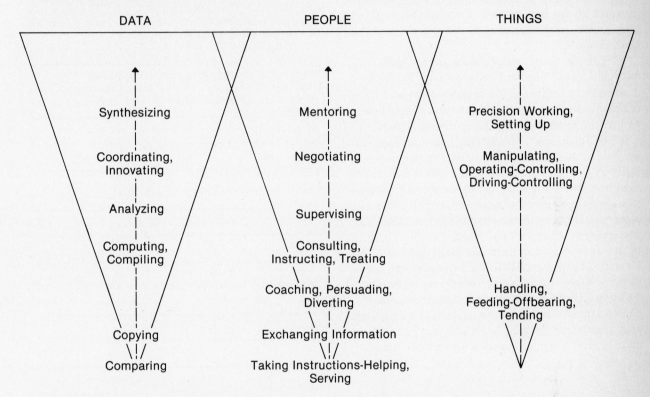

DATA / PEOPLE / THINGS

DATA: Synthesizing; Coordinating, Innovating; Analyzing; Computing, Compiling; Copying; Comparing

PEOPLE: Mentoring; Negotiating; Supervising; Consulting, Instructing, Treating; Coaching, Persuading, Diverting; Exchanging Information; Taking Instructions-Helping, Serving

THINGS: Precision Working, Setting Up; Manipulating, Operating-Controlling, Driving-Controlling; Handling, Feeding-Offbearing, Tending

Note: Each successive function reading down usually or typically involves all those that follow it. The functions separated by a comma are separate functions on the same level separately defined. They are on the same level because empirical evidence does not make a hierarchical distinction clear.

The hyphenated functions: *Taking Instructions-Helping, Operating-Controlling, Driving-Controlling,* and *Feeding-Offbearing* are single functions.

Setting Up, Operating-Controlling, Driving-Controlling, Feeding-Offbearing, and *Tending* are special cases involving machines and equipment of *Precision Working, Manipulating,* and *Handling,* (respectively, and hence are indented under them).

Fig. 2. Summary chart of worker function scales used in functional job analysis (From U.S. Department of Labor, *Handbook for Analyzing Jobs,* **Washington, D.C., U.S. Government Printing Office, 1973.)**

[6] R. E. Christal, *U.S.A.F. Occupational Research Project,* AFHRL–TR–73–75, January 1974; J. E. Morsh Job analysis in the U.S.A.F., *Personnel Psychology* (1964): 7–17.

[7] A. B. Chalupsky, "Comparative Factor Analyses of Clerical Jobs," *Journal of Applied Psychology* 46 (1962) 62–67; J. K. Hemphill, *Dimensions of executive positions.* Research Monograph Number 89, Bureau of Business Research, The Ohio State University, 1960. C. H. Lawshe, *Individual job questionnaire checklists of office operations.* Purdue University Bookstore, 1955.

[8] E. J. McCormick, P. R. Jeanneret, and R. C. Mecham, "A Study of Job Characteristics and Job Dimensions as Based on the Position Analysis Questionnaire (PAQ)," *Journal of Applied Psychology* 56 (1972): 347–367.

[9] E. A. Fleishman, On the relation between abilities, learning, and human performance. *American Psychologist,* 1972, 27, 1017–1032. E. A. Fleishman, Toward a taxonomy of human performance. *American Psychologist,* 1975, 30, 1127–1149.

[10] J. R. Hackman, and G. R. Oldham, "Development of the Job Diagnostic Survey," *Journal of Applied Psychology* 60 (1975): 159–170.

[11] J. C. Flanagan, "The Critical Incident Technique," *Psychological Bulletin* 51 (1954): 327–358.

physiological data, and numerous industrial engineering approaches.[12] Each of these stresses a different aspect of work which could be used for the analysis of a job.

The worker-oriented approach is also easier to administer (although the task-oriented approach is clearly the most popular method, but requires the development and inventory with thousands of items) because it is usually shorter than the task-oriented approach and can be compiled in a single booklet and simultaneously administered to all incumbents and across *all* jobs.

Examples of four specific techniques to gather job information will be noted from the many available.[13] These are the functional job language technique,[14] the critical incident technique,[15] the job element technique,[16] and the Position Analysis Questionnaire (PAQ).[17]

The functional job language technique (see Figure 2) is a "qualitative" way to derive job information by interviewing job incumbents and asking them to fill out forms describing what they do on the job. The emphasis here is on identifying worker activities. (We will use a variant of this method in this exercise.) The *U.S. Dictionary of Occupational Titles* (DOT), published by the federal government, is a large volume of information from over 20,000 jobs. For each job, a coded system enables analysts to describe its "functions." These functions can be viewed as the degree of complexity required by the job in terms of working with data, people, and things. The DOT is thus an excellent place to begin when conducting a job analysis. It should

be noted, however, that functional job analysis is used to summarize dimensions of job duties in a qualitative (scaled) manner and would have little use for personnel decision making because of the DOT's *very* general job specifications.

"Think of the last time you saw one of your subordinates do something that was very helpful to your group in meeting their production schedule." (Pause till he (she) indicates he (she) has much an incident in mind). "Did his (her) action result in increase in production of as much as one percent for that day, or some similar period?"

(If the answer is "no," say) "I wonder if you could think of the last time that someone did something that did have this much of an effect in increasing production." (When he (she) indicates he (she) has such a situation in mind, say) "What were the general circumstances leading up to this incident?" _____

_____

_____

"Tell me exactly what this person did that was so helpful at that time." _____

_____

_____

"Why was this so helpful in getting your group's job done?"

_____

_____

_____

"When did this incident happen?" _____

_____

_____

"What was this person's job?" _____

_____

_____

"How long has he (she) been on this job?" _____

_____

_____

"How old is he (she)?" _____

_____

[12] G. Salvendy, and W. D. Seymour, *Prediction and Development of Industrial Work Performance* (New York: Wiley, 1973).

[13] E. J. McCormick, "Job and Task Analysis," in M. D. Dunnette, ed., *Handbook of Industrial and Organizational Psychology* (Chicago: Rand McNally, 1976), pp. 652–653.

[14] Manpower Administration, U.S. Dept. of Labor, *Handbook for Analyzing Jobs* (Washington, D.C.: Superintendent of Documents, 1972), stock no. 2900–0131. See also *Guide to Writing Class Specifications,* IPPD, USCSC, Region VIII, March 1974.

[15] J. C. Flanagan, "The Critical Incident Technique," *Psychological Bulletin* 51, no. 4 (July 1954).

[16] E. S. Primoff, "How to Prepare and Conduct Job-Element Examinations," U.S. Civil Service Commission Project No. 6B531A January, 1973. See also E. S. Primoff, "The Development of Processes for Indirect or Synthetic Validity: IV. Empirical Validation of the J-Coefficient. A Symposium," *Personnel Psychology* 12 (1959): 413–418.

[17] E. J. McCormick, P. R. Jeanneret, and R. C. Mecham, "A Study of Job Characteristics and Job Dimensions as Based on the Position Analysis Questionnaire (PAQ)," *Journal of Applied Psychology* 54, no. 4 (August 1972): 347–368.

Fig. 3. Sample of form for use by an interviewer in collecting effective critical incidents (from J. C. Flanagan, "The Critical Incident Technique," *Psychological Bulletin* 51 (1954): 327–358.

The critical incident technique, a qualitative technique, requires job incumbents to be interviewed in order to ascertain what activities they perform are critical to effective or ineffective performance. Rather than identifying all relevant worker functions, as is done in the functional job language technique, only those critical to effective performance are identified. This technique often works well in the design of performance-appraisal systems, which are discussed in Exercise 4. Figure 3 shows an example of the data collection tool.

Thus far we have not discussed quantitative or structured methods of job analysis where predetermined lists of descriptions of job content are provided to incumbents, supervisors, etc., to note the frequency or importance of each aspect of a job to determine a final list of job dimensions. Such a procedure avoids the questionable reliability of the nonquantitative methods of job analysis which may not use the same verbiage to describe the same job dimensions contained in several

jobs. This creates several shortcomings in other personnel systems such as career pathing, human-resource planning, performance appraisals, selection, promotion, and wage and salary administration. Such methods also have the advantage of being less costly over time and can insure that dimensions are not redundant, are exhaustive, and can offer help in selection-exam pooling by grouping tasks across jobs for examination and validation purposes. These are usually referred to as job-inventory or task-inventory methods and consist of a list of tasks relevant to the jobs within the occupational area. Such checklists are used for job inventories, although the term "checklist" may be appropriate because it implied a "checking" of terms, whereas most job inventories require more complex responses, such as rating the importance of each job-content item on the list. Well-designed job inventories usually consist of statements of activities, omitting obvious cues (see Fig. 4).

TASKS REQUIRED	A Check (√) if required	B IMPORTANCE Criticalness of this task as relative to other tasks 1=unimportant 2=minor importance 3=important 4=very important 5=critical (insert number below)	C FREQUENCY Time spent relative to other tasks 1=much less time 2=less time 3=about the same time 4=more time 5=much more time (insert number below)	D ERROR CONSEQUENCE Probability of a serious consequence resulting if task is not done properly 1=low 2=same 3=average 4=high 5=certainty (insert number below)	E DIFFICULTY Difficulty of performing your job if you could not do this task 1=no difficulty 2=some difficulty 3=a great deal of difficulty 4=nearly impossible 5=impossible (insert number below)	F LEARNED TASK Where did you learn to perform this task? 1=doing a job I now supervise 2=in the department where I am now a supervisor, but not on the job I now supervise 3=elsewhere in the plant, outside the department 4=when I became a supervisor, but from outside this department 5=outside the plant 6=other, please specify (insert number below)
1. Install & adjust new rollers & passes.						
2. Monitor condition of rollers & other equipment.						
3. Determine when passes need to be replaced.						
4. Determine if machine breakdowns are electrical or mechanical problems.						
5. Inspect quality of product being produced.						
6. Monitor safety hazards.						
7. Monitor work of crew members.						
8. Diagnose machine/ equipment breakdowns.						
9. Instruct crew members on new jobs & safety.						

Fig. 4. A checklist of task-oriented items

A major contributor to the development of job-inventory techniques has been the Personnel Division of the U.S. Air Force Human Resources Laboratory.[18] (See Fig. 5.) Other military services have adopted them as well, and at least a few other organizations—private and governmental—have used some form of job inventory for research or operational purposes.

Listed below is a duty and the tasks which it includes. Check all tasks which you perform. Add any tasks you do which are not listed. Then rate the tasks you have checked. H. INSTALLING AND REMOVING AERIAL CABLE SYSTEMS	CHECK	TIME SPENT	IMPORTANCE
	✓ IF DONE	1. Very much below average 2. Below average 3. Slightly below average 4. About average 5. Slightly above average 6. Above average 7. Very much above average	1. Extremely unimportant 2. Very unimportant 3. Unimportant 4. About medium importance 5. Important 6. Very important 7. Extremely important
1. Attach suspension strand to pole			
2. Change and splice lasher wire			
3. Deliver materials to lineman with snatch block and handline			
4. Drill through-bolt holes and secure suspension clamps on poles			
5. Install cable pressurization systems			
6. Install distribution terminals			
7. Install pulling-in line through cable rings			
8. Load and unload cable reels			
9. Load lashing machine with lashing wire			

Fig. 5. A job inventory example for the outside wire and antenna systems career field of the U.S. Air Force (from E. J. Morse and W. B. Archer, *Procedural Guide for Conducting Occupational Surveys in the United States Air Force,* Lackland Air Force Base, Texas, Personnel Research Laboratory, Aerospace Medical Division, PRL-TR-67-11, September 1967)

The job-element technique is a quantitative procedure used to question job "experts" about important work activities.[19] Each expert is to respond to four questions about an element to determine its importance in the job to be done. It should be noted that job elements are usually human qualities or traits and not behaviors. The form used to collect job-content information requires a very complex scoring procedure, as shown in Fig. 6.

The job-inventory method has also given us the Position Analysis questionnaire (PAQ), a worker-oriented approach that is very attractive for job analysis. It assumes that, although diverse jobs may contain an infinite number of unique activities, all these activities can be characterized in terms of a finite number of common underlying process elements. It is perhaps this latter orientation that has made the PAQ popular.[20] It is a standard questionnaire which can be

[18] R. E. Christal, *U.S.A.F., Occupational Research Project,* AFHRL-TR-73-75, January 1974. See also J. E. Morse, Job Analysis in the U.S.A.F., *Personnel Psychology* 17 (1964): 7-17.

[19] E. S. Primoff, "How to Prepare and Conduct Job Element Examinations" (Washington, D.C.: U.S. Government Printing Office, 1975).

[20] L. R. Taylor, "Empirically Derived Job Families as a Foundation for the Study of Validity Generalization. Study I. The Construction of Job Families Based on the Component and Overall Dimensions of the PAQ," *Personnel Psychology* 31 (1978): 325-340; L. R. Taylor, and G. A. Colbert, "Empirically Derived Job Families as a Foundation for the Study of Validity Generalization. Study II. The Construction of Job Families Based on Company-Specific PAQ Dimensions," *Personnel Psychology* 31 (1978): 341-353.

Job:
Grade:

Date:

Rater No.

(col. 3 4 5)

Job No.

(6 7 8)

Rater Name and Grade:
Title and Location:

Page No. __ (col 1 2)   1 2

(These columns for use in hand calculation of values)

Element No. (Do not Punch)	Barely acceptable workers (B) + all have ✓ some have 0 almost none have	To pick out superior workers (S) + very important ✓ valuable 0 does not differentiate	Trouble likely if not considered (T) + much trouble ✓ some trouble 0 safe to ignore	Practical. Demanding this element, we can fill (P) + all openings ✓ some openings 0 also no openings	Columns	Item Index (IT) $S \times P$ T $SP + T$	Total Value (TV) $IT + S - B - P$	SP' (P' (+ = 0 ✓ = 1 0 = 2))	Training Value (TR) $S + T + SP' - B$
					9–12				
					13–16				
					17–20				
					21–24				
					25–28				
					29–32				
					33–36				
					37–40				
					41–44				
					45–48				
					49–52				
					53–56				
					57–60				
					61–64				
					65–68				
					69–72				
					73–76				
					77–80				

Note: for all categories except P', + counts 2, ✓ counts 1, 0 counts 0. For category P', + counts 0, ✓ counts 1, 0 counts 2.

* U.S. Civil Service Commission
Personnel Research and Development Center
Washington, D.C.

Fig. 6. Job element blank (from E. Primoff, "How to Prepare and Conduct Job Element Examinations," Washington, D.C., U.S. Government Printing Office, 1975)

Fig. 7. Summary of job dimension title* (from E. J. McCormick, "Job and Task Analysis," in M. D. Dunnette, ed., *Handbook of Characterizational and Organizational Psychology* (Chicago: Rand McNally, 1974)

JOB DIMENSIONS BASED ON JOB DATA	JOB DIMENSIONS BASED ON ATTRIBUTE PROFILE DATA

Division I: Information Input

J1–1	Perceptual interpretation	A1–1	Visual input from devices/materials
J1–2	Evaluation of sensory input	A1–2	Evaluation of visual input
J1–3	Visual input from devices/materials	A1–3	Perceptual input from processes/events
J1–4	Input from representational sources	A1–4	Verbal/auditory input/interpretation
J1–5	Environmental awareness	A1–5	Non-visual input

Division 2: Mental Processes

J2–6	Decision making	A2–6	Use of job-related knowledge
J2–7	Information processing	A2–7	Information processing

Division 3: Work Output

J3–8	Manual/control activities	A3–8	Manual control/coordination activities
J3–9	Physical coordination in control/related activities	A3–9	Control/equipment operation
J3–10	General body activity versus sedentary activities	A3–9	Control/equipment operation
J3–11	Manipulating/handling activities	A3–10	General body/handling activities
J3–12	Adjusting/operating machines/equipment	A3–11	Use of foot controls
J3–13	Skilled/technical activities		
J3–14	Use of miscellaneous equipment/devices		

Division 4: Relationships with Other Persons

J4–15	Interchange of ideas/judgments/related information	A4–12	Interpersonal communications
J4–16	Supervisory/staff activities	A4–13	Signal/code communications
J4–17	Public/related personal contact	A4–14	Serving/entertaining
J4–18	Communicating instructions/directions/related job information		
J4–19	General personal contact		
J4–20	Job-related communications		

Division 5: Job Context

J5–21	Potentially stressful/unpleasant environment	A5–15	Unpleasant physical environment
J5–22	Potentially hazardous job situations	A5–16	Personally demanding situations
J5–23	Personally demanding situations	A5–17	Hazardous physical environment

Division 6: Other Job Characteristics

J6–24	Attentive job demands	A6–18	Work schedule 1
J6–25	Vigilant/discriminating work activities	A6–19	Job responsibility
J6–26	Structured versus unstructured work activities	A6–20	Routine/Repetitive work activities
J6–27	Regular versus irregular work schedule	A6–21	Attentive/discriminating work demands
J6–28	Work/protective versus business clothing	A6–22	Work attire
J6–29	Specific versus non-specific clothing	A6–23	Work schedule II
J6–30	Continuity of work load		

General (G) Dimensions

JG–1	Decision/communication/social responsibilities	(No overall analyses made)	
JG–2	Environmental demands/general body control		
JG–3	Equipment/machine operation		
JG–4	Unnamed		
JG–5	Manual control activities		
JG–6	Office/related activities		

JG-7   Evaluation of sensory input
JG-8   General/public-related personal contact
JG-9   Use of technical/related materials
JG-10   General physical activities versus
        sedentary activities
JG-11   Hazardous/personally demanding
        situations
JG-12   Attentive/vigilant work activities
JG-13   Unnamed
JG-14   Supervision/coordination

*The dimensions based on job data and on attribute profile data are arranged by PAQ division in parallel columns for comparative purposes. Within any given division there may be dimensions based on the two sources which may be identical, or nearly so. However, the ordering and numbering of dimensions within each division is not intended to reflect corresponding dimensions.

used to build a profile of any job and rank it relative to others on such broad categories as interpersonal activity or job situation and context. The PAQ is a statistically derived instrument resulting from several years of research into the nature of work which is divided into six divisions, each of which has several job dimensions as shown in Fig. 7. Certainly one considerable problem in job analysis, reliability, can be satisfied with the PAQ.

Any of these techniques can help a job analyst to specify the behaviors or activities that encompass a particular job. Once this information is gathered, performance, education, training, and experience levels or requirements can be developed. Together with the information about actual worker activities, this additional information comprises the job description and job specification.

The frequency of use of the four methods in public personnel positions can be seen in Table 1. This table clearly indicates, based on the survey tables that in public jurisdictions the job element and functional language techniques are most commonly used.[21]

---

[21] E. L. Levine, N. Bennett, and R. A. Ash, "Evaluation and Use of Four Job Analysis Methods for Personnel Selection," *Public Personnel Management* 8, no. 3 (May–June 1979).

TABLE 1. Use of Four Methods of Job Analysis

	(N = 106)					
	% Using for j.a. study	Mean no. job analysis studies	% Using for exam plans	Mean no. exam plans	% Using for validation	Mean no. validation studies
Critical Incidents	24.5	2.6 (26)	10.4	2.5 (11)	12.3	2.0 (13)
Job Elements	57.5	15.7 (61)	54.7	17.5 (58)	22.6	8.8 (24)
PAQ	8.5	10.7 (9)	6.6	4.9 (7)	3.8	2.3 (4)
Functional Language	59.4	20.1 (63)	49.1	12.2 (52)	17.9	10.6 (19)

Source: American Compensation Association Survey, 1976.
Coverage: 275 larger U.S. corporations employing nearly 3,000,000 employees in 35 different business fields, including manufacturing, finance, food, insurance, transportation, utilities, and health care.

What Are the Uses of a Job Description?[22]   As noted previously, the information contained in a job description can be used as a basis for the essential decisions made in personnel administration. To the extent that the description is job related (i.e., oriented toward worker behavior on the job), decisions about what selection predictors are relevant can be made. For example, if through a job analysis we find that handling heavy loads is a behavior necessarily performed on the job, we may want either to ask job applicants about their strength and physical health or test it directly by having them lift something. The presumption is that the act of heavy lifting on the test will predict lifting behavior on the job.

Job descriptions may also help to tell us what our training programs should emphasize—what skills, abilities, and knowledge are needed to perform the tasks spelled out in the job description. Job dimensions can be weighted as to their importance, and performance can be evaluated by any one of a number of appraisal techniques (see Exercise 4). The job description can be used in wage and salary administration as the level of difficulty, and the contribution to organization goals of each job activity are ascertained and attached to monetary rewards (see Exercise 16).

What Is Job Performance?   As we attempt to identify what people do in their jobs, we must define job performance. *Performance* is simply behavior that has been evaluated in an organization. *Behavior,* such as setting up machinery, talking to others, or writing reports, is constantly evaluated by members of an organization as to its value to the organization. Often we develop indices, or measures of performance, to help judge whether the performance contributes to organizational outcomes. Such measures could be absenteeism ratios, profit, or sales volumes.[23] But these *effectiveness measures* can be quite removed from behavior and performance. For instance, an employee may engage in certain behaviors (e.g., calling on customers regularly), and these behaviors may be evaluated by the organization as desired performance. But effectiveness ratios based on these behaviors (e.g., sales volume) may be low because of external factors such as product demand. Thus, when we concentrate on effectiveness, we may miss some important things that people actually *do* on the job. When we select, appraise, or train people, we want to have what people do to get job results—their behaviors and or activities—clearly in mind.

It is also essential to keep in mind that job performance is multidimensional—that is, there is more than one type of activity a person performs on a job. An individual's job performance may consist of running a machine, monitoring a control panel, filling out log sheets, and instructing others. In job analysis, we must gather information on all of these types of job activities, or job dimensions, in order to make job-related decisions in the area of, for example, performance appraisal.

Job performance also involves a statement of the level of performance required. For example, how many calls per week should a salesperson make, how many subassemblies should a mechanic prepare per day, or how congenial should a bank teller be toward customers? Obviously, deciding on these performance levels is often difficult as jobs become less routine and programmable.

Job performance is not necessarily static, and this may cause problems in job analysis. Performance levels change over time and are different across job holders. New trainees and those in the lower job grades within a job group or classification would not be expected to perform at the same level as senior job holders. Job analyses must reflect these dynamic aspects of job performance.[24]

PROCEDURE

Overview. As described in the *Appendix,* variations of the functional job language technique and a quantitative technique are used to conduct a job analysis and write job descriptions. A few participants are chosen and their jobs are used in the analysis. They are interviewed, data regarding their jobs is collected and analyzed, and a job description is written.

PART A

STEP 1: Divide into small groups and designate one person from each group as the individual whose job will be analyzed. (If no one in the group holds a job, use one of the suggested jobs in Form 1 for the analysis.)

STEP 2: Form 2 gives examples of worker-oriented and task-oriented items or activities for several types of jobs. If the job to be analyzed falls into one of these groups, the examples help to show what behaviors may be typical for the job

---

[22] C. E. Schneier, "Content Validity: The Necessity of a Behavioral Job Description," *The Personnel Administrator* 21, no. 2 (February 1976): 38–44.

[23] J. P. Campbell et al., *Managerial Behavior, Performance, and Effectiveness* (New York: McGraw-Hill, 1970).

[24] C. E. Schneier, "Content Validity," 38–44.

group. These behaviors are called "items" in the functional job language technique for analyzing jobs.[25]

PART B

STEP 3: Those whose jobs are to be analyzed should fill out Form 4, noting the instructions (Form 3).

TIME: About 35 minutes, Parts A and B.

PART C

STEP 4: Other members of each group should read over the job holder's completed Position Classification Questionnaire, then interview the job holder and (1) fill out a Position Audit Form (Form 5) as the interview is conducted (see *Appendix*). Be sure to identify the major job items and duties for the job you are analyzing, or (2) complete the quantitative job inventory with each job analyst using Form 4 and the job incumbent using Form 6 directly. Job analysts should each complete Form 6. Score Form 6 for both analysts and incumbents.

TIME: About 45 minutes.

PART D

STEP 5: Next, job analysts will discuss their completed Position Audit Forms (Form 5), show them to job holders for any additions, and then develop the final Job Description (Form 7) outlining each job in a maximum 10–12 independent job dimensions.

The process of gathering information, interviewing job incumbents, discussing job information, and eventually isolating job items that appear in the job description is similar to the functional job language technique. The terms on the final description represent the "functions" or activities of the job incumbent.

If you have used the functional-language technique, try to use the following rules in writing the dimensions for each job:

1. Use verb-object explanatory phrases.
2. Use the present tense.
3. Use telegraphic style avoiding unnecessary verbs.

4. Avoid using general adjectives and adverbs.
5. Avoid using specific proprietary names.
6. Avoid any unnecessary verbiage.
7. Begin each dimension with a verb (or gerund), not nouns.
8. Use as specific terms as possible.

The action verbs provided in Form 8 may help with this effort.

TIME: About 50 minutes.

APPENDIX: GUIDELINES FOR CONDUCTING JOB ANALYSES[26]

Conducting an On-Site Job Analysis. Using the observation-interview method, the general procedure of job analysis follows several steps. The first is for the analyst to become familiar with the technologies of the jobs and characteristics of the organization to be studied. Information for these purposes may be obtained from:

1. Books, periodicals, and other literature on technical or related subjects available in libraries.
2. Catalogs, flow charts, organizational charts, and process descriptions already prepared by the establishment.
3. Technical literature on processes and job descriptions prepared by trade associations, trade unions, and professional societies.
4. Pamphlets, books, and job descriptions prepared by federal, state, and municipal government departments which have interests in the occupational area—e.g., health, agriculture, labor, or commerce.

By planning in advance for the job-analysis study, the analyst will be able to talk intelligently to management, supervisors, and workers in a language common to all. This background information will also help the analyst to observe and evaluate job tasks and processes objectively without loss of time.

Whenever possible, arrangements should be made so that the following are available to the analyst prior to the actual analysis of jobs: (1) an orientation tour of the establishment; (2) introductions to department heads and supervisors with whom he or she will deal during the study; and (3) a list of job titles, together

---

[25] In practice, it is most desirable for each organization to generate job items for each and every job. The lists in Form 2 can be helpful in attempting to derive items. However, they should never be used as a substitute for each organization's best attempts to derive its own job items.

[26] Adapted from U.S. Department of Labor, *Handbook for Analyzing Jobs* (Washington, D.C.: U.S. Government Printing Office, 1972).

with an indication of the number of men and women employed in each job.

The orientation tour is highly desirable for the analyst to obtain an overall picture of operations, to become familiar with the general processes, and to observe the flow of work within the establishment. During the tour the analyst will usually be introduced to the foreman or heads of the departments where the analyses are to be made. The analyst should take this opportunity to explain briefly the major objective of the study.

The analyst should request information regarding departmentalization, the titles of jobs in the various departments, and the number of workers employed in each job. This information will be used for the preparation of the staffing schedule and to make initial determinations as to processes and jobs involved within the scope of the study.

Good job analysis involves observing workers performing their jobs and interviewing workers, supervisors, and others who have information pertinent to the job. It is the most desirable method for job-analysis purposes because it (a) involves firsthand observation by the analyst; (b) enables the analyst to evaluate the interview data and to sift essential from nonessential facts in terms of that observation; and (c) permits the worker to demonstrate various functions of the job rather than describing the job orally or in writing.

The analyst uses the observation-interview method in two ways:

1. Observes the worker on the job performing a complete work cycle before asking any questions. During the observation, he or she takes notes of all the job activities, including those not fully understood. When the analyst is satisfied that as much information as possible has been accumulated from observation, he or she talks with workers or supervisors, or both, to supplement notes.

2. Observes and interviews simultaneously. While watching, the analyst talks with workers about what is being done and asks questions about what he or she is observing, as well as about conditions under which the job is being performed. Here, too, the analyst should take notes in order to record all the data pertinent to the job and its environment.

The interview process is subjective—a conversational interaction between individuals. Therefore, the analyst must be more than a recording device. The amount and objectivity of information received depends on how much is contributed to the situation. The analyst's contribution is one of understanding and adjusting to the worker and his or her job.

A good background preparation will enable the analyst to obtain facts quickly, accurately, and comprehensively. He or she must be able to establish friendly relations on short notice, extract all pertinent information, and yet be sufficiently detached to be objective and free of bias.

The analyst must develop skill in combining note taking with the conversational aspect of the interview, and must be able to write intelligible notes while engaged in conversation or to intersperse writing with fluent conversation. Often in deference to the analyst, the worker will stop talking while notes are being made. The analyst should make it clear whether he or she wishes the conversation continued or not in these circumstances.

Some workers object to a record being made of what they say. The analyst must decide how much the interview may be affected by this attitude and modify his or her practices accordingly. A small looseleaf book, such as a stenographer's notebook, is best suited for recording notes while observing and interviewing.

Suggestions for Effective Note Taking

1. Notes should be complete, legible, and contain data necessary for the preparation of the job-analysis schedule.

2. Notes should be organized logically, according to job tasks and the categories of information required for a complete analysis.

3. Notes should include only the facts about the job with emphasis on the work performed and worker traits involved. Use only words, phrases, and sentences that impart necessary information.

(Obviously, on-site observations are difficult in a classroom setting, but may be arranged if a student is working nearby.)

FOR FURTHER READING

Arvey, R. D., and M. E. Begalia. "Analyzing the Homemaker Job Using the Position Analysis Questionnaire (PAQ)." *Journal of Applied Psychology* 60, no 4 (1975): 315-317. (II-R)

Arvey, R. D., and K. M. Mossholder. "A Proposed Methodology for Determining Similarities and Differences among Jobs." *Personnel Psychology* 30 (1977): 363-374. (II-R)

Archer, W. B., and D. A. Frochier. "The Construction, Review and Administration of Air Force Job Inventories." Lackland Air Force Base, Texas: Personnel Research Laboratory, Aerospace Medical

Division, PRL-TDR-63-21, AD-426-755, August 1963. (II-R)

Ash, R. A., and S. L. Edgell. "A Note on the Readability of the Position Analysis Questionnaire (PAQ)." *Journal of Applied Psychology* 60 (1975): 765-766. (II-R)

Berenson, C., and H. O. Ruhnke. "Job Descriptions: How to Write and Use Them." *Personnel Journal* 48 (1969). (I)

Brumbach, G. B. "Consolidating Job Descriptions, Performance Appraisals, and Manpower Reports." *Personnel Journal* 50 (1971): 604-610. (I)

Brumbach, G. B., and J. W. Vincent. "Factor Analysis of Work-Performed Data for a Sample of Administrative, Professional and Scientific Positions." Personnel Psychology 23 (1970): 101-107. (II-R)

Campbell, J. P., M. D. Dunnette, E. E. Lawler, and C. Weick. *Managerial Behavior, Performance, and Effectiveness.* New York: McGraw-Hill, 1970, Chapters 4 and 5. (II)

Caruth, D. L. "The Trouble with Work Measurement Is . . . ." *Michigan Business Review* 24, no. 1 (January 1972): 7-15. (I)

Chalupsky, A. B. "Comparative Factor Analyses of Clerical Jobs." *Journal of Applied Psychology* 46 (1962): 62-67. (II-R)

Christal, R. E. United States Air Force Occupational Research Programs. Air Force Human Research Laboratory, January 1974. AFHRL-TR-73-75. (II-R)

Cornelius, E. T., T. J. Carron, and M. N. Collins. "Job Analysis Models and Job Classification." *Personnel Psychology* 32 (1979): 693-708. (II-R)

Cornelius, E. T.; M. D. Hakel, and P. R. Sackett. "A Methodological Approach to Job Classification for Performance Appraisal Purposes. *Personnel Psychology* 32 (1979): 283-297. (II-R)

Davis, L. E., and J. C. Taylor, eds. *The Design of Jobs.* 2d ed. Santa Monica, Calif.: Goodyear, 1979.

Dunnette, M. D. "A Note on *the* Criterion." *Journal of Applied Psychology* 47 (1963): 251-254. (II)

Dunnette, M. D., L. M. Hough, and R. L. Rosse. "Task and Job Taxonomies as a Basis for Identifying Labor Supply Sources and Evaluating Employment Qualifications." *Human Resources Planning* 2 (1979): 37-51. (II-R)

Fine, S. A. "Matching Job Requirements and Worker Qualifications." *Personnel* 35, no. 3 (May-June 1958): 52-58. (I)

Flanagan, J. C. "The Critical Incident Technique." *Psychological Bulletin* 51 (1954): 327-358. (II)

Fleishman, E. A. "On the Relation between Abilities, Learning, and Human Performance." *American Psychologist* 27 (1972): 1017-1032. (II-R)

Fleishman, E. A. "Toward a Taxonomy of Human Performance." *American Psychologist* 30 (1975): 1127-1149. (II)

Gehm, J. W. "Job Descriptions-A New Handle on an Old Tool." *Personnel Journal* 49, no. 2 (December 1970): 954-983. (I)

Ghiselli, E. E. "Dimensional Problems of Criteria." *Journal of Applied Psychology* 40 (1956): 1-4. (II)

Guion, R. M. "Synthetic Validity in a Small Company: A Demonstration." *Personnel Psychology* 18 (1965): 49-65. (II-R)

Hackman, J. R., and E. E. Lawler. "Employee Reactions to Job Characteristics." *Journal of Applied Psychology* 55 (1971): 268-286. (II-R)

Hemphill, J. K. "Job Descriptions for Executives." *Harvard Business Review* 37 (1959): 55-67. (I)

Henderson, R. I. "Job Descriptions—Critical Documents, Versatile Tools." *Supervisory Management,* Part I (December 1975), Part II (December 1975), Part III (January 1976), Part IV (February 1976). (I)

Inn, A., and C. L. Hulin. "Three Sources of Variance, Static Dimensionality, Dynamic Dimensionality, and Individual Dimensionality." *Organizational Behavior and Human Performance* 8 (1972): 53-83. (II-R)

Jenkins, G. D. et al. "Standardized Observations: An Approach to Measuring the Nature of Jobs." *Journal of Applied Psychology* 60 (1975): 171-181. (II-R)

Krzystofiak, F., and J. M. Newman. "A Quantified Approach to Measurement of Job Content: Procedures and Payoffs." *Personnel Psychology* 32 (1979). (II-R)

Lawshe, C. H. *Individual Job Questionnaire Checklists of Office Operations.* Purdue University Bookstore, 1955. (I)

Levine, E. L., N. Bennett, and R. A. Ash. "Evaluation and Use of Four Job Analysis Methods for Personnel Selection." *Public Personnel Management* 8, no. 3 (May-June 1979). (I)

McCormick, E. J. "Job and Task Analysis." In M. D. Dunnette, ed. *Handbook of Industrial and Organizational Psychology.* Chicago: Rand McNally, 1976. (II)

McCormick, E. J. "Job Information: Its Development and Applications." In D. Yoder and H. Heneman, Jr., eds. *Staffing Policies and Strategies.* Washington, D.C.: Bureau of National Affairs, Inc., 1975, pp. 35-84. (I)

McCormick, E. J., A. S. DeNisi, and J. B. Shaw. "Use of the Position Analysis Questionnaire for Establishing the Job Component Validity of Tests." *Journal of Applied Psychology* 64, no. 1 (1979): 51–56. (II–R)

McCormick, E. J., P. R. Jeanneret, and R. C. Mecham. "A Study of Job Characteristics and Job Dimensions as Based on the Position Analysis Questionnaire (PAQ)." *Journal of Applied Psychology* 56 (1972): 347–367. (II–R)

McCormick, E. J. and J. Tiffin. *Industrial Psychology.* 6th ed. Englewood Cliffs, N.J.: Prentice-Hall, 1974, Chap. 3. (I)

Morse, J. E. and W. B. Archer, *Procedural Guide for Conducting Occupational Surveys in the United States Air Force.* Lackland Air Force Base, Texas: Personnel Research Laboratory, Aerospace Medical Division, PRI–TR–67–11, September 1967. (I)

Pearlman, K. "Job Families: A Review and Discussion of Their Implications for Personnel Selection." *Psychological Bulletin* 87 (1980): 1–28. (II–R)

Pinto, P. R., and C. C. Pinder. "A Cluster Analytic Approach to the Study of Organizations." *Organizational Behavior and Human Performance* 8 (1972): 408–422. (II–R)

Prien, E. P. "Development of a Clerical Position Description Questionnaire." *Personnel Psychology* 18 (1965): 91–98.

Prien, E. P., and W. W. Ronan. "Job Analysis: A Review of Research Findings." *Personnel Psychology* 74 (1971): 371–396. (II)

Primoff, E. S. "The J-Coefficient Approach to Jobs and Tests." *Personnel Administration* (1957): 34–40. (I)

Rakich, J. S. "Job Descriptions: Key Element in the Personnel Subsystem." *Personnel Journal* 51 no. 1 (January 1972): 42–45+. (I)

Replies and rejoinders in *Personnel Psychology* 32 (1979): 507–538.

Reuter, V. G. "Work Measurement Practices." *California Management Review* 14, no. 1 (Fall 1971): 24–30. (I–R)

Schneier, C. E. "Content Validity: The Necessity of a Behavioral Job Analysis." *The Personnel Administrator* 21, no. 2 (February 1976): 38–44. (I)

Seashore, S. E., B. P. Indik, and B. S. Georgopolous. "Relationships Among Criteria of Job Performance." *Journal of Applied Psychology* 44 (1960): 195–202. (II–R)

Shartle, C. L. *Occupational Information. Its Development and Application.* 3d ed. Englewood Cliffs, N.J.: Prentice-Hall, 1959. (I)

Taylor, L. R. "Empirically Derived Job Families as a Foundation for the Study of Validity Generalization. Study I, The Constructions of Job Families Based on the Component and Overall Dimensions of the PAQ." *Personnel Psychology* 31 (1978). 325–340. (II–R)

Taylor, L. R., and G. A. Colbert. "Empirically Derived Job Families as a Foundation for the Study of Validity Generalization. Study II, The Construction of Job Families Based on Company-Specific PAQ Dimensions." *Personnel Psychology* 31 (1978): 341–353. (II–R)

Thompson, J. W. "Functional Job Descriptions." *Personnel Journal* 30, no. 10 (March 1952): 380–388. (I)

Tornow, W. W., and P. R. Pinto. "The Development of a Managerial Job Taxonomy: A System for Describing, Classifying and Evaluating Executive Office Positions." *Journal of Applied Psychology* 61 (1976): 410–418. (II–R)

Trattner, M. H. "Task Analysis in the Design of Three Concurrent Validity Studies of the Professional Administrative Career Examination." *Personnel Psychology* 32 (1979). (II–R)

Tucker, L. R. "Some Mathematical Notes on Three-Mode Factor Analysis." *Psychometrika* 31 (1966): 279–311. (II–R)

U.S. Department of Labor. *Dictionary of Occupational Titles.* 3d ed. Washington, D.C.: U.S. Government Printing Office, 1979. (I)

U.S. Department of Labor, Manpower Administration. *Task Analysis Inventories.* Washington, D.C.: U.S. Government Printing Office, 1973. (I)

Walsh, W. J. "Writing Job Descriptions: How and Why." *Supervisory Management* 17, no. 2 (February 1972): 2–8. (I)

Ward, J. H., and M. E. Hook. "Application of an Hierarchical Grouping Procedure to a Problem of Grouping Profiles." *Educational and Psychological Measurement* 23 (1963): 69–81. (II–R)

Weitz, J. "Criteria for Criteria." *American Psychologist* 16 (1961): 228–231. (II)

Wernimont, P. F., and J. P. Campbell. "Signs, Samples, and Criteria." *Journal of Applied Psychology* 52 (1968): 372–376. (II)

PART A

Form 1 Sample Jobs to Be Analyzed

MANAGER

Responsible for the efficient management of a business. Coordinates the operation of production, distribution, sales departments, and marketing. Determines administrative policies and executes through subordinate managers. Supervises about thirty-six persons.

PROGRESSIVE ASSEMBLER AND FITTER

Works on an assembly line making complex equipment, such as appliances or automobiles. Fastens one or more parts into a larger assembly by means of bolting, riveting, soldering, filing, lining up, or fitting the parts together. Passes assembly to next station on a conveyor system. This work may involve the use of electric or pneumatic drills, screwdrivers, wrenches, or riveting machines.

STENOGRAPHER

Takes dictation in shorthand for correspondence, reports, and other matters and transcribes dictated material, writing it in longhand or using a typewriter. May need to know technical language and jargon used in a particular profession. May perform a variety of related clerical duties such as filing, typing, answering the phone, etc. May take dictation on a stenotype machine or may transcribe information from a sound-producing record.

PART A

Form 2 Sample Job Items, Criteria, or Job Requirements

Sample job items (worker-oriented) for machine operators and first-line personnel:

1. Knowledge of _____ (specify equipment, machinery, structure or components)
2. Knowledge of preventive maintenance
3. Knowledge of electrical equipment
4. Knowledge of equipment assembly, installation, and repair, etc.
5. Operation of motor vehicles
6. Threading (chasing) on lathe
7. Loading, unloading, and feeding machines
8. Knowledge of cutting sheetmetal
9. Knowledge of using gas torch for cutting, etc.
10. Knowledge of painting metal
11. Knowledge of riveting
12. Knowledge of welding
13. Knowledge of forging and forge-welding
14. Work practices (includes keeping things neat, clean, and in order)
15. Ability to instruct
16. Use of measuring instruments (mechanical, electrical, electronic, as appropriate to line of work)
17. Use of test equipment (electronics)
18. Ability to plan and organize the work
19. Ability to interpret instructions, specifications, etc.
20. Ability to read electronic diagrams and schematics
21. Ability to use reference materials and manuals
22. Ability to follow directions in a shop
23. Ability to use carpenter's tools
24. Dexterity and safety
25. Ability to drive safely (motor vehicles)
26. Dexterity and eye-hand coordination
27. Reliability and dependability as a _____ (specify title of job)
28. Troubleshooting (mechanical)
29. Ability to work with others
30. Ability to work as a member of a team
31. Ability to meet deadline dates under pressure
32. Ingenuity (ability to suggest and apply new methods)
33. Ability to keep records and make reports

General job items (worker-oriented) for office personnel:

1. Ability to apply procedures
2. Ability to determine procedures for handling unique problems
3. Ability to plan and organize work
4. Ability to work independently without immediate supervision
5. Ability to check long technical reports for conformance with given principles of style and format
6. Judgment
7. Cooperative with others
8. Ability to learn new procedures
9. Ability to explain new procedures
10. Ability to help people find things in files
11. Preparing correspondence to explain material being sent in answering requests, following forms
12. Ability to work under pressure
13. Ability to meet short deadlines
14. Ability to order supplies, seeing in advance what is likely to be needed
15. Initiating telephone correspondence to answer questions or explain material being sent
16. Ability to do numerical work in budgeting and planning
17. Ability to do editorial checking for grammar
18. Ability to do editorial checking for punctuation
19. Ability to do editorial checking for spelling
20. Ability to plan coordination of work of several others, in terms of needs of particular task
21. Reliability and dependability

Form 2 (continued)

22. Ability to maintain security of confidential materials, in a room where visitors are permitted
23. Willingness to do the same detail over and over
24. Accurate typing (speed not required), cross-outs permitted
25. Accurate and rapid typing
26. Ability to interpret written instructions and regulations
27. Ability to prepare reports
28. Ability to set priorities on work
29. Ability to express oneself orally
30. Memory for procedures
31. Memory for directions
32. Practical knowledge of material and equipment used in office operation
33. Speed and accuracy of alphabetizing
34. Filing accuracy
35. Speed of simple tasks (like folding papers, or stuffing and sealing envelopes)
36. Ability to use business machines (specify which ones)
37. Tact in dealing with angry people

Descriptions of task-oriented general job items for managerial/supervisory personnel

1. *Training and preparing employees to work:* The ability to teach, train, and explain to employees thoroughly and clearly the correct methods, work and sequences, changes in methods of work, etc. Make sure they understand by questioning them. Develop skills of workers.

2. *Placing and utilizing manpower:* The ability to assign work according to abilities, so employees can work most effectively. This involves fitting the right person to the right job; matching individual interests and abilities with the job; knowing how employees feel about their assignments; being aware of employees' ambitions; and recognizing each person's individual abilities when planning assignments.

3. *Giving explicit or general directions:* The ability to select and give either detailed information to each employee about what is to be done and exactly how it is to be done, or to set up general goals and then encourage employees to do the work in the way they think best.

4. *Checking on work progress:* The ability to know the daily developments and progress of work; to keep informed about details of each employee's progress; to see that orders are being carried out; to correct and assist employees; to make certain that work is up to standard; and to know promptly when something goes wrong.

5. *Setting levels of effort and achievement:* The ability to set deadlines; to encourage employees to participate in setting deadlines; to motivate individuals to get and maintain high production; to establish standards of job performance; to encourage effective performance and an atmosphere conducive to good work.

6. *Helping individual workers with job-related problems:* The ability to help employees with their work problems; to give personal attention to individuals who have difficulty adjusting to the job; to help employees improve their job performance by explaining their mistakes to them.

7. *Giving workers feedback on their job performance:* The ability to give employees effective feedback on both good and poor performance, recognizing good performance personally and, if possible, when other employees are present; to constructively criticize poor performance privately; to give reasons for the criticism, keeping employees informed on all aspects of the job situation, including progress.

8. *Giving information to employees:* Keeping workers fully informed about things of general interest; holding meetings to discuss work activities and problems of all types, organizational direction and policies, current work schedules, employee suggestions, and general work problems. Encourage workers to talk and to think through their own opinions.

9. *Getting information from employees and acting on it:* Receiving employees' suggestions relating to their work as well as ideas for new work methods; asking for suggestions to improve production; acting upon suggestions that have merit; encouraging employees to express ideas and opinions on job improvement; listening to points of view on job matters.

10. *Establishing an appropriate work atmosphere:* Finding a balance between being a strict, business-like disciplinarian type of leader and being a friendly type.

11. *Getting support and services from outside the unit:* The ability to get needed equipment and see that employees have required work materials; to coordinate with other supervisors when group action is needed to solve a problem; and to get the full cooperation of other units.

12. *Acting as a buffer between workers and management:* The ability to clearly explain management to workers and workers to management; to define organizational goals and policies for employees; to defend, explain, and clarify these goals when they are not understood or are criticized by employees; to pass on employees' views to management; to stand up for employees as a group and as individuals.

Form 2 (continued)

13. *Helping employees with personal problems:*   Looking out for the personal welfare of subordinates, including helping employees solve personal problems; listening when employees ask for advice; settling conflicts between employees; and doing personal favors for them.

14. *Interpersonal relationships:*   The ability to talk to, understand, empathize with, work with, and be tolerant of citizens, fellow workers, and visitors.

15. *Dependability/reliability:*   The ability to be counted on to perform all duties or assignments whether or not supervision is present.

16. *Organizational ability:*   The ability to establish priorities and organize group activities into a plan of action that maximizes use of available resources and minimizes expenditures of time and energy.

17. *Adaptability:*   The ability to adjust to ideas and activities in order to cope with varying situations.

18. *Application of management principles and practices:*   The ability to apply to any given situation the management knowledge and skills which result in meeting the total needs of the organization and citizens.

19. *Initiative:*   The ability to see the need for action and then to act appropriately.

20. *Leadership:*   The ability to accept responsibility, to make decisions, to delegate responsibility (where appropriate), and to motivate people toward a coordinated effort.

21. *Teaching ability:*   The ability to explain and impart knowledge in an understandable manner and to ensure that it has the intended effect or response.

22. *Professionalism:*   The ability to conduct oneself in a manner that will be a credit to the profession.

PART B

Form 3 Classification Questionnaire Instructions for Job Incumbent

The following guides have been developed to assist you in completing Form 3.

1. *Define your job.* State briefly what is done by the unit in which you work. Explain how your job fits in with others in the organization, and make clear the purpose of your position. This should be as brief and concise as possible.

2. *List your different kinds of duties.* Describe each briefly, but in enough detail to give a clear understanding of your work. Start with the primary duties of your position. Then estimate the percentage of time for each.

3. *If you have any responsibility for the work of others, explain the nature and extent of your supervision and guidance of their work.* This includes supervision over those who report to you and their subordinates, and it also includes indirect responsibility. State by kinds of jobs the employees for whom you are responsible and to what extent.

4. *Explain the scope and effect of your work.* State how and to what extent your actions, recommendations, and decisions affect your organization, your clients, or the public. Explain the consequences of possible mistakes or errors in judgment. Describe how you influence the quality of work produced by others. Explain the extent of your authority to speak or act for your organization. Describe the effects of your work on: (1) policy, procedure, and organization; and (2) use of people, material, equipment, and funds.

5. *Describe the supervision and guidance you receive.* State what supervision and help you receive before, during, and after performance of your assignments from your supervisor, others, written guides, or practices. Describe any other guides for doing your work, such as regulations, procedures, practices, manuals, and standards, and describe how directly they affect your work.

6. *State the nature and extent of the mental demands of your position.* They may include any or all of the following:
   a) initiative—taking action without specific instruction;
   b) originality—the creativeness or inventiveness demanded by the work;
   c) judgment—the selection of the best course of action;
   d) any other significant mental demand.

7. *What are the knowledges, skills, and abilities required.* State any knowledges, skills, and abilities actually required by the job. For instance, include special manual skills, physical abilities, and aptitudes required. Identify the tasks concerned in each case and describe how and why such requirements are necessary.

8. *State the nature and purpose of the contacts you have in your work with persons other than your supervisors or subordinates.* Tell whether your work contacts are to exchange information, to make explanations, to persuade others, or to take part in group action.

9. *List anything else that affects your position.* Specify any job conditions or other considerations not covered elsewhere in your position description which affect the responsibility or difficulty of your work.

Name _____   Group Number _____

Date _____   Class Section _____   Hour _____   Score _____

PART B

Form 4 Position Classification Questionnaire for Job Incumbent

_____   _____
                                                Name of employee

_____   _____
Department name   _Position number (if applicable)_

_____   _____
Organization name   _Current position title_

Information on this form will be used to help classify and/or set the pay for your job. Please be as clear and accurate as possible.

Describe below, in sufficient detail including time spent, the work of the position, listing the different duties performed. (If more space is needed, please use additional sheets.)

_____

Percent time spent: _Duties or work performed:_

_____ %   1. _____

_____ %   2. _____

_____ %   3. _____

_____ %   4. _____

_____ %   5. _____

_____ %   6. _____

_____ %   7. _____

_____ %   8. _____

_____ %   9. _____

_____ %   10. _____

_____ %   11. _____

_____ %   12. _____

Form 4 (continued)

_____

Nature and extent of mental demands made:

_____

Nature of contacts with others besides workers and supervisor:

_____

Supervision exercised in this position (list names and job titles):

_____

Name and title of immediate supervisor/superior:

_____

Special requirements:

		Incidental or important	Percent of position's work time
Typing	_____	_____	_____
Shorthand	_____	_____	_____
Weapons (specify)	_____	_____	_____
Vehicles (specify)	_____	_____	_____

Machinery (list):

_____	_____	_____
_____	_____	_____

Other (specify):

_____	_____	_____
_____	_____	_____
_____	_____	_____
_____	_____	_____
_____	_____	_____

Other relevant information:

_____

I certify that I have read the above instructions and that entries are correct to the best of my ability.

_____   _____

Employee signature   Date

_____

To be completed by job analyst:
Name _____
Title _____
Date _____

Reviewed by: _____
Name _____
Title _____
Date _____

Name _____   Group Number _____

Date _____ Class Section _____ Hour _____ Score _____

PART C

Form 5 Position Audit Form for Job Analysts

GENERAL DATA

1. Department Unit Name _____
2. Name _____
3. Position Title _____

I. ORGANIZATION RELATIONSHIPS

4. Employees supervised and titles

A) _____

B) _____

C) _____

D) _____

E) _____

F) _____

G) _____

H) _____

I) _____

J) _____

5. Total number supervised _____
6. Supervision received

_____
_____
_____
_____
_____

7. Organization of department (sketch an organization chart for the incumbent's part of the organization):

II. DUTIES OF THE POSITION

8. A) _____
_____
_____

B) _____
_____
_____

Form 5 (continued)

C) _____
   _____
   _____

D) _____
   _____
   _____

E) _____
   _____
   _____

F) _____
   _____
   _____

G) _____
   _____
   _____

H) _____
   _____
   _____

I) _____
   _____
   _____

J) _____
   _____

9. Major outputs of the unit supervised

_____
_____
_____
_____

III. QUALIFICATIONS REQUIRED BY THE POSITION

10. Education required
_____
_____
_____
_____

11. Experience required
_____
_____
_____
_____

12. Other requirements (specify)
_____
_____
_____
_____
_____
_____
_____

13. Required knowledge, skills, and abilities
A) _____
B) _____
C) _____
D) _____
E) _____
F) _____
G) _____
H) _____
I) _____
J) _____
K) _____

PART C

Form 6 Quantitative Job Analysis Form

Item	Importance	Group Average	Frequency	Group Average
1. Analyzes financial information				
2. General and business programming				
3. Community–public relations				
4. Statistical analysis and research				
5. Trains others				
6. Makes decisions concerning _____				
7. Develops budgets				
8. Supervises management personnel				
9. Makes verbal presentations				
10. Forecasts needs				
11. Makes personnel decisions concerning _____				
12. Supervises (students, trainees, patients, subordinates, etc.)				
13. Issues directives				
14. Schedules work of others				
15. Interchanges information with prospective (employees, students or trainees)				
16. Uses hand tools				
17. Estimates sizes				
18. Uses mathematics				
19. Performs clerical tasks				
20. Uses manual force				
21. Persuades others				
22. Interchanges information with customers, clients, patients, etc.				
23. Interprets information				
24. Issues directives				

Form 6 (continued)

Item	Importance	Group Average	Frequency	Group Average
25. Controls operations				
26. Monitors work process				
27. Interprets information				
28. Develops methods				
29. Gives information				
30. Reports written information				
31. Writes _____				
32. Orally informs _____				
33. Drives motor vehicles types _____				
34. Coordinates work activities				
35. Plans work activities				
Others:				
36.				
37.				
38.				
39.				
40.				
41.				
42.				
43.				
44.				
45.				

IMPORTANCE KEY

1 = of no importance
2 = of little importance
3 = of average importance
4 = of high importance
5 = of critical importance

FREQUENCY KEY

1 = never occurs
2 = seldom occurs
3 = sometimes occurs
4 = often occurs
5 = almost always occurs

Name _____ Group Number _____

Date _____ Class Section _____ Hour _____ Score _____

PART D

Form 7 Job Description Form

Job Title: _____

Description of Work

General statement of duties:

Supervision received:

Supervision exercised:

Major Duties and Their Definitions (in order of importance):

1.

2.

3.

4.

5.

6.

7.

8.

9.

10.

PART D

Form 7 (continued)

Minimum Qualifications

Required knowledge, skills, and abilities:

Education:

Experience:

Other:

PART D

Form 8 Job Analysis—Action Verbs*

The following verbs are useful in identifying and defining job functions. Although many of the divisions may seem self-evident, we are defining each in the interest of consistency on the part of the person writing job descriptions.

Administer. Manage or direct the execution of affairs.

Adopt. Take up and practice as one's own.

Advise. Recommend a course of action; offer an informed opinion based on specialized knowledge.

Analyze. Separate into elements and critically examine.

Anticipate. Foresee and deal with in advance.

Appraise. Give an expert judgment of worth or merit.

Approve. Accept as satisfactory; exercise final authority with regard to commitment of resources.

Arrange. Make preparation for an event; put in proper order.

Assemble. Collect or gather together in a predetermined order from various sources.

Assign. Specify or designate tasks or duties to be performed by others.

Assume. Undertake; take for granted.

Assure. Give confidence, make certain of.

Authorize. Approve; empower through vested authority.

Calculate. Pass from person to person or place to place.

Clear. Gain approval of others.

Collaborate. Work jointly with, cooperate with others.

Collect. Gather.

Compile. Put together information; collect from other documents.

Concur. Agree with a position, statement, action, or opinion.

Conduct. Carry on; direct the execution of.

Confer. Consult with others to compare views.

Consolidate. Bring together.

Consult. Seek the advice of others.

Control. Measure, interpret, and evaluate actions for conformance with plans or desired results.

Coordinate. Regulate, adjust, or combine the actions of others to attain harmony.

Correlate. Establish a reciprocal relationship.

Correspond. Communicate with.

Delegate. Commission another to perform tasks or duties that may carry specific degrees of accountability.

Design. Conceive, create, and execute according to plan.

Determine. Resolve; fix conclusively or authoritatively.

Develop. Disclose, discover, perfect, or unfold a plan or idea.

Devise. Come up with something new—perhaps by combining or applying known ideas or principles.

Direct. Guide work operations through the establishment of objectives, policies, rules, practices, methods, and standards.

Discuss. Exchange views for the purpose of arriving at a conclusion.

Dispose. Get rid of.

Disseminate. Spread or disperse information.

Distribute. Deliver to proper destinations.

Draft. Prepare papers or documents in preliminary form.

Endorse. Support or recommend.

Establish. Bring into existence.

Estimate. Forecast future requirements.

Evaluate. Determine or fix the value of.

Execute. Put into effect or carry out.

Exercise. Exert.

Expedite. Accelerate the process or progress of.

Formulate. Develop or devise.

Furnish. Provide with what is needed; supply.

Implement. Carry out; execute a plan or program.

Improve. Make something better.

Initiate. Start or introduce.

Inspect. Critically examine for suitability.

Interpret. Explain something to others.

Investigate. Study through close examination and systematic inquiry.

Issue. Put forth or distribute officially.

Maintain. Keep in an existing state.

Form 8 (continued)

Monitor. Watch, observe, or check for a specific purpose.
Negotiate. Confer with others with an eye to reaching agreement.
Notify. Make known to.
Operate. Perform an activity or series of activities.
Participate. Take part in.
Perform. Fulfill or carry out some action.
Place. Locate and choose positions for.
Plan. Devise or project the realization of a course of action.
Practice. Perform work repeatedly in order to gain proficiency.
Prepare. Make ready for a particular purpose.
Proceed. Begin to carry out an action.
Process. Subject something to special treatment; handle in accordance with prescribed procedure.
Promote. Advance to a higher level or position.
Propose. Declare a plan or intention.
Provide. Supply what is needed; furnish.
Recommend. Advise or counsel a course of action; offer or suggest for adoption.
Represent. Act in the place of or for.
Report. Give an account of; furnish information or data.
Research. Inquire into a specific matter from several sources.
Review. Examine or re-examine.
Revise. Rework in order to correct or improve.
Schedule. Plan a timetable.
Secure. Gain possession of; make safe.
Select. Choose the best suited.
Sign. Formally approve a document by affixing a signature.
Specify. State precisely in detail or name explicitly.
Stimulate. Excite to activity; urge.
Submit. Yield or present for the discretion or judgment of others.
Supervise. Personally oversee, direct, inspect, or guide the work of others with responsibility for meeting standards of performance.
Train. Teach or guide others in order to bring up to a predetermined standard.
Transcribe. Transfer date from one form of record to another or from one method of preparation to another— without changing the nature of the date.
Verify. Confirm or establish authenticity; substantiate.

*From Richard I. Henderson, *Job Description, Critical Documents, Versatile Tools* (New York: American Management Association, 1975).

Name _____   Group Number _____

Date _____   Class Section _____   Hour _____   Score _____

ASSESSMENT OF LEARNING IN PERSONNEL ADMINISTRATION
EXERCISE 3

1. Try to state the purpose of this exercise in one concise sentence.

2. Specifically what did you learn from this exercise (i.e., skills, abilities, and knowledge)?

3. How might your learning influence your role and your duties as a personnel administrator?

4. What common problems are likely to be encountered as a job analyst interviews job incumbents?

5. Why is it a good idea to ask the incumbent and his or her supervisor about job duties?

6. Additional questions given by your implementor:

Section 3

IDENTIFYING, OBSERVING, AND APPRAISING PERFORMANCE IN ORGANIZATIONS

Section 3 contains two exercises that explain the process of measuring performance levels of workers. This process, typically called performance appraisal, occurs in every organization, regardless of size or type. Workers' performance is continually evaluated, whether it be informally through the judgments of others in the organization or formally through rating scales or another type of rating format.

Before a person's performance can be judged, job behaviors must be categorized and evaluated as to the degree of performance (e.g., from excellent to unacceptable) each behavior illustrates. The requirements a job makes in terms of workers' behavior is best assessed from a job analysis. Thus, the development of performance appraisal systems is a logical outgrowth of job analysis, as the analysis pinpoints what duties, responsibilities, and behaviors are required. These aspects of the job can be used as a basis for rating people. If a job analysis indicates that a major duty of a job is record keeping, record keeping becomes an appropriate performance criterion. After such a criterion is identified, the level of record keeping required, perhaps stated in terms of accuracy of the data, must be decided. There may be several levels of accuracy defined, each rated differently (e.g., excellent, average, etc.).

Once job performance is identified and evaluated, selection of people can begin, for there now exists a process for appraising the performance of those people selected based on job requirements, not on any one individual's performance level in a job.

In this view, performance objectives and standards are seen as an extension of job analysis, or as another phase of gathering job information. Two exercises are included in Section 3 to describe how this job information is translated into performance appraisal forms, or formats, used to rate people. Exercise 4 presents the general issues in performance appraisal and the advantages and disadvantages of various formats. Behaviorally Anchored Rating Scales (BARS), an appraisal system which emphasizes what behaviors are required to be considered successful on a job, are described in the *Introduction* and developed in Exercise 4. Exercise 5 allows you to design a popular and important appraisal system which emphasizes the results or outcomes of job behaviors, as opposed to the behaviors themselves. This system, often used in managerial/administrative positions, is called Management by Objectives (MBO).

Exercise 4

Appraising job performance: addressing key issues and designing behaviorally anchored rating scales (BARS)

PREVIEW

The subject of this exercise is the problem of appraising performance in organizations. Performance appraisal or evaluation is vital to every organization, as results are used for promotion decisions, wage and salary administration, and many other crucial decisions. First, performance appraisal formats, or forms, are developed for the jobs analyzed in Exercise 3 and various common performance appraisal formats are compared as to their advantages and disadvantages.

The second part of the exercise explains the advantages and disadvantages of Behaviorally Anchored Rating Scales (BARS), a potentially useful appraisal system due to its many practical benefits. BARS are described and designed.

OBJECTIVES

1. To gain an understanding of various methods and uses of performance appraisals.
2. To become aware of the difficulty in identifying, observing, and measuring job performance.
3. To gain experience in determining what criteria or job dimensions are appropriate in appraising performance.
4. To build skill in designing Behaviorally Anchored Rating Scales (BARS).

PREMEETING ASSIGNMENT

Read the entire exercise, carefully reviewing the Procedure.

INTRODUCTION

Identifying, Observing, and Appraising Job Performance

Performance appraisal (PA) is one of the most problematic areas in personnel administration. No matter whether the organization is large or small, business, governmental, or educational, the performance of its members must be evaluated in order to make decisions on wage and salary levels, on promotion, on termination, on training needs, and on many other important programs. Some PA's are quite informal, perhaps an occasional pat on the back and a few encouraging words by one's superior. Often, however, PA is a formal process relying on detailed written forms to supply information.

Performance Appraisal Objectives. PA has several objectives,[1] as indicated in Table 1. As can be seen from the table, the results of appraisals are vital for the

[1] L. L. Cummings and D. P. Schwab, *Performance in Organizations* (Glenview, Ill.: Scott Foresman, 1973); S. J. Carroll and C. E. Schneier, *Performance Appraisal and Review Systems* (Pacific Palisades, Calif.: Goodyear, 1981); C. E. Schneier and R. W. Beatty, "Performance Appraisal Revisited: Integrating Behaviorally Based and Effectiveness Based Methods. Part 1: Appraisal Objectives, Problems, and Formats," *The Personnel Administrator* 24, no. 7 (1979): 65–78.

effective operation of other human resource management programs. For example, a merit pay or bonus system would have little credibility if appraisal results were not actually used as the basis for these awards. Likewise, the appraisal system would have little credibility if its results were not seen by people in the organization as influencing such decisions as merit pay. None of the objectives listed in Table 1 can be met unless the specific appraisal system the organization uses accurately measures job performance of persons being rated. As we will see, this assumption is often problematic.

Thus, the decision for management is not whether to appraise performance, but rather how to do so. The vital questions personnel administration, as a staff function, must help answer are how often to appraise, what methods to use, which raters to use, and what to do with the results of the appraisal.

Deciding What to Measure. A first and perhaps most important decision in PA must come when management decides what to measure—what it will base the PA on. "Performance" is an elusive concept. Essentially, it is evaluated behavior or results. But which behaviors or results ought to be evaluated? In addition, should personality, appearance, or attitudes be evaluated?

Any appraisal system must help to identify what should be measured. For some jobs, such as typists, this is a straightforward process. We would measure a typist's performance primarily on accuracy and speed. But what about a manager or an accountant? Do we measure a manager on the profit of his or her unit? What if no profit is generated, as in the public sector? What if profit was obtained but the manager's behavior was so punitive that it caused the best staff members to leave the organization or seek transfers? Should the accountant be evaluated on the number of audits made, on the number of errors found in a clients' books, in interpersonal relations with clients, or on the number and size of new clients he or she secures? Obviously, all may be relevant, but some are difficult to measure.

No matter what type of appraisal format is used, a thorough analysis of each job (see Exercise 3) is typically required in order to identify those aspects of job performance that should be evaluated. These are called *criteria*. In developing a set of criteria, we must be certain to include only those aspects that have a bearing on job success and are available for measurement—the *relevant criteria*. For the accountant noted in the previous paragraph, personal appearance might have a bearing on job success, particularly as it refers to a client's willingness to trust and respect the accountant. But for the job of a research chemist working alone in a laboratory, personal appearance would not seem to be relevant to job success.

A thorough job analysis can help to identify the set of relevant criteria for a job.[2] Once they have been identified, they can be translated into *performance standards*. Standards signify the level of performance required on each aspect of job performance (e.g., verbal communication, work quantity) to attain certain ratings (e.g., excellent, average) and to qualify for particular personnel decision outcomes (e.g., promotion, merit raise). A performance standard for the criterion of sales volume for a salesperson may, for example, indicate that sales of 40,000 units per year or higher is considered excellent performance and merits a bonus. Not all criteria lend themselves so easily to quantifiable performance standards. Criteria such as interpersonal relations would have more judgmental, qualifiable standards—for example, "is tactful and contributes useful ideas in meetings."

What criteria are used and their relevance for job success not only help to determine the utility of an appraisal system, but also whether the system complies with legislation and guidelines on discrimination.

PA and the Law. Organizations often rely on three types of measures of performance: (1) personal traits—initiative or leadership ability; (2) job performance behaviors; and (3) job results—profit levels, sales volume, number of units rejected. These performance criteria provide standards against which workers' performance can be compared.

While any criteria that help account for observed differences in performance are useful, certain legal requirements now make it necessary for organizations to demonstrate that their criteria are actually related to job performance.[3] In the *Albermarle Paper Co.* v. *Moody* case the Supreme Court found that the company attempted to validate a test using ratings based on subjective and vague factors as criteria. Further, the company did not comply with the *Equal Employment Opportunity Commission (EEOC) Guidelines* (see Exercises 9 and 17) by not basing the performance ratings on a job analysis. The Court ruled that the employer could no longer use the test, and was required to pay the plaintiffs back pay and their attorneys' fees.

---

[2] See Carroll and Schneier, *Performance Appraisal and Review Systems;* Exercise 3.

[3] See W. H. Holley and H. S. Field, "Performance Appraisal and the Law," *Labor Law Journal* 26 (July 1975): 423–430; D. B. Schneier, "The Impact of EEO Legislation on Performance Appraisals," *Personnel* 55 (July–August 1978): 24–34; D. E. Thompson et al., "Performance Appraisal and the Law: Policy and Research Implications of Court Cases," *Proceedings of the Academy of Management National Meeting,* 1979; Exercises 9 and 17.

Thus, using appearance as a criteria may be disallowed if the organization cannot establish a clear relationship between a certain type of appearance and successful job performance. In addition, as discussed in Exercise 9, organizations must show that their PA's are reliable and reasonably accurate in order to use them as evidence of job success itself.

Various legal requirements and guidelines regarding equal employment opportunity (see also Exercise 17) are now beginning to affect performance appraisal practices significantly. Thus, a thorough, job-related PA form and well trained raters are becoming a necessity rather than a luxury for most larger organizations. The expenditure of time, effort, and money on PA is returned to an organization in numerous ways, such as through compliance with the law, identification of worker skill and ability deficiencies, rational promotion and merit raise decisions. However, the question for an organization becomes one of choosing from amongst the many varieties of PA formats.

Types of PA Formats. The ability of an appraisal to attain the objectives noted in Table 1 is of course determined by many factors discussed below, such as commitment from top management. The particular format or type of rating scale or system used does, however, have a significant influence on the utility and effectiveness of an appraisal system, its ability to measure performance accurately, and its ability to assist in compliance with legislation, as noted in the previous paragraph.

One of the most visible and most difficult aspects of appraisal concerns the choice of the format to use. There are innumurable varieties in use. The following categorization scheme, while not containing mutually exclusive categories, does help convey the various types of formats:[4]

1. *Comparative techniques*—the ratee is ranked against others in the same department or job class, typically on a global measure of overall performance.

2. *Absolute standards*—the ratee is rated against standards determined by company policy and

_____

[4] The categorization scheme was used in Cummings and Schwab, *Performance in Organizations.* See also R. Henderson, *Performance Appraisal: Theory to Practice* (Reston, Virginia: Reston, 1980), Chap. 8; references for specific types of formats, particularly within categories 1 and 2, can be found in *For Further Reading;* an excellent review of research of the various formats is F. J. Landy and J. L. Farr, "Performance Rating," *Psychological Bulletin* 87 (1980): 72–107.

written on the forms. This group includes "qualitative" techniques, such as critical incidents, and "quantitative" techniques, such as Behaviorally Anchored Rating Scales (BARS).

3. *Goal setting*—the ratee is rated according to the degree to which he or she attains predetermined job goals, such as Management by Objectives (MBO) (see Exercise 5).

4. *Direct indices*—the ratee is rated on the basis of such data as absenteeism, productivity, tardiness, etc.

Each of the specific methods within each general category has distinct advantages and disadvantages. Table 1 provides a general evaluation of some of the more frequently used types of systems.

One type of comparative technique is the forced-distribution ranking format. The rater must allocate a fixed percentage of ratees from a group or unit to each of several categories of performance. For example, ten percent must be allocated to the "Excellent" category, twenty percent to the "Good" category, forty percent to the "Fair" category, twenty percent to the "Poor" category, and ten percent to the "Unacceptable" category. Problems occur when raters are called upon to defend these global judgments and when comparisons across units must be made.

Personal trait scales that are not behaviorally anchored contain a list of traits (e.g., Initiative, Dependability) which may call for a rating using a numbered scale (i.e., 1 = highest performance, 2 = next highest performance, etc.) or a set of adjectives (e.g., Excellent, Very Good, etc.). This format would be considered an absolute standard type of system, although the "standards"—the numbers or adjectives—are open to varied interpretations.

Checklists are a very popular method of appraisal. Here, a group of behaviors, traits, or other characteristics is generated from persons knowledgeable about the job. Raters check those items that best describe the ratee's performance. In some systems, all items that apply are checked; in others, raters must choose only one of a group of items. Items can be standardized as to the level of performance they indicate and weighted in importance. Checklists are also absolute standard systems.

Behaviorally Anchored Rating Scales (BARS), discussed in detail later, is an absolute standard type of system that uses several aspects of job performance on which a person is rated. In addition, each scale is "anchored" at each of several points with behavioral statements, rather than merely with numbers or adjectives, which define each level of performance.

An example of a goal setting format is the ever-popular Management by Objective (MBO) system, described in detail in Exercise 5. In this system, goals or objectives are jointly set by superiors and subordinates, and the rating given is dependent upon the degree to which the objectives are attained.

Each of these methods has distinct advantages and disadvantages (see Table 1). Best results are probably obtained by matching the characteristics of each technique with the specific goal of the PA program and the characteristics of the organization involved. For example, if a single ratee is performing a certain type of job, comparative techniques would not be appropriate. If desired job behaviors have been identified, weighted, and communicated to ratees, some type of quantitative absolute standard technique may be useful. Often, techniques are used in combination. It is not unusual to combine MBO with certain indices of effectiveness (e.g., costs). The objective is to obtain as much job-relevant information as possible on which to base the PA.

The Ratees in a PA Program. Some research has found that most effective PA programs allow for ratee participation in the development of the criteria and provide for feeding back ratings to ratees.[5] This participation helps to gain ratees' commitment to the goals of the program and helps them to become aware of raters' problems. That is, as they participate in developing criteria and specific rating formats and in simply discussing the appraisal process, ratees can become more sensitive to the problems raters have in making their judgments, in reviewing the large amount of information they may have on each ratee, and in comparing ratees to each other. Participation also would help to communicate desired levels of performance—just what has to be done to receive a good PA—to ratees.

The Rater in a PA Program. The raters have a difficult task. They must observe and recall performance, they must try to fill out complex forms objectively, and they must justify their ratings to ratees. Their burden can be reduced by training them in the use of the particular format employed and by alerting them to the common types of rater biases and errors.[6]

Because performance must be observed over long periods of time (e.g., six months or one year) in a PA program, good raters often make anecdotal records of performance, being careful to include positive and negative incidents. Several raters can be used to get a more complete opinion of performance. Possible raters include the job incumbent, peers, subordinates, supervisors one and two levels above the ratee, and persons external to the organization brought in to rate performance. As long as potential raters have direct knowledge about a ratee's performance, they may be useful.

Giving Feedback to Ratees About Their Performance. Justifying a PA is one of the most difficult problems for raters. They may receive little help from the form, especially if it is a general or global rating. Ratees want to know specifically what parts of their performance need improvement and what parts were satisfactory. Only then can the appraisal objective of improving performance be attained. In addition, raters may be unsure of their ratings and/or may have based them on inadequate observation or non–job-related factors. These ratings may be difficult to justify to ratees.

Ratees often feel threatened by PA and become defensive in the appraisal interview. A "problem solving" approach to the appraisal interview, rather than a "tell and sell" approach can be useful. In the former, the rater tries to find the cause of poor performance and develop ways to remove these blocks, perhaps by training programs. The whole process is one of supportive confrontation, coaching and discussions of problems, rather than strictly evaluating.[7] Some studies have shown that criticism in the interview has a negative effect on performance, while mutual goal setting

---

[5] R. J. Burke and D. S. Wilcox, "Characteristics of Effective Employee Performance Review and Development Interviews," *Personnel Psychology* 22 (1969): 291–305; R. J. Burke, W. Weitzel, and T. Weir, "Characteristics of Effective Employee Performance Review and Development Interviews: Replication and Extension," *Personnel Psychology* 31 (1978): 903–920; D. Warmke and R. Billings, "A Comparison of Training Methods for Altering the Psychometric Properties of Experimental and Administrative Performance Ratings," *Journal of Applied Psychology* 64 (1979): 124–131.

[6] H. J. Bernardin and C. S. Walter, "Effects of Rater Training and Diary-Keeping on Psychometric Error in Ratings," *Journal of Applied Psychology* 62 (1977): 64–69; H. J. Bernardin and E. C. Pence, "Effects of Rater Training: Creating New Response Sets and Decreasing Accuracy," *Journal of Applied Psychology* 65 (1980): 60–66; an excellent review relevant to this issue is M. D. Spool, "Training Programs for Observers of Behavior: A Review," *Personnel Psychology* 31 (1978): 853–888.

[7] See, e.g., N. R. F. Maier, *The Appraisal Interview,* 2d ed. (LaJolla, Calif.: University Associates, 1976); Carroll and Schneier, *Performance Appraisal and Review Systems;* Henderson, *Performance Appraisal: Theory to Practice.*

Table 1. Relative Ability of Performance Appraisal Methods to Attain Appraisal System Objectives.*

Performance appraisal objectives	Forced-distribution ranking	Personal trait scales (numerical or objective anchors)	Checklists	Behaviorally anchored rating scales (BARS)	Management by objectives (MBO)
Validation of Selection Techniques Requires: Job relatedness, comprehensive list of dimensions tapping behavioral domain of the job; systematic job analysis to derive criteria; assessment of inter-rater reliability; professional, objective administration of format; continual observation of ratee performance by raters.	Poor	Poor	Good to Very Good	Very Good to Excellent	Fair to Good
A Rationale for Personnel Decision Making (e.g., identifying promotion potential, job assignments, demotions and terminations, etc.) Requires: Job-related criteria; job dimensions dealing with ability to assume increasingly difficult assignments built into form; ability to rank ratees comparatively; measurement of contribution to organization/department objectives; assessment of ratee's career aspirations and long-range goals.	Fair to Good (Varies)	Poor to Fair	Fair to Very Good (Varies)	Good (Varies)	Fair to Good
Measuring Performance Accurately Requires: Lessening of rater response set errors (e.g., leniency, halo); agreement with other performance measures not on the format (e.g., direct indices, such as salary, sales volume); reliability across multiple raters; flexibility to reflect changes in job environment; job-related criteria; commitment of raters to observe ratee performance frequently and complete format seriously; the use of the same standards across raters.	Poor to Fair	Fair to Poor	Good to Very Good	Good	Good to Excellent
Feedback and Development Requires: Specific, behavioral terminology on the format; setting behavioral targets for ratees to work toward; participation of raters and ratees in development; job relatedness; problem-solving performance review which ends with a plan for performance improvement; reduction of ambiguity/anxiety of ratees regarding job performance required and expected by raters/organizations.	Poor	Poor	Good to Excellent	Very Good to Excellent	Fair to Good

Table 1. (Continued)

Performance appraisal objectives	Forced-distribution ranking	Personal trait scales (numerical or objective anchors)	Checklists	Behaviorally anchored rating scales (BARS)	Management by objectives (MBO)
Assessing Training Needs Requires: Specifying deficiencies in behavioral terms; incorporating all relevant job dimensions; eliminating motivation/attitude and environmental conditions as causes of inadequate performance.	Poor	Poor to Fair	Good to Very Good	Very Good	Fair to Good
Rewards Allocation Requires: Ability to rank order ratees or results in quantifiable performance score; facilitating a variance or spread of scores to discriminate between good, bad, fair, etc., ratees; measuring contributions to organizational/departmental objectives; perception of accuracy and credibility by employees.	Good to Very Good	Fair	Very Good to Excellent	Very Good to Excellent	Good to Excellent

*Each method's ability to attain the objectives would, of course, depend on several issues particular to each rating situation, such as rater biases, number of raters available, care taken to develop the format, reward structure in the organization, etc.

has a positive effect on future performance and reduces anxiety and defensive behavior in the appraisal interview.[8]

These suggestions can be helpful, but telling people how they are doing, especially when they are doing poorly, is still a difficult and anxiety-producing process for most raters and ratees. However, ratees want to know where they stand and what they must do to improve their performance. Thus, feedback is vital to them.

Problems in PA. Beside the difficult nature of judging others in general, some particular problems in the PA process can lessen its effectiveness. Raters may make certain types of errors in their ratings. They may rate all ratees too high (leniency error), or they may not discriminate sufficiently across ratees, but instead "bunch up" PA scores by giving everyone a similar, average rating (central tendency error). They may base their rating on one key trait or aspect of job performance, rather than rating all of the important aspects of per-

formance separately (halo error). For example, because a ratee is often tardy, he or she is rated low overall, even if performance is good when at work.

Another problem of PA programs is lack of agreement between raters and ratees on the standards of good performance. Many ratees may not know what is required of them. Often, they may not know what the important aspects of job performance are and/or what the desired level of performance is on these dimensions of their job. This ambiguity may come from the lack of any organizational policy in this area, or the lack of communication of this policy to the raters or ratees.

These problems in PA require careful consideration by the personnel administrator. The first step is often a thorough job analysis. No matter what PA format is used, the critical elements of performance to be rated—or the job *items*—must be identified. Only then can we make useful *ratings,* or evaluations of employee performance.

Factors Contributing to Successful Implementation of Appraisal Systems. Even in cases where a detailed job-related appraisal form has been developed with the participation of ratee and where raters have been trained in alleviating common rater errors, the effectiveness of the appraisal system is by no means assured.

[8] See, e.g., H. H. Meyer et al., "Split Roles in Performance Appraisal," *Harvard Business Review* 43 (January–February 1965): 123–129; Burke, Weitzel, and Weir, "Effective Employee Performance Reviews."

While the choice of format is important, it can be overshadowed by the power of various policies and beliefs about appraisal in an organization.

First, raters must be rewarded for accurately and thoroughly assessing their subordinates' performance, for completing the forms conscientiously, and for communicating their judgments to subordinates. In short, a vital aspect of any supervisor's job is *performance management,* an activity which includes making ratings, but also extends to monitoring and improving subordinates' performance and providing ongoing coaching and counseling to subordinates on performance-related matters.[9] If superiors are rewarded for effective performance management activities, and the organization fosters the belief that time spent on these activities is legitimate, then appraisal has a much higher probability of being an effective human resource management system.

Second, the results of the appraisals must actually be used in decisions that affect people's jobs, rewards, and careers. If appraisal results are not used in rewards decisions, promotion decisions, job-assignment decisions, etc., the system loses credibility very quickly. Managers will not spend time to make ratings when they are not tied to important consequences for both themselves and their subordinates.[10]

Third, it must be remembered that performance appraisal is essentially a judgment and information-processing task.[11] The raters must evaluate and judge behavior as to its appropriateness; they must judge its relevance. Raters must also process an enormous

amount of information about ratee behavior, observing, recalling, assimilating, and weighing. How accurately they perform this difficult task says perhaps more about the effectiveness of the appraisal systems than the particular characteristics of the forms. The forms can assist raters in this group of judgmental, information-processing activities they must engage in as they make their rating. Specificity of criteria, as well as job-relatedness and thoroughness, is a crucial characteristic of forms, and of course the forms must be understandable to users and no more lengthy and complex than necessary. But even a form exhibiting these characteristics does not preclude judgment or take the place of a serious and conscientious rater who has knowledge of both the job and the ratee's behavior.

Human judgment and information-processing are neither completely objective nor infallible. Raters should be assisted in their efforts not only by the rating form itself but also through training and opportunities to practice and develop the skills required to evaluate others' behavior.

BEHAVIORALLY ANCHORED RATING SCALES

A performance appraisal (PA) technique that many believe to be one of the most useful currently available is Behaviorally Anchored Rating Scales (BARS). BARS have been credited with success because they have been found to assist in attaining the major objectives of PA, namely, accurate measurement of job performance and improvement of job performance through feedback to ratees.

What Are BARS? BARS[12] are a PA format in which the rater is provided with statements of standards against which to evaluate the performance of ratees. These standards are placed on the scales in BARS, one scale for each important broad performance area, or job dimension. The dimensions can be identified by several methods, including those often used to analyze jobs (see Exercise 3). When BARS are developed, small group discussions can be held with potential

[9] See Carroll and Schneier, *Performance Appraisal and Review Systems.*

[10] The Civil Service Reform Act (CSRA) of 1978 (Public Law 95-454, Oct. 13, 1978, 95th Congress) specifically states that performance appraisals based on performance standards be used for merit pay decisions and other personnel actions in the federal government. This new emphasis on tying performance to rewards in the public sector will no doubt increase the importance and visibility of performance appraisals in government agencies (see, e.g., C. A. Newland, "Performance Appraisal of Public Administrators: According to Which Criteria?" *Public Personnel Management* 8 (1978): 294-304.

[11] See Carroll and Schneier, *Performance Appraisal and Review Systems;* Landy and Farr, "Performance Rating;" A. Lewin and S. Layman, "Information Processing Models of Peer Nominations," *Personnel Psychology* 32 (1979): 63-81; C. Banks, "An Experimental Study of the Rating Process: Correlates of Rating Behavior," paper presented at Annual Meeting, Western Psychological Association, San Diego, 1979; W. Borman, "Individual Differences Correlates of Accuracy in Evaluating Others' Performance Effectiveness," *Applied Psychological Measurement* 3 (1979): 103-115; M. Hakel, "Normative Personality Factors Recovered from Ratings of Personality Descriptors: The Beholder's Eye," *Personnel Psychology* 27 (1974): 409-421.

[12] For an excellent discussion of the rationale and procedure for BARS, see P. C. Smith and L. M. Kendall, "Retranslation of Expectations: An Approach to the Construction of Unambiguous Anchors for Rating Scales," *Journal of Applied Psychology* 47 (1963): 149-155. See also Landy and Farr, "Performance Rating"; P. S. Burgar, "Have Behavioral Expectation Scales Fulfilled Our Expectations? Theoretical and Empirical Review," *JSAS Catalogue of Selected Documents in Psychology* 8 (1978): 76; C. E. Schneier and R. W. Beatty, "Performance Appraisal Revisited, Part II: Developing Behaviorally Anchored Rating Scales," *The Personnel Administrator* 24, no. 8 (1979): 59-70.

raters and ratees in order to identify the important aspects of the job which should be evaluated in PA.

Each job dimension identified in these group discussions eventually becomes one of the behaviorally anchored scales. The scale is typically presented vertically on a page with "Excellent" or "Very Good" performance at the top of the page and "Unacceptable" or "Very Poor" performance at the bottom of the page. Between these two extreme values are a number of scale points, usually five, seven or nine in number (examples appear as Form 7 in this exercise).

While initial BARS formats often had one or more statements or behavioral examples at each scale value to "anchor" the scale, recent research has concluded that this format does not adequately alleviate rater errors, such as reliability or leniency.[13] Thus, the statements can be placed anywhere on the form, at or between scale values, which best represents the level of performance they were developed to illustrate (see Form 7). If six job dimensions have been identified for a job, six scales will be used as the appraisal format, each with several anchors illustrating various degrees of performance along the scale. The scales might also contain statements to help clarify and define the job dimension being rated. For each scale, the rater indicates what level of performance he or she feels is indicated by the ratee's typical job behavior, using the behavioral anchors and dimension-clarification statements as guidelines and cues to recall. Because behavioral statements covering all aspects of job performance cannot typically be placed on the scales, raters can write in specific behavioral examples they recall for each ratee at appropriate levels on the scale. These added anchors would be their own examples and rationale for a rating at a specific level.

Why Are BARS Useful? BARS are useful because of their unique PA characteristics, the first such feature being their behavioral orientation. BARS rely on job behavior, or what people actually *do* on their jobs. This behavioral emphasis takes into account only those things under control of the individual ratee, not overall measures of effectiveness which may not be related to job behavior (see *Introduction,* Exercise 3).

By attaching behavioral anchors to scales, BARS can help to specify what people must do to receive good, fair, or poor ratings. This is often more useful than simply indicating the job dimensions on which people will be evaluated, as is true of many of the for-

mats in Form 1. This specificity of BARS allows raters to give feedback to ratees regarding why they received the ratings they did and can help to define what they must do to improve their performance. This type of feedback not only helps to make PA less subjective and based more on actual observed behavior, but also helps ratees to overcome anxiety associated with PA.

In addition, BARS allows for ratee and rater participation in their development. In the small group meetings where the job dimensions and anchors are developed for BARS, raters and ratees give much thought to their jobs and the important aspects of job performance are thus made explicit. This awareness can be useful to raters, as they now have a guide to use when observing performance. Ratees would be better able to judge their superiors' expectations. Any ambiguities or conflicts regarding duties, responsibilities, or differences between raters' and ratees' ideas of desired performance could be cleared up in the discussion sessions. Finally, the participation of the ultimate users in BARS' design and the retention of actual language used by the job holders help to assure rater and ratee commitment to the PA technique.

Because BARS can provide a quantitative rating, appraisal scores can be related to current wage and salary structure to determine what behaviors are being highly rewarded with monetary rewards. Ranges of scores on BARS could be tied to different levels of merit raises. Certain job dimensions could be singled out, given high weights relative to other dimensions and used for bonus administration, etc.

Several "spin-off" effects of BARS make them useful for several personnel programs.[14] BARS can be used to identify the behavioral criteria on which to make selection decisions and design selection tests. BARS can also help to specify behavioral training objectives (see Exercise 10). Eventually, the broad content of training courses would be the job dimensions in BARS and the specific behaviors to be learned in each content area could be derived from the behavioral anchors. Motivation techniques may benefit from BARS, as certain behaviors are identified which could be areas of poor performance for the organization. These could be pinpointed and linked to rewards to help improve performance.

BARS is a rather recent PA technique. Although it shows promise, it is used by only a small portion of organizations, and the research available to date is not conclusive regarding the ability of BARS to eliminate

[13] See, e.g., H. J. Bernardin et al., "Behavioral Expectation Scales: Effects of Developmental Procedures and Formats," *Journal of Applied Psychology* 61 (1976): 75–79.

[14] M. R. Blood, "Spin-Offs from Behavioral Expectation Scale Procedures," *Journal of Applied Psychology* 59 (1974): 513–515.

certain types of rater errors.[15] BARS is a time-consuming technique to develop, requiring much effort of raters. They must observe actual job behavior closely and make many, often difficult judgments. But BARS' advantages as a PA system seem to be considerable, and more organizations are adopting them each year. They satisfy the demands of performance evaluation in terms of providing specific feedback to employees, identifying training needs, forming a basis for promotion decisions and wage and salary administration, and helping to develop valid selection criteria.

Some Terminology. The meaning of certain terms used in the previous discussion and in the exercise should be clarified at this point. *Job dimensions* are those broad content areas of job performance that describe what duties, skills, responsibilities, or activities are performed. In BARS, each scale has as its title a job dimension, derived from some type of job analysis technique. *Anchors* are specific statements that illustrate actual job behavior, or worker activity. These anchors are attached at various points on the scales of BARS and are the standard against which raters evaluate ratee behavior.

Writing effective behavioral anchors is a difficult and time-consuming process. Many anchors are needed as some are discarded when BARS are designed due to ambiguity (see *Procedure*). The best anchors are those that describe behavior in specific terms and avoid adjectives which can be interpreted differently by different raters (e.g., occasionally, usually, best, etc.). Figure 1 contains a few suggestions for writing effective anchors and Figure 2 contains sample behaviors for managerial jobs.

Remember the distinction between these anchors, which describe *behavior,* and *performance,* which is measured or evaluated behavior. In BARS, we concentrate (a) on the behaviors essential for success in a particular job as described in the anchors, and (b) on the performance as an evaluation or measurement of an individual on the behaviors specified. We do not directly measure *effectiveness,* or contribution to organizational goals with BARS. *Effectiveness measures* are summary indices of performance which often contain some factors not within the direct control of the person we are rating. Examples would be cost overruns, profit, or productivity (see Exercise 5).

15 See D. P. Schwab, H. G. Heneman, and T. A. Decotiis, "Behaviorally Anchored Rating Scales: A Review of the Literature," *Personnel Psychology* 28 (1975): 549–562; M. D. Dunnette and W. C. Borman, "Personnel Selection and Classification Systems," *Annual Review of Psychology* 30 (1979): 477–535; Burgar, "Behavioral Expectation Scales."

Is a Separate BARS System Needed for Each Job in an Organization? The procedures advocated here to implement BARS are designed to be based on the needs of the specific job. Thus, effective BARS performance evaluation systems would often require extensive participation of the job incumbent in their design. Cooperation is critical if the performance evaluations are to be "situation specific." In other words, the greater generality that is obtained by making performance evaluations fit wider and wider ranges of jobs, the more the people in those jobs are measured abstractly and not specifically. Thus, we lose specific job relatedness of the performance appraisal criteria as we attempt to make performance evaluations fit several groups of jobs, unless, of course they are quite similar. Obviously, greater generality detracts from the usefulness of a performance evaluation for the purposes of employee feedback, identifying training needs, making promotion decisions, wage and salary decisions, and selection validation.

If we are going to reduce rater errors and subjectivity when evaluating an employee's performance, attempts must be made to make performance evaluations as specific and as job related as possible. Obviously systems can be devised which are generally applicable, but the errors created by general applicability, although meeting short-run needs, can only open the door to criticism, dissatisfaction, subsequent rater and ratee criticisms and dissatisfaction, as well as litigation by not being job specific. But job relatedness can only be achieved if serious commitment on the part of the organization is obtained, for BARS require an indepth analysis of job content, a time-consuming process.

It is difficult to judge the number of job incumbents required in a position in order to develop a BARS system. Obviously, the larger the number of incumbents, the more behavioral anchors that can be generated and the smaller the burden on each incumbent rating anchor would be. A larger pool of anchors can make the resultant system more thorough and descriptive. A system could be developed for as few as ten incumbents, however, providing they are given time to participate.

Some job dimensions may be applicable to more than one job, thus cutting developmental time and cost. Great care must be taken to assure that dimensions used across jobs or positions are in fact applicable.

Toward a Dynamic PA System. PA formats, including BARS, are static in nature. That is, they cannot change over time. However, job performance, job environments, and job holders are all dynamic in

Fig. 1. Suggestions for writing useful behaviors

1. Use specific examples of behavior, *not conclusions* about the "goodness" or "badness" of behavior.

    Use this: This supervisor tells a secretary when the work was to be completed, the degree of perfection required, the amount of space it must be typed within, and the kind of paper necessary.

    Not this: This supervisor could be expected to give very good instructions to a secretary. Instructions would be clear and concise.

2. Avoid using *adjective qualifiers* in the anchor statements; use descriptions of actual behavior.

    Use this: This supervisor understands employees such that the supervisor can repeat both the employee's communication and the intent of the message. They also make certain they talk in private when necessary and do not repeat the conversation to others.

    Not this: When supervising associates, this supervisor does a good job of understanding their problems. This supervisor is kind and friendly.

3. Avoid using anchors that make assumptions about employee *knowledge* about the job; use descriptions of behavior.

    Use this: This employee performs the disassembly procedure for rebuilding a carburetor by first removing the cap and then proceeding with the internal components, gaskets, etc. If in doubt about the procedure, the mechanic will refer to the appropriate manual.

    Not this: This mechanic knows how to dissassemble a carburetor and will do so in an efficient and effective manner.

4. Avoid using *frequencies* in anchor statements; use descriptions of behavior.

    Use this: This officer performs the search procedure by first informing those arrested of their rights, asks them to assume the search position and then proceeds to conduct the search by touching the arrested in the prescribed places. When the search is complete, the officer informs the arrested and proceeds to the next step in the arrest procedure.

    Not this: This officer always does a good job in performing the search procedure.

5. Avoid using *quantitative values* (numbers) within anchors.

    Use this: This accountant submits reports on time which contain no misinformation or mistakes. If discrepancies occur on reports from the last period, this accountant identifies the cause.

    Not this: This accountant could be expected to meet 90% of deadlines with 95% accuracy.

nature—they do change over time. For example, assume that a PA system was developed in January and certain performance standards were set to be used to evaluate job performance of ratees at the end of the current appraisal period (i.e., July). During the six-month appraisal period, new equipment or technology may be introduced to make the job easier, duties and responsibilities may be added or deleted from the job, and/or the job holder's ability may improve due to experience. Any of these occurrences could make the static performance standards and the PA format based on them obsolete. In order to prevent this problem, PA formats must constantly be updated, revised, and redesigned in light of the dynamic nature of jobs and worker abilities. BARS are no exception. New anchors would have to be written periodically in order to keep the system up to date.

PROCEDURE

Overview. Various performance appraisal techniques, or formats, are compared in order to point out their strengths and weaknesses. A BARS appraisal format is designed for the job analyzed in Exercise 3, or one of the jobs for which job descriptions appear in Exercise 14.

PART A

STEP 1: Compare and contrast the six different types of formats in Forms 1–6 as to their ability to meet the basic appraisal objectives outlined in the exercise *Introduction*. Be very specific as to *why* each format would facilitate or deter the attainment of each objective.

TIME: About one hour.

Fig. 2. Examples of behaviors for managerial jobs

Planning Behaviors
  Analyzes situations and seeks input to develop plans.
  Develops measurable objectives consistent with organizational objectives.
  Designs use of resources to accomplish objectives.
  Anticipates crises and makes changes to avert problems.

Organizing Behaviors
  Assigns/delegates tasks.
  Identifies alternative approaches to resource uses.
  Coordinates human, financial, and material resource uses.
  Divides unit objectives into identifiable tasks and sets due dates.

Controlling Behaviors
  Monitors/reviews unit performance.
  Takes corrective action when needed.
  Develops efficiency/effectiveness approaches/alternatives as needed.
  Anticipates/avoids problems.
  Monitors budget, policies, and procedures while maintaining quality and productivity.
  Knows current status of all resources (human, financial, material).

Leadership Behavior
  Involves/encourages subordinates in decision making.
  Provides or makes needed training available.
  Offers individual counseling regarding tasks or objectives.
  Makes decisions promptly and with necessary information.
  Sets example by being on time, visible, and available.
  Develops subordinates to assume manager's responsibility in his/her absence.

Supervisory Behaviors
  Records critical work behaviors/instances.
  Clarifies expectations of work performance for employees.
  Works with employees to set developmental/individual performance objectives.
  Provides regular feedback to employees based upon observation of work behavior.
  Reviews annual performance appraisals with employee.

Communication Behaviors
  Conveys ideas and information in understandable manner (checks it out).
  Listens to others and comprehends messages.
  Reports accurate information, written and oral, using correct English.
  Reacts promptly to communications.
  Keeps administration and employees informed of changes and future actions or issues.

Cooperation/Coordination

  Lets others know of plans in advance.
  Supports joint or multidepartmental objectives.
  Shares available resources with other units needing resources.
  Meets with other managers to become informed and avoid problems.
  Initiates efforts to implement cooperative solutions to problems.

PART B

STEP 2: Become familiar with the BARS appraisal format by briefly reviewing those contained in Forms 7–12. Notice all are behaviorally anchored, often with more than one anchor, or statement, for each scale value. Many different forms of the scales are in use, but all are in the incumbent's job language.

TIME: About 20 minutes.

STEP 3: Now that you have been introduced to the BARS format, you are ready to develop a set of BARS. Here you are to derive a set of job dimensions from a typical job analysis form of a job description. You may use the job you analyzed in Exercise 3, or use any of the job descriptions in Exercise 14, to derive a set of job dimensions which will each become a behaviorally anchored scale.

In an organization developing BARS,

job or position descriptions could be used as a starting point for the development of behavioral anchors and dimensions. Of course, small group discussions with incumbents and their supervisors, or any of the job analysis techniques noted in Exercise 3, would help to generate information about jobs. Typically, small-group discussions with supervisors and subordinates are used in a BARS program to obtain job information and to generate commitment to the program.

TIME: About one hour.

STEP 4: Review the possible errors involved in writing BARS by using Form 13.

TIME: About 30 minutes.

STEP 5: Several supervisors and job incumbents would be asked to write anchors for each job dimension illustrative of various degrees of performance. These anchors will eventually appear on the final BARS form after "retranslation" (see Step 6). Write two or more behavioral anchors for each of the five levels of performance on Form 14. Make sure *each* group member writes a set of anchors for *each* job dimension, as a very large number of anchors is required.

You may find it more convenient to write each anchor on a 5 × 7 index card, since each group member will be called upon to retranslate the anchors in Step 6. Develop a list of the job dimensions for the job you are using and give each a numerical or alphabetic code. When group members originally write their anchors, they can put the job dimension code on one side and write the anchor on the reverse. Each person will write several anchors on cards for *each* job dimension.

TIME: About two hours per person.

STEP 6: A large pool of anchors now exists for each of the five performance levels and for each job dimension. The group's consensus must now be attained as to (a) what job dimension they feel each anchor best illustrates, and (b) what level of performance each anchor defines.

In order to decide under which job dimension an anchor best fits, all of the anchors written for a job are put on a list in random order and several people with knowledge of the job then indicate which job dimension they feel the anchor was originally meant to illustrate. Thus, the anchors are "retranslated" back to the original set of dimensions. If high

agreement is reached among those performing this step as to what dimension an anchor best illustrates, the anchor can be placed on that job dimension scale in the final BARS form. If people do not agree as to which dimension an anchor belongs, it is probably ambiguous and should be discarded. Further, if, after all of the anchors are retranslated, one or a few original job dimensions have not been used (i.e., few or no anchors have been translated to them), it may mean that these dimensions were too broad or ambiguous and they should be discarded or combined into other dimensions. If 70 percent or more of the group agree on the placement of an anchor, it should be retained.

Next, each anchor is given a scale value of 1 through 5. These values indicate the level of performance the anchor illustrates. The values can be averaged among all those participating, and the mean is a good approximation of the group's feeling as to where the anchor should be on the scale.[16] The retranslation procedure can be facilitated by using Form 15. All of the anchors written can be numbered consecutively. Each person will review each anchor written, including those they wrote, indicating which job dimension is best illustrated and what scale value, or level of performance, the anchor best represents. Each anchor's identifying number can be placed on each group member's Form 15, rather than writing out each anchor on the form. The anchor work sheets (Form 14), or index cards containing the anchors, can then be passed to each group member in order for them each to complete Form 15.

TIME: Time varies with size of group and complexity of job, but it should take no more than one hour per person for Step 5.

STEP 7: After each group member has completed Form 15, compute the percentage of the group that placed an anchor under each of the dimensions. Do this for each anchor. Retain any anchor for which about 70 percent of the group members agree as to placement under a job dimension.

For those anchors now remaining, compute the mean scale value given by the group.

---

[16] Standard deviations can also be computed for the anchors, with large standard deviations indicating poor agreement among people. Anchors with standard deviations of greater than 1.75 could be discarded.

TIME: About one to two hours, with a calculator.

STEP 8: After percentages of agreement and means are calculated in Step 7, discard those anchors that have low agreement as to job dimension. Discard job dimensions for which no anchors seem to belong. Then attach the remaining anchors for each dimension on the final BARS form (Form 16) at the appropriate point on the scale indicated by the mean value given to the anchor by the group.[17] You will have one scale for each job dimension. Weights can be assigned to each job dimension. The weights could be used to derive a final PA score (i.e., the score [1–5] on each dimension times the weight of the dimension, summed across all dimensions). Such scores could then be linked to merit raises or used to compare ratees for promotion decisions.

The dimension weights could be written on each job dimension scale. The set of scales, one scale for each job dimension, each with their behavioral anchors, makes up the final performance-appraisal format called BARS.

TIME: About two hours.

FOR FURTHER READING

Allen, P., and R. Rosenberg. "The Development of a Task-Oriented Approach to Performance Evaluation...." *Public Personnel Management* (January–February 1978): 26–32. (I)

"Appraising the Performance Appraisal." *Business Week* (May 19, 1980). (I)

Atkin, R. S., and E. T. Conlon. "Behaviorally Anchored Rating Scales: Some Theoretical Issues." *Academy of Management Review* 3 (1978): 119–128. (II)

Barrett, R. S. *Performance Rating.* Chicago: Science Research Associates, 1966. (II)

---

[17] After you have retranslated and weighted the remaining anchors and completed one Form 16 for each job dimension, you will probably notice that anchors are not attached along the scale at equal intervals. This is acceptable since raters use the anchors to cue them to ratee behavior and to help decide what level of performance ratee behavior represents. All possible ratee behaviors cannot be placed on the form. As they rate, raters can add some behavioral anchors, indicating actual behaviors they observed the ratee exhibiting, at appropriate places on the scale to assist them in making their judgment. In addition, descriptions of the job dimension can be added to the left side of the scale to assist raters. If too much of the scale is void of anchors, however, more should be written.

Beatty, R. W., C. E. Schneier, and J. R. Beatty. "An Empirical Investigation of Perceptions of Ratee Behavior Frequency and Ratee Behavior Change Using Behavioral Expectation Scales (BES)." *Personnel Psychology* 30 (1977): 647–658. (II–R)

Beer, M. et al. "A Performance Management System: Research, Design, Introduction, and Evaluation." *Personnel Psychology* 31 (1978): 505–135. (II)

Bernardin, H. J. "The Effects of Rater Training on Leniency and Halo Errors in Student Rating of Instruction." *Journal of Applied Psychology* 63 (1978): 301–308. (II–R)

Bernardin, H. J., and E. C. Pence. "Effects of Rater Training: Creating New Response Sets and Reducing Accuracy." *Journal of Applied Psychology* 15 (1980): 60–66. (II–R)

Bernardin, H. J., M. B. LaShells, P. C. Smith, and K. M. Alvares. "Behavioral Expectation Scales: Effects of Developmental Procedures and Formats." *Journal of Applied Psychology* 61 (1976): 75–79. (II–R)

Bigoness, W. J. "Effects of Applicant's Sex, Race, and Performance Ratings: Some Additional Findings." *Journal of Applied Psychology* 61, no. 1 (1976): 80–84. (II–R)

Blanz, F., and E. E. Ghiselli. "The Mixed Standard Scale: A New Rating System." *Personnel Psychology* 25 (1972): 185–199. (II–R)

Blood, M. R. "Spin-Offs from Behavioral Expectation Scale Procedures." *Journal of Applied Psychology* 59 (1974): 513–515. (II)

Blum, M. L., and J. C. Naylor. *Industrial Psychology,* rev. ed. New York: Harper & Row, 1968. (II)

Borman, W. C. "Individual Difference Correlates of Accuracy in Evaluating Others' Performance Effectiveness." *Applied Psychological Measurement* 3 (1979): 103–115. (II–R)

Borman, W. C. "Exploring the Upper Limits of Reliability and Validity in Job Performance Ratings." *Journal of Applied Psychology* 63 (1978): 135–144. (II–R)

Borman, W. C. "The Rating of Individuals in Organizations: An Alternate Approach." *Organizational Behavior and Human Performance* 12 (1974): 105–124. (II–R)

Borman, W. C., and M. D. Dunnette. "Behavior-Based Versus Trait-Oriented Performance Ratings: An Empirical Study." *Journal of Applied Psychology* 60 (1975): 561–565. (II–R)

Borman, W. C., and W. R. Vallon. "A View of What Can Happen When Behavioral Expectation Scales Are Developed in One Setting and Used in Another." *Journal of Applied Psychology* 59 (1974): 197–201. (II–R)

Burgar, P. S. "Have Behavioral Expectation Scales Fulfilled Our Expectations? Theoretical and Empirical Review." *JSAS Catalogue of Selected Documents in Psychology* 8 (1978): 76. (II)

Burke, R. J., W. Weitzel, and T. Weir. "Characteristics of Effective Performance Review and Development Interviews: Replication and Extension." *Personnel Psychology* 31 (1978): 903–920. (II–R)

Campbell, J. P., M. D. Dunnette, R. D. Arvey, and L. N. Hellervick. "The Development of Behaviorally Based Rating Scales." *Journal of Applied Psychology* 57 (1973): 15–22. (II–R)

Carroll, S. J., and C. E. Schneier. *Performance Appraisal and Review Systems.* Pacific Palisades, Calif.: Goodyear, 1981. (II)

Cummings, L. L. "A Field Experimental Study of the Effects of Two Performance Appraisal Systems." *Personnel Psychology* 26 (1973): 489–502. (II–R)

Cummings, L. L., and D. P. Schwab. "Designing Appraisal Systems for Information Yield." *California Management Review* 20, no. 4 (1978): 18–25. (I)

Cummings, L. L., and D. P. Schwab. *Performance in Organizations: Determinants and Appraisal.* Glenview, Ill.: Scott Foresman, 1973. (II)

Dailey, C. A., and A. M. Madsen. *How to Evaluate People in Business.* New York: McGraw-Hill, 1980. (I)

Davies, C., and A. Francis. "The Many Dimensions of Performance Measurement: There is More to Performance than Profits or Growth." *Organizational Dynamics* 3, no. 3 (Winter 1975): 51–65. (I)

DeCotiis, T. A. "An Analysis of the External Validity and Applied Relevance of Three Rating Formats." *Organizational Behavior and Human Performance* 19 (1977): 247–266. (II–R)

DeCotiis, T. A., and A. Petit. "The Performance Appraisal Process: A Model and Some Testable Hypotheses," *Academy of Management Review* 3 (1978): 635–646. (II)

Dickinson, T. L., and P. M. Zellinger. "A Comparison of the Behaviorally Anchored Rating and Mixed Standard Scale Formats." *Journal of Applied Psychology* 65 (1980): 147–154. (II–R)

Dickinson, T. L., and T. E. Tice. "A Multitrait-Multimethod Analysis of Scales Developed by Retranslation." *Organizational Behavior and Human Performance* 9 (1973): 421–438.

Dunnette, M. D., and W. C. Borman. "Personnel Selection and Classification Systems." *Annual Review of Psychology* 30 (1979): 477–525. (II)

Emerson, L. V. *Evaluating Your Staff.* Washington, D.C.: National Association of Regional Councils, 1978).

Flanagan, J. C. "The Critical Incident Technique." *Psychological Bulletin* 51 (1954): 327–358. (II–R)

Flanagan, J. C. "A New Approach to Evaluating Personnel." *Personnel* 26 (1949): 35–42. (I)

Fulmer, W. E. "Tailoring Employee Evaluation Forms to Your Organization's Needs." *Personnel* 55 (January–February 1978): 65–72. (I)

Fogli, L., C. L. Hulin, and M. R. Blood. "Development of First-Level Behavioral Job Criteria." *Journal of Applied Psychology* 55 (1971): 3–8. (II–R)

Friedman, B. A., and E. T. Cornelius, III. "Effect of Rater Participation in Scale Construction of the Psychometric Characteristics of Two Ratings Scale Formats." *Journal of Applied Psychology* 61, no. 2 (1976): 210–216. (II–R)

Hakel, M. "Normative Personality Factors Recovered from Ratings of Personality Descriptions: The Beholder's Eye." *Personnel Psychology* 27 (1974): 409–421. (II–R)

Harari, O., and S. Zedeck. "Development of Behaviorally Anchored Rating Scales for the Evaluation of Faculty Teaching." *Journal of Applied Psychology* 58 (1973): 261–265. (II–R)

Henderson, R. *Performance Appraisal: Theory to Practice.* Reston, Virginia: Reston, 1980.

Holley, W. H., and H. S. Feild. "Performance Appraisal and the Law." *Labor Law Journal* 27 (July 1975): 423–430. (I)

Ivancevich, J. M. "A Longitudinal Study of Behavioral Expectation Scales: Attitudes and Performance." *Journal of Applied Psychology* 65 (1980): 139–146. (II–R)

Kane, J. S., and E. E. Lawler, "Performance Appraisal Effectiveness: Its Assessment and Determinations." *Research in Organizational Behavior* 1 (1979): 425–478. (II)

Kane, J. S., and E. E. Lawler, "Methods of Peer Assessment." *Psychological Bulletin* 85 (1978): 555–586.

Kavanagh, M. J. "The Content Issue in Performance Appraisal: A Review." *Personnel Psychology* 24 (1971): 653–668. (II)

Kleine, B. H. "How to Give and Receive Criticism Effectively." *Supervisory Management* 24 (March 1979): 37–41. (I)

Koontz, H. "Making Managerial Appraisal Effective." *California Management Review* 15 (1972): 46–55. (I)

Korman, A. "The Prediction of Managerial Performance: A Review." *Personnel Psychology* 21 (1968): 295–322. (II)

LaBraque, M. "On Making Sounder Judgments, Strategies and Snares." *Psychology Today* 14 (June 1980): 30–40. (I)

Landy, F. J., and J. L. Farr. "Performance Rating." *Psychological Bulletin* 87 (1980): 72–107. (II)

Landy, F. J., and R. M. Guion. "Development of Scales for the Measurement of Work Motivation." *Organizational Behavior and Human Performance* 5 (1970): 93–103. (II–R)

Latham, G. P., K. H. Fay, and L. M. Saari. "The Development of Behavior Organization Scales for Appraising Performance of Foremen." *Personnel Psychology* 32 (1979): 299–311. (II–R)

Latham, G. P., and K. N. Wesley. *Performance Appraisal and Goal Setting.* Reading, Mass.: Addison-Wesley, in press. (I)

Lawler, E. E. "Performance Appraisal and Merit Pay." *Civil Service Journal* (April–June 1979): 14–18. (I)

Lefton, R. E. et al. *Effective Motivation Through Performance Appraisal.* New York: Wiley, 1977. (I)

Levinson, H. "Appraisal of What Performance?" *Harvard Business Review* 54 (July–August 1976): 30–47. (I)

Lewin, A., and S. Layman. "Information Processing Models of Peer Nominations." *Personnel Psychology* 32 (1979): 63–81. (II–R)

London, M., and J. R. Paplawski. "Effects of Information on Stereotype Development in Performance Appraisal and Interview Contexts." *Journal of Applied Psychology* 61, no. 2 (1976): 199–205. (II–R)

Lopez, F. M. *Evaluating Employee Performance.* Chicago: Public Personnel Association, 1968. (I)

Maier, N. R. F. *The Appraisal Interview.* 2d ed. La Jolla, Calif.: University Associates, 1976. (I)

Mayfield, E. C. "Management Selection: Buddy Nominations Revisited." *Personnel Psychology* 23 (1970): 377–391. (II–R)

McGregor, D. "An Uneasy Look at Performance Appraisal." *Harvard Business Review* 34 (1957): 89–94. (I)

Meyer, H. E. "The Science of Telling Executives How They're Doing." *Fortune* 89, no. 1 (January 1974): 102–106+. (I)

Meyer, H. H., E. Kay, and J. R. P. French. "Split Roles in Performance Appraisal." *Harvard Business Review* 43 (1965): 123–129. (I–R)

Miner, J. B. "Bridging the Gulf in Organizational Performance." *Harvard Business Review* 46 (1968): 102–110. (I)

Miner, J. B. "Management Appraisal: A Capsule Review and Current References." *Business Horizons* 11, no. 5 (1968): 83–96. (I)

Newland, C. A. "Performance Appraisal of Public Administrators: According to Which Criteria?" *Public Personnel Management* 8 (1979): 294–304. (I)

Nieva, V. F., and B. A. Gutek. "Sex Effects, an Evaluation." *Academy of Management Review* 5 (1980): 267–276. (II)

Polster, H., and H. S. Rosen. "Use of Statistical Analysis in Performance Review." *Personnel Journal* 53, no. 7 (July 1974): 498–406+. (II)

Prien, E. P., M. A. Jones, and L. M. Miller. "A Job Related Performance Rating System." *The Personnel Administrator* 22 (November 1977): 37–41. (I–R)

Rieder, G. A. "Performance Review—A Mixed Bag." *Harvard Business Review* 51, no. 4 (July–August 1973): 61–67. (I)

Schaffer, R. H. "Demand Better Results—and Get Them." *Harvard Business Review* 52, no. 6 (November–December 1974): 91–98. (I)

Schneier, C. E. "Raters' Preferences for Performance Appraisal Criteria as a Function of Their Cognitive Structure." *Psychological Reports* 45 (1979): 459–467. (II–R)

Schneier, C. E. "Operational Utility and Psychometric Soundness of Behavioral Expectation Scales (BES): A Cognitive Reinterpretation." *Journal of Applied Psychology* 62 (1977): 541–548. (II–R)

Schneier, C. E., and R. W. Beatty. "Performance Appraisal Revisited." Series of three articles, *The Personnel Administrator* 24 (July, August, and September 1979). (I)

Schneier, C. E., and R. W. Beatty. "The Influence of Role Prescriptions on the Performance Appraisal Process." *Academy of Management Journal* 21 (1978): 129–134. (II–R)

Schneier, C. E., and R. W. Beatty. "Performance Appraisal in Organizations: An Empirical Study of the Effects of Raters' Level in the Hierarchy." *Proceedings of the Thirteenth Eastern Academy of Management Meetings.* Washington, D.C., 1976. (II–R)

Schneier, C. E., and R. W. Beatty. "Toward a Cognitive Theory of the Performance Appraisal (PA) Process: A Field Investigation of the Effects of Matching Rater Cognitive Structure with Cognitive Requirements of PA Formats." Paper delivered at the National Meetings of the Academy of Management, Kansas City, 1976. (II–R)

Schneier, D. B. "The Impact of EEO Legislation on Performance Appraisal." *Personnel* 55 (July–August 1978): 24–34. (I)

Schwab, D. P., H. Heneman, and T. A. Decotiis. "Behaviorally Anchored Rating Scales: A Review of the Literature." *Personnel Psychology* 28 (1975): 549–562.

Scott, W. E., and Hamner, W. C. "The Influence of

Variations in Performance Profiles in the Performance Evaluation Process: An Examination of the Validity of the Criterion." *Organizational Behavior and Human Performance* 14 (1975): 360-370. (II-R)

Smith, H. P., and P. J. Brouwer. *Performance Appraisal and Human Development.* Reading, Mass.: Addison-Wesley, 1977. (I)

Smith, M. "Documenting Employee Performance." *Supervisory Management* 24 (September 1979): 30-36. (I)

Smith, P. C. "Behaviors, Results, and Organizational Effectiveness: The Problem of Criteria." In M. Dunnette, ed., *Handbook of Industrial Organizational Psychology.* Chicago: Rand McNally, 1976. (II)

Smith, P. C., and L. M. Kendall. "Retranslating of Expectations: An Approach to the Construction of Unambiguous Anchors for Rating Scales." *Journal of Applied Psychology* 47 (1963): 149-155. (II-R)

Spool, M. D. "Training Programs for Observers of Behavior: A Review." *Personnel Psychology* 31 (1978): 853-888. (II)

Stevens, G. E., and A. S. DeNisi. "Women as Managers: Attitudes and Attributions for Performance by Men and Women." *Academy of Management Journal* 23 (1980): 355-361. (II-R)

The Bureau of National Affairs, Inc. *Management Performance Appraisal Programs.* PPF Survey No. 104. Washington, D. C.: The Bureau of National Affairs, Inc., January 1974. (I-R)

The Conference Board. *Appraising Managerial Performance.* New York: Conference Board, 1977. (I)

Thompson, E. E. et al. "Performance Appraisal and the Law: Policy and Research Implications." Proceedings, Academy of Management National Meeting, 1979. (II)

Thompson, P. H., and G. W. Dalton. "Performance Appraisal: Managers Beware." *Harvard Business Review* 48, no. 1 (1979): 149-157. (I)

Whisler, T. L., and S. F. Harper, eds. *Performance Appraisal.* New York: Holt, Rinehart and Winston, 1962. (II)

Williams, M. R. *Performance Appraisal in Management.* New York: Crane Russak, 1972. (I)

Williams, W. E., and D. A. Seiler. "Relationships Between Measures of Effort and Job Performance." *Journal of Applied Psychology* 57 (1973): 49-54. (II-R)

Zedeck, S., and H. T. Baker. "Nursing Performance as Measured by Behavioral Expectation Scales: A Multitrait-Multirater Analysis." *Organizational Behavior and Human Performance* 7 (1972): 457-466. (II-R)

Zedeck, S., and M. R. Blood. *Foundations of Behavioral Science Research in Organizations.* Monterey, Calif.: Brooks/Cole, 1974. (I)

Zedeck, S., R. Jacobs, and D. Kafry. "Behavioral Expectations: Development of Parallel Forms and Analysis of Scale Assumptions." *Journal of Applied Psychology* 61 (1976): 112-115. (II-R)

PART A

Form 1 Performance Appraisal Formats—Sample A, Overall Effectiveness Rating

Instructions: This evaluation form asks you to evaluate a subordinate's current level of job performance. You are requested to think of someone else (doing the same job as the subordinate being evaluated) who you feel is an "average" performer and compare your subordinate to this "average" performer on the scale below. Please place an X along the scale to describe what you believe is your subordinate's overall level of performance compared to the "average" performer.

Rater _____ Title _____ Date _____

Ratee _____ Title _____

Unsatis-factory	Well below average	Somewhat below average	A little below average	Average	A little above average	Somewhat above average	Well above average	Extremely successful
1 2	3 4	5 6	7 8	9 10	11 12	13 14	15 16	17 18

← Lower evaluation   Higher evaluation →

PART A

Form 2 Performance Appraisal Formats—Sample B

Job Police Dispatcher

Supervisor _____ Title _____

Rating Period _____

Subordinate _____ Job Class and Grade _____

Instructions: Rate the subordinate by comparing him or her to all others in your unit performing the same job.

	Rank Relative to Other Ratees in This Job Class				
Job Dimension	*Better than 90% of ratees*	*Better than 70–90% of ratees*	*Better than 30–70% of ratees*	*Better than 10–30% of ratees*	*Better than 0–10% of ratees*
Dispatches emergency equipment.					
Performs matron duties as required.					
Performs public relations work.					
Files reports.					
Types reports.					
Operates console and other equipment.					
Provides technical/legal assistance to officers.					
Edits and interprets information.					
Supervises dispatching operations and personnel.					
Orients and trains all newly hired dispatchers and reserves.					
Overall Performance					

PART A

Form 3 Performance Appraisal Formats—Sample C

MAGICO	EMPLOYEE PERFORMANCE APPRAISAL

IDENTIFICATION DATA

NAME OF EMPLOYEE	NO.	DIVISION	EMPLOYEE CLASSIFICATION	CODE

EDUCATION

HIGH SCHOOL DIPLOMA	COLLEGE	DEGREE(S)
☐ YES ☐ NO	YRS.	

PROFESSIONAL & TECHNICAL REGISTRATION

PROFESSIONAL REGISTERED	TYPE OF REGISTRATION	STATES WHICH REGISTERED
☐ YES ☐ NO	☐ EIT ☐ P.E. ☐ LAND SURVEYOR ☐ OTHER:	

EXPERIENCE				ABSENTEEISM			
YEARS EMPLOYED	PREVIOUS	PRESENT ASGN	(SICK)	(CAUSE)	(WITHOUT PAY)	TOTAL	
	YRS. MO.	YRS. MO.		HOURS	HOURS	HOURS	

REASON FOR EVALUATION	PERIOD OF REVIEW	
☐ 6 MONTHS REVIEW ☐ ANNUAL REVIEW ☐ OTHER:	FROM	THRU

PERSONAL CHARACTERISTICS		NEEDS IMPROVEMENT				AVERAGE		GOOD		EXCEL.	
ENTHUSIASM: *Excitement brought to the job, eagerness to achieve, desire to excel, pride of accomplishment.*	Reviewing Supervisor	0	1	2	3	4	5	6	7	8	9
	Endorsing Supervisor										
AMBITION: *Desire to succeed and accomplish goals.*	Reviewing Supervisor	0	1	2	3	4	5	6	7	8	9
	Endorsing supervisor										
PERSERVERANCE: *Persistence to achieve positive results, diligence.*	Reviewing Supervisor	0	1	2	3	4	5	6	7	8	9
	Endorsing Supervisor										
INITIATIVE: *Gets things started, desires to achieve, to improve, to seek knowledge, to display innovative thought.*	Reviewing Supervisor	0	1	2	3	4	5	6	7	8	9
	Endorsing Supervisor										
ATTITUDE: *Willingness, disposition, emotional reaction, moods, and temperament.*	Reviewing Supervisor	0	1	2	3	4	5	6	7	8	9
	Endorsing Supervisor										
COOPERATION: *Desire and ability to work with others toward common organizational goal.*	Reviewing Supervisor	0	1	2	3	4	5	6	7	8	9
	Endorsing Supervisor										
HUMAN RELATIONS: *Ability to achieve amiable reactions from peers, supervisors and subordinates.*	Reviewing Supervisor	0	1	2	3	4	5	6	7	8	9
	Endorsing Supervisor										
LEADERSHIP: *Ability to inspire and effectively direct others.*	Reviewing Supervisor	0	1	2	3	4	5	6	7	8	9
	Endorsing Supervisor										
COMPLIANCE WITH COMPANY POLICIES: *Ability to adapt, accept and respect.*	Reviewing Supervisor	0	1	2	3	4	5	6	7	8	9
	Endorsing Supervisor										

PART A

Form 4 Performance Appraisal Formats—Sample D

Name _____   Job Class _____

Date Employed _____   Location or Dept. _____

Carefully analyze employee's performance. Study each **factor** and the description of each **degree**. Place an X in the square which most clearly fits the employee's performance. Where necessary, make comments below the factor to explain your evaluation. After completion, discuss review with employee and summarize on back.

Part I—Ability & Application

Initiative (ability to exercise self-reliance and enterprise)	Grasps situation and ☐ goes to work without hesitation	Works independently ☐ often; seldom waits for orders	Usually waits for instruc- ☐ tions; follows others	Does only what is specif- ☐ ically instructed to do
Comments on Initiative:				
Quality of work (accuracy and effectiveness of work; freedom from errors)	Consistently good quali- ☐ ty; errors rare	Usually good quality; few ☐ errors	Passable work if closely ☐ supervised	Frequent errors; cannot ☐ be depended upon to be accurate
Comments on Quality:				
Quantity of work (output of work; performance speed)	Works consistently and ☐ with excellent output	Works consistently with ☐ above average output	Maintains group average ☐ output	Below average output; ☐ slow
Comments on Quantity:				
Job knowledge (technical knowledge of job; ability to apply it)	Knows job thoroughly; ☐ rarely needs help	Knows job well; seldom ☐ needs help	Knows job fairly well; ☐ requires instructions	Little knowledge of job; ☐ requires constant help
Comments on Knowledge:				
Attitude (enthusiasm, coop- erativeness, willingness)	Enthusiastic; outstand- ☐ ing in cooperation; tries new ideas	Responsive; cooperates ☐ well; meets others more than half-way	Usually cooperates; ☐ does not resist new ideas	Uncooperative; resents ☐ new ideas; displays little interest
Comments on Attitude:				
Dependability (willingness to accept responsibility; to follow through)	Outstanding ability to ☐ perform with little super- vision	Willing and able to ac- ☐ cept responsibility; little checking required	Usually follows instruc- ☐ tions; normal follow-up	Refuses or unable to car- ☐ ry responsibility; needs constant follow-up
Comments on Dependability:				
Attendance (reliability to be on the job)	Always can be relied ☐ upon to be at work on time; absent only when real emergency	Usually can be relied ☐ upon to be at work on time; explained ab- sences occur occasion- ally	Comes in late with rea- ☐ sonable excuses; fairly frequent explained ab- sences	Frequent unexplained ☐ lateness and/or ab- sences
Comments on Attendance:				
Leadership (ability to guide, direct others)	Others naturally follow ☐ his example or direction; obtains good results from others	Willingly assumes guid- ☐ ance of others; is fairly well accepted in this role	Is accepted reluctantly ☐ by his group as a guide or example; gets fluc- tuating results	Shows no aptitude or ☐ skill in leadership
Comments on Leadership:				

Form 4 (continued)

Part II—Capacity & Ambition for Advancement

Check (√) applicable sections (more than one section may apply):

REGRESSING	NOT SUITED TO JOB	NOT LIKELY TO ADVANCE	PROGRESSING	SATISFACTORY	MAXIMUM PERFORMANCE ON JOB	READY FOR PROMOTION

Review your ratings and comments; then briefly outline what actions you will take or suggest to maintain, to improve, or to correct the behavior and/or output of this employee.

_____

_____

_____

_____

_____

Time set for necessary
improvement to take place: _____

Discuss your rating results with the employee:

Date _____ Signature _____
                                             Employee

Employee's reaction to review and suggestions was: (check one)

Appreciation
(Completely willing to
strive for improvement) ☐

Interest
(Will try to
follow suggestions) ☐

Disinterest
(Satisfied with
present status) ☐

Resentment
(Feels review
is imposition) ☐

Other (explain) _____

_____

Conclusions drawn from interview _____

_____

_____

_____

Date _____ Signature _____
                                             (Reviewer)

PART A

Form 5 Performance Appraisal Formats—Sample E, Dimensional Performance Appraisal Format

Job Title _____ Date _____

Dimension	Weight %	Unac-ceptable 1	Poor 2	Below Avg. 3	Average 4	Above Avg. 5	Good 6	Excellent 7
1.								
2.								
3.								
4.								
5.								
6.								
7.								
8.								
9.								
10.								
11.								
12.								
Points (weights X rating)	100%	___	___	___	___	___	___	___
		___	___	___	___	___	___	___

Total Points _____

Form 5 (continued)

After reviewing the description for this job, supervisors and subordinates should have agreed on the dimensions to be included and the weights assigned to each dimension. Both raters and ratees are to review the job-related work behaviors of the ratee. These job-related work behaviors are to be described for each dimension in the spaces provided below. This behavior is to be descriptive and typical of the ratee on this dimension during the rating period. Once this behavior has been described, it is to be evaluated for each dimension on the scale provided earlier.

JOB-RELATED BEHAVIORS

DIMENSION : _____ : _____
_____
_____
_____

DIMENSION : _____ : _____
_____
_____
_____

DIMENSION : _____ : _____
_____
_____
_____

DIMENSION : _____ : _____
_____
_____
_____

DIMENSION : _____ : _____
_____
_____
_____

DIMENSION : _____ : _____
_____
_____
_____

Form 5 (continued)

JOB-RELATED BEHAVIORS (continued)

DIMENSION : _____ : _____

_____

_____

_____

DIMENSION : _____ : _____

_____

_____

_____

DIMENSION : _____ : _____

_____

_____

_____

DIMENSION : _____ : _____

_____

_____

_____

DIMENSION : _____ : _____

_____

_____

_____

DIMENSION : _____ : _____

_____

_____

_____

☐ SUPERVISOR'S EVALUATION

☐ EMPLOYEE'S SELF-EVALUATION

☐ _____ EVALUATION

SIGNATURE: _____

DATE: _____

PART A

Form 6 Performance Appraisal Formats—Sample F

Job Title   District Advisor   Date _____

Job Objective   Collections   Name _____

Measurement Method   Cost   District _____

Carryovers	Present	Date	Target	Date	Actual	Date
Delinquent balances carried over (final readout)						
Dollar amount of bad debt losses submitted to bonding company						

Instructions: Below, please indicate what you believe to be the typical behavior of this DA based on your observation of his/her job performance.

Check One

___   *Excellent:*   Ensures that all D/MR/Cs* have correct route books; makes certain all bills are out on time; puts rack money in bank; all records are up to date and collection incentives are thoroughly explained; pays company account by due date.

___   *Very Good:*   Makes sure all statements are made out correctly, all racks are emptied and money banked; ensures that statement dates are observed; makes every effort to pay company account by due date.

___   *Good:*   Follows up with all D/MR/Cs to ensure that collections are accurate and prompt; seldom fails to pay company account by due date.

___   *Average:*   Accounts are advised of collection procedures and D/MR/Cs are encouraged to make collections on time; sometimes fails to pay company account by due date.

___   *Below Average:*   Does not *push* to ensure that D/MR/Cs are instructed on collection procedures and billing dates.

___   *Poor:*   *Unaware* of delinquent accounts; does not provide adequate billing instructions to D/MR/Cs.

___   *Unacceptable:*   Does not talk to D/MR/Cs about collection or personally follow up on collection problems.

How could this manager improve his or her performance in the area of collection cost that is not included in the above description? _____

_____

*Abbreviations for the three positions supervised by the District Advisor.

PART B

Form 7 Examples of BARS—Sample A*

Position _____Police Dispatcher_____

Job Dimension _____Dispatching emergency equipment._____

Excellent performance: Information is clearly communicated and sites are accurate when given to officers. In the event the ambulance doesn't know direction to a particular location, the dispatcher accurately gives directions. Gathers relevant information and dispatches emergency equipment to appropriate site. Gathers and relays all vital information to hospital to patrol unit accurately and clearly. Asks caller vital questions and relays accurate information to patrol car. This person can be expected to correctly use appropriate department codes and languages in radio and phone conversations. Calmly relates information—able to decide when some codes are not enough.

Very good performance: Can be expected to give clear, distinct information to officers. Information is accurate and understandable when responding to officers. Responds to an emergency in a calm, collected manner, never losing control of the situation. Advises other departments of an ambulance running through their city. Advises other units of emergency equipment that is running hot and gives accurate locations and direction of traffic. Able to distinguish priorities. Keeps self informed on any changes made in the codes.

Good performance: Both the message and sites specified are accurate. Takes what information possible over phone and relays to officer.

Fair performance: Information is accurate and well understood. This employee can be expected to make a sound evaluation of information gathered and dispatch patrol car only when necessary. Sends patrol car immediately to scene after receiving call if patrol car is available. This person can be expected to use all the appropriate codes and languages, but on occasion will forget the right code or language to use.

Poor performance: Is difficult to understand, but gives accurate sites. Becomes upset and nervous. Can be expected to dispatch patrol unit regardless of the nature and importance of the information gathered. This person will substitute one code or language for another, causing some confusion, but immediately corrects the same as soon as an error is detected.

Very poor performance: Is clearly understood, but fails to give appropriate sites. Mixes up information and, as a result, emergency equipment is delayed in arrival. Responds in a nervous manner in emergencies and has a difficult time disguising lack of control. During periods of peak workload, this employee can be expected to forget to dispatch patrol car when one is needed. Gives erroneous and confusing information to the dispatched officer.

Unacceptable performance: Fails to dispatch emergency equipment in an immediate and efficient manner. Neglects to relay relevant information to patrol unit. Relays information to patrol unit in a garbled and stuttered fashion. Fails to observe proper FCC regulations in performing dispatch duties.

*These examples were chosen as they are scales actually developed and used in organizations. However, not all of these particular BARS formats or their anchors conform to the guidelines discussed in the exercise *Introduction* and Fig. 1.

PART B

Form 8 Examples of BARS—Sample B

Position   Chemical Equipment Operator

Job Dimension   Verbal Communications

7   ☐   This operator could be expected to:
check verbal instructions against written procedures; check to make sure he or she heard others correctly; brief replacements quickly and accurately, giving only relevant information.

6   ☐   This operator could be expected to:
inform superiors immediately if problems arise; listen to others carefully and ask questions if he or she does not understand; give information, instructions, etc., in a calm, clear voice.

5   ☐   This operator could be expected to:
inform others of his or her location in the plant; avoid discussing non–work-related subjects when relating plant status to others; inform others of all delays that took place on the shift.

4   ☐   This operator could be expected to:
give others a detailed account of what needs to be done, but not to establish priorities; mumble when speaking to others; not face the person communicating with him or her and act disinterested.

3   ☐   This operator could be expected to:
fail to relate necessary details to those relieving him or her at break or shift change; not seek information and only offer it when asked; guess at status of pots when relaying information; not check to be sure he or she has heard others correctly, but rely on what he or she thought the person said; leave out information about his or her own errors when talking to others.

2   ☐   This operator could be expected to:
never ask for help if unsure of something or if errors are made; refuse to listen to others; continually yell at others and use abusive language.

1   ☐   This operator could be expected to:
not answer when called; refuse to brief replacements; give person relieving him or her inaccurate information deliberately.

PART B

Form 9 Examples of BARS—Sample C

Job Title _____ Center Director

Job Dimension _____ Maintenance and operation of equipment

Instructions: Preface each anchor with "The director can be expected to . . . ."

1. Excellent performance

    1.17 maintain a full inventory of recreational equipment.

2. Very good performance

    2.33 make personal daily checks of the operational status of all equipment.

    2.5 maintain 75% inventory of recreational equipment.

    2.83 arrange training for each new employee on the use of equipment.

3. Good performance

    3.0 promptly order replacements or repairs for equipment.

    3.0 utilize an established reporting system as well as occasional personal checks for the operational status of equipment.

    3.33 establish a procedure for training new employees to use equipment.

    3.5 check the operational status of all equipment.

4. Fair or average performance

5. Poor performance

    5.33 rely on employees to tell him or her of equipment failures.

    5.5 fail to establish a method of determining operational status of equipment.

6. Very poor performance

    6.33 fail to train new employees on use of equipment.

    6.5 fail to replace or repair equipment.

    6.5 ignore the operational status of equipment.

7. Unacceptable performance

PART B

Form 10 Examples of BARS—Sample D

Position   Computer Programmer/Systems Analyst

Job Dimension   Professional Growth

Excellent	Keeps abreast of changes and additions to existing software and hardware. Modifies programs and programming methods to increase efficiency. Takes initiative to use home study, extracurricular classes, discussions, and meetings as means to upgrade performance.
Very good	On the job, works toward development of long-term potential; off the job, reads and studies in areas of work and professionally oriented material. Constantly exploring books and manuals for new techniques and applications.
Good	Has plans for finding and filling in any professional gaps that will hinder professional development. Takes special classes or training if it deals with the job. Concerned mainly with knowledge of specified configuration of software and hardware. Studies only material applicable to own circumstances but strives to maintain high level of competence in specific areas.
Average	Will accept new techniques and is desirous of improvement if minimum effort and time are required.
Slightly less than average	This person is willing to spend some time on self-improvement but waits until ordered into the situation by a superior.
Poor	The programmer resists any kind of learning experience related to professional growth. May take special training if asked but will not participate.
Very poor	Dislikes learning new material and has to be continually reminded about self-improvement. Does nothing to promote professional growth.
Unacceptable	Reads and does nothing related to improving work activities.

PART B

Form 11 Examples of BARS—Sample E

Position ___Management Auditor___

Job Dimension ___Job Planning___

Exceptional

1. Modifies plans in response to problems that would have substantially delayed the job.
2. Develops a detailed report outline which fully addresses the objectives and scope of the review.
3. Lays out entire task in a systematic and orderly fashion which identifies all the critical stages.
4. Develops detailed approaches to evaluate segments within major issue areas by using planning techniques, such as Program Evaluation, Review Techniques, Critical Path Analysis, and Decision Tables, for alternate approaches.

Superior

1. Anticipates a data-gathering problem and prepares a contingency plan ready to overcome it.
2. Recognizes changes in priorities and modifies assignment/task schedules accordingly.
3. Develops a flow chart showing procedures for performing the specific audit steps.
4. Identifies a potential area of review based on information obtained in a literature search for another job.

Proficient

1. Accurately estimates how long it takes to accomplish a given audit step.
2. Thinks through problems thoroughly before taking action, thereby avoiding the necessity to repeat steps.
3. Follows audit plans developed and supported by other team members.

Borderline

1. Produces a job plan that is inadequate, due to insufficient background research.
2. Allows deadlines to get too near before initiating action, typically resulting in delays.
3. Promises more than he/she is able to deliver in a given time frame.
4. Causes delay in job efforts by gathering and assembling unnecessary data.
5. Needs to have constant guidance to be able to follow audit steps.
6. After determining that OTA has ongoing work in the general area of the job, the employee does not follow up to get the results of their study.

Unacceptable

1. Does not summarize information gathered into logical order as related to audit steps.
2. Form 100 prepared by employee is incomplete.
3. Follows individual plan without any coordination with fellow team members, to the detriment of team efforts.
4. Identifies potential areas of review which are not congruent with the overall job objective.

PART B

Form 12 Examples of BARS—Sample F

Position ___Manager___

Job Dimension ___Scale for Organization of Work Activities___

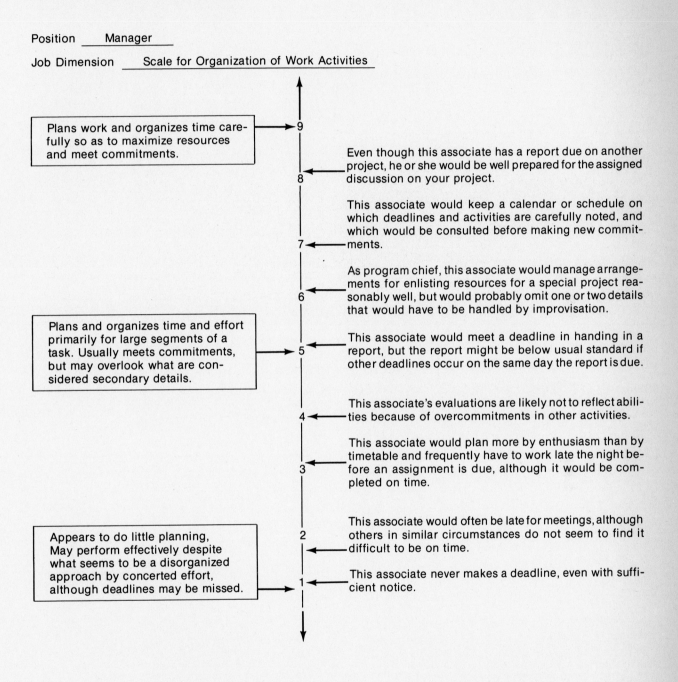

Plans work and organizes time carefully so as to maximize resources and meet commitments. → 9

8 ← Even though this associate has a report due on another project, he or she would be well prepared for the assigned discussion on your project.

7 ← This associate would keep a calendar or schedule on which deadlines and activities are carefully noted, and which would be consulted before making new commitments.

6 ← As program chief, this associate would manage arrangements for enlisting resources for a special project reasonably well, but would probably omit one or two details that would have to be handled by improvisation.

Plans and organizes time and effort primarily for large segments of a task. Usually meets commitments, but may overlook what are considered secondary details. → 5 ← This associate would meet a deadline in handing in a report, but the report might be below usual standard if other deadlines occur on the same day the report is due.

4 ← This associate's evaluations are likely not to reflect abilities because of overcommitments in other activities.

3 ← This associate would plan more by enthusiasm than by timetable and frequently have to work late the night before an assignment is due, although it would be completed on time.

2 ← This associate would often be late for meetings, although others in similar circumstances do not seem to find it difficult to be on time.

Appears to do little planning, May perform effectively despite what seems to be a disorganized approach by concerted effort, although deadlines may be missed. → 1 ← This associate never makes a deadline, even with sufficient notice.

Name _____ Group Number _____

Date _____ Class Section _____ Hour _____ Score _____

PART B

Form 13 Behavioral Anchor Review Sheet

Instructions: Please review the examples listed. Then read each of the anchors and determine if the anchor has any of the problems cited.

Use the following key to note the problem in the anchor beside each anchor and *underline* the problem in the anchor.

> C — a <u>conclusion</u> about a behavior is used.
>
> Q — a <u>quantitative</u> value is used.
>
> A — an <u>adjective</u> qualifier is used.
>
> K — a <u>knowledge</u> about a job rather than a behavior is used.
>
> F — the <u>frequency</u> that a behavior occurs is used.
>
> N — <u>none</u> of the above problems is shown.

_____ 1. Could be expected to give employees confidence and a strong sense of responsibility by delegating many important jobs to them.

_____ 2. Could be expected to exhibit courtesy and respect toward employees.

_____ 3. Could be expected to be rather critical of departmental standards in front of employees, thereby risking the development of poor attitudes.

_____ 4. Could be expected to renege on promises to employees who were told they could transfer back into their previous department if they didn't like the new one.

_____ 5. Could be expected to conduct a full day's clinic with new employees and develop them into top associates in the area.

_____ 6. Could be expected *never* to fail to conduct training meetings weekly at a scheduled hour and to convey exactly what is expected.

_____ 7. Could be expected to remind employees to wait on customers instead of conversing with each other.

_____ 8. Could be expected to tell employees to come in anyway even though they called in to say they were ill.

_____ 9. Could be expected to make promises to employees about salary being based on work output, knowing such a practice was against company policy.

_____ 10. Could be expected to be supportive of employees and to spend time with them, assisting where possible.

_____ 11. Could be expected to introduce himself or herself to all employees not acquainted with.

_____ 12. Could be expected to say hello to employees and visitors.

_____ 13. Could be expected to answer questions, but is abrupt in manner.

_____ 14. Could be expected to tell employees that their complaints are unfounded.

_____ 15. Reports by this manager would be clear and well organized, whether oral or written. Language is used well to convey ideas.

_____ 16. This manager's written work is usually interesting and easy to read, with few errors in construction or usage.

Form 13 (continued)

_____ 17. This manager would be asked to make oral reports on group projects because of an ability to present findings concisely and clearly.

_____ 18. This manager's reports would be well organized, with ideas clearly expressed; but oral reports and spontaneous comments might be less coherent and not very convincing.

_____ 19. This manager talks reasonably well, but is hard to follow. A position on an issue is occasionally misunderstood.

_____ 20. This manager can be expected to hand in reports that contain the essential ideas, but quality of written expression and construction is below average.

_____ 21. This manager might begin discussing a problem in the middle so that the interested parties have a difficult time understanding what he or she is talking about.

_____ 22. This manager has trouble speaking and writing in a manner that others can understand.

_____ 23. This manager would be careful to criticize action or suggested action rather than the individual involved.

_____ 24. When another employee did not understand a point in a discussion, this manager would spend a lot of time trying to explain the point.

_____ 25. This manager would usually apologize before asking a supervisor to repeat a statement not understood.

_____ 26. This manager would insist on having the roles in a group effort defined and would be careful to do his or her part, even to seeing that others did what he or she thought was their fair share.

_____ 27. This manager would agree to help with an extra task if asked, but usually would find some excuse not to help for very long.

_____ 28. This manager would be occasionally sarcastic to those who ask for help.

_____ 29. This manager would almost always interrupt a discussion with questions and comments and would not be deterred by the open annoyance of other employees.

_____ 30. This manager would be late, sprawl in the back of the room, and talk out of turn to others during meetings.

_____ 31. This manager could be expected, whenever possible, to sit down and talk with an employee who is considered to be "demanding."

_____ 32. If two employees asked this manager whether they could exchange assignments because of rapport problems, one would expect this manager to discuss the problem with the employees and make certain changes that would be satisfying to them.

_____ 33. If this manager were interviewing an employee who talks rapidly and continuously of unrelated problems, he or she could be expected to look interested and listen.

_____ 34. If this manager were assigned for the first time to supervise a group who insists upon having their supervisor treat them in a certain way, he or she could be expected to do as the group wishes without making an issue about it.

_____ 35. If spouse of an employee who has been injured asks whether the employee is in good condition, this manager could be expected to reply as follows: "His or her condition is good."

_____ 36. If a customer complained about the service, this manager is likely to tell the customer that the organization is short of employees and the needs of the customers who were there earlier have to be met first.

_____ 37. In the presence of an employee who is crying because his or her spouse is dangerously ill, this manager would be expected to tell the employee not to cry.

Name _____ Group Number _____

Date _____ Class Section _____ Hour _____ Score _____

PART B

Form 14 Behavioral Anchor Work Sheet*

Job title:

Job dimension:

Behavioral Anchor Statements:

Instructions: On this sheet please provide two or more behavioral anchor statements for each performance level. You will complete one "Behavioral Anchor Sheet" for each job dimension for the job.

1. Excellent performance:

2. Good performance:

3. Fair or average performance:

4. Poor performance:

5. Unacceptable performance:

*Make up similar sheets as required for each job dimension.

Name _____   Group Number _____

Date _____ Class Section _____ Hour _____ Score _____

PART B

Form 15 Worksheet for Retranslating Behavioral Anchors

Anchor number and/or abbreviation	Job dimension	Anchor scale value (1 to 5)
1.		
2.		
3.		
4.		
5.		
6.		
7.		
8.		
9.		
10.		
11.		
12.		
13.		
14.		
15.		
16.		
17.		
18.		
19.		
20.		
21.		
22.		
23.		
24.		
25.		
26.		
27.		
28.		
29.		
30.		
31.		
32.		
33.		
34.		
35.		
36.		
37.		
38.		
39.		
40.		
41.		
42.		
43.		
44.		
45.		
46.		
47.		
48.		

Form 15 (continued)

Anchor number and/or abbreviation	Job dimension	Anchor scale value (1 to 5)
49.		
50.		
51.		
52.		
53.		
54.		
55.		
56.		
57.		
58.		
59.		
60.		
61.		
62.		
63.		
64.		
65.		
66.		
67.		
68.		
69.		
70.		
71.		
72.		
73.		
74.		
75.		
76.		
77.		
78.		
79.		
80.		
81.		
82.		
83.		
84.		
85.		
86.		
87.		
88.		
89.		
90.		
91.		
92.		
93.		
94.		
95.		
96.		
97.		
98.		
99.		
100.		

* Each person in your group will need to fill out a sheet like this one; use additional sheets if necessary.

Name _____ Group Number _____

Date _____ Class Section _____ Hour _____ Score _____

PART B

Form 16 Final Behaviorally Anchored Rating Scale*

Job Title _____

Job Dimension _____

1. Excellent
   performance

2. Good performance:

3. Fair or
   average performance:

4. Poor performance:

5. Unacceptable
   performance:

*Make up similar sheets as required for each job dimension.

Name _____ Group Number _____

Date _____ Class Section _____ Hour _____ Score _____

ASSESSMENT OF LEARNING IN PERSONNEL ADMINISTRATION
EXERCISE 4

1. Try to state the purpose of this exercise in one concise sentence.

2. Specifically what did you learn from this exercise (i.e., skills, abilities, and knowledge)?

3. How might your learning influence your role and your duties as a personnel administrator?

4. Why is performance appraisal such an important human resource management program? What is its relationship to other human resource management programs?

5. What characteristics of jobs, departments, or entire organizations should be considered before a decision to implement an appraisal system is made?

EXERCISE 4 (continued)

6. Why do supervisors (and subordinates) often find appraisal a difficult and anxiety-producing activity?

7. How could a BARS system be evaluated as to its cost effectiveness?

8. What advantages would BARS seem to have over other appraisal systems? What disadvantages?

Exercise 5

Designing and implementing a management by objectives (MBO) program: measuring employee contributions

PREVIEW

One widely used performance appraisal technique is Management by Objectives (MBO). MBO has been used effectively in many types of organizations and is based on setting objectives or goals and evaluating people based on the degree to which they attain the objectives. MBO is not only used as a performance appraisal system, but also as a basic management planning and control tool. It helps to focus effort of people on important organizational goals and emphasizes results of their efforts and their contributions to organizational success. In this exercise MBO is discussed and you are able to assess your own understanding of MBO via a quiz. You also design an MBO program and conduct and evaluate a performance-review session.

OBJECTIVES

1. To become familiar with the advantages of MBO as a performance appraisal and a general planning and control technique.

2. To become familiar with the actual design and implementation process of MBO, including an appreciation for problems typically encountered and the type of forms used in MBO.

3. To gain skill in conducting an MBO performance review session and in giving people feedback about their performance.

PREMEETING ASSIGNMENT

Read the entire exercise.

INTRODUCTION

Management by Objectives

Management by Objectives (MBO) is perhaps best described by McConkie in his extensive review of the MBO literature:

> A managerial process whereby organizational purposes are diagnosed and met by joining superiors and subordinates in the pursuit of mutually agreed upon goals and objectives which are specific, measurable, time bounded, and joined to an action plan; progress and goal attainment are measured and monitored in appraisal sessions which center on mutually determined objective standards of performance.[1]

MBO is a management technique and process whereby *objectives* or goals may be estabished for: (1) the organization; (2) each department; (3) each manager within each department; and (4) each employee who works in an area where the establishment of objectives would be practical and valuable. MBO is

---

[1] M. C. McConkie, "A Clarification of the Goal Setting and Appraisal Processes in MBO," *Academy of Management Review* 4 (1979): 29.

not a measure of employee behavior, but is an attempt to measure employee *effectiveness,* or contribution to organizational success and goal attainment.

Establishing objectives usually consists of having the key people affected by the objectives meet to agree on the major objectives for a given time period (e.g., one year), develop plans for how and when the objectives will be accomplished, and decide on the criteria for determining if the objectives have been met. Once objectives have been established, progress reviews are made regularly until the end of the period for which the objectives were established. At that time the people who established the objectives at each level in the organization meet to evaluate actual results and then agree on the objectives for the next period.

The most important tool a manager has in setting and achieving forward-looking goals is people, and to achieve results with this tool he or she must be able, first, to instill in workers a sense of commitment and desire to contribute to organizational goals; second, control and coordinate the efforts of workers toward goal accomplishment; and third, help subordinates to improve their ability to make ever greater contributions to the organization. Often the personnel department plays a vital role in this process by helping managers understand and implement MBO and reviewing employees' progress in appraisal interviews or review sessions.

MBO: Some History. The MBO approach, in the sense that it requires managers to set specific objectives to be achieved in the future and encourages them to continually ask what more can be done, is offered as a partial answer to the question of maintaining organizational vitality and creativity. Management by Objectives was introduced first by Peter Drucker in 1954. As a management approach, it has been further developed by many management practitioners and theoreticians, among them Douglas McGregor, George Odiorne, and John Humble. Essentially MBO is a process or system in which a superior and subordinates sit down and jointly set specific objectives to be accomplished within a set time frame and for which the subordinate is then held directly responsible.

All organizations exist for a purpose, whether it be, for example, to make steel products or to educate others. To achieve that purpose top management sets goals and objectives that are common to the whole organization. In organizations not using MBO, most planning and objective setting to achieve these common organizational goals are directed from the top down. Plans and objectives are passed from one managerial level to another and subordinates are told both what to do and what their responsibilities are. The MBO approach injects an element of negotiation and dialogue into this process. The superior may bring specific goals and measures for his or her subordinate to a meeting with this subordinate, who also brings specific objectives and measures which he or she sees as appropriate or as contributing to better accomplishment on the job. Together they develop a group of specific goals, measures of achievement, and time frames. The subordinate commits himself or herself to the accomplishment of those goals and is then held responsible for them within some tolerance limits. The manager and subordinate may have occasional progress reviews and reevaluation meetings, but at the end of the set period of time the subordinate is judged on the results achieved. He or she may be rewarded for success by salary, praise, or promotion. If objectives were not met, the employee may receive additional training or be transferred to a job that will give needed training or supervision. Whatever the outcome, it will be based on accomplishment of the goals people had some part in setting and were hopefully committed to achieving.

Varieties of MBO. In practice, this MBO approach of necessity varies widely, especially in regard to how formalized and structured it is in a given organization and to what degree subordinates are allowed to set their own goals. In fact it has been said that "MBO like ice cream comes in 29 flavors."[2]

In some organizations MBO is a very formal management system with precise scheduling of performance reviews, formal evaluation techniques, and specific formats in which objectives and measures must be presented for review and discussion. In other organizations it may be so informal as to be described simply as the process of getting together and deciding what we've done and what we're going to do in the future. However, in most organizations using MBO it takes the form of formal objective-setting and appraisal meetings held on a regular basis, often quarterly, semiannually, or annually.

Even more variable than the degree of formality and structure in MBO is the degree to which subordinates are allowed to set their own goals. In this regard the kind of work that an organization does plays a large part in determining how much and on what level a subordinate will be allowed to participate in formulating his or her own goals. In some organizations subordinates are almost told what they need to do and simply asked if they will commit themselves to achieve this goal, while in others they are given a great latitude and room for innovation.

2 Hodgson, J. S. "Management By Objectives: The Experience of a Federal Government Department." *Canadian Public Administration* 16, no. 4 (1974) 422–431.

The MBO Process. Regardless of the type of organization, however, the MBO process usually consists of three steps:

1. Mutual goal setting;

2. Freedom for the subordinate to perform;

3. Reviewing performance.

These steps are detailed as follows:

Step 1: Setting Objectives. Individual managers determine what specific outcomes they plan to produce as a result of their efforts. They also carefully plan how these results will be produced, but the emphasis is on the *result*. The objectives are stated as precisely as possible. For most organizations, this means in quantitative terms, whenever feasible. Finding the right measure to use for an objective has proven to be as hard as finding the right objective in the first place (see Fig. 1). Organizations have also discovered that they must ensure that the objectives of one manager merge, rather than conflict, with those of other managers who may share in the accomplishment of some larger organizational goal. Providing for this "interlock" of objectives both vertically and horizontally has also proved difficult. While individual managers initiate the process of setting objectives, the proposals they originate are reviewed by their supervisors to ensure that subordinate goals are in support of the goals of higher levels in the organization and that, ultimately, the organizational objectives will be achieved. This has meant, in most organizations, that information about the view of the future from the top has had to be transmitted downward in the organization, so that individual managers have a meaningful context within which to formulate their goals. Organizations have developed a variety of means for achieving this two-way flow of information and objectives, including committee meetings, conferences, and memoranda.

Step 2: Working Toward the Goals: Action Planning. Organizations often report pleasant surprises at the genuine commitment employees bring to their work in an MBO system. Achieving the objectives they have helped to develop seems really to matter to managers. Subordinates are typically given latitude regarding how they will meet objectives. While specific behaviors are seldom spelled out as they would be in a BARS system (see Exercise 4), the subordinate must still behave within limits set by resources available, law, or ethics.[3]

Step 3: Reviewing Performance. Objectives not only serve to point effort in the right direction, they

serve in measuring progress as well. This review of progress is the performance appraisal aspect of MBO. It takes the form of normal managerial controls which attempt to measure effectiveness, but may facilitate greater effectiveness because of clearer goals and more detailed advanced planning concerning how to achieve them. While the types of objectives may be changed as a result of these reviews, most organizations do so reluctantly and only if it is clearly necessary. On the other hand, the levels of objective accomplishment may be mediated depending on extraneous factors, or those external to the organization (e.g., interest rates or general product demand). Thus, performance must be evaluated with this in mind.

MBO: What Can Go Wrong. While the basic MBO process seems simple enough, there are several problems associated with the actual implementation of MBO which can prevent it from being an effective process. Because many organizations have attempted MBO and/or are currently using it, the problems that manifest themselves in implementation are reasonably well known and have been catalogued in several published articles.[4] A brief listing and explanation of the more common problems follow:

1. Overemphasis on objectives (ends) at the expense of specifying how these objectives are to be attained (means). This can lead to ambiguity; lack of recognition for effort, creativity, and motivation; and a "results at any price philosophy" that may be harmful to an organization in the long run.

2. Too much paperwork reduces commitment and overloads managers.

3. Lack of commitment from top management often makes MBO just another fad.

4. Lack of proper training and knowledge in goal setting, MBO philosophy and methods, and in holding review sessions can deter MBO efforts.

5. No genuine participation by superior and subordinate in goal setting due to personality, supervisory style, or status differences precludes subordinates from seeing any real effort on the part of managers to include them and thus their commitment is lost.

---

[3] See C. E. Schneier and R. W. Beatty, "Developing Behaviorally Anchored Rating Scales (BARS). *The Personnel Administrator* 24 (August 1979): 59–70.

[4] See C. E. Schneier and R. W. Beatty, "Integrating Behavior-Based and Effectiveness-Based Methods," *The Personnel Administrator* 24 (Sept. 1979): 51–62. A. P. Raia, *Managing by Objectives* (Glenview, Ill.: Scott Foresman, 1974), Chap. 9; H. Levinson, "Management by Whose Objectives?", *Harvard Business Review,* July–August 1970, pp. 125–134; B. D. Jamieson, "Behavioral Problems with Management by Objectives," *Academy of Management Journal* 16 (1973): 496–505.

6. Failure to recognize that many aspects of performance are group efforts and that MBO for a single worker may hurt group cohesiveness unless the entire group shares in rewards from goal attainment. Likewise, failure to meet one's goals in MBO may be due to the performance of others on whose work one depends.

7. Relying only on performance goals reduces incentive to improve certain skills and ability. Training goals, staff and self-development goals, etc., are helpful.

8. Goal-setting difficulty, especially for higher-level, unprogrammed positions, can thwart MBO. Data on job performance and discussions with others familiar with job performance may help.

In summary, MBO has been an effective system in several organizations. However, attention must be paid to details. Advance planning and education are required, an assessment of an organization's willingness to accept MBO is necessary, and continual evaluation, analysis, and redesign can help improve MBO effectiveness.

Research has generally supported the effectiveness of MBO efforts to improve performance.[5] Various problems have been noted with such research, one of which is that when an organization adopts MBO, it typically makes other changes in policy, planning, and control techniques, and/or in supervisory practices as well. It is therefore difficult to isolate MBO from these other changes as direct causes of any subsequent improvement in organizational effectiveness.

MBO and Behaviorally Anchored Rating Scales (BARS). MBO is a system that specifies the desired results or *ends* for a task, department, or organization. However, there may be a need to specify the *means* or methods available and desired to attain these results. That is, while MBO derives much of its motivational

---

[5] For a review of MBO research, see G. P. Latham and G. A. Yukl, "A Review of Research on the Application of Goal Setting in Organizations," *Academy of Management Journal* 18 (1975): 824–843 and M. L. McConkie, "A Clarification of the Goal Setting and Appraisal Process in MBO," *Academy of Management Review* 4 (1979): 29–40. Since much of the effectiveness of MBO can be traced to the effect of goal setting on performance, Edwin Locke's theory of goal setting, and its related body of supporting research, is also a relevant aspect of the MBO literature. Locke's theory is explained in E. A. Locke, "Toward a Theory of Task Motivation and Incentives," *Organizational Behavior and Human Performance* 3 (1968): 157–189. Research on the theory is reviewed in the Latham and Yukl article cited in this note.

ability by providing for the delegation of discretion and authority to people in order that they may carry out their objectives, it may permit too much freedom for some and not specify methods of goal attainment in enough detail for others.

Experienced job incumbents may know of several methods for goal attainment. With no formal guidelines available to define those accepted methods, however, incumbents may be so anxious to attain their objectives that they adopt a "results at any price" philosophy. Thus, they might go beyond the bounds of ethics (or the law) to meet their sales quota, lower their costs, increase their profit, win an election, or develop a new product, service, or program. Inexperienced incumbents, on the other hand, may need to have methods for goal attainment specified due to their lack of experience or their interest in attempting to find more effective approaches to goal attainment.

Behaviorally anchored rating scales (BARS, see Exercise 4) can be very helpful in this regard, as they enable incumbents to become aware of the types of behaviors thought to be instrumental for goal attainment. The behavioral anchors used in BARS pinpoint desired performance. They thus can be used to give ratees ideas on how to obtain objectives and can cue ratees as to the judgment the organization has made on the utility or ethics of certain behaviors (see page 127).

For example, an objective in MBO may be to increase the effectiveness of one's communications with subordinates. It is to be measured by increases in satisfaction scores obtained from questionnaires submitted to subordinates. If a BARS system were implemented for the job in question before MBO is attempted, the anchors on the BARS for the dimension called Communications Skills could inform a job incumbent that effective communications would come about through such behaviors as the solicitation of subordinates' views, holding frequent, regularly scheduled departmental meetings, and/or developing a system of memoranda sent to all staff members. These behaviors would be the anchors which indicate desired performance on the BARS form for the Communications Skill dimension. The BARS would tell job incumbents *how* to attain their objectives in behavioral terms,[6] while an MBO system would help decide what the objectives should be.

MBO and BARS can thus be seen as very compatible performance appraisal systems, with BARS a useful prerequisite to implementing an MBO program.

---

[6] See Schneier and Beatty, "Integrating Behavior-Based and Effectiveness-Based Methods"; and Exercise 4.

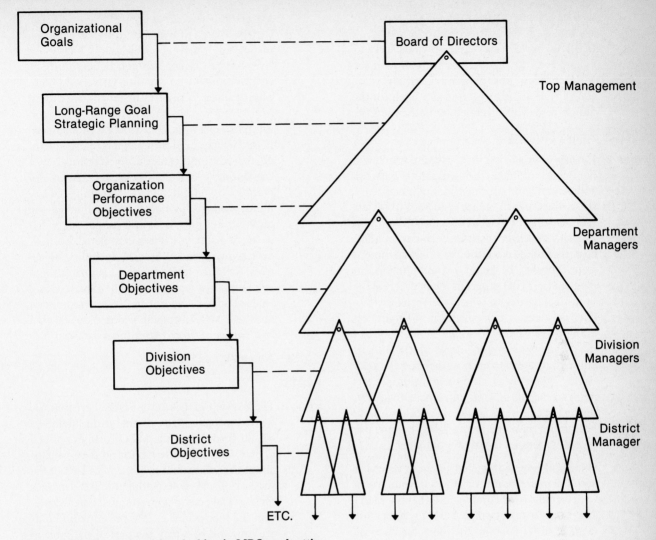

Fig. 1. Vertical and lateral interlocking in MBO goal setting

PROCEDURE

Overview. MBO is a process of evaluating performance which focuses on the individual's effectiveness or contributions to the organization and not their behavior or evaluations of behavior. Thus, MBO attempts to determine what people at work are to contribute and measures this in terms of quantity, quality, cost, timeliness of output, etc. In this exercise you are given an opportunity to measure contributions to effectiveness.

First, a checklist is used to review your understanding of MBO concepts. Examples of MBO information and a few typical MBO forms are presented next. A task follows in which various measures of effectiveness, or indices, are linked to appropriate methods of measuring these effectiveness indices. An

MBO form is then developed for a familiar job. Finally, an MBO performance review session is conducted and evaluated.

PART A

STEP 1: Form 1 provides a brief review of your understanding of MBO. Complete the form and review your answers with those given by the implementor or discuss them in small groups.

TIME: 15 minutes.

PART B

STEP 2: In Forms 2 and 3 there are two examples of forms used in MBO programs. These contain job *objectives,* along with the *methods* used to assess performance on these objectives. Study these forms so that you are familiar with the type of objectives used in MBO and how they are assessed. Also provided are a few blank MBO forms (Forms 4 and 5) which serve as examples to further familiarize you with the MBO process and paperwork. Study these carefully, as they can be used as models for the MBO forms you develop later in the exercise.

TIME: About 15 minutes.

STEP 3: Form 6 consists of a brief exercise which will help you to make the distinction between "objectives" and the "methods of measuring" these objectives. You are requested to review the measures of objective accomplishment in Form 6. This list consists of quantity, quality, cost, timeliness dimensions, and other dimensions that may be useful in attempting to implement an MBO program. They describe the broad categories to which the specific effectiveness measures, or results, in the right column of Form 6 might belong. You are to take the "what is measured" items (A through J) and assign them to each of the "specific outcomes" items by placing the appropriate letter(s) to the left of each outcome. Obviously, several of the items in the right column may need more than one letter; thus, you may use several letters for a specific outcome.

Once you have completed Form 6, review it with the implementor or others in your group to determine if you understand that the MBO approach is an attempt both to determine *what* is to be done on the job (objectives or specific outcomes) *and* to provide some *means of measuring* what level of accomplishment was achieved.

TIME: About 30 minutes.

PART C

STEP 4: After you understand the concepts in Form 6, you are ready to design an MBO program for a job with which you have some familiarity. Form into groups of not more than six people and choose one member whose job will be used for the MBO system. The remaining group members will interview the job holder and construct an MBO form. Any type of job may be used. You may want to use the job the group has used in the past (Exercises 3 or 4). If you do not use a job one of the group members now holds or has held in the past, use one of the jobs for which job descriptions

are given in Exercises 3 or 17. Fill out Form 7 first. It is a worksheet to be used as you decide upon goals or objectives. The objectives used in Form 7 should be set *jointly* by the job holder and the interviewers. In completing Form 7, be certain that you have listed *objectives, not methods* in the objectives column. For example, scheduling is often placed in the objective column, but it is really a method for accomplishing an objective, as better scheduling will lead to reduced costs, complaints, or maintenance. Generally, many items, such as planning or organizing, are methods not objectives and should be treated as such. After you have completed Form 7, devise your own MBO form, including objectives, actions planned, etc. This form should be placed on a separate sheet of paper and will be used below. Use Forms 2–5 as examples of how your MBO form might look. You will need two copies of your MBO form for Step 5.

TIME: About 40 minutes.

PART D

STEP 5: The last step in the exercise is the Performance Review process. One of the group members who helped design the MBO form developed in Step 4 and who also has the most knowledge about the job should role-play the part of the supervisor who will conduct the performance review. The person who supplied the information for the form (i.e., the person who holds the job) will role-play the part of the ratee in the review. If jobs were chosen which do not belong to any of the group members, any member who has some knowledge of the job chosen can act as the ratee.

Two separate reviews will be held. First, the rater and ratee should assume that the ratee had only fair performance. That is, he or she did not meet all of the objectives and/or did not meet them at the level of performance specified. One copy of the MBO form designed for the job in Step 4 can be filled out to reflect this degree of performance. Then the review is held and the remaining group members act as observers and complete Form 8. They each answer each question and mark their answers in the answer row designed for the "fair performance" review. The rater's job, of course, would be to discuss the ratee's performance: its pros and cons, its relation to set goals, reasons for poor performance, and what can be done to improve performance. The ratee's job would be to respond in a way he or she feels appropriate, given fair performance.

The second performance review is conducted in the same manner; however, this time the assumption is that the ratee's performance has been very good. The MBO form can be filled out to reflect this level of performance and the review proceeds with the rater giving the feedback and the ratee responding. Again, remaining group members complete Form 8, but this time mark their answers in the answer row designated for the "very good performance" review.

When both reviews are complete, the observers can each compare their observations on Form 8 and discuss them with the rater and ratee. What patterns emerged in the two reviews? What were the major differences and similarities? Which was most constructive for the ratee? The group could also critique the performance of the rater and ratee. Was a "problem-solving" focus or a "criticism" focus used?

TIME: About 7 minutes per review and about 20 minutes for discussion.

FOR FURTHER READING

Beck, A. C., and E. D. Hillman. "OD to MBO or MBO to OD: Does It Make a Difference?" *Personnel Journal* 51 (1972): 827–34. (I)

Brumback, G. B. "Toward a New Theory and System of Performance Evaluation: A Standardized MBO-Oriented Approach," *Public Personnel Management* 7, no. 4 (1978): 205–211. (I)

Bryan, J. F., and E. A. Locke. "Goal Setting as a Means of Increasing Motivation." *Journal of Applied Psychology* 51 (1967): 274–277. (II–R)

Carroll, S. J., and C. E. Schneier. *Performance Appraisal and Review Systems.* Pacific Palisades, Calif.: Goodyear, 1981, in press.

Carroll, S. J., and H. L. Tosi. *Management by Objectives: Application and Research.* New York: Macmillan, 1973. (I)

Carroll, S. J., and H. L. Tosi. "The Relationship of Characteristics of the Viewed Process as Moderated by Personality and Situation Factors to the Success of Management by Objectives Approach." *Proceedings, Academy of Management National Meeting,* 1969. (II–R)

Drucker, Peter. *The Practice of Management.* New York: Harper, 1954. (I)

French, W. L., and R. W. Hollmann. "Management by Objectives: Team Approach." *California Management Review* 17 (Spring 1975): 13–22. (I)

Humble, J. W. *Management by Objectives in Action,* London: McGraw-Hill, 1970. (I)

Humble, J. W. *Improving Business Results.* London: McGraw-Hill, 1968. (I)

Humble, J. W. *Management by Objectives.* London: Industrial Education and Research Foundation, 1967. (I)

Ivancevich, J. M. "Changes in Performance in a Management by Objectives Program." *Administrative Science Quarterly* 19 (1974): 563–574. (II–R)

Ivancevich, J. M. "A Longitudinal Assessment of MBO." *Administrative Science Quarterly* 17 (1972): 126–138. (II–R)

Ivancevich, J. M., J. H. Donnelly, and H. L. Lyon. "A Study of the Impact of Management by Objectives on Perceived Need Satisfaction." *Personnel Psychology* 23 (1970): 139–151. (II–R)

Ivancevich, J. M., J. T. McMahan, J. W. Streidl, and A. D. Szilagyi. "Goal Setting: The Tenneco Approach to Personnel Development and Management Effectiveness." *Organizational Dynamics* 6 (Winter 1978): 58–79. (I)

Jamieson, B. D. "Behavioral Problems with Management by Objectives." *Academy of Management Journal* 16, no. 3 (1973): 496–505. (II)

Klinger, D. E. "Does Your MBO Porgram Include Clear Performance Contracts?" *The Personnel Administrator* 24, no. 5 (1979): 65–68. (I)

Latham, G. P., and L. M. Saari. "Importance of Supportive Relationships in Goal Setting," *Journal of Applied Psychology* 64 (1979): 151–156. (II–R)

Latham, G. P., and G. A. Yukl. *Increasing Productivity Through Performance Appraisal.* Reading, Mass.: Addison-Wesley, 1981. (I)

Latham, G. P., and G. A. Yukl. "Effects of Assigned and Participation Goal-Setting on Performance and Job Satisfaction." *Journal of Applied Psychology* 61 (1976): 199–205. (II–R)

Latham, G. P., and G. A. Yukl. "A Review of Research on the Application of Goal-Setting in Organizations." *Academy of Management Journal* 18 (1975): 824–845. (II)

Levinson, J. "Management by Whose Objectives?" *Harvard Business Review* 48 (July–August 1970): 125–134. (I)

Locke, E. A. "Toward a Theory of Task Motivation and Incentives." *Organizational Behaviors and Human Performance* 3 (1968): 157–189. (II)

Locke, E. A. "Performance Goals as Determinants of Level of Performance and Boredom." *Journal of Applied Psychology* 51 (1957): 120–130. (II–R)

Mager, R. F. *Preparing Objectives for Programmed Instruction.* San Francisco: Learon, 1962. (I)

MBO Symposium. *Training and Development Journal* 26, no. 4 (April 1972): 2–23. (I)

McConkie, M. L. "A Clarification of the Goal Setting and Appraisal Processes in MBO." *Academy of Management Journal* 4 (1979): 29–40. (II–R)

McGregor, D. *The Human Side of Enterprise.* New York: McGraw-Hill, 1960. (I)

McGregor, D. *Leadership and Motivation.* Cambridge: The MIT Press, 1966. (I)

McGregor, D. "An Uneasy Look at Performance Appraisal." *Harvard Business Review* 35 (1957): 80–94. (I)

Odiorne, G. S. *Personnel Administration by Objectives.* Homewood, Ill.: Irwin, 1971. (I)

Odiorne, G. S. *Training by Objectives: Economic Approach to Management Training.* New York: Macmillan, 1970. (I)

Odiorne, G. S. *Management by Objectives.* New York: Pitman, 1964. (I)

"Public Sector MBO." (Special feature.) *Public Personnel Management* 5 (March–April 1976): 83–102 (3 articles). (I)

Raia, A. P. *Managing by Objectives.* Glenview, Ill.: Scott Foresman, 1972. (I)

Raia, A. P. "Goal Setting and Self Control." *Journal of Management Studies* 2 (1965): 34–53. (I)

Reddin, W. J. *Managerial Effectiveness.* London: McGraw-Hill, 1971. (I)

Schleh, E. C. *Management by Results.* New York: McGraw-Hill, 1961. (I)

Schneier, C. E., and R. W. Beatty, "Integrating Behavior-Based and Effectiveness-Based Methods," *The Personnel Administrator* 24, no. 9 (1979): 51–62. (I)

Stedary, A. C. *Budget Control and Cost Behavior.* Englewood Cliffs, New Jersey: Prentice-Hall, 1960. (I)

Steers, R. M. "Factors Affecting Job Attitudes in a Goal-Setting Environment." *Academy of Management Journal* 19 (1976): 6–16. (II–R)

Steers, R. M. and D. G. Spencer. "Achievement Needs and MBO Goal-Setting," *Personnel Journal* 57 (1978): 26–28. (I)

Tosi, H. L., and S. J. Carroll. "Managerial Reaction to Management by Objectives." *Academy of Management Journal* 11 (1968): 415–425. (II–R)

Wickens, J. S. "Management by Objectives: An Appraisal." *Journal of Management Studies* 5 (1968): 365–370. (I)

Wikstrom, W. S. *Managing by and with Objectives. Studies in Personnel Policy, No. 212.* New York: Conference Board, 1968. (I)

Name _____   Group Number _____

Date _____   Class Section _____   Hour _____   Score _____

PART A

Form 1 MBO Review List

1. Which of the following are the *major* focuses of MBO?
   ____ results (or output)
   ____ employee on-the-job activities
   ____ the goal-setting process
   ____ the performance review process
   ____ advising employees how to do their job
   ____ leaving people alone to do their job

2. Which of the following terms may typically be used to measure MBO *results*?

____ timeliness/dependability	____ lost time
____ quality	____ training
____ cost reduction	____ maintenance
____ innovations	____ employee satisfaction
____ profit realization	____ technical accomplishments
____ quantity	____ employee turnover

3. What factors can we assume to be responsible for motivating people to perform well through an MBO system?
   ____ mutual goal setting
   ____ freedom to perform
   ____ feedback on performance
   ____ annual review procedures
   ____ changes in job content

PART B

Form 2 Sample Job Objectives of a Paper Carrier

Job Objectives of a Paper Deliverer

Objectives	Measure	Measures		Time frame	Methods
		Present level	Desired level		
1. Deliver papers	quantity	90% 1½ hrs. after received	95% 1½ hrs. after received	2 mos.	Bike, car, walk
	quality	4 complaints per 1000	1 complaint per 1000	1 mo.	Good service (i.e., dry, porched, accurate delivery)
	cost	1.00 (25¢ per complaint)	0.25	1 mo.	
2. Sales	quantity	1 new customer per month	2 new customers per month	6 mos.	Make more calls Good service (i.e., dry, porched, accurate delivery)
	quality	maintained for 6 months	maintain for one year		
3. Profit	quantity	75¢ per customer per month	1.00 per customer per month	2 mos.	Reduce costs
	cost	3.25 per month	3.00 per month	2 mos.	Control expenses (i.e., rubber bands, plastic sleeves, delinquent accounts)
4. Collections	quantity	90% of customers pay in one week of month end	95% of customers paid in one week of month end	1 mo.	Make more follow-ups, use the telephone, use stamped envelopes
5. Paying for papers	cost	5% delinquency charge	2% delinquency charge	2 mos.	Develop working capital, increase payment of accounts receiveable

PART B

Form 3 Sample Managerial Job Objectives

Sam Speedy		General manager	Progress reviews
Prepared by manager	Date	Position title	1st _____
Harry Slow		Production manager	2nd _____
Reviewed by supervisor	Date	Position title	3rd _____
			Date

Major job objectives	% WT		Measures of results	Std. of perf.	Results		Dates	
					Target	Actual	Target	Actual
1. Product delivery (May be broken down by products)	25%	a.	Percent of on-schedule delivery	94%	Increase to 98%		8/31	
		b.	Number of customer complaints as a % of monthly purchase orders	4%	Decrease to 3%		9/30	
2. Product quality (May be broken down by products)	30%	a.	Percent of rejects per total monthly volume	6%	Decrease to 4%		7/31	
		b.	Ratio of factory repair time to total production hours/month.	7%	Decrease to 4%		9/31	
		c.	Number of units service free during warranty period	73%	Increase to 86%		10/31	
3. Operating efficiency	25%	a.	Cost per unit of output per month	$35.75/unit	Reduce to $35.50/unit		2/1	
		b.	Equipment utilization time as a % of monthly available hours	86%	Increase to 95%		11/15	
4. Other key objectives	20%							

PART B

Form 4 A Goal-Setting-Program Form

Level of objective	*Type of objective*
1. Organizational	1. Routine responsibilities
2. Departmental	2. Problem solving
3. Divisional	3. Innovative
4. Managerial employee or individual	4. Personal or organizational development
	5. Other

	1	2	3	4
R A N K	*Objectives* (What must I/we accomplish in order for the organization to function?)*	*How will the attainment of objectives be measured?* (How will I/we know when the objective is accomplished?)	*Time frame for objective*	*Plan for obtaining the objective* (What must be done to accomplish the objective?)
		Quantity measure: Quality measure: Cost measure: Other measures (please describe):		

*Add codes for level and type of objective after each objective is stated.

PART B

Form 5 Performance Plan and Review

Employee name: _____ Position title: _____ Appraisal period: _____

Department _____ Date _____ Reviewed by _____

PERFORMANCE PLAN

1 List responsibilities (Key words to describe the major elements of this employee's job.)	2 List performance objectives and/or results to be achieved (A more specific statement of the employee's key responsibilities and/or goals he can reasonably be expected to achieve in the coming period.)	3 Determine relative importance (Rank order)	PERFORMANCE REVIEW 6 Note actual achievements, comment on performance

4 Long-range goals	Work goals beyond this appraisal period and/or career goals.	Supervisor's comments
5 What help is required from your supervisor or others to achieve goals for this appraisal period and/or long range goals?		Supervisor's comments

Name _____   Group Number _____

Date _____ Class Section _____ Hour _____ Score _____

PART B

Form 6 MBO Measurement of Unit or Individual Outputs

Instructions: Place one or more of the letters A through D beside each of the items in the right hand column.

What is measured (in MBO)

A. Quantity
B. Quality
C. Cost control
D. Timeliness/dependability

Specific outcomes or results used as measures (ways of measuring)

_____ Type A units sold
_____ Transfers due to unsatisfactory performance
_____ Training programs held
_____ Minority persons hired
_____ Warranty claims filed
_____ Items entered in a ledger
_____ Days off the job
_____ Mileage per replacement vehicle
_____ Turnover
_____ Sales
_____ Tools replaced
_____ Reduction in expenses from previous period
_____ Extent of contribution and amount of innovation in the project (i.e., highly creative ideas)
_____ Rejected products
_____ Pedestrian-vehicle accidents
_____ Visits to the first-aid room
_____ Cost of material used in training
_____ Reports completed by X date
_____ Community complaints received
_____ Maintenance budget plus or minus
_____ Grievances received
_____ Profit by product line
_____ Mileage per replacement tire
_____ Potential contribution to total sales and profits
_____ Returned goods
_____ Research projects completed on time and within budget
_____ Traffic accidents
_____ The rate at which individuals advance
_____ Transfers at employee's request
_____ Employees ready for assignment
_____ Units constructed
_____ Days tardy
_____ Earnings on commissions
_____ Length of service
_____ EEOC complaints received
_____ Units produced
_____ Claims received and processed
_____ Complaints from employees
_____ Containers filled to capacity
_____ Discharges
_____ Plus or minus budget

Form 6 (continued)

____ Dollars of savings realized from project

____ Burglaries

____ Errors in filing

____ Housing units occupied

____ Cost of each research project against budget

____ Damaged units shipped

____ Value of new cost-reducing procedures

____ Days sick

____ Percentage of profits to sales

____ Garbage cans emptied

____ Contributions and suggestions made via the suggestion program

____ Ratio of maintenance cost to production cost

____ Calls per day

____ Penetration of the market

____ Number of repairs on warranty

____ Time to reach expected results

____ Length of frequency of unauthorized visits

____ Injury accidents

____ Type L units sold

____ Letters typed

____ Minority persons trained

____ Cost of maintenance per machine

____ Number of promotable persons

____ Number of new units sold vs. old

____ Successful completion of a course

____ Number of crimes against persons

____ Number of disgruntled customers

____ Results of a morale or attitude survey

____ Cost of spoiled work

____ Calls answered

____ Quits

____ Return of invested capital

____ Gallons used per vehicle

____ Amount of downtime

____ Complaints per 1000

____ New customers per month

____ Customers maintained for one year

____ Customers paid by end of month

____ Delinquency charges

____ Percent of on-schedule delivery

____ Number of customer complaints as a % of monthly purchase orders

____ Percent of rejects per total monthly volume

____ Ratio of factory repair time to total production hours/month

____ Number of units service free during warranty period

____ Cost per unit of output per month

____ Equipment utilization time as a percent of monthly available hours

Name _____ Group Number _____

Date _____ Class Section _____ Hour _____ Score _____

PART C

Form 7 Management by Objectives Worksheet for Joint Goal Setting

Job Title: _____

Objectives (What?)	Levels of Accomplishment (How measured?) Type of measure	Time Frame (When?) Present level (baseline)	Target level	Actual level	Methods used to Meet Objectives (How?)
1.					
2.					
3.					
4.					
5.					
6.					
7.					
8.					
9.					
10.					
11.					
12.					

Name _____   Group Number _____

Date _____ Class Section _____ Hour _____ Score _____

PART D

Form 8 Evaluation of MBO Performance Review Session

Record your opinions about the conduct of each MBO review session below:

Criteria	Review agenda*	Level of performance (please circle) ←Not at all→ ←Average→ ←Very much→
1. Did the ratee clearly understand the objectives? Did they agree with them?	F:	0 1 2 3 4 5 6 7 8 9 10
	VG:	0 1 2 3 4 5 6 7 8 9 10
2. Was the rater willing to give the subordinate the freedom to perform the job and seem interested in having them do it their own way?	F:	0 1 2 3 4 5 6 7 8 9 10
	VG:	0 1 2 3 4 5 6 7 8 9 10
3. Did the rater stick to the MBO items and not wander into new items or personal characteristics?	F:	0 1 2 3 4 5 6 7 8 9 10
	VG:	0 1 2 3 4 5 6 7 8 9 10
4. Was the rater very supportive of the ratee?	F:	0 1 2 3 4 5 6 7 8 9 10
	VG:	0 1 2 3 4 5 6 7 8 9 10
5. Did the rater listen and clearly understand what the ratee was saying?	F:	0 1 2 3 4 5 6 7 8 9 10
	VG:	0 1 2 3 4 5 6 7 8 9 10
6. Did the ratee leave feeling he or she had been fairly reviewed?	F:	0 1 2 3 4 5 6 7 8 9 10
	VG:	0 1 2 3 4 5 6 7 8 9 10
7. Did the rater become defensive?	F:	10 9 8 7 6 5 4 3 2 1 0
	VG:	10 9 8 7 6 5 4 3 2 1 0
8. Did the ratee become defensive?	F:	10 9 8 7 6 5 4 3 2 1 0
	VG:	10 9 8 7 6 5 4 3 2 1 0
9. Overall, was the review effective in helping improve performance?	F:	0 1 2 3 4 5 6 7 8 9 10
	VG:	0 1 2 3 4 5 6 7 8 9 10

*   F = Review session based on ratee having fair performance.
   VG = Review session based on ratee having very good performance.

Name _____ Group Number _____

Date _____ Class Section _____ Hour _____ Score _____

ASSESSMENT OF LEARNING IN PERSONNEL ADMINISTRATION
EXERCISE 5

1. Try to state the purpose of this exercise in one concise sentence.

2. Specifically what did you learn from this exercise (i.e., skills, abilities, and knowledge)?

3. How might your learning influence your role and your duties as a personnel administrator?

4. What are the major strengths and weaknesses of MBO as a performance appraisal system?

EXERCISE 5 (continued)

5. How would you go about convincing line managers that MBO was necessary?

6. How could an MBO system be evaluated in a cost-benefit analysis?

Section 4

HUMAN RESOURCE SELECTION AND STAFFING

After the groundwork for a human resource program has been laid through planning and forecasting of future needs, job analyses, and performance definition and appraisal (see Sections 2 and 3), the procurement process can begin. Selection of people to fill various positions, due to attrition, succession, and expansion, is of obvious importance to an organization, particularly in a dynamic and mobile post-industrial society in which organizations and people change rapidly. However, selection can be much more efficient if a clear statement of human resource needs, job duties and responsibilities, and desired performance are developed first. That is, the selection system can only be as effective as the foundation on which it is built. Only after we have, for example, thoroughly analyzed a job and decided what requirements successful performance demands in terms of human knowledge, ability, skill, personal characteristics, and experience, can we hope to find the best person to fill that job.

Selection is thus a matching problem—to find the best person for a job, given constraints of time, money, and the supply and characteristics of available human resources. Further, selection is decision making under uncertainty. We can never be sure a person is "right" for a job until after he or she performs it for some time, but we do not have the luxury of such hindsight in organizations. Therefore, we must attempt to predict future job performance from past and present information. As in any risky decision, we would attempt to reduce the degree of uncertainty and the consequences

of error—or increase our odds of winning—by gathering as much relevant information as is practical on which to base the decision.

Several types of information we gather in the human resource selection and staffing process and certain techniques have proven to be effective in predicting future performance. In this section, the following four different techniques, each concentrating on a different type of information, are presented: (1) biographical data (Exercise 6); (2) interviewing (Exercise 7); (3) work sampling and simulation (Exercise 8); and (4) testing (Exercise 9). Each of these techniques has certain advantages and disadvantages as selection devices, and they are best employed in combination rather than singly, as each facilitates the gathering of a different type of information. When all of the information gathered from the various techniques is combined, the odds on making an incorrect selection decision can be reduced. However, gathering such information is not without cost in terms of organizational resources. Those making the selection decision must be convinced that the cost involved in gathering each additional piece of information is outweighed by the benefit of using it in selection decision making. The basic selection validation procedure, the method whereby each selection system is evaluated for its success in selecting effective employees, is illustrated in Fig. 1.

The four exercises in Section 4 explain the major selection techniques and enable you to design them in order to better understand their objectives and operation.

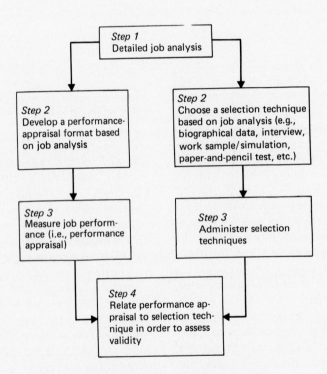

Fig. 1. The basic selection validation procedure

Exercise 6

Biographical data as a predictor of job success

PREVIEW

Numerous organizations use an applicant's organizational memberships, previous work experiences, education, and other biographical information to help make their selection decisions. The assumption behind this practice is that certain bits of biographical data are good predictors of job success. That is, those whose backgrounds contain these items will eventually perform well on the job. This exercise examines the assumption that biographical data predicts job performance, as well as typical personnel practices dealing with the use of biographical data as a selection strategy. The predictive accuracy of various types of biographical data is discussed, resumes are evaluated, and job application blanks are developed and assessed as to their validity in this exercise.

OBJECTIVES

1. To become familiar with current personnel practices regarding the use of biographical data in selection decisions.
2. To become familiar with the advantages and disadvantages of using biographical data to help make seleciton decisions.
3. To develop skill in evaluating resumes and references and in drafting application blanks.
4. To begin to develop skill in assessing the validity of biographical data in selection.

PREMEETING ASSIGNMENT

Read the *Introduction* and *Procedure* only. Do not read through any of the forms, with the exception of Form 1, until told to do so by your implementor.

INTRODUCTION
Using Biographical Data to Make Selection Decisions

Application blanks and an applicant's personal resume appear to be used nearly as widely as interviewing to help make selection decisions in organizations. Obviously, the greatest relevance of the application blank is for selecting people from outside the organization, as biographical data for people currently inside an organization would typically be on record already. Recently, attention in personnel administration has been refocused on biographical data as a predictor of future job success. Systematic scoring and weighting techniques have been developed and, in some cases, long biographical-data forms which may superficially resemble personality or interest tests in content. But most biographical forms still include at least questions about age, education, marital status, experience, and references.

Uses of Biographical Data. Biographical data has typically been used to aid in the selection process in the following ways:

1. To facilitate an initial screening out of applicants who are obviously not qualified for the job;

2. To furnish information useful in planning an upcoming selection interview with the applicant;

3. To obtain names of references that may be contacted for additional data about the applicant's work experience and general character;

4. To collect information for administration of personnel programs (i.e., social security number, number of dependents, etc.); and

5. To collect sophisticated "behavioral histories" of applicants.

"Hard" versus "Soft" Items.[1] Many have advocated that only an individual's previous experiences that are directly and easily verifiable should be classified as biographical items, since many other items are "fakable." Examples of verifiable items are "rank in high school graduating class" or "prior jobs with inclusive dates." These items can be checked with other records.

Verifiable items are called "hard" items, while those that are not verifiable are called "soft" items. The latter are often expressed in abstract value judgments rather than realistic behavior. An example of a soft item would be, "What high school subject did you enjoy most?" There is, of course, no reasonable way to check the truthfulness of such an item. An applicant could indicate any subject he or she thinks the organization is looking for.

While an enlarged classification of biographical items (i.e., hard *and* soft) obviously expands the amount of personal information collected, a more constrained classification may reduce the tendency towards fictionalization. Items that are historical and verifiable may result in a narrow, but representative, set of data about the individual, while an enlarged classification may be quite unrepresentative. For example, even when applicants tend to respond honestly, items calling for conjecture, interpretation, and supposition may have enough ambiguity to enable an individual to respond in a way that is either an exaggeration or a misrepresentation of the facts. However, the most predictive items are those which require an individual to summarize his or her feelings regarding a whole set of experiences.

Despite these shortcomings of biographical data, they seem to have accuracy in predicting job performance. One explanation is that the weighted or scorable application blank (in which each question is given a numerical weight)[2] is representative of an individual's history, while other predictors, especially the unstructured selection interview, may be but a caricature based on the perceptions of an interviewer. The most effective scorable application blank also should contain only "relevant" items—that is, only those directly related to job performance, or to qualifying dispositions such as,

As a child, where did you and your friends play?

(a) In the street (research jobs)

(b) On the playground (research jobs)

(c) At someone else's house (sales jobs)

(d) At my house (sales jobs).

Further, the scorable weighted application blank (WAB) may work because it escapes the fallacy of attempting to predict future job performance by measuring general items, such as overall ability or formal education, as opposed to more specific, quantifiable items, such as specific job skills. See Table 1 for a list of personal history items which may be predictive of job success. Table 2 shows how such items may be scored.

Developing Biographical-Data Items. Several suggestions could be valuable as aids in developing biographical-data questions. Questions should be concise; they should be expressed such that responses can be given in numbers; and options given to respondents in a question should contain *all* reasonable alternatives, or if this is not possible, then an "escape" option (i.e., "other") should be provided. Further, questions should convey a neutral or pleasant connotation to the respondent and should not be threatening.

Biographical Data as a Predictor of Job Success. The application blank itself can be used as a predictor of future job performance in two ways. First, in scored application forms each item of information on the form is examined to determine if it is actually predictive of some aspect of job performance, such as tenure or quality and quantity of work output. Items that actually discriminate between successful and unsuccessful employees (i.e., a strong positive correlation exists between those whose performance is high and those who respond in a certain way to an item) are usually scored quantitatively. In other words, each item is assigned a weight or score and the score is awarded if the item is answered in the way found most

---

[1] Many of the ideas discussed here were adapted from J. J. Asher, "The Biographical Item: Can It be Improved?" *Personnel Psychology* 25 (1972).

[2] See, e.g., G. W. England, *Development and Use of Weighted Application Blanks* (University of Minnesota-Industrial Relations Center, 1971).

Table 1. Personal history items found to be predictive of "job success"

PERSONAL

1. Age
2. Age at hiring
3. Marital status
4. Number of years married
5. Dependents, number of
6. Children, number of
7. Age when first child born
8. Physical health
9. Recent illnesses, operations
10. Time lost from job for certain previous period (last 2 years, etc.)
11. Living conditions, general
12. Domicile, whether alone, rooming house, keep own house, etc.
13. Residence, location of
14. Size of home town
15. Number of times moved in recent period
16. Length of time at last address
17. Nationality
18. Birth place
19. Weight and height
20. Sex

BACKGROUND, GENERAL

21. Occupation of father
22. Occupation of mother
23. Occupation of brothers, sisters, other relatives
24. Military service and rank
25. Military discharge record
26. Early family responsibility
27. Parental family adjustment
28. Professionally successful parents
29. Stable or transient home life
30. Spouse does not work outside home

EDUCATION

31. Education
32. Educational level of spouse
33. Educational level of family, relatives
34. Education finances—extent of dependence on parents
35. Type of course studied—grammar school
36. Major field of study—high school
37. Specific courses taken in high school or college
38. Subjects liked, disliked in high school
39. Years since leaving high school
40. Type of school attended, private/state
41. College grades
42. Scholarship level, grammar school and high school
43. Graduated at early age compared with classmates

EMPLOYMENT EXPERIENCE

44. Educational—vocational consistency
45. Previous occupations (general type of work)
46. Held job in high school (type of job)
47. Number of previous jobs
48. Specific work experience (specific jobs)
49. Previous selling experience
50. Previous life insurance sales experience
51. Total length of work experience (total years, months)

From G. W. England, *Development and Use of Weighted Application Blanks* (University of Minnesota-Industrial Relations Center, 1971).

52. Being in business for self
53. Previous employee of company now considering application
54. Seniority in present employment
55. Tenure on previous job
56. Employment status at time of application (employed, unemployed)
57. Reason for quitting last job
58. Length of time unemployed
59. Previous salary earned, or salary earned at present employment

SKILLS

60. Ability to read blueprints
61. Does repair work on own car
62. Amount of previous training for applicant job
63. Amount of previous training for any other job
64. Possesses specific skills required for job
65. Number of machines that a person can operate

SOCIOECONOMIC LEVEL—FINANCIAL STATUS

66. Financial responsibility
67. Number of creditors
68. Number of accounts with finance companies
69. Number of accounts with stores
70. Amount of loan as a proportion of total income
71. Monthly mortgage payment
72. Highest pay received
73. Debts
74. Net worth
75. Savings
76. Amount of life insurance carried
77. Amount of other insurance carried
78. Kinds of and number of investments
79. Real estate owned (own home, etc.)
80. Owns automobile
81. Make, age of auto owned
82. Owns furniture
83. Has telephone in home
84. Minimum current living expenses
85. Salary requests, limits set for accepting job
86. Earnings expected (in future, 2 years, 5 years, etc.)

SOCIAL

87. Club memberships (social, community, campus, high school)
88. Frequency of attendance at group meetings
89. Offices held in clubs
90. Experience as a group leader
91. Church membership

INTERESTS

92. Prefer outside to inside labor
93. Hobbies
94. Number of hobbies
95. Specific type of hobbies, leisure time activities preferred
96. Sports
97. Number of sports active in
98. Most important source of entertainment

PERSONAL CHARACTERISTICS, ATTITUDES EXPRESSED

99. Willingness to relocate or transfer
100. Confidence (as expressed by applicant)
101. Basic personality needs (5 types) as expressed by applicant in reply to question on application blank

102. Drive
103. Stated job preferences

MISCELLANEOUS

104. Time taken for hiring negotiations between applicant and company
105. Former employer's estimate of applicant
106. Interviewer's estimate of applicant's success, based on health, social personality, relationships, etc.
107. Source of reference to company for job application
108. Has relatives or acquaintances presently working for company
109. Number of character references listed
110. Availability for entire season of work stated
111. Availability—can start immediately, can't start immediately
112. Manner of filling out application blank (time taken, method used, way information stated, etc.)
113. Restrictions on hours available for duty

Table 2. Sample responses

Group I Long Tenure Saleswomen NAME*		Age	Marital Status	No. of Dependent Children	Living Arrangements	Highest School Grade Completed	Length of Residence (Years)	Amount of Previous Sales Experience	TOTAL SCORE
Adams, Mary	Responses:	49	Wid	0	Rent	7	26	0	
	Weights:	2	2	0	2	0	2	0	8
Coe, Hilda		29	Div	1	Rent	8	13	0	
		1	1	1	2	1	2	0	8
Doe, Mary		29	Sing	0	Room	12	22	2y 4m	
		1	0	0	1	2	2	1	7
Hale, Joan		42	Mar	0	Rent	14	4	1y 3m	
		2	1	0	2	4	1	1	11
Jones, Sue		19	Mar	0	Room	11	19	0	
		0	1	0	1	1	2	0	5
Little, Betty		65	Sing	0	Room	10	20	6	
		2	0	0	1	1	2	2	8
O'Shea, Helen		43	Mar	0	Own	13	24	0	
		2	1	0	3	3	2	0	11
Roe, Matilda		40	Mar	0	Own	14	6	0	
		1	1	0	3	4	1	0	10
Sellers, Doris		38	Mar	1	Own	11	8	0	
		1	1	1	3	1	2	0	9
Smith, Jane		46	Wid	0	W/Rel	7	40	16	
		2	2	0	1	0	3	4	12

*The names used in this example are fictitious.

appropriate for the organization. All of the scores awarded are then summed so that a numerical total score can be used as a basis for making selection decisions—in the same manner as scores of aptitude tests are used. For example, for some jobs a certain cutoff or minimum score might be decided on. The application blanks are scored and those job applicants scoring above the cutoff score are hired or sent to the next step in the selection process, while those scoring below the cutoff are eliminated.[3]

One of the virtues of biographical data is that it has tended to have high criterion validity. For example, Williams, with only 21 items, was able to predict AFROTC volunteering vs. nonvolunteering with an r of 0.72 in a cross-validation sample of over 200 cases.[4]

Among the Standard Oil Co. (N.J.), studies the following sorts of evidence of validity were obtained:

1. For skilled craftsmen, correlations with overall job performance ranged from .27 to .46.

2. For engineering and technical personnel, correlations with overall job performance were .39 and .27.

3. For commercial type office personnel, correlations with overall job performance were .40, .38, and .47.

4. For supervisors, correlations were .43 and .38 with overall performance.

5. From the Standard Oil of New Jersey Early Identification of Management Potential Study, a correlation range of .14 to .63 was obtained with various criteria of managerial success. The mean correlation was .37.

Owens has also cited average Biographical Information Blank (BIB) correlations across several studies in predicting various outcomes such as sales success (.35), clerical performance (.48), credit risk (.62), and high-level talent or creativity (.48).[5]

Table 3. Additional BIB validities taken from large samples

BIB	CRITERION		JOB FUNCTION	N	r
	Job grade	Job success			
Background BIB	.39	.44	Marketing	896	.44
Perception Test	.17	.20	Refining	90	.57
Judgment Test	.32	.27	Production	245	.44
Total	.46	.46	Exploration	146	.16
			Staff	86	.40
N =	304	1745	Other	282	.43
			Female	50	.50
			Black	57	.40
			Total	1745	.44

Source: C. P. Sparks, "Biographical Data as a Predictor of Job Success." Paper presented at the 38th meeting of the Academy of Management, San Francisco, August, 1978.

Table 3 shows other evidence of the empirical validity of BIB's for predicting job success.

Examples of various types of BIB questions are provided in Table 4. Notice that there are many types of questions which may be used to capture the type of data desired. Also it should be noted that the reliabilities of BIB's are high, ranging from .60 to .93 in the various factors BIB's attempt to measure (e.g., from

introverted personalities to successful trade skills).[6] However, it has been noted, as would be expected, that shortening a BIB to include only the "predictive" questions may increase its fallability and thus reduce its reliability.[7] It is thus suggested that some of the unrelated questions be retained to reduce this occurrence.

In reviewing BIB's it may be noted that these instruments should attempt to collect measurable historical data in the preferred format of single-choice continuum items with an escape option (see Table 4). They can be combined with a Weighted Application Blank

[3] A scored application form is validated by procedures similar to those employed in the validation of tests (see Exercise 9 and England, *Development and Use of Weighted Application Blanks*). The discussion of weighted application blanks and validation of biographical items above is meant only as a brief introduction to a complex process. Detailed discussions can be found in the England text.

[4] W. E. Williams, "Life History Antecedents of Volunteers vs. Non-Volunteers for an A.F.R.O.T.C. Program." Paper Read at Midwestern Psychological Association, Chicago, 1961.

[5] W. A. Owens, "Background Data." In M. D. Dunnette, ed., *Handbook of Industrial and Organizational Psychology* (Chicago: Rand McNally, 1976).

[6] W. A. Owens, Ibid.

[7] J. S. Zalinski, and N. M. Abrahams, "The Effects of Item Context in Faking Personnel Selection Inventories," *Personnel Psychology* 32 (1979).

Table 4. Some Types of Biodata Items*

1. *Yes-No*
   Have you found your life to date to be pleasant and satisfying?
2. *Continuum, single choice*
   What is your weight?
   (a) under 135 pounds
   (b) 136 to 155 pounds
   (c) 156 to 175 pounds
   (d) 176 to 195 pounds
   (e) over 195 pounds
3. *Non-continuum, single choice*
   What was your marital status at college graduation?
   (a) single
   (b) married, no children
   (c) married, one or more children
   (d) widowed
   (e) separated or divorced
4. *Non-continuum, multiple choice*
   Check each of the following from which you have ever suffered.
   (a) allergics
   (b) asthma
   (c) high blood pressure
   (d) ulcers
   (e) headaches
   (f) gastrointestinal upsets
   (g) arthritis
5. *Continuum, plus "escape option"*
   What was your length of service in your most recent full-time job?
   (a) less than 6 months
   (b) between 6 months and 1 year
   (c) 1 to 2 years
   (d) 2 to 5 years
   (e) more than 5 years
   (f) no previous full-time job
6. *Non-continuum, plus "escape option"*
   When are you most likely to have a headache?
   (a) when I strain my eyes
   (b) when I don't eat on schedule
   (c) when I am under tension
   (d) January first
   (e) never have headaches
7. *Common stem, multiple continua*
   Over the past 5 years, *how much* have you enjoyed each of the following? (Use continuum 1 to 4 at right below.)
   (a) loafing or watching TV
   (b) reading
   (c) constructive hobbies
   (d) home improvement
   (e) outdoor recreation
   (f) music, art, or dramatics, etc.
           (1) very much
           (2) some
           (3) very little
           (4) not at all

*From W. A. Owens, "Background Data," in M. D. Dunnette, ed., *Handbook of Industrial and Organizational Psychology* (Chicago, Rand McNally, 1976).

and collect information that the WAB has not obtained. They work because they have predictability due to their clean criterion (we should know our own past), they can be scanned, and because the answers to the questions do not change if the questions are restated. Although no standard BIB's exist, a catalog of BIB items may be obtained from the Scientific Affairs Committee of Division 14 of the American Psychological Association. In constructing a BIB, many factors (areas of questioning) should be used for each job, and of course the answers should be similar for each job family and be different across job families. The size of a BIB can vary with 40–50 questions sufficient with a mixed criterion and no weighting of questions up to 200 questions. However, since BIB items are very heterogeneous, it may take at least 50 criterion-keyed items to generate any reasonable reliability. On the other hand, if 200 to 300 items can be factored, scales composed of the 10 or 12 highest loading items on a factor will yield reliabilities in the 0.80s. The cutting score to use for hiring should be in the top 75 percent of applicant scores and can be adjusted to minimize hiring errors. BIB's are scored in various ways with bar graphs by quantiles preferred. BIB's are validated item by item using a criterion-related item analysis.[8]

Biographical data is also used to predict job success, as judgments based on the applicant's total personal history are used in situations where the applicant cannot be interviewed. Thus, selection decisions are sometimes based primarily on personal history data.

Reference Checks. Typically, applicants are asked to furnish a few names of references on an application blank. These are often past employers or supervisors, teachers or professors, or friends and associates. Sometimes, an applicant blank will specify the inclusion of one professional or academic reference and a personal one. These persons may then be contacted in order to provide additional information about an applicant's background, work experience, or character and integrity. In addition, they are used to verify certain statements made on an application blank.

Some jobs require applicants to ask references to submit a letter of recommendation or fill out a form giving their opinion of the applicant. Others simply require an applicant to furnish names of references. In either case, the use of references can be useful only if the references are honest in their evaluation and if the

[8] See W. A. Owens, "Background Data." In M. D. Dunnette, ed., *Handbook of Industrial and Organizational Psychology* (Chicago: Rand McNally, 1976) for a more detailed discussion of these statistical issues.

organization actually makes the reference check.

Many people tend to exaggerate when writing references, as they do not wish to say negative things about someone or fear the applicant will be penalized if they give anything but the most favorable judgment. Further, references may provide a biased view of the applicant, as an applicant would only request references from persons he or she felt would give a favorable response.

Despite these problems, references can be useful in providing data for selection decisions. Their credibility, and hence their utility, can be increased: (1) if they are contacted by phone instead of in writing; (2) if they have bothered to write an unsolicited personal letter rather than filling out a recommendation form; and (3) if certain methods of asking questions are used which can reduce leniency in responses. One such method is a forced-choice format in which the reference must read through several groups of statements and mark only those in each group representative of the applicant.[9]

This is obviously forcing the reference to make a simple choice about the applicant. Most reference checks look more like the questions asked in Table 5. When you study Exercises 9 and 17 you may have some questions about the validity and discrimination possibilities of these questions.

The Law and Biographical Data. Equal employment opportunity laws and various guidelines of federal agencies restrict the types of information that can be asked on application blanks in certain situations. For example, it may not be legal to ask if a person has ever been arrested, but only if they have ever been convicted of a crime. All arrests do not lead to convictions and there is typically a higher percentage of minority-group persons arrested than nonminorities—thus, the question may be discriminatory.[10] All biographical-data-collection devices must be checked for compliance with the various laws and guidelines (see Table 2, Exercise 17).

In addition, certain other laws, such as the Fair Credit Reporting Act of 1970, restrict and control the gathering of additional specific types of information. The Fair Credit Reporting Act requires that if credit-rating organizations are used to furnish information about an applicant, the applicant is entitled to disclosure and must be notified in writing that the information is being sought. Such organizations gather infor-

mation about indebtedness, character, alcohol and drug use, etc. This information can be useful in selection decisions, but should be gathered only with the knowledge of the applicant and should be restricted to those types of information shown to have a direct impact on job performance. The abuses possible from gathering such personal information are obvious.

A Note on Recruitment. Before selection decisions are made, regardless of the selection tool used, the organization must attract job applicants. This is called recruitment. Recruitment of human resources refers to an organization's positive efforts to seek out qualified job applicants. Of course, the degree of recruitment activity depends on several factors. Among these are the human-resource requirements of the organization, characteristics of the job, the labor supply, geographic location of the organization relative to the labor supply,

Table 5. Questions to Ask in a Reference Interview

1. What were the candidate's responsibilities in order of importance?

2. How would you rate the candidate's quality and volume of work?

3. How would you describe the candidate's attitude?

4. How would you characterize the relationship between the candidate and his or her staff?

5. What were the candidate's principal strengths, outstanding successes, and significant failures?

6. What was the most effective way to motivate the candidate?

7. How would you compare the candidate's performance to the performance of others with similar responsibilities?

8. How did the candidate work with other people and what were the reasons?

9. How did you feel about the candidate's management practices?

10. How would you describe the candidate's success in training, developing, and motivating subordinates?

11. What could the candidate have done to produce even better results?

12. What company did the candidate work for prior to joining you and what company did he or she join after leaving?

13. What would subordinates say about the candidate?

14. What does the candidate need to do for continued professional growth and development?

15. What other information do you have that would help to develop a more complete picture of the candidate?

Source: From P. A. Rabinowitz, "Reference Auditing, an Essential Management Tool," *Personnel Administrator* 24, no. 1 (1979): 37.

[9] See A. N. Nash and S. J. Carroll, "A Hard Look at the Reference Check," *Business Horizons* 13, no. 5 (1970): 43–49.
[10] See R. L. Minter, "Human Rights and Pre-employment Injuries," *Personnel Journal* 51 (1972): 431–433. The laws on equal employment opportunity affecting selection are discussed in Exercise 17.

general economic conditions and unemployment rates, ability to staff positions from internal human resources (i.e., people who are already members of the organization), and affirmative action plans (see Exercise 17). Typically, an organization will actively recruit or seek job applicants in order to increase the numbers of women and minorities in their labor pool (affirmative action plans); to find a person with particular skills, ability, etc.; or to improve the mix and diversity of their work force to enable it to solve future problems and implement future plans.

Several external contacts for human resources can be tapped. These include: advertising in newspapers, professional publications, educational organizations, public and private employment agencies, professional organizations, and labor unions. Each of these offers unique advantages and can prove to be a valuable source of personnel. For example, the placement office of a university is a source of younger, typically inexperienced people with specialized education, which makes them appropriate for entry-level managerial and administrative positions. Employment agencies charge employers (and/or job seekers) a fee for their service, but may be able to locate someone to fill a job that requires unusual education and experience. Unions sometimes are able to control supply, especially skilled and craft labor, through apprenticeship programs and agreements with employers. In the construction industry, for example, the union will furnish the organization with the entire skilled labor pool and funnel workers to organizations through their own recruiting and placement process. This can be very economical to an employer.

Any recruiting efforts, or lack of them, provide publicity for an organization. As part of the overall selection and staffing process, this publicity can be positive or negative, useful in making better selection decisions or not useful. In recruiting activities, therefore, an organization must be cognizant of the utility of recruiting or selection decisions, as well as of the effects such activity might have on the people already employed and on the general public. Finally, recruiting efforts must be subjected to a rigorous cost/benefit analysis. In certain occupations, geographical areas, and industries, little recruiting is necessary, perhaps due to general economic conditions and the supply of labor. The costs and benefits can be economic as well as intangible, such as goodwill. Both need to be considered as recruitment activities are planned and implemented.

PROCEDURE

Overview. First, the many types of data that are possible to collect via an application blank are reviewed; then, sample resumes are presented for a job of administrative officer. You will evaluate these resumes and choose the best candidate for the job based on the information in the resumes. Completed application blanks for the same job are then compared to the resumes. Finally, you will develop an application blank for a job based on information gathered in a job analysis.

PART A

STEP 1: Work individually or in small groups. Form 1 provides a set of sixteen statements, along with eight pairs of adjectives which each describe a type of information that can be obtained from an application blank. First, each person in the group will determine which of the two adjectives in each number (1–8) is best described by each of the sixteen statements. Next, each person chooses which adjectives in the list appearing at the end of Form 1 provide the type of information most useful for predicting job success via an application blank. Be sure to discuss your responses with the other group members and try to reach consensus on this group task.

TIME: About 20 minutes.

PART B

STEP 2: Forms 2, 3, and 4 contain resumes of three applicants for the job of an administrative officer. The officer reports to the president of a manufacturing firm which employs 200 people. See the job description, Form 5. Information about the organization is given in Form 6. Rank the applicants in the order you believe represents their probable success with the company. Then, compare your choices with other members of your group and answer the following questions:

a) Why did you assign this order? Can you justify your decisions?

b) What questions would you like to ask each candidate in an interview and what additional information would you like about each candidate in order to improve your decision making?

TIME: About 25 minutes.

PART C

STEP 3: Forms 7, 8, and 9 contain completed job-application blanks for the three candidates in Step 2. Read over these applications carefully and then answer the following questions in your group discussion:

a) What are the benefits of the completed application blanks over merely using resumes in making selection decisions?

b) What do you notice now about the applicants that you missed previously when you read only the resumes?

c) Did the use of the application blank provide answers to any of the questions you may have developed in question b of Step 2?

d) What is your ranking of the three candidates now? If it has changed, why has it?

TIME: About 25 minutes.

PART D

STEP 4: In Form 10 you have a BIB that has been constructed and validated for all managerial jobs in Palms Pacific Corporation. For each question, the number of successful managers (those in the top 25% of all managerial performance appraisals) have responded to each alternative as indicated by the percentages shown. You are to decide on the weight you wish to give each question and/or each response category and then multiply these weights by the alternatives chosen by the three candidates to obtain a total score for each candidate. After tabulating the BIB, have your group respond to these questions:

a) What decision would you reach now having the BIB as well as the application blank?

b) What new information do you now have that you did not obtain by the information blank?

c) What areas of assessment of the candidates do you believe you now have captured that were not in hand previously?

d) Do you believe the use of the BIB was a fair and nondiscriminatory procedure for making a hiring decision?

TIME: About 40 minutes.

PART E

STEP 5: This task is to develop a job-application blank to gather biographical data based on job-analysis information. Form 5 contains the job description for the job of Administrative Officer. From this information you are asked first to determine a set of criteria to be used in selecting among candidates for this job. That is, what would be the qualifications, education, etc., you would look for when selecting a person for the job? Then you are asked to:

a) Design an application blank that captures the selection criteria your group has developed. Be sure the items (questions) are presented with enough alternatives to cover the possible responses to them.

b) Determine a scoring or weighting system for evaluating the application blank. Go through all of the items and give each a weight that reflects its relative importance as a predictor of future job success. Decide how each item should be answered in order for the applicant to receive, for example, all of the points assigned to the item, half the points, etc. Then develop a cutoff score which would be the minimum total score an applicant could get and still be considered for the job.

c) Complete your new application blank for each of the three candidates, using their resumes and the application blanks in Forms 2–4 and 7–9 as the basis for the information required. Then score the application blank according to the scoring system you devised in (b) above.

d) Select the new administrative officer based on the new application blank. Was it the same person as your group had chosen in Step 2, Step 3, or Step 4?

e) Prepare a brief rationale for your choice such that you could defend it to the unsuccessful applicants and to other parties.

f) What information do you still not have about the applicants that you feel is necessary for making a good selection decision? How would you ascertain this information?

TIME: About two and one-half hours.

FOR FURTHER READING

Ash, P. and F. P. Krocker. "Personnel Selection, Classification, and Placement." *Annual Review of Psychology* 26 (1975): 481–507. (II)

Asher, J. J. "The Biographical Item: Can It Be Improved?" *Personnel Psychology* 25 (1972): 251–269. (II–R)

Baker, B. L. *The Use of Biographic Factors to Moderate Prediction and Predict Salary Level.* Unpublished doctoral dissertation, Purdue University, 1967. (II–R)

Beason, G. M. and J. A. Belt. "Verifying Job Applicants' Backgrounds." *Personnel Administrator* 19 (1974): 29–32. (I)

Blashfield, R. K. "Mixture Model Tests of Cluster Analysis: Accuracy of Four Agglomerative Hierarchical Methods." *Psychological Bulletin* 83 (1976): 377–388. (II)

Block, J. *Lives Through Time.* Berkeley: Bancroft Books, 1971. (I)

Brousseau, K. R. *Effects of Job Experience on Personality.* Unpublished doctoral dissertation, Yale University, 1976. (II)

Browning, R. C. "Validity of Reference Ratings from Previous Employers." *Personnel Psychology* 21 (1968): 389–393. (II–R)

Cassens, R. P. *Cross Cultural Dimensions of Executive Life History Antecedents.* Greensboro, N.C.: The Creativity Research Institute, Inc., The Richardson Foundation, 1966. (II–R)

Cherry, R. L. *Socioeconomic Level and Race as Biographical Data Moderators.* Unpublished doctoral dissertation, Louisiana State University, 1969. (II–R)

Clark, E., "Holding Government Accountable: The Amended Freedom of Information Act." *Yale Law Journal* 84 (March 1975): 741–769. (II)

Clarke, J. R. "Landing that Right Executive Job." *Management Review* 69 (August 1975): 31–36. (I)

Cronbach, L. J. "The Two Disciplines of Scientific Psychology." *American Psychologist* 12 (1957): 671–684. (II)

Cronbach, L. J. "Beyond the Two Disciplines of Scientific Psychology." *American Psychologist* 30 (1975): 116–127. (I)

Cronbach, L. J. and G. Gleser. "Assessing Similarity Between Profiles." *Psychological Bulletin* 50 (1953): 456–473. (II–R)

Davies, G. K. "Needed: A National Job Matching Network." *Harvard Business Review* 47, no. 5 (1969): 63–72. (I)

Dornon, J. M. *Identification of Long-Tenure Hourly Factory Workers Using a Weighted Application Blank.* (Experimental Publication System Ms. No. 276-2) Washington, D. C.: American Psychological Association, 1970. (II–R)

Dunnette, M. D. "A Modified Model for Test Validation and Selection Research." *Journal of Applied Psychology* 47 (1963): 317–323. (II–R)

England, G. W. *Development and Use of Weighted Application Blanks.* Minneapolis: University of Minnesota, Industrial Relations Center, 1971. (I)

Feild, H. S. and L. P. Schoenfeldt. "Ward and Hook Revisited: A Two-Part Procedure for Overcoming a Deficiency in the Grouping of Persons." *Educational and Psychological Measurement* 35 (1975): 171–173. (II)

Fleishman, E. A. and J. Berniger. "One Way to Reduce Office Turnover." *Personnel Psychology* 37 (1960) 63–69. (I)

Frank, B. A. *A Comparison of an Actuarial and a Linear Model for Predicting Managerial Behavior.* Unpublished doctoral dissertation, University of Houston, 1976. (II–R)

Frisch, M. H. *Biographical Information and Personality: Toward a Better Understanding of Biodata.* Unpublished doctoral dissertation, Rice University, 1978. (II–R)

Gaudreau, P. A. *Investigation of Sex Differences Across Job Levels.* Unpublished doctoral dissertation, Rice University, 1975. (II)

Goldstein, L. L. "The Application Blank: How Honest Are the Responses?" *Journal of Applied Psychology* 55 (1971): 491–492. (II–R)

Guion, R. M. "Recruiting, Selection, and Job Placement," In M.D. Dunnette, ed., *Handbook of Industrial and Organizational Psychology.* Chicago: Rand McNally, 1976. (II)

Hawk, R. *The Recruitment Function.* New York: Amacom, 1967. (I)

Henry, F. R. *Research Conference on the Use of Autobiographical Data as Psychological Predictors.* Greensboro, N.C.: The Creativity Research Institute, Inc., The Richardson Foundation, 1965. (II–R)

Herring, J. W. *Predictive Validity of a Management Aptitude Test Battery.* Unpublished doctoral dissertation, University of Houston, 1969. (I)

Jernigan, L. R. *A Principal Components Analysis of the Guilford-Zimmerman Temperament Survey.* Unpublished doctoral dissertation, Texas Christian University, 1970. (II–R)

Kavanaugh, M. J. and D. Y. York. "Biographical Correlates of Middle Managers' Performance." *Personnel Psychology* 25 (1972): 319–332. (II–R)

Kessler, C. C. and G. J. Gibbs. "Getting the Most from Application Blanks and Refernces." *Personnel* 52 (January–February 1975): 53–62. (I)

Lee, R. and J. M. Booth. "A Utility Analysis of a Weighted Application Blank Designed to Predict Turnover for Clerical Employees." *Journal of Applied Psychology* 59 (1974): 516–518. (II–R)

Lopresto, R. "Recruitment Sources and Techniques." In J. Famidaro, ed., *Handbook of Modern Personnel Administration.* New York: McGraw-Hill, 1972. (I)

Lunnenborg, C. A. "Biographic Variables in Differential vs. Absolute Prediction." *Journal of Educational and Psychological Measurement* 5 (1968): 207–210. (II–R)

Manese, W. R. *Correlates of Organizational Tenure.* Unpublished doctoral dissertation, University of Houston, 1971. (II)

Maslin, H. L. "How to Avoid Discrimination in Your Help-Wanted Ads." *Supervisory Management* 21 (February 1976): 2–5. (I)

Matteson, M. T. *An Exploratory Investigation of a Methodology for Constructing Homogeneous Keys for a Biographical Inventory.* Unpublished doctoral dissertation, University of Houston, 1969. (II)

McClelland, J. N. and F. Rhodes. "Prediction of Job Success for Hospital Aides and Orderlies from MMPI Scores and Personal History Data." *Journal of Applied Psychology* 46 (1962): 281–284. (II–R)

Minter, R. L. "Human Rights Laws and Preemployment Inquiries." *Personnel Journal* 51 (June 1972): 431–433. (I)

Moore, C. L. *An Exploratory Investigation of Ethnic Differences Within an Industrial Selection Battery.* Unpublished master's thesis, University of Houston, 1966. (II)

Moore, C. L. *Ethnic Differences as Measured by a Biographical Inventory Questionnaire.* Unpublished doctoral dissertation, University of Houston, 1968. (II–R)

Morrison, R. R., W. A. Owens, J. R. Glennon, and L. E. Albright. "Factored Life History Antecedents of Industrial Research Performance." *Journal of Applied Psychology* 46 (1962): 281–284. (II–R)

Mosel, J. N. and R. R. Wade. "A Weighted Application Blank for Reduction of Turnover in Department Store Sales Clerks." *Personnel Psychology* 4 (1951): 177–184. (II–R)

Nash, A. J. and S. J. Carroll. "A Hard Look at the Reference Check." *Business Horizons* 13, no. 5 (1970): 43–49. (I)

Nevo, B. "Using Biographical Information to Predict Success of Men and Women in the Army." *Journal of Applied Psychology* 61 (1976): 106–108. (II–R)

Novack, S. R. "Developing an Effective Application Blank." *Personnel Journal* 49 (May 1970): 419–423. (I)

Owens, W. A. "Toward One Discipline of Scientific Psychology." *American Psychologist* 23 (1968): 782–785. (II)

Owens, W. A. "A Quasi Actuarial Prospect for Individiual Assessment." *American Psychologist* 26 (1971): 992–999. (II)

Owens, W. A. "Background Data." in M. D. Dunnette (ed.) *Handbook of Industrial and Organizational Psychology.* Chicago: Rand McNally, 1976. (II)

Owens, W. A., J. R. Glennon, and L. W. Albright. "American Psychological Association Scientific Affairs Committee, Division 14." *A Catalog of Life History Items.* Greensboro, N.C.: The Creativity Research Institute, Inc., The Richardson Foundation, 1966. (I)

Owens, W. A., and E. R. Henry. *Biographical Data in Industrial Psychology, A Review and Evaluation.* Greensboro, N.C.: The Creativity Research Institute, Inc., The Richardson Foundation, Inc., 1966. (II)

Owens, W. A. and L. F. Schoenfeldt. "Toward a Classification of Persons." *Journal of Applied Psychology.* (Monograph) 64 (1979): 569–608. (II)

Rosenbaum, R. W. "Predictability of Employee Theft Using Weighted Application Blanks." *Journal of Applied Psychology* 61 (1976): 94–98. (II–R)

Rosenfeld, C., "Job Seeking Methods Used by American Workers." *Monthly Labor Review* 98 (August 1975): 39–42. (I–R)

Schmitt, N., B. W. Coyle, J. K. White and J. Rauschenberger, "Background, Needs, Job Perceptions, and Job Satisfaction: A Causal Model." *Personnel Psychology* 31 (1978): 889–901. (II)

Schoenfeldt, L. F., "Utilization of Manpower: Development and Evaluation of an Assessment-Classification Model for Matching Individuals with Jobs." *Journal of Applied Psychology* 59 (1974): 583–595. (I–R)

Schrader, A. D., *An Investigation of the Fakability of an Empirically Scored Biographical Inventory with Variations in the Subtleness and Specificity of Subject Response Set.* Unpublished master's thesis, University of Houston, 1975. (II–R)

Schrader, A. D., *A Comparison of the Relative Utility of Several Rational and Empirical Strategies for Forming Biodata Dimensions.* Unpublished doctoral dissertation, University of Houston, 1968. (I–R)

Scott, R. D. and R. W. Johnson, "Use of the Weighted Application Blank in Selecting Unskilled Employees." *Journal of Applied Psychology* 51 (1967): 393–395. (II–R)

Schuh, A. J., "Application Blank Items and Intelligence as Predictors of Turnover." *Personnel Psychology* 20 (1967): 59–63. (II–R)

Sparks, C. P. *Prediction of Cognitive Test Scores by Life History Items, Comparison Across Two Different Ethnic Groups.* Houston: Author, 1963. (I–R)

Sweet, D. H. *The Job Hunter's Manual.* Reading, Mass.: Addision-Wesley, 1975. (I)

Tanofsky, R., R. R. Shepps, and P. J. O'Neill. "Pattern Analysis of Biographical Predictors of Success as an Insurance Salesman." *Journal of*

Applied Psychology 53 (1969): 136–139. (II–R)

Taylor, L. R. *A Quasi-Actuarial Approach to Assessment.* Unpublished doctoral dissertation, Purdue University, 1968. (II–R)

Tucker, M. F., V. B. Cline, and J. R. Schmitt. "Prediction of Creativity and Other Performance Measures from Biographical Information Among Pharmaceutical Scientists." *Journal of Applied Psychology* 51 (1967): 131–138. (II–R)

Wanous, J. P. "Tell It Like It Is at Realistic Job Previews." *Personnel* 52 (July–August 1975): 50–60. (I)

Wanous, J. P. *Organizational Entry: Recruitment, Selection, and Socialization of Newcomers.* Reading, Mass.: Addison-Wesley, 1980. (I)

Ward, J. H. and N. E. Hook. "Application of an Hierarchical Grouping Procedure to a Problem of Grouping Profiles." *Educational and Psychological Measurement* 23 (1963): 69–81. (II–R)

Webb, S. C. "The Comparative Validity of Two Biographical Inventory Keys." *Journal of Applied Psychology* 44 (1960): 177–183. (II–R)

Wessel, M. R. *Freedon's Edge: The Computer Threat to Society.* Reading, Mass.: Addison-Wesley, 1974. (I)

Zalinski, J. S. and N. M. Abrahams. "The Effects of Item Context in Faking Personnel Selection Inventories." *Personnel Psychology* 32 (1979). (II–R)

Name _____ Group Number _____

Date _____ Class Section _____ Hour _____ Score _____

PART A

Form 1 Categories of Biographical Data

A. Circle the word that best describes each statement below.

1a. Verifiable—Unverifiable

How many full-time jobs have you had in the past five years?

1b. Verifiable—Unverifiable

What aspect of your last full-time job did you find most interesting?

2a. Historical—Futuristic

List your three best subjects in high school.

2b. Historical—Futuristic

Do you intend to further your education?

3a. Actual behavior—Hypothetical behavior

Did you ever build a model airplane that flew?

3b. Actual behavior—Hypothetical behavior

If you had the training, do you think you would enjoy building innovative model airplanes for a toy manufacturer?

4a. Memory—Conjecture

Before you were twelve years old, did you ever try to perform chemistry experiments at home?

4b. Memory—Conjecture

If your father had been a chemist, do you think you would have performed chemistry experiments at home before you were twelve years old?

5a. Factual—Interpretive

Do you repair mechanical things around your home, such as appliances?

5b. Factual—Interpretive

If you had the training, how would you estimate your performance as an appliance repairperson?

6a. Specific—General

As a child, did you collect stamps?

6b. Specific—General

As a child, were you an avid collector of things?

7a. Actual response—Response tendency

Which of the following types of cameras do you own?

7b. Actual response—Response tendency

In buying a new camera, would you most likely purchase one with automatic features.

Form 1 (continued)

8a. External event—Internal event

Did you ever have private tutoring lessons in any school subject?

8b. External event—Internal event

How important did you view homework when you were in high school?

B. Which of the following words seem to describe the best type of data to collect on an application blank? Why?

____ Verifiable	____ Memory	____ General
____ Unverifiable	____ Conjecture	____ Actual response
____ Historical	____ Factual	____ Response tendency
____ Futuristic	____ Interpretive	____ External event
____ Actual behavior	____ Specific	____ Internal event
____ Hypothetical behavior		

PART B

Form 2 Resume No. 1

Merle Wonder
9680 Willow
Bigville, USA

JOB OBJECTIVE

Position in Administration Heading a Major Department

EDUCATION

1962-1965:   Harding College, Harding, Vermont
               Majors: Music History and Literature; Voice
               Degree: B. Mus., June 1966, cum laude   G.P.A.: 3.75
               Honors: Independent Study Honors in Music History & Literature
               Member: Omega Alpha National Scholastic Honorary Fraternity

1973-1974:   University of the West, Western, Arizona
               Major: Business Administration; Emphasis: Organizational Behavior
               Degree: M.B.A. June, 1974   G.P.A. 3.95
               Member: Who's Who Among Students in American Universities & Colleges

Other: While employed at New York University (1971-1972), completed two
               graduate courses in guidance and counseling.
               While employed at the University of Missouri (1972-1973), completed
               six graduate fundamentals courses in business administration in
               preparation for M.B.A. program.

EMPLOYMENT

2/72-8/73:   Planters International, Columbia, Missouri
               Administrative Assistant to Head of Budget Department

8/71-1/72:   New York University, New York, New York
               Administrative Assistant to Director of Planning and Director
               of Exhibitions

9/70-2/71:   Heckl and Dunover, 355 Madison Avenue, New York, N.Y.
               Assistant to Sales Manager, Upbeat Books Division

10/66-9/70:   G. Whiz, Inc. 76 Third Avenue, New York, N. Y.
               Assistant to Head of Performance Department in Record Compilation

12/65-10/66:   Peter A. Flop & Co., Inc., 101 Grand Street, New York, N. Y.
               Record Clerk

Prior: Please see amplification.

PERSONAL

Born: 2/3/42 in Minneapolis, Minnesota   Height: 5'8"; wt.: 135 lbs.
Health: Good; no physical limitations   Marital Status: married; no children
Residence: Rents apartment; willing to relocate
Finances: Good order; no debt encumbrance
Hobbies: Music, creative writing, travel, swimming, hiking

Form 2 (continued)

EDUCATION

Graduate courses in business administration and guidance and counseling completed include the following:

Management and Organization
Administrative Theory and Practice
Organizational Behavior
Labor Relations
Personnel Management
Behavior of Task Groups
Administrative Controls
Business Policy

Accounting
Financial Accounting
Managerial Accounting

Methods
Business Statistics
Introduction to Management Science
Business Research

Marketing
Fundamentals of Marketing
Consumer Behavior

Business Law
Fundamentals of Business Law

Finance
Fundamentals of Finance

Economics
Fundamentals of Economics
Business and Economic Analysis
Business and Its Environment

Guidance and Counseling
Principles and Practices of Counseling
Tests and Measurements

EMPLOYMENT HIGHLIGHTS

2/72-8/73:
PLANTERS INTERNATIONAL

Employed as Director of Budget Department. Duties and responsibilities included:

Monitoring departmental budgets and grants and initiating budget changes; researching and preparing annual reports; preparing weekly, monthly and quarterly payroll forms; supervising secretarial and office personnel and delegating assignments; handling and coordinating administrative matters for 25 employees and research assistants; ordering and procuring equipment and supplies; managing department in manager's absence; arranging conferences, and meetings.

Reason for leaving: To return to school on a full-time basis to get my M.B.A.

8/71-1/72:
NEW YORK UNIVERSITY

Employed as Administrative Assistant to Director of Planning and Director of Exhibitions. Duties and responsibilities included:

Reading and interpreting mail and reports and advising employer as to appropriate action; initiating and following up various matters by telephone; writing own correspondence; scheduling and arranging art exhibitions on campus; coordinating art department; scheduling courses, helping draft course proposals, and preparing teaching schedules for art department; preparing press releases and publicity material for art department and exhibitions; advising students; creating new forms and initiating new procedures; organizing and maintaining a complex filing system; delegating tasks to junior secretary and student assistants; keeping employer informed of relevant campus matters; ordering office equipment and supplies for art department, exhibitions department, and libraries.

Reason for leaving: Moving to Columbia, Missouri

Form 2 (continued)

<u>9/70-2/71</u>:
HECKL AND DUNOVER (book publishing company)

Employed as Assistant to Sales Manager, Upbeat Books Division. Duties and responsibilities included:

Writing own correspondence and memos; making travel arrangements; reorganizing and maintaining filing system; keeping sales records; ordering and sending books; coordinating about 100 salesmen and keeping personnel records; utilizing computer printouts; preparing kits for new salesmen.

<u>Reason for leaving</u>: Injury to elbow.

<u>10/66-9/70</u>:
G. WHIZ, INC.

Employed as Assistant to Head of Performance Department. Duties and responsibilities included:

Preparing reports, promotional material involving research and compilation; duties involved much public contact, both in person and on telephone; making many decisions on own; much high pressure work involving deadlines. Writing own correspondence; handling telephone and written orders; handling all routine Performance Department matters.

<u>Reason for leaving</u>: No opportunity for advancement

<u>12/65-10/66</u>:
PETER A. FLOP & CO., INC. (construction materials distributing company)

Employed as Record clerk in Personnel Department. Duties and responsibilities included:

Processing invoices; keeping personnel records; interviewing applicants for screening; administering aptitude tests to applicants. Typing correspondence, forms, reports; various clerical duties.

<u>Reason for leaving</u>: To accept better position.

<u>Prior Employment</u>:

Part-time and summer employment during school and college years included receptionist (Franklin-Hall, Harding College); cashier (Globe Theater, Green, Nebraska); and stock work, clerical duties, and some sales work (Green Shoe Company, Green, Nebraska).

REFERENCES

Available on request.

PART B

Form 3 Resume No. 2

Gaylord Golden   2825 E. Closer Dr.
Born: February 18, 1937   Phoenix, Arizona
Married: Three children

I.   Educational Background   GPA

        BA-United College, Schenectady, New York   1959   2.31
           -University of Maine, Portland, Maine   1966   3.0
        MBA-University of Colorado   1971   3.58

II. Engineering

     The first two years of undergraduate work were in the mechanical engineering
     program. This program included two years of physics, one year of chemistry, the
     basic courses from ME, CE, and EE as well as English and German.

     At the end of sophomore year, transferred into the Industrial Administration
     program. Utilizing engineering credits and majoring in economics.

III. Mathematics and Quantitative Courses

        Analytical Geometry and Algebra   United College
        Differential Calculus   United College
        Integral Calculus   United College
        Business Statistics   United College
        Quantitative Methods II (chi Square, ANOVA) University of Colorado
        Business Decision Theory (in progress)   University of Colorado
        Computer Programming (Fortran IV)   University of Colorado
        General Math Review (Algebra and Calculus)   University of Colorado
        Persons in Society   University of Colorado
        Introduction to Management Science   University of Colorado

IV. Accounting and Finance

        Principles of Accounting I and II   United College
        Using Accounting Information   University of Colorado
        Corporation Finance   United College
        Public Finance   United College
        Financial Administration   University of Colorado

V.   Economics

        Elementary Economics I and II   United College
        Development of Economic Thought
           (Price and Income Theory)   United College
        Money and Banking   United College
        Economics of Transportation   United College

VI. Management

        Problems of Business and Industry   United College
        Human Relations   University of Colorado

Form 3 (continued)

Administrative Problems	University of Colorado
Business Problems	University of Colorado
Public Administrative Systems	University of Colorado
Administrative Policies	University of Maine
Persons in Society	University of Colorado
Social Psychology	University of Colorado

VII. Marketing

Marketing Concepts and Issues	University of Colorado
Marketing Policies	University of Colorado
Global Marketing Problem	University of Colorado

VIII. Other

Advanced Business Law	University of Colorado

IX. Experience

Chief Mountain Community College (enrollment 4,000)   Nov. 1970 to present
Assistant to the President and Member of Marketing Department.
Duties: Administrative officer to oversee internal operation of entire college including
budgets, promotions and personnel procedures. Instructor in Retail Merchandising Pro-
gram.
Courses Taught: Principles of Management, Personnel Management, Retailing, Basic
Marketing, Salesmanship, Cooperative Work Experience.

Other Activities: Involved in program design and development; conducted an Institutional
Research and Development Program; member of the Community College Curriculum Committee.

Sweetwell, Inc. Residential Div.   Jan. 1967 to Oct. 1970
Product: Residential temperature controls and accessories. Gas valves, thermostats,
limit switches, electronic aircleaners, combustion safeguard equipment, zone valves.
Position and Duties: Sales Engineer. Responsible for selling all division products
and promotional programs to dealers and wholesalers. Also, heavily involved with technical training of dealer service personnel. A major portion of effort was devoted to
resolving constant channel conflicts.
Customers: Heating, plumbing and air conditioning wholesalers and their associated
dealers and service organizations. Also, called on OEMS and "quasi" OEMS (Wards, other
chains). Occasionally called on architects, mechanical engineers, city engineers,
inspectors, building owners and utilities.

Territory: Portions of Western Colorado, and Montana.

Volume: Approximately 450,000 per year

Reasons for change: Left to begin work on MBA and to enter the education field.

L.D. Jones Systems and Metering Division   May 1966 to Nov. 1967

Product: Meters and valves for the petroleum and petrochemical industry. Also, service
station pumps and other marketing equipment.

Position and duties: District Sales Manager. Working with customers on technical appl
cation of meters and valves, contacting major oil companies to sell pumps, working with
local representatives and distributors on sales problems. Finding and evaluating
service representatives.

Form 3 (continued)

Customers: Production engineers, project engineers, PA's terminal superintendents, Major oil companies, pipelines, jobbers and chemical companies.

Territory: Rocky Mountain States

Volume: Approximately $100,000.

Reason for change: This division is eliminating direct sales force.

Hedena Electrical Agencies   April 1962 to May 1966

Product: Capacitors, Resistors, Semiconductors, Integrated circuits.

Position and duties: 8/65-6/66 Sales Account Manager at main plant. Handled all customer problems, e.g. order processing, quoting, expediting, engineering liason. Processed approximately $5 million/year. 6/62-8/65 Sales Engineer in Houston office. Sold all company products in territory. Included technical application work, attaining account control and liason with the factory.

Contacts: Component and Project engineers, buyers and PA's

Territory: Texas, Kansas, New Mexico

Volume: Approximately $85,000. Helped achieve 35% increase in '65.

Accomplishments: Obtained largest order ever taken in territory ($9,000).

Reason for change: Limited future in the inside sales position.

Circle Fast Corp., Cinch Division   May 1959 to April 1962

Products: Electrical connectors, ignition systems, specialized capacitors.

Position and duties: Applications Engineer. Handled inside and outside sales work. Sold concept, pushed design thru engineering, costing, manufacturing. Worked on sales and advertising programs.

Customers: OEM manufacturers of electronics equipment.

Contacts: Component and Project Engineers, buyers.

Territory: No specific assignment-where demand required.

Reason for change: Greater opportunity with Hedena Electrical Agencies.

PART B

Form 4 Resume No. 3

CHARLOTTE PYLE

Health: Excellent
Interests: Tennis, swimming, reading, photography

<u>Home</u>   <u>Office</u>

2121 S. Broadway   Two West Exposition Place
Muncie, Indiana   Muncie, Indiana

<u>Professional Experience</u>

Skyline Management Corp., Muncie, Indiana

1971-present   Vice President and Member of the
                                Board of Directors

1966-1971   Senior Consulting Associate

Skyline Management Corp. is a research, consulting, and executive development company devoted primarily to retailers, wholesalers, and manufacturers with distribution, marketing and administrative problems. The firm also provides consulting services to Skyline Data Systems. The latter is a subsidiary of Towncorp and a major supplier of on-line computer services in the field of distribution. In the aggregate, these companies employ over 150 professional associates, most of whom have advanced degrees in a variety of fields, including economics, accounting, finance, quantitative business analysis, management, and marketing. Background materials on Skyline Management and the company's annual reports are available upon request.

Directed or provided major support for over 80 industry studies on the changing structure and economics of distribution. These studies covered emerging developments in virtually all lines of retail and wholesale trade.

Designed and/or participated in over 30 management development programs sponsored by individual companies or trade associations. All programs were based on a substantial amount of corporate and industry research, and most of the programs involved specialized seminars for senior and middle management executives.

Served as a featured speaker at over 30 national conferences. Each presentation was based on the findings of original or ongoing research.

The following activities are illustrative of the types of assignments completed during this time period.

- Authored a major research report on the applicability of quantitative marketing concepts to retailing and the implications of the hypermarket for manufacturers, wholesalers, and retailers.

- Conducted management audits of several companies to determine their capability to meet long-run company objectives. The firms analyzed include two of the largest discount department store firms and one of the largest department store firms in the United States and several of the largest retailing organizations in Europe.

Form 4 (continued)

- Developed step-by-step profit planning and management-by-objectives systems for numerous firms and trade associations. Clients in this area include firms in wholesale and retail distribution in the United States and Canada.

- Prepared a detailed market potential analysis for a leading drygoods wholesaler. This study evaluated sales potential on a county-by-county basis utilizing multiple regression analysis techniques.

- Developed systems for determining the profitability of individual merchandise items, suppliers, and customers for a leading wholesaler trade association.

- Assisted several major retailing corporations in developing long-run budgeting programs. These analyses were based on a detailed understanding of the company's strengths and reactions and related factors.

Education

MBA (1966) -- University of Wisconsin

- Ford Foundation Fellowship
- NCR Thesis Grant
- Teaching Associate

BA (1964) -- University of Indiana - Ft. Wayne -- Graduated with honors/earned 100 percent of undergraduate expenses.

PART B

Form 5 Job Description

ADMINISTRATIVE OFFICER'S JOB—Palms Pacific Corporation, Inc.

DESCRIPTION OF WORK:

General Statement of Duties: Supervises and coordinates responsible administrative work of a complex nature involving program responsibility; does related work as required.

Supervision Received: Receives policy guidance from an administrative superior or board members.

Supervision Exercised: Plans, organizes, develops, coordinates, and directs a staff of administrative and clerical personnel. Total at all levels exceeds twenty.

EXAMPLE OF DUTIES: (Any one position may not include all of the duties listed, nor do the listed examples include all tasks that may be found in positions.)

Administers, coordinates, and directs a complex administrative management program involving program responsibility for a department or equivalent; organizes and directs the work of personnel in day-to-day operation, and conducts long-range planning.

Establishes working methods and procedures and develops departmental procedures and policies related to administrative functions.

Directs major staff services, including budget, training, record keeping, and personnel and general administrative services. Develops supporting data and presents budget estimates and requests.

Directs or performs studies on efficiency, work flow, procedures, work standards, and research and planning.

Develops and compiles comprehensive reports.

Develops and implements immediate and long-range plans for administrative areas of the organization.

Performs related work as required.

REQUIRED KNOWLEDGE, SKILLS, AND ABILITIES:

Extensive and broad knowledge of complex administrative management programs. Skill and ability in administering, planning, and directing personnel in day-to-day programs appropriate to the position to be filled. Ability to interpret and apply laws, rules, regulations, and industry practices. Ability to relate with and coordinate department activities with employees, other departments, and the general public.

QUALIFICATIONS FOR APPOINTMENT:

Education: Graduation from a college or university with major course work in public or business administration or related field.

Experience: Six years progressively responsible experience in a supervisory, technical, or professional area related to management or administration; familiarity with computer software very helpful.

OR

Any equivalent combination of education and experience.

PART B

Form 6 The Palms Pacific Corporation, Inc.

Palms Pacific Corporation (PPC) is a small organization whose primary objectives are the following: to manufacture specialized electronics equipment, including meters, scopes, scanners, etc.; to manufacture certain medical/electronic products, such as "heart pacers" (devices implanted into a person's chest cavity through surgery in order to help stimulate and regulate their heartbeat); to engage in research and development in the electronics field; and to provide technical assistance in a consulting capacity to other organizations, including government and educational clients. PPC is located in a large West Coast city in the United States. It is only ten years old and has grown rapidly since its founding by an electrical engineer, a heart specialist, a former designer of computer hardware, and a lawyer. These four founders still own over eighty percent of the stock in this closed corporation, although not in equal shares.

PPC had about two million dollars in gross sales last year, brought in another $750,000 from government contracts, and about $300,000 from consulting contracts. PPC has finally gotten to the point where the four principals noted above no longer take part in day-to-day operations. Their expertise is better spent on planning and strategy making, on securing new business and clients, and on consulting activities. They hired an administrative vice president a year ago to oversee the operations, but soon realized that this person was overburdened as well. They thus decided to look for an administrative officer who would be responsible for the clerical and some technical aspects of the operations, while the administrative vice president, to whom the officer would report, would still oversee the major functional areas. The four principals of PPC are actually board members, but still do take part in some operating-level decisions in their area of expertise (see organization chart, Figure 1).

The administrative vice president is a 45-year-old white male who has a bachelor's degree from a major California university in management. He had had twenty years of administrative experience and was considered a "good catch" by the directors of PPC. He is a native of the West Coast, married, no children, and an avid environmentalist. He takes pride in his frequent returns to his alma mater and other schools to take courses, attend seminars and workshops, etc., in order to learn of new techniques in budgeting, training, motivation, leadership, and interpersonal relations. He is knowledgeable and competent and has the respect of those who work with and for him. His leadership style is quite structured and authoritarian and he finds it difficult to delegate work without checking it over closely.

The administrative officer would be in charge of such activities as government-contract administration, personnel record keeping, training and development, state and federal government relations, wage and salary administration, and coordinating efforts of the scientific/technical and manufacturing personnel. Report writing, planning, and policymaking are additional duties. Selection and staffing are currently handled by each individual division of PPC, as are performance appraisal, wage and salary administration, and motivation programs. There is currently no union in PPC. Most of its employees are professionals in law, medicine, management, or engineering. Operating-level persons are highly skilled.

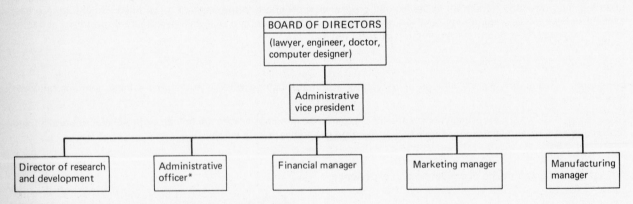

*Position being sought by three applicants in this exercise.

Fig. 1. Organization Chart for Palms Pacific Corporation (top management levels only; doctor is current president and board chairman)

PART C

Form 7 Application 1 for Job of Administrative Assistant

FOR OFFICE USE ONLY	
Possible Work Locations	Possible Positions

APPLICATION FOR EMPLOYMENT

(PLEASE PRINT PLAINLY)

FOR OFFICE USE ONLY	
Work Location _____	Rate _____
Position _____	Date _____

To Applicant: We deeply appreciate your interest in our organization and assure you that we are sincerely interested in your qualifications. A clear understanding of your background and work history will aid us in placing you in the position that best meets your qualifications and may assist us in possible future upgrading.

PERSONAL   Date: __June 18__

Name __Wonder__   __M.__   Social Security No. __821-34-6063__
    Last   First Initial   Middle Initial

Present address __9680__ __Willow__ __Bigville__ __USA__ Telephone No. __482-3668__
    No.   Street   City   State   Zip

How long have you lived at above address? __one year__

Previous address __616__ __31st__ __New York__ __N.Y.__ How long did you live there? __5 mo.__
    No.   Street   City   State   Zip

To Applicant: READ THIS INTRODUCTION CAREFULLY BEFORE ANSWERING ANY QUESTIONS IN THIS BLOCKED-OFF AREA. The Civil Rights Act of 1964 prohibits discrimination in employment practice because of race, color, religion, sex or national origin. P.L. 90-202 prohibits discrimination on the basis of age with respect to individuals who are at least 40 but less than 65 years of age. The laws of some States also prohibit some or all of the above types of discrimination.
DO NOT ANSWER ANY QUESTION CONTAINED IN THIS BLOCKED-OFF AREA UNLESS THE EMPLOYER HAS CHECKED THE BOX NEXT TO THE QUESTION, thereby indicating that the requested information is needed for a bona fide occupational qualification, national security laws, or other legally permissible reasons.

☒ Are you over the age of twenty-one? __yes__ If no, hire is subject to verification that you are of minimum legal age.

☒ Sex: M __x__ F _____   ☒ Height: __5__ ft. __8__ in.   ☒ Weight: __142__ lbs.

☒ Marital Status: Single _____ Engaged _____ Married __xx__ Separated _____ Divorced _____ Widowed _____

☒ Date of Marriage __1971__   ☒ Number of dependents including yourself __1__   ☒ Are you a citizen of the U.S.A.? __yes__

☒ What is your present Selective Service classification? __1-Y__

☒ Indicate dates you attended school:

Elementary __1948 - 1956__ High School __1956 - 1960__ College __1962 - 1966__
    From   To   From   To   From   To

Other (Specify type of school) __M.B.A. Graduate Degree in Business Administration__ __1973 - 1974__
    From   To

☒ Have you ever been bonded? __no__ If yes, on what jobs? _____

Employer may list other bona fide occupational questions on lines below:

☐ _____
☐ _____

What method of transportation will you use to get to work? __Drive__

Position(s) applied for __Administrative Officer__ Rate of pay expected $ __300__ per week

Would you work Full-Time __yes__ Part-Time _____ Specify days and hours if part-time _____

Were you previously employed by us? _____ If yes, when? _____

List any friends or relatives working for us __none__
                                          Name(s)

If your application is considered favorably, on what date will you be available for work? __July__ 19 ___

Are there any other experiences, skills, or qualifications which you feel would especially fit you for work with the Company? _____
__I feel my extensive administrative experience uniquely qualifies me for the position of an administrative assistant.__

Form 7 (continued)

Do you have any physical defects which preclude you from performing certain kinds of work? __none__   If yes, describe such defects and specific work limitations._____

Have you been convicted of a crime in the past ten years, excluding misdemeanors and summary offenses? ___no___   If yes, describe in full _____

Have you had a major illness in the past 5 years? _____ If yes, describe _____

Have you received compensation for injuries? __yes__ If yes, describe __injury to elbow__
_____

RECORD OF EDUCATION

School	Name and Address of School	Course of Study	Check Last Year Completed				Did You Graduate?	List Diploma or Degree
Elementary	Lincoln Elementary Minneapolis, Minn.		5	6	7	X̶	[X] Yes [ ] No	
High	Dungan High School Minnespolis, Minn.	music	1	2	3	X̶	[X] Yes [ ] No	Diploma
College	Harding College Harding, Vermont	music	1	2	3	X̶	[X] Yes [ ] No	B.Mus.
Other (Specify)	University of the West Western, Arizona	Business Administration	1	X̶	3	4	[X] Yes [ ] No	M.B.A.

MILITARY SERVICE RECORD

Were you in U.S. Armed Forces?   Yes _____ No ___XX___ If yes, what Branch? _____

Dates of duty: From _____ To _____ Rank at discharge _____
              Month   Day   Year   Month   Day   Year

List duties in the Service including special training _____
_____

Have you taken any training under the G.I. Bill of Rights? _____ If yes, what training did you take? _____

PERSONAL REFERENCES (Not Former Employers or Relatives)

Name and Occupation	Address	Phone Number
Sam Dow	Minneapolis	461-3822
Helen Sapp	Minneapolis	436-4916
Doris Paulsen	New York	834-9006

Form 8 (continued)

List below all present and past employment, beginning with your most recent

I

Name and Address of Company and Type of Business	From Mo.	From Yr.	To Mo.	To Yr.	Describe in detail the work you did	Weekly Starting Salary	Weekly Last Salary	Reason for Leaving	Name of Supervisor
Planters Int'l Columbia, Mo.	2	72	8	73	Administrative Assistant	225	225	to get MBA	Phyllis Dorn

II

Name and Address of Company and Type of Business	From Mo.	From Yr.	To Mo.	To Yr.	Describe in detail the work you did	Weekly Starting Salary	Weekly Last Salary	Reason for Leaving	Name of Supervisor
New York University New York	8	71	1	72	Administrative Assistant	183	209	moving	Helen Gurgle

III

Name and Address of Company and Type of Business	From Mo.	From Yr.	To Mo.	To Yr.	Describe in detail the work you did	Weekly Starting Salary	Weekly Last Salary	Reason for Leaving	Name of Supervisor
Heckl & Dunover New York	9	70	2	71	Assistant to Sales Manager	126	143	Injury to elbow	J. Paul Handsom

IV

Name and Address of Company and Type of Business	From Mo.	From Yr.	To Mo.	To Yr.	Describe in detail the work you did	Weekly Starting Salary	Weekly Last Salary	Reason for Leaving	Name of Supervisor
G. Whiz, Inc. New York	10	66	9	70	Assistant to Head of Performance Dept.	113	141	no opportunity	Dan Block

V

Name and Address of Company and Type of Business	From Mo.	From Yr.	To Mo.	To Yr.	Describe in detail the work you did	Weekly Starting Salary	Weekly Last Salary	Reason for Leaving	Name of Supervisor
Peter A. Flop & Co. New York	12	65	10	66	Glorified record clerk	86	94	to obtain better position	Laurence R. Dunn

May we contact the employers listed above? __yes__ If not, indicate by No. which one(s) you do not wish us to contact _____

The facts set forth above in my application for employment are true and complete. I understand that if employed, false statements on this application shall be considered sufficient cause for dismissal. You are hereby authorized to make any investigation of my personal history and financial and credit record through any investigative or credit agencies or bureaus of your choice.*

—3— Signature of Applicant

*To Employer: The requirements of the Fair Credit Reporting Act may be applicable if a credit report on the applicant is obtained and considered.

PART C

Form 8 Application 2 for Job of Administrative Assistant

FOR OFFICE USE ONLY	
Possible Work Locations	Possible Positions

APPLICATION FOR EMPLOYMENT

(PLEASE PRINT PLAINLY)

FOR OFFICE USE ONLY	
Work Location _____	Rate _____
Position _____	Date _____

To Applicant: We deeply appreciate your interest in our organization and assure you that we are sincerely interested in your qualifications. A clear understanding of your background and work history will aid us in placing you in the position that best meets your qualifications and may assist us in possible future upgrading.

PERSONAL   Date: June 1

Name __Golden_____G_____ Social Security No. _322-10-0003_
        Last   First Initial   Middle Initial

Present address __2825 Closer Dr.____Minute____U.S.A._____ Telephone No. _632-4242_
                 No.   Street   City   State   Zip

How long have you lived at above address? ___4 years_____

Previous address _123____Main_____Yuma____Co._____ How long did you live there? _3 yrs._
                 No.   Street   City   State   Zip

To Applicant: READ THIS INTRODUCTION CAREFULLY BEFORE ANSWERING ANY QUESTIONS IN THIS BLOCKED-OFF AREA. The Civil Rights Act of 1964 prohibits discrimination in employment practice because of race, color, religion, sex or national origin. P.L. 90-202 prohibits discrimination on the basis of age with respect to individuals who are at least 40 but less than 65 years of age. The laws of some States also prohibit some or all of the above types of discrimination.
   DO NOT ANSWER ANY QUESTION CONTAINED IN THIS BLOCKED-OFF AREA UNLESS THE EMPLOYER HAS CHECKED THE BOX NEXT TO THE QUESTION, thereby indicating that the requested information is needed for a bona fide occupational qualification, national security laws, or other legally permissible reasons.

☒ Are you over the age of twenty-one? _yes_____ If no, hire is subject to verification that you are of minimum legal age.

☒ Sex: M _M___ F _____ ☒ Height: _6_ ft. _4_ In. ☒ Weight: _185_ lbs.

☒ Marital Status: Single _____ Engaged _____ Married _XX_ Separated _____ Divorced _____ Widowed _____

☒ Date of Marriage _1963_ ☐ Number of dependents including yourself _4_ ☒ Are you a citizen of the U.S.A.? _yes_

☒ What is your present Selective Service classification? _2-D_

☒ Indicate dates you attended school:

Elementary _1945_ _1951_ High School _1951_ _1955_ College _1955_ _1959_
          From   To   From   To   From   To

Other (Specify type of school) _____
                                              From   To

☒ Have you ever been bonded? _no_ If yes, on what jobs? _____

Employer may list other bona fide occupational questions on lines below:

☐ _____

☐ _____

What method of transportation will you use to get to work? _Drive_____

Position(s) applied for _Administrative Officer_____ Rate of pay expected $ _350_ per week

Would you work Full-Time _yes_ Part-Time _____ Specify days and hours if part-time _____

Were you previously employed by us? _no_ If yes, when? _____

List any friends or relatives working for us __no_____
                                                         Name(s)

If your application is considered favorably, on what date will you be available for work? _August_ _1_ 19__

Are there any other experiences, skills, or qualifications which you feel would especially fit you for work with the Company? _____
   All of my work experience and education appears directly related to the job of the

Administrative Officer

Form 8 (continued)

Do you have any physical defects which preclude you from performing certain kinds of work? __no__   If yes, describe such defects

and specific work limitations._____

Have you been convicted of a crime in the past ten years, excluding misdemeanors and summary offenses? _no_   If yes, describe

in full _____

Have you had a major illness in the past 5 years? __no__ If yes, describe _____

Have you received compensation for injuries? ___no___ If yes, describe _____

RECORD OF EDUCATION

School	Name and Address of School	Course of Study	Check Last Year Completed				Did You Graduate?	List Diploma or Degree
Elementary	Linwood Elementary South Bend, Indiana	✕	5	6	7	⑧	☒ Yes ☐ No	✕
High	Jefferson High School South Bend, Indiana	Sciences	1	2	3	④	☒ Yes ☐ No	Diploma
College	United College Schenectady, New York	Industrial Administration		2	3	④	☒ Yes ☐ No	B.A.
Other (Specify)	University of Maine Portland, Maine University of Colorado	Business Administration	②		3	4	☒ Yes ☐ No	MBA

MILITARY SERVICE RECORD

Were you in U.S. Armed Forces?   Yes _____   No ___no___   If yes, what Branch? _____

Dates of duty: From _____ To _____ Rank at discharge _____
        Month   Day   Year   Month   Day   Year

List duties in the Service including special training _____

_____

Have you taken any training under the G.I. Bill of Rights? _____ If yes, what training did you take? _____

PERSONAL REFERENCES (Not Former Employers or Relatives)

Name and Occupation	Address	Phone Number
Helen Hope	South Bend, Indiana	443-2821
Paul Bean	Schenectady, N.Y.	211-0348
Horace West	Yuma, Colorado	866-4328

Form 8 (continued)

List below all present and past employment, beginning with your most recent

	Name and Address of Company and Type of Business	From Mo.	Yr.	To Mo.	Yr.	Describe in detail the work you did	Weekly Starting Salary	Weekly Last Salary	Reason for Leaving	Name of Supervisor
I	Chief College Eduction Phoenix, Arizona	11	70	pres.		Instructing in Business Administration Courses and Adminis. Officer	275	340	want to return to industry	Hank Low, President

	Name and Address of Company and Type of Business	From Mo.	Yr.	To Mo.	Yr.	Describe in detail the work you did	Weekly Starting Salary	Weekly Last Salary	Reason for Leaving	Name of Supervisor
II	Sweetwell Thermostatic Controls Phoenix, Arizona	1	67	10	70	Sales Engineer	230	460 (with bonus)	wanted to try college teaching	Ray Bones President

	Name and Address of Company and Type of Business	From Mo.	Yr.	To Mo.	Yr.	Describe in detail the work you did	Weekly Starting Salary	Weekly Last Salary	Reason for Leaving	Name of Supervisor
III	L.D. Jones Petroleum Meters & Valves Peublo, Colorado	5	66	11	67	District Sales Manager	200	265	to take better opportunity	Dan I. Davis

	Name and Address of Company and Type of Business	From Mo.	Yr.	To Mo.	Yr.	Describe in detail the work you did	Weekly Starting Salary	Weekly Last Salary	Reason for Leaving	Name of Supervisor
IV	Hedena Electrical Capacitors, etc. Dallas, Texas	4	62	5	66	Sales Account Manager	160	218	for better opportunity	William H. Rue

	Name and Address of Company and Type of Business	From Mo.	Yr.	To Mo.	Yr.	Describe in detail the work you did	Weekly Starting Salary	Weekly Last Salary	Reason for Leaving	Name of Supervisor
V	Circle Fast Cor. Electrical Connectors Ft. Worth, Texas	5	59	4	62	Applications Engineer	130	156	to get a better job	Edward Hanson

May we contact the employers listed above? __yes__ If not, indicate by No. which one(s) you do not wish us to contact _____

The facts set forth above in my application for employment are true and complete. I understand that if employed, false statements on this application shall be considered sufficient cause for dismissal. You are hereby authorized to make any investigation of my personal history and financial and credit record through any investigative of credit agencies or bureaus of your choice.*

—3— *Signature of Applicant*

*To Employer: The requirements of the Fair Credit Reporting Act may be applicable if a credit report on the applicant is obtained and considered.

PART C

Form 9 Application 3 for Job of Administrative Assistant

FOR OFFICE USE ONLY	
Possible Work Locations	Possible Positions

APPLICATION
FOR
EMPLOYMENT

(PLEASE PRINT PLAINLY)

FOR OFFICE USE ONLY	
Work Location _____	Rate _____
Position _____	Date _____

To Applicant: We deeply appreciate your interest in our organization and assure you that we are sincerely interested in your qualifications. A clear understanding of your background and work history will aid us in placing you in the position that best meets your qualifications and may assist us in possible future upgrading.

PERSONAL   Date: May 16

Name __Pyle__ _____ __C.__ _____ Social Security No. 388-42-6066
        Last   First Initial   Middle Initial

Present address __2121 S. Broadway__ __Muncie__ __Indiana__ ____ Telephone No. 322-0367
        No.   Street   City   State   Zip

How long have you lived at above address? __three years__

Previous address __1414 South Continental__ __Muncie, Indiana__ ____ How long did you live there? __3 yr__
        No.   Street   City   State   Zip

To Applicant: READ THIS INTRODUCTION CAREFULLY BEFORE ANSWERING ANY QUESTIONS IN THIS BLOCKED-OFF AREA. The Civil Rights Act of 1964 prohibits discrimination in employment practice because of race, color, religion, sex or national origin. P.L. 90-202 prohibits discrimination on the basis of age with respect to individuals who are at least 40 but less than 65 years of age. The laws of some States also prohibit some or all of the above types of discrimination.

DO NOT ANSWER ANY QUESTION CONTAINED IN THIS BLOCKED OFF AREA UNLESS THE EMPLOYER HAS CHECKED THE BOX NEXT TO THE QUESTION, thereby indicating that the requested information is needed for a bona fide occupational qualification, national security laws, or other legally permissible reasons.

☒ Are you over the age of twenty-one? _____ If no, hire is subject to verification that you are of minimum legal age.

☒ Sex: M _____ F _____   ☒ Height: ____ ft. ____ in.   ☒ Weight: ____ lbs.

☒ Marital Status: Single ____ Engaged ____ Married ____ Separated ____ Divorced ____ Widowed ____

☒ Date of Marriage ____ ☒ Number of dependents including yourself ____ ☒ Are you a citizen of the U.S.A.? __yes__

☒ What is your present Selective Service classification? _____

☒ Indicate dates you attended school:

Elementary _____ High School _____ College __1961 - 1966__
    From   To   From   To   From   To

Other (Specify type of school) _____
               From   To

☒ Have you ever been bonded? __no__ If yes, on what jobs? _____

Employer may list other bona fide occupational questions on lines below:

☐ _____

☐ _____

What method of transportation will you use to get to work? __Bus__

Position(s) applied for __Administrative Officer__ ____ Rate of pay expected $ __280 to start__ per week

Would you work Full-Time __xx__ Part-Time ____ Specify days and hours if part-time _____

Were you previously employed by us? __no__ If yes, when? _____

List any friends or relatives working for us __none__ _____
               Name(s)

If your application is considered favorably, on what date will you be available for work? __June 30__ ____ 19__

Are there any other experiences, skills, or qualifications which you feel would especially fit you for work with the Company? ____

__This job looks as if it was made for me! It seems a most logical step in my__

__professional development.__

(Turn to Next Page)

Form 9 (continued)

Do you have any physical defects which preclude you from performing certain kinds of work? ____none____ If yes, describe such defects

and specific work limitations. _____

Have you been convicted of a crime in the past ten years, excluding misdemeanors and summary offenses? ___no___ If yes, describe

in full _____

Have you had a major illness in the past 5 years? ___no___ If yes, describe _____

Have you received compensation for injuries? ___no___ If yes, describe _____

RECORD OF EDUCATION

School	Name and Address of School	Course of Study	Check Last Year Completed				Did You Graduate?	List Diploma or Degree
Elementary	Pure Grade School Houston, Texas	✕	5	6	7	⑧	☒ Yes ☐ No	✕
High	Lafayette Central Hobart, Indiana		1	2	3	④	☒ Yes ☐ No	Diploma
College	University of Indiana Ft. Wayne, Indiana		1	2	3	④	☒ Yes ☐ No	BA
Other (Specify)	University of Wisconsin		①	2	3	4	☒ Yes ☐ No	MBA

MILITARY SERVICE RECORD

Were you in U.S. Armed Forces? Yes _____ No ___no___ If yes, what Branch? _____

Dates of duty: From _____ To _____ Rank at discharge _____

            Month   Day   Year   Month   Day   Year

List duties in the Service including special training _____

_____

Have you taken any training under the G.I. Bill of Rights? _____ If yes, what training did you take? _____

PERSONAL REFERENCES (Not Former Employers or Relatives)

Name and Occupation	Address	Phone Number
David L. Good	Muncie, Indiana	442-4046
Harold E. Luba	Muncie, Indiana	442-4046
Frank Curtis	Hobart, Indiana	863-6023

Form 9 (continued)

List below all present and past employment, beginning with your most recent

	Name and Address of Company and Type of Business	From Mo.	From Yr.	To Mo.	To Yr.	Describe in detail the work you did	Weekly Starting Salary	Weekly Last Salary	Reason for Leaving	Name of Supervisor
I	Skyline Management Corp. Research and Consulting Firm Muncie, Indiana	6	66	present		Vice President	160	300 (with options)	I want to move into a purely administrative position in preparation for top management of a major corporation.	David L. Good, President
II										
III										
IV										
V										

May we contact the employers listed above? __yes__ If not, indicate by No. which one(s) you do not wish us to contact _____

The facts set forth above in my application for employment are true and complete. I understand that if employed, false statements on this application shall be considered sufficient cause for dismissal. You are hereby authorized to make any investigation of my personal history and financial and credit record through any investigative or credit agencies or bureaus of your choice.*

Charlotte Pyle

—3—
        Signature of Applicant

*To Employer: The requirements of the Fair Credit Reporting Act may be applicable if a credit report on the applicant is obtained and considered.

PART D

Form 10 Biographical Data Form: Pacific Palms Corporation

Question and/or response category weight	Question	Merle	Gaylord	Charlotte	% of successful managers selecting this response[1]	
	1. My present marital status is (<u>mark all that apply</u>)					
	A. single			X	A	14
	B. married	X	X		B	84
	C. separated				C	1
	D. divorced				D	1
	E. widowed				E	*
	F. remarried				F	1
	2. The highest education level that my father attained was					
	A. eighth grade or lower			X	A	19
	B. some high school but did not graduate				B	17
	C. high school graduate		X		C	25
	D. some college but did not graduate				D	16
	E. college graduate				E	16
	F. master's degree or equivalent				F	4
	G. doctoral degree or equivalent	X			G	3
					Omit	*
	* Less than 1%					
	3. The occupation which my father followed for most of his life may be best described as					
	A. business executive	X			A	17
	B. clerical worker				B	6
	C. farmer or rancher				C	9
	D. professional man				D	15
	E. salesman			X	E	10
	F. store or shop owner		X		F	8
	G. service worker (barber, chauffeur, etc.)				G	2
	H. skilled craftsman (carpenter, machinist, etc.)				H	19
	I. unskilled or semi-skilled worker				I	7
	J. other				J	7
					Omit	1
	4. The highest educational level that my mother attained was					
	A. eighth grade or lower			X	A	11
	B. some high school but did not graduate				B	16
	C. high school graduate		X		C	38
	D. some college but did not graduate				D	18
	E. college graduate				E	15
	F. master's degree or equivalent				F	2
	G. doctoral degree or equivalent	X			G	
					Omit	*

[1] Will not equal 100% due to incomplete sampling, rounding, omitted responses, duplicated responses obtained over time. The relative percentages for each response category in a question, as opposed to the absolute percentage, is relevant.

Form 10 (continued)

Question weight	Question	Merle	Gaylord	Charlotte	% of successful managers selecting this response	
	5. At some time during her life my mother was employed for a substantial period of time in (<u>mark all that apply</u>)					
	A. a profession such as law or medicine				A	1
	B. business				B	11
	C. clerical or stenographic work				C	25
	D. factory work				D	8
	E. house work				E	21
	F. laboratory work				F	1
	G. library work		X		G	1
	H. musical work				H	2
	I. nursing				I	5
	J. sales work				J	14
	K. service work such as cook or beautician				K	6
	L. sewing			X	L	5
	M. teaching	X			M	16
	N. some other work				N	8
	O. she was never employed				O	24
	6. While I was growing up, my mother was employed outside of our home (<u>mark all that apply</u>)					
	A. never				A	53
	B. before I started to school			X	B	14
	C. when I was in grammar school	X			C	25
	D. when I was in high school		X		D	35
	7. Of the children in my family I was					
	A. oldest	X			A	36
	B. youngest by a few years				B	22
	C. youngest by many years			X	C	5
	D. neither oldest nor youngest		X		D	23
	E. I was an only child				E	14
					Omit	*
	8. My childhood family situation was					
	A. unusually happy		X		A	33
	B. average			X	B	64
	C. not particularly happy	X			C	3
					Omit	*
	9. During my teens my parents and I got along					
	A. very well; we agreed on almost everything	X			A	11
	B. better than most; we rarely had disagreements			X	B	40
	C. about average; as well as other family groups				C	46
	D. not very well; we had many disagreements				D	*
	E. not at all; we almost never agreed		X		E	*
					Omit	*

Form 10 (continued)

Question weight	Question	Merle	Gaylord	Charlotte	% of successful managers selecting this response	
	10. When I was a boy, my father helped me in (mark all that apply)					
	A. learning to use tools		X		A	69
	B. learning sports			X	B	57
	C. school work				C	45
	D. selecting school subjects	X			D	24
	E. selecting a job				E	30
	F. learning to drive a car				F	72
	G. none of these				G	7
	11. When I was a boy, my mother helped me in (mark all that apply)					
	A. choosing clothes		X		A	73
	B. choosing girl friends			X	B	3
	C. music				C	17
	D. school work	X			D	57
	E. selecting school subjects				E	25
	F. selecting reading material				F	21
	G. none of these				G	9
	12. As a young man, when I returned home from a date, my parents usually (mark all that apply)					
	A. were very inquisitive			X	A	3
	B. scolded me because I did not come home earlier				B	4
	C. were waiting up when I came in				C	15
	D. were interested but did not ask many questions	X			D	61
	E. teased or kidded me about the evening				E	5
	F. had retired for the night		X		F	49
	13. The one of the following statements which was most characteristic of my father when I was growing up is					
	A. a strict person with strong moral principles		X	X	A	39
	B. a very stern person but not too moralistic				B	8
	C. a fairly principled person				C	45
	D. a person who was forced by circumstances to modify his principles				D	2
	E. a rather ineffectual person compared with what he might have been	X			E	5
	14. As a boy, when I misbehaved at home or in the neighborhood, I was usually disciplined by					
	A. my mother				A	42
	B. my father		X	X	B	54
	C. someone else				C	1
	D. no one	X			D	*
	E. I did not misbehave enough to need discipline				E	3
					Omit	1

Form 10 (continued)

Question weight	Question	Merle	Gaylord	Charlotte	% of successful managers selecting this response
	15. During my teens my parents permitted me to make the final decisions concerning (mark all that apply)				
	A. attending religious services				A 54
	B. courses I took in school				B 88
	C. decorating my room				C 52
	D. drinking				D 30
	E. selecting my clothes				E 82
	F. smoking				F 45
	G. taking music lessons	X			G 48
	H. the hour I should be home				H 30
	I. use of my spare time				I 76
	J. use of the automobile				J 17
	K. whom I dated				K 97
	L. none of these		X	X	L 1
	16. I seriously considered quitting school				
	A. frequently		X		A 1
	B. occasionally			X	B 6
	C. seldom				C 12
	D. almost never	X			D 81
					Omit *
	17. The highest educational level that I attained was				
	A. less than high school graduate				A *
	B. high school graduate				B 2
	C. high school graduate plus formal training other than college				C 2
	D. two years of college or less				D 4
	E. more than two years of college but did not graduate				E 4
	F. college graduate		X	X	F 65
	G. master's degree or equivalent	X			G 20
	H. doctoral degree or equivalent				H 2
					Omit *
	18. At the time I graduated from high school, my age was				
	A. 15 or younger				A 1
	B. 16				B 7
	C. 17	X		X	C 50
	D. 18				D 38
	E. 19		X		E 3
	F. 20 or older				F 1
	G. I did not graduate from high school				G 1
					Omit *

Form 10 (continued)

Question weight	Question	Merle	Gaylord	Charlotte	% of successful managers selecting this response
	19. The high school subjects which I took and *liked* very much were (mark all that apply)				
	A. agriculture				A 7
	B. art				B 11
	C. biological sciences				C 41
	D. bookkeeping				D 15
	E. chemistry			X	E 47
	F. civics				Ḟ 38
	G. English or literature			X	G 43
	H. foreign language				H 22
	I. history				I 59
	J. mathematics		X		J 72
	K. mechanical drawing				K 31
	L. music	X			L 18
	M. physical education			X	M 67
	N. physics				N 43
	O. religion				O 7
	P. shop		X		P 28
	Q. shorthand				Q 1
	R. speech				R 23
	S. typing	X			S 20
	T. none of these				T *
	20. The number of students in the high school I attended for the longest period of time was				
	A. less than 100			X	A 4
	B. 100 to 500				B 34
	C. 500 to 1000		X		C 24
	D. 1000 to 2000	X			D 24
	E. more than 2000				E 13
					Omit *
	21. My usual scholastic standing in high school was in the				
	A. top 5%	X			A 27
	B. upper third but not top 5%			X	B 45
	C. middle third				C 22
	D. lower third		X		D 2
	E. I do not know				E 4
					Omit *
	22. When I was in school, I felt that the best way to get good marks in my subjects was to				
	A. keep my homework up to date and of high quality			X	A 64
	B. cram before exams				B 4
	C. ask for and complete additional assignments				C 1
	D. take a very active part in class discussions				D 17
	E. make myself popular with the teachers				E *
	F. find out what each teacher emphasized and concentrate on that				F 8
	G. do something else				G 1
	H. I was not especially interested in getting good marks		X		H 4
					Omit 1

Form 10 (continued)

Question weight	Question	Merle	Gaylord	Charlotte	% of successful managers selecting this response	
	23. During my high school days when I found problems hard to understand, I usually					
	A. asked teachers or parents for help	X			A	49
	B. asked schoolmates for help		X		B	11
	C. gave closer attention in class				C	6
	D. planned and carried out background study				D	5
	E. studied until the problem was solved			X	E	27
	F. none of these				F	1
	24. The number of full-time students in the undergraduate college which I attended the longest was					
	A. 400 or less	X			A	2
	B. 400 to 1000				B	9
	C. 1000 to 2000				C	13
	D. 2000 to 5000				D	24
	E. 5000 to 10,000			X	E	25
	F. more than 10,000		X		F	22
					Omit	*
	25. During my last full-time year of undergraduate college, the number of hours per week that I spent in study outside of class was about					
	A. 5 or less		X		A	2
	B. 6 to 10				B	12
	C. 11 to 15				C	23
	D. 16 to 20			X	D	28
	E. more than 20	X			E	29
					Omit	*
	26. My scholastic standing when I graduated from (or left) undergraduate college was					
	A. upper 5% of my class	X			A	12
	B. upper 15% (but not top 5%)				B	22
	C. upper 30% (but not top 15%)			X	C	25
	D. upper half (but not top 30%)				D	24
	E. lower half of my class		X		E	10
					Omit	*
	27. While in high school or college, I earned a school letter as a (mark all that apply)					
	A. baseball player				A	19
	B. basketball player			X	B	26
	C. boxer		X		C	1
	D. football player				D	32
	E. swimmer				E	3
	F. tennis player				F	5
	G. trackman				G	19
	H. wrestler				H	3
	I. participant in some other sport				I	11
	J. none of these	X			J	34

Form 10 (continued)

Question weight	Question	Merle	Gaylord	Charlotte	% of successful managers selecting this response	
	28. During my undergraduate years I partici-pated in (mark all that apply)					
	A. a social club or fraternity	X			A	56
	B. political clubs			X	B	16
	C. a school paper or yearbook				C	14
	D. dramatics	X			D	5
	E. musical activities	X			E	11
	F. forensics				F	2
	G. athletic activities		X	X	G	56
	H. some other school-sponsored activity				H	51
	I. none of these				I	10
	29. The part of the money for my support which I personally earned during my last couple of years of undergraduate college was					
	A. less than 10%	X			A	14
	B. 10% to 30%			X	B	20
	C. 30% to 60%				C	21
	D. 60% to 90%				D	17
	E. about all of it		X		E	23
					Omit	*
	30. While I earned my first money on a regu-lar job (other than from members of my family), my age was					
	A. younger than 8		X		A	3
	B. 8 to 10				B	15
	C. 11 to 12				C	29
	D. 13 to 14			X	D	26
	E. older than 14	X			Omit	*
	31. In thinking about my career in the busi-ness world and my abilities in administra-tive and supervisory activities on the one hand and in technical and scientific activi-ties on the other, I believe that I have the greatest chances for success in positions which are					
	A. entirely administrative and super-visory	X			A	31
	B. primarily administrative with some technical work				B	36
	C. about equally divided between ad-ministrative and technical work				C	26
	D. primary technical with some admin-istrative work		X	X	D	7
	E. entirely technical and scientific				E	1
					Omit	*

Form 10 (continued)

Question weight	Question	Merle	Gaylord	Charlotte	% of successful managers selecting this response
	32. In terms of my own executive ability or potential executive ability (not just in this one but in any company) I think I stand in the A. top 5% B. upper 20% but not in the top 5% C. upper half but not in the top 20% D. in the lower half E. I don't know	 X	 X	 X	 A 31 B 49 C 14 D 1 E 6 Omit *
	33. The speed at which I usually work is A. much faster than most people B. somewhat faster than most people C. somewhat slower than most people D. much slower than most people E. I am unable to tell	 X	 X	 X	 A 13 B 70 C 12 D * E 6 Omit *
	34. By the time I had graduated from high school I had been (mark all that apply) A. captain of an athletic team B. manager of an athletic team C. editor of the school paper or year-book D. president of a school club E. president of my class or the student council F. chairman of an important student committee G. none of these	 X	 X	 X	 A 29 B 8 C 8 D 30 E 23 F 31 G 35
	35. During my last year in high school the number of evenings a week that I would go out socially was A. less than 1 B. 1 C. 2 D. 3 E. 4 or more	 X	 X	 X	 A 7 B 20 C 46 D 20 E 7 Omit *
	36. When I have a free afternoon or evening to spend alone, I am most likely to A. attend a movie B. watch television C. listen to music D. lounge around and relax E. read F. work on a hobby G. do something else	 X	 X	 X	 A 2 B 11 C 4 D 7 E 38 F 28 G 10 Omit *

Form 10 (continued)

Question weight	Question	Merle	Gaylord	Charlotte	% of successful managers selecting this response	
	37. I was able to go to school as long as I did because (mark all that apply)					
	A. I was supported by my family	X			A	42
	B. I worked and paid part of my expenses			X	B	59
	C. I worked and paid all of my expenses		X		C	15
	D. I received a scholarship, fellowship, or assistantship				D	32
	E. I obtained a loan				E	13
	F. I received assistance from a government agency				F	17
	38. When I had a very difficult task to do during my teens, I would usually					
	A. ask someone else to do it for me				A	*
	B. ask someone else to show me or help me	X			B	34
	C. look up methods in a book or manual			X	C	17
	D. try to work it out alone		X		D	45
	E. look for some other approach				E	3
					Omit	*
	39. During my last year in high school I had					
	A. no close friends				A	*
	B. one or two close friends			X	B	12
	C. a small group of close friends		X		C	62
	D. a great many close friends				D	23
	E. almost everyone in my class as a close friend	X			E	3
					Omit	*
	40. I believe that most of my associates tend to think of me as					
	A. quite different from them in emotional make-up			X	A	7
	B. only slightly different from them in emotional make-up	X			B	23
	C. very much like them in emotional make-up				C	43
	D. I haven't given it much thought		X		D	28
					Omit	*
	41. The way I act at the present time when I become angry is					
	A. storm around for a while letting off steam				A	10
	B. try not to show that I am angry at all			X	B	25
	C. talk it over with someone	X			C	27
	D. try to keep away from everybody for a while		X		D	13
	E. I never let my temper get the best of me				E	25
					Omit	*
	Total Score					

Name _____   Group Number _____

Date _____ Class Section _____ Hour _____ Score _____

ASSESSMENT OF LEARNING IN PERSONNEL ADMINISTRATION

EXERCISE 6

1. Try to state the purpose of this exercise in one concise sentence.

2. Specifically what did you learn from this exercise (i.e., skills, abilities, and knowledge)?

3. How might your learning influence your role and your duties as a personnel administrator?

4. What type of data is available from an application blank that is not typically available from personal resume's?

5. What advantages do weighted, or scorable application blanks have over traditional ones?

Exercise 7
Interviewing as a predictor of job success

PREVIEW

In this exercise a pervasive selection technique, the interview, is explored. Although the selection interview is used very widely, it can easily become a very subjective and biased selection tool. Not only are interviewers able to inject their own personal prejudices into the selection decision process via the interview, but they may not be furnished with relevant questions that can differentiate between successful and unsuccessful job holders. This exercise is designed to acquaint you with the interview process and to build your skills in conducting interviews. Applicants are interviewed in role-playing episodes and a group selects the most qualified from among three candidates. A structured or patterned employment interview is also designed from job analysis information.

OBJECTIVES

1. To become aware of the uses of the interview as a device to predict future job success.
2. To become aware of the types of information that can be gathered from the interview, the limitations and typical errors in the interviewing process, and ways to improve the effectiveness of the interview.
3. To build skills in interviewing for selection purposes and in designing structured forms to record interviewer comments.

PREMEETING ASSIGNMENT

Read the entire exercise.

INTRODUCTION
The Interviewing Process

A Key Selection Device. Very few people are hired in any organization without at least one interview. Because it is used so often, the interview is a crucial part of the selection process. But is it an effective one?

In an article entitled "Confessions of An Interviewer," the following remarks were made:

> Most of the corporate recruiters with whom I've had contact are decent, well-intentioned people. But I've yet to meet anyone, including myself, who knows what he (or she) is doing. Many interviewers seem to have absolute faith in their omniscience, but I suspect that their "Perceptiveness" is based more upon preconceived untested assumptions than upon objectively derived data.[1]

Dunnette and Bass summed up the interviewing process by stating that:

> The personnel interview continues to be the most widely used method for selecting employees, despite the fact that it is a costly, inefficient, and usually invalid procedure. It is often used to the exclusion of far more thoroughly researched and validated procedures. Even when the interview is used in conjunction with other procedures, it is almost always treated as the final hurdle in the selection process. In fact, other selection methods

---

[1] R. A. Martin, "Confessions of an Interviewer," *MBA* (January 1975) 8.

(e.g., psychological tests) are often regarded simply as supplements to the interview.[2]

It would seem that the interview remains the key selection instrument for most organizations, but an imperfect one. The popularity of the interview continues, and its importance has not suffered from the increased use of tests and other selection devices. Insistence on selecting people on the basis of interviews can best be explained by reference to the needs of the interviewer to talk to a candidate face-to-face, rather than on the grounds of its demonstrated efficacy as a selection device to predict subsequent job performance.

Validity Problems. Like all selection devices, the interview must demonstrate its worth by predicting successful versus unsuccessful eventual performers from amongst interviewees. To the extent that specific responses to questions posed in an interview later predict job success, we can describe the hiring decisions made on the basis of interviews as having a certain degree of validity.[3]

Furthermore, the formal selection interview, like an application blank, is typically considered a "test" under government guidelines on employment practices. Selection techniques other than pencil-and-paper tests may also be improperly used so as to have the effect of discriminating against minority groups. Such techniques include, but are not restricted to, unscored interviews, unscored application forms, and records of educational and work history.[4]

Decisions made on the basis of interviews thus can, under certain conditions (see also Exercise 17), be judged as discriminatory. While considerable research on the validity of the interview has been conducted lately, a recent review was not optimistic.[5]

Analyses of the outcomes of lawsuits indicated that most found the interview to be vulnerable to charges of discrimination. Several factors, including stereotyping and differential behavior of interviewers, have been shown to lead to subjectivity in the interview. Earlier research has reinforced these conclusions, casting doubt on the ability of the interview to predict future job performance.[6]

Sources of Error in Interviews. Information-gathering interviews used in the context of selection are measurement devices. They attempt to measure the appropriateness of an interviewee for a position. But because they rely so heavily on human judgment, they are susceptible to many errors. Among the most common are the following:[7]

1. **Overemphasis on negative information**—the interview has been called a search for negative information, and often the finding of even a small amount of negative information can lead to the rejection of an interviewee.

2. **Interviewer stereotypes**—often interviewers develop a stereotype of the ideal job candidate; successful interviewees are thus not necessarily the ones best qualified, but the ones who conform to the stereotype; if different interviewers have different stereotypes, an interviewee could be evaluated positively by one and negatively by another.

3. **Job information**—lack of relevant job information can increase the use of irrelevant attributes of interviewees in decision making.

4. **Differential use of cues by interviewers**—some interviewers may place more weight on certain attributes than others, or they may combine attributes differently as they make their overall decisions.

5. **Visual cues**—interviewees' appearance and nonverbal behavior (e.g., whether they "look" interested) can influence their evaluation in an interview greatly, yet perhaps be unrelated to job success.

6. **Similarity to interviewer**—sex, race, and/or attitude similarity to interviewers may lead to favorable evaluations.

7. **Contrast effects**—the order of interviewees influences ratings; for example, strong candidates who succeed weak ones look even stronger by contrast.

[2] M. D. Dunnette and B. M. Bass, "Behavioral Scientists and Personnel Management," *Industrial Relations* 2, no. 3 (1963): 115–130.

[3] See Exercise 9 for a discussion of validity.

[4] Office of Federal Contract Compliance, Employee Testing and Other Selection Devices, *Federal Register* 36, no. 77 (1971): 7532–7535; see also "Uniform Guidelines in Employee Selection Procedures," *Federal Register* 43, no. 166 (1978): 38290–38315.

[5] R. D. Arvey, "Unfair Discrimination in the Employment Interview: Legal and Psychological Aspects," *Psychological Bulletin* 86 (1979): 736–765; see also N. Schmitt, "Social and Situational Determinants of Interview Decisions: Implications for the Employment Interview," *Personnel Psychology* 29 (1976): 99–102.

[6] E. C. Mayfield, "The Selection Interview—A Re-Evaluation of Published Research," *Personnel Psychology* 17 (1964): 239–260; R. Wagner, "The Employment Interview, A Critical Summary," *Personnel Psychology* 2 (1949): 17–46.

[7] See Schmitt, "Social and Situational Determinants of Interview Decisions."

Effective Interviewing. Good interviewing requires more thought, structure, and planning than it typically receives and, as noted earlier, effective interviews are those that help to identify interviewees who will succeed on the job. Interviews should be structured (e.g., a specific set of predetermined questions is used) in order to provide a consistent measure of applicants. Interviews should emphasize the evaluation of characteristics, such as verbal skills, which cannot easily be assessed through other selection techniques. Because of validity problems, interviews are best utilized as one predictor amongst several which together provide a rationale for selection or rejection of a candidate. This is also important because not all successful job performers are good interviewees, and not all jobs require the type of characteristics that would be evident in an interview.

Interviewing Skills. Interviewing is a very complex task, requiring a set of skills beyond friendliness or the ability to communicate verbally. Professor Milton Hakel has provided a list of the skills required for effective interviewing (see Tables 1 and 2). As the figure notes, obtaining information is only one aspect of interviewing. A complex interplay of two personalities is at work.

Table 1. Basic Interviewing Skills*

I. *Planning the Interview.* Examination of the application blank, the job requirements, and also mapping out areas to be covered in the interview. Planning and organizing questions pertinent to these areas. Insuring that the interview will be held in an optimal environment, free from interruption.

II. *Getting Information.* Use of appropriate questioning techniques to elicit relevant information in the same sequence over all interviewees. Probing incomplete answers and problem areas while maintaining an atmosphere of trust. Structuring the interview. Comprehensive questions and follow-up comments.

III. *Giving Information.* Effectiveness in communicating appropriate and accurate information about the organization and available jobs for which the applicant would qualify, and in answering the applicant's questions. Closing the interview.

IV. *Personal Impact.* The total effect the interviewer has on the applicant, both as an individual and as a representative of the organization. This includes the applicant's first impression of the interviewer, given to the applicant through the interviewer's tone of voice, eye contact, personal appearance and grooming, postures and gestures, as well as the interviewer's impact throughout the interview.

V. *Responding to the Applicant.* Concern for the applicant's feelings while maintaining control over the interview. Reacting appropriately to the applicant's comments, questions, and nonverbal behaviors. Convey a feeling of interest in the applicant, encourage an atmosphere of warmth and trust, and make use of encouragement and praise.

VI. *Information Processing.* Gathering, integrating, and analyzing interview information, culminating in a final placement decision. Identifying personal characteristics and judging them in the context of the job requirements. Skill in assimilating, remembering, and integrating all information relevant to the final evaluation.

*Contributed by Milton D. Hakel, Department of Psychology, Ohio State University.

Table 2. Effective Intervieiwng: Guidelines for Interviewees

Dress appropriately.

Be punctual.

Know the interviewer's name and correct pronunciation.

Make sure your "body language" communicates your interest and attentiveness.

Do some research regarding the organization and the interviewer to ask pertinent questions.

Pause briefly and pensively before answering complex questions.

Try not to discuss salary in preliminary interviews.

Be responsive to each part of each question.

Ask how any personal or potentially illegal questions are related to job performance before responding.

Bring pencil and paper in case some information (e.g., a telephone number) must be recorded.

Make some notes regarding high (and low) points of interview shortly after it ends in order to follow up in subsequent interviews.

Thank the interviewer for his/her time.

Be certain that any responses on application blanks or resumes are consonant with those provided in the interview.

The Interviewer Report Form. In some instances, it may be desirable to construct a form for interviewers to use in order to record their evaluations of the interviewee. This would help achieve interviewer agreement as each interviewer would have the same standards of judgment. The form, of course, should be tailored to the specific needs of the organization. The following are suggestions for using interview recording forms:

1. The dimensions of the job should be carefully defined and made specific to facilitate interviewer

reliability as interviewees' performance in the interview is evaluated on each dimension.

2. The interviewer's judgments should be made such that they reflect predictions of how an interviewee would actually perform on the job. Thus, the criteria used to evaluate the performance of those currently holding the job should be assessed and interviewees could be evaluated on those criteria which can be addressed via an interview. (See the performance appraisal procedures discussed in Exercises 4 and 5.)

3. Any number of varieties of forms can be used to evaluate interviewees (see, for example, Forms 2–4 of this exercise). Ease in completion and completion immediately following the interview help to assure their utility.

4. The use of a written form to document interviewers' judgments enables the predictability of those judgments to be assessed. The written record of judgments made by each interviewer can be compared either to the overall assessment of a candidate on all predictors or to whether selected interviewees succeed on the job.

Tapping Social and Motivational Factors. Because it is generally agreed that the interview can assess social and motivational factors, it may be possible for interviewers to predict such factors on the basis of the interview, in addition to the job dimensions relative to the applicant's work experience, abilities, knowledge, and skills. However, such social and motivational factors may not emerge from a job analysis which focused on the tasks required to perform the job, as opposed to personal characteristics required. Therefore, an interview may be limited to explorations of an applicant's education and specific vocational training questions that could indicate possession of knowledge and skills required by the job.

In most cases, preemployment tests measuring basic abilities and basic job skills will better indicate potential to learn and to understand the operations required by the job than the interview. The interview may be more likely than most selection tools to be influenced by non–job-related factors in making selection decisions, and the interviewer must be alert to the dangers of overstepping legal bounds.

Keeping the above caveats about job relatedness and the dangers of subjective, perceptually determined evaluations in mind, social and motivational factors are still worthy of consideration. The following types of social and motivational factors are often used to help predict future job success in an interview:

1. Does this interviewee appear to be dependable? Will he or she demonstrate and maintain good work habits and attendance records and require a minimum of supervision? Experience indicates that many individuals who have ability and aptitude still do not seem able to maintain good work habits. This latter factor is frequently labeled poor "motivation" (see Exercises 14 and 15).

2. Will this individual assume responsibility for the job to be done? Will he or she take the initiative where appropriate and seek assistance when it is needed? While this factor is related closely to the preceding one, it has the added dimensions of leadership, judgment, and understanding.

3. Will this interviewee be willing and able to work with others? Will he or she accept and understand the need for coordination and communication? Here the emphasis on interpersonal relations is in maintaining work flow rather than specific personality characteristics.

4. Will this interviewee be sincerely interested in the job and its possibilities? Will he or she be motivated by and obtain personal satisfaction from the job? Here the emphasis is on the "fit" between the interests of the interviewee and the position requirements of the job.

5. Will the interviewee be a relatively adaptable employee, one who does not lose his or her head in emergencies? A common complaint of supervisors is the fact that some individuals go to pieces when the routine is disturbed.

6. Are the goals and aspirations of this interviewee consonant with the available opportunities? Turnover among nonprofessionals was relatively unheard of several years ago. Today each individual seems to have a personal timetable of accomplishments which the organization is expected to support.

7. Is the manner and appearance of this interviewee consistent with job requirements? Manner and appearance are important for some types of jobs, and they should be considered in the light of job requirements.

8. Considering the interviewee's qualifications as a whole in relation to job requirements, is overall work performance likely to be satisfactory?

Interviewer Accuracy and Reliability. It has been recommended here that interviewers' judgments be recorded in the form of predictions of the applicant's job performance. That is, particular responses made by interviewees to questions should each be analyzed in relation to whether persons giving certain responses are later successful on the job. Predictions should be made with respect to such aspects of job performance as interpersonal relations and motivation to work.

To help make the interview more "objective," the interviewer should write an applicant evaluation report and should also be required to select applicants in such a way that those selected and rejected will be judged to have differing degrees of predicted job success on the various dimensions. To validate interviewer predictions, it is also necessary to have such variations in predicted future success among those actually hired, for the variations enable the interviewer's predictions to be related to subsequent measures of actual job performance. If the interviewer's predictions of high success, for example, are consistently confirmed by actual job performance evaluations, the predictive ability of the interviewer is evidenced to be high.

The reliability of interviewer judgments can also be measured by the degree of agreement between the judgments of two or more independent interviewers who have interviewed the same applicants. Interviewer reliability can be faulty for several reasons: (a) the recording form may be ambiguous or otherwise faulty, making it difficult to obtain agreement between independent interviewers (a remedy is, of course, to revise the form), and (b) interviewers may have varying frames of reference for making predictions about job performance (the remedy may be interviewer training).

It is usually possible to distinguish between these sources of unreliability by analyzing the nature of disagreement among interviewers. Of course, both factors noted above may be present. In checking reliability between two or more interviewers, the following procedures are recommended:

1. Each interviewer should independently interview and rate the same sample of applicants. An adequate sample would be at least thirty to fifty applicants, but preferably many more.

2. The mean rating assigned by each interviewer and the standard deviation[8] of these ratings should be calculated for each job dimension.

3. The product-moment correlation coefficient[9] between the ratings assigned by two interviewers should be calculated for each dimension. In general, if the correlation coefficient is less than 0.60, there is cause for concern about the degree of agreement between the two interviewers.

---

[8] See *Appendix,* Exercise 9.

[9] Ibid.

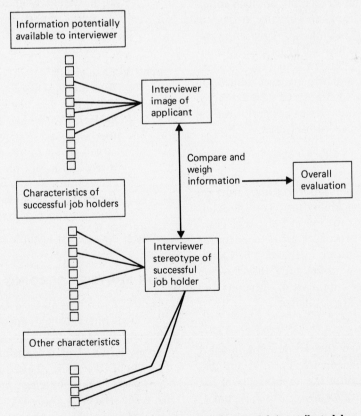

Fig. 1. Interviewer information-processing model (contributed by Milton D. Hakel, Department of Psychology, Ohio State University.)

Interviewing as Information Processing. Fig. 1 depicts the information-processing procedure typically used by interviewers as they make their evaluation of an interviewee. Each small box represents a specific type of information. For example, skill in communicating verbally, previous experience, and education would be types of information available about a job candidate. The interviewer also uses information describing successful job holders (e.g., very knowledgeable in technical matters, considerable previous supervisory experience, etc.) and "other" information (e.g., current plans regarding expansion in the unit). Some information from each category is used to form the interviewer's image of the interviewee and his or her perception or stereotype of the "ideal" job holder. Comparing these two types of information, interviewers make an evaluation. The evaluation could be erroneous if any of the information or perceptions used to form it are incorrect or biased. As Fig. 1 shows, the process is necessarily subjective, as individual judgment and perception play such an important role.

Training in the techniques of interviewing involves methods of establishing rapport with an interviewee, developing lines of questioning, and the desire of a means to achieve thorough coverage of an applicant's background. Training in these areas can be accomplished by recording practice interviews or role plays of interviews on tape recorders or video equipment. Tape playback affords an objective analysis of interviewer technique. Training to predict applicant job performance is best conducted by having two interviewers independently interview and rate the same applicant. The ratings and the evidence utilized in making the resulting predictions are then examined and discussed after the interviewee has performed on the job and job success can be measured.

PROCEDURE

Overview. First, interviewer report (rating) forms are assessed as to their applicability for recording interviewer's observations for the job of Personnel Technician III. An interview procedure is developed for the job of Administrative Officer in Exercise 6. Candidates are interviewed by groups after they develop interviewer report forms, and a set of questions and final selection decisions are compared.

PART A

STEP 1: You are to review the job description for a Personnel Technician III (Form 1) and discuss in small groups the applicability of the interviewer rating forms (Forms 2, 3, and 4)

for evaluating candidates for this job. Assess whether you feel each form helps the interviewer to be more objective and gain more information and describe why you feel the way you do.

TIME: About one hour.

PART B

STEP 2: Divide into small groups and design an interviewing procedure (i.e., interviewer report form and specific questions to ask interviewees) for the job of the Administrative Officer of Palms Pacific Corporation (refer back to the organization description, job description, resumes, application blank, etc., for this job in Exercise 6.) Those persons playing the roles of Charlotte, Gaylord, and Merle should not be involved in this activity as they will be interviewees. The interviewing procedure should adhere to the following criteria:

a) It should address and go beyond the information obtained on the biographical data sheets or application blanks.

b) It should attempt to assess social and motivational factors deemed important for job success (see *Introduction* to this exercise).

c) It should be quantifiable; i.e., the interviewer report form should be scorable in order to check the form's reliability and validity.

STEP 3: Each group is then to interview the three persons playing the roles of Merle, Gaylord, and Charlotte for the job of Administrative Officer. (They have already been chosen for the last exercise or will be chosen from the larger group by the implementor.) Once all three applicants have been interviewed by each group, interview report forms are completed, and the choices of all groups are to be revealed and compared.

TIME: About two to three hours.

FOR FURTHER READING

Andler, E. C. "Preplanned Question Areas for Efficient Interviewing." *Personnel Journal* 55 (January 1976): 8–10. (I)

Arvey, R. D. "Unfair Discrimination in the Employment Interview: Legal and Psychological Aspects." *Psychological Bulletin* 86 (1979): 736–765. (II–R)

Bucalo, J. "The Balanced Approach to Successful Screening Interviews." *Personnel Journal* 57 (1978): 420–426+. (I)

Carlson, R. E. "Selection Interview Decisions: The Effect of Interviewer Experience, Relative Quota Situation, and Applicant Sample on Interviewer Decisions." *Personnel Psychology* 20 (1967): 259–280. (II–R)

Carlson, R. E., and E. C. Mayfield. "Evaluating Interview and Employment Application Data." *Personnel Psychology* 20 (1967): 221–460. (II–R)

Dipboye, R. L., and I. W. Wiley. "Reactions of Male Raters to Interviewee Self-Presentation, Style, and Sex: Extensions of Previous Research." *Journal of Vocational Behavior* 13 (1978): 192–203. (II–R)

Drake, J. D. *Interviewing for Managers.* New York: Amacom, 1972. (I)

Dunnette, M. D., and B. M. Bass. "Behavioral Scientists and Personnel Management." *Industrial Relations* 2 (1963): 115–130. (I)

Embrey, W. R., W. Mondy, and R. M. Noe. "Exit Interview: A Tool for Personnel Development." *Personnel Administrator* 24 (1979): 43–48. (I)

Fear, R. A. *The Evaluation Interview.* 2d ed., rev. New York: McGraw-Hill, 1978. (I)

Galassi, J. P., and M. D. Galassi. "Preparing Individuals for Job Interviews: Suggestions from More than 60 Years of Research." *Personnel and Guidance Journal* 57 (1978): 188–192. (I)

Goodale, J. A. "The Success of the Selection Interview Lies in the Interviewer's Willingness to Make Eight Simple Decisions." *Journal of College Placement* 39 (1979): 33–38. (I)

Gordon, R. L. *Interviewing.* Rev. ed. Homewood, Ill.: Dorsey, 1975. (I)

Gorman, C. D., W. H. Clover, and M. E. Doherty. "Can We Learn Anything About Interviewing Real People from 'Interviewers' of Paper People? Two Studies of the External Validity of a Paradigm." *Organizational Behavior and Human Performance* 22 (1978): 165–192. (II–R)

Guion, R. M. "Recruiting, Selection, and Job Placement." In M. D. Dunnette, ed. *Handbook of Industrial and Organizational Psychology.* Chicago: Rand McNally, 1976. (II)

Hakel, M. D. "Similarity of Post-Interview Trait Rating Intercorrelations as a Contributor to Interrater Agreement in a Structured Employment Interview." *Journal of Applied Psychology* 55 (1971): 443–448. (II–R)

Heneman, H. G. et al. "Interviewer Validity as a Function of Interview Structure, Biographical Data and Interviewee Order." *Journal of Applied Psychology* 60 (1975): 748–753. (II–R)

Hollandsworth, L. G., Jr. et al. "Relative Contributions of Verbal, Articulative, and Non-Verbal Communication to Employment Decisions in the Job Interview Setting." *Personnel Psychology* 32 (1979): 359–367. (II–R)

Kleinke, C. L. *First Impressions.* Englewood Cliffs, New Jersey: Prentice-Hall, 1975. (I)

Landy, F. J. "The Validity of the Interview in Police Officer Selection." *Journal of Applied Psychology* 61 (1976): 193–198. (II–R)

London, M., and J. R. Popolawski. "Effects of Information on Stereotype Development in Performance Appraisal and Interview Contexts." *Journal of Applied Psychology* 61 (1976): 199–205. (II–R)

Lopez, F. M. *Personnel Interviewing.* 2d ed. New York: McGraw-Hill, 1975. (I)

Mayfield, E. C., and R. E. Carlson. "Selection Interview Decisions: First Results from a Long-Term Research Project." *Personnel Psychology* 19 (1966): 41–53. (II–R)

Mayfield, E. C. "The Selection Interview—A Re-Evaluation of Published Research." *Personnel Psychology* 17 (1964): 239–260. (II)

McGovern, T. V., and H. E. Tinsley. "Interviewer Evaluations of Interviewee Nonverbal Behavior." *Journal of Vocational Behavior* 13 (1978): 163–171. (II–R)

Medley, H. A. *Sweaty Palms: The Neglected Art of Being Interviewed.* Belmont, Cal.: Lifetime Learning, 1978. (I)

Moffatt, T. L. *Selection Interviewing for Managers.* New York: Harper & Row, 1979. (I)

Osborn, H. O., and W. R. Manese. *How to Install and Validate Selection Techniques.* Houston: American Petroleum Institute, 1971. (I)

Robertson, J. *How to Win a Job Interview.* Englewood Cliffs, New Jersey: Prentice-Hall, 1978. (I)

Schmitt, N. "Social and Situational Determinants of Interview Decisions: Implications for the Employment Interview." *Personnel Psychology* 29 (1976): 79–102. (II)

Schmitt, N., and B. W. Coyle. "Applicant Decisions in the Employment Interview." *Journal of Applied Psychology* 61 (1976): 184–192. (II–R)

Serafini, C. R. "Interviewer Listening." *Personnel Journal* 54 (1975): 398–399+. (I)

Short, L. O., and L. E. Taber. "The Selection Interview: An Interim Approach." *Public Personnel Management* 7 (1978): 143–147.

Steward, C. J., and W. B. Cash, Jr. *Interviewing: Prin-*

ciples and Practices. 2d ed. Dubuque, Iowa: W. C. Brown, 1978. (I)

Tucker, D. H., and P. M. Rowe. "Relationship Between Expectancy, Causal Attributions, and Final Decisions in the Employment Interview." *Journal of Applied Psychology* 64 (1979): 27–34. (II–R)

Ulrich, L., and D. Trumbo. "The Selection Interview Since 1949." *Psychological Bulletin* 63 (1965): 100–116. (II)

Webster, E. C. *Decision-Making in the Employment Interview.* Montreal: Industrial Relations Center, McGill University, 1964. (I) (II–R)

Weiner, Y., and M. Schneiderman. "Use of Job Information as a Criterion in Employment Decisions of Interviewers." *Journal of Applied Psychology* 59 (1974): 699–704. (II–R)

PART A

Form 1 Job Description

PERSONNEL TECHNICIAN III

DESCRIPTION OF WORK:

General Statement of Duties: Performs complex technical work in recruitment, examination, classification, wage and salary administration, training, and other functions of a personnel program.

Supervision Received: Works under general supervision of an administrative or technical superior.

Supervision Exercised: Exercises supervision over assigned personnel.

EXAMPLES OF DUTIES: (Any one position may not include all of the duties listed, nor do the listed examples include all tasks which may be found in positions of this class.)

Conducts position audits on departmental and classwide basis and recommends human-resource allocations; interviews employees, supervisors, and department heads; observes work performed; studies department organization and work assignments; and reviews other factors affecting classification and class relationships. Reviews, analyzes, and recommends class-specification revisions and drafts new class specifications.

Assists in obtaining, assembling, and computing wage and salary data; collects pay data through personal interviews with private and public employers; determines comparability of job duties and responsibilities between community and city positions. Collects, tabulates, and computes wage and salary data collected on national pay surveys.

Analyzes personnel requisitions. Conducts recruitment; drafts promotional and employment announcements and composes classified advertising. Interviews and advises applicants of job opportunities. Reviews experience, education, test scores, and other factors regarding eligibles with appointing authorities.

Selects and recommends standardized aptitude, intelligence, achievement, performance, and other tests; determines cutoff scores. Selects, revises and constructs test items and prepares tests; develops rating patterns. Evaluates experience and education of applicants; interviews, evaluates, and certifies eligibles. Organizes oral panel interviews.

Performs related work as assigned.

QUALIFICATIONS FOR APPOINTMENT:

Knowledges, Skills, and Abilities: Considerable knowledge of the principles of personnel administration, including working knowledge of examination processes and job-evaluation methods and techniques. Some knowledge of statistics and ability to make statistical computations. Ability to organize and present effective oral and written reports. Ability to establish and maintain effective working relationships with employees, department heads, officials, and the general public.

Education: Graduation from a four-year college with major course work in business administration, public administration, public administration, or related fields.

Experience: Three years experience in technical personnel work involving recruitment, examination, classification, pay administration, training or other personnel functions at the professional level.

    OR

Any equivalent combination of education and experience.

PART A

Form 2 Interviewer Report Form

Job Title:	Candidate's Name:	Date:

Rating factors

Consider all factors in relation to the position for which the examination is being given.

Rating

Mark your tentative rating in pencil by checking the appropriate boxes. Mark your final rating in ink after all candidates have been interviewed.

	Below acceptable level						Accept-able	Good	Outstanding		WT	SCORE
	10	20	30	40	50	60	70	80	90	100		
1. Appearance, physical condition												
2. Ability to communicate ideas												
3. Ability to understand and respond to questions												
4. Attitude, manner, interest and willingness to work and learn												
5. Knowledges, skills, and abilities required by job specification												
6. Add other rating factors as required:												
7.												
8.												

Examiner's signature _____

PART A

Form 3 Interviewer Report Form

Interviewee name: _____ Date: _____

Interviewer name: _____ Title: _____

Position applying for: _____ Department: _____

Instructions: Read over this form carefully *before* the interview to familiarize yourself with the type of information it contains. Try to cover all areas on the form either through direct or indirect questions of interviewee. Immediately after the interview, complete the form.

1. Discrepancies between application blank/resume and interview responses? How were they handled?

   _____
   _____
   _____

2. Why is applicant applying for the position?

   _____
   _____
   _____

3. Summarize previous job experience.

   _____
   _____
   _____

4. Personal attributes which qualify interviewee for job?

   _____
   _____
   _____

5. Enthusiasm, leadership, verbal skill, intelligence displayed (if required on job)?

   _____
   _____
   _____

6. Salary and fringe benefit expectations.

   _____
   _____
   _____

Form 3 (continued)

7. Formal education, professional development, plans for future education?

_____

_____

_____

8. Reasons given for any problems with previous employers (supervisors, subordinates, peers).

_____

_____

_____

9. Other information brought out in interview not covered above, yet related to job.

_____

_____

_____

10. Provide an overall assessment of interviewee, specifically indicating your prediction of successful job performance if hired. Provide a rationale for your judgment. Should applicant be rejected now? If not, are further interviews necessary?

_____

_____

_____

_____

_____

PART A

Form 4 Interviewer Report Form*

Candidate for: _____ Interviewer: _____

Name of applicant: _____ Date: _____

Please record your conclusions after the interview is completed. Notice the extent to which the interviewee possesses or will probably demonstrate the qualities listed below. The specific items under each category are intended to direct your attention to the kinds of evidence you may need to consider as you make your judgments. Check all relevant items, based on information gathered only from the interview, under each broad category.

1. *Cooperation*—Will applicant get along with others and work as member of team?

Overall rating on this item

Lowest	Low	Below average	Average	Above average	High	Highest
☐	☐	☐	☐	☐	☐	☐

Check below those items applicable.
- ☐ Evidence of previous friction with supervisors, peers, subordinates.
- ☐ Preference for solitary work assignments.
- ☐ Tendency to be a "loner" in social activities.
- ☐ Evidence of involvement in community, religious, and/or athletic activities.
- ☐ Openness and candidness in the interview.
- ☐ Evidence of excessive reactions to criticisms.

2. *Need for achievement*—Are the goals and aspirations of this applicant consistent with available opportunities?

Overall rating on this item

Lowest	Low	Below average	Average	Above average	High	Highest
☐	☐	☐	☐	☐	☐	☐

Check below those items applicable
- ☐ Level of abilities and qualifications consistent with available opportunities.
- ☐ Level of ambition consistent with available opportunities in the company.
- ☐ Is easily discouraged by obstacles and setbacks.

3. *Job satisfaction*—Will applicant be involved in and derive personal satisfaction from job?

Overall rating on this item

Lowest	Low	Below average	Average	Above average	High	Highest
☐	☐	☐	☐	☐	☐	☐

Check below those items applicable.
- ☐ Has participated in job-related activities (clubs, societies, etc.)
- ☐ Has taken advantage of company-sponsored opportunities to develop skills related to job.
- ☐ Evidence of success in school or work situations.
- ☐ Hobbies, interests, and personal goals are in line with job activities.

4. *Rewards needed*—Does applicant give evidence that he or she will find the rewards offered by the organization in terms of financial rewards and supervisory recognition compatible with the opportunities provided by the company?

Overall rating on this item

Lowest	Low	Below average	Average	Above average	High	Highest
☐	☐	☐	☐	☐	☐	☐

Check below those items applicable.
- ☐ Needs too much constant recognition by others.
- ☐ Seems to get much satisfaction from the job itself.
- ☐ Will soon demand more in financial rewards than we are in a position to offer.

Form 4 (continued)

5. *Work experience*—Does applicant's work history indicate the ability to learn and understand the operations required?

Overall rating on this item

Lowest	Low	Below average	Average	Above average	High	Highest
☐	☐	☐	☐	☐	☐	☐

Check below those items applicable.
☐ Has experience in performing similar tasks.
☐ Evidence of job failure due to lack of ability.
☐ Has knowledge of tools, equipment, and work procedures.
☐ Evidence of job progression.
☐ Assignment to special projects or task forces.

6. *Responsibility and initiative*—Will applicant exercise judgment in getting the job done, taking initiative where appropriate and seeking assistance when needed?

Overall rating on this item

Lowest	Low	Below average	Average	Above average	High	Highest
☐	☐	☐	☐	☐	☐	☐

Check below those items applicable.
☐ Evidence of capacity for independent thought and action to meet work standards.
☐ Evidence of ability to assume leadership role when required.
☐ Instances of seeking easy way out to meet work deadlines.
☐ Tendency to blame others for work delays and interruptions.
☐ Evidence of sticking it out till the job is done.

7. *Manner and appearance*—Will others react favorably to applicant?

Overall rating on this item

Lowest	Low	Below average	Average	Above average	High	Highest
☐	☐	☐	☐	☐	☐	☐

Check below those items applicable.
☐ Over-all appearance favorable.
☐ Shows interpersonal tact.
☐ Adequate level of self-confidence.
☐ Has ability to present and communicate ideas.
☐ Is sensitive to the needs of others.

8. *Composure*—Will applicant maintain composure under pressure, keeping head in emergencies?

Overall rating on this item

Lowest	Low	Below average	Average	Above average	High	Highest
☐	☐	☐	☐	☐	☐	☐

Check below those items applicable.
☐ Evidence of ability to adjust to changes in work environment (work interruptions, machine failure, other disruptions of routine schedule).
☐ Evidence of reacting impulsively in emergencies.
☐ Evidence that the quality of his or her work suffers in emergencies.
☐ Evidence of ability to adjust to changes in work procedures.

9. *Dependability*—Will applicant have a good attendance record and maintain good work habits?

Overall rating on this item

Lowest	Low	Below average	Average	Above average	High	Highest
☐	☐	☐	☐	☐	☐	☐

Check below those items applicable.
☐ Attendance record: times sick, late or otherwise absent from work.
☐ Evidence of reprimands for poor work performance.
☐ Safety record: evidence of responsibility for or involvement in accidents or work interruptions.
☐ Evidence of good work habits.

Form 4 (continued)

10. *Training*—Does applicant's experience give him or her an edge over other applicants?

Overall rating on this item

Lowest	Low	Below average	Average	Above average	High	Highest
☐	☐	☐	☐	☐	☐	☐

Check below those items applicable.
☐ Adequate level of educational attainment.
☐ Evidence of relevant on-the-job training.
☐ Evidence of relevant vocational school training.
☐ Has participated in workshops, continuing-education classes.
☐ Evidence of self-initiated skill development (e.g., correspondence school, programmed instruction, etc.).

Should applicant be hired for the job stated? Yes ＿＿ No ＿＿

If yes, state reason. ＿＿＿

If no, state reason. ＿＿

COMMENTS: ＿＿

＿＿＿＿＿＿＿＿＿

* Adapted from H. G. Osborn and W. R. Manese, *How to Install and Validate Employee Selection Techniques.* (Washington, D.C.: American Petroleum Institute, 1971).

Name _____   Group Number _____

Date _____ Class Section _____ Hour _____ Score _____

ASSESSMENT OF LEARNING IN PERSONNEL ADMINISTRATION

EXERCISE 7

1. Try to state the purpose of this exercise in one concise sentence.

2. Specifically what did you learn from this exercise (i.e., skills, abilities, and knowledge)?

3. How might your learning influence your role and your duties as a personnel administrator?

4. What are your own strengths and weaknesses as an interviewer and an interviewee?

5. What type of information about job applicants can be obtained from an interview which cannot be obtained via application blanks and reference checks?

6. Summarize the problems which plague many interview situations.

7. How would you evaluate the effectiveness of an interview program? Could you subject such a program to a cost/benefit analysis?

8. Should a line manager who would be an interviewee's superior conduct final-selection interviews, should the personnel specialists conduct them, or should both be involved? Under what conditions might each of these three strategies be effective?

Exercise 8

Work sampling and simulation as predictors of job success

PREVIEW

There has been a trend in personnel administration toward devising selection techniques that allow job applicants to perform activities during selection which closely parallel those they will actually perform on the job. The assumption is, of course, that the best predictor of job performance is job performance itself, rather than previous education, test scores, or interview data. These devices are called "situational" tests when used as selection tools because they present applicants with situations similar to those actually found on the job. Their performance in these situations is assumed to represent their performance in the actual job situation. Two types of techniques have been used in this regard. In the first, work sampling, prospective applicants are asked to perform a sample activity of the job to gauge their ability to perform the entire job. The second technique, simulation, utilizes activities designed to simulate actual job performance through a variety of techniques. For example, a role-playing activity would give selection specialists an idea of how an applicant would act in a supervisory role. In this exercise, you design a work sample and participate in two common types of simulations, an in-basket test and a leaderless group discussion.

OBJECTIVES

1. To become familiar with work sampling and simulation as selection devices and with their advantages over more traditional selection tools (e.g., interviews and biographical data).

2. To gain skill in designing a work sample that could be used to aid in selection decisions.

3. To learn how assessment centers are designed and implemented and to build skill as assessors and assessees in an assessment center.

4. To receive feedback on your own potential for success in administrative positions and task groups as you participate as an assessee in an in-basket test and a leaderless group discussion.

PREMEETING ASSIGNMENT

Read the entire exercise, except procedure and forms of Parts C and D until asked to do so, paying particular attention to the parts of the *Procedure* you are asked to read.

INTRODUCTION

Assessing Future Job Behavior at the Time of Selection

Beyond the measuring of historical information (biographical data) and responses to verbal questions (interviewing) as selection techniques, there have re-cently been attempts to measure behavior similar to that observed on the job. Obviously, if we can measure an applicant's behavior in situations that are very close

233

to those actually found on the job, we can perhaps obtain indications of ability and skill levels far better than inferences about ability and skill levels obtained from biographical data, interviews, or even psychological testing.[1]

Work Sampling. The first of the methods designed to approximate job content closely, work sampling (see also Fig. 4, Exercise 9), should provide a good measure of an applicant's suitability for a job, for it requires applicants to perform actual segments of the job before a final hiring decision is made. Wernimont and Campbell have proposed such a procedure and advocate what they refer to as the "behavioral consistency" of such a technique.[2] They believe that the behavioral consistency approach to selection (i.e., allowing candidates to evidence behaviors actually required on the job and inferring future job behavior from past job behavior or present behavior on a work sample) would have several immediate advantages, such as diminishing the problem of faking and reducing charges of discrimination and invasion of privacy which often accompany testing. As we have become more proficient with these measures, we can sample the underlying behaviors and focus on these rather than on other "signs" of candidates' job skills.

Campion[3] studied the job of an auto mechanic with work sampling. He developed a work sample for a few aspects of the mechanic's job by having subjects actually perform some of the typical tasks performed by mechanics and then observing and scoring their performance. This scoring was done via a scale for each task which gave a certain number of points for each response subjects made. For example, when prospective mechanics were asked to measure radial misalignment, they received ten points if they used a dial indicator, three points if they used a straightedge, one point if they relied only on "feel," and zero points if they used any other method. A similar scoring procedure was developed for several other automobile mechanic tasks (e.g., installing pulleys and gears, etc.)

When performance on work samples was compared with that on paper-and-pencil tests, the mechanics' performance on the work-sample measure was in all instances significantly and positively related to supervisory evaluations of their actual subsequent performance on the job. However, none of the relationships between actual job performance and the paper-and-pencil tests reached statistical significance. Successful performance on the work sample was more accurately able to predict subsequent successful performance on the job than were traditional ability tests.

Thus, it seems that personnel selection could often be improved by a strategy that used a behavioral consistency assumption. Of course, some additional factors, such as a candidate's anxiety level during the sample performance or lack of ability to perform the sample in the case of new workers, would have to be considered when work sampling was used as a selection device.

Often, work samples are categorized as motor and verbal samples. The "verbal" samples, however, can more easily be explored as simulations in the assessment center topic to follow. The many reports of "motor" work samples can be seen as follows:[4]

A carving dexterity test for dental students (Anderson and Friedman, 1952; Layton, 1953; Moore and Peel, 1951; Webb, 1956; Weiss, 1952).

A blueprint reading and tool identification test (Anonymous, 1954).

Shorthand and stenographic tests (Bender and Loveless, 1958).

A lathe test, a drill press test, and a tool dexterity test for machine operators (Bennett and Fear, 1943; Long and Lawshe, 1947; Tiffin and Greenly, 1939).

A sewing machine test for sewing machine operators (Blum, 1943; Inskeep, 1971).

A meat weighing test for meat scalers and packers (Bridgman, Spaethe, and Dignan, 1958).

Test for mechanics such as installing belts and pulleys, disassembling and repair of a gear box, installing and aligning a motor, pressing a bushing into a sprocket and reaming it to fit a shaft (Campion, 1972).

Vehicle repairman test (Carpenter et al., 1954).

A clothesmaking test (Croft, 1959).

Motions tests for bench assembly jobs (Drewes, 1961).

Two hand coordination test for mine operators (Durrett, 1961).

[1] See R. M. Guion, "Open A New Window: Validities and Values in Psychological Measurement," *American Psychologist* 29 (1974): 287–296.

[2] P. F. Wernimont, and J. P. Campbell, "Signs and Samples, and Criteria," *Journal of Applied Psychology* 52 (1968): 372–376.

[3] J. E. Campion, "Work Sampling for Personnel Selection," *Journal of Applied Psychology* 56 (1972): 40–44.

[4] J. J. Asher and J. A. Sciannino, "Realistic Work Sample Tests: A Review," *Personnel Psychology* 27 (1974): 519–533.

A screw board test for machine operators in a register manufacturing company (Ekberg, 1947).

A rudder control test for pilots (Fleishman, 1953; Melton, 1947).

A direction control test for pilots (Fleishman, 1955).

A complex coordination test for pilots (Fleishman, 1956).

A realistic typing test for office personnel (Giese, 1949; Skula and Spillane, 1954; West and Bolanovich, 1963; Ash, 1960).

A stitching test for sewing machine operators (Glanz, 1949).

A test for tracing trouble in a complex circuit (Grant and Bray, 1970).

A mechanical assembly test for loom fixers and spinning frame fixers (Harrell, 1937).

A test for the inspection of electronic defects (Harris, 1964).

A programming test for computer operators (Hollenbeck and McNamara, 1965; McNamara and Hughes, 1961).

A driver's test (Lauer, 1955).

A tool dexterity test involving fastening or unfastening bolt, washer, and nut with wrenches and/or screw drivers. Designed for machine tool operators and aircraft construction riveters (Lawshe, 1949).

A map reading test for traffic control officers (Naylor, 1954).

An electrical and radio information test for radio receivers and transmitter repairmen (Personnel Research Branch, 1958).

A punched card test for computer machine operators (Saunders, Seil, and Rosensteel, 1956).

An optical test for relay adjusters who work with small parts and tools (Speer, 1957).

An electronics test for electronics technician trainees (Thorndike and Hagen, 1955).

A packaging test for production machine operators (Uhlmann, 1962).

Work samples, because they focus on actual job behaviors, may not racially discriminate when carefully developed and based on good job analysis.[5] One word of caution should be noted, however. This is the uniformity with which the scoring procedure is to be applied. Obviously, scoring must be based on the same work sample performed in the same time frame (e.g., not asking one mechanic applicant to repair a trans-

mission and another to work on a carburetor). But even with standardized administration procedures, the methods of determining the scores of each applicant during the work sample must be the same. For example, for a lathe operator the items scored might be number of units produced per period of time, waste rates, number of items passing quality control, etc. The procedure used to determine the applicant's score not only should have reliable information on these relatively objective criteria, but it should also have reliable scoring on any overall scores given each applicant, and any judgment of scoring procedures should also have the dimensions outlined very specifically, as well as what behaviors one expected for each level of scoring.[6] Benchmarks on actual examples of work samples constituting at least acceptable levels of performance are also recommended, especially in more complex and creative jobs (e.g., designer, illustrator, graphic designer, photographer).

One interesting variant on actually conducting work samples is to capture what applicants believe they can actually do in the work sample. Such self-assessments do offer some promise of a faster and cheaper data-collection tool with some success in predicting later job success. However, these approaches have shown that minority groups are generally less accurate in self-assessment of work skills than non-minorities. Thus, self-assessment of skills in lieu of actually conducting a work sample (e.g., for typing) may not be practical in some instances.[7]

Simulations and Assessment Centers. The second type of measure of actual job behavior is simulation, often used in assessment centers. This measure differs from work sampling in that it uses simulation of job content, rather than a sample of actual job content, as well as multiple sources of data, as input to the selection process. However, for our purposes here, the use of simulations will be focused upon more heavily than other assessment-center techniques. The technique has gained considerable acceptance in recent years, especially for predicting success in managerial jobs.

The assessment-center concept evolved around the time of World War II to evaluate candidates for assignments in America's intelligence organization, the Office of Strategic Services (OSS). Assessees ex-

[5] G. A. Bragnoli, J. E. Campion, and J. A. Basen. "Racial Bias in the Use of Work Samples for Personnel Selection." *Journal of Applied Psychology* 64, no. 2 (1979): 119–123.

[6] J. R. Caplan, "Using Work Samples to Select Creative and Design Professionals." Paper presented at the American Psychological Association, Toronto, Canada, 1978.

[7] R. A. Ash, "Self-Assessments of Five Types of Typing Ability." Paper presented at the American Psychological Association, Toronto, Canada, 1978.

perienced a series of interviews, tests, and performance simulations designed to reveal whether they possessed the qualities for intelligence work. The candidates were examined not only for mental ability and motivation, but for physical stamina, emotional stability, resistance to stress, and other characteristics. To this end they were sent over obstacle courses, attacked in "stress" interviews, and observed when they were falsely told that they had "flunked out." The program was designed to reveal every asset and weakness they possessed which could affect their subsequent job performance.

This assessment center was staffed by psychologists and psychiatrists under the direction of Dr. Henry A. Murray of Harvard University. Murray's pioneering work in the 1930s had paved the way for evaluations of human characteristics and potential. Murray felt it necessary to observe candidates for several days and to put them through elaborate individual and group performance situations, based on the conviction that ordinary interviews and standard paper-and-pencil psychological tests were insufficient to assess potential for successful job performance.

A large number of organizations are now using simulations in determining management potential. Studies indicate that assessment centers are often superior to other techniques in identifying management potential.[8] They are used at all levels of management, from the first level of supervision to top corporate management. Organizations using centers may be found in every major industry, in government, and in almost all the industrialized nations of the world.

Proponents of assessment centers argue that they are more accurate in measuring potential for job success than traditional tests because they sample actual behavior, not what the applicant says he or she would do. For years, managers have observed that applicants can often talk a better story than they can perform. The assessment center checks on actual performance. The assessment-center method appears to provide validities (i.e., correlations of assessment-center performance with actual job performance) above those normally associated with tests or panel interviews. Reviews of published validity studies of the assessment-center process have recently been published.[9]

The most-publicized and largest research study on the assessment center is AT&T's Management Progress Study. Results of assessments of several groups of managers were retained for research purposes only and not released to the assessees or their superiors so as to preclude influencing subsequent promotion decisions regarding the assessees. The researchers administered an assessment center to 422 male employees of Bell Telephone companies beginning in 1956 and waited eight years before obtaining information on the assessees' success. Comparisons made in 1965 of the management level attained by people assessed several years earlier demonstrated that of the total number who reached middle management, 78 percent were correctly predicted to do so by the assessment staff. Among those who had not progressed further than first-level management within ten years, 95 percent were predicted not to do so by the assessors. Later communications indicate that similar accuracy was achieved after a longer time from original assessment to subsequent performance.[10]

From the studies to date, overall ratings of potential or performance from assessment-center procedures generally have shown impressive predictive power in determining future job success. Unfortunately, the use of the ratings in decision making about assessee's careers somewhat inhibits total acceptance of some findings. A "self-fulfilling prophecy" is argued (i.e., those branded as successful in assessment centers may attain success because of the label and not competence) when unvalidated assessment center results are used for career planning, etc. Nevertheless, predictive accuracy has been demonstrated in a few studies.[11]

Some of the criticisms that have been leveled at assessment center research are important to note. First, the criterion measure may be contaminated. Klimoski and Strickland argue that perhaps assessors merely duplicate decisions already made by using the preferences of organizational decision makers in assessing candidates.[12] In any case, the use of assessment centers, at least, helps to clarify an organizational policy on advancement. However, there must still be more work done on capturing and relating information on advancement, promotion, and performance with

[8] See J. R. Huck, "Assessment Centers: A Review of the External and Internal Validities," *Personnel Psychology* 26 (1973): 191–212.

[9] See also A. Howard, "An Assessment of Assessment Centers," *Academy of Management Journal* 17 (1974): 115–134.

[10] D. W. Bray, et al., *Formative Years in Business: A Long Term AT&T Study of Managerial Lives* (New York: Wiley, 1974). See also A. Howard, "An Assessment of Assessment Centers," *Academy of Management Journal* 17 (1974): 115–134. See also J. R. Hinrichs, "An Eight-Year Follow-Up of a Management Assessment Center," *Journal of Applied Psychology* 63, no. 5 (1978): 596–601.

[11] Ibid.

[12] R. J. Klimoski and W. J. Strickland, "Assessment Centers —Valid or Merely Prescient," *Personnel Psychology* 30 (1977): 353–361.

assessment center outcomes. Regrettably, the relationship between actual assessment center behaviors and on-the-job behaviors has not been substantiated as yet, although there have been several correlational studies.[13] A second criterion is the racial and sex effects of assessment centers. One study has demonstrated differences in race in the assessment center (as well as in criterion measures) on dimensions such as administrative skills, sensitivity, and effective intelligence, with black females scoring lower than white females. There was no racial effect for interpersonal effectiveness, however. There was also no significant difference in the overall ratings.[14]

Organizational Policy. Assessment Centers need to operate as a part of a management system. Prior to the introduction of a center into an organization, a policy statement should be prepared and approved by the organization. This policy statement should address the following areas:

1. **Objective**—This may be selection, development, early identification, affirmative action, evaluation of potential, evaluation of competency, or any combination of these.
2. **Assessees**—The population to be assessed, the method of selecting, procedures for notification, and policy related to re-assessing should be specified.
3. **Assessors**—The assessor population, limitations on use of assessors, number of times assigned, evaluation of assessor performance, and certification requirements where applicable should be specified.
4. **Use of Data**—The flow of assessment reports, who receives reports, restrictions on access to information, procedures and controls for research and program evaluation purposes, feedback procedures to management and employee, and the length of time data will be maintained in files should be specified.
5. **Job Analysis**—The job analysis of the target position or positions should be included or referenced. The analysis should include the method of data collection, description of job elements, and the derived skills, knowledge and dimensions that are being assessed.

6. **Qualification of Consultant**—The internal or external consultants responsible for the development of the center should be identified and their professional qualifications and related training listed.
7. **Validation**—There should be a statement of the validation model that is being used. There should be a time schedule of when a validation report should be available.[15]

Assessment Center Design. The first stage in developing an assessment center is a thorough job analysis to determine major job elements and define dimensions to be measured in the assessment center. A list of dimensions for a managerial job is not a list of the characteristics of a perfect manager. Rather, the job analysis defines areas about which the assessment should be concerned—areas that should be evaluated in making a selection decision. Very few are expected to be rated high on all of the dimensions.

The dimensions used thus depend on the job, as the objective is to simulate job content. The dimensions listed below are examples. Notice that some of these may not be found through a job analysis (e.g., energy) and others are felt necessary for successful performance in almost any job (e.g., high level of motivation). Generalizing from managerial dimensions selected in assessment centers, the following seem to be important dimensions of managerial work in addition to knowledge, abilities, and specific skills:

1. Energy
2. Organizing and planning*
3. Use of delegation*
4. Overall potential
5. Oral and written communications skills*
6. Behavior flexibility
7. Controlling*
8. Decision making*
9. Human relations competence*
10. Initiative
11. Self-direction
12. Analytical ability*
13. Resistance to stress
14. Originality

[13] J. R. Huck and D. W. Bray, "Management Assessment Center Evaluation and Subsequent Job Performance for White and Black Females," *Personnel Psychology* 29 (1976): 13–30.
[14] Ibid.

[15] J. L. Moses and F. M. McIntyre, "Standards and Ethical Considerations for Assessment Center Operations." Paper prepared for the 6th International Congress on Assessment Center Method, White Sulphur Springs, West Virginia, April 1978.

15. Leadership*
16. Perception of threshold social cues
17. Personal impact

Obviously, many of these dimensions may not be said to be job relevant, an important consideration when contemplating using assessment centers for selection procedures (also see Exercises 3 and 9 for discussions regarding legal restrictions placed on job analyses and selection tests or techniques). Therefore, designing the assessment dimensions around actual job content may not only be good practice, but also safe practice in that it may reduce the probability of violating equal opportunity laws or guidelines. When using assessment centers as a selection method, it may be helpful to consult the list above. The dimensions of managerial jobs which may be more closely tied to the content of managerial jobs are indicated with an asterisk (*).

Types of Assessments. Common types of simulations of job content used in assessment centers include:

In-baskets: This is the most frequently used technique and is usually considered the most important. The most relevant simulations are developed from actual "in-basket items" in the organization. The candidate is usually faced with an accumulation of memos, reports, notes of incoming telephone calls, letters, and other materials typically collected in the in-basket of the job incumbent. The candidate is asked to dispose of these materials in the most appropriate manner by writing letters, notes, delegating, self-reminders, agenda for meetings, etc. Often the in-basket is followed by a questionnaire or an interview by an assessor, in which the candidate is asked to justify decisions, actions, or nonactions. Ratings of performance may be narrative comments or highly standardized checklists.

Leaderless group discussions: The participants in leaderless group discussions are usually given a discussion question and instructed to arrive at a group decision. No one in the group is designated as its leader. Topics often include promotion decisions, disciplinary actions, or production expansion problems. Participants may be given a particular point of view to defend, although they know the group must eventually come to a mutually agreeable decision. Dimensions that can be revealed in the leaderless group discussion include interpersonal skills, acceptance by a group, individual influence, and leadership.

Management games: Management games usually require participants to solve problems, either cooperatively or competitively. Stock market tasks, manufacturing exercises, merger negotiations, or acquisitions are common. Games often use a computer to simulate the consequences of decisions. The games may bring out leadership and organizational abilities or interpersonal skills. Some games also permit observations under stress, especially when conditions suddenly change or when competition stiffens. The games are often used as a "warm-up" exercise in assessment centers.

Presentation: Assessees are often given time to make an oral presentation on a management topic or theme. Assessors observe oral communications skills, persuasiveness, poise, and reaction to the stress of making a group presentation. Often the presentation is short (5–10 minutes) but based on an extensive analysis of a problem that they have taken an hour or more to prepare. The formal presentation usually requires recommendations. At times the presentation is based on the assessee obtaining more information to be able to make decisions than is provided in the instructions to the presentation. In these situations fact-finding, tolerance of ambiguity, and decision making may be measured.

Supplementary Data Used in the Assessment Center

Tests: All types of paper-and-pencil tests of mental ability, personality, interests, and achievement (e.g., reading, arithmetic, general knowledge) are often used as supplements to other selection methods. The tests are generally standardized instruments, although organizations have developed their own. Some are more objective tests while others are more projective (e.g., candidates respond to different stimuli, such as pictures). Seldom do organizations select the same tests, as jobs vary within and between organizations.

Interviews: Most assessment centers have at least one interview with the assessee. Current interests and motivation, as well as general background and comments on past performance are assessed. The interview varies in terms of structure, standardization of interpretation, and the general climate in which it is conducted.

Other assessments: Often written exercises, such as autobiographical essays or personal-history questionnaires, are completed before entering the center. Creative writing assignments may also be required of assessees.

The Assessment Center Procedure. The general procedure begins with an analysis of the job to be performed, as noted earlier. Next is the selection of the simulations most appropriate, then the training of assessors, conduct of the simulations, and finally the evaluation report of each assessee is written.

The training of assessors usually focuses on interviewing, managing the in-basket exercises, and observing behavior. Almost all of the assessment center simulations call for some combination of these skills. Assessors are often managers two or more levels above the level being assessed. A typical assessment center will have four to six assessors in anywhere from a 4:1 to 1:1 ratio to assessees. The assessors may be psychologists, members of management, or both.

Assessors become familiar with the exercises by participating themselves, watching videotapes, or observing actual assessee performances as nonvoting (trained) members of an assessment team. The job dimensions to be assessed are defined and assessors are given practice and instruction in how to recognize varying degrees of performance on them. Assessor training varies widely in duration, from brief orientations to two or three weeks of intensive training. Companies highly interested in training managers in appraisal techniques may change assessors frequently, while those most interested in producing a stable selection program or in saving money on assessor training may make changes less often.

Perhaps the most critical aspect of using the assessment center method is the evaluation report. Usually, a large body of data for each assessee is ultimately reduced to a few reported test scores and booklets containing judgments and comments. A formal written report summarizing the assessment findings and recommendations is needed (see Form 6 of this exercise) in order to summarize the data.

Peer and self-ratings and rank orderings of assessees may also be part of the evaluation process. But assessors typically write reports, skill by skill, exercise by exercise, and candidate by candidate. The reports are read aloud in a final evaluation meeting where each assessee is rated by every assessor on each dimension. Meaningful differences of opinion are discussed and either resolved or noted. Final reports are usually written in a narrative style, relating remarks to specific behaviors and specifying the candidate's strengths, weaknesses, and developmental needs.

Feedback of results to candidates is handled differently in various organizations according to the original objectives of the program. Those highly concerned with management development emphasize the directions in which the candidate should move in the future. Others concerned with training may stop in the middle of the assessment program and offer feedback and discussion of particular exercises. Oral feedback is much more frequent than written. Line management or assessment center personnel may provide feedback either automatically or on request only.

The assessment center concept is important as a selection device because of its close relationship to actual job performance and its accuracy in measuring potential and predicting future job success. However, it is as yet a comparatively new selection tool and much research is required. Further, it is a complex and costly selection device, requiring considerable planning and expertise. Its potential uses, however, offer great promise for the future. These include information for:

—employment

—human resource planning

—entry into training programs

—feedback on strengths and weaknesses

—criterion measures

—promotion decisions

—early identification of management potential

—demotion decisions

—transfer decisions

One final statement about assessment centers should be noted; it is that the items measured should be limited to skills, knowledge, and preferences as constructs. Straying far from these is too tempting in the opportunities that an assessment center presents, and should be avoided because it requires inferences of questionable scientific quality in predicting job success.[16]

PROCEDURE

Overview. First, you are asked to design a work sample that could be used as a selection aid. Next, you will actually conduct an assessment center. A sample report made by assessors is provided to acquaint you with the evaluations made in assessment centers. In-basket and leaderless-group-discussion simulations are used to assess the three candidates for the job of administrative officer.

PART A

STEP 1: Forms 1 and 2 contain two job descriptions, one for the job of heavy-duty mechanic and one for the job of clerk typist III. Form into

---

16 M. L. Tenopyr, "Content–Construct Confusion," *Personnel Psychology* 30 (1977): 47–54.

groups of four or five and design a work-sampling procedure for one of the jobs. That is, develop activities similar to those actually performed on the job which prospective job applicants could be asked to perform in order to assess their suitability for the job. Your work sample must include a specific method for scoring or evaluating applicants. Use the examples of work samples for a mechanic's job given in the *Introduction* to this exercise as a guide. Why would the sample offer better data about an applicant than an application blank or interview?

TIME: About 35 minutes.

PART B

STEP 2: This part contains instructions for *assessees* and assessors for an assessment center simulation with the option of an in-basket, a leaderless group discussion (LGD), and two presentation/fact-finding situations. Read only the appropriate instructions below, depending on whether you were chosen to be an assessor or an assessee.

Instructions for assessees. If you were chosen to play the role of an *assessee,* reacquaint yourself with the job of administrative officer of Palms Pacific Corp. (see the job description in Form 5 of Exercise 6 repeated as Form 3 of this exercise; also see the organization's description, appropriate resume, and application for your role in Exercise 6). The implementor may give you additional instructions for your role. Use all of this information as a jumping-off point to choose the simulations you feel appropriate to elicit the behavior appropriate for the job. The instructions for the simulations are given in Parts C and D at the end of this exercise. Do *not* read these until you are instructed to do so. You will be given a time limit for each of these activities.

Instruction for assessors. Below is an outline of the assessment center procedure. Your group of assessors will be assessing three candidates for the job of administrative officer for Palms Pacific Corp., used in Exercises 6 and 7.

A. Form into small groups. Review both the job description for administrative officer (first appearing in Exercise 6 and reproduced as Form 3 here) and the other information about the job first given in Exercise 6. Then develop a set of job dimensions for the job which should be assessed in an assessment center. You may have such lists from previous exercises which can be amended, if necessary, and used here. Be sure to weight your dimensions in order of importance for success on the job.

Select the appropriate simulation activities. Half of your group will be assessors for each simulation (e.g., in-basket or LGD) and will assess a group of candidates for the job, but as a group you will write three assessor reports, and choose the best candidate for the job. Each assessor should read through the simulations, including the instructions, very carefully. These situations simulate realistic administrative problems. They yield insights into performance dimensions common to many management positions. The situations are ones that might be expected regardless of organizational type. The assessees must determine many courses of action, such as planning meetings, gathering reports, and delegating. Suitability for the job would be determined by performance in these situations, coupled with other selection tools.

Although the simulations yield many insights, an interview with the assessee, when conducted as soon as possible after the simulation is completed, is also quite valuable. This interview can probe into the reasons for each action taken, perceptions, values, etc., and thus provide more information on which to base the selection decision. The simulations may yield information on the following job dimensions:

Written communication

Interpersonal skills

Leadership skills

Influence

Coordination

Analytical ability

Planning, organizing, controlling

Delegation skills

Problem-analysis skills

Judgment

Decision making

The interview may add information on the above dimensions, but also permits assessment on the following dimensions:

Initiative

Oral-communication skill

Flexibility

Independence

Leadership

B. In order to conduct a valid assessment, compare the job dimensions you identify as relevant from the job description of administrative officer with those listed in Form 4 and weight the importance of each dimension as a percentage of the total job as shown in Form 5. The Assessor's Report Form (Form 5) can be used to help you decide how to judge the assessees' performance in the simulations. Place a mark by all of the relevant dimensions you have identified, both from the job description and the lists given in Step A above, on Form 5. Add any dimensions not on the form you feel are relevant. These become the dimensions on which you will evaluate assessees. Try to define each dimension and cite an example of assessee behavior which would illustrate performance on that dimension.

TIME: About 45 minutes.

C. Once you have identified the relevant dimensions on which to assess candidates for the job of administrative officer and noted them on Form 5, you are ready to begin the assessment. Three people who have assumed the roles of the three job applicants (Merle Wonder, Gaylord Golden, and Charlotte Pyle) in Exercises 6 and 7 will play the roles of assessees. They will be assessed by each group of assessors on each dimension noted on Form 5 as you fill it out. Now divide your group in half so one half can concentrate on each assessment. Three more persons will join the three job applicants for the job of administrative officer in order to form a group of six assessees. Together these six people will form a discussion group and complete the LGD exercise.

TIME: About 15 minutes.

PART C AND D

STEP 3: Administer first the in-basket (Form 7) or one of the fact-finding simulations (Forms 8 and 9) and then the group discussion to the asses-

sees. Instructions and time limits for both simulations are given at the end. Be sure to time the assessees as they perform these tasks, and observe them very closely.

The in-basket or fact finding exercises cannot be scored until completed. Therefore, since the assessor groups have already been split into those who have primary responsibility for scoring the in-basket and those who have primary responsibility for scoring the LGD (Form 10), the in-basket should be conducted first so that it can be scored while the LGD is conducted. Be sure to fill out Form 5 while your part of the assessor group reads the in-basket results. (You will have to share the in-basket and fact-finding results with other assessor groups, as only one set of these results are available for each of three assessees.)

Observe and record assessee behavior on the in-basket and LGD (see the forms for specific instructions). Assess each person on dimensions selected using the scale below. Report your rating on the right-hand side of Form 5.

5—extremely favorable behavior on this dimension was demonstrated (excellent)

4—considerable favorable behavior on this dimension was demonstrated (above average)

3—some favorable behavior on this dimension was demonstrated (average)

2—little favorable behavior on this dimension was demonstrated (below average)

1—very little favorable behavior on this dimension was demonstrated (poor)

0—no behavior on this dimension was demonstrated

After the simulations are finished, prepare and conduct an interview with assessees to obtain additional relevant information, if you feel it necessary. You may want to score the in-basket and fact-finding exercises before holding these interviews. Be sure to revise the scores on the Assessor's Report Form after the interview to reflect the additional information.

TIME: The in-basket and fact-finding exercises require 45 minutes and the LGD requires 30 minutes. Postexercise interviews would, of course, require additional time.

STEP 4: The in-basket and fact-finding exercises should now be scored and the LGD completed and scored. Each assessor team is to have the team members who had primary responsibility for scoring performance in the in-basket and fact finding discuss assessees' performance on the in-basket, while the team members who observed and scored the discussion group are to discuss the performance on the LGD. The entire group should then reach agreement on each assessee's performance and compose the Assessor's Overall Report, or "Management Report," for each of the three assessees. A sample report is included as Form 6 of this exercise.

TIME: About one hour to two hours.

FOR FURTHER READING

Abt, L. E. "A Test Battery for Selecting Technical Magazine Editors." *Personnel Psychology* 2 (1949): 75–91. (II–R)

Adams, W. M. "Prediction of Scholastic Success in Colleges of Law: 1. The Experimental Edition of the Iowa Legal Aptitude Test." *Educational and Psychological Measurement* 3 (1943): 291–305. (II–R)

Anderson, A. V., and S. Friedman. "Prediction of Performance in a Navy Dental Prosthetic Technician Training Course (Abstract)." *American Psychologist* 7 (1952): 288. (II)

Anonymous. "Validity Information Exchange." No. 7–094. *Personnel Psychology* 7 (1954): 572. (II–R)

Arbous, A. G., and J. Maree. "Contribution of Two Group Discussion Techniques to a Validated Test Battery." *Occupational Psychology* 25 (1951): 73–89. (II–R)

Ash, P. "Validity Information Exchange." No. 13–07. *Personnel Psychology* 13 (1960): 456. (II–R)

Ash, R. A. "Self-Assessments of Five Types of Typing Ability." Paper presented at the American Psychological Association, Toronto, Canada, 1978. (II–R)

Asher, J. J., and J. A. Scarrino. "Realistic Work Sample Tests: A Review." *Personnel Psychology* 27 (1974): 519–533. (II)

Asher, J. J. "The Biographical Item: Can it be Improved?" *Personnel Psychology* 25 (1972): 251–269. (II)

"Assessment Centers." *Public Personnel Management* 3, no. 5 (September–October 1974), symposium of three articles. (I)

Baier, D. E., and R. D. Dugan, "Tests and Performance in a Sales Organization." *Personnel Psychology* 9 (1956): 17–26. (II–R)

Bass, B. M. "The Leaderless Group Discussion as a Leadership Evaluation Instrument." *Personnel Psychology* 7 (1954): 470–477. (II–R)

Bass, B. M., and C. H. Coates. "Validity Information Exchange." No. 7–082. *Personnel Psychology* 7 (1954): 553–554. (II–R)

Bender, W. R. G., and H. E. Loveless. "Validation Studies Involving Successive Classes of Trainee Stenographers." *Personnel Psychology* 11 (1958): 491–508. (II–R)

Bennett, G. K., and R. A. Fear. "Mechanical Comprehension and Dexterity." *Personnel Journal* 22 (1943): 12–17. (I–R)

Blum, M. L. "Selection of Sewing Machine Operators." *Journal of Applied Psychology* 27 (1943): 35–40. (II–R)

Bragnoli, G. A., J. E. Campion, and J. A. Basen. "Racial Bias in the Use of Work Samples for Personnel Selection." *Journal of Applied Psychology* 64, (1979): 119–123. (II–R)

Bray, D. W., and R. J. Campbell. "Selection of Salesmen by Means of an Assessment Center." *Journal of Applied Psychology* 52 (1968): 36–41. (II–R)

Bray, D. W., R. J. Campbell, and D. L. Grant. *Formative Years in Business: A Long-Term AT&T Study of Managerial Lives.* New York: Wiley, 1974. (I–R)

Bray, D. W., and D. L. Grant. "The Assessment Center in the Measurement of Potential for Business Management." *Psychological Monographs* 80 (1966). (II–R)

Bray, D. W., and J. L. Moses. "Personnel Selection." *Annual Review of Psychology* 23 (1972): 545–576. (II)

Breslow, E. "The Predictive Efficiency of the Law School Admission Test at the New York University School of Law." *Psychology Newsletter* 9 (1957): 13–22. (II–R)

Bridgman, C. S., M. Spaethe, and F. Dignan. "Validity Information Exchange." No. 11–21. *Personnel Psychology* 11 (1958): 264–265. (II–R)

Brown, D. D., and E. E. Ghiselli. "The Relationship Between the Predictive Power of Aptitude Tests for Trainability and for Job Proficiency." *Journal of Applied Psychology* 36 (1952): 370–377. (II–R)

Byham, E. C. "Assessment Center for Spotting Future Managers." *Harvard Business Review* 48, no. 4 (1970): 150–160. (I)

Byham, W. C. "The Assessment Center as an Aid in Management Development." *Training and Development Journal* (December 1971): 10–22. (I)

Campbell, R. J., and D. W. Bray. "Assessment Centers: An Aid in Management Selection." *Personnel Administration* 30, no. 2 (1967): 6–13. (I)

Campion, J. E. "Work Sampling for Personnel Selection." *Journal of Applied Psychology* 56 (1972): 40–44. (II–R)

Caplan, J. R. "Using Work Samples to Select Creative and Design Professionals." Paper presented at the American Psychological Association, Toronto, Canada, 1978. (II–R)

Carpenter, C. R. et al. "The Development of a Sound Motion Picture Proficiency Test." *Personnel Psychology* 7 (1954): 509–523. (II–R)

Castle, P. F. C., and F. I. de la P. Garforth. "Selection, Training, and Status of Supervisors: I. Selection." *Occupational Psychology* 25 (1951): 109–123. (II–R)

Catalog of Assessment and Development Exercises. Pittsburgh: Development Dimensions, 1975. (I)

Cohen, B. M. "What the Supervisor Should Know About Assessment Centers." *Supervisory Management* 20 (June 1974): 30–34. (I)

Cowan, J., and M. Kurtz. "Internal Assessment Center: An Organization Development Approach to Selecting Supervisors." *Public Personnel Management* 5 (January–February 1976): 15–23. (II)

Croft, E. J. "Prediction of Clothing Construction Achievement of High School Girls." *Educational and Psychological Measurement* 19 (1959): 653–655. (II–R)

Davis, F. B., ed. "Army Air Forces Aviation Psychology Program Research Reports." *The AAF Qualifying Examination Report No. 6.* Washington, D.C.: U.S. Government Printing Office, 1917, Chapter 6. (I)

Dodd, W. E., A. O. Kraut, and S. H. Simonetti. "Selected Annotated Bibliography on Identification and Assessment of Management Talent." *Professional Psychology* 3 (1972): 193–199. (I)

Drewes, D. W. "Development and Validation of Synthetic Dexterity Tests Based on Elemental Motion Analysis." *Journal of Applied Psychology* 45 (1961): 179–185. (II–R)

DuBois, P. H., and R. I. Watson. "The Selection of Patrolmen." *Journal of Applied Psychology* 34 (1950): 90–95. (II–R)

Dunnette, M. D. "Personnel Selection and Placement." Belmont, Cal.: Wadsworth, 1966. (I)

Durrett, H. L. "Validity Information Exchange." No. 14–03. *Personnel Psychology* 14 (1961): 453–455. (II–R)

Ekberg, D. L. "A Study in Tool Usage." *Educational and Psychological Measurement* 7 (1947): 421–427. (II–R)

Finkle, R. B. "Managerial Assessment Centers." In M. D. Dunnette, ed., *Handbook of Industrial and Organizational Psychology.* Chicago: Rand McNally, 1976. (II)

Finkle, R., and W. S. Jones. *Assessing Corporate Talent,* New York: Wiley, 1970. (I)

Fleishman, E. A. "Individual Differences and Motor Learning." In R. M. Gagne, ed., *Learning and Individual Differences.* Columbus, Ohio: Merrill, 1967. (II)

Fleishman, E. A. "Psychomotor Selection Tests: Research and Application in the U.S. Air Force." *Personnel Psychology* 9 (1956): 449–467. (II–R)

Fleishman, E. A. "Predicting Code Proficiency of Radio Telegraphers by Means of Aural Tests." *Journal of Applied Psychology* 39 (1955): 150–155. (II–R)

Fleishman, E. A. "Evaluations of Psychomotor Tests for Pilot Selection: The Direction Control and Compensatory Balance Tests." *Technical Report* (AFPTRC–TR–54–131). Lackland Air Force Base, Texas: Air Force Personnel and Training Research Center, December 1954. (II–R)

Fleishman, E. A. "Testing for Psychomotor Abilities by Means of Apparatus Tests." *Psychological Bulletin* 50 (1954): 241–262. (II–R)

Fleishman, E. A. "An Evaluation of Two Psychomotor Tests for the Prediction of Success in Primary Flying Training." *Research Bulletin* (53–9). Lackland Air Force Base, Texas: Human Resources Research Center, May 1953. (II–R)

Fleishman, E. A., and W. E. Hempel. "A Factor Analysis of Dexterity Tests." *Personnel Psychology* 7 (1954): 15–32. (II–R)

Forehand, G. A., and H. Guetzkow, "The Administrative Judgment Test as Related to Descriptions of Executive Judgment Behaviors." *Journal of Applied Psychology* 45 (1961): 257–261. (II–R)

Frederikson, M. "Validation of a Simulation Technique." *Organizational Behavior and Human Performance* 1 (1966): 87–109. (II–R)

Frederikson, M., O. Jensen, A. Beaton, and B. Bloxom. *Prediction of Organizational Behavior.* New York: Pergamon, 1972. (II)

Gael, S. and D. L. Grant. "Employment Test Validation for Minority and Nonminority Telephone Company Service Representatives." *Journal of Applied Psychology* 56 (1972): 135–139. (II–R)

Ghiselli, E. E., and R. R. Barthol. "The Validity of Personality Inventories in the Selection of Employees." *Journal of Applied Psychology* 37 (1953): 18–20. (II–R)

Giese, W. J. "A Tested Method for the Selection of Office Personnel." *Personnel Psychology* 2 (1949): 525–545. (II–R)

Glanz, E. "A Grade Test for Power Sewing Machine Operators." *Journal of Applied Psychology* 33

(1949): 436–441. (II-R)

Glaser, R., P. A. Schwarz, and J. C. Flanagan. "The Contribution of Interview and Situational Performance Procedures to the Selection of Supervisory Personnel." *Journal of Applied Psychology* 42 (1958): 69–73. (II-R)

Gleason, W. J. "Predicting Army Leadership Ability by Modified Leaderless Group Discussion." *Journal of Applied Psychology* 41 (1957): 231–235. (II-R)

Glickman, A. S. "The Naval Knowledge Test." *Journal of Applied Psychology* 40 (1956): 389–392. (II-R)

Gordon, L. V. "Clinical, Psychometric, and Work Sample Approaches in the Prediction of Success in Peace Corps Training." *Journal of Applied Psychology* 51 (1967): 111–119. (II-R)

Grant, D. L., and D. W. Bray, "Validation of Employment Tests for Telephone Company Installation and Repair Occupations." *Journal of Applied Psychology* 54 (1970): 7–14. (II-R)

Grant, D. L., W. Kathovsky, and D. W. Bray. "Contributions of Projective Techniques to Assessment of Management Potential." *Journal of Applied Psychology* 32 (1948): 452–455. (II-R)

Guion, R. M. "Open A New Window: Validities and Values in Psychological Measurement." *American Psychologist* 29 (1974): 287–296. (II)

Hamner, W. C. et al. "Race and Sex as Determinants of Ratings by Potential Employers in a Simulated Work-Sampling Task." *Journal of Applied Psychology* 59 (1974): 705–711. (II-R)

Handyside, J. D., and D. C. Duncan. "Four Years Later: A Follow-up of an Experiment in Selecting Supervisors." *Occupational Psychology* 28 (1951): 9–23. (II-R)

Harrell, W. "The Validity of Certain Mechanical Ability Tests for Selecting Cotton Mill Machine Fixers." *Journal of Social Psychology* 8 (1937): 279–282. (II-R)

Harris, D. H. "Development and Validation of an Aptitude Test for Inspectors of Electronic Equipment." *Journal of Industrial Psychology* 2 (1964): 29–35. (II-R)

Henry, E. R. *Research Conference on the Use of Autobiographical Data as Psychological Predictors.* Greensboro, N.C.: The Richardson Foundation, 1965. (II)

Hinrichs, J. R. "Comparison of 'Real Life' Assessments of Management Potential with Situation Exercises, Paper and Pencil Ability Tests, and Personality Inventories." *Journal of Applied Psychology* 53 (1969): 425–432. (II-R)

Hinrichs, J. R., and S. Haanpera. "Reliability of Measurement in Situational Exercises: An Assessment of the Assessment Center Method." *Personnel Psychology* 29 (1976): 31–40. (II)

Hinrichs, J. R. "An Eight-Year Follow-up of a Management Assessment Center." *Journal of Applied Psychology* 63 (1978): 596–601. (II-R)

Hollenbeck, G. P., and W. J. McNamara, "CUCPAT and Programming Aptitude." *Personnel Psychology* 18 (1965): 101–106. (II-R)

Howard, A. "An Assessment of Assessment Centers." *Academy of Management Journal* 17 (1974): 115–134. (I)

Huck, J. R. "Assessment Centers: A Review of the External and Internal Validities." *Personnel Psychology* 26 (1973): 191–212. (II)

Huck, J. R., and D. W. Bray. "Management Assessment Assessment Center Evaluations and Subsequent Job Performance of White and Black Females." *Personnel Psychology* 29 (1976): 13–30. (II-R)

Inskeep, G. C. "The Use of Psychomotor Tests to Select Sewing Machine Operators—Some Negative Findings." *Personnel Psychology* 24 (1971): 707–714. (II-R)

Jaffee, C. L. *Effective Management Selection: An Analysis of Behavior by Simulation Techniques.* Reading, Mass.: Addison-Wesley, 1971. (I)

Jaffee, C. L., J. Bender, and C. Calvert. "The Assessment Center Technique: A Validation Study." *Management of Personnel Quarterly* (Fall 1970): 9–14. (I-R)

Jones, R. A., and W. B. Michael. "The Validity of a Battery of Tests in Communication Skills for Foreign Students Attending an American University." *Educational and Psychological Measurement* 21 (1961): 493–496. (II-R)

Klimoski, R. J., and W. J. Strickland. "Assessment Centers—Valid or Merely Prescient." *Personnel Psychology* 30, (1977): 353–361. (II-R)

Knauft, E. B. "Validity Information Exchange." No. 7-070. *Personnel Psychology* 7 (1954): 405–406. (II-R)

Knauft, E. B. "A Selection Battery for Bake Shop Managers." *Journal of Applied Psychology* 33 (1949): 304–315. (II-R)

Korman, A. L. "The Prediction of Managerial Performance. A Review." *Personnel Psychology* 21 (1968): 295–322. (II)

Kraut, A. I., and G. J. Scott. "Validation of an Operational Management Assessment Program." *Journal of Applied Psychology* 56 (1972): 124–129. (II-R)

Kriedt, P. H. "Validation of a Correspondence Aptitude Test." *Journal of Applied Psychology* 36

(1952): 5–7. (II-R)

Lauer, A. R. "Comparison of Group Paper-and-Pencil Tests With Certain Psycho-Physical Tests for Measuring Driving Aptitude of Army Personnel." *Journal of Applied Psychology* 39 (1955): 318–321. (II-R)

Lawshe, C. H. "Hand-tool Dexterity Test." In O. K. Buros, ed., *The Third Mental Measurements Yearbook.* New Brunswick: Rutgers University Press, 1949. (II)

Layton, W. L. "Predicting Success in Dental School." *Journal of Applied Psychology* 37 (1953): 251–255. (II-R)

Long, W. F., and C. H. Lawshe. "The Effective Use of Manipulative Tests in Industry." *Psychological Bulletin* 44 (1947): 130–148. (II-R)

MacKinnon, D. W. *How Assessment Centers Got Started in the United States.* Pittsburgh: Development Dimensions Press, 1974. (I)

MacKinnon, D. W. *An Overview of Assessment Centers* (Technical Report No. 1). Greensboro, N. C.: Center for Creative Leadership, 1975. (I)

Mandell, M. M. "Validity Information Exchange." No. 9–2. *Personnel Psychology* 9 (1956): 105. (II-R)

Mandell, M. M. "The Administrative Judgment Test." *Journal of Applied Psychology* 34 (1950): 145–147. (a) (II-R)

Mandell, M. M. "Scientific Selection of Engineers." *Personnel* 26 (1950): 296–298. (b) (II-R)

Mandell, M. M. "Selecting Chemists for the Federal Government." *Personnel Psychology* 3 (1950): 53–56. (c) (II-R)

Mandell, M. M. "Validation of Group and Performance Test." *Personnel Psychology* 3 (1950): 179–186. (d) (II-R)

Mandell, M. M. "The Selection of Foremen." *Educational and Psychological Measurement* 7 (1947): 385–397. (II-R)

Mandell, M. M., and S. Adams. "Selection of Physical Scientists." *Educational and Psychological Measurement* 8 (1948): 575–581. (II-R)

McNamara, W. J., and J. L. Hughes. "A Review of Research on the Selection of Computer Programmers." *Personnel Psychology* 14 (1961): 39–51. (II-R)

Melton, A. W., ed., "Army Air Forces Aviation Psychology Program Research Reports." *Apparatus Tests,* Report No. 4., Chapter 8. Washington, D.C.: U.S. Government Printing Office, 1947. (II-R)

Merenda, P. F. "Navy Petty Officer Promotion Examinations as Predictors of On-the-Job Performance." *Educational and Psychological Mea-surement* 19 (1959): 657–661. (II-R)

Moore, B. G. R., and E. A. Peel. "Predicting Aptitude for Dentistry." *Occupational Psychology* 25 (1951): 192–199. (II-R)

Moses, J. L. "The Development of an Assessment Center for the Early Identification of Supervisory Potential." *Personnel Psychology* 26 (1973): 569–580. (II-R)

Moses, J. L. "Assessment Center Performance and Management Progress." *Studies in Personnel Psychology* 4 (1972): 7–12. (I)

Moses, J. L., and V. R. Boehm. "Relationship of Asessment Center Performance to Management Progress of Women." *Journal of Applied Psychology* 60 (1975): 527–529. (II)

Moses, J. L., and W. C. Byham, eds. *Applying the Assessment Center Method.* New York: Pergamon, 1976. (I)

Naylor, G. F. K. "Aptitude Tests for Air Traffic Control Officers." *Occupational Psychology* 28 (1954): 209–217. (II-R)

OSS Staff. *The Assessment of Men.* New York: Rinehart, 1948. (I)

Personnel Research Branch, The Adjutant General's Office, Department of the Army. "Validity Information Exchange." No. 11–18. *Personnel Psychology* 11 (1958): 257–259.

Personnel Research Branch, The Adjutant General's Office, Department of the Army. "Validity Information Exchange." No. 10–41. *Personnel Psychology* 10 (1957): 485–486. (a) (II-R)

Personnel Research Branch, The Adjutant General's Office, Department of the Army. "Validity Information Exchange." No. 10–42. *Personnel Psychology* 10 (1957): 487–489. (b) (II-R)

Poruben, A. "A Test Battery for Actuarial Clerks." *Journal of Applied Psychology* 34 (1950): 159–162. (II-R)

Rubenowitz, S. "Predicting Academic Success: A Follow-up Study." *Occupational Psychology* 32 (1958): 162–170. (II-R)

Saunders, W. J., W. R. Seil, and R. K. Rosensteel. "Validity Information Exchange." No. 9–31. *Personnel Psychology* 9 (1956): 379. (II-R)

Seashore, R. H. "Work Methods: An Often Neglected Factor Underlying Individual Differences." *Psychological Review* 46 (1939): 123–141. (II-R)

Shultz, M. "Validity Information Exchange." No. 8–09. *Personnel Psychology* 8 (1955): 118–119. (II-R)

Skula, M., and R. F. Spillane. "Validity Information Exchange." No. 7–016. *Personnel Psychology* 7 (1954): 147–148. (II-R)

Snyder, R. "Validity Information Exchange." No. 8–

14. *Personnel Psychology* 8 (1955): 263. (II-R)

Speer, G. S. "Validity Information Exchange." No. 10-5. *Personnel Psychology* 10 (1957): 80. (II-R)

Stern, F., and L. Gordon. "Ability to Follow Instructions as a Predictor of Success in Recruit Training." *Journal of Applied Psychology* 45 (1961): 22-24. (II-R)

Tenopyr, M. L. "Content-Construct Confusion." *Personnel Psychology* 30 (1977): 47-54. (II)

Thorndike, R. L., and E. Hagen. "Validation of the Electronics Technician Selection Test at Selected Class 'A' Schools." Bureau of Naval Personnel. *Technical Bulletin* (April 15, 1955): 3-53. (II-R)

Tiffin, J., and R. J. Greenly. "Experiments in the Operation of a Punch Press." *Journal of Applied Psychology* 23 (1939): 450-460. (II-R)

Tracy, W. "The Empty In-Basket Trick." *Personnel Journal* 52 (1973): 36-40. (I)

Uhlmann, F. W. "A Selection Test for Production Machine Operators." *Personnel Psychology* 15 (1962): 287-293. (II-R)

Warren, N. D., and A. A. Canfield. "An Optometric Aptitude Test." *Educational and Psychological Measurement* 8 (1948): 183-191. (II-R)

Webb, S. C. "The Prediction of Achievement for First Year Dental Students." *Educational and Psychological Measurement* 16 (1956): 543-548. (II-R)

Weislogel, R. L. "Development of Situational Tests for Military Personnel." *Personnel Psychology* 7 (1954): 492-497. (II-R)

Weiss, I. "Prediction of Achievement Success in Dental School." *Journal of Applied Psychology* 36 (1952): 11-14. (II-R)

Wernimont, P. F., and J. P. Campbell. "Signs and Samples, and Criteria." *Journal of Applied Psychology* 52 (1968): 372-376. (II-R)

West, L., and D. J. Bolanovich. "Evaluation of Typewriting Proficiency: Preliminary Test Development." *Journal of Applied Psychology* 47 (1963): 403-407. (II-R)

Williams, S. B., and H. J. Leavitt. "Prediction of Success in Learning Japanese." *Journal of Applied Psychology* 31 (1947): 164-168. (II-R)

Wollowick, H., and W. McNamara. "Relationship of the Components of an Assessment Center to Management Success." *Journal of Applied Psychology* 53 (1969): 348-352. (II-R)

Zoll, A. A. *Dynamic Management Education,* 2d ed. Reading, Mass.: Addison-Wesley, 1969. (I)

PART A

Form 1 Job Description

HEAVY-DUTY MECHANIC

DESCRIPTION OF WORK:

General Statement of Duties: Performs skilled work in the repair and maintenance of automotive and heavy-duty equipment.

Supervision Received: Works under the supervision of a foreman.

Supervision Exercised: None.

EXAMPLE OF DUTIES: (Any one position may not include all of the duties listed nor do the listed examples include all tasks that may be found in positions of this class.)

Overhauls, repairs, and maintains cars, trucks, earth moving, road-construction, and heavy-duty equipment.

Performs major repairs on gasoline, semi-diesel, and diesel engines; transmissions; differentials; drive units; brakes; suspension systems, chassis; front and rear ends; cooling systems, fuel systems; instruments; electrical systems; hydraulic systems; and accessory power equipment. Rebuilds engines, carburetors, ignition systems, and radiators.

Performs general tune-up, using testing machines.

Performs emergency road service.

Performs welding as required.

Performs related work as required.

REQUIRED KNOWLEDGES, SKILLS, AND ABILITIES:

Considerable knowledge of the standard practices, methods, materials, and tools used in the automotive mechanic trade. Working knowledge of the hazards and safety precautions peculiar to the trade. Working knowledge of the design, operation, and repair of light- and heavy-duty gasoline and diesel equipment, hydraulic systems, and accessory power equipment. Skill in the use of mechanics tools, materials, welding equipment, and testing equipment. Ability to diagnose mechanical defects and determine parts and adjustments necessary to put equipment into proper operating condition. Ability to follow written and oral instructions. Ability to establish and maintain effective working relationships with employees and the public.

QUALIFICATIONS FOR APPOINTMENT:

Education: Eighth-grade completion or equivalent.

Experience: Four years experience in the repair and maintenance of automotive equipment, including one year on heavy-duty and construction equipment.

　　　OR

Any equivalent combination of education and experience.

PART A

Form 2 Job Description

CLERK TYPIST III

DESCRIPTION OF WORK:

General Statement of Duties: Performs a variety of clerical and typing work requiring the exercise of some independent judgment.

Supervision Received: Works under general supervision of a clerical or technical superior.

Supervision Exercised: Exercises supervision over personnel as assigned, or full supervision incidental to the other duties.

EXAMPLES OF DUTIES: (Any one position may not include all of the duties listed nor do the listed examples include all tasks that may be found in positions of this class.)

Types correspondence, reports, and other office forms requiring some independence of judgment as to content, accuracy, and completeness.

Reviews correspondence and reports, determines what information is to be cross-filed and/or included in other files or reports in order that a ready and complete history or file is available; determines routing and filing.

Compiles, computes, and tabulates data for reports requiring judgment as to content.

Locates source material, edits, and coordinates material for inclusion into research-and-development reports, recognizing variations and verifies completeness of report.

Furnishes the public with information and advice in areas where the public is generally uninformed (such as auto theft, and where time is of the essence), which requires a working knowledge of both agency policies and procedures and applicable laws.

Determines and collects amount of fees, where some degree of personal judgment is involved in the decision, issues receipts, keeps records of transactions.

Performs related work as required.

REQUIRED KNOWLEDGES, SKILLS, AND ABILITIES:

Considerable knowledge of grammar, spelling, and punctuation. Working knowledge of office practices and procedures. Skill in operating a typewriter. Ability to follow written or oral instructions. Ability to make mathematical computations. Ability to establish and maintain effective working relationships with employees, the public, and other agencies.

QUALIFICATIONS FOR APPOINTMENT:

Education: High-school graduation or equivalent.

Experience: Two years experience in general clerical work involving typing.

   OR

Any equivalent combination of education and experience.

PART B

Form 3 Job Description

ADMINISTRATIVE OFFICER'S JOB—PALMS PACIFIC CORPORATION, INC.

DESCRIPTION OF WORK:

General Statement of Duties: Supervises and coordinates responsible administrative work of a complex nature involving program responsibility; does related work as required.

Supervision Received: Receives policy guidance from an administrative superior or board members.

Supervision Exercised: Plans, organizes, develops, coordinates, and directs a staff of administrative and clerical personnel. Total at all levels exceeds twenty.

EXAMPLE OF DUTIES: (Any one position may not include all of the duties listed, nor do the listed examples include all tasks that may be found in positions.)

Administers, coordinates, and directs a complex administrative management program involving program responsibility for a department or equivalent; organizes and directs the work of personnel in day-to-day operation, and conducts long-range planning.

Establishes working methods and procedures and develops departmental procedures and policies related to administrative functions.

Directs major staff services, including budget, training, record keeping, and personnel and general administrative services. Develops supporting data and presents budget estimates and requests.

Directs or performs studies on efficiency, work flow, procedures, work standards, and research and planning.

Develops and compiles comprehensive reports.

Develops and implements immediate and long-range plans for administrative areas of the organization.

Performs related work as required.

REQUIRED KNOWLEDGES, SKILLS, AND ABILITIES:

Extensive and broad knowledge of complex administrative management programs. Skill and ability in administering, planning, and directing personnel in day-to-day programs appropriate to the position to be filled. Ability to interpret and apply laws, rules, regulations, and industry practices. Ability to relate with and coordinate department activities with employees, other departments, and the general public.

QUALIFICATIONS FOR APPOINTMENT:

Education: Graduation from a college or university with major course work in public or business administration or related field.

Experience: Six years progressively responsible experience in a supervisory, technical, or professional area related to management or administration; familiarity with computer software very helpful.

    OR

Any equivalent combination of education and experience.

PART B

Form 4 Glossary of Assessment Center Dimensions

Analytical skills
> Skill to oversee complex nuances in decision-making situations.

Communication skills
> Conveys ideas and information in understandable manner (checks it out); listens to others and comprehends messages; reports accurate information, written and oral, using correct English; reacts promptly to communications; keeps administration and employees informed of changes and future actions or issues.

Controlling
> Establishes standards and maintenance of feedback from processes; monitors/reviews unit performance; takes corrective action when needed; develops efficiency/effectiveness approaches/alternatives as needed; anticipates/avoids problems; monitors budget, policies, and procedures while maintaining quality and productivity; knows current status of all resources (human, financial, material).

Cooperation/coordination
> Lets others know of plans in advance; supports joint, or multidepartmental objectives; shares available resources with other units needing resources; meets with other managers to become informed and avoid problems; initiates efforts to implement cooperative solutions to problems.

Decision making
> Makes effective decisions and renders judgment. Skill to reach logical conclusions based on evidence at hand.

Leadership
> Skill in motivating and integrating the interests of a group to resolve job-related problems. Involves/encourages subordinates in decision-making; provides or makes needed training available; offers individual counseling regarding tasks or objectives; makes decisions promptly and with necessary information; sets example by being on time, visible, and available; develops subordinates to assume responsibility in manager's absence.

Oral communication skills
> Effectiveness of expression in individual or group situations.

Organizing skills
> Assigns/delegates tasks; identifies alternative approaches to resource uses; coordinates human, financial, and material resource uses; divides unit objectives into identifiable tasks and sets due dates.

Planning skills
> Effective in forecasting and proceduralizing own activities and those of a group; analyzes situations and seeks input to develop plans; develops measurable objectives consistent with organizational objectives; designs use of resources to accomplish objectives; anticipates crises and makes changes to avert problems.

Problem-analysis skills
> Effective in seeking out pertinent data and determining the source of the problem.

Openness to influence
> Willing to consider ideas and new methods and accept criticism, suggestions, or advice from others; does not object to ideas before they are explained; does not refuse to accept suggestions or advice from others; does not try to avoid criticism by blaming others for mistakes.

Priority setting
> Distinguishes between important and unimportant problems; consciously establishes priorities; establishes priorities and takes action on the basis of the importance of the problem; considers alternative courses of action before arriving at a final decision.

Work accomplishment
> Is able to meet deadlines and doesn't have to be pushed to get the job finished; does not have difficulty in meeting project deadlines; performs a large amount of work in the time available.

Supervisory skills
> Records critical work behaviors/instances; clarifies expectations of work performance for employees; works with employees to set development/individual performance objectives; provides regular feedback to employees based upon observation of work behavior; reviews annual performance appraisals with employee.

Form 4 (continued)

Delegation skills
Effectively uses subordinates and understands where a decision can best be made.

Written communication skills
Skill in expressing ideas clearly in writing, in good grammatical, concise form.

Constructive initiative
Takes the initiative in acquiring and sharing constructive ideas through involvement with conviction; takes the initiative in group meetings; offers constructive ideas to others outside manager's organizational unit; attempts to expand technical or administrative knowledge in areas where he or she is not fully competent; communicates ideas with conviction.

Thoroughness and accuracy
Is thorough, accurate, and logical in his or her work; gives sufficient attention to detail when seeking problem solutions; is accurate in work; uses a scientific approach to problem solution (i.e., observe, analyze, evaluate, decide, implement, follow up); is not thorough in approach to work assignments; makes unwarranted or illogical assumptions in solving problems.

Formal communications
Speaks clearly, concisely, and interestingly before groups; prepares complete reports; gives clear presentations; never uses a steady, dull monotone in speech.

Organizational perspective
Considers the total organization when making decisions in his or her own organizational unit; involves people from other departments in his or her work; sees problems in light of the problems of others (i.e., does not limit thinking to his or her own position or organizational unit); never fails to communicate across department lines.

Credibility
People react favorably toward, and have confidence in, this person; behaves in a way that causes people to react favorably towards him or her; has the confidence of superiors; has the confidence of peers.

Flexibility
Is flexible and will attempt new methods and keeps up with current developments in his field; will attempt new methods and not be limited by old ways of doing things; adapts readily to new situations; keeps up with current developments in his field; enthusiastic in carrying out new work assignments.

Subordinate participation
Delegates authority and involves subordinates in decisions and setting objectives; involves subordinates in decision-making process; permits subordinates to participate in decision-making process when appropriate; consults with subordinates in setting their performance objectives; delegates authority to his subordinates.

Support for organization
Operates and communicates with concern for the best interests of the total company; takes action to reduce operating budgets in time of general economic decline; builds favorable attitudes about organization in minds of subordinates; expects appropriate benefits and values for money spent; makes a special effort to explain policies and methods to those who do not understand them.

Team building
Inspires enthusiasm and confidence through personal contact and the development of a cohesive group; has the confidence of subordinates; molds a cohesive work group; inspires enthusiasm for a project among subordinates; budgets time to allow for sufficient direct contact with subordinates; holds regular briefing sessions with subordinates.

Control
Maintains necessary discipline among subordinates and follows up on work assignments and takes corrective action if necessary; never fails to follow up on work assignments given to others; takes action when errors or faulty work are observed in his subordinates; never permits subordinates to make poor presentations before other organizational units or higher level management; maintains necessary discipline.

Unit improvement
Established long-range goals for unit, and is improvement oriented; establishes definite long-range goals for organizational unit; works closely with subordinates who lack motivation; provides incentives for improving performance; offers creative and logical suggestions to higher management for improving his or her operation; establishes definite short-range goals for organizational unit.

Form 4 (continued)

Supportiveness

Supports his or her subordinates through appropriate utilization and development of their capacities; builds confidence in subordinates by supporting their actions; understands the capabilities and limitations of subordinates; selects and places qualified personnel; gives adequate instructions to subordinates when new methods are initiated or new work assigned.

Units productivity

Subordinates maintain a high level of quality in their work and accomplish large amounts of work; subordinates accomplish a large amount of work; maintain a high level of quality in their work; subordinates never tend to be lax in their work, to the point of poor quality results.

Conflict resolution

Maintains cooperative and cohesive work group by effectively communicating company objectives and helping to resolve conflict; takes action to settle conflicts among subordinates; communicates objectives of company and organizational unit to subordinates; help subordinates settle their differences; communicates with subordinates by providing vital information affecting organizational unit and its members.

PARTS B, C, and D

Form 5 Assessor's Report Form

Assessor's name _____ Date _____

Job title _____ Group no. _____

PART I

Instructions: Select job dimensions from the glossary of dimensions at the end of this form that you believe are relevant performance criteria for the job of administrative officer; provide an example of behavior which would illustrate each dimension selected (as indicated in the example below). Indicate from which simulation(s) the performance on the dimension being rated originated (i.e., In-basket, LDG, or both). Score on a scale of 0–5 for each of the assessees against each dimension. Make additional copies of this section as required.

Scale

5—extremely favorable behavior on the dimension was demonstrated   (Excellent)
4—considerable favorable behavior on the dimension was demonstrated   (Above Average)
3—some favorable behavior on the dimension was demonstrated   (Average)
2—a little favorable behavior on the dimension was demonstrated   (Below Average)
1—very little favorable behavior on the dimension was demonstrated   (Poor)
0—no behavior on the dimension was demonstrated

Relevant dimension	*Simulation assessed*	*Assessees'* *performance rating*
EXAMPLE: *Impact:* Example: On first meeting rest of the assessee group, how he/she handles getting-to-know-them procedures, establishes rapport and respect, etc.	In-Basket ____ LGD __X__ Fact Finding ____ All ____	No. 1 _5_ No. 4 _3_ No. 2 _0_ No. 5 _3_ No. 3 _2_ No. 6 _1_ Dimension weight ____%
1. _____ Example of extremely favorable behavior	In-Basket ____ LGD ____ Fact Finding ____ All ____	No. 1 ____ No. 4 ____ No. 2 ____ No. 5 ____ No. 3 ____ No. 6 ____ Dimension weight ____%
2. _____ Example of extremely favorable behavior	In-Basket ____ LGD ____ Fact Finding ____ All ____	No. 1 ____ No. 4 ____ No. 2 ____ No. 5 ____ No. 3 ____ No. 6 ____ Dimension weight ____%
3. _____ Example of extremely favorable behavior	In-Basket ____ LGD ____ Fact Finding ____ All ____	No. 1 ____ No. 4 ____ No. 2 ____ No. 5 ____ No. 3 ____ No. 6 ____ Dimension weight ____%
4. _____ Example of extremely favorable behavior	In-Basket ____ LGD ____ Fact Finding ____ All ____	No. 1 ____ No. 4 ____ No. 2 ____ No. 5 ____ No. 3 ____ No. 6 ____ Dimension weight ____%

Form 5 (continued)

5. _____
Example of extremely favorable behavior

In-Basket ____	No. 1 ____ No. 4 ____
LGD ____	No. 2 ____ No. 5 ____
Fact Finding ____	No. 3 ____ No. 6 ____
All ____	Dimension weight ____%

6. _____
Example of extremely favorable behavior

In-Basket ____	No. 1 ____ No. 4 ____
LGD ____	No. 2 ____ No. 5 ____
Fact Finding ____	No. 3 ____ No. 6 ____
All ____	Dimension weight ____%

7. _____
Example of extremely favorable behavior

In-Basket ____	No. 1 ____ No. 4 ____
LGD ____	No. 2 ____ No. 5 ____
Fact Finding ____	No. 3 ____ No. 6 ____
All ____	Dimension weight ____%

8. _____
Example of extremely favorable behavior

In-Basket ____	No. 1 ____ No. 4 ____
LGD ____	No. 2 ____ No. 5 ____
Fact Finding ____	No. 3 ____ No. 6 ____
All ____	Dimension weight ____%

9. _____
Example of extremely favorable behavior

In-Basket ____	No. 1 ____ No. 4 ____
LGD ____	No. 2 ____ No. 5 ____
Fact Finding ____	No. 3 ____ No. 6 ____
All ____	Dimension weight ____%

10. _____
Example of extremely favorable behavior

In-Basket ____	No. 1 ____ No. 4 ____
LGD ____	No. 2 ____ No. 5 ____
Fact Finding ____	No. 3 ____ No. 6 ____
All ____	Dimension weight ____%

PART II

Dimensions not included in the Glossary of Dimensions, but considered relevant:

Relevant dimension	Simulation assessed	Assessees' performance rating

1. _____
Example of extremely favorable behavior

In-Basket ____	No. 1 ____ No. 4 ____
LGD ____	No. 2 ____ No. 5 ____
Fact Finding ____	No. 3 ____ No. 6 ____
All ____	Dimension weight ____%

2. _____
Example of extremely favorable behavior

In-Basket ____	No. 1 ____ No. 4 ____
LGD ____	No. 2 ____ No. 5 ____
Fact Finding ____	No. 3 ____ No. 6 ____
All ____	Dimension weight ____%

FORM 5 (continued)

3. _____

Example of extremely favorable behavior

In-Basket ____
LGD   ____
Fact Finding ____
All ____

No. 1 ____   No. 4 ____
No. 2 ____   No. 5 ____
No. 3 ____   No. 6 ____
Dimension weight ____%

4. _____

Example of extremely favorable behavior

In-Basket ____
LGD   ____
Fact Finding ____
All ____

No. 1 ____   No. 4 ____
No. 2 ____   No. 5 ____
No. 3 ____   No. 6 ____
Dimension weight ____%

5. _____

Example of extremely favorable behavior

In-Basket ____
LGD   ____
Fact Finding ____
All ____

No. 1 ____   No. 4 ____
No. 2 ____   No. 5 ____
No. 3 ____   No. 6 ____
Dimension weight ____%

6. _____

Example of extremely favorable behavior

In-Basket ____
LGD   ____
Fact Finding ____
All ____

No. 1 ____   No. 4 ____
No. 2 ____   No. 5 ____
No. 3 ____   No. 6 ____
Dimension weight ____%

7. _____

Example of extremely favorable behavior

In-Basket ____
LGD   ____
Fact Finding ____
All ____

No. 1 ____   No. 4 ____
No. 2 ____   No. 5 ____
No. 3 ____   No. 6 ____
Dimension weight ____%

PARTS C and D

Form 6

Date: October 12

Assessee: Joel Harris

On October 12 Joel Harris attended the Assessment Center

Harris's overall performance in the Assessment Center was average or above average on most exercises. He showed strengths in energy and initiative.

Observers see his as having definite potential for a middle-manager position but as requiring development. The odds of his actually being a middle manager were seen as good.

In the background interview, Harris was extremely open in discussing his problems and hopes in detail. He came across as a loyal, hardworking, highly-motivated person who has a strong desire to do a good job, but he could use work in creativity, initiative, independence, and leadership skills. He appeared to be tenacious and have a high stress tolerance and to be good in problem analysis. He struck the assessors as being in charge of his job but his efforts are not bearing the fruit he would like. Delegation seemed strong as was subordinate development. Believes the only way to train is to teach by example. Sensing poor morale, however, he doesn't quite know how to improve it.

Harris participated energetically in the exercises and appeared to be intent on doing well. In the group discussion exercises, he showed initiative in starting the group on its task and providing initial organization. His oral communications were somewhat hampered by his use of slang, but in general he spoke in a clear, articulate, fluent manner. His voice was low in volume. On the negative side, he tended to be a bit repetitive in speech and have a great need to summarize and then resummarize. He did not seem overly stressed.

Harris's impact on exercise groups was high. Others quickly took control only after a fight from Harris. Peer and self-ratings indicated he was never a group leader. His overall contribution was usually in the middle. His principal difficulty in group exercises came from his inability to completely convince the group. Rather than pursue an argument until he won, he would give in too quickly.

Harris's financial analysis presentation in the LGD was excellent, but he had a few flaws in his analysis. His presentation in the group discussion was good and he was able to convince the group. He was also an effective secretary for the group.

Questioning in the "Research Budget" fact-finding exercise was well organized and effective. He appeared sometimes to find decision making difficult, but once the decision was made, he stuck to his idea. Slightly nervous, he was not stressed by the resource person.

Writing seems to be a strong area. Harris's Financial presentation was very easy to read and well organized. Similar observations were made about his creative writing assignment and his in-basket. He showed promise in technical knowledge of finance.

In the in-basket exercise, he did quite well, organizing material, setting priorities. He did handle all of the material and on several occasions displayed outstanding judgment.

Form 6 (continued)

STRENGTHS:
Work standards: Tried hard in every exercise; works very hard on job; does not want to personnally settle for less than the best. Was somewhat disappointed by own performance as indicated by his self-evaluation.
Intelligence: Fast reader, catches on fast.
Corporate Thinking: A company person, very loyal.
Integrity: Will not compromise convictions, e.g., copy machine discussion.
Energy: Active in all exercises.
Stress Tolerance: Except for management game, showed little stress.
Interest in Self-Development: Welcomes help; worked his way through college, willing to move. While interest seemed very high, there was some doubt about strength of drive for self-development.
Level of Aspiration: Seems to be unhappy without winning or doing the best possible.

WEAKNESSES:
Creativity: Not seen in approach to current job or in exercises - nothing shown in creative writing exercise.
Leadership: After an initial positive impact, influence in group lessened a bit.
Independence: In present job, seems to do what his boss wants; same attitude expressed in in-basket where he tended to delegate up and to follow "what boss wants."
Use of Delegation: Average in in-basket. He reports he does mail that should be done by subordinates.
Problem Analysis: Did not see all facets of Pretzel Company problem.
Financial Analytical Ability: Missed only a few opportunities to change product mix.
Range of Interest: Could be broader.
Flexibility: Seemed to approach most cases and situations in a similar way (was flexible in accepting ideas of others).
Temper: When did not get his way in compensation committee discussion, he became a bit of an obstruction to the leader's efforts.

MIXED FINDINGS:
Impact: Good first impression - after that would stand out in a crowd.
Oral Communication Skill: Fluent, articulate, talks a bit too much.
Oral Presentation Skill: Formal presentations very good, e.g., financial presentation. Seems to depend on preparation.
Written Communication Skill: English ability adequate, hard to read writing.
Salesmanship: For the formal financial presentation, showed salesmanship; in the "Compensation Committee" exercise he tried for too much money but did convince peers; in group situations could sell well under opposition.
Sensitivity: Assessors described him variously as sensitive, very sensitive, too sensitive and insensitive during the center. There was a general feeling that he might be somewhat soft, e.g., his delay in firing one of his subordinates he admitted should have been fired sooner. Yet he seemed sensitive to people problems in in-basket cases and to needs of individuals in discussion groups.
Tenacity: When ego is involved or he feels there is an ethical problem, Harris can be very tenacious, e.g. fighting for doing right by customer regarding the photocopier. On the other hand, he did not follow up on a few points in group discussions.
Management Style: Expressed concern for "subordinate training;" tends to delegate up - may let people "over-lead" him. Realizes need to be more "tough-minded."
Planning & Organizing: Attempted to organize most groups and did attempt to maintain organization. In-basket organization of work and priorities good.

Form 6 (continued)

<u>Management Control</u>:   Interview indicated some weaknesses in this area: felt Harris
would have a tendency to overcontrol too far down, but in in-basket he did an above
average job of controlling, using due dates, etc.
<u>Judgment</u>:   Showed good judgment in marketing-related problems; weak in judgment in
other areas.

While Harris did poorly in many areas, it was felt that he is definitely trainable. He
was also seen as needing a lot of support and guidance and an understanding, "fatherly"
supervisor, but one that would force him to make decisions. It was felt he would develop
best in a highly structured job with slowly increasing planning and organizing responsibility as his skills develop. An assignment in Illinois as a product manager might be
good.

Some priority development challenges: -management through others
                                               -problem analysis
                                               -organization
                                               -administrative skills

Harris should be easy to communicate with regarding his assessment. He is extremely
open and was accurate in his self-appraisals. A potential difficulty may be his inse-
curity causing him to view "help" as a threat.

PARTS C and D

In-Basket Exercise

ANALYZING SITUATIONS AND TAKING ACTION

Instructions. This exercise is called an in-basket because the materials are correspondence waiting on your desk for your attention and action. This is a means of capturing your responses to issues, problems, and opportunities with which you are confronted in a managerial situation. After you have spent *45 minutes* responding to the ten items and stated *exactly* how you would handle *each* one on the bottom of the items, you may be interviewed by the assessor team, at which time you will have an opportunity to further explain your decisions and actions.

Situation. Assume you are the executive officer of a manufacturing company that employs about 2000 people. You report directly to the president and founder of the company. The organization primarily manufactures relatively standard electronics components, but still must have technical people on board for routine product updating and the design of new products. The business has now begun to prosper and last year sales topped four million dollars and earned a return on investment of 11.2 percent. Your employees will be described below and an organization chart of the company is also enclosed.

For the first three days of this week you were attending a management development conference and your duties were assigned to Mr. Rogers, but he had an emergency appendectomy. The work was then given to Mr. Sloane, but his father suffered a heart attack and he flew home. You were called three hours ago and arrived five minutes ago. The time is 1:15 on Wednesday (3/6). The ten items in this packet are on your desk waiting for your attention. Ms. Pitts is not at her desk.

Assignment. Go through the entire packet of in-basket items making decisions and taking any appropriate action you feel is necessary. Write down *exactly* what you would do on each item. If some items are to be handled later, decide what you would do then. Your sequence of handling the items is important, so note how you would prioritize them.

Reminder. You are the next to the top person in the organization, you have been gone, and there are only two working days remaining in this week for all of the production units. Don't forget to *write down* your responses to each item itself.

Description of Some Key Employees.

Gladys Pitts: Executive secretary; 38 years old. A widow, quite aware of company communication lines and procedures. She is putting her son through college.

Buster Rogers: Administrative assistant; 58 years old. An old friend of "Hap" Seer. He was given his present job based on "Hap's" strong insistence. Although he has not always met your expectations, he has been a valuable source of information and knows most of the company's employees well.

Fred Sloane: Production manager; 57 years old. Another long-time company employee who began to work for "Hap" when he was testing the first component in his garage.

Harold "Hap" Seer: President; 54 years old. Owner and principal stockholder of the company. He is also the designer of the company's biggest selling product, although most of the design work is now left to others as he primarily interfaces with clients and the local community.

Jack Thompson: Head of New Product Development; 33 years old. Very bright and a good team leader.

Tom Vaughn: Purchasing manager; 41 years old. Always thought to be a "nervous nellie," overreacts in many situations.

Note: Other lower-level employees may be named in the items that follow.

ORGANIZATION CHART

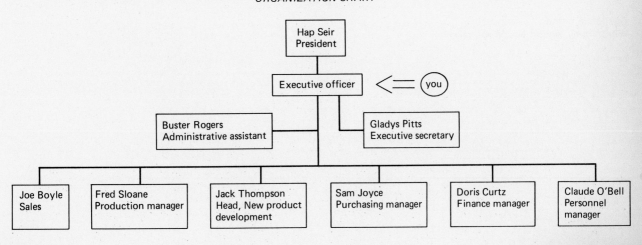

Urgent !
Call from Los
Angeles — Operator
56.

Assessee name:
What, if any, action would you take?   (Both a major client and your mother live in Los Angeles.)

To: Boss

From: Gladys

Time: 1:00   (3/6)

Ms. Flakey (clerk in Finance Dept.) is in the Woman's Lounge, claiming to be sick. She wants your permission to go home.

Assessee name:
What, if any, action would you take?

PRIORITY

From: *Hap Leir*

To: *Executive Officer*

Time: *9:45 (3/6)*

dee me immediately!

Assessee name:
What, if any, action would you take?

PRIORITY

To: Executive Officer

From: Personnel Manager

Got word Jack Thompson has been interviewing for other jobs.
We can't lose him. Will you talk to him?

Assessee name:
What, if any, action would you take?

PRIORITY

Executive Officer
Capacitor Plant
City

Dear_____

　　As we agreed last month, you are to address the group next Friday on
"Management Leadership in Times of Economic Cutbacks." Because the
talk is next week we need your Outline by Friday to get it to our members.

　　　　　　　　　　　　　As Always,

　　　　　　　　　　　　　Paul
　　　　　　　　　　　　　President

Assessee name:
What, if any, action would you take?

To: Executive Officer   PRIORITY

From: Boyle

Just wanted to let you know that my idea of inviting some of the big
contractors out for a drink is really paying off. Ralph Victor, Henry
Aris, and Pete Hiskin were here last month. And Pete placed a nice
order on the spot!

That crab Doris won't pay for the booze, though. She says that it
isn't a legitimate business expense. Will you set her straight?

                                                    Joe

Assessee name:
What, if any, action would you take?

                                                                 PRIORITY

To: Executive Officer

From: Doris

        Something must be done about teaching Hanson and Williams
about credit risks. They tried to get me to approve a new account order
from General Instruments for $110,900. I would not approve it. They
argued with me even after I showed them the company owed six firms a
total of $115,000 in past-due notes.

        Also, something must be done about the wild parties that go
on around here on Saturdays. Monday morning there were cigar and
cigarette butts all over the back room and even a whisky bottle!

        I am not to be expected to work in a place where such things
are tolerated.

Assessee name:
What, if any, action would you take?

To: Executive Officer   PRIORITY

From: Buster

      I thought you ought to know that Fred told me the other day a man
came into the plant pretending to be a customer. I say "pretending"
because he left after a half hour without buying anything. But he did
talk quite a bit to Mr. White and Mr. Hyde out in the plant.
      I think that he is an organizer for the Union.
      I thought you would like to know. Maybe we should review our plant
security?

B

Assessee name:
What, if any, action would you take?

PRIORITY

TO: Executive Officer

From: Fred

            Someone has been stealing building materials over the
weekend. I first noticed this three weeks ago when I helped a fellow
load some last Saturday. On Monday, the pile was much smaller. The
next Saturday I took a count and wrote it down. Sure enough, on Monday
there were 25 less. They got away with 30 the next weekend.

            If you okay it, here's what I propose to do. I will
come back to the yard late Saturday afternoon with a shotgun and some
of my pals from the police department (who will be off duty) and stand
watch. Then if we have "visitors," they will have a big surprise.

            Is this all right with you?

Fred

Assessee name:
What, if any, action would you take?

To: Executive Officer   PRIORITY

From: Doris

        Do you want these sent to Mr. Seer? What explanation
        should be included?

                                Results

SALES DATA

1. Current sales/sales last year   87.8%
2. Sales percentages:
     Lumber & building materials   60.4%
     Hardware,tools, home & garden   15.3%
     Paint & painting supplies   8.0%
     Remodeling contracts   16.2%
3. New sales per full employee $7,500.00
4. Net sales/average net worth   1.9
5. Net sales/average net working capital   2.5

OPERATING DATA

Net sales divided into:

6. Net cost of materials sold   72.9%
7. Gross wages excluding management's   15.6%
8. Depreciation expense   1.8%
9. Auto and truck expense   1.0%
10. Advertising expense   1.2%
11. Bad debts less recoveries   2.8%

FINANCIAL STATISTICS

12. Current ratio   1.8
13. Inventory turnover (on cost)   2.1
14. Accounts-receivable turnover   4.9
15. Long-term debts/total assets   12.0%
16. Net worth/total assets   38.1%

REPORTED PROFITABILITY (before taxes)

17. As percent of net sales   3.8%
18. As percent of tangible assets   4.4%
19. As percent of net worth   7.2%

Assessee name:
What, if any, action would you take?

PARTS C and D

Fact-Finding Exercise 1

Instructions: You have 30 minutes to complete this exercise. You are to read the enclosed memo and respond first in terms of your reactions or feelings if you were Mr. Burke. Second, describe the actions you would take if you were Burke. At the end of the 30 minutes, someone will pick up your response.

Memorandum:

Attention:	Jones and Burke
From:	Jack Larson
Subject:	Questions and thoughts concerning my performance review to be conducted on December 15, 1980.
Date:	November 15, 1980

1. What do you expect as a back-up Machinist for Clem (Jack's co-worker)?

2. When are you willing to advance me to Machinist A?

3. Why shouldn't I have the same respect as Clem? For what reason?

4. Are you aware of my capabilities as a *quality* Machinist?

   a. confidence in my work
   b. positive attitude about the company
   c. ability to learn any job quickly
   d. ability to work well with Harold
   e. ability to adapt to Burke's way of thinking, even if different from my own

Comments:

So as to better understand my attitude, here are a few of my thoughts.

I like working for Ogilvy and Ryan Corporation. For the most part, people here are friendly and nice. You give me the right to be an individual and I appreciate it. I would like to continue to work here for the next few years. But, I don't intend to be a Machinist forever. But for now, this is my bread and butter. I am prepared to give 100 percent—if I can have some reciprocation. By this I mean respect as an individual person. I am extremely ambitious and haven't begun to show my true capabilities. I am willing to make every effort if I can expect reciprocation. All I ask is for you to clarify *my worth* to the company.

I have a future planned and I know what I need over the next few years. My *main* question is, can the company give me what I want, "if" I first show how good I am?

One other problem. I acknowledge that Burke and I have had some misunderstandings. These can be worked out quite easily, if he can accept me as me and open his mind up to the fact that I am more of a humane person than a mechanical robot. But sometimes, Mr. Jones, when I am not treated as such, I speak up.

I thank you for taking time to read this. Please think about it. That way you will be better prepared to discuss these things with me when I am reviewed.

ASSESSEE NAME _____

Role played:

Merle	A	B	C
Gaylord	A	B	C
Charlotte	A	B	C

Assessee Name _____

Exercise 1 (continued)

1. Describe your reactions or feelings as if you were Mr. Burke in the memo.

_____

_____

_____

_____

_____

_____

_____

_____

_____

_____

_____

_____

2. What actions would you take if you were Mr. Burke in the memo?

_____

_____

_____

_____

_____

_____

_____

_____

_____

_____

_____

_____

_____

Assessee Name _____

PARTS C and D

Form 9 Fact-Finding Exercise 2

Header Corporation manufactures assembly equipment for manufacturers of furniture which have an average selling price of $12,000. Business has been declining for the last several years, primarily because competitors with
newer equipment can undersell Header. In the past, Header has distributed profits as dividends instead of investing
in new equipment, as did its competitors. Header now has no profits to distribute and must sell a subsidiary in order
to survive the year. However, someone in the plant has just developed what they believe is a totally new assembly. In
trial runs, production has been faster than ever before. Better yet, it appears as if the old machines can be converted
to the new method. It is estimated that it will take six months to convert the old equipment to the new process and require another six months to obtain an accurate picture of the efficiency and effectiveness of the new operation.

1. Write a brief problem statement.

_____

_____

_____

_____

2. Give several detailed alternative solutions to the problem.

_____

_____

_____

_____

_____

_____

_____

_____

_____

3. State your decision and provide supporting rationale for its choice.

_____

_____

_____

_____

_____

_____

Form 9 (continued)

4. Describe, in detail, your plan for implementing and evaluating the decision you have made.

_____

_____

_____

_____

_____

_____

_____

_____

_____

_____

_____

PARTS C and D

Form 10 Leaderless Group Discussion: Bonus Allocation Problem

There are six people required for this problem. Each of you is a representative to the Bonus Allocation Committee of an organization. A total of forty employees have been recommended for bonuses by their supervisors. For this purpose, the company has allocated $50,000. Today you are to make decisions on six of these people. About twenty-eight of the forty workers have already been allocated their bonuses and you have allocated about $38,500 of the $50,000 for them.

The date is November 1, 1981. Your assignment during the committee meeting is to help the committee make the most equitable use of the available funds. You have 45 minutes to do this task. Remember that five other people will be working with you and the group must decide on an exact bonus figure (or zero bonus) for each of the six workers about whom you have data sheets (data sheets follow). The sheets discuss the reasons behind the supervisors' nominations for the bonuses and contain some data from the worker's personnel file to assist you in his group decision.

TO: Bonus Allocation Committee

FROM: Wilson Harvey

SUBJECT: Bonus for Sam Dulle

DATE: 10/30/81

The position of head custodian has traditionally been underestimated in our firm, but last month, based on recommendations of consultants, it was elevated to a higher level of compensation. I personnally feel that Sam's contributions also have been underestimated for many years. His quiet, unassuming manner might be the reason that he is not noticed, but his work clearly speaks for itself.

We have a flawless custodial staff that has a low turnover rate and few union grievances. Sam has developed this group and it has functioned nearly perfectly since its inception, quite an exception in our industry.

Because Sam was at the top of his previous job class, he was overlooked for a salary increase last time around (6/15/81). In light of his new job class, relation to range, survey data, and performance, I highly recommend a substantial increase for Sam.

PERSONNEL FILE ON ___Sam Dulle___

Job Title...Head Custodian

1. Date of employment...................................6/15/65

2. Starting salary......................................$4,000

3. Education..High-school diploma

4. Experience in job class..............................27 years

5. Age..51

6. Number in family.....................................7

7. Date of next merit review............................6/15/82

8. Last increase..$250 (12/1/80)

9. Present salary.......................................$18,000

10. Salary comparison with employer's council survey*....Lowest quartile

*This recent survey consisted of twenty local organizations in the same industry.

Form 10 (continued)

TO: Budget Allocation Committee

FROM: Swede Hagen, Manager

SUBJECT: Harry Slack's Bonus

DATE: 10/18/81

I am recommending a special increase for Harry at this time to recognize increased responsibilities in the company's research center in the last six months. Harry was a "bargain" when we hired him a few years ago. He had worked as a research analyst in the Coast Guard and our offer was noticeably higher than his service pay, so Harry accepted this offer on the spot. The data shows that he is underpaid for the job, while his duties have reflected a heavier workload and increased responsibilities. The nearest qualified applicant for a similar job is asking $28,000.

   Harry has demonstrated total competence in his job, which he performs much better than some of my longer-service analysts.

PERSONNEL FILE ON ___Harry Slack_____

Job Title...Research Analyst

1. Date of employment..3/18/77

2. Starting salary...$8,500

3. Education...B.S.

4. Experience in job class..4 years

5. Age..27 years

6. Number in family...2

7. Date of next merit review..3/18/82

8. Last increase..$575 (3/15/80)

9. Present salary...$26,500

10. Salary comparison with employer's council survey..............Lowest fifth

Comments:

Form 10 (continued)

TO: Bonus Allocation Committee

FROM: Fel A. T. Eldora, Manager Corporate Data Analysis

SUBJECT: Bonus for Flo Pfannensteil

DATE: 10/31/81

Flo's contributions have exceeded expectations such that she has now completed three projects several months before deadline. Despite her age (28) and limited experience, her academic tools and analytical approach to problems are far better than I have witnessed in years. She has not only received critical praise from her team members, but has received several lucrative offers from competitive firms.

Flo receives about the same compensation as two associates with more seniority with the company (with less potential and education), but her productivity is second to none.

She has also shown definite leadership potential. At this time, we cannot offer her an advanced supervisory position that would meet her need for more autonomy and status, but I feel she is already qualified. (I am hoping to offer her a promotion within a year.)

In the meantime, I believe we can recognize her value with a handsome special increase that would indicate our pleasure with her performance and offset the substantially higher salary ($34,000) and status (Systems Manager) offered to her by competitors.

PERSONNEL FILE ON   Flo Pfannensteil

Job Title..Computer Systems Analyst

1. Date of employment.....................................7/11/75

2. Starting salary...$20,100

3. Education...Ph.D.

4. Experience in job class................................4 years

5. Age..28

6. Number in family.......................................1

7. Date of next merit review..............................7/11/82

8. Last increase..$350 (3/15/80)

9. Present salary...$26,500

10. Salary comparison with employer's council survey.......50th percentile

Comments:

Form 10 (continued)

TO: Bonus Allocation Committee

FROM: Maggie Hard, Head Accounts Manager

SUBJECT: Special Increase/ R. W. Good

DATE: 10/27/81

Bud did not receive a merit increase in August principally because he is near the maximum of his job class, a most unfair ceiling. He is the only "manager" who is not in the next higher grade (range $22,500-$25,100). His position is to be reclassified but I don't know when. I don't think we should downgrade positions in the middle-management range when they are as important as this one. I'm sure Bud's patience is becoming shorter because of his "second-class citizen" standing. In fact, he may be already looking for another job.

I recommended an increase at the last bonus time because (1) the cost-of-living rate of increase has been 11 percent in this area; (2) his performance has been more than satisfactory; (3) he came in early from his vacation to finish a priority project when his assistant was hospitalized. The president sent him a letter of commendation for the materials he prepared for the stockholders' meeting. In addition, his staff has increased from two to five.

PERSONNEL FILE ON ___R. W. Good___

Job Title..Head of Accounts Payable

1. Date of employment.......................................8/4/67

2. Starting salary...$8,250

3. Education.. ...HS diploma

4. Experience in job class..................................15 years

5. Age...43

6. Number in family..4

7. Date of next merit review................................8/4/82

8. Last increase...$1000 (1/1/80)

9. Present salary..$19,375

10. Salary comparison with employer's council survey.......80th percentile

Comments:

Form 10 (continued)

TO: Bonus Allocation Committee

FROM: Larry Snyder, VP for Personnel and Public Relations

SUBJECT: Bonus for A. M. Jones, Personnel Administrator

DATE: 10/18/81

A. M. was very unhappy with the size of the salary increase awarded last time, which was a smaller percentage than he had been getting. I feel it is imperative that we at least match it now. Normally I would oppose this type of action (as my record shows), if it were only for the reason of being contrary to corporate policy. However, A. M. has matured in his job so rapidly that he truly deserves a larger raise than he was given. In addition, his rapport with our two most important departments is unmatched by anyone on our staff. In fact, one has recently advised me that his relationship with A. M. was the only reason his department is willing to attempt our job-enrichment program.

  Purely for financial reasons, A. M. is prepared to accept an offer of $29,000 from another firm, but told me he will remain with us if we grant him a good increase. We desperately need him, at least until I can develop a potential replacement to gain the confidence of our most important departments (which should take about 12-18 months).

PERSONNEL FILE ON ___A. M. Jones_____

Job Title...Personnel Administrator

 1. Date of employment....................................5/12/71

 2. Starting salary.......................................$9,500

 3. Education...LLB

 4. Experience in job class...............................11 years

 5. Age...38

 6. Number in family.....................................3

 7. Date of next merit review............................5/12/82

 8. Last increase..$850 (3/15/80)

 9. Present salary.......................................$26,250

10. Salary comparison with employer's council survey.......50th percentile

Comments:

Form 10 (continued)

```
TO:        Bonus Team

FROM:      Sally Headdy, District Head, Technical Planning

SUBJECT:   Delores Hopes's Bonus
           Supervisor of Technical Writing

DATE:      10/31/81
```

Delores was granted a three-month paid leave of absence to complete her master's thesis. When she returned in December, I submitted a recommendation for a merit salary increase for which she was scheduled, according to normal company policy. At that time management decided to defer her increase for six months, since her "time on the job" was three months short of other staff members for the year, who were also eligible and indeed received increases, and also since she had been on paid leave. As I stated before, I cannot agree with a company policy that encourages an employee to seek academic attainment, but penalizes her financially when she does so. Delores's loyalty to the firm and her work are no problem in terms of her leaving us, but I feel it is only fair that she receive her "normal" increase at this time, retroactive to its regularly scheduled date.

   She should also receive an additional increase in recognition of her academic attainment. It should be noted that her recent academic development, plus extensive experience, make her rather marketable, should she choose to "shop around." In fact, awareness of her skills may be increasing as she just received a government award for her work on the "Red Herring" Project.

PERSONNEL FILE ON ___Delores Hopes___

```
Job Title..........................................Supervisor of Technical Writing

 1.  Date of employment...............................12/12/73

 2.  Starting salary...................................$4,650

 3.  Education.........................................M.S.

 4.  Experience in job class..........................17 years

 5.  Age...............................................41

 6.  Number in family.................................1

 7.  Date of next merit review........................6/12/82

 8.  Last increase....................................$750 (6/15/80)

 9.  Present salary...................................$17,850

10.  Salary comparison with employer's council
     survey.*.........................................40th percentile
```

*This recent survey consisted of twenty local organizations in the same industry.

<u>Comments:</u>

Name _____ Group Number _____

Date _____ Class Section _____ Hour _____ Score _____

ASSESSMENT OF LEARNING IN PERSONNEL ADMINISTRATION
EXERCISE 8

1. Try to state the purpose of this exercise in one concise sentence.

2. Specifically what did you learn from this exercise (i.e., skills, abilities, and knowledge)?

3. How might your learning influence your role and your duties as a personnel administrator?

4. What job and organizational characteristics would seem to signal the use of assessment centers for selection in addition to interviews and biographical data?

5. How can objectivity of assessors be improved?

6. Should assessors be managers in the same departments or functional areas as assessees? Why or why not?

7. How could you evaluate the effectiveness of a work sampling or simulation selection device? (You may wish to refer to Exercise 9 for help in answering this question.)

Exercise 9

Testing personnel and validating selection procedures

PREVIEW

This exercise is designed to facilitate understanding of psychological testing as a selection device and the use of statistics to analyze test results and make effective selection decisions. Thus, the *interpretation of test results,* rather than test construction or design, is the focus of the exercise.

Two of the most important concepts in selection are validity and reliability. The former term has been noted briefly in previous exercises and defined as the relationship between a predictor or selection device (such as an applicant's response to an interview question) and job performance. Reliability has been defined as consistency of a measure over time or across raters (such as many raters' agreement on one person's performance appraisal). However, validity and reliability are much broader concepts which serve as the basis for much of the personnel selection. This exercise explores these concepts in more depth.

OBJECTIVES

1. To become aware of the advantages and disadvantages of the use of tests as personnel selection devices.

2. To gain an understanding of the importance of validity and reliability in personnel selection.

3. To build skill in applying basic statistics that enable validity and reliability to be assessed.

PREMEETING PREPARATION

Read the entire exercise. The *Introduction* should be read very carefully. Review elementary regression and correlation computations, as well as the measures of central tendency (i.e., standard deviation and mean) which are used in these computations. See the *Appendix* to this exercise for such a discussion.[1]

INTRODUCTION
Basic Issues in Personnel Testing

When discussing personnel testing, we generally are referring to the use of paper-and-pencil methods of assessing individuals for employment. However, testing can also mean the use of any method (even an informal interview) for collecting information used in making selection decisions. Thus, although in this exercise we will be focusing primarily on psychological paper-and-pencil tests, the methodology of reliability and validity—which will be discussed—can be applied to all of the selection techniques treated in Exercises 6, 7, and 8.

---

[1] Most statistics textbooks would also contain a discussion of basic regression, correlation, and measures of central tendency.

Two Perspectives on Testing. In looking at the issues involved in personnel testing and selection, two perspectives must be kept in mind. The first perspective concerns the accurate use of all procedures available when an organization is seeking to substantiate the validity of a selection procedure. This may be referred to as the "ideal" practice and should be consistent with the statements various professional groups have made in this regard. These include the combined pronouncements of the American Psychological Association (APA), the American Education Research Association, and the National Council on Measurement in Education on ethics and the use of tests, and APA Division 14's (Industrial and Organizational Psychology) statement on validation and personnel selection procedures.[2] The profession of psychology, through these groups, can be viewed as seeking the "best" methodology possible. See Fig. 1 for an example.

The second perspective concerning testing seeks "fairness," or the elimination of discriminatory hiring practices. This perspective will be referred to as the "legal" status of tests which emerges from various government pronouncements and court cases.[3] A set of minimum standards to be used as guides in the design of selection procedures may eventually come from the courts and legislatures. Although these two perspectives on testing may be viewed somewhat differently in terms of their objectives, they are not necessarily inconsistent with each other in actual practice. The differences are largely in the degree to which selection procedures should be assessed as to validity, etc. (i.e., the exhaustiveness to which the method of selection is examined). In this exercise, both perspectives will be discussed. Obviously, it would be very difficult to discuss one without the other, as what the first states in the ideal sense, the second amends for the practical sense. A glossary of terminology pertaining to psychological and legal jargon is presented in Exercise 17.

Validity.[4] The ability of an instrument (e.g., a test, a questionnaire, an interview, etc.) to actually measure

the quality or characteristic it was originally intended to measure is called validity. Unfortunately, validity is rather difficult to pin down precisely because it may vary depending on the method used. Therefore, it is necessary to predetermine standards that can be used as guidelines for ascertaining the absence or presence of validity evidence. Since there is no one definite measure of validity, it is important to evaluate all the available measures. If all such evaluations of validity point in one direction—either the presence of or lack of validity—then the decision may not be difficult. If, on the other hand, the results from different assessments vary, it becomes more difficult to determine the degree of validity actually present from the evidence. Also, there is always the problem of making a wrong decision as a result of chance or random error, despite the precautions taken.

Empirical, or Data-Based, Validity Models. In order to assess whether a measure, say a certain test, is actually measuring what it was originally intended to measure, several sets of procedures are currently in use. These procedures are called validity models or strategies and can be based on actual statistical data or on

---

[2] *Principles for the Validation and Use of Personnel Selection Procedures* (Washington, D.C.: American Psychological Association, 1975); and *Standards for Educational and Psychological Tests,* (Washington, D.C.: American Psychological Association, 1975).

[3] The discussion of the legal aspects (i.e., the second perspective) will focus on validation based on job relatedness and not the statistical procedures for the determination of discrimination (called adverse impact). Discrimination or adverse impact is the target of discussion in Exercise 17.

[4] The following discussions are meant only to introduce the topics. More rigorous discussions can be obtained in several entries in the *For Further Reading* section of this exercise.

```
┌─────────────────────────────────┐
│          PERSONNEL               │
│       ADMINISTRATOR'S            │
│          JOB SKILLS              │
│                                  │
│  1. Administration               │
│     planning                     │
│     organizing                   │
│     budgeting            ALTERNATIVE
│     supervising          SELECTION
│                          METHODS
│  2. Interpersonal
│     communication        Biodata
│     motivation           Interview
│     leadership           Work samples
│                          Simulation
│  3. Technical            Paper-and-Pencil
│     systems design         Tests
│     human-resource planning
│        and forecasting
│     job analysis
│     performance appraisal
│        recruiting, selecting
│     test development and
│        validation
│     training and development
│     motivation systems
│     wage, salary, and
│        benefit administration
│     labor relations
│     research
└─────────────────────────────────┘
```

Fig. 1. Selection methods available to assess a candidate's skills for the job of personnel administrator

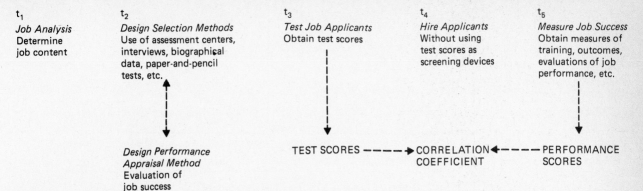

t_1	t_2	t_3	t_4	t_5
Job Analysis Determine job content	*Design Selection Methods* Use of assessment centers, interviews, biographical data, paper-and-pencil tests, etc.	*Test Job Applicants* Obtain test scores	*Hire Applicants* Without using test scores as screening devices	*Measure Job Success* Obtain measures of training, outcomes, evaluations of job performance, etc.

Design Performance Appraisal Method Evaluation of job success

TEST SCORES - - - → CORRELATION COEFFICIENT ← - - - PERFORMANCE SCORES

Fig. 2. The predictive validation model

judgment. Faced with the problem of actually measuring validity, personnel administrators or others may choose one of the models discussed below, relying on statistical techniques to guide their assessment of validity.

Of the two models noted briefly here, the most basic and preferred model is the *predictive validity* model. In using this model, one would attempt to show the results of a test (or some other selection tool) would accurately predict actual job success. Here, a test's results are called a *predictor* and the actual job success, the *criterion,* or that which we are attempting to relate the predictor to. In a predictive validity study (Fig. 2), we would try to assess the relationship between a test (predictor) and job success (the criterion) by analyzing the job (t_1), designing an appropriate test and methods of performance appraisal (t_2), and then administering the test to a group of job applicants (t_3), but not using their test scores as a basis for selection decisions. We could perhaps select on the basis of another "predictor," like high-school grades, or simply hire everyone until the positions are filled (t_4). Then we would evaluate the newly hired applicants' performance, perhaps by using some measure of effectiveness, such as number of cost overruns during a period, or by some type of performance appraisal system, perhaps using supervisory ratings. After the performance measure is used to evaluate the recently hired applicants (t_5) who have had time to perform their jobs, the results of the test administered at t_3 are related to the performance of the group at t_5 by means of a correlation coefficient. The correlation coefficient (r) is a statistical measure of association between two groups of paired numbers (see Figs. 3 and 4 and the *Appendix*). If the coefficient indicates that those who did well on the test also later did well on the job, then we could assume that a high score on the test would *predict* later job success. Further, we might infer that the results of the study described above indicate validity of the test, because it

seemed to measure or predict what it was intended to measure—job success.

Although a predictive validity study as described above is sound in a scientific and statistical sense, it is sometimes difficult in a practical sense. For example, a reasonably large sample of workers (at least thirty or so) would be required in order to make firm conclusions from the statistical analysis. In addition, predictive validity studies take some time as we must wait until a sufficient period of time has passed before performance can be ascertained (i.e., t_4 to t_5). Finally, we cannot use the test we may have developed or purchased (both at considerable cost) to make selection decisions for the *initial* applicants because we must hire them first in order to assess the test's validity. We could use the test scores as a rationale for selection of *future* applicants, however, if the predictive validity of the test was shown.

Due to these problems, a second validity strategy, *concurrent validity* (Fig. 5) is sometimes used. Here current employees rather than new hirees are used as the sample on which to base the validity study. As Fig. 5 indicates, some type of test (or other selection technique) for which the validity must be assessed is developed, and performance appraisal methods are also developed if they are not already in existence (t_1). Then the test (the predictor) is given to the sample of workers on the job and their performance is appraised (t_2). The statistical association between the predictor (test score) and the criterion (job performance) is shown again by the simple correlation coefficient. As in predictive validity, if high test scores are associated with high job performance, the test can be assumed to be valid, provided certain precautions were taken, such as randomly selecting the sample, use of a large enough sample, proper testing environment, an accurate performance measure, etc. If the test predicts high performance for people currently on the job, it may be used to select new workers.

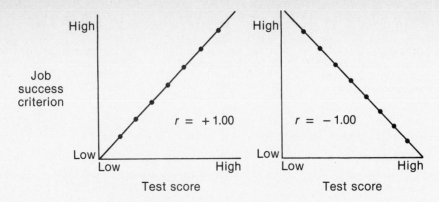

Fig. 3. Perfect positive and negative correlations

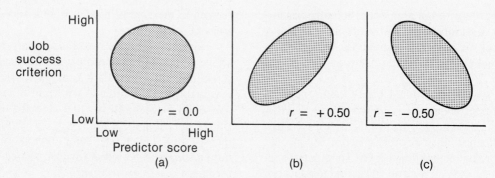

Fig. 4. Examples of correlations varying in magnitude and direction

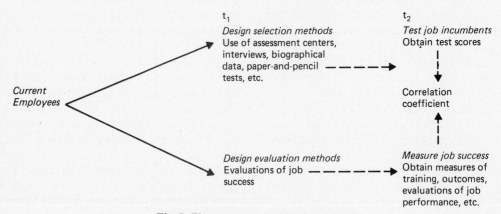

Fig. 5. The concurrent validation model

The study is called a concurrent study because test scores and performance scores can be obtained concurrently (t_2) for a group of current job holders. Thus, this method can be quicker than predictive validity and enables the organization to use the predictor on all future hirees. No future employees would be hired without using their test scores, as in predictive validity. Of course, we run the risk of measuring a group of current employees who may already have high test scores as they are the remainder of a larger group previously screened by some other selection method when they were hired. In addition, they may have learned, or developed, while on the job and could thus get high test scores. When we use the same test on a group of applicants, they may get lower scores simply because they have not yet been able to learn what the original sample was able to while on the job, rather than because they would not be good future performers.

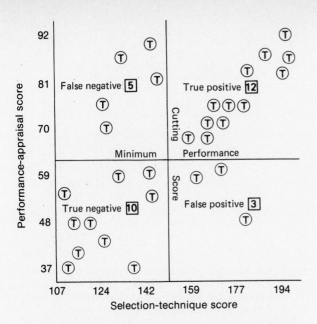

Fig. 6. Restriction of range and other validity problems

Concurrent validity studies readily illustrate another problem of validity (which may also be found with predictive studies). This is the restriction-of-range problem. Fig. 6 shows a plot of a relationship between selection test scores and performance appraisal scores when persons are hired irrespective of scores on the selection test. Notice that the scores are divided into four quadrants by "minimum performance" scores of about 60 and a "cutting score" on the selection instrument of about 150. Of the total of thirty scores, twenty-two are "hits" because they indicate that twelve of the people who pass the cutting score also perform well (true positives). Ten persons also did not perform well or exceed the cutting score (true negatives). However 26.6 percent of the scores (eight of thirty) are "misses" because these people either passed the cutting score but did not perform well (false positives), or did not pass the cutting score but exceeded the minimum performance standard. This last quadrant, false negatives, is often the concern when using traditional tests to select minionity employees (i.e., excluding employees who could do the job because of a culturally biased test). The restriction-of-range problem is created when the cutting score is used without first using the full range of potential employees to do the job. Thus, in Fig. 6 when the test was not validated, only the fifteen candidates who passed the cutting score would be employed and thus included in the calculation of the correlation coefficient. In a concurrent study the scores would be only the seventeen persons who presumably maintained minimum performances. Now contrast the distributions of (1) the use of an unvalidated test, and

(2) the use of a concurrent study, with (3) the entire distribution. Which would have a higher correlation coefficient? Because of this restriction in range, the correlation coefficient would be depressed. Such a finding often calls for an explanation of "differential validity" in which different selection methods may be required for different segments of the applicant population. Each of these tests must then be validated for the appropriate applicant groups. However it may be found that using well-designed selection techniques eliminates the need for differential-validity measures, although this issue is under considerable debate in professional journals.[5]

Nonempirical, or Logical, Validity Models. The second major strategy for validation is rational (or logical) methods. These methods are permissible under the official guidelines used by the federal government[6] when empirical validation is not feasible, largely because of small sample sizes. These methods concern what is called *content validity* and require a thorough knowledge of job demands based on a careful job analysis.

Content validity refers to the extent to which a test actually measures some aspect of the job itself, or has content similar to job content. As the content of the test approaches the content of the job, performance on the test would approach performance on the job. Of course, in selection, the more closely a selection test or predictor calls for performance which is similar to actual job performance, the better we would be able to predict job performance from test performance. The selection techniques discussed in Exercise 8, work sampling and simulation, were designed to be content-valid because, in the case of the former, a sample of actual job content is used as the test. In the latter, actual job content is simulated.

Figure 7 shows how closely various selection techniques approximate actual job content. Of course, the closest selection technique to actual job content would be performing the job itself before final hiring, as in a probation period. The furthest type of predictor from

[5] For example, see V. B. Bohem, "Negro-White Differences in Validity of Employment and Training Selection Procedures," *Journal of Applied Psychology* 56 (1972): 33–39; and P. Bobko and C. J. Bartlett, "Subgroup Validities: Differential Definitions and Differential Predictions," *Journal of Applied Psychology* 63 (1978): 12–14.

[6] Guidelines have been issued by the Equal Employment Opportunity Commission, Civil Service Commission (now Office of Personnel Management), Department of Labor, and Department of Justice Uniform Guidelines on Employee Selection Procedures, *Federal Register,* August 25, 1978.

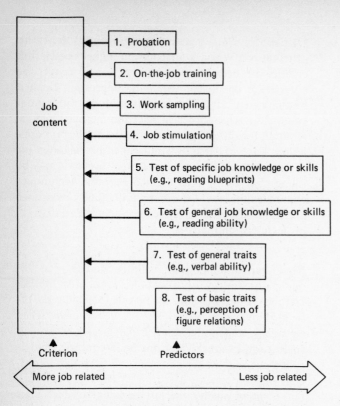

Fig. 7. Selection procedures and their relation to job content
(Adapted from R. M. Guion, "Open a New Window:
Validities and Values in Psychological Measurement,"
American Psychologist 29 (1974): 291.)

actual job content would be a test of general traits, such as perception of figural relations.

In content validation, inferences about the usefulness of the test or predictor are often made by assessing how the test is constructed and whether it actually taps the behavioral content or domain of the job. Content validity is thus established by a systematic observation of job content via a very thorough job analysis (see Exercise 3). Then selection devices are designed which actually assess or sample knowledge, skills, and behaviors required for job success. For example, typing tests are content-valid measures to use in hiring stenographers, because stenographers type. The same can be said for a shorthand test. When both are used together, we obtain more complete sampling of job content than when each is used alone. The more completely we tap the entire behavioral set or "domain" of the job, the more content-valid the selection process would be. Note that statistical procedures are seldom used in content validity; only expert judgment that the predictor taps the content of the job is really necessary here, as well as a thorough job analysis. However, this does not mean that content samples could not be scored and therefore empirically validated.[7] Thus, although content validity

is often called a nonempirical approach, it can be empirically validated with a sufficient sample size if the content sample is scored.

Two additional types of validity should also be mentioned because they are suggested by the *APA Division 14 Principles for the Validation and Use of Selection Procedures*. These are construct and synthetic validity. Construct validity is the degree to which a formally articulated concept of a trait (e.g., perceptual speed, spatial ability, empathy) may be measured by a test and related to job performance. This is difficult to do and requires more than a single criterion-related study. Synthetic validity is where the validity may be inferred from prior research relating predictors to specific relevant criterion elements.

Content and construct validity are applicable in many situations. Excluding these methods would seriously handicap organizations with few employees in a job class—for example, in the selection of astronauts, where they have proved most effective. Such organizations cannot use elegant empirical validation designs which are dependent on large sample sizes. Fortunately, Title VII of the 1964 Civil Rights Act, as interpreted by the 1978 *Guidelines,* allows these methods where predictive and concurrent validation strategies are not technically feasible.

Reliability. The reliability of a measure refers to its trustworthiness. In other words, it expresses the repeatability, stability, or consistency of the measure. The reliability coefficient, which is typically obtained

---

[7] This scoring of content samples has been widely discussed by Robert M. Guion. He prefers that the method be referred to as "content-oriented" validation and that the samples be scored with a standardized system. References to Guion's concerns are in *For Further Reading* at the end of the exercise.

Table 1. Allocation of Variance in Different Estimates of Reliability

	Sources of variance						
	I	II A	II B	III	IV A	IV B	V
Reliability procedure	Lasting general characteristics	Lasting specific characteristics (specific to whole test)	Lasting specific characteristics (specific to particular test items)	Temporary general characteristics	Temporary specific characteristics (specific to whole test)	Temporary specific characteristics (specific to particular test items)	Variance not otherwise accounted for
Immediate test-retest	S*	S	S	S	S	E	E
Delayed test-retest	S	S	S	E	E	E	E
Immediate alternate form	S	S	E†	S	S	E	E
Delayed alternate form	S	S	E	E	E	E	E
Split-half	S	S	E	S	S	S	E

* S = systematic variance
† E = error variance
Source: Adapted from R. M. Guion, *Personnel Testing* (New York: McGraw-Hill, 1965), p. 39.

through use of the simple correlation coefficient (although other methods of computing reliability are possible), indicates how consistent the scores obtained on a measure are.

Four basic types of reliability are used in psychological testing. The first is called the *test-retest* method and is expressed as the correlation between the scores from two different administrations of the same test to the same people. The administrations should be fairly close together so as not to allow learning or maturation to influence the scores too heavily. This method would result in an index of stability.

The second type of reliability estimate is the *alternate forms* method. Here two different forms of the same test can be developed by drawing two different random samples of questions from a larger population of questions, all of which were designed to measure the same idea. This method may be a little more useful than test-retest because the same items do not appear on both tests.

The third type of reliability, the *split-half* method, assesses the internal consistency of a measure. Here, for example, a test would be split into odd and even items or questions and a correlation coefficient computed for the two sets of scores. If all of the test items were measuring a similar idea or concept, we would expect the relationship between the two halves to be high.

The fourth type of reliability estimate is the *internal consistency* method. This technique is concerned with the average correlation of a set of items and reflects the degree of homogeneity within the measure. Coefficient alpha and the Kuder-Richardson Formula "20" coefficient (KR-20) are the most commonly used formulas for estimating the internal consistency of a test. (A presentation of the KR-20 formula is available in Exercise 10, Part B.)

Table 1 shows the sources of variance with alternative methods of estimating reliability. The two types of variance are systematic and error. Systematic variance arises when the characteristics of an individual are repeatedly measured. This increases the correlation coefficient. Error variance occurs when there exist different levels of performance on a test (inconsistency). This lowers the correlation coefficient.

Test Construction. Tests are constructed by sampling job content, whether a predictive, concurrent, content, or other validity study is to be used. This is true for both the predictor and the criterion. Any "test" must be constructed from samples of job content that must be performed; from specific items, such as job knowledge or skills; or from constructs, such as leadership, dexterity, spatial ability, etc. Obviously, the further from actual job samples, the greater the inferences that serve as hypotheses to be tested in terms of job relatedness. In any case, a test must represent a sample of actual job content randomly selected and presented in such a way that the test can differentiate high performers from low performers (i.e., varying level of difficulty of test questions) on the dimensions measured by the test and can be clearly related to job performance. The example used in Exercise 8 (the selection of an auto mechanic) which asks questions about installing pulleys and belts, disassembling gear boxes, aligning a motor, and pressing a bushing illustrates a sampling of job content in the construction of a test. The items within any test should also be checked for reliability and validity by conducting an item analysis to determine if the test actually discriminates in the way intended. For example, will applicants in the top half of the test-score distribution also tend to have a certain question "right" and applicants in the bottom half tend to get the question "wrong?" If this occurs, the item has favorable discriminating power and contributes to the overall reliability and validity of the test.[8] The statistical techniques used to determine usable items in test construction are chi square (χ^2) and point biserial correlation.

Practical Usefulness of Tests. A critical question that is often unanswered, yet is a major issue in the validation process, is: How high must a correlation be for it to be useful in predicting success?

> Tests with a coefficient of validity less than 0.50 are practically useless, except in distinguishing between extreme cases, since at that value of *r* the forecasting efficiency is only 13.4 percent.[9]

This statement, paraphrased from a statistical text, can be found in many other texts as well. Relatively few validity coefficients, however, especially in personnel studies, exceed 0.50.[10] In fact, the 0.30 level may become the accepted standard of practical significance, based on the decision in a recent court case.[11] The following statement is from footnote 13 of the First Circuit decision, which was appealed and cited by the District Court in that case:

> The objective portion of the study produced several correlations which were statistically significant (likely to occur by chance in fewer than five of one hundred similar cases) and practically significant (correlation of +0.3 or higher, thus explaining 9% or more of the observed variation). Of the seven statistically significant correlations, four were not practically significant. . . .[12]

Because the higher court cited the lower court's opinion regarding 0.30 being the level of correlation necessary to establish the *practical* utility of a test, it may become an accepted standard.

Why are tests being used even though they generally fall into this "practically useless" class? Is it because of ignorance on the part of test users? Not at all. The "index of forecasting efficiency,"[13] as formulated in statistics texts, is concerned with a precision of prediction much finer than that required in most practical situations. As a measure of the real practical utility of a test, the effectiveness index may be grossly misleading.[14]

The difference between the two concepts of *practical utility* and the *statistical index of efficiency* can be seen more clearly if we consider the predictions, in two different situations, of how far people can broad jump. If the occasion is an athletic contest, we might want to predict just how many feet and inches each person will cover by giving some sort of a test, let's say of strength in their legs. The average difference between our estimated distances based on the test results and the actual jumps will serve as a crude indicator of our test's index of forecasting efficiency—the better (i.e., the more valid) the basis on which we make our predictions, the smaller this average difference will become. But, suppose we move from the athletic contest to a situation in which practical values are more important, say one in which it is necessary to leap across a brook. Those who fail by a fraction of an inch to make the jump will get their feet just as wet as will those who miss by six inches. And those who just clear it will be as successful in staying dry as those who sail over with a few feet to spare. Now the "efficiency" of our predictive test of leg strength does not lie in how close we can predict the exact length of a person's jump, as in the athletic contest, but in the confidence with which our predictive test permits us to say, "Of people who score above a certain point, nine out of ten will make the jump, but of those whose scores are below a certain point, only three out of ten will get across."

Of course, the absolute dichotomy (those who make it across the stream versus those who did not) is as extreme in its way as the pinpoint precision estimate is at the other extreme. That is, in trying to predict job performance from tests (or any predictors), we do not attempt to pinpoint performance exactly, as we did in the athletic contest, nor do we often assume that there are only two categories, success and failure, as we did in the jump across the brook. But typically, in selection, we are attempting to guess in which of a few general categories of success (e.g., high, middle, low) our job candidates will eventually fall. Thus, the real situation is much more like the brook jump than the athletic contest; therefore cruder approximations and *practical*

---

[8] Statistical tables are available to show how large a correlation coefficient must be, given a certain sample size, in order to have various degrees of certainty (e.g., one error out of 20 trials or $p < 0.05$) that the relationship obtained was not due to chance (see *Appendix*).

[9] J. P. Guilford, *Psychometric Methods* (New York: McGraw-Hill, 1936, p. 364). The index of forecasting efficiency $= 100\,(1 - \sqrt{1 - r^2})$ where *r* is the validity coefficient, the correlation between the predictor and the criterion. When the number of cases is small, a correction term $\frac{N-1}{N-2}$ is inserted under the square root sign.

[10] The correlation coefficient's range is $+1.00$ to -1.00.

[11] *N.A.A.C.P., Inc.* v. *Beecher*, U.S. District Court, Dist. of Mass., Feb. 1974.

[12] Ibid, n. 13

[13] J. P. Guilford, "Reliability and Validity of Measures," in J. P. Guilford, *Psychometric Methods* (New York: McGraw-Hill, 1954), Chap. 14.

[14] Many of the following comments are reproduced with permission from the Psychological Corporation's *Test Service Bulletins,* nos. 43 and 45.

significance become important. We thus typically do not attempt to predict specific success levels from test scores; rather, we try to predict with some validity the percentages of people above or below a certain score that will subsequently be high, or middle, or low performers.

Percent of improvement over chance, as used with the index of forecasting efficiency, refers to the narrowing of a zone of error around a predicted score. When the validity coefficient (or correlation coefficient) is zero (i.e., no relationship is indicated between a test score and job performance), knowledge of the test score does not permit us to predict an individual's score on the criterion with any accuracy at all. The best guess we can make with respect to any individual, regardless of how s/he scored on such a test, is that they will be average on the criterion. Here, the band of error (the standard error of estimate) is as large as the spread (the standard deviation) of the ratings on the criterion (job performance) for the entire group (see *Appendix*). As the correlation between the test scores and the criterion ratings increases, our precision in predicting ratings of individuals on the criterion also increases. We may predict with some degree of confidence, for example, that a person who scores in the top quarter of the test will be rated in the top quarter on the criterion as well. Of course, some of our predictions will be in error (i.e., some of those whose scores are in the top quarter on the test will be rated in the second quarter on performance, a smaller number in the third quarter, and a few may even be rated in the lowest quarter). The larger the validity coefficient, the fewer misplaced persons there will be; furthermore, the smaller will be the amount of displacement. In other words, if the validity coefficient is very high (i.e., close to + 1.00), we may expect most of those who score in the top quarter on the test to be rated in the top quarter on performance as well, a very few to be rated in the second quarter, and fewer still (or perhaps none at all) to be rated in the third or fourth quarters. This is because the relationship between the two sets of scores is so nearly perfect as to almost appear in ascending or descending order. The person with the fifth highest predictor score may have the sixth highest criterion score. Therefore, if we take the top fourth of the predictor scores, we may get very close to the top fourth of the criterion scores as well.

Accuracy and the Standard Error of the Estimate. The number of persons for whom statistically calculated predictions are wrong, and the amount by which estimates are in error, are reflected in the standard error of estimate. When validity is perfect, the standard error of estimate is zero; when validity is reduced, the stan-

dard error of estimate increases. The degree to which the standard error of estimate is reduced concerns an improvement over a chance occurrence of a prediction. In this sense, large validity coefficients (i.e., correlation coefficients—r's) are necessary; it takes a very large r to reduce the standard error of estimate enough to get, for example, a 50 percent improvement in the probability that a prediction was due to a real association between a predictor and a criterion and was not due to chance.

What permits us to use tests effectively even though their validity coefficients are considerably lower than we would like? First there is the matter of precision. The standard error of the estimate refers to the amount of error around predictions of precise, specific rankings of each individual on the criterion. In most practical work, such precision is unnecessary. We do not ordinarily need to predict that John Jones will be the nineteenth best performer of a group of twenty-five engineering apprentices. We are far more likely to be concerned with whether or not Jones will be one of the satisfactory apprentices. For these purposes, whether Jones is nineteenth or twenty-third is of little consequence; we can, however, make a confident prediction that he may or may not succeed, even though there may be a large standard error of estimate applicable to the specific rank our formula predicts.

A related factor working in our favor in the practical use of tests is that, as the above explanations note, predictions are most accurately made at the extremes—and it is the extremes that are of greatest interest to us. Few organizations fire as many as half of those they hire. More often, the failures are the bottom 10 percent, 20 percent, or possibly 30 percent, the extremes. In organizational selection, a test of "moderate" validity can be efficient in quickly screening out the "clearly ineligible" from the "clearly eligible." There will remain an indifferent zone of test scores for persons in the "eligible" range; for them, other considerations than paper-and-pencil test scores may determine whether they should be hired. These could include scores on biographical data items, interviews, work samples or simulation, although the statistical progresses remain the same for all scored selection procedures.

Formal tables are available which can be used to estimate expectancies when the validity coefficient is of a given size and the percent of on-the-job successes and failures is known. Table 2 has been constructed from these formal tables to illustrate the usefulness of coefficients of various magnitudes.

The first part of Table 2 is based on a failure rate of 20 percent. It shows the percent of individuals at different levels on a predictor or test who are successful

Table 2. Percent of Successful Individuals in Each Decile on Test Score

Standing on the test		When the total percent of failures is 20%, and				When the total percent of failures is 30%, and				When the total percent of failures is 50%, and			
Percentile	Decile	$r = 0.30$	$r = 0.40$	$r = 0.50$	$r = 0.60$	$r = 0.30$	$r = 0.40$	$r = 0.50$	$r = 0.60$	$r = 0.30$	$r = 0.40$	$r = 0.50$	$r = 0.60$
90–99th	10	92%	95%	97%	99%	86%	91%	94%	97%	71%	78%	84%	90%
80–89th	9	89	91	94	97	81	85	89	92	63	68	73	78
70–79th	8	86	89	91	94	78	81	84	88	59	62	65	69
60–69th	7	84	86	88	91	75	77	80	83	55	57	59	61
50–59th	6	82	84	85	87	72	74	75	77	52	52	53	54
40–49th	5	80	81	82	83	70	70	70	71	48	48	47	46
30–39th	4	78	77	77	78	67	66	65	64	45	43	41	39
20–29th	3	75	73	72	71	63	61	59	56	42	38	35	31
10–19th	2	71	68	64	61	59	55	50	45	37	33	28	22
1–9th	1	63	56	49	40	50	43	35	27	29	23	16	10

Source: The Psychological Corporation, *Test Service Bulletin* 45, p. 11. Reprinted by permission.

performers (in marks earned, or dollar sales, or merit rating, or number of widgets assembled, or whatever we are trying to predict) when the validity coefficient is 0.30, 0.40, 0.50, or 0.60. The columns at the left show the decile rank on the test. Individuals with percentile ranks of 90 to 99 are in the tenth decile or top 10 percent, those with percentile ranks from 80 to 89 are in the next (ninth decile), etc. The first decile includes the individuals between the first and ninth percentiles on the test—the 10 percent who scored lowest. In the third column from the left is shown the percent of persons in each decile who may be expected to succeed when the validity coefficient (r) is 0.30. The next column to the right presents similar expectancy information when r = 0.40, the next column is for r = 0.50, and the last column for a validity coefficient of 0.60.

What does this table tell us? Assume a selection test is given and a correlation of 0.30 is found between scores on the test and success in the first year of work. Ninety-two percent of those who score in the top 10 percent of the group on the test may be expected to succeed, while only 63 percent in the bottom decile (10 percent) can expect to survive the first year. If the validity coefficient is 0.40, ninety-five percent in the top decile may be expected to survive; of the lowest-scoring applicants, 56 percent are likely to survive. The survival rate when r = 0.60 is almost perfect (99 percent) for the top group; it is only 40 percent for the lowest scorers. Notice how the amount of error, or discriminating ability of the test, decreases as the validity coefficient increases, as was explained above. As the validity coefficient approaches evidence of a perfect relationship (i.e. +1.00), between the test scorer and performance, the percentage of people who score highest on the test and who will succeed on the job goes up while the percentage of people who score lowest on the test and will succeed on the job goes down. That is, the higher validity coefficient has a lower error asso-

ciated with it and is evidence that the test scores are better able to discriminate between successful and unsuccessful performers.

The last two sections of Table 2 present similar information for validity coefficients of 0.30, 0.40, 0.50, and 0.60 when failure rates are 30 percent and 50 percent. The last column at the right shows, for example, that if only 50 percent of a total group is successful and the validity coefficient is 0.60, the top scoring individuals will have a survival rate of 90 percent; of those in the bottom decile on the test, only one out of ten is likely to succeed.

It is interesting to compare the figures in the column headed r = 0.50 (when failures total 20 percent) with the quotation stated above regarding the low practical utility of tests with validity coefficients of less than 0.50 which thus have forecasting efficiency of only 13.4 percent. The "only 13.4 percent" sort of statement may be (and often has been) misinterpreted as indicating that the test can tell us little. Actually, the test with an r of 0.50 has improved our picture dramatically. Without it, we could say only that for every person the odds are four chances to one they will succeed because 20 percent is the total percent of failures. With the test of r = 0.50, we can sort the candidates into groups and say that some have distinctly better prospects for success than others. If three people score, respectively, in the tenth, the seventh, and the lowest deciles, we can give odds on their success, as shown in Tables 2 and 3.

What are the practical implications of these facts? Most apparent is the potential utility of validity coefficients of 0.60, 0.50, 0.40, and even 0.30; the information they provide is far from useless. For personnel people in organizations, data such as these provide information with respect to the selection ratios or the percentage of successful applicants to the total hired. The number hired or assessed to assure a certain mini-

Table 3. Estimates of Job Success With and Without Testing

	Our estimate of chances of success without test information (failure rate = 20%)	Our estimate of chances of success with knowledge of test scores ($r = 0.50$; failure rate = 20%)
Person in 10th decile	4 to 1 (80%/20%)	32 to 1 (97%/3%)
Person in 7th decile	4 to 1 (80%/20%)	7 to 1 (88%/12%)
Person in 1st decile	4 to 1 (80%/20%)	1 to 1 (49%/51%)

mum number of successes later can be estimated.

As do all other statistics, standard errors of estimate and validity coefficients require full understanding. Our errors of estimate may always be greater than we would like. The precision of our estimates may be less than perfect and we shall aim constantly to increase that precision. At the same time, if a test will increase appreciably our ability to predict performance (even though broadly), we can still use it—with caution, but with an appreciation for the additional information it supplies. Finally, statistics are *not* a substitute for thinking. A rating or a grade represents a judgment; a test score is a statement of accomplishment on a specified set of tasks. Regardless of how high or how low a coefficient of correlation may be, the following issues always demand consideration:

1. How the judgments were determined;

2. The nature of the test and its relation on the job; and

3. The behaviors, skills, and abilities of the particular group of individuals being studied.

The validity (or correlation) coefficient has been likened to a three-legged stool. One leg is the predictor (frequently a test), another is the criterion (ratings of job performance), and the third is the population on which the coefficient is obtained (grade level, job, family, sex, spread of ability, etc.). One who uses a three-legged stool without ascertaining that all three legs warrant confidence is very likely to be floored!

Personnel Testing and the Law. Recent legislation in the area of equal employment opportunity and discrimination in employment have probably had as great an effect on personnel testing as any personnel program. The general impact of these laws on personnel is noted in various exercises, most notably Exercise 17. Regarding personnel testing, however, the *Myart* v. *Motorola* case, which involved the charge of discrimination against a black job applicant on the basis of intelligence, pointed out the possible misuse of personnel testing.

Along with several other important factors, such as the racial tension and violence in this country during the 1960s, the disposition of Congress and the administration, and the general social climate, the above-mentioned case helped to spawn the passage of the Civil Rights of 1964. This act protected employers' rights to use tests, but not to discriminate with them on the basis of race, color, religion, sex, or national origin. As a result of this law, guidelines issued by federal agencies (e.g., Equal Employment Opportunity Commission [EEOC] and Office of Federal Contract Compliance [OFCC]), and court cases, several standards regarding testing have been set. Certainly many more will be developed through precedent and others changed.

Most of these standards deal with validity, explained above to mean the relation of a test's content to job content or the ability of a test to predict job performance. The laws state that tests are illegal which discriminate on the basis of race, etc., rather than on the basis of ability or merit. A problem is that, due to past differences in opportunity and education, certain groups of people may score low on certain types of tests which are related to job performance—thus these applicants would be kept out of certain jobs (see Fig. 6). In these cases validity data may be required for each such group and often lower cutoff scores are used for certain groups.

The Equal Employment Opportunity Commission (EEOC) has specifically advocated for a considerable period of time the following types of procedures to help avoid discrimination:

1. A total personnel assessment system that is nondiscriminatory within the spirit of the law and places special emphasis on the following:
   a) careful *job analysis* to define skill requirements
   b) special efforts in *recruiting minorities*
   c) *screening and interviewing* related to job requirements
   d) *tests* selected on the basis of specified job-related criteria
   e) comparison of test performance versus *job performance*
   f) *retesting*
   g) tests should be *validated for minorities.*

2. *Objective administration of tests.* It is essential that tests be administered by personnel who are skilled not only in technical details, but also in

establishing proper conditions for test taking. Members of disadvantaged groups tend to be particularly sensitive in test situations and those giving tests should be aware of this and be able to alleviate a certain amount of anxiety.[15]

Besides the *Myart* v. *Motorola* case, the United States Supreme Court has heard three major employment cases. Two of these have affirmed the use of previous *EEOC Guidelines (Griggs* v. *Duke Power* and *Albermarle Paper Co.* v. *Moody)* for both predictor and criterion variables. A more recent case *(Washington, D.C.* v. *Davis)* indicated that empirical validity may not be required if the test appears to be job related (although the test in question did correlate significantly with training success as a criterion).

The controversies surrounding employment testing are certainly continuing and impact on an organization's selection processes greatly. Affirmative action programs—explicit attempts to hire certain groups (Exercise 17)—as well as special training programs are extremely helpful. The most effective procedures for compliance with the laws regarding testing, however, are rigorous validation practices to insure that each test is predictive of job performance in a certain job and for a certain group of job applicants.

Summary. In this *Introduction* we have attempted to present the basic issues regarding validity and reliability of personnel selection tests. It is obvious that even the most basic explanation must involve the use of some statistical terms and concepts, for much of the definition of validity is formulated in these terms.

The selection techniques used by an organization, including psychological test scores, interview responses, etc., in order to form a rationale for selection decisions must be validated in some way, not only due to legal requirements, but also due to the needs of the organization to have a clear picture of the relationship of responses from selection techniques to actual job performance and the accuracy of its techniques to predict subsequent performance. Only then can rational cost/ benefit analyses be conducted as to the "worth" of each selection device or, for example, the logic of allocating resources to develop a certain test. The effectiveness of any predictor is measured, in the final analysis, by its predictive accuracy as compared to other competing predictors, or to using none at all. For some jobs and some applicant populations, a very accurate predictor

would not seem economical to develop. For example, for some entry-level, unskilled jobs, very gross predictors, such as physical ability, might be sufficient and resources would be better allocated to training and motivation programs in order to assure successful performance once hired. But in selecting a vice-president of finance or a chief of neurosurgery, sophisticated and more costly selection devices would seem warranted. We typically would attempt to select the best vice-president of finance from among all candidates and then assume he or she has the ability to succeed without formal training. But we might select those people among candidates for a stock clerk job with the minimum qualifications and then train them to perform successfully on the job.

The key issues in any discussion regarding validity and testing are the predictors (i.e., test scores, interview responses, biographical items, etc.) and their relation to the criteria (i.e., job success as measured by performance appraisal formats, profit, sales, number of accidents, etc.) via a validity coefficient (i.e., a correlation coefficient of range -1.00 to $+1.00$). Validity can be calculated using empirical data in the predictive and concurrent models explained earlier, or by expert judgment in the content-validity model. Reliability of a selection device refers not only to its ability to produce consistent results over time, but also to its ability to predict accurately. Accurate prediction, of course, is a relative concept which depends on many factors, such as the nature and size of the sample of applicants, the cost and nature of the predictor(s), the size of the validity coefficient, the nature and importance of the job, the degree to which we can accurately define and identify job success, and other factors of a judgmental nature. Thus, as was noted above, the statistical techniques briefly reviewed here are seen merely as tools that may help us to improve our predictive ability in personnel selection, point out weaknesses in our predictors, and help us make practical decisions regarding the number of job applicants to assess.

As Fig. 7 depicts, regardless of any statistical analysis at all, we would, of course, be more confident that our predictor is useful the closer its content approaches the actual job content. Thus the predictors near the top of Fig. 7 would, from a practical viewpoint, seem to be very useful because performance on them is so close to performance on the job. Of course, developing job-content-related predictors is sometimes difficult (i.e., for very technical jobs requiring specific skills not possessed by most applicants) and costly, and the other predictors, such as general traits and abilities, are also important determinants of job success.

The selection strategy thus typically reduces to

[15] Equal Employment Opportunity Commission, *Guidelines on Employment Testing Procedures,* August 24, 1966, pp. 3–4. United States Government Printing Office, 1967, 0–302–505(403).

the process of gathering as much relevant, job-related information as possible regarding a job applicant, while considering the cost of developing each additional selection device or predictor, its predictive accuracy, the nature and importance of the job itself, and the relative costs of a sophisticated training versus selection program.

It should be repeated that the selection strategies outlined here, the validity and reliability considerations, and the statistical concepts all also apply to interviews, biographical items, work sampling, simulations, and other predictors or selection devices, as well as to psychological tests, as shown in the figure on page 168. Finally, the *Introduction* of this exercise has concentrated not only on psychological (e.g., pencil-and-paper) tests in its discussions of validity and accuracy, but has concentrated on test-score interpretation rather than test design. The latter, of course, is also a very important issue and must be dealt with as questions for tests are developed from job-analysis data in order to be job-related, and hence relevant and credible, as well as predictive of subsequent job success.

Finally, we close this section on employee selection by stating three basic reasons for doing the best selection job possible. First, we believe it is right and fair to all who may apply for a position in an organization. Second, the organization will benefit in terms of productivity by having the most-capable employees (and, ultimately, consumers will benefit also). Third, by not giving proper attention to selection decisions, an organization opens itself to costly litigation.

PROCEDURE

Overview. In Part A you will make scatter diagrams showing relations between test scores and performance. In Part B you will calculate the reliability of a test using sample data provided. In Part C you will compute the standard error of measurement, estimate "true" scores, and develop confidence intervals for true scores. In Part D you will be asked to determine the criterion-related validity of a test. The statistical computations to be used in this exercise are explained in the *Appendix*.

PART A

STEP 1: Form 1 describes the subscales which may be obtained from the GATB (General Aptitude Test Battery), an instrument developed by the United States Employment Service and used by many state employment offices. Form 2 contains fictitious GATB scores for 45 persons on four of these subscales: Finger Dex-

terity, Computations, Arithmetic, and Three-Dimensional Space. The persons hold the position of Draftsperson I. At the time that the tests were administered, each employee was also rated on job performance by his or her supervisor. For each test, make a scatter diagram showing the relation between the test score and performance. Be sure to number and title each figure. Then convert each scatter diagram into a quadrant chart (see Fig. 6) by drawing appropriate vertical and horizontal lines on each chart at the medians of the predictor and criterion variables. Label and number each chart.

STEP 2: Write responses about Step 1 in preparation for presenting these to the organization's Vice President for Administration.
a) What is the purpose of the project?
b) Describe the sample, and tell what we do not know about the sample.
c) Describe the tests given.
d) Explain the criterion measure used.
e) Discuss the type of validity investigated.
f) Discuss the results for validity of each test. Which tests would you use for actual selection based on the results?
g) How much error is there in these predictions? How would it be calculated? How could it be reduced?

TIME: About 1 hour.

PART B

STEP 3: Form 3 contains the test results of a 40-item, tailor-made test given to a group of machinists. The scores have been divided into results on the 20 odd and the 20 even items. You are to apply the split-half method of test reliability and the Spearman–Brown prophecy formula (discussed in the *Appendix*) to the data and present a brief report on whether the test is reliable enough to use as a selection tool. (Hint: assess the probability that your resulting reliability was due to chance.)

STEP 4: There is also a formula, given in the *Appendix*, that is to be used with the split-half reliability method which would indicate the number of questions that should be added to a test in order to obtain a desired level of reliability. You are to calculate the desired number of questions needed on a test to give a reliability of .90.

TIME: About 1½ hours.

PART C

STEP 5: After reliability coefficients of tests have been calculated, the tester is often interested in the standard error of measurement (SE_{meas}). Because there is always some error involved in testing (i.e., from poor questions, poor conditions, characteristics of the test taker's effort, etc.), we know that the test score a person gets may not be their "true" score—their score if the test, the conditions, etc., were perfect. We often want to know how far away the obtained test score might be from this "true" score and what probability we could assign to the event of the true score being within a certain range around the obtained score. The SE_{meas} is a value, based on the variance (s^2) and the reliability (r) of a test, which helps to determine an interval about the "true" score.

Form 4 asks you to compute the standard error of measurement, based on the Spearman–Brown corrected reliability coefficient obtained in Part B. Then, you are to compute estimated "true" scores and are to use the SE_{meas} to compute intervals for these "true" scores.

TIME: About 1 hour.

PART D

STEP 6: Using Form 5 you are to validate a test. Machinists' supervisors have appraised them on a performance-appraisal scale ranging from 0 (lowest performance) to 100 (highest performance). The results of the performance evaluation and scores on a 40-item selection test for a group of machinists appear as Form 5. Using these sample data and the information in the *Introduction* and *Appendix,* answer the questions on Form 5.

TIME: About 1 hour.

EXERCISE 10 APPENDIX

Learning to Use Statistics in Personnel Decision-Making

1. When one desires to know the average of any group of values the *arithmetic mean* ($\bar{x}$) can be applied.

2. If, however, one desires to know the *middle* value of a group of values, the *median* (X_{50}) is used. (When a group of values contains extreme cases at the low or high ends of the distribution, the median is a more meaningful measure than the arithmetic mean for the distribution of items.)

3. The *standard deviation* ($\underline{s}$) is used to determine the degree of *dispersion* of values about a sample mean. Approximately 68 percent of the values will fall with one standard deviation above and below the mean of a group of values when the values within the group approximate a normal distribution. Two standard deviations above and below the mean will include approximately 95 percent of the values; and three standard deviations on either side of the mean will include over 99 percent of the values in the distribution.

4. The *standard error of the mean* (SE_{mean}) can be used when one is testing the adequacy or representativeness of a sample, since it indicates how far the *sample arithmetic mean* can be (not *is*) away from the *true mean* of the entire population. Hence, it, like all standard error statistics, is a quality control statistic similar to the standard deviation in that one standard error above and below any statistic involves a predictive range of 68 percent; two above and below, 95 percent; and three above and below, 99 percent, assuming normality.

5. The *standard error of the difference* (SE_{diff}) is used to indicate how far the *difference* between *sample means* can be away from the *true difference* between two population means. Hence, it, too, performs a quality-control function.

6. The *standard error measurement* (SE_{meas}) is used to determine measurement error within a testing instrument. As the reliability of the measure increases, the standard error of measurement decreases. The SE_{meas} can also be used to develop confidence intervals "true" scores.

7. To determine the degree of relationship existing between two paired variables—a *correlation* (r)—a product moment coefficient is used. Its range is + 1.00 (perfect positive association) to − 1.00 (perfect negative correlation). Zero indicates no statistical association.

8. Just as standard error formulas for other statistics have been used for quality-control purposes, so is the *standard error of estimate* (SE_{est}) used to determine how far a predicted point *can be* away from the true estimated point for the entire population.

9. The *regression equation*

$$Y' = a_{yx} + b_{yx}X$$

and/or *line* is used to facilitate the prediction of an unknown point or value within one group of values from a particular known point or value within another set of values.

Statistical Formulas

1. To find the *arithmetic mean (x) of ungrouped information*, which may or may not be arrayed, you:
   a) Add all of the individual values.
   b) Divide the total by the number of individual values.

   These steps are briefly expressed using the symbols below:

   $$\bar{x} = \frac{\Sigma X}{N};$$

   where:

   $\bar{x}$ = Arithmetic Mean

   Σ = Sum of

   X = Values, such as items or test scores

   N = Total number of values

2. To find the *arithmetic mean (x̄) of grouped data:*
   a) Determine the midpoint of each class interval.
   b) Multiply the midpoint of each class interval by the frequency for that specific class interval.
   c) Add all the products found in step b.
   d) Divide the total by the number of individual values.

   These steps are expressed by the following formula:

   $$\bar{x} = \frac{\Sigma(f \cdot MP)}{N};$$

   where:

   $\bar{x}$ = Arithmetic mean

   Σ = Sum of

   f = Frequency (number of values in each class interval)

   $\cdot$ = Multiply

   MP = Midpoint of class interval

   N = Total number of values

3. To find the sample *standard deviation (s) of ungrouped data:*
   a) Calculate the arithmetic mean.
   b) Find the difference between each individual value and the $\bar{x}$. (It does not matter whether the difference is a positive or negative value, since the differences are squared in the next step.)
   c) Square each of the differences obtained.

d) Add these squared values and find their average.
e) Extract the square root of the resulting number.

The formula for the standard deviation of ungrouped information is:

$$s = \sqrt{\frac{\Sigma D^2}{N-1}};$$

where:

s = Standard deviation

Σ = Sum of

D^2 = Individual differences squared

N = Total number of values

$\sqrt{}$ = Square root sign

4. To calculate the sample standard deviation (s) from a frequency distribution:
   a) Find the arithmetic mean.
   b) Find the difference between the midpoint of each class interval and the $\bar{x}$. (It is assumed that the midpoint will represent the average difference of each individual item in the class interval from the $\bar{x}$.)
   c) Square each of the differences obtained.
   d) Multiply the squared results by the frequency for that class interval.
   e) Add the numbers obtained in step d, and then find the average.
   f) Extract the square root of the average.

The formula for the standard deviation of grouped data is:

$$s = \sqrt{\frac{\Sigma f(D^2)}{N-1}};$$

where:

s = Standard deviation

Σ = Sum of

f = Frequency of occurrence

D^2 = Differences squared

N = Total number of values

$\sqrt{}$ = Square root sign

5. To find the *standard error of the mean* (SE_{mean}):

Divide the standard deviation of the distribution by the square root of the number of values in the sample.

The formula for the standard error of the mean is:

$$SE_{mean} = \frac{s}{\sqrt{N}};$$

where:

SE_{mean} = Standard error of the mean

s = Standard deviation

N = Total number of values in the sample

$\sqrt{}$ = Square root sign

6. To compute the standard error of the difference (SE_{diff}):

a) Find the standard error of the mean for each of the two groups.
b) Square each standard error of the mean.
c) Add the squared results of step b.
d) Extract the square root of the resulting number.

Putting these steps into a formula, we have:

$$SE_{diff} = \sqrt{(SE_{mean\ 1})^2 + (SE_{mean\ 2})^2}$$

where:

SE_{diff} = Standard error of the difference

$(SE_{mean\ 1})^2$ = Standard error of the mean of group 1 squared

$(SE_{mean\ 2})^2$ = Standard error of the mean of group 2 squared

The above formula for the SE_{diff} is adequate when the number of values in each group are the same (i.e., when $N_1 = N_2$). When the two groups are of unequal size, the following formula is necessary.

$$SE_{diff} = \sqrt{\left[\frac{\Sigma D_1^2 + \Sigma D_2^2}{N_1 + N_2 - 2}\right]\left[\frac{1}{N_1} + \frac{1}{N_2}\right]}$$

where the subscripts for ΣD_1^2, ΣD_2^2, N_1, and N_2 indicate that group one (1) is being used to find ΣD_1^2 and N_1, while group two (2) is being used to find ΣD_2^2 and N_2.

7. The formula for the t test is:

(1) $t = \dfrac{\bar{x}_1 - \bar{x}_2}{SE_{diff}}$

$= \dfrac{D}{SE_{diff}}$;

(2) $t = \dfrac{D}{SE_{diff}}$;

where:

t = Value of t

$\bar{x}_1$ = Arithmetic mean of group 2

$\bar{x}_2$ = Arithmetic mean of group 2

SE_{diff} = Standard error of the difference

8. To calculate a *median* (X_{50}) from grouped information:

a) Determine the position of the median value by dividing the total number of values by 2. This will tell you in which class interval the median value will be found.
b) Then, use the following formula:

$$X_{50} = L + \frac{n_1}{n_2}\ (i);$$

where:

X_{50} = Median

L = Lower limit of class interval containing the median value

n_1 = Number of values which must be covered in the median class in order to reach the median value

n_2 = Number of values in the median class itself or the frequency

i = Width of the median value

9. The definitional formula for *Pearson Product Moment Correlation* (r) is:

$$r = \frac{\sum_{i=1}^{n}(X_i - \bar{X})(Y_i - \bar{Y})}{\sqrt{\sum_{i=1}^{n}(X_i - \bar{X})^2 \sum_{i=1}^{n}(Y_i - \bar{Y})^2}}$$

A computational formula is:

$$r = \frac{N\Sigma XY - (\Sigma X)(\Sigma Y)}{\sqrt{[N\Sigma X^2 - (\Sigma X)^2][N\Sigma Y^2 - (\Sigma Y)^2]}}$$

10. The basic formula for calculating the *regression line* is:

$$Y' = a_{yx} + b_{yx} \cdot X$$

where:

    Y' = A predicted value on the regression line (the "criterion")

    a_{yx} = A measure of the height of the line on the y axis when $X = 0$

    b_{yx} = The measure of the slope of the line (the coefficient of regression)

    X = The known value (the "predictor")

Computational formulae are:

$$b_{yx} = \frac{N\Sigma XY - (\Sigma X)(\Sigma Y)}{N\Sigma X^2 - (\Sigma X)^2} \; ;$$

$$a_{yx} = \overline{Y} - b_{yx} \cdot \overline{X}$$

Many of you will recognize $Y' = a + bX$ as the algebraic formula for computing a simple straight line. In order to locate the line on a graph, the values of a and b must be calculated. The discovery of these values then makes it possible to find either the height of the line or the predicted Y value merely by inserting the appropriate X value in the equation. Since the formula contains two unknown values, a and b, it is technically known as a simultaneous equation. As such, its solution lies in two steps; for the value of either a or b must be found before the remaining value can be calculated.

However, we can also find the value for b by using standard deviations.

This formula for b is:

$$b_{yx} = r \, \frac{s_y}{s_x}$$

where:

    b_{yx} = The value of b for the regression of Y on X

    r = The coefficient of correlation

    s_y = The standard deviation of the Y variable

    s_x = The standard deviation of the X variable

11. The *standard error of the estimate* SE_{est} is an estimate of the standard deviation of a set of Y's (criteria) which are conditional on a set of X's (predictors). To calculate the SE_{est} we assume that the standard deviations of all the single Y distributions are the same and then compute this standard deviation based on all the scores in the entire distribution. The formulae are as follows:

$$SE_{est} = s_y \sqrt{1 - (r)^2}$$
    (for predicting Y values from known X values)

or

$$SE_{est} = s_x \sqrt{1 - (r)^2}$$
    (for predicting X values from known Y values)

The SE_{est} value allows us to set confidence intervals around a regression line. For example, given any X value, we could predict the corresponding Y value on the basis of the computed regression line. Since we assume that around any such *obtained* Y variable (signified by Y') the *actual* Y values will lie in a normal distribution. The SE_{est} is an estimate of the standard deviation of the original estimate of Y derived from the regression equation. Our estimates of Y' thus can be made within certain limits defined by the value of the SE_{est} and the probability level we choose, indicating our risk of error. If we have chosen the 0.05 level, any estimate of Y' will be within ± 1.96 times the value of SE_{est} from the Y' value obtained from the original regression equation. (This is, of course, because for a normal distribution 95 percent [i.e., 1.00 – 0.05] of the values lie between plus and minus 1.96 standard deviations from the population mean—here the obtained regression line.)

The SE_{est} allows us to compute *actual* maximum and minimum values, at specified probability levels, from *obtained* values for predictors (or criteria) in a regression requation. This is important since the obtained value from a regression equation is always an *estimate* and we might want to know within what range around the estimate the true value would lie (at different probability levels).

12. The formula for the standard error of measurement is:

$$SE_{meas} = s \sqrt{1 - r}$$

where:

    SE_{meas} = the standard error of measurement

    s = the sample standard deviation for the total test (not the standard deviation for either half-test, but the standard deviation for the full test)

r = the reliability estimate for the total test (use r_{SB} if the reliability estimate is based upon the split-half method; see below for an explanation of r_{SB})

13. The Spearman-Brown prophecy formula (r_{SB}) corrects the reliability estimate when it is based upon the split-half method of reliability. It is necessary since the size of each subset of items is only half as large as the original test. Since longer tests are generally more reliable than shorter tests (other factors remaining constant), the full-length test will be more reliable than one of half that length. Thus, to make such a correction, the Spearman-Brown prophecy formula (r_{SB}) is used:

$$r_{SB} = \frac{2 \cdot r_0}{1 + r_0}$$

where:

r_{SB} = Spearman-Brown prophecy formula for reliability

r_0 = the original reliability estimate, calculated by computing a correlation coefficient for the two half-test scores

14. When a particular reliability is desired, more items may be added to the length of the test in an effort to increase the original reliability. Rather than having to immediately develop new items, one can estimate how many items must be added in order to increase the original reliability figure to the desired reliability figure. The formula which gives this estimate is as follows:

$$k = \frac{r_D (1 - r_{SB})}{r_{SB} (1 - r_D)}$$

where:

k = a factor by which the original length of the test must be multiplied to obtain the desired level of reliability. Once k is determined, one must multiply the original length of the test, N, by k to determine the necessary new length of the test.

r_D = the desired reliability of the test.

15. "True" test scores may be estimated from a knowledge of the observed test score. The formula for calculating a true score is as follows:

$$T^{I} = (r) \cdot (X - \overline{X}) + \overline{X}$$

where:

T^{I} = estimated "true" score

r = estimated reliability coefficient (use r_{SB} when appropriate)

X = observed test score

$\overline{X}$ = mean of the set of observed test scores

16. Confidence intervals which estimate a range of "true" scores can also be developed. The intervals are based on the degree of confidence that one wants to have regarding the possible range of the "true" score. Naturally, if a great deal of confidence is desired, the range of the interval will become large. When a test is *perfectly* reliable, the observed value, X, is equal to the "true" score, T. To develop a confidence interval for "true" scores, the following formula is employed:

$$T^{I} - (z) \cdot (SE_{meas}) \leqslant T \leqslant T^{I} + (z) \cdot (SE_{meas})$$

where:

T^{I} = estimated "true" score, defined above

T = actual true score

SE_{meas} = the standard error of measurement

z = a z-value obtained from the standard normal distribution table. Usually, the desired confidence will be .90, .95, or .99, in which case the corresponding value for z will be 1.64, 1.96, or 2.58, respectively.

Table of t Values[a], [b]

Degrees of freedom N^c	Probability Values		
	0.10	0.05	0.01
15	1.75	2.13	2.95
15	1.75	2.13	2.95
16	1.75	2.12	2.92
17	1.74	2.11	2.90
18	1.73	2.10	2.88
19	1.73	2.09	2.86
20	1.72	2.09	2.84
21	1.72	2.08	2.83
22	1.72	2.07	2.82
23	1.71	2.07	2.81
24	1.71	2.06	2.80
24	1.71	2.06	2.80
25	1.71	2.06	2.79
26	1.71	2.06	2.78
27	1.70	2.05	2.77
28	*1.70*	*2.05*	*2.75*
28	1.70	2.05	2.76
29	1.70	2.04	2.76
30	1.70	2.04	2.75
35	1.69	2.03	2.72
40	1.68	2.02	2.71
45	1.68	2.02	2.69
50	1.68	2.01	2.68
60	1.67	2.00	2.66
70	1.67	2.00	2.65
80	1.66	1.99	2.64
90	1.66	1.99	2.63
100	1.66	1.98	2.63
125	1.66	1.98	2.62

[a] Same as critical ratio.
[b] Derived from R. A. Fisher's *Statistical Methods for Research Workers*.
[c] DF = $N^1 - 1 + N_2 - 1$.
Note: This is a two-tail test. For directional probability (one-tail), divide the probability value by 2. Above 50 degrees of freedom this table becomes a z table.

Table of r Values (two variables)

N	Probability Values*	
	0.05	0.01
10	0.63	0.75
15	0.51	0.63
20	0.44	0.57
25	0.39	0.51
30	0.36	0.46
35	0.33	0.43
40	0.31	0.40
45	0.29	0.38
50	0.28	0.29
50	0.28	0.29
75	0.23	0.29
100	0.19	0.25
200	0.15	0.18

*r values listed are statistically significant for the appropriate N and confidence level on a one-tail test.

Table of Squares and Square Roots of the Numbers from 1 to 100

Number	Square	Square root	Number	Square	Square root	Number	Square	Square root
1	1	1.000	41	16 81	6.403	81	65 61	9.000
2	4	1.414	42	17 64	6.481	82	67 24	9.055
3	9	1.732	43	18 49	6.557	83	68 89	9.110
4	16	2.000	44	19 36	6.633	84	70 56	9.165
5	25	2.236	45	20 25	6.708	85	72 25	9.220
6	36	2.449	46	21 16	6.782	86	73 96	9.274
7	49	2.646	47	22 09	6.856	87	75 69	9.327
8	64	2.828	48	23 04	6.928	88	77 44	9.381
9	81	3.000	49	24 01	7.000	89	79 21	9.434
10	1 00	3.162	50	25 00	7.071	90	81 00	9.487
11	1 21	3.317	51	26 01	7.141	91	82 81	9.539
12	1 44	3.464	52	27 04	7.211	92	84 64	9.592
13	1 69	3.606	53	28 09	7.280	93	86 49	9.644
14	1 96	3.742	54	29 16	7.348	94	88 36	9.695
15	2 25	3.873	55	30 25	7.416	95	90 25	9.747
16	2 56	4.000	56	31 36	7.483	96	92 16	9.798
17	2 89	4.123	57	32 49	7.550	97	94 09	9.849
18	3 24	4.243	58	33 64	7.616	98	96 04	9.899
19	3 61	4.359	59	34 81	7.681	99	98 01	9.950
20	4 00	4.472	60	36 00	7.746	100	100 00	10.000
21	4 41	4.583	61	37 21	7.810			
22	4 84	4.690	62	38 44	7.874			
23	5 29	4.796	63	39 69	7.937			
24	5 76	4.899	64	40 96	8.000			
25	6 25	5.000	65	42 25	8.062			
26	6 76	5.099	66	43 56	8.124			
27	7 29	5.196	67	44 89	8.185			
28	7 84	5.292	68	46 24	8.246			
29	8 41	5.385	69	47 61	8.307			
30	9 00	5.477	70	49 00	8.367			
31	9 61	5.568	71	50 41	8.426			
32	10 24	5.657	72	51 84	8.485			
33	10 89	5.745	73	53 29	8.544			
34	11 56	5.831	74	54 76	8.602			
35	12 25	5.916	75	56 25	8.660			
36	12 96	6.000	76	57 76	8.718			
37	13 69	6.083	77	59 29	8.775			
38	14 44	6.164	78	60 84	8.832			
39	15 21	6.245	79	62 41	8.888			
40	16 00	6.325	80	64 00	8.944			

FOR FURTHER READING[16]

American Psychological Association and American Educational Research Association, National Council on Measurement in Education. *Standards for Educational and Psychological Tests*. Washington, D.C.: The American Psychological Association, 1975. (II)

American Psychological Association, *Principles for the Validation and Use of Personnel Selection Procedures*. Washington, D.C.: The American Psychological Association, 1975. (II)

Anastasi, A. *Psychological Testing*. 3d ed. New York: Macmillan, 1975. (II)

Anvey, R. D. Fairness in Selecting Employees. Reading, Mass.: Addison-Wesley, 1979. (II)

Ash, D., and L. P. Kroeker. "Personnel Selection, Classification and Placement," *Annual Review of Psychology* 26 (1975): 481–501. (II)

Barrett, R. S. "Gray Areas in Black and White Testing." *Harvard Business Review* 46 (January–February 1968): 92–95. (I)

Bartlett, C. J., and B. S. O'Leary. "A Differential Prediction Model to Moderate the Effects of Heterogeneous Groups in Personnel Selection and Classification." *Personnel Psychology* 22 (1969): 1–17. (II–R)

Bobko, P., and C. J. Bartlett. "Subgroup Validities: Differential Definitions and Differential Prediction," *Journal of Applied Psychology* 63, no. 1 (1979): 12–14. (II–R)

Boehm, V. R. "Populations, Preselection, and Practicalities: A Reply to Hunter and Schmidt," *Journal of Applied Psychology* 63, no. 1 (1979): 15–18. (II–R)

Bray, D. W., and J. L. Moses. "Personnel Selection." *Annual Review of Psychology* 23 (1972): 545–576. (II)

Brown, S. H. "Validity Distortions Associated with a Test in Use." *Journal of Applied Psychology* 64, no. 4 (1979): 460–462. (II–R)

Buros, O. K., ed. *The Seventh Mental Measurements Yearbook*. Highland Park, New Jersey: Gryphon, 1972. (II)

Byham, W. C., and M. E. Spitzer. *The Law and Personnel Testing*. New York: Amacom, 1971. (I)

Campbell, D. T., and D. W. Fiske. "Convergent and Discriminant Validation by the Multitrait-Multimethod Matrix." *Psychological Bulletin* 56 (1959): 81–105. (II)

Civil Rights Act of 1964, Title VII. (II)

Cronbach, L. J., and G. C. Gleser. *Psychological Tests and Personnel Decisions*. Urbana: University of Illinois Press, 1965. (II)

Cronbach, L. J., and P. E. Meehl. "Construct Validity in Psychological Tests." *Psychological Bulletin* 52 (1955): 281–302. (II–R)

Dick, W., and N. Hagerty. *Topics in Measurement: Reliability and Validity*. New York: McGraw-Hill, 1971. (I)

Dunnette, M. D. "A Modified Model for Test Validation and Selection Research." *Journal of Applied Psychology* 47 (1963): 317–323. (II)

Dunnette, M. D., and W. C. Borman. "Personnel Selection and Classification Systems." *Annual Review of Psychology* 30 (1979): 477–525. (II)

Equal Employment Opportunity Commission. "Guidelines on Employment Selection Procedures." *Federal Register* 35 (1970): 48–52. (I)

Fincher, C. "Differential Validity and Test Bias." *Personnel Psychology* 43, no. 166 (1978): 38290–38315. (II)

Fincher, C. "Personnel Testing and the Law." *American Psychologist* 28 (1973): 489–497. (II)

French, W. "Psychological Testing: Some Problems and Solutions." *Personnel Administration* (March–April 1966): 19–24. (I)

Gael, S., D. L. Grant, and R. J. Ritche. "Employment Test Validation for Minority and Nonminority Clerks with Work Sample Criteria." *Journal of Applied Psychology* 60 (1975): 420–426. (II–R)

Ghiselli, E. E. *The Validity of Occupational Aptitude Tests*. New York: Wiley, 1966. (II–R)

Grant, D. L. *Issues in Personnel Psychology* 11 (1980): 369–384. (II)

Gross, A. L., and S. Wen-Lerey. "Defining "Fair" or "Unbiased" Selection Models: A Question of Utilities." *Journal of Applied Psychology* 60, no. 3 (1975): 345–351. (II–R)

Guilford, J. P. "Reliability and Validity of Measures." In J. P. Guilford, *Psychometric Methods*. New York: McGraw-Hill, 1954, Chap. 14. (II–R)

Guion, R. M. "'Content Validity' in Moderation." *Personnel Psychology* 31 (1978): 205–213. (II)

Guion, R. M. "Scoring of Content Domain Samples: The Problem of Fairness." *Journal of Applied Psychology* 63 (1978): 499–506. (II–R)

Guion, R. M. "Content Validity—The Source of My Discontent." *Applied Psychological Measurement* 1, no. 1 (1977): 1–10. (II)

Guion, R. M. "Open a New Window: Validities and Values in Psychological Measurement." *American Psychologist* 29 (1974): 287–296. (II)

Guion, R. M. *Personnel Testing*. New York: McGraw-Hill, 1965. (II)

---

[16] See also, *For Further Reading*, Exercise 13.

Guion, R. M. "Synthetic Validity in a Small Company: A Demonstration." *Personnel Psychology* 18 (1965): 49–63. (II–R)

Hess, L. R. "Synthetic Validity: A Means of Meeting EEOC Test Validation Requirements:" *Training and Development Journal* 27, no. 2 (1973): 48–52. (II–R)

Hills, F. S. "Job Relatedness vs. Adverse Impact in Personal Decision Making." *Personnel Journal* 59 (March 1980): 211–216. (I)

International Personnel Management Association. *Catalogue of Personnel Tests.* Chicago: IPMA, 1975. (I)

Koenig, P. "They Just Changed the Rules on How To Get Ahead. Field Report on Psychological Testing and Job Applicants." *Psychology Today* 8 (June 1974): 87–96+. (I)

Kulhovy, R. W. "Personnel Testing: Validating Selection Instruments." *Personnel* 48 (September–October 1971): 20–24. (I)

Lawshe, C. H., and M. J. Balma. *Principles of Personnel Testing.* New York: McGraw-Hill, 1966. (II)

McNemar, A. "On So-Called Test Bias." *American Psychologist* 30 (1975): 848–851. (II)

Miner, M. G., and J. B. Miner. *Employee Selection Within the Law.* Washington, D.C.: Bureau of National Affairs, 1978. (II)

Mobley, W. H. "Meeting Government Guidelines on Testing and Selection." *The Personnel Administrator* 19, no. 8 (1974): 42–48. (I)

Nunnally, J. C. *Psychometric Theory.* 2d ed. New York: McGraw-Hill, 1978. (II)

O'Conner, E. J., K. N. Wexley, and R. A. Alexander. "Single-Group Validity: Fact or Fallacy." *Journal of Applied Psychology* 60 (1975): 352–355. (II–R)

O'Leary, L. R. "Fair Employment, Sound Psychometric Practice, and Reality." *American Psychologist* 28 (1973): 147–150. (II)

Osburn, H. G., and W. R. Manese. *How to Install and Validate Employee Selection Techniques.* Washington, D.C.: American Petroleum Institute, 1971. (I)

Punke, H. H. "The Relevance and Broadening Use of Personal Testing." *Labor Law Journal* 25 (March 1974): 173–187. (I)

Rawls, J. E., and D. J. Rawls. "Recent Trends in Management Selection." *Personnel Journal* 53, no. 2 (1974): 104–109. (I)

Reilly, R. R., Zedeck, and M. L. Tenopyr. "Validity and Fairness of Physical Ability Tests for Predicting Performance in Craft Jobs," *Journal of Applied Psychology* 64 (1979): 262–274. (II–R)

Robertson, D. E. "Employment Testing and Discrimination." *Personnel Journal* 54, no. 1 (1975): 18–21+. (I)

Sandman, B., and F. Urban. "Formal Testing and the Law." *Labor Law Review,* January 1976. (I)

Schmidt, F. L. et al. "Further Tests of the Schmidt-Hunter Bayesian Validity Generalization Procedure." *Personnel Psychology* 32 (1979): 257–281. (II–R)

Schneier, C. E. "Content Validity: The Necessity of a Behavioral Job Description." *The Personnel Administrator* 21 (February 1976): 38–44. (I)

Thyne, J. M. *Principles of Examining.* New York: Wiley, 1974. (II)

Wallace, S. R. "How High the Validity." *Personnel Psychology* 27 (1974): 397–407. (II)

Walsh, R. J., and L. R. Hess. "The Small Company, EEOC, and Test Validation Alternatives: Do You Know Your Options?" *Personnel Journal* 53, no. 11 (1974): 840–845. (I)

Whyte, W. H. *The Organization Man.* New York: Simon and Schuster, 1956. (I)

Wiener, J., and M. L. Schneiderman. "Use of Job Information as a Criterion in Employment Decisions of Interviewers." *Journal of Applied Psychology* 59 (1974): 699–704. (II–R)

PART A

Form 1 Aptitudes Measured by the GATB

The nine aptitudes measured by the GATB are listed below. The letter used as symbol to identify each aptitude and the part or parts of the GATB measuring each aptitude are also shown.

Aptitude	Tests
G—Intelligence	Part 3—Three-Dimensional Space Part 4—Vocabulary Part 6—Arithmetic Reason
V—Verbal Aptitude	Part 4—Vocabulary
N—Numerical Aptitude	Part 2—Computation Part 6—Arithmetic Reason
S—Spatial Aptitude	Part 3—Three-Dimensional Space
P—Form Perception	Part 5—Tool Matching Part 7—Form Matching
Q—Clerical Perception	Part 1—Name Comparison
K—Motor Coordination	Part 8—Mark Making
F—Finger Dexterity	Part 11—Assemble Part 12—Disassemble
M—Manual Dexterity	Part 9—Place Part 10—Turn

The following are the definitions of the nine aptitudes measured by the GATB:

G—Intelligence—General learning ability. The ability to "catch on" or understand instructions and underlying principles; the ability to reason and make judgments. Closely related to doing well in school. Measured by Parts 3, 4, and 6.

V—Verbal Aptitude—The ability to understand meaning of words and to use them effectively. The ability to comprehend language, to understand relationships between words and to understand meanings of whole sentences and paragraphs. Measured by Part 4.

N—Numerical Aptitude—Ability to perform arithmetic operations quickly and accurately. Measured by Parts 2 and 6.

S—Spatial Aptitude—Ability to think visually of geometric forms and to comprehend the two-dimensional objects. The ability to recognize the relationships resulting from the movement of objects in space. Measured by Part 3.

P—Form Perception—Ability to perceive pertinent detail in objects or in pictorial or graphic material. Ability to make visual comparisons and discriminations and see slight differences in shapes and shadings of figures and widths and lengths of lines. Measured by Parts 5 and 7.

Q—Clerical Perception—Ability to perceive pertinent detail in verbal or tabular material. Ability to observe differences in copy, to proofread words and numbers, and to avoid perceptual errors in arithmetic computation. A measure of speed of perception which is required in many industrial jobs even when the job does not have verbal or numerical content. Measured by Part 1.

K—Motor Coordination—Ability to coordinate eyes and hands or fingers rapidly and accurately in making precise movements with speed. Ability to make a movement response accurately and swiftly. Measured by Part 8.

F—Finger Dexterity—Ability to move the fingers, and manipulate small objects with the fingers, rapidly or accurately. Measured by Parts 11 and 12.

M—Manual Dexterity—Ability to move the hands easily and skillfully. Ability to work with the hands in placing and turning motions. Measured by Parts 9 and 10.

PART A

Form 1 (continued)

GENERAL APTITUDE TEST BATTERY — Parts

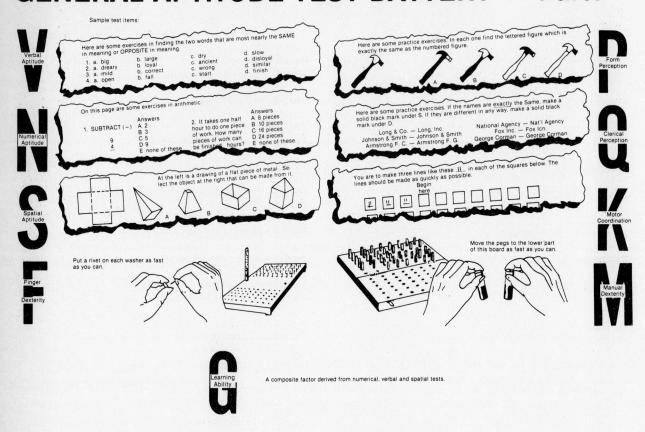

Sample test items:

Verbal Aptitude — Here are some exercises in finding the two words that are most nearly the SAME in meaning or OPPOSITE in meaning.

1. a. big	b. large	c. dry	d. slow
2. a. dreary	b. loyal	c. ancient	d. disloyal
3. a. mild	b. correct	c. wrong	d. similar
4. a. open	b. fall	c. start	d. finish

Form Perception — Here are some practice exercises. In each one find the lettered figure which is exactly the same as the numbered figure.

Numerical Aptitude — On this page are some exercises in arithmetic.

1. SUBTRACT (−)
9
4

Answers
A 2
B 3
C 5
D 9
E none of these

2. It takes one half hour to do one piece of work. How many pieces of work can be finished hours?

Answers
A 8 pieces
B 10 pieces
C 16 pieces
D 24 pieces
E none of these

Clerical Perception — Here are some practice exercises. If the names are exactly the Same, make a solid black mark under S. If they are different in any way, make a solid black mark under D.

Long & Co. — Long, Inc.
Johnson & Smith — Johnson & Smith
Armstrong F. C. — Armstrong F. G.

National Agency — Nat'l Agency
Fox Inc. — Fox Icn.
George Corman — George Corman

Spatial Aptitude — At the left is a drawing of a flat piece of metal. Select the object at the right that can be made from it.

Motor Coordination — You are to make three lines like these in each of the squares below. The lines should be made as quickly as possible. Begin here

Finger Dexterity — Put a rivet on each washer as fast as you can.

Manual Dexterity — Move the pegs to the lower part of this board as fast as you can.

Learning Ability (G) — A composite factor derived from numerical, verbal and spatial tests.

Source: *Test Development Guide*, U.S. Dept. of Labor Manpower Admin.

PART A

Form 2 GATB Scores and Employee Performance

Subject #	Job performance	Test			
		Finger dexterity	Compu-tation	Arithmetic reasoning	Three-dimensional space
1	24	22	11	33	2.4
2	30	23	11	28	2.0
3	28	16	14	40	2.8
4	22	16	18	34	3.1
5	14	21	17	41	3.0
6	36	21	17	41	3.7
7	27	20	18	38	3.2
8	28	10	11	33	3.5
9	26	17	11	26	1.4
10	24	15	17	36	2.8
11	22	23	12	38	2.8
12	26	25	12	38	2.7
13	26	29	13	38	2.2
14	26	15	16	43	3.0
15	21	11	15	39	1.7
16	26	28	20	35	2.6
17	20	14	16	38	2.8
18	18	09	14	38	2.0
19	30	17	23	46	2.6
20	31	29	07	27	1.3
21	25	17	15	44	3.8
22	19	17	16	42	2.6
23	22	23	15	40	2.4
24	23	24	13	29	1.6
25	35	15	10	30	2.0
26	14	06	03	35	1.6
27	23	27	18	39	2.8
28	16	15	13	33	1.8
29	30	23	18	41	3.5
30	34	14	18	36	2.8
31	24	29	17	31	4.0
32	24	21	23	42	3.3
33	26	23	15	36	3.6
34	32	13	18	41	2.8
35	24	16	14	40	2.7
36	21	24	06	23	1.3
37	21	15	18	41	3.3
38	36	23	17	33	3.0
39	23	17	05	29	2.7
40	27	27	21	37	2.4
41	26	25	23	40	3.4
42	23	17	17	37	3.0
43	29	27	14	37	2.5
44	30	30	12	31	2.3

PART B

Form 3 Sample Data for Split-Half Reliability Computation

Employee	Odd scores (20 items)	Even scores (20 items)	Totals
A	90	80	170
B	85	65	150
C	84	80	164
D	83	75	158
E	81	75	156
F	95	60	155
G	92	80	172
H	94	70	164
I	93	90	183
J	98	90	188
K	97	95	192
L	97	90	187
M	60	60	120
N	66	50	116
O	68	60	128
P	70	68	138
Q	74	70	144
R	74	36	110
S	81	75	156
T	81	80	161

Split-Half Reliability Estimates:

1. Find the sample means and standard deviations for the odd and even scores given above.

2. Find the correlation between the two sets of scores using the correlation coefficient (*r*) formula given in the *Appendix*. This correlation becomes your *initial* split-half reliability estimate for the test.

3. Find the reliability estimate for the total test as corrected by the Spearman–Brown Prophecy Formula, also given in the *Appendix*.

4. Determine the number of items the test should be increased to in order to achieve a reliability coefficient of .90. See the *Appendix* for the necessary formula for determining the number of items.

Name _____ Group Number _____

Date _____ Class Section _____ Hour _____ Score _____

PART C

Form 4 Standard Error of Measurement, "True" Scores, and Confidence Intervals

1. Find the standard error of measurement (SE_{meas}) for the total test scores (after combining the odd and even scores for each of the individuals for the full set of 40 items). Use the sample standard deviation for the total test results and the r_{SB} estimate of reliability in calculating the SE_{meas}, the formula for which is given in the *Appendix*.

2. For an obtained total test score of 170, determine the estimated "true" score for this same individual. Use the formula given in the *Appendix* for this estimation.

3. For an obtained total test score of 170, determine a 95 percent confidence interval about the estimated "true" score.

Name _____ Group Number _____

Date _____ Class Section _____ Hour _____ Score _____

PART D

Form 5 Sample Data for Analysis of the Validity of a Test

Employees	Test scores	Performance rating
A	170	75
B	150	52
C	164	50
D	158	60
E	156	75
F	155	70
G	172	80
H	164	75
I	183	85
J	188	82
K	192	90
L	187	80
M	120	50
N	116	50
O	128	60
P	138	40
Q	144	70
R	110	55
S	156	60
T	161	70

Answer the following questions.

1. What is the criterion-related validity for the above test?

2. Using the formula given in the *Appendix*, determine the slope (b_{yx}) of the regression equation for predicting performance ratings from a knowledge of the total test scores.

3. Using the formula given in the *Appendix*, determine the intercept (a_{yx}) where the regression line crosses the y axis.

4. Using the formula given in the *Appendix*, find the standard error of estimate (SE_{est}).

5. Given that a person's test score is 170, determine the performance score that would be predicted for that person, using the regression equation computed above.

Name _____   Group Number _____

Date _____ Class Section _____ Hour _____ Score _____

ASSESSMENT OF LEARNING IN PERSONNEL ADMINISTRATION
EXERCISE 9

1. Try to state the purpose of this exercise in one concise sentence.

2. Specifically what did you learn from this exercise (i.e., skills, abilities, and knowledge)?

3. How might your learning influence your role and your duties as a personnel administrator?

4. What is the difference between statistical and practical significance?

5. Why are reliability and validity such important concepts in personnel administration?

6. How could you evaluate an organization's personnel testing program from a legal perspective? From a cost/benefit perspective? What would be the relationship between these two types of evaluations?

Section 5

BUILDING HUMAN RESOURCE SKILLS: TRAINING AND DEVELOPMENT

Once individuals assume their positions, know what is expected of them (i.e., performance appraisal), and have been chosen with *basic* skills and abilities to do the job (i.e., selection), their performance may not be satisfactory. Training is one method of improving performance, as is motivation (see Section 6). The purpose of training is to provide or upgrade skills to improve performance, and a diagnosis should be conducted to determine if training is needed to resolve present, or avoid future, performance criticisms.

Training and development, like selection, is an activity made necessary because of the dynamic nature of the environment in which organizations exist, as well as by the changes that occur in its human resources. The organization, through its members, must develop new skills over time to remain viable.

Often, training is required immediately after selection, as a selection strategy may have required that applicants be hired and then trained on the job. Perhaps the training-after-hiring decision was made from an economic standpoint. That is, it was thought to be more economical to train after hiring than to commit funds to selection in order to find those applicants who did not require training. Perhaps such applicants would command too high a wage or salary; perhaps they simply did not exist in the labor market.

An organization may also initiate training in order to add skills, abilities, and knowledge to workers, which may be required as technology changes, as a job's scope changes, or as products or services the organization offers change. Perhaps a worker's performance is deficient and remedial training is called for to improve present job performance. Training is also used to improve future job performance as workers are prepared, or "groomed," for promotions. This latter situation is often referred to as the development process—an individual or organization's efforts to upgrade skills, ability, or knowledge in order to facilitate the individual's personal growth in any one of a number of areas. Of course, from the organization's standpoint, it is counting on this investment in employee development to be returned in terms of the person's ability to make greater contributions to the organization in the future.

The organization *and* the individual share responsibility for career development and management. The organization, to protect and enhance its investment in its human resources, must design career "ladders," or paths people can take to assume greater amounts of responsibility, to develop new skills and abilities, and/or to attain promotions. Special training programs to add to a person's skills, abilities, and knowledge, given they are performing their current job satisfactorily, are required. Developmental assignments and staffing decisions may also be used.

The individual, of course, must take initiative in planning his or her own career. A realistic self-analysis to uncover one's strengths, weaknesses, and career interests and objectives is a good first step. Enrolling in various types of training programs, seminars, or workshops is another. Asking for assignments that use or develop additional abilities is also required. An organization can do no more to manage persons' careers than they are willing to do themselves. But increased labor pool mobility, rapidly changing job environments, technological obsolescence, specialization, "professionalism" of many types of occupations, and rising expectations and aspirations of workers make career management and development a necessity for individuals and organizations.

Training is defined most basically as learning; as such, a criterion for effective training is often behavioral change. Whether the organization initiates a skill-development program for entry-level workers operating a punch press or a two-week sensitivity–training session for its top managers as part of an Organization Development (OD) program, behavior change is an ultimate objective. In the former case it could be an increased frequency of punched parts, while in the latter it could be a higher percentage of correct strategic planning decisions.

Training and development are further viewed as a sequential three-phase process. First, training needs must be assessed in order to ascertain whether training would be an effective strategy for the problem at hand (e.g., poor performance, a need for people to fill new positions, etc.). Diagnoses are used to decide who needs training, who would benefit the most from training, and what type of training is required (Exercise 10). Second, training-program objectives are established, hopefully in behavioral terms, training-program content is decided on, training methods are chosen and/or designed, and the programs are implemented (Exercise 10). Finally, training programs must be evaluated as to their effectiveness. Here, the vital question becomes: Did job behavior change as a result of the training and/or development program, and was training implemented at the least possible cost? (Exercise 11). While this question is often a difficult and costly one to answer, it is necessary, for it provides the data used to redesign programs or to argue for their continued use. Careers must be analyzed and managed such that an organization's human resources are developed and utilized effectively (Exercise 12).

Exercise 10
Training and development programs: needs assessment, design, and implementation

PREVIEW

In order for an organization to grow and remain viable in light of changing conditions in its environment, its human resources must adapt to that dynamic environment by continually adding new skills, knowledge, and abilities to their repertoire. In addition, the organization must maintain an internal pool of human resources capable of moving into higher-level positions. It is through training and development programs that the personnel department is able to help upgrade and add to the existing competence level of an organization's labor pool. However, before any training and development program is begun, a thorough assessment of training needs is required. Here the needs of the organization in terms of human resources are made explicit and the current skill and ability levels of people are measured against these needs. Specific deficiencies found would signify not only who needs training, but also exactly what type of training is required.

Once training needs have been assessed, those responsible for training still have many important decisions to make. Among these are the methods to be used in training (e.g., lecture, on-the-job coaching, etc.), the length of the program, who the trainers shall be and how they will be trained, and whether training will take place in the organization or at an external site. These decisions can all be grouped under the category of training-program design and implementation considerations.

In this exercise, data are furnished to enable you to learn how training needs are assessed, and various methods used to train people in organizations are explored.

OBJECTIVES

1. To become familiar with the process and purposes of assessing training needs available.

2. To build skill in diagnosing workers' deficiencies amenable to training and in making decisions as to who should receive training.

3. To increase your awareness of the many types of training methods and their relative strengths and weaknesses.

4. To learn how to identify and write behavioral training objectives and specific target training behaviors.

5. To build skill in training and/or teaching others and evaluating their learning.

6. To build skill in designing effective training programs for entry-level jobs.

PREMEETING ASSIGNMENT

Read the *Introduction* and *Procedure.* Do *not* read beyond Form 6 until told to do so by the Implementor.

INTRODUCTION

Training and Development Programs: Needs Assessment and Design and Implementation

NEEDS ASSESSMENT

Organization, Job, and Person Analyses. If we have defined desired performance in a job and a worker does not perform at the desired level, a possible remedy for the situation may be training. That is, if the person has the basic ability and willingness to do a job well but has not yet acquired the specific skills necessary, training may be required. Before a training program is designed, several vital tasks must be carried out. First, an analysis of the organization's objectives must be conducted in order to determine its short- and long-run goals and needs (see Exercise 2). These goals can then be translated into the performance and skill levels of human resources required in order to meet them. Second, a job analysis (see Exercise 3) is conducted to determine the tasks required to meet goals and the important dimensions of the tasks. Third, current performance levels of workers must be measured by using some type of performance-appraisal technique (see Exercises 4 and 5) in order to pinpoint any deviance from standards and to identify precise areas of performance deficiency. Once these performance measures are made, any deficiencies uncovered are used as the rationale for designing specific training programs to overcome the deficiencies.[1]

Unfortunately, many training programs seem doomed to fail because trainers may be more interested in conducting the training program itself than in first assessing the needs of their organizations and the workers. Educators and trainers in organizations often seem to be seduced by such techniques as programmed instruction or sensitivity training. Because of sophisticated equipment fads, or other inducements, trainers may be willing to use techniques before they have determined the needs of their organization and whether the techniques will meet those needs. Thus, a thorough assessment of both the needs of the organization and current levels of performance is required before a training program's content or training method is decided. Only after the specific deficiencies have been uncovered should funds be committed to training.

Crucial Training Decisions and Alternatives. Typically, the primary concern of the personnel department is not with assessing the organization to determine its overall goals and objectives; this is a responsibility of top management. Personnel specialists would, however, take responsibility for measuring current performance levels in order to identify deficiencies amenable to training. Through appropriate observation, supervisors' evaluations, and diagnostic testing, we can determine whether performance is substandard, whether current employees are capable of benefitting from training, and the specific areas in which they may require training. Also, we need to determine whether current employees with substandard performance can improve their performance through training, or if they should be transferred or terminated to make room for those who can do the job without training. This type of decision involves the weighing of monetary, personal, union contractual, and other considerations. There are alternatives to training that would always be considered. We must consider: (a) whether changes in job design (see Exercise 14) may bring employee performance up to standards; (b) whether new equipment or processes may be a solution; (c) whether incentive programs are needed because employees are able but not willing to perform well (see Exercise 15); (d) whether transfer, demotion, layoff, termination, or some other form of discipline (e.g., a pay cut) is required; or (e) whether training itself is the best course of action.

Job-knowledge tests, work samples, diagnostic psychological tests, performance-appraisal reports, union contract provisions, and workers' employment histories provide the kind of information needed to make these decisions. Of course, assessments of the job and physical environment are also required. For example, one study has shown how tests could accurately identify potential fast and slow workers within one week after beginning work.[2] Thus, those predicted to perform below standard could be trained before their poor performance became detrimental to productivity. But perhaps more importantly, through this type of diagnostic work the organization identified those new workers for whom training was not necessary, and thus saved much in training time and cost.

Another actual example of the importance and utility of training needs assessment involved workers

---

[1] See I. L. Goldstein, *Training: Program Development and Evaluation* (Monterey, Cal.: Brooks/Cole, 1974); D. F. Michalak and E. G. Yager, *Making the Training Process Work* (New York: Harper & Row, 1979).

[2] See W. McGehee, "Cutting Training Waste," *Personnel Psychology* 1 (1948): 331–340.

using precision measuring instruments.[3] These workers were all sent to a specially designed diagnostic center where their proficiencies in the use of a set of these instruments were measured via work samples (see Exercise 8). Following their assessment, only those workers lacking required skills were sent to training, and even these received training only in those particular areas in which they were deficient. Thus, training dollars went to those specific areas where they would be of the most value. Close scrutiny of funds spent on training is an ever-increasing practice as organizations realize the real expense of training programs when all direct and indirect costs are considered (e.g., trainers' salaries, equipment, space, trainees' time, planning time, publicity for the program, evaluation of the program, etc.).

Assessing the Training Needs of New Workers. An instructional or training program must be based on the characteristics of the group to be trained. If the program is intended for those persons already on the job, data from a job analysis, the specification of critical job dimensions, and performance appraisals provide required information. However, if the target population is a new group of employees, performance appraisals would not be available. Thus, it is difficult to assess the performance deficiencies amenable to training of an incoming group of employees. Potential solutions might consist of administering work samples and/or simulations, such as the type discussed in Exercise 8, to hirees, examining employers who have recently hired similar trainees. The latter procedure must be performed carefully, because small differences between organizations can radically change the make-up of the entering population. Thus, two corporations with the same characteristics, but in differing locales or with different reputations, may draw significantly different employees with dissimilar training needs.

Assessment of training needs of new hires can still be made, however, by allowing them to perform on the job for a short period of time and then assessing deficiencies, and/or by inferring from selection data their need for training. For example, the amount of previous experience and formal education might indicate that, if hired, a new worker would require some training.

Of course, the remedy in these cases could also be one of better selection. An organization might decide that rather than hire people who seem minimally qualified, assess their training needs, and train them soon after hiring, they should improve selection procedures in order to attempt to select persons who do not require initial training. This latter strategy is typically adopted in selection for upper-level organizational positions more often than in lower-level positions. We would thus probably expect to select a vice-president who does not require much formal training, but to select clerks or maintenance persons who do.

A further consideration in regard to selection versus training strategies obviously includes the supply of qualified labor in the geographical area in which an organization can attract persons. In areas where qualified labor is in short supply, training and development naturally may become more important. In addition, an organization's Equal Employment Opportunity (EEO) and Affirmative Action Program (AAP) strategies would impact selection versus training decisions (see Exercise 17). For example, if an increase in the proportion of women or minorities is sought in certain managerial job categories, selection may be the only viable strategy in the short run. Training and development would, however, be an effective long-run strategy, as those in lower-level positions would be developed over time to take the managerial positions as they become available.

An analysis of specific training needs is critical—training-program objectives, design, methods, cost, and time frame depend on such an assessment. If organizations are to expect a quick return on their training expenditures, they must know who they are training and why they are being trained. A careful assessment of training needs, backed by a thorough job analysis and performance-appraisal system, provides such information.

DESIGN AND IMPLEMENTATION CONSIDERATIONS

Why Training is Important. Training, defined most basically, is simply an activity to facilitate learning in organizations. While many training activities in organizations may not appear to be similar to classrooms or schools where we assume learning traditionally takes place, their basic objective is the same: to teach or to transmit information, to build skills and abilities, and/ or to change behavior.

Training has become an even more important organization activity in the last few decades. One reason is that the many advances in technology have greatly influenced the work people do in organizations. Because more jobs have become automated and spe-

[3] Lawshe, C. H., Jr., R. A. Bolda, and R. L. Brune, "Studies in Management Training Evaluation: I. Scaling Responses to Human Relations Training Cases," *Journal of Applied Psychology* 42 (1958): 396–398.

cialized and because sophisticated machinery is now often used, workers must possess very specific knowledge and abilities to perform their jobs. Further, as organizations become more complex, jobs become more specialized at all organizational levels. Also, as organizations become more interested in providing a career orientation for their members, skills, ability, and knowledge must be added periodically to members' repertoires through formal training programs to enable individuals to assume higher-level positions as their careers advance. Training and development are vital due to the consequences of age and obsolescence. Rapid changes in technology cause current skills to be outdated, and advances in age can lead to obsolescence unless skills are continually updated through development programs. Finally, to achieve success in many jobs, experience alone is no longer sufficient. As organizations develop their own unique procedures and work processes, employees often must be retained to perform the same job in a new organization that they held in a previous one. This fact, coupled with the high degree of mobility in much of the labor market, makes training increasingly important.

Training as Learning. Organizations do use some training at most job levels to add to or improve members' skills and abilities. Often programs are quite formal and structured, such as entry-level skill training, training for clerical positions, or management training for new college graduates. At other times training is quite unstructured, meant to help participants become aware of their own behavior and its impact on others in groups.[4] If training is essentially learning, even the most informal learning processes—such as a colleague informing someone of the whereabouts of the cafeteria or which secretary not to use for dictation—are essentially training. Discovering new work methods through one's own mistakes or self-study programs could also be considered training. As organizations and job content change and as people aspire to move ahead in organizations, exposure to the proper experience (and people) and adding skills, abilities, and knowledge are important training considerations in anyone's career plans.

Behavioral Objectives. Learning can be defined as "a relatively permanent change in behavior that occurs as a result of practice or experience.[5] The emphasis on

behavioral change is the vital aspect of this definition. In formal organizational training programs, we are interested in facilitating behavioral change—changing poor performance to good performance; adding certain behaviors and perhaps removing others. The key question to ask when considering what a training program's content should be is: What should the trainee be able to do upon completion of the program? Thus, training-program designers must set behavioral objectives for their programs. These objectives would specify what trainees would be able to do if training were successful.[6]

Behavioral objectives help planners focus on the end result of training: behavioral change. Even though the aim of many programs is to transmit information to the trainees (e.g., by lectures and reading programs), the ultimate purpose of even this training is to change trainee behavior on the job as a result of the exposure to new information. Of course, at higher levels of organizations, the exact changes in behavior desired of trainees may be difficult to pinpoint, as jobs are unprogrammed and thus identification of desired job behaviors is difficult and time consuming. For example, we may not always be sure exactly what behaviors we would like managers to change as a result of a seminar on human-relations training. Analysis can produce specific behavioral objectives, even at this level.[7] These might include a reduction in interruptions of subordinates when they are asking questions, giving verbal praise more often, or inquiring whether subordinates are having problems more frequently.

Transfer of Training. If behavioral objectives are set prior to training and if these objectives are similar to those behaviors actually performed on the job, transfer of learning from training environment to job environment is more easily facilitated. Of course, learning is transferred most readily by designing a training program that teaches behaviors *identical* to those required in the job—that is, if report writing is required on the job, training would attempt to build skill in report writing. Transfer is also facilitated by training for understanding of principles; after training, these principles can be applied to actual job situations.

Transfer is further aided if what is learned in training is reinforced on the job. For example, if workers had just finished a training program that taught them how to be more assertive and offered suggestions on

---

[4] See, for example, R. T. Golembiewski and A. Blumberg, eds., *Sensitivity Training and the Laboratory Approach* (Itasca, Ill.: Peacock, 1970).

[5] B. M. Bass and J. A. Vaughan, *Training in Industry: The Management of Learning* (Belmont, Cal.: Wadsworth, 1966), p. 8.

[6] See R. F. Mager, *Preparing Instructional Objectives* (Belmont, Cal.: Fearson, 1962); Michalak and Yager, *Making the Training Process Work.*

[7] See D. Yoder and H. G. Heneman, eds., *ASPA Handbook of Personnel and Industrial Relations,* Vol. 5 (Washington, D. C.: Bureau of National Affairs, Inc., 1977), Chap. 5.

how to perform their jobs better, they may not be able to transfer this learning to the job if their supervisor dictates job procedure and allows no deviance. Clearly, what was learned in training will not be reinforced on the job; new behaviors cannot realistically be transferred. In these cases, training efforts obviously are very inefficient and indicate an improper assessment. That is, the supervisor may be the one who needs training!

Training and Learning Theory. Because training is essentially learning, much learning research and theory is relevant for those designing training programs. Learning theory and research have much to offer trainers regarding the following aspects of learning: (1) the structure of the training environment, (2) the role of the teacher/trainer, (3) the influence of the individual characteristics of the trainee on learning, (4) basic human learning processes, (5) reinforcement and punishment, (6) retention and transfer of learning, and (7) the role of practice in learning.[8] Trainers can become familiar with this research as they develop training course designs and incorporate recommendations based on their findings.

Some of the specific learning principles or concepts that are important considerations in training are:

1. *Practice:* Practice in training is simply performing the training tasks after learning in order to improve proficiency. Practice should be taken seriously by trainees, and inducements to motivate trainees may improve the benefits of practice. Practice should typically be distributed over periods of time, rather than be "massed" at one time, and should include requiring trainees to make responses to stimuli other than those encountered in training, so as to "generalize" their learning.

2. *Feedback:* Feedback, or the knowledge of results of one's effort, is vital in training. Feedback can be positive or negative, but trainees need to know where they stand and whether they are on the right track. Tests, programmed learning, evaluations of trainees by trainers, and observing one's own performance (i.e., by videotape) provide feedback.[9]

3. *Reinforcement:* In operant learning theory, reinstatement is the change in one's environment, or a consequence of behavior, which strengthens the probability of the future occurrence of the behavior that produced the reinforcer. For example, if performing a new task correctly (behavior) produces verbal praise from a trainer, the correct performance may be associated with the (pleasant) outcome and perhaps occur in the future if the verbal praise was rewarding to the person receiving it. Among the many outcomes of behavior occurring in organizations are recognition, money, verbal praise, grades, prizes, and successful completion of the training itself.[10]

4. *Shaping behavior:* Behavior shaping refers to the selective reinforcement of successively approximate performance of a target behavior until the target is duplicated. For example, if a certain task is to be learned, it can be broken into small component behaviors. Each of these is reinforced when it is observed as the trainees come closer and closer to the total completion of the task, until they are finally able to complete the task. In this way, behaviors not previously in one's repertoire can be added to existing behaviors.[11]

5. *Modeling:* Behavior modeling refers to a process beyond reinforcement whereby behavior occurring in others (e.g., supervisors) in the trainee's environment is initiated by the trainee. An assumption is made that many behaviors are learned, either intentionally or unintentionally, for example. Trainees have been shown to learn very quickly from exposure to a model performing the desired target behavior. Videotapes are extremely well suited as a method for this type of approach. Trainees can observe a model or themselves performing, critique the performance, and then attempt the behavior. In addition, trainees receive vicarious reinforcement when the model's behavior is reinforced (e.g., a peer used as a model receives verbal praise for engaging in a behavior being taught in a training program.)[12] Modeling is,

---

[8] See C. E. Schneier, "Training and Development Programs: What Learning Theory and Research Have to Offer," *Personnel Journal* 53 (1974): 288–293, 300; Goldstein, *Training: Program Development and Evaluation.*

[9] See C. P. Latham and J. J. Blades, "The Practical Significance of Locke's Theory of Goal Setting," *Journal of Applied Psychology* 60 (1975): 122–124; A. P. Goldstein and M. Sorcher, *Changing Supervisor Behavior* (New York: Pergamon, 1974).

[10] See Exercise 15 for a more thorough discussion of reinforcement.

[11] C. E. Schneier, "Behavior Modification in Management: A Review and Critique," *Academy of Management Journal* 17 (1974): 528–548; F. Luthans and R. Krietner, *Organizational Behavior Modification* (Glenview, Ill.: Scott Foresman, 1975).

[12] Goldstein and Sorcher, *Changing Supervisory Behavior;* Yoder and Heneman, *ASPA Handbook of Personnel and Industrial Relations,* Chap. 5; T. O'Connor, "How to Set Up, Run, and Evaluate a Training Program Based on Behavior Modeling Principles," *Training* 16 (January 1979): 64–67.

of course, more appropriate for observable psychomotor tasks than for cognitive knowledge.

Obviously, many other relevant issues in learning are also vital to training. Among these are punishment, schedules of reinforcement, verbalization of learning, testing, retention and transfer, and the role of the learning environment. The key point for trainers and personnel administrators designing training programs is that training is learning. Thus, what we know about how people learn should be incorporated into training programs. As a start, training programs for most jobs could be designed which rely on positive reinforcement, allow for practice at proper intervals, break complex tasks into smaller components used as intermediate learning goals, and assess and facilitate trainee interest and motivation.

Training Methods. Many methods can be employed in training programs to facilitate learning. At the managerial level, these have been grouped into information-processing methods, simulation methods, and on-the-job methods.[13] Each category contains several specific methods, including the following:

Information-Processing
    lecture
    conference
    t-group
    laboratory training
    observation
    closed-circuit TV
    programmed instruction
    correspondence courses
    motion pictures
    reading lists

Simulation
    cases
    incidents
    role playing
    business games
    in-baskets

On-the-Job
    job rotation
    committee assignments or Junior Boards
    on-the-job coaching
    feedback from performance appraisal
    apprenticeships

Obviously, some methods are more time consuming, costly, and appropriate for certain jobs than are others. Therefore, how does a training-program designer choose a training method from this large list?

Some of the factors that signal the use of one method over others are the training objectives, trainee characteristics, trainer skill, cost, time, and nature of the job. In addition, the type of learning that will take place (e.g., concept learning, rule learning, problem-solving) would determine the type of method to be chosen. Clearly, a sensitivity-training group or a week-long conference may not be appropriate for a group of unskilled laborers learning simple maintenance jobs—on-the-job coaching may be applicable here. Job rotation, in which some time is spent learning several jobs, could be useful for the young management trainee. Programmed instruction has been found quite effective for learning a complex set of rules or procedures.[14]

Each of the three general types of training methods previously listed has advantages as well as limitations. For example, on-the-job methods are usually inexpensive, as they require no special personnel equipment or space. They are also practical, offer flexibility and control to the organization, and allow for practice. Off-the-job methods eliminate the pressures and restrictions of the work environment. However, transfer of learning is often difficult to assess with these methods.

The Training-Program Designer's Task. The trainers or training-program designers thus have a large task. They must first assess training needs, then formulate behavioral objectives for the training program. Next, they must consider such operating constraints as time, space, and physical and human resources. Their selection of a training method would depend on such factors as nature of trainer, trainees, and the job. Personnel administrators must also decide, in conjunction with others close to the job, the relative amount of organizational time, energy, and money that should be given to training as opposed to selection. Here, other variables, such as labor-market composition, must be taken into account. Administrators must determine when to train—before the job begins, early in the job, periodically as additional skills are needed, and/or at promotion-decision time? Clearly, with a task as multi-faceted as this, no easy answers or guidelines realistically can be offered. Careful thought, analysis, and learning from experience are required.

[13] J. P. Campbell, M. D. Dunnette, E. E. Lawler, and K. Weick, *Management Behavior, Performance, and Effectiveness* (New York: McGraw-Hill, 1970), Chap. 10.

[14] See S. J. Carroll, F. T. Paine, and J. J. Ivancevich. "The Relative Effectiveness of Training Methods: Expert Opinion and Research." *Personnel Psychology* 25 (1972): 495–509.

PROCEDURE

Overview. First, you are asked to review both a description of a training program and four workers' performance records. The candidates are assessed as to their potential to benefit from the training program, and the candidates who are thought to benefit most from the training program are identified. Next, simple tasks are used to compare the effectiveness of two different training methods.

PART A

STEP 1: Divide into small groups. Review the outline of the "Success in Middle Management" training program (Form 1), as well as the information about the middle-management position given in Form 2. Then think about what successful job performance is, as well as what skills would be needed by persons in order to be successful in the middle-management job described in Form 2. For example, does this middle manager need to write many reports? If so, an assumption you would make would be that report writing is a prerequisite for successful performance. Next, determine a set of selection criteria for prospective trainees which would help you decide who should be trained. For example, one such criterion could be that anyone with three years or less of experience could not be considered for training. You will probably want to look over the information about the job given in Form 2, the training program outline (Form 1), and the information about prospective trainees (Forms 3–6) before you develop the criteria.

TIME: About 40 minutes.

STEP 2: In Forms 3–6 you are given fact sheets on four employees who have been recommended by their superior for training for the middle-management position described in Form 2. The position would be a promotion for these employees. Consider each of these candidates and make decisions as to whether each should attend the training program described in Form 1. The two-week program (trainees fly home for the weekend) will cost $550 per week, plus expenses, or a total of about $1,850 per person. The budget will permit only two of the four persons to attend at this time.

The training program is being conducted by a well-known management group (Training Specialists, Inc.) in a resort/retreat setting.

There will be extensive use of many types of techniques, including an assessment center (see Exercise 8). Each participant will also receive a review of his or her performance from the training-program committee. Your organization has used the program in the past, and the participants have been very enthusiastic about it. In fact, the "rumor mill" indicates that entry into this program is almost a sure step to the top.

Make a decision as to whether to send each candidate to the training program and provide reasons for your decisions on Forms 3–6. Assume you will have to present your reasons to each candidate and to his or her superior in a meeting to be scheduled later. Your written rationale (using the bottom of each candidate's fact sheet as a worksheet for your decision making) will also be placed in the candidate's personnel file. Note what additional information, if any, you would require before making this decision, but make the decision on the basis of the information presented. Recommend a different type of training for those candidates whom you feel could benefit from training but not from the program described here.

TIME: About one hour.

PART B

STEP 3: Here you will form into groups of about 6–8 members and compare two methods of training for two simple tasks. First, complete Form 7 which asks for general and specific behavioral objectives for two tasks: tying a necktie and using the Kuder-Richardson formula [K-R] for reliability. Also, specify how you would assess trainee learning on these tasks (e.g., a quiz, by observation, etc.) in column 3 of Form 7.

STEP 4: After you have filled in Form 7, pick four members of your group to act as trainees and then ask them to leave the room or area. You will teach two of them how to do each task by the "on-the-job coaching method." That is, explain to them how to do the tasks according to the objectives you have specified. Show them each step, allow them to perform the step, and critique them, working closely (preferably on a one-to-one basis) with them until they have learned the task.

Teach the other two trainees how to perform the same two tasks by the "lecture" method. That is, write out a set of instructions which trainees read and which explains how to perform each task (tying a tie and using the Kuder-Richardson formula [K–R]) in detail. Use Form 8 or separate sheets to prepare your "lectures." Then present the lecture to the two trainees being trained by the lecture method and allow them to perform the task. An explanation of the second training task (use the Kuder-Richardson formula) is provided (for trainers only) in Form 9. Trainees should be able to use the formula to compute the reliability of a test after training. Trainers may have to supply additional numerical examples for trainees to use the K–R formula.

TIME: About two hours.

STEP 5: Now allow each trainee to perform the tasks while you observe him or her. Record your observations on Form 10. Be sure to score trainees on accuracy, speed, and/or any other criteria you feel relevant. After trainees are evaluated and the evaluations have been recorded on Form 10, answer the questions at the bottom of Form 10 in your small groups. Trainers can compare and contrast the two methods used to train group members.

TIME: About one hour.

FOR FURTHER READING

Addison-Wesley Series in Organization Development. E. H. Schein, R. Beckhard, and W. G. Bennis, eds; various authors. Reading, Mass.: Addison-Wesley. (I)

Aldefer, C. "Change Processes in Organizations." In M. D. Dunnette, ed., *Handbook of Industrial and Organizational Psychology*. Chicago: Rand McNally, 1976. (II)

Argyris, C., and D. A. Schoen, *Organizational Learning: A Theory of Action Perspective,* Reading, Mass.: Addison-Wesley, 1978. (II)

Babb, H. W., and D. G. Kopp. "Applications of Behavior Modification in Organizations: A Review and Critique." *Academy of Management Review* 3 (1978): 281–292. (II)

Bass, B. M. "Quality Standards for 'Ready-to-Use' Training and Development Programs." *Journal of Applied Behavioral Science* 13 (1977): 518–532.

Bass, B. M., and J. A. Vaughn. *Training in Industry: The Management of Learning.* Belmont, Cal.: Wadsworth, 1966, Chap. 6. (II)

Beatty, R. W. "Personnel Systems and Human Performance." *Personnel Journal* 52 (1973): 307–312. (I)

Beatty, R. W., and C. E. Schneier. "Training the Hard-Core Unemployed through Positive Reinforcement." *Human Resource Management* 11, no. 4 (Winter 1972): 11–17. (I)

Beer, M. "The Technology of Organization Development." In M. D. Dunnette, ed., *Handbook of Industrial and Organizational Psychology.* Chicago: Rand McNally, 1976. (II)

Bell, C. R., and F. H. Margolis. "Blending Didactic and Experiential Learning Methods." *Training and Development Journal* 32 (August 1978): 16–21. (I)

Berg, I. *Education and Jobs: The Great Training Robery.* New York: Praeger, 1970. (I)

Blake, R. R., and J. S. Mouton. *Corporate Excellence through Grid Organization Development.* Houston: Gulf, 1964. (I)

Brown, F. B., and K. R. Wedel. *Assessing Training Needs.* Washington, D.C.: Washington National Training and Development Service Press, 1974. (I)

Bugelski, B. R. *The Psychology of Teaching.* 2d ed. Indianapolis: Bobbs-Merrill, 1971. (I)

Burris, R. W. "Human Learning." In M. D. Dunnette, ed., *Handbook of Industrial and Organizational Psychology.* Chicago: Rand McNally, 1976. (II)

Byers, K. T., ed. *Employee Training and Development in the Public Sector.* Rev. ed. Chicago: International Personnel Management Association, 1974. (I)

Campbell, J. P. "Personnel Training and Development." *Annual Review of Psychology* 22 (1971): 565–602. (II)

Campbell, J., M. D. Dunnette, E. E. Lawler, and C. Weick. *Managerial Behavior, Performance and Effectiveness.* New York: McGraw-Hill, 1970. (II)

Catalenello, R. F., and D. L. Kirkpatrick. "Evaluating Training Programs—The State of the Art." *Training and Development Journal* 20, no. 8 (1966): 38–44. (I)

Carroll, S. J., F. T. Paine, and J. M. Ivancevich. "The Relative Effectiveness of Training Methods: Expert Opinion and Research." *Personnel Psychology* 25 (1972): 495–509. (II–R)

Cascio, W. F., and W. F. Phillips. "Performance Testing: A Rose Among Thorns." *Personnel Psychology* 32 (1979): 751–766. (II–R)

Donaldson, L., and E. E. Scannell. *Human Resource Development: The New Trainer's Guide.* Reading, Mass.: Addison-Wesley, 1978. (I)

Dubin, R., ed. *Professional Obsolescence.* Lexington, Mass.: Heath, 1972. (I)

Farr, J. L., B. S. O'Leary, and C. J. Bartlett. "Effect of Work Sample Tests Upon Self-Selection and Turnover of Job Applicants." *Journal of Applied Psychology* 58 (1973): 283-285. (II-R)

Fordyce, J. K., and R. Weil. *Managing with People.* Reading, Mass.: Addison-Wesley, 1971. (I)

Fournier, F. F. *Coaching for Improved Work Performance.* 2d ed. Englewood Cliffs, New Jersey: Prentice-Hall, 1978. (I)

Gagne, R. M. *Learning and Individual Differences.* Columbus: Merrill, 1967. (II)

Gagne, R. M. "Military Training and Principles of Learning." *American Psychologist* 17 (1962): 83-91. (II)

Gallegos, R. C., and J. G. Phelan. "Using Behavioral Objectives in Industrial Training." *Training and Development Journal* 28, no. 4 (April 1974): 42-48. (I)

Goldstein, A. P., and M. Sorcher. *Changing Supervisor Behavior.* New York: Pergamon, 1974. (I)

Goldstein, I. L. "Training in Work Organizations." *Annual Review of Psychology* 31 (1980).

Goldstein, I. L. *Training: Program Development and Design.* Monterey, Cal.: Brooks/Cole, 1974. (I)

Golembiewski, R. T., and A. Blumberg, eds. *Sensitivity Training and the Laboratory Approach.* Itasca, Ill.: Peacock, 1970. (I)

Goodman, P. S., P. Salipante, and H. Paransky. "Hiring, Training, and Retraining the Hard-Core Unemployed: A Selected Review." *Journal of Applied Psychology* 58 (1973): 23-33. (II)

Gordon, M. E. "Planning Training Activity." *Training and Development Journal* 27, no. 1 (1973): 3-6. (I)

Gordon, M. E., and S. L. Cohen. "Training Behavior as a Predictor of Trainability." *Personnel Psychology* 26 (1973): 261-272. (II-R)

Hand, H. H., and J. W. Solcum. "A Longitudinal Study of the Effects of a Human Relations Training Program on Managerial Effectiveness." *Journal of Applied Psychology* 56 (1972): 412-417. (II-R)

Hautaluoma, J. E., and J. F. Gavin. "Effects of Organizational Diagnosis and Intervention on Blue-Collar 'Blues.'" *Journal of Applied Behavioral Science* 11 (1975): 475-496. (II)

Hinrichs, J. R. "Personnel Training." In M. D. Dunnette, ed., *Handbook of Industrial and Organizational Psychology.* Chicago: Rand McNally, 1976. (II)

Huse, E. F. *Organizational Development and Change.* 2d ed. St. Paul: West, 1979. (I)

Johnson, R. B. "Determining Training Needs." In R. L. Craig and L. R. Bittel, eds., *Training and Development Handbook.* New York: McGraw-Hill, 1967, Chap. 2. (I)

Keys, B. "The Management of Learning Grid for Management Development." *Academy of Management Review* 2 (1977): 289-297. (II-R)

Langford, H. "Needs Analysis in the Training Department." *Supervisory Management* 23 (August 1978): 18-25. (I)

Levinson, H. et al. *Diagnosing Organizations.* Cambridge, Mass.: Harvard University Press, 1972. (II)

Mager, R. *Preparing Objectives for Programmed Instruction.* San Francisco: Fearon, 1962. (I)

McGehee, W., and P. W. Thayer. *Training in Business and Industry.* New York: Wiley, 1961. (I)

Mechner, F. "Engineering Supervisory Job-Performance Change." *Training* 15 (6 October 1978): 65-70. (I)

Michalak, D. F., and E. G. Yager. *Making the Training Process Work.* New York: Harper & Row, 1979. (I)

Morgan, C. P., C. E. Schneier, and R. W. Beatty. "Diagnosing Organizations: New Fad or New Technology in Management Consulting?" *Proceedings of the Thirty-Fourth Annual Meeting of the Academy of Management,* Seattle, 1974 (abstract). (II)

Nash, A. N., J. P. Muczyk, and F. L. Veltoni. "The Relative Practical Effectiveness of Programmed Instruction." *Personnel Psychology* 24 (1971): 397-418. (I-R)

Odiorne, C. S. *Training by Objectives.* New York: Macmillan, 1970. (I)

O'Reilly, A. "What Value is Job Analysis in Training?" *Personnel Review* (Great Britain) 2, no. 3 (1973): 50-60. (I)

Pfeiffer, J. W., and J. E. Jones, eds. *Structured Exercises for Group Facilitators.* Iowa City, Iowa: University Associates Press (Annual). (I)

Pinto, P. R. "Your Trainers and the Law." *Training* 15 (October 1978): 71-73+. (I)

Raphael, M. A. "Work Previews Can Reduce Turnover and Improve Performance." *Personnel Journal* 54 (1975): 97-98. (I)

Rummler, G. A., J. P. Yaney, and A. W. Schrader, eds., *Managing the Instructional Programming Effort.* Ann Arbor, Mich.: Bureau of Industrial

Relations, 1967. (I)

Salipante, P., and P. Goodman. "Training, Counseling, and Retention of the Hard-Core Unemployed." *Journal of Applied Psychology* 61 (1976): 1–11. (II–R)

Schein, E. H. "The First Job Dilemma." *Psychology Today* 1 (March 1968): 27–37. (I)

Schneier, C. E., and R. W. Beatty, eds. *Personnel Administration Today.* Reading, Mass.: Addison-Wesley, 1970. (I)

Schneier, E. C. "Training and Development Programs: What Learning Theory and Research Have to Offer." *Personnel Journal* 53 (1974): 288–293. (I)

Skinner, B. F. *The Technology of Teaching.* New York: Appleton-Century-Crofts, 1968. (II)

Spool, M. "Training Programs for Observers of Behavior: A Review." *Personal Psychology* 31 (1978): 853–888. (II)

Triandis, H., J. Feldman, D. Weldon, and W. Harvey. "Ecosystems Distrust and the Hard-to-Employ." *Journal of Applied Psychology* 60 (1975): 303–307. (II–R)

U.S. National Technical Information Service. *Management Games: A Bibliography with Abstracts.* Springfield, Virginia: NTIS, 1975. (I)

Yoder, D., and H. G. Heneman, eds. *ASPA Handbook of Personnel and Industrial Relations* 5 Washington, D.C. Bureau of National Affairs, Inc. 1977. (I)

Zeira, Y. "An Evaluation of a Planned Change Effort through Top Management Training." *Industrial Relations Journal* 6 (1975): 42–52. (I–R)

Zoll, A. *Dynamic Management Education.* 2d ed. Reading, Mass.: Addison-Wesley, 1969. (I)

PART A

Form 1 Training Program Outline for the Course Offered by Training Specialists, Inc. Entitled "Success in Middle Management: An Intensive Training Program for Managers"

PROGRAM OUTLINE

I. *Management Techniques*
- **The Art of Management**
  What is Management?
  Roles of a Manager

- **Planning and Organizing Your Work**
  Planning
      Setting objectives
      Developing a strategy
  Organization
      Principles of organization
      Line vs. staff
      Formal vs. informal

- **Managing Your Time and Delegating Your Work**
  Time
      Cost of poor time management
      Guidelines for good time management
  Delegation
      Factors causing delegation problems
      How to make delegation work

- **Standards of Performance**
  Definition of Standards
  Types of Standards
      Positive
      Negative

- **Performance Appraisal—An Aid to Control**
  Key Questions which Require Answers
  Tools and Techniques of Effective Appraisal

- **The Making of a Decision**

- **Motivation and the Human Side of Management**
  Understanding Human Behavior
  Developing Employee Attitudes
  Motivational Needs of Today's Employees

- **Elements of Effective Communications**
  Written vs. Verbal
  Barriers to Effective Communication

- **How to Further Yourself as a Manager**
  Developing Self-Direction
  Is There a Formula?

- **Union Management Relations**

II. *Special Topics in Operations Analysis*
- **Production Scheduling**

- **Production Standards and Quotas**

- **Establishing a General Maintenance Policy**

- **Inventory Control**

- **Inspection Systems**

- **The Occupational Safety and Health Act (OSHA)**

PART A

Form 2 Middle-Management Position Information

This job is one in a medium-sized publishing and printing organization. There are about thirty upper middle managers, each typically supervising about fifty people each and reporting to vice presidents. They are often plant or division managers. The managers are almost exclusively concerned with the administrative, technical, and manufacturing aspects of the organization. The journalists, writers, editors, and salespersons are separated administratively from these managers. It is a very responsible job, typically one most managers in the organization aspire to, and commands a good salary and excellent benefits, including stock options. These positions are the training ground for those few who reach top management. The middle managers prepare budgets, hire and fire subordinates, supervise other managers, including professional people, and develop new administrative or operating procedures and/or new products. They also develop policies and plans and see to it that the plans are implemented.

Since many of the departments, divisions, or plants operate as "profit centers," these managers would be responsible for profit and cost of their units and for making most strategic decisions regarding production scheduling and standards. A few different unions (e.g., typesetters) are represented, but their contracts with the company are settled centrally, not on a plant-by-plant or divisional basis.

The managers have varied backgrounds and amount of experience. The organization sometimes promotes those young people who show great promise to this position quite early in their careers. However, for those who fail to reach top management positions after being promoted, there is a good chance of "early retirement." Turnover is also high in these positions and they are considered to be quite stress-producing. They typically mean relocation, often in small towns or cities. The move back to corporate headquarters, if it is made, of course involves another relocation to a major East Coast city.

PART A

Form 3 Fact Sheets for Prospective Trainee

Worker No. 1

Name: Sam Horn

Present job: Credit manager and assistant to finance director

Number of subordinates: 6

Years in present job: 2

Years in managerial position: 3

Years with the organization: 5

Age: 38

Education: B.A. in finance

Performance evaluation: Overall, rated "Very Good" (highest level possible).

Rated high in planning, flexibility, motivating others, and

oral communication.

Test scores (based on company norms): High in "initiating structure" (LOQ)*, and

medium to high in "consideration." (LOQ)*

Very high in intelligence.

Assessment center report: Excellent in budgeting, planning, organization, and coordination.

Low on creativity, leadership, and delegation.

Aspiration level: Wants to be president of the company.

Decision: ____ send ____ not send

Reasons:

Alternative type of training recommended:

Other information desired:

* Note: The LOQ (Leadership Opinion Questionnaire) is a widely used instrument to measure leadership style. Initiating structure refers generally to the degree to which a leader feels it important to structure work and tasks for subordinates. Consideration refers generally to the degree to which a leader feels it is important to show warmth, empathy, or support for subordinates.

PART A

Form 4 Fact Sheets for Prospective Trainees

Worker No. 2

Name: Joyce Juice

Present job: Assistant personnel director

Number of subordinates: 51

Years in present job: 4

Years in managerial position: 8

Years with the organization: 15

Age: 39

Education: Business College plus 92 university hours, still working on degree in business management.

Performance evaluation: Highest overall rating possible.

High in interpersonal skills, motivation of others, problem solving.

Very low in coordination and organization.

Test scores: (based on company norms) Typing: 105 wpm.

Intelligence: upper 1/3.

Consideration: top 10%.

Initiating structure: lowest 25%.

Assessment center report: None available (was ill, has been rescheduled).

Aspiration level: Has decided she wants to go as far as she can with the company.

Decision: ____ send ____ not send

Reasons:

Alternative type of training recommended:

Other information desired:

PART A

Form 5 Fact Sheets for Prospective Trainees

Worker No. 3

Name: Helen O'Cool

Present job: Advertising manager; chief of layout and product design

Number of subordinates: 13

Years in present job: 2

Years in managerial position: 3

Years with the organization: 8

Age: 36

Education: B.A., advertising; M.F.A., drawing; M.B.A., marketing

Performance evaluation: Very good on planning, organization, and verbal communication.

Average in delegation.

Low in budgeting, team work. Superior indicated she was very creative.

Test scores: (based on company norms) High in intelligence.

High in initiating structure.

Low in consideration.

Assessment center report: High in risk taking, planning, and organization.

Average to low in flexibility, stress tolerance, problem analysis, and sensitivity.

Aspiration level: She feels she is long past consideration for promotion and is quite dissatisfied with her progress to date.

Decision: ____ send ____ not send

Reasons:

Alternative type of training recommended:

Other information desired:

PART A

Form 6 Fact Sheets for Prospective Trainees

Worker No. 4

Name: Hercule P. Rowe

Present job: Assistant to Vice President of Manufacturing

Number of subordinates: 22

Years in present job: 5

Years in managerial position: 9

Years with the organization: 12

Age: 33

Education: B.A. in English; M.B.A. in management science.

Performance evaluation: High in interpersonal skills, working with others, communication, flexibility, delegation.
Average in planning and organization.
Low in control and budgeting.
Overall rating was "average."

Test scores: (based on company norms) High in consideration.
High in initiating structure.
Above average in intelligence.

Assessment center report: Excellent in sensitivity and creativity.
High in flexibility, energy, risk taking, decision making, independence.
Average in planning and organization.

Aspiration level: Wants to make V.P. in five years.

Decision: ____ send ____ not send

Reasons:

Alternative type of training recommended:

Other information desired:

Name _____   Group Number _____

Date _____   Class Section _____   Hour _____   Score _____

PART B

Form 7 Comparison of Training Methods

General behavioral training objective 1	Specific target training behaviors 2	How will trainee learning be assessed on each target training behavior? 3
Training task 1: Tying a tie		
Tying a knot in a necktie.	1.	
	2.	
	3.	
Training Task 2: Using the Kuder-Richardson 20 (K–R 20) formula for test reliability*		
Learning the K¬R 20 formula and using it to assess the reliability of tests.	1.	
	2.	
	3.	

* See Form 9 for an explanation of the K-R 20.

PART B

Form 8 Worksheet for Lectures

Write your "lectures" for Training Task 1 (Tying a tie) and Training Task 2 (Using the Kuder-Richardson 20 formula for reliability) on the reverse side and/or on additional sheets if necessary.

PART B

Form 9 (for trainers only) The Kuder–Richardson Formula 20 (K–R 20) for Estimating Test Reliability[1]

The reliability of a test refers to its consistency or repeatability. Responses to questions should form a similar pattern across test takers or over time. This would lead to the inference that the test was measuring something stable over time or throughout all of its questions. Several methods are available for assessing reliability,[2] but one common method is split-half reliability. Reliability scores are obtained by correlating two sets of scores on one administration of a test in order to assess the relationship of scores on one portion of the test to those on another portion. The reliability coefficient is thus a correlation coefficient with range of +1 (perfect positive relationship), to 0 (no relationship), to −1 (perfect negative relationship). After the test is split in half, scores on one "half" are compared to the other. The first half versus the last half, or odd-numbered items or questions versus even-numbered questions, can be used as the two "halves." Obviously, items of a test can be split in many other ways to complete split-half reliability (e.g., first and third versus second and fourth quarters, etc.). But for each such split, a different correlation coefficient for the two sets of scores could be obtained as different questions or items are used. Therefore, which one is the best estimate of reliability?

Kuder and Richardson have developed a computational procedure that is equivalent to assessing the average of all possible split-half reliability coefficients that could be computed for a given test. This formula is easy to use and gives an excellent estimate of reliability, as it accounts for all possible splits and thus reduces the chances of obtaining a biased reliability coefficient due to one particular pattern of questions used in one split.

The formula, typically referred to as the K–R 20, is as follows:

$$r_{KR} = \left(\frac{k}{k-1}\right)\left(\frac{\sigma_o^2 - \sum p_i q_i}{\sigma_o^2}\right).$$

The meanings of the symbols are:

k = number of items in the test;
p_i = proportion of students responding correctly to item i;
q_i = $1 - p$ (the proportion of students responding incorrectly);
σ_o^2 = the test variance;
$\sum p_i q_i$ = sum of p times q for all test items.

The term $k(k-1)$ is a correction factor permitting r to equal 1.0. The term $p_i q_i$ is actually the difficulty of item i multiplied by 1 minus the difficulty of the item. To get $\sum p_i q_i$, all of the $p_i q_i$ for each item must be summed. The assumptions of the K–R 20 are that items can be scored either right or wrong and that the total score on the test is the sum of the scores on each item. Thus, on items where partial credit is given, the K–R 20 is not applicable.

Example: Below is a table showing the responses of five students on each item of a six-item test. A "0" indicates that the incorrect response was given and a "1" indicates that a correct response was given.

			Item				
Student	1	2	3	4	5	6	Total no. correct responses per student (X)
1	1	0	0	1	1	1	4
2	1	0	1	1	1	1	5
3	0	0	1	1	0	1	3
4	1	0	1	0	0	0	2
5	1	1	0	1	1	1	5
							19

Form 9 (continued)

The K–R reliability estimate for this test is computed below.

		Item						
		1	2	3	4	5	6	
Total number of correct responses per item		4	1	3	4	3	4	$\bar{X}$ = Mean correct responses per student, 3.8
Proportion of correct responses per item	(p)	0.8	0.2	0.6	0.8	0.6	0.8	σ_0^{2*} = 1.36 (variance)
Proportion of incorrect responses per item	(q)	0.2	0.8	0.4	0.2	0.4	0.2	$\imath_{KR} = \left(\dfrac{6}{5}\right)\left(\dfrac{1.36 - 1.12}{1.36}\right)$
pq		0.16	0.16	0.24	0.16	0.24	0.16	$\imath_{KR}$ = 0.212 = KR20 reliability coefficient
$\sum pq$	1.12							

* Variance = $\dfrac{\sum(X - \bar{X})^2}{N}$

---

[1] Adapted from W. Dick and N. Hagerty, *Topics in Measurement, Reliability and Validity* (New York: McGraw-Hill, 1971), pp. 23–24, 31–33.

[2] See Exercise 9 and R. Guion, *Personnel Testing* (New York: McGraw-Hill, 1965); W. Dick and N. Hagerty, *Topics in Measurement, Reliability and Validity;* and J. Guilford, *Psychometric Methods* (New York: McGraw-Hill, 1954).

Name _____ Group Number _____

Date _____ Class Section _____ Hour _____ Score _____

PART B
Form 10 Evaluation of Trainee Learning

Criteria for evaluation of trainee learning		Task	
		No. 1 (Tying tie)	No. 2 (K–R 20)

Method 1 (Lecture)

Criteria	Trainee		
Speed	Trainee 1		
	Trainee 2		
Accuracy	Trainee 1		
	Trainee 2		
Other:	Trainee 1		
	Trainee 2		

Method 2 (Coaching)

Criteria	Trainee		
Speed	Trainee 1		
	Trainee 2		
Accuracy	Trainee 1		
	Trainee 2		
Other:	Trainee 1		
	Trainee 2		

After the training programs have been designed and trainees have used them and have been evaluated, discuss the following issues and briefly summarize your discussions:

1. Which method best satisfied the criterion speed for each task? Under which method for each task were trainees most accurate?

2. How did the ratees feel about learning under each of the methods? Which method did they prefer? Why?

3. What are the advantages and disadvantages of each method?

4. For what type of training task would each of the methods seem to be most appropriate?

5. What training method would be most effective for each of these tasks? Why?

Name _____ Group Number _____

Date _____ Class Section _____ Hour _____ Score _____

ASSESSMENT OF LEARNING IN PERSONNEL ADMINISTRATION

EXERCISE 10

1. Try to state the purpose of this exercise in one concise sentence.

2. Specifically what did you learn from this exercise (i.e., skills, abilities, and knowledge)?

3. How might your learning influence your role and your duties as a personnel administrator?

4. What skills, abilities, and knowledge must one possess in order to be successful at assessment of training needs?

5. What are the most effective training/learning methods for your own learning? Why?

6. What are the major differences between assessing training needs at entry-level, versus managerial-level, jobs?

7. Why is behavior change such an important objective of training and development programs?

8. How are job analyses, performance appraisal, and human-resource planning related to assessment of training needs?

Exercise 11

Evaluating the effectiveness of training and development programs

PREVIEW

As with all personnel programs, training and development programs should be evaluated for their effectiveness. Since training and development programs are expensive, time-consuming, and often developed to attain specific objectives, it seems reasonable to inquire whether or not the money and time have been used wisely and the objectives met. This is accomplished most easily by asking the question: Was there any change in behavior in the desired direction after training? Often, however, this question is not asked or the answer is obscured by faulty measurement, inappropriate questions, and/or lack of pretraining data for comparison with posttraining data.

In this exercise, the importance of systematically and rigorously evaluating the effectiveness of training and development programs is discussed. Several activities are designed to enable you to select the criteria for your evaluation and to develop the evaluation instruments needed to gather appropriate data.

OBJECTIVES

1. To become aware of the importance of evaluating training and development program effectiveness as a vital process in administering programs.

2. To become familiar with the types of data required to evaluate a training program rigorously.

3. To become familiar with the more common types of experimental designs that can be used to assess systematically differences in groups of trainees before and after training and/or differences between groups who have received training and those who have not.

4. To begin to build skill in designing instruments to gather the data needed in training-program evaluation.

PREMEETING ASSIGNMENT

Read the entire exercise. Review Exercises 4 and 5 as well as the *Appendix* to Exercise 9 covering *t*-tests for differences between means, or a statistics text on the same topic.

INTRODUCTION

A Rationale, a Method, and Criteria for Training-and-Development-Program Evaluation

Evaluating training and development programs is a complex task. Basically, it involves determining what, if anything, the training program actually accomplished. The task is difficult because many aspects of the training situation (i.e., content, duration, etc.), as well as individual characteristics of trainers and trainees, can influence the outcomes of programs. Evaluators thus must design an assessment procedure that is sensitive to such differences. They must determine training goals, which include a complex array of possible changes in knowledge and behavior after training. Further, evaluators must define these goals very specifically and explain their interrelationships before training can be evaluated with confidence.

Surprisingly, few organizations seriously attempt to evaluate their training programs, frequently because of the difficulty in measuring job performance itself in order to assess whether performance was enhanced by training. Given the expense of training programs, the scant amount of research devoted to evaluating the impact of training is astonishing. A major question at this point is how long organizations will follow a policy of spending millions for training but not one penny for training evaluation.

A Rationale for Evaluation. Evaluation is frequently deferred because training programs are designed with little or no thought as to how they will subsequently be evaluated. The prescribed training techniques of a program are *assumed* to be capable of moving the trainee toward the stated training objectives, but we never know what a particular program *actually* accomplished without evaluation. Often, if evaluation is attempted, the criterion of training-program accomplishment is merely a statement by the trainees indicating whether they *think* they have learned something, or whether the trainees' superiors *think* the trainees learned something. Only occasionally is the criterion how much trainees *actually* learned (i.e., changes in behavior). Evaluation of training should be planned and evaluated as carefully as the training program itself, for careful evaluation is the only means we have for assessing the value of such programs and determining the nature of the changes that are necessary to make future programs more effective.

A Method for Evaluating Training Programs. One common error in evaluating training programs is omitting the indirect or less visible costs, such as instructors' preparation time or trainees' salaries. A first consideration in evaluation should thus be a detailed analysis of all costs. Fig. 1 contains a list of the more common costs.

Once costs have been assessed, each type of program, whether developed and delivered in-house or outside, could be prioritized as to its perceived value to the organization. This would be a somewhat subjective evaluation, but it could be made by gathering input from several relevant persons (e.g., trainers, trainees, managers of trainees, etc.) and assessing the impact of each program on behavior, performance, or results

(see Evaluation Criteria). When each of the prioritized programs' costs is assessed relative to perceived importance and impact, some programs will emerge as having a low cost/benefit ratio. These should be investigated more fully. They could perhaps be increased in frequency of delivery or expanded in content or trainee population. Other programs will emerge as being of only marginal benefit after their costs and priority are assessed.

The costs of the evaluation process (e.g., evaluators' time, costs of producing a report and supplying data on the program's effectiveness, etc.) for each training program must also be considered in a cost/benefit analysis. In some cases, the cost of evaluation may be similar to or higher than the cost of the program itself. Each evaluation process should be of a level of complexity appropriate for the program to which it will be applied.

Trainees' salaries
Trainers' salaries
Transportation costs—trainees and trainers
Per diem expenses—trainees and trainers
Tuition to program
Materials and supplies
Preparation time for trainers
Rental cost for facilities
Improvements to space
Equipment purchase or rental
Developmental time for trainers, planners
Cost of evaluation

---

* After B. S. Deming, "A System for Evaluating Training Programs," *Personnel,* November–December 1979, pp. 33–41.

Fig. 1. Possible costs associated with training programs*

Evaluation Criteria. It has been suggested that evaluation procedures include the following four criteria: reaction, learning, behavior, and results.[1] *Reaction* is defined as what the trainees thought of the particular program (i.e., their opinions). It does not include a measure of the learning that takes place. Following are some guidelines for gauging participant reaction to a training program (see also Exercise 20).

1. Design a questionnaire based on information directly related to program design and methods. The questionnaire should be validated by carefully standardized procedures to ensure that the

---

[1] D. L. Kirkpatrick, "Techniques for Evaluating Training Programs," *Journal of American Society of Training Directors* 13 (1959): 3–9; D. L. Kirkpatrick, "Evaluating Training and Development Programs: Evidence vs. Proof," *Training and Development Journal* 31 (November 1977): 9–12.

responses actually reflect the participants' opinions.

2. Design the instrument so that the responses can be tabulated and qualified easily (e.g., by using an answer sheet for responses).

3. To obtain more honest opinions, provide for the anonymity of the participants.

4. Provide space for opinions about items that are not covered in the questionnaire. This procedure often leads to the collection of important information that is useful in the subsequent redesign of the questionnaire (e.g., a space for "other comments or reactions to the program").

5. Pretest the questionnaire on a sample of participants to determine its completeness, the time necessary for completion, and participant reactions to the questions themselves.[2]

The reaction of the majority of participants is often a critical factor in the continuance of training programs; decisions should not turn on the comments of only a few very satisfied or disgruntled participants who choose to be vocal. Receptivity to a program (i.e., positive reactions) provides a good atmosphere for learning; it does not, however, necessarily *cause* high levels of learning.

In *learning,* the second aspect of training to be evaluated, the training analyst is concerned with measuring principles, facts, techniques, and attitudes that were specified as training objectives. The measures must be objective and quantifiable indicators of the learning that has taken place in the training program. There are many different measures of learning, including paper-and-pencil tests and learning curves. The original training objectives help to determine the choice of the most appropriate measure. Of course, it is best if learning is assessed both before *and* after training in order to determine changes.

Behavior measures refer to actual job performance. Just as favorable reaction does not necessarily mean that learning has occurred in the training program, superior training performance (i.e., learning) does not always result in similar behavior in the job setting. The measurement of learning does not always correlate with performance on the job and should not be substituted for studies of on-the-job behavior without first determining that a strong relationship exists between the two. Behavior on the job is often measured with such performance-appraisal techniques as behaviorally anchored rating scales (BARS) (see Exercise 4). Again, before-and-after training measures of performance levels should be taken to see whether learning from training has transferred to job performance.

The fourth criterion for training effectiveness, the *results* of a training program, refers to a program's impact on organizational objectives. Some of the results that could be examined include costs, turnover, absenteeism, grievances, and morale. These data are easily gathered by examining company financial and personnel records. Hopefully, all of the previous three criteria would affect results. That is, if we design a training program that people felt was useful, that they learned something from, and that improved their own individual job performance, we would hope organizational performance would improve also.

Although great disparities show up in the kinds of training evaluation reported in the literature and in the degree of scientific rigor with which evaluation is performed, general agreement seems to exist concerning the following principles:[3]

1. Evaluation should be planned at the same time as the training program and should constitute an integral part of the total program from beginning to end.

2. Evaluation should be carried out at several levels and at several times.

3. Evaluation should follow the most rigorous experimental design possible.

Conducting Research on Training-Program Effectiveness. There are many possible experimental designs or ways in which trainees are (a) grouped, (b) administered training programs and evaluation questionnaires, and (c) compared to other groups (see Fig. 2). Most such designs, however, are of the "after-only" variety, that is, the trainees' reactions, learning, or behavior are observed or measured only after their exposure to training. It is thus impossible to tell whether, for example, knowledge was developed as a result of training or existed before training. A slight improvement over this single-measure method is a comparable measure of a matched "control" group that does not receive training but is similar in education, age, experience, etc., to the experimental group. This latter design can be further improved if evaluation includes both before-and-after measures of the experimental (i.e., training) group and a matched con-

[2] D. A. Nadler, *Feedback and Organization Development* (Reading, Mass.: Addison-Wesley, 1977).

[3] B. M. Bass and J. A. Vaughan, *Training in Industry: The Management of Learning* (Belmont, Cal.: Wadsworth, 1968), Chap. 8.

	Design A: "Before" and "After" with no control group	Design B: "After" only with one control group		Design C: "Before-After" with one control group	
		Experimental group	Control group	Experimental group	Control group
"Before" training measurement taken:	Yes (X_1)	No	No	Yes (X_1)	Yes (Y_1)
Training given:	Yes	Yes	No	Yes	No
"After" training measurement taken:	Yes (X_2)	Yes (X_2)	Yes (Y_2)	Yes (X_2)	Yes (Y_2)
Change due to training assumed by measuring difference (D) between:	$D = X_2 - X_1$	$D = X_2 - Y_2$		$D_1 = X_2 - X_1$ $D_1 = X_2 - Y_2$ (if $X_1 = Y_1$)	

Source: Adopted from B. Bass and J. Vaughan, *Training in Industry: The Management of Learning* (Belmont, Cal.: Wadsworth, 1968), p. 146.

Fig. 2. Sample training design

trol group. The use of two or more control groups permits even more sophistication in design and allows isolation of possible events occurring simultaneously with training (i.e., maturational processes and the initial measurement itself) from training effects. The utility of the basic experimental designs can be compared in Fig. 2.

In Design A, no control group is used and each subject serves as his or her own control. The difference between the before and after measures might indicate change due to training. However, as there is no control group, change may simply be due to maturation, learning on the job over time, or increased motivation.

To avoid this, Design B employs a control group. Neither group is measured before training, but if the subjects in the two groups are randomly assigned and each group is fairly large (e.g., thirty or more people), we can be reasonably confident that if the after measure for the experimental group is significantly greater than that of the control group (i.e., $X_2 > Y_2$), training has had an effect. Of course, we still do not know whether learning, knowledge, etc., increased for either group from before to after the training without a before measure.

Thus, a still more rigorous design is Design C, which uses both a before and after measure and a control group. If we randomly assign people to each of the groups and note that they are at about the same level of performance or learning before training (i.e., $X_1 = Y_1$), then differences in the experimental group over the control group after training would indicate that training had an effect (i.e., $X_2 > X_1$), indicating change due to training for the experimental group. More sophisticated designs are available which account for such factors as changes due to the measuring instrument or process itself, and these allow us to be even more con-

fident that results are due to training.[4] However, the more sophisticated the design, the more costly evaluation becomes. Design C in Fig. 2 should be used as a minimally rigorous design when possible.[5]

The Training Subsystem. The entire training process, or subsystem of the larger personnel system, can be represented as a systematic program to assess training needs, design and implement training programs (Exercise 10), and evaluate training effectiveness (Exercise 11). This entire process can be represented in a schematic, such as the one in Fig. 3.

In Fig. 3, it is obvious that all aspects of training are sequentially related. In addition, the development of criterion measures—that is, the standards against which trainees and the program itself will be assessed—comes early in the sequential process. The feedback loops suggest that after trainees have graduated from the program and been assessed on the criteria, training content, methods, and/or materials may have to be changed to reflect new requirements of trainees or inadequacies of the existing program. This redesign after evaluation enables training programs to remain not only relevant to the needs of trainees, but also flexible enough to accommodate changes in jobs.

PROCEDURE

Overview. In this exercise, you build skill in designing instruments to assess the four criteria that can be used

4 See D. Campbell and J. Stanley, *Experimental and Quasi-experimental Designs for Research* (Chicago: Rand McNally, 1967); and Bass and Vaughan, *Training in Industry*.

5 See also Exercises 19 and 20.

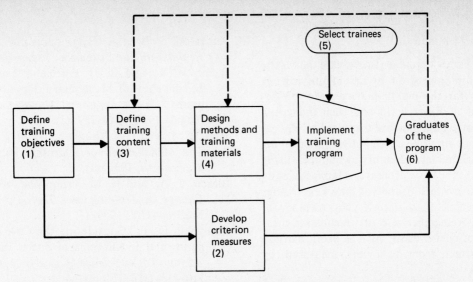

Fig. 3. The training subsystem (Adapted from G. A. Eckstrand, "Current Status of the Technology of Training," *AMRL Document Technical Report 64–86,* September 1964, p. 3; see also, R. W. Beatty, "Personnel Systems and Human Performance," *Personnel Journal* 52 (1973): 307–312.)

in evaluating training programs: reactions, learning, behavior, and results. Techniques discussed in Exercises 4 and 5 on performance appraisal are utilized.

PART A

STEP 1: You are to break into groups of about four to six members and determine how you would measure an individual's reactions to the middle-management training program described in Exercise 10. You are to design a questionnaire to measure these reactions (Form 1). Give careful thought to precisely how you would define the term "reactions." Make sure the questions are clearly worded and allow for proper response alternatives. Remember that reactions include opinions and attitudes about various aspects of the program.

TIME: About 45 minutes.

STEP 2: Each group is to design a questionnaire to evaluate learning that might have taken place in the middle-management training program presented in Exercise 10. First, devise questions that would provide data on what knowledge the trainees gained. They might have gained knowledge in the areas noted in the training-program outline, such as communications, etc. What questions could you ask in a pencil-and-paper test to assess this knowledge? Tell how you would score the answers to these questions. In order to do this, you must, of course, formulate your own answers

to the questions. Next, discuss how you would actually measure the trainees' learning that resulted from the program by comparing, for example, their answers to your questions before and after training (see Fig. 1, *Introduction*) and/or using a control group. What statistic(s) would you use to measure this type of change and how could you be assured that any change you detect is not merely due to chance (refer to *Appendix,* Exercise 9). Finally, how would you determine if any change that did occur was due to the training program itself (even if you felt it was not due to chance)? Answer these questions as a group and write your answers in the spaces provided on Form 2.

TIME: About one hour.

STEP 3: Here you evaluate behavioral change as a result of training. You are to choose among the skills being taught in the training program in Exercise 10 and design one Behaviorally Anchored Rating Scale (BARS) to measure behavior on this skill. Use Form 3 for your BARS. You may want to refer to Exercise 4 (you can simply write in a set of anchors without performing the retranslation procedure). BARS, as you remember, was argued to be an excellent performance appraisal system, as it was developed to measure behavior. If we measure behavior change as a result of training, we can thus rate performance change as indicated by the various levels of performance on the BARS scale.

TIME: About 45 minutes.

STEP 4: Using Form 4, you are to evaluate the results of a training program by first identifying key results for the middle-management job described in Exercise 10 and then indicating how you would measure these results. The results can either be on an individual or an organizational level. Identifying and measuring results is the basic process in Management by Objectives (MBO), and you may want to refer to Exercise 5 to refresh your memory of MBO. Remember also that results are measures of effectiveness, such as profit margin, as distinct from behaviors measured by BARS.

TIME: About 50 minutes.

PART B

STEP 5: Form 5 contains data from an experimental and a control group which have been used in a "JIT Plus" (Job Instruction Training) program that you, as personnel administrator, have developed and implemented. The JIT Plus training program was used for twenty-five randomly selected new employees of the fifty currently holding Assembler I jobs. You have randomly selected twenty-five remaining assemblers who have completed the regular JIT training program as a control group and you are now in a position to compare the JIT with the JIT Plus in a cost/benefit analysis. Your group is to do the following:

a) Evaluate the experimental JIT Plus program by assessing production changes one year after the training and determine whether or not the JIT Plus approach makes enough difference to warrant its extra costs. If a difference was observed, can you say it was due primarily to the JIT Plus program?

b) Prepare a brief report on the statistical analyses you used and recommendations relative to instituting one of the training programs for all new Assemblers I, based on the results of your analysis.

(The *Appendix* to Exercise 9 may help with the statistical analysis.)

TIME: About one hour.

FOR FURTHER READING

Alden, J. "Evaluation in Focus." *Training and Development Journal* 32 (October 1978): 46–50. (I)

Anderson, S. B. et al. *Encyclopedia of Educational Evaluation.* San Francisco: Jossey Bass, 1975. (I)

Baker, H. K., and R. H. Gorman. "Evaluating the Effectiveness of Management Development Programs." *Public Personnel Management* 7 (July-August 1978): 249–257. (I)

Bass, B. M., and J. A. Vaughan. *Training in Industry: The Management of Learning.* Belmont, Cal.: Wadsworth, 1966. (I)

Blasco, J. A., and H. M. Trice. *The Assessment of Change in Training and Therapy.* New York: McGraw-Hill, 1969. (I)

Campbell, D. T. "Considering the Case against Experimental Evaluations of Social Innovations." *Administrative Science Quarterly* 15, no. 1 (1970): 110–113. (II)

Campbell, D. T., and J. Stanley. *Experimental and Quasiexperimental Designs for Research.* Chicago: Rand McNally, 1966). (II)

Catalenello, R. F., and D. L. Kirkpatrick. "Evaluating Training Programs—The State of the Art." *Training and Development Journal* 23, no. 5 (1968): 2–9. (I)

Cook, T. D., and D. T. Campbell. "The Design and Conduct of Quasi-Experiments and True Experiments in Field Settings." In M. D. Dunnette, ed., *Handbook of Industrial and Organizational Psychology,* Chicago: Rand McNally, 1976. (II)

Deming, B. S. "A System for Evaluating Training Programs." *Personnel* 57 (November–December 1979): 33–41.

Form, W. H., and A. L. Form. "Unanticipated Results of a Foreman Training Program." *Personnel Journal* 32 (1953): 207–212. (I)

Goldstein, J. L. *Training Program Development and Evaluation.* Monterey, Cal.: Brooks/Cole, 1974. (I)

Goldstein, I. L. "Training in Work Organizations." *Annual Review of Psychology* 31 (1980). (II)

Hamblin, A. C. *Evaluation and Control of Training.* New York: McGraw-Hill, 1974. (I)

Hughes, J. L. "The Effectiveness of Programmed Instruction: Experimental Findings." In S. Marfulies and L. D. Eigen, eds., *Applied Programmed Instruction.* New York: Wiley, 1962. (II)

Keller, R. T. "A Longitudinal Assessment of a Managerial Grid Seminar Training Program." *Group and Organization Studies* 3 (1978): 343–355. (II-R)

Kirkpatrick, D. L. "Evaluating Training Programs: Evidence vs. Programs." *Training and Development Journal* 31 (November 1977): 9–12. (I)

Kirkpatrick, D. L. "Techniques for Evaluating Training Programs." *Journal of American Society of Training Directors* 13 (1959): 3–9, 21–26. (I)

Kohn, W., and T. Parker. "Some Guidelines for Evaluating Management Development Seminars." *Training and Development Journal* 23, no. 7 (1968): 18-22. (I)

McKenney, J. L. "An Evaluation of a Business Game in an MBA Curriculum." *Business Journal* 35, no. 3 (1962): 278-286. (I-R)

MacKinney, A. C. "Progressive Levels in the Evaluation of Training Programs." *Personnel* 34 (1957): 72-77. (I)

Moursund, J. P. *Evaluation: An Introduction to Research Design.* Monterey, Cal.: Brooks/Cole, 1973. (II)

Nadler, D. A. *Feedback and Organization Development: Using Data-Based Methods.* Reading, Mass.: Addison-Wesley, 1977. (I)

Nixon, G. *People, Evaluation, and Achievement.* Houston: Gulf, 1973. (I)

Oberg, E. "Top Management Assesses University Executive Programs." *Business Topics* 2, no. 2 (1963): 7-27. (I)

Odiorne, G. S. "The Need for an Economic Approach to Training." *Journal of the American Society of Training Directors* 18, no. 3 (1964): 3-12. (I)

Rader, M. H. "Evaluating a Management Development Program for Women." *Public Personnel Management* 8 (May-June 1979): 138-145. (I-R)

Randall, L. K. "Evaluation: A Training Dilemma." *Journal of American Society of Training Directors* 19, no. 1 (1965): 34-42. (I)

Selltiz, C., M. Jahoda, M. Deutsch, and S. W. Cook. *Research Methods in Social Relations.* New York: Holt, Rinehart and Winston, 1962. (II)

Spitzer, D. "Remember These Do's and Don'ts of Questionnaire Design." *Training* 16 (May 1979): 34-37. (I)

Stone, E. *Research Methods in Organizational Behavior.* Santa Monica, Cal.: Goodyear, 1978. (II)

Woodward, N. "The Economic Evaluation of Supervisor Training." *Journal of European Training* 4 (1975): 134-141. (I)

Name _____   Group Number _____

Date _____   Class Section _____   Hour _____   Score _____

PART A

Form 1 Evaluating Reactions to the "Success in Middle Management" Training Program (See Exercise 10)

A Reactions Questionnaire

Questions:

1.

_____

2.

_____

3.

_____

4.

_____

5.

_____

6.

_____

7.

_____

8.

_____

9.

_____

10.

_____

11.

_____

12.

_____

13.

_____

14.

_____

15.

_____

Name _____ Group Number _____

Date _____ Class Section _____ Hour _____ Score _____

PART A

Form 2 Evaluating Learning in the "Success in Middle Management Training Program" (See Exercise 10)

I. List several sample questions (along with their answers) that could be used in a pencil-and-paper test to evaluate what knowledge trainees have gained as a result of the training.

Question:

1.

    Answer:

_____

2.

    Answer:

_____

3.

    Answer:

_____

4.

    Answer:

_____

5.

    Answer:

_____

6.

    Answer:

_____

7.

    Answer:

_____

8.

    Answer:

_____

II. Develop a design that will allow you to indicate whether or not the training program actually led to changes in knowledge (see Fig. 1, Exercise 11). Explain the statistics you would use to decide whether or not your answer was due to change (see *Appendix* to Exercise 9 or a statistics text).

Name _____ Group Number _____

Date _____ Class Section _____ Hour _____ Score _____

PART A

Form 3 Evaluating Behavior Change in the "Success in Middle-Management" Training Program (see Exercise 10) with BARS (see Exercise 4).

Middle-management skill chosen _____

Performance or skill level   *Behavioral description or anchors:*

Excellent	7	
Very good	6	
Good	5	
Average	4	
Fair	3	
Poor	2	
Unacceptable	1	

Name _____ Group Number _____

Date _____ Class Section _____ Hour _____ Score _____

PART A

Form 4 Evaluating Results of the "Success in Middle Management" Training Program (see Exercise 10) with MBO (see Exercise 5).

Key result area to be measured (e.g., quantity, cost, etc.)	Measure used to assess key result area (e.g., profit margin, etc.)
1.	
2.	
3.	
4.	
5.	
6.	
7.	
8.	

PART B

Form 5 Assessing the Worth of a Training Program via a Cost/Benefit Analysis

Using the data presented below concerning an experimental training program (JIT Plus) and the traditional program (JIT) for persons holding the job of Assembler I, calculate which program is economically and statistically most beneficial to the organization during a six-month period after training for a group of 25 Assemblers.

	JIT Plus program (experimental—E)	JIT program (control—C)
Sample size (N)	$N_E = 25$	$N_C = 25$
Average no. of units produced before training for entire group of trainees (per month)	$\bar{X}_{E1} = 47$	$\bar{X}_{C1} = 47$
Average no. of units produced after training for entire group of trainees (per month)	$\bar{X}_{E2} = 52$	$\bar{Y}_{C2} = 50$
Cost of training program (per trainee)	$150.00	$100.00

Additional information: The total profit from units produced is $50.00 per unit produced. The *t*-statistic computed for the difference between the mean production of the experimental and training groups after training is 1.77. (Refer to *Appendix*, Exercise 9 or any statistics text for explanation of *t* statistic and appropriate tables.) The basic difference in cost per trainee between the two programs is due to additional instructional equipment necessary in the JIT Plus program. However, training times are quite short and equal for the two programs. The same number and type of trainers are required for each program.

Name _____   Group Number _____

Date _____ Class Section _____ Hour _____ Score _____

ASSESSMENT OF LEARNING IN PERSONNEL ADMINISTRATION
EXERCISE 11

1. Try to state the purpose of this exercise in one concise sentence.

2. Specifically what did you learn from this exercise (i.e., skills, abilities, and knowledge)?

3. How might your learning influence your role and your duties as a personnel administrator?

4. What skills and knowledge are required in order to evaluate training and development programs effectively?

5. When during training and development program design and implementation should evaluation be considered? Why?

6. What problems might you encounter as you attempt to develop behavioral criteria for management development programs?

Exercise 12
Career Development and career management

PREVIEW

Career development concerns the readiness for progression through a series of positions during a person's working life. With organizations' increasing interest in developing their human resources, career issues have become very visible. In addition, employees' expectations regarding what an organization should do to facilitate career growth rise as they become more educated. This exercise examines the nature of careers in organizations, particularly professional careers. The different responsibilities of the individual and the organization for the development and management of careers are detailed. Career stages and their relationship to performance are also discussed, as is the interdependency of career development programs and human-resource planning and forecasting systems, training programs, and appraisal systems. Exercise activities focus on self-assessment, career planning, conducting a career development interview, and developing a career path within an organization. A detailed case study is included to provide a context for the interview and career path activities.

OBJECTIVES

1. To provide participants with feedback about their knowledge, skills, abilities, and experience in order to develop a realistic assessment of their suitability for various careers.

2. To develop career goals and action plans for short- and longer-term periods based upon self-assessment data.

3. To begin to gain skill in conducting a career planning and development review session, utilizing communication, counseling, and feedback skills.

4. To develop appreciation for the organization's interests in career pathing by designing routes through an organization for a young professional.

PREMEETING ASSIGNMENT

Read the entire exercise.

INTRODUCTION
Careers: Individual and Organizational Perspectives

Several years ago certain expectations prevailed among most people entering organizations in this country to begin their careers. The economy was growing and business was expanding rapidly to meet pent-up demand from large numbers of consumers held back during World War II. Thus, there seemed to be plenty of room at the top for ambitious, bright people. Promotions and career advancement were commonplace.

People also felt that "being at the right place at the right time" was largely responsible for career moves. Little management or planning of one's career, other than remaining competent and adding new skills and experience, seemed necessary. Upon interviewing the middle-aged people who rose during the expansion decades and are now in responsible organizational positions, one hears the following comments over and over: "I never would have guessed I would end up doing this!" "No, I didn't start out in this type of work, it just turned out this way." Further, what little career planning was done was limited to the personnel departments of the largest organizations.

Today these expectations have been called myths.[1] In many organizations there simply is no more room at the top! All careers do not progress steadily upward in the 1980s. Many organizations have imposed hiring freezes and ceilings on positions at higher levels. Others have cut back to "trim the fat." As the mean age of the employed population increases and medical advances push back the retirement age, more people will remain in top positions longer. The attrition rates will decrease since people attained their positions at early ages. Further, their effectiveness may decline over time or they may "burn out" unless they are given new responsibilities and opportunities.

Those who are obtaining promotions and rising in an organization are not able to leave their futures to fate. They plan to be in the right place at the right time through carefully chosen career paths, visible and challenging assignments, well-calculated job changes, and strategically placed bursts of formal education and skill development. It is much more common now to hear the following comments: "I'll take this position for a year or two in order to build up my resume." "No one gets the VP jobs without a brief stint in the field, so I'll pay my dues out there as early in my career as I can."

Finally, people realize that attending to their careers is as much their responsibility as it is that of their organization. The personnel department must share this responsibility with each employee and each manager. *Individuals must take the initiative for career planning* and for readying themselves for future assignments and positions through training and experience. Because an integral part of managing is staff assessment and development, *each manager must be sensitive to the career interest of his or her subordinates,* as well as the human-resource needs of the organization. He or she must therefore become proficient at coaching, counseling, and assisting people to meet individual and organizational objectives. It seems few managers are now skilled in these areas. The personnel department thus augments the capability of line managers and employees through its own career development programs, but line managers remain the key resource.

The following discussion of careers is centered around two themes. The first is that career development must be placed in a realistic context, reflecting today's organizational environment. The volatility and uncertainty of that environment, coupled with a shifting emphasis toward professionalism among workers, makes expectations of automatic advancement largely a myth. The competition is too great. Planning, mastering a variety of skills, and informed decision making are required to manage careers today.

Second, the notion of career development and management is viable only if both the individual and the organization—through supervisors and personnel departments—participate. Responsibility lies with both the individual and the organization, and each has a particular vantage point suggesting certain activities.

What is Career Management and Development and Why Is It So Important? Career has been defined as:

> ... the individually perceived sequence of attitudes and behaviors associated with work-related experiences and activities over the span of person's life.[2]

This definition emphasizes the particular perception a person has of his or her career since we each view our work experiences differently. In addition, career is a process, a sequence of activities that takes place as a person's work life unfolds. It is important to note that the notion of success or failure is not included in the definition. While many people think of career as something positive and successful, containing only promotions and a steady rise in status, career is a much broader concept. Success and failure are values imposed on a person's activities. A career as a fisherman may denote success to one person and failure to another, as may a career as an executive.

Career development, as a general term, refers to the systematic process of guiding the *movement* of the organization's human resources through various positions and layers of the hierarchy. *Career planning* consists specifically of the activities that assist in making choices as to occupation, organization, job assignment, and engaging in various forms of self-development (e.g., formal education or training programs). Planning requires the gathering and analysis of information and the development of plans to guide behavior. *Career management* refers to specific human resource management activities, such as recruitment, selection, placement and appraisal, designed to facilitate career development.[3]

[1] E. Staats, "Career Planning and Development: Which Way is Up?" *Public Administration Review* 37 (1977): 73–76.

[2] D. Hall, *Careers in Organizations* (Santa Monica, Cal.: Goodyear, 1976), p. 4.

[3] T. Gutteridge, "Organizational Career Development: State of the Practice." Symposium, National Meeting of the Academy of Management, Kansas City, 1976.

Both career planning and career management have a broad focus and contain individual as well as organizational perspectives. For example, a person would develop his or her own plan for selecting a particular job assignment in order to fulfill certain career objectives related to gaining experience for future advancement. The organization would provide certain job opportunities in order to fulfill its objectives of preparing people to assume greater amounts of responsibility. As the individual and organizational objectives mesh, utilization of human resources becomes effective.

The importance of individual and organizational attention to career development and management is due to several factors noted above. These include the possible limits to promotions and advancement caused by lack of economic growth and/or the increasing age of workers. Development and management are also vital due to the uncertainty an organization faces as it attempts to remain viable in an ever-changing and increasingly competitive environment. An organization must continue to anticipate its human resource needs through human resource planning and forecasting (see Exercise 2) in order that it might ready its members to meet any number of possible problems it might face.

Aspirations of people entering organizations have steadily risen with their educational levels. While the notion of career cited above includes attitudes and experiences over a person's work life, most people conceive of career as upward movement. Their expectation for a career orientation is a progression through various positions of increasing responsibility, challenge, and rewards rather than merely a position. An interest in quality of life and life planning, including career planning, is becoming more evident. Employees constantly look to the future, and the organization must help them develop their skills and abilities in order to retain them.

The ever-increasing interest in Equal Employment Opportunity (EEO), along with other legislation in this area (see Exercise 17), requires organizations to develop mechanisms for facilitating their members' movement along career paths and offering new opportunities, positions, and training to assure such movement.

Finally, a viable career development and management system is crucial to an organization for the same reasons its other human resource programs, such as selection and reward administration, are vital. An organization's human resources are primary assets. Their cost is enormous, both in terms of direct outlays for wages, salaries, and benefits and in terms of consequences of decisions people make on behalf of the

organization. Effective utilization of the human assets is thus very important.

Career Development and Management from the Individual's Perspective—Sources of Career Behavior. There are, of course, numerous theories explaining why people behave as they do, both on and off the job.[4] A simple model appears as Fig. 1. Basic personality and developmental characteristics do determine to some extent why certain behaviors are exhibited, as well as how these behaviors may influence career interests and choices. In addition, a person's *heredity,* particular *age* or *stage* in life, and *environment* help determine some basic perceptions and values. These, in turn, shape one's *self-concept.*

For example, persons with certain physical characteristics (determined partially by heredity), whose early experiences emphasized and rewarded successful competition with siblings and peers, may eventually develop a self-concept characterized by confidence and considerable physical ability. One's aspiration level might thus be high. Needs for success, visibility, and the opportunity to interact with others develop. Behaviors, such as keeping in excellent physical condition and participating in athletics, which enable this person to prepare for a particular career, would be evidenced. Successful career outcomes in sports could result. As depicted in Fig. 1, such outcomes would influence both one's experience and self-concept. Future behavior and outcomes would in turn be influenced through revisions in aspiration level and needs.[5]

Interests, Personality, and Careers. It is easy to understand, through studying Fig. 1, why people with poor verbal skills seldom choose politics, a career that emphasizes public speaking. The choice and success of careers are not quite as simple or linear as Fig. 1 might suggest, however. Interests play a large part in determining the compatibility between a person and a career. Measuring interests has been the subject of much work in vocational and developmental psychology. The Strong Vocational Interest Blank (SVIB)[6] is a very sophisticated and frequently used instrument on which responses are obtained from questions about

[4] See, e.g., W. Mischel, *Introduction to Personality,* 2d ed. (New York: Holt, Rinehart and Winston, 1976).

[5] See J. Leach, "The Notion and Nature of Careers," *Personnel Administration* (September 1977): 49–55.

[6] See E. K. Strong, *The Vocational Interests of Men and Women* (Stanford: Stanford University Press, 1943); *Careers in Organizations,* p. 4.

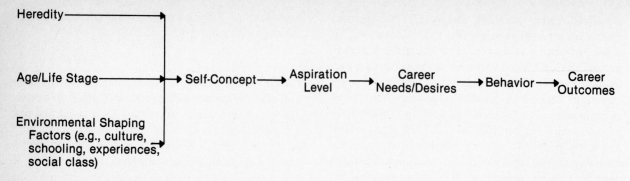

Fig. 1. Determinants of career behavior (see J. Leach, "The Notion and Nature of Careers," *Personnel Administration* (September 1977): 49–55).

Personality group	Sample interests	Sample personal traits	Sample characteristic occupations
Realistic	Precise use of objects—mechanical, electrical, animals, manual	Practical, shy, conforming, thing-oriented	Engineering, technician, skilled trades
Investigative	Exploration and examination of physical, biological, cultural things	Rational, introverted, analytical, intellectual	Scientific and analytical occupations
Artistic	Use of various materials to create art forms; language, music, drama	Creative, expressive, non-conforming	Music, art, literary occupations
Social	Interaction with others to train, educate, cure them	Friendly, outgoing, tactful	Teaching, social welfare
Enterprising	Interaction with others to attain organizational goals; leadership	Aggressive, ambitious, persuasive	Sales, administration
Conventional	Use of data; clerical, organizing, computational activities	Practical, efficient, orderly	Accounting, secretarial

Fig. 2. Holland's personality groups and compatible occupations (See J. Holland, *Making Vocational Choices: A Theory of Careers* (Englewood Cliffs, New Jersey: Prentice-Hall, 1973).

one's interests and preferences. These can then be compared to characteristics of responses of people in certain occupations and their positions on similar questions. A high interest in data, as opposed to people, would suggest certain occupations conceptually. Career choices will be more effective if persons are able to utilize their current interests in their jobs although they might over time develop other interests as well.

Personality is, of course, a determinant of career behavior and several theorists have attempted to relate the two. Holland[7] has developed six personality types

which correspond to six career environments. Various occupations can be named to illustrate the use of specific personal traits belonging to those in each personality type (see Fig. 2). Once one's personality has been categorized into one of the six groups, the assumption is made that he or she would develop career aspirations and make career choices that are compatible.

Career Stages. In addition to various theories relating personal characteristics, personality, or interests to careers, individual career choices and behavior can sometimes be predicted by assessing which career stage a person occupies at any given point in their lives. This emphasis is compatible with the definition of career as a dynamic process and as a sequence of activities.

[7] Holland, *Making Vocational Choices: A Theory of Careers* (Englewood Cliffs, New Jersey: Prentice-Hall, 1973).

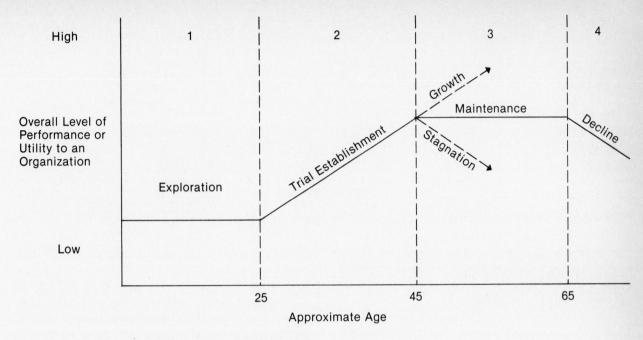

Fig. 3. Career Stages (After Hall, *Careers in Organizations*)

Several well-developed notions of careers as a series of *stages* have been proposed.[8] They can be summarized into the following general states: exploration and trial, growth, a stable period, and decline (see Fig. 3). Hall[9] has noted that the mid-career stage is often the most problematic and stressful. It is at this stage that people have an awareness of advancing age and may search for new life goals and be concerned about obsolescence, security, and marketability in their field. In addition, family relationships may change significantly during this period (e.g., children leave home). As Fig. 3 depicts, growth, stagnation, or maintenance are possible from this stage. Predicting the path taken is an important endeavor for both the organization and the individual. Each is preparing to offset stagnation or obsolescence and facilitate growth and movement.

Certain individual and organizational activities, concerns, and outcomes are related to each of the general states depicted in Fig. 3. The following is an example of a sequential list of such activities, concerns, etc., that might follow the general career stages depicted in Fig. 3 for those in an administrative/managerial career:

Stage 1: School-to-work transition; counseling from parents, professionals, internships during summers; subprofessional training.

Stage 2: Challenging first job; supervisory training and experience; development of more realistic attitudes toward work and organizations; support from mentors in the organization.

Stage 3: Realization that some career goals are unattainable; visibility and responsibility in an organization; needs for security, perhaps due to family responsibilities; development of a comfortable life-style, prestige, and position; a feeling of success.

Stage 4: Anxiety about retirement; being called on to engage in mentoring activities and to play an "elder statesman role"; retirement planning; feelings of absolescence, perhaps a lack of motivation.

The activities for these stages are a mixture of the ideal (i.e., a challenging, as opposed to a "dead end," first job) and the real (i.e., retirement planning). Each person's attitudes, experiences, and outcomes as he or she moves through career and life stages would, of course, differ.

Yet there are some commonalities. For many people the activities noted above mirror their own experience. Writers in the area of career and life stages have performed a valuable service because the description of developmental stages, albeit general, are able to provide people who are assessing their own situations with models and ideas. Sometimes simply knowing that others are going through a similar "crisis" enables

[8] Hall, *Careers in Organizations*, p. 4.
[9] Ibid., p. 4.

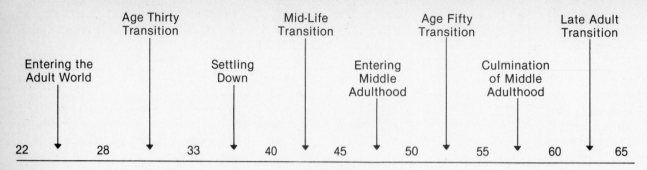

Approximate Age

Fig. 4. Levinson's adult male life stages (D. J. Levinson, *The Seasons of a Man's Life* (New York: Knopf, 1978.)

one to cope better. Levinson's life stages provide an interesting description of adult development which, along with other models presented here, can assist in self-assessment and planning.

Levinson's Life Stages. Levinson[10] has developed an interesting, useful theory of adult male life stages which could assist persons to assess and understand their own career movement. Levinson uses the notion of life structure to define the basic pattern or design of a person's life, including how an individual is attached to society through such mechanisms as religion and to self through, for example, values. Life structure is determined by choices people make about the relative centrality or importance of occupation, marriage and family, friendships and peer relationships, leisure, etc.

The life structure evolves through the adult years, consisting of alternating periods of stable and transitional periods. The latter are bridges or boundary zones between stable periods. Choices made in these periods lead to change in life structure. For example, divorce would perhaps decrease the importance of family relative to occupation or civic activities; career choices emphasizing work might thus prevail subsequent to divorce or may have led to divorce. Levinson's theory is thus concerned with all domains, not simply work, as a man's life unfolds, with his activities in other areas affecting career choice and behavior.

Levinson's stages and their approximate ages are listed in Fig. 4. As noted earlier, the mid-life transition is a particularly difficult period. At around forty years of age, various physical, social, and other changes lead men to assess their lives. Successes are evaluated and one's "Dream" is reappraised for reality. Fundamental life choices are open to question. Changes and dissatisfaction can occur.

Schein's Career Stages and Anchors. Schein[11] has advanced a theory of career development that speaks more specifically to career stages than life stages. According to Schein, each stage has particular vocational issues and tasks for the person to accomplish in order to progress. The stages (i.e., growth/fantasy/exploration, entry, basic training, full member/early career, and full member/midcareer) correspond roughly to ages and follow the general pattern of entry, peak performance, and an eventual leveling off or performance plateau. The tasks associated with each stage refer to such activities as looking for a job (entry stage) and overcoming insecurities (basic training stage), while the vocational issues refer to such issues as balancing individual and organizational needs (full member/early career stage).

Schein[12] has also developed the concept of "career anchors" to shed further light on the progression through career stages. The anchors shape decisions, goals, and movement. They are composed of three components—talents and abilities, motives and needs, and attitudes and values. Anchors develop as a result of experience and interaction between the individual and the work environment. They form a set of "driving and constraining forces on career decisions and choices."[13] The following five broad "anchors" have been identified:

1. Management competence;
2. Technical and functional competence;
3. Security;
4. Creativity; and
5. Autonomy and independence.

[10] D. J. Levinson, *The Season's of a Man's Life* (New York: Knopf, 1978).

[11] E. G. Schein, *Career Dynamics* (Reading, Mass.: Addison-Wesley, 1978).
[12] Ibid.
[13] Ibid.

Once something is known about a person's dominant anchor, career choices become understandable and perhaps predictable to some degree. If, for example, security is the result of one's talents, abilities, motives, needs, attitudes, and values, we would not expect the person to become so dissatisfied at mid-career as to leave a job at a large organization and begin his or her own small company. The person anchored by creativity or autonomy and independence, however, might do just that.

Self-Assessment and Career Planning. The theories and notions of career and life stages discussed above are useful from the individual's perspective as they provide a conceptual framework for understanding one's own career behavior and hence facilitating self-assessment. Along with several specific assessment activities (e.g., determining one's skills, abilities, interests, strengths, weaknesses, peak experiences, etc.),[14] the theories facilitate career planning.

While the process should be shared with the organization, career planning involves individual assessment, analysis, decision making, and eventual action on the individual's part. Career objectives must be formulated in light of a realistic appraisal of one's self, and action must be taken that reflects organizational realities.

Career Development and Management from the Organization's Perspective. The organization's perspective on careers is a bit different than the individual's. It also, however, should be concerned with career planning, development, and management. Those responsible for career development on behalf of the organization must gather and analyze data, make decisions, and act. These activities, however, are often carried out for groups of people at a time, such as secretaries, engineers, or middle managers. The perspective becomes one of utilizing human resources most effectively to attain organizational objectives and meet future organizational needs. Career development and management specialists realize that, in the long run, organizational objectives are best attained when individual and organizational objectives coincide.

While every policy or action (e.g., a pay raise or a shift in product lines) affects several persons' careers, the organization acts in the area of careers chiefly through its supervisors and its personnel or human resource department. Each has primary responsibility for various programs.

Supervisors are responsible for assessment and development of their subordinates. This could include the management of careers through assistance in attaining desired positions, in assessing strengths and weaknesses, and in counseling to help subordinates plan and realize career objectives consistent with those of the organization. The supervisor's job in career development is a very difficult one. Many supervisors do not possess the skills required to counsel and coach others. Neither are they comfortable with providing feedback to subordinates concerning job performance. Further, suppose a subordinate is interested in developing a skill or receiving training in an area not needed by the organization? Denying the subordinate any opportunity to widen his or her scope of skills could be career-limiting to the individual, but may not be beneficial to the organization in the short run as it is unable to use skills.

The personnel department helps to develop career paths (a series of related positions to which people aspire) to ensure that human resource needs are met. It addresses department-level or organization-level human-resources problems, such as turnover, which may be related to career movement (e.g., good people leave because no advancement is offered). The personnel department often takes the lead in providing career planning assistance to employees, helping to train supervisors in career management techniques, and ensuring that career development programs are coordinated with other human resource programs. Each of these functions of the supervisor and personnel department is discussed below.

The Supervisor as Career Counselor. While supervisors should help provide developmental assignments for subordinates and provide them with feedback through performance appraisal (see Exercises 4 and 5), their day-to-day involvement in career development and management comes primarily in the form of counseling.

Counseling can be defined as assisting employees to solve what they perceive to be a problem—any problem which may affect their work (e.g., poor performance, attendance, personal conduct, apathy, anxiety, etc.). After the problem has been identified by the subordinate and the supervisor, a sensitive and competent supervisor can be very effective at problem solving on a one-to-one basis. The supervisor's knowledge and interpersonal/helping skills are required, as is the subordinate's trust. Vocational and career coun-

---

[14] See activities in this exercise, as well as P. P. Kotter et al., *Self-Assessment and Career Development* (Englewood Cliffs, New Jersey: Prentice-Hall, 1978); N. Weiler, *Reality and Career Planning* (Reading, Mass.: Addison-Wesley, 1977).

seling can be seen as more specialized versions of problem recognition and solution on the job.[15]

There are several theoretical positions and resultant approaches prevalent in the broad area of counseling. These include trait-factor, client-centered, psychodynamic, and developmental approaches.[16] Each offers a different manner of interacting with subordinates to diagnose problems and assist in their solution. For example, the popular client-centered approach, patterned largely after the work of Carl Rogers,[17] translates quite well to the work setting. Very briefly, using the client-centered approach, as problems are addressed and career decisions are made, the counselor (supervisor) facilitates openness on the part of the subordinate, providing a supportive attitude. Rather than attempt to prescribe specific solutions, the counselor would hope to facilitate the subordinate in reaching his or her own solutions and taking "ownership" of the problems. The supervisor, however, may feel a conflict in loyalties (i.e., to the organization or to the subordinate) in such interactions. The example noted above of the subordinate desiring training in a skill not required by the organization is relevant here.

Certain skills are required of supervisors in order to be effective counselors, regardless of which counseling approach is taken. Verbal, communication/listening, and helping skills are crucial. The subordinate who is unwilling to discuss him or herself and is insecure or shy would probably not open up about career aspirations or interests with an overbearing, abrupt supervisor. Sensitivity and patience are necessary. Fig. 5 lists a few pointers regarding the often difficult process of communicating with subordinates about performance and career issues.

A supervisor does not need to be a professional counselor to be effective in career development. But he or she must realize that career development and management is a viable and integral part of managing and that various skills and techniques are required to be effective.

The Role of the Personnel Department. Much of the organization-wide interest and activity in career development and management originate in the personnel or human resource management departments or in specific career development subunits within these units.

Hall and Hall[18] have catalogued several problems related to career management which can be addressed in a macro or organization-wide sense. Fig. 6 summarizes these problems and suggests some potential solutions. As can be seen, various other human-resource programs (e.g., job enrichment [see Exercise 14] and assessment centers [see Exercise 8]) can in themselves be viable solutions to career-related problems.

In addition to these strategies, the organization, through its policies and the entire range of its human resource programs, can facilitate career development in a number of ways. The organization might enhance recruitment, selection, and placement programs to better match persons to positions, thereby lessening dissatisfaction after entry. Improvements in appraisal systems could provide more accurate and detailed feedback about strengths and weaknesses so that career moves could be planned more realistically. Supervisors could be rewarded for their efforts and skills in counseling, coaching, and helping subordinates to plan career moves that attempt to fulfill organizational human-resource needs. Human-resource planning and job-analysis programs could be augmented to provide accurate estimates of numbers and types of positions required in the future, enabling employees to ascertain whether positions they might desire are anticipated to materialize.[19] Career information centers could be established to centralize data about potential positions and offer workshops to help sensitize and train persons in the areas of life and career stages, career growth and development, and the design of individual career development plans.[20] Creative strategies such as sabbaticals have also been used successfully to facilitate career development, personal commitment to careers, and hence improved performance and a higher probability of retention.

Women and Careers. Several societal shifts have altered the role of women in the work force and affected their career development, particularly in occupations previously dominated by males. This has posed an especially challenging and visible problem for organizations. There has been a decline in housewifery as a full-time occupation. Women are marrying later and hav-

[15] See H. J. Peters and J. C. Hansen, eds., *Vocational Guidance and Career Development* (New York: Macmillan, 1977).

[16] See J. O. Crites, "Career Counseling: A Review of Major Approaches," in Peters and Hansen, *Vocational Guidance and Career Development*.

[17] See, e.g., C. Rogers, *On Becoming a Person* (Boston: Houghton Mifflin, 1961).

[18] D. Hall and F. Hall, "What's New in Career Management?" *Organizational Dynamics* 12 (1976): 17–33.

[19] J. W. Walker, "Personal and Career Development," in D. Yoder and H. G. Heneman, eds., *ASPA Handbook of Personnel and Industrial Relations,* Vol. 5 (Washington, D.C.: Bureau of National Affairs, Inc., 1977).

[20] Gutteridge, "Organizational Career Development."

Fig. 5. Communication skills (From I. V. Emerson, *Evaluating Your Staff,* Washington, D.C.: National Association of Regional Councils, 1978.)

Ways to Tune in Other People

- Listen full blast—pay full, active attention to the person speaking. Take notes if you find your mind wandering.

- Let the other person know that you hear and understand by nodding, smiling, or reacting in words.

- Probe with questions to make sure you're getting the full picture, all the information you need, all sides of the story.

- Empathize with the person you're listening to by letting him or her know that you have problems and shortcomings, too, and you know how it feels.

- Check out your understanding of what the other person is saying by paraphrasing and asking if that's what he or she meant: "In other words you're saying..." or "If I understand you correctly you mean...."

- Summarize at the end of the conversation to make sure that you and the person you're talking with will both leave with the same impressions of what was said.

- Learn to ask questions and give evaluations using descriptive rather than evaluative language. Even a fairly serious criticism can be accepted by an employee if the language you use is straightforward and focused on the performance rather than the individual.

- Be aware of your style of communication and situation in which you are using it. Sometimes it's appropriate to be assertive. At other times it works best to be reassuring. Sometimes you should lead a discussion, and at other times you should fade into the background as much as possible.

Fig. 6. Career-related problems and potential solutions involving human-resource programs (D. Hall and F. Hall, "What's New in Career Management," *Organizational Dynamics* 12 (1976): 17–33.)

Problem	*Programs/potential solutions*
High turnover	Provide challenging first jobs
	Provide job enrichment
	Provide realistic job previews
Develop high-potential candidates quickly	Develop assessment centers
	Develop clear job paths
Increase promotion opportunities in stable or contrasting environment	Provide cross-functional (lateral) moves
	Provide fall-back positions for promotions and transfers that do not work out
	Provide downward moves at the same pay

ing fewer children, later in their lives. They are more educated and are participating in even greater numbers in the work force.[21] In addition, Equal Employment Opportunity (EEO) (see Exercise 17) legislation has banned discrepancies between women's and men's reward and career structures which have been discriminatory.

There has thus been an enormous amount written recently concerning the management of women's careers.[22] Numerous guidelines have been offered. The solutions to long-standing attitudinal barriers against women will not be easy or quick ones. Recognizing that some male supervisor's negative perceptions concerning women's perceived competence and the in-

appropriateness of their personality or temperament for managerial positions are myths, and noting women's low self-concepts and fear of failure are keys to solving the problems.[23] The solutions begin with sound human-resource programs that select and promote on the basis of merit, not sex, and with equitable reward and appraisal systems. In addition, training is required to help identify and alleviate negative attitudes or perceptions that lead to covert discrimination.

Simply hiring a manager because she is a woman is not sufficient. Designing a recruiting system that locates qualified women, as well as other human-resource systems that ensure the systematic integration of women into all organizational levels, is required. Eventually women (and minorities) will be dealt with equitably by human-resource programs in order to eliminate discrimination. Then the career

---

[21] R. A. VanDusen and E. B. Sheldon, "The Changing Status of American Women," in Peters and Hansen, *Vocational Guidance.*

[22] See, e.g., B. A. Stead, ed., *Women in Management* (Englewood Cliffs, N.J.: Prentice-Hall, 1978).

[23] V. O'Leary, "Some Attitudinal Barriers to Occupational Aspirations in Women," *Psychological Bulletin* 81 (1974): 809–826.

development and management process becomes one of effectively dealing with careers of "managers" or "scientists," or "employees," not of "women managers," or "women scientists" or "women employees."

Retirement Planning and Career Development. Some of the same societal factors affecting values and concerns of women also affect retirees. Retirement planning has also become more visible lately. The work force is more educated, and it is aging. Gains in medicine have enabled many people to remain in the work force longer. Economic necessity, interest, and motivation have also kept people working.[24] Age discrimination legislation has also been passed (see Exercise 17).

The organization has a responsibility to its older workers as well as to its younger ones. Challenging first jobs are as important to younger workers as are final positions which stimulate and utilize them with dignity to older workers. In addition, the organization might structure jobs to lessen travel or physical exertion for older workers. Varying the ages in occupational groups to take advantage of more experienced workers' knowledge can be useful. Training and development programs to reduce tensions and foster understanding between older and younger workers could reduce anxieties of all workers. Certainly some specific changes such as those in benefits, including for example, credit toward pensions for accumulated sick leave, are very attractive to older workers.

Perhaps the worst mistake the organization can make is to assume that performance always declines with age or that careers are over simply because of technological changes in jobs held by older workers. In fact, beginning a second career at middle age now seems to be quite popular. Career development strategies to anticipate what skills need to be acquired might keep people productive throughout their careers. Career paths, transfer, rotational assignments, and changes in job duties to emphasize advising and mentoring roles are all important career considerations for workers near retirement.

The Relation of Career Development and Management to Other Human Resource Programs. The preceding discussion emphasized the interrelationship between career-related programs and activities and other human resource programs.[25] The overall organizational objective with all programs is, of course, the effective use of human resources, which requires a fully integrated system. Each aspect of the career management process assumes that another human-resource program has provided it with appropriate inputs or will use its outputs to manage human resources.

For example, the development of career paths—series of positions, perhaps with increasing skill and responsibilities, through which persons are able to move over time—is effective only if job analysis and human-resource planning systems have accurately identified numbers and types of positions that will be required. In addition, once career paths are designed, training and development systems use the information for designing programs to teach skills required to move along the path. Reward systems use the information to evaluate the jobs' relative complexity and set appropriate salary levels. Career activities, like other facets of the human resource program, are related to all other programs and hence must be properly integrated with them.

Summary. The preceding discussion of career planning, development, and management has only scratched the surface of an increasingly important and far-reaching human-resource management issue. We have emphasized the roles that individuals and organizations must take in the area of careers, through supervisors and personnel departments. While the perspective of individuals and organizations differ in scope, many of their activities, such as assessment of career potential and interests, understanding of career behavior, and the development of strategies to further careers, are similar. The objectives from each perspective must be compatible. Satisfying the organization's long-term needs for talent, commitment, and performance can best be achieved through satisfying the individual's needs for growth, challenge, and a fulfilling career.

Intensive work in personnel departments on careers is relatively new. It has been spurred simultaneously by organizations' realization of the importance of developing a long-lasting commitment from people via a career orientation and the elevated expectations of employees. As with many programs, however, career development programs raise expectations even further. Organizations must be able to act on these expectations to remain credible.

Regardless of the specifics of any career development activity, the foregoing discussion points out certain suggestions which can be made to facilitate effectiveness. First, career development is related to training programs but differs in that it is an effort to facilitate movement through a series of positions over a relatively long period of time. Second, career problems

[24] J. Sonnerfeld, "Dealing with the Aging Workforce," *Harvard Business Review* 56 (November–December 1978): 81–92.

[25] Human-resource programs referred to in this section are discussed in detail in separate exercises elsewhere in this volume.

and strategies have general applicability but must essentially be designed for each individual, taking into account his or her unique interests, past experiences, abilities, personality, and life stage. Third, organizations must attempt to show that career ladders and each position within them have some intrinsic value to the organization and to the right person. Jobs must be seen as satisfying in their own right, not simply as a means to a higher position. The only road to improvement and development is not straight up! Fourth, organizations that are serious about career development and management must train and reward supervisors for demonstrating skills related to counseling, communicating, career planning, providing performance feedback, and planning. Each supervisor must see these tasks as an important, integral part of managing.

Payoffs to the organization as a result of an effective career planning, development, and management system come in the form of increased commitment to job and organization, improved performance, and ability to predict and meet human-resource requirements. For individual employees, enhanced self-worth, job satisfaction, and the opportunity to continue to develop their skills and abilities are potential benefits. Each party must take responsibility and commit their resources in order to reap these benefits.

PROCEDURE

Overview. Forms are provided to use in each person's assessment of their own background, interests, knowledge, skills, abilities, and experience. Then career objectives and plans are developed for each individual. Groups are asked to conduct and observe a role play of a career development review session, providing feedback on communication skills and effective problem-solving behavior. A career path is designed for the same person in the role play.

PART A

STEP 1: In Form 1, *each* person should answer each of the various types of questions, providing a realistic self-assessment. Be deliberate and serious in order to provide useful data for yourself. After you have completed the form, look over your responses, reflect upon them, look for trends, patterns, or surprises. Discuss some responses with others who completed the form.

TIME: About two hours.

STEP 2: Now that you have a basis for reflecting upon your own career interests, complete Form 2

and develop *specific* career plans and objectives. Then note some actions you plan to take as you begin to attain these goals. Make them realistic, personal, and useful for goal attainment. If you have not yet begun a career in a formal sense, your goals and action plans will probably reflect those required for an effective job search and information-gathering process. If you are currently in one of the various career stages, your plans would reflect next steps to further your career.

TIME: About one to two hours.

PART B

STEP 3: Form 3 provides background on a conglomerate in the fashion industry, Paris Fashions, Inc., and one of its subsidiaries, Corky Craig, Ltd. Information is also given about one of Corky Craig's employees, J. Harris, to be combined with an Assessor's Report on Harris found in the Assessment Center (Exercise 8). Choose a male or female to be his (or her) supervisor. Then conduct a career development discussion with Harris as each plays their respective roles. Be sure to cover the issues noted on Form 4 and complete this form as you conduct the role play. The *Appendix* to the exercise provides some hints for effective communication and feedback, important issues in this type of interaction. The remaining group members act as observers, completing Form 5. After the role play, designed to last 20 to 30 minutes, observers should discuss their observations with the participants, providing feedback on the effectiveness of the behavior of each in such a situation.

TIME: About one hour.

STEP 4: Form 6 asks for the development of a career path for Harris. A career path can be defined as a series of related positions that together help form a career for a person in an organization. As you develop the career path, note all of the potential routes Harris could take in Corky Craig within the three departments described in detail on the Corky Craig organization chart. Be sure your path reflects Harris's strengths and weaknesses, the requirements you assume for each particular position, and the probability that the positions would become available at the time Harris would be ready for them. A career path is a forecast, resting upon various uncertainties and assumptions. Try to be creative as you develop a path that attains individual and organizational objectives.

TIME: About one hour.

FOR FURTHER READING

Bartol, K. M. "The Sex Structuring of Organizations: A Search for Possible Causes." *Academy of Management Review* 3 (1978): 805–815. (II–R)

Benson, P., and G. Thornton. "A Model Career Planning Program." *Personnel* 55 (1978): 31–39. (I)

Berlew, D., and D. T. Hall. "The Socialization of Managers." *Administrative Science Quarterly* II (1966): 207–223. (II–R)

Bolles, R. *What Color Is Your Parachute?* Berkeley, Cal.: Ten Speed, 1973. (I)

Bowen, D. D., and D. T. Hall. "Career Planning for Employee Development." *California Management Review* 20 (Winter 1977): 23–35. (I)

Bray, D. et al. *Formative Years in Business.* New York: Wiley, 1974. (I–R)

Brennan, L. D. et al. *Resumes for Better Jobs.* New York: Simon & Schuster, 1973. (I)

Bright, W. "How One Company Manages Its Human Resources." *Harvard Business Review* 54 (January–February 1976): 81–92. (I)

Burack, E. H. "Self-Assessment: A Strategy of Growing Importance." *Training and Development Journal* 41 (April 1979): 48–52. (I)

Cassell, F. H. "The Increasing Complexity of Retirement Decisions." *MSU Business Topics* 27 (Winter 1979): 15–24. (I)

Corey, G. *I Never Knew I Had a Choice.* Monterey, Cal.: Brooks/Cole, 1979. (I)

Cotton, C. C., and R. F. Fraser. "On-the-Job Career Planning: One Organization's Approach." *Training and Development Journal* 32 (February 1978): 20–24. (I)

Cox, A. J. *Confessions of a Corporate Headhunter.* New York: Trident, 1973. (I)

Criter, J. "Work and Careers." In R. Dubin, ed. *Handbook of Work, Organization, and Society.* Chicago: Rand McNally, 1977. (II)

Crystal, J. C., and R. N. Bolles. *Where Do I Go From Here With My Life?* New York: Seabury, 1974. (I)

Downs, S. et al. "Self-Appraisal: A Convergence of Selection and Guidance." *Journal of Occupational Psychology* 51 (1976): 271–278. (II–R)

"Dual-Career Couples." *Psychology of Women Quarterly,* special issue, 1978. (II–R)

Glueck, W. F. *Personnel.* rev. ed. Dallas: Business Publications, Inc., 1978. (I)

Grass, D. "A Guide to R & D Career Pathing." *Personnel Journal* 58 (1979): 227–231. (I)

Gutteridge, J. "Organizational Career Development: State of the Practice." *Annual Academy of Management National Meeting,* Kansas City, August 1976. (II)

Hackman, J. R., and L. L. Suttle. *Improving Life at Work.* Santa Monica, Cal.: Goodyear, 1977. (I)

Hall, D. *Careers in Organizations.* Santa Monica, Cal.: Goodyear, 1976. (I)

Hall, D., and F. Hall. "What's New in Career Management." *Organization Dynamics* 12 (1976): 17–33.

Hall, D., and D. Super. "Career Development: Exploration and Planning." *Annual Review Psychology* 29 (1978): 333–372. (II)

Hall, D. T. "A Theoretical Model of Career Subidentity Development in Organizational Settings." *Organizational Behavior and Human Performance* 6 (1971): 50–76. (II–R)

Hall, D. T. "Potential for Career Growth." *Personnel Administration* 34 (May–June 1971): 18–30. (I)

Hall, D. T., and F. S. Hall. *The Two-Career Couple.* Reading, Mass.: Addison-Wesley, 1979. (I)

Heilman, M. E., and L. R. Saruvatari. "When Beauty is Beastly: The Effects of Appearance and Sex on Evaluations of Applicants for Managerial and Nonmanagerial Jobs." *Organizational Behavior and Human Performance* 23 (1979): 360–372. (II–R)

Hennings, M., and A. Jardim. "Women Executives in the Old Boy Network." *Psychology Today* 11 (January 1977): 76–81. (I)

Holland, J. *Making Vocational Choices: A Theory of Careers.* Englewood Cliffs, New Jersey: Prentice-Hall, 1973. (II)

Jelinek, M. *Career Management for the Individual and the Organization.* St. Clair: Wiley, 1979. (I)

Jelinek, M. *Career Management and Women.* Paper presented at the International Communications Association Conference. Berlin, West Germany, 1976. (I)

Jelinek, M., and A. Harlan. *MBA Goals and Aspirations.* Given at a national meeting of the Academy of Management. Detroit, Mich., 1980. (I–R)

Jennings, E. E. "Mobicentric Man." *Psychology Today* 4 (July 1970): 35–40. (I)

Kellogg, M. S. *Career Management.* New York: American Management Association, Inc., 1972. (I)

Kay, M. J. "Employee Counseling." In D. Yoder and H. G. Heneman, Jr., eds. *ASPA Handbook of Personnel and Industrial Relations.* Vol. 5. Washington, D.C.: BNA, 1977. (I)

Kotter, J. P. et al. *Self-Assessment and Career Development.* Englewood Cliffs, New Jersey: Prentice-Hall, 1978. (I)

Leach, J. "The Notion and Nature of Careers." *The Personnel Administrator* 22 (Sept. 1977): 49–55. (I)

Levinson, D. J. *The Seasons of a Man's Life.* New York: Knopf, 1978. (I)

Levinson, H. "On Being a Middle-Aged Manager." *Harvard Business Review* 47 (1969): 51–60. (I)

Lippitt, G. "Developing Life Plans." *Training and Development Journal* 33 (1979): 2–7. (I)

Maanen, J. Van, ed. *Organizational Careers.* New York: Wiley, 1977. (I)

Maccoby, M. *The Gamesman.* New York: Simon & Schuster, 1976. (I)

Mardon, J., and R. Hopkins. "The Eight-Year Career Development Plan." *Training and Development Journal* 23 (1969): 10–15. (I)

Marsh, P. "The Career Development Workshop." *Training and Development Journal* 27 (1973): 38–45. (I)

May, R. *Man's Search For Himself.* New York: Dell, 1973. (I)

Morgan, M. A., D. T. Hall, and A. Martier. "Career Development Strategies in Industry—Where We Are and Where We Should Be." *Personnel* 56 (March–April 1979): 13–30. (I)

Muller, D. H. "A Model for Human Resources Development." *Personnel Journal* 55 (1976): 238–243. (I)

O'Leary, V. "Some Attitudinal Barriers to Occupational Aspiration in Women." *Psychological Bulletin* 81 (1974): 809–826. (II)

Osipow, S. *Theories of Career Development.* New York: Appleton-Century-Crofts, 1968. (II)

Palmer, W. "An Integrated Program for Career Development." *Personnel Journal* 51 (1972): 398–451. (I)

Peters, H. J., and J. C. Hansen, eds. *Vocational Guidance and Career Development.* 3d ed. New York: Macmillan, 1977. (II) See also J. O. Crites, "Career Counseling: A Review of Major Approaches." *The Counseling Psychologist* 4 (1974): 3–23. (II)

"Plotting a Route to the Top." *Business Week* (October 12, 1974). (I)

Quinn, J. E. "Job Characteristics and Early Retirement." *Industrial Relations* 17 (1978): 315–323. (II–R)

Reha, R. K. "Preparing Women for Management Roles." *Business Horizons* 22 (April 1979): 68–71. (I)

Roe, A. *The Psychology of Occupations.* New York: Wiley, 1956. (II)

Rogers, C. *On Becoming a Person.* Boston: Houghton Mifflin, 1961. (I)

Sargent, A. G., ed. *Beyond Sex Roles.* St. Paul: West, 1977. (I)

Schein, E. G. *Career Dynamics.* Reading, Mass.: Addison-Wesley, 1978. (II)

Sheehy, G. *Passages: Predictable Crises of Adult Life.* New York: Dutton, 1976. (I)

Shingleton, J., and R. Bao. *College to Career.* New York: McGraw-Hill, 1977. (I)

Slocum, W. *Occupational Careers.* Chicago: Aldine, 1974. (I)

Sonnenfeld, J. "Dealing with the Aging Work Force." *Harvard Business Review* 56 (November–December 1978): 81–92. (I)

Sperry, L., and L. Hess. *Contact Counseling: Developing People in Organizations.* Reading, Mass.: Addison-Wesley, 1974. (I)

Souerwine, A. H. *Career Strategies.* New York: Amacom, 1978. (I)

Staats, E. "Career Planning and Development: Which Way Is Up?" *Public Administration Review* 37 (1977): 73–76. (I)

Stead, B. A., ed. *Women in Management.* Englewood Cliffs, New Jersey: Prentice-Hall, 1978. (I)

Sullivan, D. E. "Never Too Old." *Personnel Administrator* 23 (June 1978): 54–58. (I)

Super, D. E. *The Psychology of Careers.* New York: Harper & Row, 1957. (II)

Terkel, S. *On Working.* New York: Random House, 1974. (I)

Thornton, G. C. "Differential Effects of Career Planning on Internals and Externals." *Personnel Psychology* 31 (1978): 471–476. (II–R)

Valliant, G. E. *Adaptation to Life.* Boston: Little Brown, 1977. (I)

Walker, J. W. "Individual Career Planning." *Business Horizons* 16 (1973): 65–72. (I)

Walker, J. W. "Personal and Career Development." In D. Yoder and H. G. Heneman, Jr., eds., *ASPA Handbook of Personnel and Industrial Relations,* vol. 5. Washington, D.C.: Bureau of National Affairs, Inc., 1977. (I)

Walter, V. "Self-Motivated Personal Career Planning: A Breakthrough in Human Resource Management." *Personnel Journal* 55 (1976): 162–167. (I)

Warneth, C. F. "Vocational Theories: Direction to Nowhere." In J. O. Crites, "Career Counseling:

A Review of Major Approaches. *The Counseling Psychologist* 4 (1974): 3–23. (II)

Weiler, N. *Reality and Career Planning*. Reading, Mass.: Addison-Wesley, 1977. (I)

Wellbank, H. et al. "Planning Job Progression for Effective Career Development and Human Resource Management." *Personnel* 55 (1978): 55–64. (I)

APPENDIX
Communication Skills*

Good communication skills embody several characteristics:

1. Seeking to clarify your ideas before communicating;
2. Examining the true purpose of each communication;
3. Considering the total physical human setting whenever you communicate;
4. Consulting with others, when appropriate, in planning communications;
5. Being mindful, while you communicate, of the overtones as well as the basic content of your message;
6. Taking the opportunity, when it arises, to convey something of help or value to the employee;
7. Following up your communication;
8. Communicating for tomorrow as well as today;
9. Being sure your actions support your communications;

10. Seeking not only to be understood but to understand—being a good listener.

Efficient and effective listening skills are:

1. Action listening;
2. Listening for total meaning;
3. Listening to feelings;
4. Avoiding stumbling blocks to listening which include:
   - Prejudging,
   - Jumping to conclusions,
   - Assuming that others think as you do,
   - The wandering mind,
   - The closed mind,
   - Wishful hearing,
   - Plural meanings,
   - Excessive talking,
   - Absence of humility,
   - Fear, and
   - Absence of good feedback.

The characteristics of good feedback are being:

1. Specific rather than general;
2. Focused on the behavior, not the person;
3. Considerate of the needs of receiver;
4. Directed at behavior that the receiver can do something about;
5. Solicited rather than imposed;
6. Involved with sharing of information rather than giving advice;
7. Well-timed;
8. Involved with the amount of communication the receiver can use;
9. Concerned with what is said or done, not why; and
10. Checked to ensure clear communication.

* From R. S. Schuler, "Effective Use of Communication to Minimize Employee Stress," *The Personnel Administrator* 24, no. 4 (June 1979): 43–44.

PART A

Form 1 Self-Assessment Activities*

In order to obtain a more realistic and complete data base about yourself upon which to base career plans, complete the following activities.

A.   *Who Am I?*
     List ten statements below that answer the question, "Who am I?"

1.

2.

3.

4.

5.

6.

7.

8.

9.

10.

B.   *Life Line*
     Draw a line below representing your life. Peaks, valleys, and slopes represent various positive and negative events and periods. The length of the line between changes in its slope signifies the length of various periods in your life. Extend the line outward beyond the point at which you are now and label events and periods all along the line that you feel are significant. Use additional sheets if necessary.

* See also G. L. Lippitt, "Developing Life Plans," *Training and Development Journal* (May 1970): 2–7; J. H. Zenger et al., *How to Work for a Living and Like It* (Reading, Mass.: Addison-Wesley, 1977); D. T. Hall et al., *Experiences in Management and Organizational Behavior* (Chicago: St. Clair, 1975); J. P. Kotler et al., *Self-Assessment and Career Development* (Englewood Cliffs, New Jersey: Prentice-Hall, 1978).

Form 1 (continued)

C. *Ranking Values*

Rank order the values below to reflect their relative importance to you. The definitions are general and not exhaustive, but are meant as illustrations of what the values could mean.

Rank

1. *Kindness*
    Being kind, loving, tender, affectionate to people; helping others; forgiving.
    _____

2. *Intellectualism*
    Interest in current affairs; intellectual curiosity; appreciation for art, music, literature, etc.; enjoyment of books; reflection; intelligence.
    _____

3. *Loyalty*
    Defending honor; helping organize group activity; working to improve prestige of group; staying committed to group, person, organization.
    _____

4. *Honesty*
    Never cheating or breaking the law; truthfulness; representing self truthfully; sincerity.
    _____

5. *Religiousness*
    Being devout; living one's religion on a day-to-day basis; belief in God or a being greater than people; prayer; seeking comfort in religion.
    _____

6. *Independence*
    Being outspoken, freethinking, frank; living own life free from control of others when given a choice; stripping self of social restraints, pressures; independent financially; self-reliant, self-sufficient.
    _____

7. *Acceptance of Authority*
    Obedient, respectful, deferent to authority figures; abiding by rules, policies voluntarily; will follow orders; dutiful.
    _____

8. *Pleasure*
    Enjoyment; leisurely life; doing what one prefers in choice situations; "giving in" to self.
    _____

9. *Equality*
    Fairness; equal opportunity; lack of prejudice, bigotry, favoritisms; brotherhood/sisterhood.
    _____

10. *Ambition*
    Achievement, getting ahead, having high goals and wants; taking action to better self and situation; hard-working.
    _____

11. *Family*
    Close familial ties; interest in family and family relationships; helping family; parenting.
    _____

12. *Adventure*
    Daring, stimulation-seeking; creative, imaginative; active.
    _____

13. *Affluence*
    Wealth, material goods; ability to consume; acquisition of material things; ability to live comfortably.
    _____

Form 1 (continued)

D. Skills/Abilities/Knowledge Inventory
    1. *Education* (degrees working toward, obtained; courses taken; training programs; certificates, etc.)

    _____

    _____

    _____

    _____

    _____

    2. *Experience*
        Jobs

        _____

        _____

        _____

        _____

        Experience other than jobs

        _____

        _____

        _____

        _____

        _____

        What I *learned* and/or can now *do* as a result of the above experience

        _____

        _____

        _____

        _____

        _____

Form 1 (continued)

Skill Level Ratings
Use the scale below to select the number that best represents your assessment of yourself on each item.

5 Exceptionally skilled—outstanding competence

4 Highly skilled—a strength

3 Generally competent—proficient

2 Limited competence—an area of difficulty or little experience/training

1 Minimal competence—definite problem area or no experience/training

Self-assessment

PEOPLE SKILLS

A. Supervising, overseeing, managing, directing others _____

B. Coaching, counseling, helping, training, advising, mentoring others _____

C. Persuading, convincing, selling, influencing others _____

D. Evaluating, judging, appraising, rating, setting goals for others _____

E. Entertaining, joking, telling stories; stimulating, captivating, engaging others _____

F. Organizing, cooperating, integrating, coordinating others _____

THINKING SKILLS

A. Fixing, diagnosing problems _____

B. Inventing, developing, setting up _____

C. Operating, running _____

D. Monitoring, inspecting, organizing _____

E. General mechanical ability _____

DATA SKILLS

A. Communicating data verbally _____

B. Communicating data orally _____

C. Compiling, integrating, coordinating, summarizing, synthesizing _____

D. Computing, calculating, figuring, analyzing _____

E. Conceiving, problem solving, abstract reasoning _____

Form 1 (continued)

E. *Preferred Job Outcomes*
Rate each of the following potential outcomes from a job in importance to you.

	Most important			Least important	
	5	4	3	2	1
A. Status, recognition					
B. Money, material rewards					
C. Opportunity to learn, grow, and develop					
D. Opportunity to work with others					
E. Opportunity to supervise others					
F. Security					
G. Working conditions (physical)					
H. Geographically desirable location					
I. Autonomy					
J. Variety					
K. Challenge					
L. Travel					
M. Respect of peers, professional colleagues					
N. Accomplish socially important work					

PART A

Form 2 Career Planning

After you have completed Form 1, analyze your responses to uncover any surprises and note any patterns. For example, you ranked ambition highly as a value in Part C above and also described yourself in Part A above patterns. Summarize the information. You could begin to make some career plans based upon your self-assessment. Such plans are useful whether you currently hold a position or are entering the job market in the near future. The purpose of the plan is simply to focus your thinking about a viable set of career options, goals, and preferences.

A. *Career Options*
    Given the data generated in Form 1, what occupational groups, specific positions, and types of organizations seem suitable for you?

    _____

    _____

    _____

B. *Career Goals*
    State career goals (e.g., jobs you would like to hold, skills/abilities/knowledge you would like to acquire, outcomes you anticipate from your working life, further education you are planning) for the three time periods indicated below. Try to be realistic. For example, if you have a goal to be a vice president of a specific bank five years after you begin work, have you checked to see that vice presidents are ever chosen with five years' experience?

    Immediate Goals (in the next year)

    _____

    _____

    _____

    Intermediate Goals (two to five years)

    _____

    _____

    _____

    Long-range Goals (after five years)

    _____

    _____

    _____

C. *Action Planning*
    Once some broad goals have been identified, action steps are required to attain them. List a few of these below for your immediate career goals. Also indicate what you plan to do to remove any obstacles that inhibit you from realizing your goals. Be very specific and realistic. State actions in concrete terms—what you really plan to *do*. An example would be to enroll in a computer programming course in order to gain experience in that area and enhance your marketability for a personnel job in that industry. An obstacle might be your fear of quantitative topics, including computers. It could be removed by talking to people who have taken the course or the instructor, looking over the materials required for the course and perhaps beginning to review them before the course begins, and scheduling your time and course load next semester to allow for extra work on the computer course. Perhaps revision of the goal would be in order.

Form 2 (continued)

What I plan to do	How I plan to do it	When I plan to do it	Obstacles	Plan to remove obstacles
Action 1				
Action 2				
Action 3				

PART B

Form 3 Background on Paris Fashions, Inc., Corky Craig, Ltd., and J. Harris

Paris Fashions, Inc. This is a large conglomerate in the fashion industry, controlling various specific organizations that produce, market, and distribute women's clothing. Among the larger subsidiaries are the following: Paris Media, Inc. (a twenty-million-dollar-a-year firm handling most of Paris's print and nonprint media advertising; Corky Craig, Ltd. (a manufacturing firm that produces several lines of clothing), and Paris Wholesale (a wholesaling firm that distributes various labels to retailers).

Paris itself employs about 8000 persons in all of its divisions and has a total combined sales of 94 million dollars annually. The organization is young, begun in 1947 through a consolidation of a few older garment houses in New York, and aggressive. Paris now prides itself on modern financial planning, diversification across markets, the very latest automated equipment, vertically integrated manufacturing, and sophisticated human resource management. Paris is recognized as a leader in the fashion industry through its successful efforts at hiring and developing new designers, its marketing and advertising ability which allows its clothing to have a significant impact on fashion, and its prudent financial management. The headquarters of the organization are in Washington, D.C., but the headquarters of its large divisions are in New York, Boston, Chicago, and Atlanta. Paris is traded in the New York Stock Exchange and is a widely held corporation. It is now moving into related fashion business, such as publishing a newspaper to compete with *Women's Wear Daily*, producing television shows on fashion and health for women, and developing a book publishing organization to sign authors writing in the fashion field.

As noted above, Paris is very concerned with human-resource management issues. Each of its subsidiaries and/or divisions has a top management group who is committed to employee development. Training, career management, human-resource planning, and appraisal systems are formalized and credible. In fact, Paris has management progression charts and skills inventories (see Exercise 2) for all of its units and uses the data from these systems to make such personnel decisions as promotion.

Corky Craig, Ltd. Corky Craig, Ltd. is one of the largest manufacturing divisions of Paris Fashions. It employs about 1100 persons in its suburban Atlanta location. Corky Craig produces women's clothing, primarily sportswear (e.g., blouses, slacks, casual dresses, outerwear) under the Corky Craig, Ltd. label. The clothing is very well-made, stylish, and priced to compete with the foreign designer labels. In fact, marketing and advertising strategies developed by Paris Media emphasizing Corky Craig, Ltd. as the "American Designer for the American Woman" have done very well. Annual sales topped eighty million dollars last year. The company was begun in 1964.

Corky Craig, Ltd. is a very sophisticated operation, employing the latest in technology, financial planning, and management techniques. The top management, consistent with the emphasis of its parent company, Paris Fashions, Inc., has developed successful employee training, development, and appraisal systems. Careers are developed and managed at Corky Craig, Ltd. with considerable success, particularly at the supervisory levels. All Corky Craig, Ltd. managers are required to attend self-assessment and career development workshops and individual career development plans are prepared annually as part of the performance appraisal process. Results of such plans are fed into human resource forecasts and training programs. An interesting feature of this system is that all managers are themselves appraised on how well they develop and manage the careers of their subordinates. Their skill in this area is thus one of the factors considered in their own appraisal. Bonus awards and merit increases, as well as promotions, go to the most highly skilled human resource managers. Persons who have risen in the corporate hierarchy in the last decade have demonstrated such skills.

Corky Craig, Ltd. has a traditional hierarchical organizational structure, displayed in the following charts. The vice presidents are chosen with the approval of the Paris Fashions, Inc. Human Resource Development group and often come from other Paris subsidiaries. Positions below the vice president level are typically chosen from within Corky Craig, Ltd. by its own management.

Form 3 (continued)

Corky Craig, Ltd. Organization Chart*

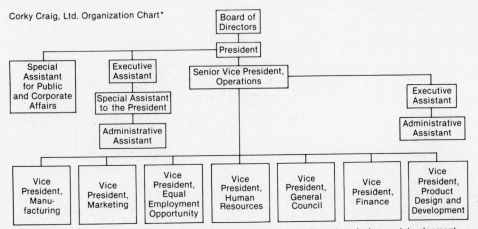

* Clerical positions omitted; details of human resources, general council, product design and development units omitted

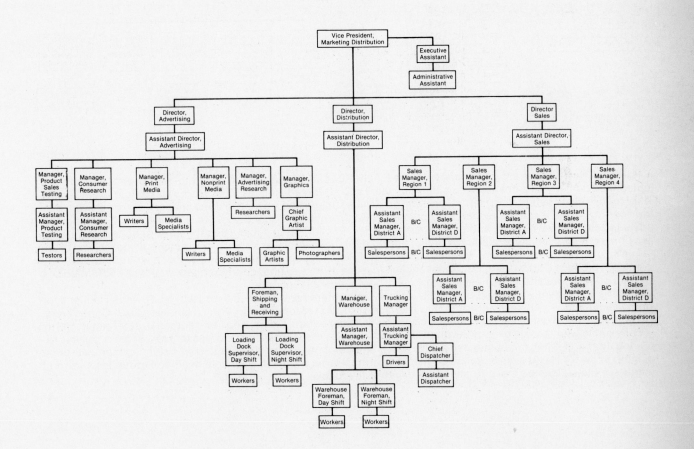

Form 3 (continued)

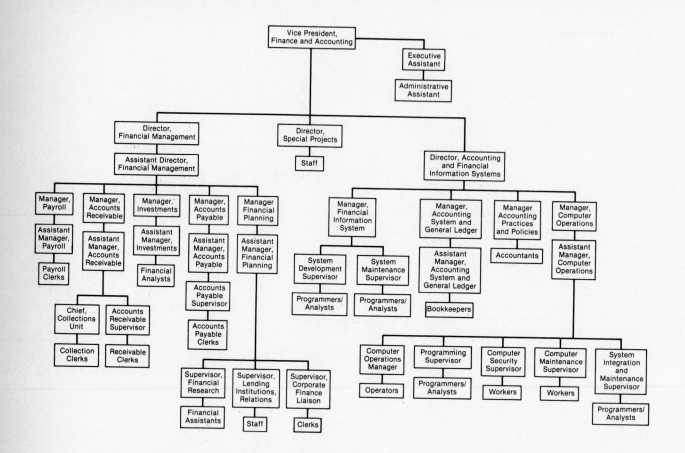

J. Harris. J. Harris is currently a supervisor in the Finance Department at Corky Craig, Ltd. Harris is 31 years old and joined the company as a financial assistant four years ago after receiving his MBA. Harris was employed as a bank teller for five years before that. Harris's present job entails supervising a group of three financial assistants who perform various tasks including research on potential investments for Corky Craig, Ltd.'s cash, sources of funds for financing capital investments, and other assorted duties. In addition to supervising the three subordinates, Harris has primary responsibility for pulling together information the financial assistant group obtains at the request of the group's supervisor, the assistant manager of Financial Planning; and for presenting oral and written reports. Any very large projects Corky Craig, Ltd. might engage in, such as how to finance a new plant, would be coordinated by Harris's supervisors and Paris Fashions, Inc.'s corporate financial people.

Harris has recently attended one of the assessment centers (see Exercise 8) developed by Paris Fashions for Corky Craig, Ltd. The results appear in that exercise as the Assessors' Report Form. Harris is a loyal Corky Craig, Ltd. employee who is interested in career advancement. In appearance, demeanor, and personal preferences, Harris is compatible with fashion executives and Corky Craig, Ltd.'s managers, but the assessors saw some problems requiring attention. They recommended a stint with a line function in Paris's Chicago men's clothing manufacturing plant to allow for Harris's development in manufacturing. Harris seems to want help but is somewhat insecure and might see the suggested move to Illinois as negative feedback.

Form 3 (continued)

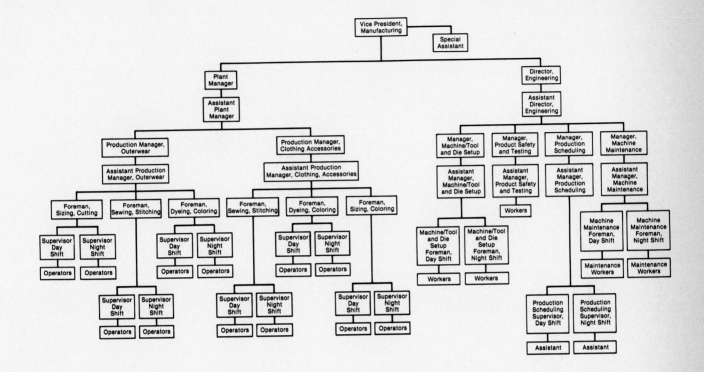

PART B

Form 4 Developmental Discussion and Career Planning with J. Harris

Developmental Discussion

I.   Review of Past Performance

II. Discussion of Potential

III. Discussion of Strengths and Weaknesses

IV. Discussion of Career Goals and Objectives

Individual Career Development Plan

I.   Immediate Career Objectives

_____

_____

_____

I.   Longer-Range Career Objectives

_____

_____

_____

III. Required Steps for Improvement of Performance in Current Job

Individual's Responsibilities and Planned Actions _____   To by done by:

_____   _____

_____   _____

_____   _____

Supervisor's and Organization's Responsibilities and Planned Actions _____   To be done by:

_____   _____

_____   _____

_____   _____

Form 4 (continued)

IV.   Required Steps for Career Advancement

____Individual's Responsibilities and Planned Actions_____   To be done by:

_____   _____

_____   _____

_____   _____

____Supervisor's and Organization's Responsibilities and Planned Actions____   To be done by:

_____   _____

_____   _____

_____   _____

____Plans for Review of Progress on Action Plans_____

_____

_____

V.   Remaining Problems, Roadblocks to Address in Next Discussion

_____

_____

_____

PART B

Form 5 Observer's Record of Developmental Discussion

I.   Comment on the supervisor's communication skills.

_____

_____

II. Comment on the supervisor's feedback skills.

_____

_____

III. Comment on the supervisor's problem-solving ability and creativity.

_____

_____

IV. Comment on the supervisor's ability to build a feeling of trust and put the subordinate
     at ease.

_____

_____

V.   Comment on the subordinate's willingness to be honest, realistic, and accept help.

_____

_____

VI. What feedback do you have for the:

     Supervisor _____

     _____

     Subordinate _____

     _____

PART B

Form 6 Career Pathing

Job incumbent _____ Title _____ Unit_____

Supervisor _____ Title _____ Unit _____

Position titles in order of movement	Rationale for particular position suggested	Time until ready to move	Summary of developmental needs to be addressed before movement	"Fallback position"

ASSESSMENT OF LEARNING IN PERSONNEL ADMINISTRATION
EXERCISE 12

1. Try to state the purpose of this exercise in one concise sentence.

2. Specifically what did you learn for this exercise (i.e., skills, abilities, and knowledge)?

3. How might your learning influence your duties and role as a personnel administrator?

4. How could an organization develop its supervisors to be more effective career developers, planners, and managers?

5. Briefly review the responsibilities of individuals and of organizations in career development. What should each be prepared to do?

6. What could or should a line manager do if one of his or her subordinates wanted to advance his or her career, for example, receiving training in a skill or knowledge area not deemed to be needed by the organization?

Section

MAINTAINING AND IMPROVING COMMITMENT, PERFORMANCE, AND PRODUCTIVITY

An effective human-resource-management system does not end with the selection and training of people. Once these procurement and development functions are completed, human resources must be utilized to their fullest capacity for the mutual benefit of the organization and the individual. Here, the role of personnel administrators, directors of human resources, and their staffs of specialists is to gather data in order to ascertain the degree of commitment, satisfaction, and performance of their human resources. Deficiencies in these areas can thereby be pinpointed and programs aimed at improvement intiated. However, even when no glaring deficiencies are uncovered through investigation and diagnosis, programs must be developed to maintain current levels of performance and commitment.

Section 6 begins with Exercise 13, which demonstrates the uses of an effective research and diagnostic scale, the Job Descriptive Index (JDI). The JDI has been used extensively due to its brevity yet comprehensiveness, and its validity. The data obtained from an instrument such as the JDI would form the rationale for developing specific programs aimed at maintaining and improving commitment, performance, and productivity.

Innumerable performance improvement programs are in use. Many seem to be based on such rewards as challenge, variety, autonomy, and recognition available from the work itself. Exercise 14 deals with job redesign programs, specifically job enrichment, aimed at providing this type of reward. The exercise provides activities designed to build skill in the design and implementation of job enrichment programs.

Other motivation or incentive programs aim to improve performance through more tangible rewards dispensed by the organization or others. The use of such extrinsic rewards as money, verbal praise, feedback, time off from work, etc., is discussed in Exercise 15. Their utility is explained by their ability to modify behavior as they are systematically dispensed and withdrawn in the work environment.

Programs designed to make the most effective use of that single pervasive organizational reward—money—are discussed in detail in Exercise 16, "Job Evaluation and Wage and Salary Administration." This exercise begins with job-evaluation techniques used to rank *jobs* (not people) in order of their relative value or worth to the organization. Subsequent to such a ranking, different wage or salary levels can be attached to each job type in a rational manner in order to develop a wage and salary system.

Exercise 13
Job satisfaction: its meaning and its measurement

PREVIEW

In this exercise the causes of positive and negative feelings or attitudes about one's work are discussed. Negative feelings toward a job, often broadly called job dissatisfaction, have been linked to absences, turnover, strikes, and other problems, in addition to poor mental health. Thus, the assessment of the extent of job dissatisfaction in organizations could be an important first step in improving organizational performance. The exercise provides experiences that build skill in assessing and alleviating job dissatisfaction. A widely used and validated questionnaire, the Job Descriptive Index (JDI), is explained as a technique to measure job satisfaction.

OBJECTIVES

1. To become aware of the possible causes, sequences, and remedies for job dissatisfaction.
2. To build skill in diagnosing those particular aspects of jobs that might lead to dissatisfaction.
3. To build skill in designing and using instruments for assessing the degree of job satisfaction-dissatisfaction within an organization and for interpreting their results.

PREMEETING ASSIGNMENT

Read the entire exercise.

INTRODUCTION
Job Satisfaction as an Indicator of Performance Problems

There has been much publicity lately regarding worker discontent in America.[1] It seems that "blue collar blues" and "white collar woes" have become familiar phrases, not only in the media and among academics, but in the work force itself. Many workers are generally dissatisfied with the boring, routine work they do. They feel they are mere "cogs in a wheel," unable to see the impact of their labor on society. Absenteeism, high turnover, strikes, sabotage, and resistance to change are cited as evidence of widespread worker discontent.

The task for the personal administrator and his or her staff is first to define specifically the extent of this type of discontent and then to assess whether or not it is a problem in the organization. If workers are dissatisfied and deleterious consequences for both themselves and the organization can be pinpointed, remedies must be devised. These remedies are typically within the responsibilities assigned to the personnel division in an organization.

What is Job Satisfaction (JS)? After a thorough analysis of the concept of JS, Edwin Locke offered the

---

[1] One of the most publicized documents is *Work in America* (Cambridge, Mass.: MIT, 1973) prepared by a special task force for the Secretary of Health, Education and Welfare.

following definition: "Job satisfaction is the pleasurable emotional state resulting from the appraisal of one's job as achieving or facilitating one's job values."[2] Thus JS is an emotional concept, a feeling—not a behavior or activity. Research has shown that this feeling is related to behavioral outcomes that are counterproductive when it is negative (i.e., job dissatisfaction or JD).[3] Most importantly, a negative feeling towards one's job is a symptom, a cue that something is wrong. It may simply be disenchantment with one's own lot in life, or it may be psychological frustrations resulting from a feeling of uselessness because one's job offers no challenge.

Causes of Job Dissatisfaction (JD). Many theories as to the nature and causes of job dissatisfaction have been advanced.[4] Negative feelings can arise from lack of variety, autonomy, or challenge, as well as the perceived inadequacy of rewards. They may be traced to the inability of one's work to offer a chance for promotion and recognition, or to the fact that workers are unable to see the impact of their work. Those aspects of jobs that deal with job content are called "motivators" by Frederick Herzberg,[5] an advocate of job enrichment (see Exercise 14) as a way of redesigning jobs to add satisfaction and improve performance.

The absence of motivators leads to JD only if workers want and need challenge, autonomy, etc., from their job. Some workers may be dissatisfied with environmental aspects of their jobs, such as relations with their supervisors and co-workers, pay, fringe benefits, and working conditions (called "hygiene" factors by Herzberg), in addition to content factors or motivators. Thus, any one of a number of aspects of one's job could lead to discontent, depending of course on each worker's own needs, experience, and expectations.

Job Satisfaction and Stress. An increasing amount of work is done each year on the causes and effects of stress and anxiety on the job.[6] Low morale or dissatisfaction can be one factor in the development of stress. Other factors such as management policies, general economic conditions, and needs for security also contribute to stress. These contextual factors interact with a person's degree of vulnerability to produce stress. Certain personality, age, occupation, and physical health profiles would help determine one's vulnerability to job stress. Finally, certain "stressors," such as changes on or off the job, trigger the stress.[7] In one study[8] those managers with low job satisfaction were found to have higher job stress.

Three types of remedies can be effective for reducing job stress.[9] These include self-management (e.g., good nutrition, exercise), the creation and use of supporting relationships on and off the job, and certain organizational improvements (e.g., team building, free flow of information, setting realistic deadlines). While the exact nature of the relationship between job satisfaction and job stress is unknown at this time, enough evidence exists to link these two emotional states both to job-related causes and outcomes. Because stress and satisfaction are both experiential in nature and may have observable, physical consequences, each individual's perception and expectations can contribute to their causes and remedies.

Expectations and JS. The emotional feelings we have defined as JS are perceptually determined by each individual. A certain level of pay may not be dissatisfying until it is perceived to be too low by the worker. People decide on the degree to which their own value standards, aspirations, and aspects of jobs that fall short can cause discontent.

But how are these expectations set? Often people compare their perceptions of what a job offers to their perceptions of what others' jobs offer. If a worker's subjective evaluation or perception of his or her ratio

[2] E. A. Locke, "What is Job Satisfaction," *Organizational Behavior and Human Performance* 4 (1969): 316. The conceptual development and research instruments for job satisfaction were initially developed by P. C. Smith and her associates. See P. C. Smith, L. M. Kendall, and C. L. Hulin, *The Measurement of Satisfaction in Work and Retirement: A Strategy for the Study of Attitudes,* Chicago: Rand McNally, 1969).

[3] See L. Porter and R. M. Steers, "Organizational, Work, and Personal Factors in Employee Turnover and Satisfaction," *Psychological Bulletin* 50 (1973): 151-176.

[4] J. P. Wanous and E. E. Lawler, "Measurement and Meaning of Job Satisfaction," *Journal of Applied Psychology* 36 (1972): 95-105.

[5] See F. Herzberg, "One More Time: How Do You Motivate Workers?" *Harvard Business Review* 46 (1968): 53-62. See also Exercise 15.

[6] See e.g., "Stress: The Breaking Point," special issue, *The Personnel Administrator* 23 (November 1978); J. E. Newman and T. A. Beehr, "Personal and Organizational Strategies for Handling Job Stress: A Review of Research and Opinion, *Personnel Psychology* 32 (1979): 1-43; R. S. Schuler, "Conceptual Unclarity: What is Stress Anyway?" *Proceedings,* Eastern Academy of Management, 1980.

[7] A. A. McLean, "Job Stress and the Psychosocial Pressures of Change," *Personnel* 53 (January-February 1976).

[8] McLean, "Job Stress," 1976.

[9] J. D. Adams, "Guidelines for Stress Management and Life Style Changes," *The Personnel Administrator* 24 (June 1979): 35-38+.

of inputs (e.g., effort) to output (e.g., pay) is lower than, for example, a brother-in-law's or a similarly employed friend's, he or she is very likely to feel short-changed and dissatisfied. In other words, discrepancies between what people feel they should receive—based on their past experience, comparisons with significant others, what they feel they need—and what they are receiving will generate dissatisfaction.

It should be noted, however, that these expectations and comparisons may be subjective, and are often biased or erroneous. For example, if a worker makes $18,000 per year and perceives that a neighbor makes $25,000 per year working at a similar job, the worker may be dissatisfied and hence reduce his or her effort on the job. It makes no difference if the neighbor actually only makes $18,000 or if the neighbor must also work evenings; what counts is the worker's perception of the neighbor's situation. Since we are often dealing with individual perceptions when discussing JS, the many possible causes and consequences of JD are difficult to pin down.

A more difficult problem occurs when people receive erroneous information about others' salaries in their own organization. If a worker feels that others with essentially the same jobs receive more money or other rewards, the worker may be dissatisfied through a lack of perceived equity. Differences in job performance or complexity and rationales for differences in rewards may not be known to all workers, or the rumors may be inaccurate. Satisfaction levels are based to some degree on our perceptions and relative amounts of rewards, as opposed to absolute amounts.

Consequences of JD. When workers feel that one or more aspects of jobs are inadequate and other aspects of the jobs do not make up for these inadequacies, they may resort to any number of actions. They can seek other jobs, thereby causing the organization to select and train replacements, often a costly process. They can come to work late or stay away the entire day, thus causing higher costs and slower production due to incomplete work crews, etc. Or dissatisfied workers may come to work, but withdraw psychologically, i.e., not concentrate, do no more than absolutely necessary, and have no interest or initiative. As a result, machines requiring maintenance go unattended, possible problems do not get reported to superiors, or accidents occur due to carelessness. Workers can also actively engage in behavior either to "get back" at the company (e.g., sabotage) or inject challenge into an unchallenging job (e.g., by trying to see how little work they can do without getting caught). Finally, discontent can be harmful to the workers' own mental health, for it can

lead to feelings of depression, inadequacy, and powerlessness.

Any of the consequences of dissatisfaction are costly not only financially, but also in terms of wasting human resources. If people are not utilized to their capacity, both they and the organization suffer. Because these consequences of JD can be so grave, the assessment and remedy of JD are important tasks of the personnel administrator.

Remedies for JD. Before remedies can be developed, the extent of dissatisfaction must be carefully determined. Questionnaires, observation, interviews, and assessment of company records can help to provide this type of information. The personnel administrator must tap attitudes, expectations, and discrepencies between what workers get and what they feel they deserve. This can be a time-consuming and costly activity, and distorted data are a danger. However, several questionnaires, scales, and other pencil-and-paper instruments have been designed and used for these purposes.[10] Of course, they must be tailored to the needs of each organization.

Once the extent and degree of dissatisfaction, the specific nature of the discontent (e.g., regarding pay, promotions, etc.), and the seriousness of the consequences have all been determined, a decision can be made as to whether or not anything should be done and if so, what.

Remedies obviously depend on the specific nature of discontent. For example, if job content is a cause of dissatisfaction, Job Enrichment (JE) or job redesign may be required (see Exercise 14). If jobs and roles are ambiguous and lacking in structure, Management by Objectives (MBO) may be called for (see Exercise 5). If workers feel they do not have the required skills to perform their jobs adequately or to get promotions, training may be signaled (see Exercises 10 and 11). If they feel they are locked into dead-end jobs with no mobility, career programs may be useful (see Exercise 12). If workers are dissatisfied with pay and extrinsic rewards, new motivational programs could be implemented (see Exercises 15 and 16). Changes in working conditions and fringe benefits, such as four-day work weeks, flexible working hours, time off with pay for good performance, modernization of facilities, offering prizes and bonuses, and even playing music and

---

[10] The Institute of Social Research of the University of Michigan has been a leader in the development and compilation of these instruments. Catalogues and specific instruments appear in *For Further Reading.*

adding bright colors and art work to plants are all possible programs for improving JS.[11]

But for the personnel administrator and concerned others, the decision is not merely determining how innovative one can be in devising remedies, which may be merely fads. The task is first to assess the extent and specific nature of dissatisfaction; second, to identify and evaluate the seriousness of its consequencies; third, to decide whether or not anything should be done to remedy problems; and fourth, to design specific remedies and assess both their cost and probable benefit. Rushing to change jobs or other aspects of work without determining the extent and nature of the problem is a primary reason for the failure of some of the remedies to job dissatisfaction.

Job Satisfaction and Quality of Work Life (QWL). Like job stress, QWL is a concept that has been given considerable attention of late and linked to job satisfaction.[12] QWL is a broad topic, covering satisfaction and morale, job design (see Exercise 14), career development (see Exercise 12), compensation (see Exercise 16), and other aspects of the working environment that help determine the actual, overall quality of the job situation.

Satisfaction/dissatisfaction can be thought of as a result or appraisal of the actual job situation by each person. QWL thus determines one's appraisal.[13] Therefore, it is helpful to consider those perceptions and emotions one has about a job in an attempt to estimate the QWL.

PROCEDURE

Overview. Jobs are assessed to identify possible job characteristics leading to JD. Data on the JS of members of an organization are provided, the extent of dissatisfaction is thereby assessed, and possible remedies are proposed. Finally, you are to detail the steps you, as a personnel administrator or personnel staff member, would take to increase JS.

PART A

STEP 1: Choose at least one type of job listed at the top of Form 1 and determine what you believe are the major aspects of the job, its content, its environment, etc., or those "variables influencing JS/JD" in that job (column 1). Also determine what could be done to enhance satisfaction in each area (column 2). For example, one "variable" may be "the chance for participation in decision making," an important factor because it leads to a feeling of worth and autonomy, which might make one feel positive (satisfied) about the job. Thus, to improve participation in decision making, and hence improve satisfaction, you could hold open meetings or request employee input regarding organizational decisions.

TIME: About 50 minutes.

PART B

STEP 2: In Form 2 you are given a sample set of data, the result of a job-satisfaction survey in an organization. The instrument used to gather the data was the Job Descriptive Index (JDI) (Form 3), a very useful JS measuring tool.[14] Review both the JDI itself and the score provided. Determine what the consequences of JD might be and what specific action you would take for each of the types of jobs listed (based on the JDI scores) to improve satisfaction in those cases where you feel action is necessary. (Pay particular attention to information given on Form 2 for males versus females.) Record this information on Form 4. For example, for production workers the average JDI score for "satisfaction with supervision" is 26.24. Since the norm or average response on this scale for men is 40.87 and most production workers in the hypothetical organization are men, the 26.24 obtained would indicate very low satisfaction. On Form 4, you would thus indicate low satisfaction on supervision for production workers in column 2. Indicate what negative consequences this could have (column 3) and what steps could be taken to remedy the low satisfaction (column 4).

---

[11] See *For Further Reading* for case studies of these various techniques.

[12] See, e.g., C. Kerr and J. M. Rosow, eds., *Work in America: The Decade Ahead.* Work in America Institute, Inc., 1979.

[13] The authors acknowledge the assistance of Edwin A. Locke in making this distinction.

---

[14] Each of the five subscales of the JDI is given a different score. Within each subscale, each positive item marked "Y" (see Form 3) receives three points, each item marked "?" receives one point, and each item marked "N" receives zero points. Negative items are scored in the opposite manner (i.e., Y = 0 points, ? = 1 point, N = 3 points). Points are summed for all items within a subscale to compute the JDI for the subscale.

FOR FURTHER READING

Abdel-Halim, A. A. "Employee Affective Responses to Organizational Stress: Moderating Effects of Job Characteristics." *Personnel Psychology* 31 (1978): 561–579. (II–R)

Adams, J. D. "Guidelines for Stress Management and Life Style Changes." *Personnel Administrator* 24 (June 1979): 35–39. (I)

Aldag, R. J., and A. P. Brief. "Examination of Alternative Models of Job Satisfaction." *Human Relations* 31 (1978): 91–98. (II–R)

Allen, A. D. "The Topeka System—Beating the Blue Collar Blues." *The Personnel Administrator* 19, no. 1 (1974): 49–52. (I)

Andrisani, P. J., and M. B. Shapiro. "Women's Attitudes Towards Their Jobs: Some Longitudinal Data on a National Sample." *Personnel Psychology* 31 (1978): 15–34. (II–R)

Beehr, T. A. "Job Stress: A New Managerial Concern." In K. M. Rowland et al., eds., *Current Issues in Personnel Management*. Boston: Allyn and Bacon, 1979. (I)

Beehr, T. A., and J. E. Newman. "Job Stress, Employee Health, and Organizational Effectiveness: A Facet Analysis, Model and Literature Review." *Personnel Psychology* 31 (1978): 665–699. (II–R)

Cherns, A. "Perspectives on the Quality of Working Life." *Journal of Occupational Psychology* 40 (1975): 155–167. (II)

Cooper, C. L., and R. Payne, eds. *Stress at Work*. New York: Wiley, 1978. (I)

Cooper, M. R. et al. "Changing Employee Values: Deepening Discontent?" *Harvard Business Review* 57 (1979): 117–125. (I)

Deci, E. L. "Work—Who Does Not Like It and Why." *Psychology Today* 5 (1972): 57–84+. (I)

Dunnette, M. D., ed. *Work and Nonwork in the Year 2001*. Monterey, Cal.: Brooks/Cole, 1973. (I)

Fairfield, R. P., ed. *Humanizing the Workplace*. Buffalo: Prometheus, 1974. (I)

Garson, B. *All the Livelong Day: The Meaning and Demeaning of Routine Work*. Garden City, N.J.: Doubleday, 1975. (I)

Golembiewski, R. T., and S. Yeager. "Testing the Applicability of the DI to Various Demographic Groupings." *Academy of Management Journal* 21 (1978): 514–519. (II—R)

Gould, S. "Age, Job Complexity, Satisfaction, and Performance." *Journal of Vocational Behavior* 14 (1979): 209–223. (II–R)

Greene, C. N. "The Satisfaction-Performance Controversy." *Business Horizons* 15 (1972): 31–42. (I)

Hackman, J. R., and G. R. Oldham. "Development of the Job Diagnostic Survey." *Journal of Applied Psychology* 60 (1975): 159–170. (II–R)

Herzberg, F. "The Wise Old Turk." *Harvard Business Review* 52 (1974): 70–80. (I)

Hulin, C. L., and M. R. Blood. "Job Enlargement, Individual Differences and Worker Responses." *Psychological Bulletin* 69 (1968): 41–55. (II)

Hulin, C. L., and P. C. Smith. "A Linear Model of Job Satisfaction." *Journal of Applied Psychology* 49 (1965): 209–216. (II–R)

Hunt, J. W., and P. N. Saul. "The Relationship of Age, Tenure, and Job Satisfaction in Males and Females." *Academy of Management Journal* 18 (1975): 690–702. (II–R)

Ivancevich, J. M. "The Performance to Satisfaction Relationship: A Causal Analysis of Stimulating and Nonstimulating Jobs." *Organizational Behavior and Human Performance* 22 (1978): 350–365. (II–R)

Kahn, R. L. "The Work Module—A Tonic for Lunchpail Lassitude." *Psychology Today* 6 (1973): 35–39+. (I)

Keller, R. T. "Role Conflict and Ambiguity: Correlates with Job Satisfaction and Values." *Personnel Psychology* 28 (1975): 57–64. (I)

Landy, F. J. "An Opponent Process Theory of Job Satisfaction." *Journal of Applied Psychology* 63 (1978): 533–547. (II–R)

Lawler, E. E. "Should the Quality of Work Life Be Legislated?" *Personnel Administrator* 21, no. 1 (January 1976): 17–21. (I)

Locke, E. A. "What Is Job Satisfaction?" *Organizational Behavior and Human Performance* 5 (1970): 484–500. (II)

Locke, E. A. "The Nature and Causes of Job Satisfaction." In M. D. Dunnette, ed., *Handbook of Industrial and Organizational Psychology*. Chicago: Rand McNally, 1976. (II)

Mayo, Elton. *The Social Problems of an Industrial Civilization*. Cambridge, Mass.: Harvard University Press, 1945. (I)

McGrath, J. E. "Stress and Behavior in Organizations." In M. D. Dunnette, ed., *Handbook of Industrial and Organizational Psychology*. Chicago: Rand McNally, 1976. (II)

McLean, A. A. "Job Stress and the Psychosocial Pressures of Change." *Personnel* 53 (January–February 1976): 40–49. (I)

O'Connor, E. J., L. H. Peters, and S. M. Gordon. "The Measurement of Job Satisfaction: Current Practices and Future Considerations." *Journal of Management* 4 (1978): 17–26. (I–R)

Organ, D. W. "The Meanings of Stress." *Business Horizons* 22 (1979): 32–40. (I)

Paine, F. T., and M. J. Gannon. "Job Attitudes of Supervisors and Managers." *Personnel Psychology* 26 (1973): 521-530. (II-R)

Porter, L. W., and K. H. Roberts. "Communication in Organizations." In M. D. Dunnette, ed., *Handbook of Industrial and Organizational Psychology*. Chicago: Rand McNally, 1976. (II)

Porter, L. W., and R. M. Steers. "Organizational, Work, and Personal Factors in Employee Turnover and Satisfaction." *Psychological Bulletin* 50 (1973): 151-176. (II)

Pritchard, R. D., and B. W. Karasick. "The Effects of Organizational Climate on Managerial Job Performance and Job Satisfaction." *Organizational Behavior and Human Performance* 9 (1973): 126-146. (II-R)

Quinn, R. P., and L. J. Shepard. *The 1972-73 Quality of Employment Survey*. Ann Arbor, Mich.: Survey Research Center, 1974. (I-R)

Quinn, R. P., and G. L. Staines. *The 1977 Quality of Employment Survey: Descriptive Statistics, with Comparison Data from the 1969-70 and the 1972-73 Surveys*. Ann Arbor: University of Michigan, 1979. (I-R)

Robinson, J. P., R. Athanasiou, and K. B. Head. *Measures of Occupational Attitudes and Occupational Characteristics*. Ann Arbor, Mich.: Survey Research Center, 1973. (II)

Sauser, W. I., Jr., and C. M. Yoric. "Sex Differences in Job Satisfaction: A Reexamination." *Personnel Psychology* 31 (1978): 537-547. (II-R)

Seeman, M. "On the Meaning of Alienation." *American Sociological Review* 24 (1959): 783-791. (I)

Sims, H. P., and A. D. Szilagyi. "Leader Reward Behavior and Subordinate Satisfaction and Performance." *Organizational Behavior and Human Performance* 14 (1975): 426-438. (II-R)

Skinner, W. "The Anachronistic Factory." *Harvard Business Review* 49 (1971): 61-70. (I)

Smith, P. C., L. M. Kendall, and C. L. Hulin. *The Measurement of Satisfaction in Work and Retirement: A Strategy for the Study of Attitudes*. Chicago: Rand McNally, 1969. (II-R)

Special Task Force to the Secretary of Health, Education, and Welfare and W. E. Upjohn Institute. *Work in America*. Cambridge, Mass.: MIT Press, 1973. (I)

Stone, E. F., and L. W. Porter. "Job Characteristics and Job Attitudes: A Multivariate Study." *Journal of Applied Psychology* 60 (1975): 57-64. (II-R)

Student, K. R. "Personnel's Newest Challenge: Helping to Cope with Greater Stress." *The Personnel Administrator* 23 (November 1978): 26-34. (I)

Taylor, J. C. "Job Satisfaction and Quality of Working Life: A Reassessment." *Journal of Occupational Psychology* 50, no. 4 (1977): 243-252. (II)

Taylor, J. C., and P. R. Shaver. *Measures of Social Psychological Attitudes*. Ann Arbor, Mich.: Survey Research Center, 1973. (II)

Terkel, S. *Working*. New York: Pantheon, 1974. (I)

"The Job Blahs: Who Wants to Work?" *Newsweek*, LXXXI, no. 13 (1973): 79-82, 84, 89. (I)

U.S. Department of Labor. *Job Satisfaction: Is There a Trend?* Washington, D.C.: U.S. Government Printing Office, 1974. (I)

U.S. National Technical Information Service (NTIS). *Job Satisfaction: A Bibliography with Abstracts*. Springfield, Virginia: NTIS, 1975. (I)

Valenzi, E., and G. Desser. "Relationships of Leader Behavior, Subordinate Role Ambiguity and Subordinate Job Satisfaction." *Academy of Management Journal* 21 (1978): 671-678. (II-R)

Wanous, J. P., and E. E. Lawler. "Measurement and Meaning of Job Satisfaction." *Journal of Applied Psychology* 56 (1972): 95-105. (II)

Weaver, C. N. "Correlates of Job Satisfaction: Some Evidence from the National Surveys." *Academy of Management Journal* 17 (1974): 373-375. (I-R)

Wernimont, P. F. "A Systems View of Job Satisfaction." *Journal of Applied Psychology* 56 (1972): 173-176. (II)

"Why So Many Congressmen Are Quitting." *U.S. News & World Report* 84 (1978): 37-38. (I)

Williams, L. K., J. W. Seybolt, and C. C. Pinder. "On Administering Questionnaires in Organizational Settings." *Personnel Psychology* 28 (1975): 93-103. (II)

Wool, H. "What's Wrong with Work in America? A Review Essay." *Monthly Labor Review* 96, no. 3 (1973): 38-44. (I)

Zimbardo, P. *Influencing Attitudes and Changing Behavior*. Reading, Mass.: Addison-Wesley, 1969. (I)

Name _____   Group Number _____

Date _____ Class Section _____ Hour _____ Score _____

PART A

Form 1 Diagnosing Determinants of Satisfaction-Dissatisfaction in Various Job Types

Type of job (check one)*

____ machine operator

____ clerical worker

____ executive

____ sales staff

____ research and development scientist

____ other (please specify)

List the major job characteristics that could influence satisfaction in a positive or a negative direction. 1	What, if anything, could be done to enhance worker satisfaction on this variable? 2
1.	
2.	
3.	
4.	
5.	

* Use a separate form if more than one job is to be analyzed.

Form 1 (Continued)

Type of job (check one)

___ machine operator

___ clerical worker

___ executive

___ sales staff

___ research and development scientist

___ other (please specify)

List the major "variables" related to worker job satisfaction for the job checked above. 1	What could be done to enhance worker satisfaction on this variable? 2
6.	
7.	
8.	
9.	
10.	

PART B

Form 2 Sample Results of the JDI for an Organization by Department and JDI Norms for Males and Females

I. Sample results for an organization (hypothetical data).

Subscale of the JDI*	Management			Production workers			Clerical workers			Sales staff			Research and development			Finance department		
	N (Sample size)	$\bar{X}$ (Mean)	SD (Std. deviation)	N	$\bar{X}$	SD	N	$\bar{X}$	SD	N	$\bar{X}$	SD	N	$\bar{X}$	SD	N	$\bar{X}$	SD
Work	118	51.43	6.23	189	31.68	5.43	58	43.28	4.88	12	51.38	4.66	14	52.57	7.61	23	19.44	4.37
Pay	143	23.24	10.06	189	20.28	3.66	58	16.23	5.67	13	25.46	1.32	14	23.11	6.61	23	16.87	3.24
Promotions	117	18.36	5.24	168	24.37	4.28	58	20.47	3.21	13	23.62	4.33	14	18.88	3.32	23	11.43	3.97
Supervision	126	30.37	10.28	187	26.24	18.11	58	42.43	6.74	13	35.57	6.72	14	35.61	4.67	23	30.88	4.68
Co-workers	118	26.32	11.46	189	46.23	11.36	58	46.29	9.53	13	40.25	7.36	14	38.23	11.29	23	36.24	3.61

II. Information about males and females in organization referred to in I above.

1. The number of females in each department is as follows:

Management	6
Production	28
Clerical	54
Sales	3
Research and development	2
Finance	3

2. Despite a lively Affirmative Action Program (AAP) (see Exercise 17 for a discussion of such plans), the organization has few women in managerial, professional, or technical positions. Furthermore, for the subsample of women within each group of workers, scores on all subscales of the JDI are lower than those for males with two exceptions. The male clerical workers' JDI scores on work, supervision, and co-workers are well below both those of the females in the group and those of females and males in the table in III below for these subscales. In the management group, the females' scores on work, promotions, and pay are considerably higher than those for males in the group and for both males and females in the table in III below for these subscales.

III. Male and female norms for the JDI based on large, diverse samples (hypothetical data).

Subscale of the JDI*	Males			Females		
	N	$\bar{X}$	SD	N	$\bar{X}$	SD
Work	2150	35.56	11.53	2077	34.68	8.87
Pay	1997	17.90	15.92	1876	19.60	16.62
Promotions	3153	21.64	16.76	3026	20.31	17.83
Supervision	1952	40.87	11.85	1771	42.82	10.36
Co-workers	1947	44.44	9.63	1631	45.90	8.47

* Maximum scores by subscale are work—54, pay—27, promotion—27, supervision—54, people—54.

PART B
Form 3

THE JOB DESCRIPTIVE INDEX

Code Number _____

Company _____

City _____

Think of your present work. What is it like most of the time? In the blank beside each word given below, write

_y_ for "Yes" if it describes your work

_N_ for "No" if it does NOT describe it

_?_ if you cannot decide

WORK ON PRESENT JOB

_____ Fascinating

_____ Routine

_____ Satisfying

_____ Boring

_____ Good

_____ Creative

_____ Respected

_____ Hot

_____ Pleasant

_____ Useful

_____ Tiresome

_____ Healthful

_____ Challenging

_____ On your feet

_____ Frustrating

_____ Simple

_____ Endless

_____ Gives sense of accomplishment

Form 3 (continued)

Think of the pay you get now. How well does each of the following words describe your present pay? In the blank beside each word, put

_y_ if it describes your pay

_N_ if it does NOT describe it

_?_ if you cannot decide

PRESENT PAY

____ Income adequate for normal expenses

____ Satisfactory profit sharing

____ Barely live on income

____ Bad

____ Income provides luxuries

____ Insecure

____ Less than I deserve

____ Highly paid

____ Underpaid

Think of the kind of supervision that you get on your job. How well does each of the following words describe this supervision? In the blank beside each word below, put

_y_ if it describes the supervision you get on your job

_N_ if it does NOT describe it

_?_ if you cannot decide

SUPERVISION ON PRESENT JOB

____ Asks my advice

____ Hard to please

____ Impolite

____ Praises good work

____ Tactful

____ Influential

____ Up-to-date

____ Doesn't supervise enough

____ Quick tempered

____ Tells me where I stand

____ Annoying

____ Stubborn

____ Knows job well

____ Bad

____ Intelligent

____ Leaves me on my own

____ Around when needed

____ Lazy

Think of the opportunities for promotion that you have now. How well does each of the following words describe these? In the blank beside each word put

_y_ for "Yes" if it describes your opportunities for promotion

_N_ for "No" if it does NOT describe them

_?_ if you cannot decide

OPPORTUNITIES FOR PROMOTION

____ Good opportunities for promotion

____ Opportunity somewhat limited

____ Promotion on ability

____ Dead-end job

____ Good chance for promotion

____ Unfair promotion policy

____ Infrequent promotions

____ Regular promotions

____ Fairly good chance for promotion

Think of the majority of the people that you work with now or the people you meet in connection with your work. How well does each of the following words describe these people? In the blank beside each word below, put

_y_ if it describes the people you work with

_N_ if it does NOT describe them

_?_ if you cannot decide

PEOPLE ON YOUR PRESENT JOB

____ Stimulating

____ Boring

____ Slow

____ Ambitious

____ Stupid

____ Responsible

____ Fast

____ Intelligent

____ Easy to make enemies

____ Talk too much

____ Smart

____ Lazy

____ Unpleasant

____ No privacy

____ Active

____ Narrow interests

____ Loyal

____ Hard to meet

Name _____ Group Number _____

Date _____ Class Section _____ Hour _____ Score _____

PART B

Form 4 Record Form for Identifying Areas of Job Dissatisfaction and Planning Courses of Action

Job group (Refer to Form 2) 1	Particular area(s) of highest job dissatisfaction (i.e., work, pay, etc.) 2	Possible negative or deleterious consequences to the organization and/or worker if dissatisfaction persists 3	Specific possible steps to be taken to remedy the situation 4
Management	1.	a. b.	a. b. c.
	2.	a. b.	a. b. c.
	3.	a. b.	a. b. c.
Production workers	1.	a. b.	a. b. c.
	2.	a. b.	a. b. c.
	3.	a. b.	a. b. c.

Form 4 (continued)

Job group 1	Particular area(s) of highest job dissatisfaction (i.e., work, pay, etc.) 2	Possible negative or deleterious consequences to the organization and/or worker if dissatisfaction persists 3	Specific possible steps to be taken to remedy the situation 4
Clerical workers	1.	a. b.	a. b. c.
	2.	a. b.	a. b. c.
	3.	a. b.	a. b. c.
Sales staff	1.	a. b.	a. b. c.
	2.	a. b.	a. b. c.
	3.	a. b.	a. b. c.

Form 4 (continued)

Job group 1	Particular area(s) of highest job dissatisfaction (i.e., work, pay, etc.) 2	Possible negative or deleterious consequences to the organization and/or worker if dissatisfaction persists 3	Specific possible steps to be taken to remedy the situation 4
Research and development	1.	a. b.	a. b. c.
	2.	a. b.	a. b. c.
	3.	a. b.	a. b. c.
Finance department	1.	a. b.	a. b. c.
	2.	a. b.	a. b. c.

Name _____   Group Number _____

Date _____   Class Section _____   Hour _____   Score _____

ASSESSMENT OF LEARNING IN PERSONNEL ADMINISTRATION
EXERCISE 13

1. Try to state the purpose of this exercise in one concise sentence.

2. Specifically what did you learn from this exercise (i.e., skills, abilities, and knowledge)?

3. How might your learning influence your role and your duties as a personnel administrator?

4. Do you feel job dissatisfaction is a major organizational problem in this country? Why or why not?

5. Could you translate job satisfaction scores on the JDI to actual dollar amounts representing various costs to an organization? What type of cost data would you need to do this?

6. What additional information would you need before translating the JDI scores into (new) organizational policies?

7. Assume there is very high job dissatisfaction among janitorial workers in a hospital. What are some of the specific possible consequences for the organization, its patients, and the rest of its staff?

8. Why might managers be dissatisfied? What are possible remedies? Can individual employees' and the organization's needs *both* really be satisfied?

Exercise 14
Designing and implementing job enrichment programs

OVERVIEW

Often problems of poor performance cannot be remedied by training. In these cases, workers have the skill and ability to perform well but may be unwilling to do so. The reasons are many and complex. Several techniques have been developed to "motivate" workers or induce them to choose those behaviors that lead to successful performance. One such technique to improve worker performance and satisfaction is Job Enrichment (JE). In JE, the content of jobs is changed in order to provide such rewards as recognition, challenge, and autonomy for workers. These types of rewards are referred to as "intrinsic" rewards because they are feelings that people give to themselves (e.g., a worker feels pride from accomplishing a complex task). The work itself, rather than what is gained by doing the work (e.g., money), is rewarding. JE is a technique designed to improve performance and productivity by offering intrinsic awards. The *Introduction* to the exercise explains JE and its assumptions and discusses the implementation of JE programs.

You are asked to assess jobs as to their applicability for JE and to role play in a situation where a JE program is being considered.

OBJECTIVES

1. To gain knowledge about the motivational strategy of JE, improving performance through intrinsic rewards, and its theoretical basis.
2. To build skill in identifying both job and situational characteristics that could lead to effective or ineffective JE programs.
3. To build skill in working with groups to perform a task and in JE program design and implementation.

PREMEETING ASSIGNMENT

Read the entire exercise, except for Part C. Do not read this part until instructed to do so by your implementor.

INTRODUCTION
Job Enrichment as a Motivation Technique

As noted in Exercise 13, well-publicized surveys[1] of blue-collar and white-collar workers suggest that many are dissatisfied with their jobs; they view their jobs as "dead ends" and feel no pride in their work.

Several reasons can be suggested to account for these feelings. The high degree of specialization in industry has fractionalized tasks and precluded workers' seeing the relationship of their work to the whole. Also, workers' expectations regarding what they want from work are ever increasing. In addition, educational levels of the work force have risen steadily, and this

---

[1] The HEW Special Task Force Report called *Work in America* (Boston, Mass.: MIT Press, 1973).

increase may lead people to expect more from their jobs than merely the receipt of economic rewards. They may desire to develop their own skills and abilities and grow emotionally and intellectually.

Frederick Herzberg's Work. A management response to this situation of dissatisfaction has been to change dull, routine, and unchallenging jobs to ones that offer challenge and a chance for growth and recognition. Frederick Herzberg[2] has developed a theory that views a job situation as offering to workers both hygiene factors, which relate to the job context or environment (i.e., pay, supervision, interpersonal relations, security, etc.), and motivator factors, which concern the job content (i.e., growth, recognition, challenge, autonomy, variety, etc.). In Herzberg's thesis, job satisfaction and, hence, desired job performance can only come from the motivators; hygiene factors cause job dissatisfaction when they are absent, but do not lead to job satisfaction when they are present. Only by changing jobs to include motivators can we motivate workers. In other words, the absence of dissatisfaction (i.e., hygiene factors are present) does not necessarily ensure the presence of job satisfaction. Motivators must be built into the job for job satisfaction, and Herzberg sees satisfaction as a prerequisite to successful performance.

Herzberg's ideas are based on certain assumptions about work and workers. One assumption is that workers require and expect satisfaction on the job through meaningful work (i.e., enriched with motivators), rather than off the job. Hygiene factors, if they motivate people at all, do so only in the short run; motivators are needed for long-run commitment and good performance.

Another Approach to Job Design. Many have criticized Herzberg's work, particularly his method for testing the theory. By asking people to explain incidents that made them feel very good or bad on the job, a biased view could be obtained. That is, people may have a tendency to cite others or external causes (hygiene factors) for their negative feelings and themselves or internal causes (motivators) for their positive feelings about their job.[3] These responses would be given regardless of the real causes of job satisfaction.

Perhaps both motivators and hygiene factors can lead to satisfaction.

A group of researchers[4] has recently advanced and tested concepts that are both similar to and different than Herzberg's. The distinction between motivators and hygiene factors is not made, and an emphasis is placed on diagnosing the extent to which jobs' content can be realistically changed. Essentially, workers are seen as motivated to perform and willing to enjoy their work if they feel that it is *meaningful* to them, they are *responsible* for completing it, and they receive *feedback* on their performance. Further, the following "core job dimensions" determine whether or not a person will perceive that meaningfulness, responsibility, and feedback are operating:

1. Skill variety—job challenges worker's skills and abilities;

2. Task identity—a "whole" piece of work is completed;

3. Task significance—job has significant effect on people, society;

4. Autonomy—considerable discretion and independence are offered; and

5. Knowledge of results—information about performance is obtained.

Vertical Job Loading. The management strategy that follows from these ideas is to redesign jobs to provide motivators—in short, to "enrich" jobs. Job enrichment (JE) has been attempted in some organizations by increasing the degree of worker autonomy, achievement, and so on. This is usually accomplished by vertical job loading. For example, an assembler's job would be increased in a vertical fashion by allowing the assembler to perform the tasks necessary to produce an entire subassembly rather than merely making one small addition to a half-completed subassembly. The job is thus loaded vertically to encompass tasks that previously preceded and succeeded the task, rather than loaded horizontally to simply add tasks at the same level (job enlargement). The worker now feels more of a sense of accomplishment and may feel increased pride as a result of the change. By building in these rewards; from the job content, the job has been enriched.

An additional technique utilized to enrich jobs uses natural work groups to give people the feeling

---

[2] See F. Herzberg, *Work and the Nature of Man* (Cleveland: World, 1966); or F. Herzberg, "One More Time: How Do You Motivate Workers?" *Harvard Business Review* 46, no. 1 (1968): 53–62.

[3] See E. A. Locke, "The Nature and Causes of Job Satisfaction." In M. D. Dunnette, ed., *Handbook of Industrial and Organizational Psychology* (Chicago: Rand McNally, 1976).

[4] See, e.g., J. R. Hackman et al., "A New Strategy for Job Enrichment," *California Management Review* 17, no. 1 (1975): 51–71; J. R. Hackman and G. Oldham, "Motivation Through the Design of Work: Test of a Theory," *Organizational Behavior and Human Performance* 16 (1976): 250–279.

they are responsible for or "own" an identifiable portion of work. Allowing each personnel specialist to "service" one department in an organization would be an example. Allowing workers to have frequent contact with clients and assisting workers in obtaining feedback in their performance may also be effective enrichment techniques.[5]

The objective in JE is to motivate workers by the work itself by providing work that is interesting and challenging, rather than motivating by means of larger and larger job content factors (such as monetary inducements to perform monotonous jobs).

Applicability of JE. Thus, JE would seem most appropriate for dull, routine jobs where there is considerable worker dissatisfaction, absenteeism, turnover, or sabotage.[6] JE would be best applied where a measure of productivity is available or where desired performance has been specified such that improvement in work output as a result of JE can be identified. JE is also effective in jobs where the cost of hygiene factors is very high, feedback mechanisms can be developed, responsibilities assigned to a job can be changed, and investment in machine-paced technology is not too high to redesign. Finally, the program would be most beneficial for those jobs that have a significant impact on overall organizational goal attainment. It is in these jobs that poor attitudes, lack of motivation, and poor performance are obviously most problematic and costly.

Implementing JE. A typical JE program should be carefully planned and coupled with specific organizational needs.[7] Perhaps one of the most common failures of JE programs is selecting for enrichment a job that does not fit the profile suggested here. Another problem is failing to account for workers' sociological and psychological makeup—their cultural background, age, and personal needs; for example, rural workers, as opposed to those with urban backgrounds, may desire more interesting work with more variety and autonomy due to their previous employment history (e.g., as self-employed farmers). Younger workers may have higher job expectations than older workers and, particularly if they do not have families to support, may value money and job security less than autonomy and challenge at work. These individual and group disparities could spell the difference between success and failure of a JE program.

Although JE is a complex system which exists in many varieties in actual practice,[8] typical steps in the implementation procedure can be summarized as follows:

1. Select an appropriate job—one in which there is now poor performance and in which successful performance is crucial to organizational or departmental goal attainment. The job must be amenable to JE by having potential for content change.

2. Assess worker attitudes, values, and expectations regarding work.

3. Determine measures of performance in order to note any changes after JE and direction of the changes.

4. Identify changes in job content that would be required to enrich the job, as well as changes in discretion or amount of "say" the worker has.

5. Make sure the changes are feasible and practical and represent vertical, rather than horizontal, job loading.

6. Implement the job-content changes and enlist the cooperation of job holders and supervisors by encouraging them to participate in program design.

7. Assess the effects of the program over time to note changes in actual performance.

Costs of Job Enrichment. An authentic program designed to add autonomy, variety, challenge, etc., to jobs is often a costly one. While there are certainly benefits to be gained, as noted above, there are numerous costs which are not obvious and yet must be considered. Fig. 1 outlines the types of costs identified through a recent survey of organizations that have implemented JE programs.[9]

It must be pointed out, however, that not every cost identified in Fig. 1 will occur, or will persist if it does occur. The type of organization and JE program, as well as several aspects of implementation (e.g., readiness of workers for changes), determines costs. Choos-

---

[5] See, e.g., Hackman et al, "Job Enrichment"; G. Dessler, *Human Behavior, Improving Performance at Work* (Reston, Virginia: Reston, 1980).

[6] R. W. Beatty and C. E. Schneier, "A Case for Positive Reinforcement," *Business Horizons* 18, no. 2 (1975): 71–78.

[7] J. R. Hackman and his colleagues have been developing an extremely useful procedure which explains those aspects of jobs leading to poor performance and offers a diagnostic system that facilitates the identification of specific problems that could be amenable to JE programs. See, e.g., Hackman et al., "Job Enrichment."

[8] For examples of JE programs in organizations, see W. Reif, D. Ferrazzi, and R. Evans, "Job Enrichment: Who Uses It and Why," *Business Horizons* 17, no. 1 (1974): 71–74.

[9] A. F. Alber, "The Real Cost of Job Enrichment," *Business Horizons* 22 (February 1979): 60–72.

ing appropriate jobs that facilitate a program's early success, stressing the importance of a more challenging job content as opposed to financial benefits, and continually analyzing the impact of JE on people and the organization can all facilitate cost reduction.

Fig. 1. Cost associated with job enrichment programs (A. F. Alber, "The Real Cost of Job Enrichment," *Business Horizons* (February 1979): 60–72).

Design-Related Costs

Wage and salary increases—acquisition of additional skills and responsibilities can put workers in higher wage/salary classes.

Facility costs—duplication of equipment and/or additional floor space for more complex jobs; changes in assembly lines, work-flow processes.

Inventory costs—when sequentially arranged work stations are separated to enrich jobs by adding responsibilities, inventory of raw materials, etc., may be required for each work station.

Implementation costs—time and money for staff persons, consultants, and others who design and implement the program.

Training costs—training of incumbents to add knowledge, skills, abilities to perform more complex tasks.

Performance-Related Costs

Quality—costs associated with reaching higher quality standards.

Resource utilization—output may fall as employees learn their new, more complex tasks; paper work may increase to record progress on the program; for some employees who are resistant to change, absenteeism, turnover, and dissatisfaction may result.

Is JE a Cure-All? JE is not the remedy to all motivation problems. Its effectiveness is limited by assumptions that are not universally applicable, by practical and cost considerations, and by the fact that relatively few organizations have used JE and, therefore, a large amount of data is not yet available regarding its effectiveness. For individuals interested in obtaining rewards (i.e., money) that enable them to satisfy any needs they might have for autonomy and challenge off the job, JE would not seem appropriate; these workers may want simply to be paid. Further, some jobs cannot be enriched feasibly; the economic costs of changes required in equipment and work flow may be great enough to offset the potential gains of JE.[10] Until more data are available on the merits of JE, some organizations may be reluctant to try it. A review of the literature,[11] although now some years old, concluded that the case

for JE had been overstated. Not enough conclusive data were available, and the positive results seemed to apply only to certain segments of the labor force.

More recently, an extensive review of the JE literature, concentrating on studies with actual performance data, was undertaken.[12] Most job enrichment studies were confounded with other changes that could have accounted for their results (e.g., modification of tools, use of goal-setting, use of incentives). Those that were felt to have been designed such that the effect of the JE itself could be assessed were used in the analysis. Positive increases in performance were found in 92% of the studies. This result is encouraging. Additional benefits of JE programs that do not translate directly and immediately to performance improvement (e.g., increased commitment to the organization) were also cited by the authors of the review. Further research is certainly required before definitive conclusions on JE can be made, but these results are promising.

Despite limitations, JE remains potentially an extremely useful strategy for motivation problems, as it enables workers to perform challenging jobs that provide variety, autonomy, and a chance for personal growth and achievement. If workers can be motivated "through the work itself," rather than by other types of rewards, certain long-run motivation problems can possibly be alleviated. Behind the JE programs lies the assumption, noted by Herzberg and others, that if people are not utilized to their fullest capacity in their jobs, motivation problems will eventually surface. The difficult task for managers is to design jobs that lead to high productivity. Rather than being productive because they are satisfied or happy, workers can gain satisfaction from high performance and productivity when jobs are enriched.

PROCEDURE

Overview. Aspects of the work situation that could lead to effective or ineffective JE efforts are reviewed in Part A. In Part B, jobs are analyzed for their enrichment potential through a JE program, and in Part C, a JE program is discussed by workers in a role-playing situation.

PART A

STEP 1: Because job enrichment, or vertical job loading, is a method designed to build motivators

[10] S. A. Levitan and W. B. Johnson, "Job Redesign, Reform, Enrichment—Exploring the Limitations," *Monthly Labor Review* 96 (1973): 36–41.

[11] C. L. Hulin and M. R. Blood, "Job Enlargement, Individual Differences and Worker Happiness," *Psychological Bulletin* 69 (1968): 41–55.

[12] E. A. Locke, D. B. Feren, V. M. McCaleb, K. N. Shaw, and A. T. Denny, "The Relative Effectiveness of Four Methods of Motivating Employee Performance." Paper presented at National Convention of American Psychological Association, New York, 1979.

into jobs, it is typically used to implement Herzberg's theory. But certain considerations are important in this process of job redesign. Listed in Form 1 are considerations regarding the job, the people involved, and particular aspects of an organization. Below each consideration briefly note whether or not it would facilitate or deter a job enrichment program's effectiveness and why. In your small groups, discuss what the items in each of the two categories (i.e., deterrents and facilitators) have in common.

TIME: About one hour.

PART B

STEP 2: Certain jobs are more amenable to vertical job loading or job enrichment than others. Before a job enrichment program is begun, the target job should be assessed for its applicability to job enrichment. A questionnaire (Form 2) and tally sheet (Form 3) are provided, which enable you to evaluate or "score" various jobs according to their potential for job enrichment. Remember: usually those jobs most amenable to job enrichment are dull, repetitive, and narrow. They are characterized by poor performance, high turnover, and/or absenteeism. Also performance in such jobs is critical to organizational success. It should also be remembered that high set-up costs for sophisticated machinery or high fixed costs in work flow might outweigh positive motivation considerations and preclude an economical change over to JE.

After reading each of the job descriptions provided in Forms 4–8, score each of the jobs with the questionnaire. A job with high potential for job enrichment will receive an average score of 4.0 to 5.0; jobs of low potential will receive scores of 1.0 to 2.0. "Potential" refers to the probability of positive return in terms of performance for the investment in a job enrichment program. What do the jobs with high potential have in common? What do the jobs with low potential have in common?

TIME: About one and a half hours.

PART C

STEP 3: In order to implement a job enrichment program and observe the process of changing job content, a role-playing situation is provided (Form 9). Each member of a small group takes part in the role play. There are six workers and one or more observers. Do not read any of the roles until your implementor has told you to do so.

One person assumes the role of J. Jaguar, the manager, and another assumes the role of L. Hooper, the personnel director. There are roles for four workers, and one or more observers is also used. Each person reads *only* their own role instructions and the general instructions to the role play. Then the roles are enacted in a group discussion involving the workers and their supervisor. Observers record their observations on the form provided (Form 10). Observers should read their instructions carefully before they fill out the form. After this group discussion, J. Jaguar can briefly meet alone with L. Hooper to relay the decision made by the group, and the final decision as to any change can, therefore, be made between Jaguar and Hooper. After your group has completed the role play, discuss the solution you reached in light of what you now know about job enrichment. Discuss the observers' comments and the feedback given to the person who played the role of the manager. Was your group's solution job enrichment? Who in the group was satisfied? Why?

TIME: About 25 minutes for role plays and 30 minutes for discussion.

FURTHER READING

Abdel-Halim, A. A. "Individual and Interpersonal Moderators of Employee Reactions to Job Characteristics: A Reexamination." *Personnel Psychology* 32 (1979): 121–137. (II–R)

Alber, A. F. "The Real Cost of Job Enrichment." *Business Horizons* 22 (February 1979): 60–72. (I–R)

Alber, A. "Job Enrichment for Profit." *Human Resource Management* 18 (1979): 15–25. (I)

Aldag, R. J., and A. P. Brief. *Task Design and Employee Motivation.* Glenview, Ill.: Scott Foresman, 1979. (I)

Allen, A. D. "The Topeka System—Beating the Blue Collar Blues." *Personnel Administrator* 19, no. 1 (1974): 49–52. (I)

Beatty, R. W., and C. E. Schneier. "A Case for Positive Reinforcement." *Business Horizons* 18, no. 2 (April 1975): 71–78. (I)

Campbell, J. P. "Motivation Theory in Industrial and Organizational Psychology." In M. D. Dunnette, ed., *Handbook of Industrial and Organizational Psychology.* Chicago: Rand McNally, 1976. (II)

Champagne, P. J., and C. Tausky. "When Job Enrichment Doesn't Pay." *Personnel* 55 (1978): 30–40.

Davis, L. E., and J. C. Taylor, eds. *Design of Jobs,* 2d ed. Santa Monica, Cal.: Goodyear, 1979. (II–R)

Dunham, R. B. "Relationships of Perceived Job Design Characteristics to Job Ability Requirements and Job Value." *Journal of Applied Psychology* 62 (1977): 760–763. (II–R)

Dyer, L., and D. F. Parker. "Classifying Outcomes in Work Motivation Research: An Examination of the Intrinsic–Extrinsic Dichotomy." *Journal of Applied Psychology* 60 (1975): 455–458. (II–R)

Ford, R. N. *Why Jobs Die and What To Do About It: Job Redesign and Future Productivity.* New York: Amacom, 1979. (I)

Ford, R. N. "Job Enrichment Lessons at AT&T. *Harvard Business Review* 51, no. 1 (1973): 96–106. (I)

Ford, R. N. *Motivation through the Work Itself.* New York: American Management Association, 1969. (I)

Frank, L. L., and J. R. Hackman. "A Failure of Job Enrichment: The Case of the Change That Wasn't." *Journal of Applied Behavioral Science* 11 (October–December 1975): 413–436. (II–R)

Gibson, C. H. "Volvo Increases Productivity through Job Enrichment." *California Management Review* 15, no. 4 (Summer 1973): 64–66. (I)

Hackman, J. R. "Group Influences on Individuals." In M. D. Dunnette, ed., *Handbook of Industrial and Organizational Psychology.* Chicago: Rand McNally, 1976. (II)

Hackman, J. R. et al. "A New Strategy for Job Enrichment." *California Management Review* 17 (Summer 1975): 57–71. (I)

Hackman, J. R., and E. E. Lawler. "Employee Reactions to Job Characteristics." *Journal of Applied Psychology Monograph* 55 (1971): 259–286. (II–R)

Hackman, J. R., J. L. Pearce, and J. C. Wolfe. "Effects of Changes in Job Characteristics on Work Attitudes and Behaviors: A Naturally Occurring Quasi-Experiment." *Organizational Behavior and Human Performance* 21 (1978): 289–304. (II–R)

Herzberg, F. "Motivation–Hygiene Profiles." *Organization Dynamics* 3, no. 2 (Fall 1974): 18–29. (I)

Herzberg, F. "New Perspectives on the Will to Work." *Personnel Administrator* 19 (July–August 1974): 21–25. (I)

Herzberg, F. "One More Time: How Do You Motivate Workers?" *Harvard Business Review* 46, no. 1 (1968): 53–62. (I)

Herzberg, F. *Work and the Nature of Man.* Cleveland: World, 1966. (I)

Herzberg, F. et al. *The Motivation to Work.* New York: Wiley, 1959. (I)

Hinrichs, J. R. *Practical Management for Productivity.* Scarsdale, New York: Work in America Institute, 1979. (I)

House, R. J., and L. A. Wigdor. "Herzberg's Dual-Factor Theory of Job Satisfaction and Motivation: A Review of the Evidence and a Criticism." *Personnel Psychology* 20 (1967): 369–389. (II)

Hulin, C. L., and M. R. Blood. "Job Enlargement, Individual Differences, and Worker Responses." *Psychological Bulletin* 69 (1968): 41–55. (II)

Kahn, R. L. "The Work Module—A Tonic for Lunchpail Lassitude." *Psychology Today* 6 (February 1973): 35–39. (I)

Ken, C., and J. M. Rosow, eds. *Work in America: The Decade Ahead.* Scarsdale, New York: Work in America Institute, 1979. (I)

Lawler, E. E., J. R. Hackman, and S. Kaufman. "Effects of Job Redesign: A Field Experiment." *Journal of Applied Social Psychology* 3 (1973): 49–62. (II–R)

Levitan, S. A., and W. B. Johnson. "Job Redesign, Reform, and Enrichment: Exploring the Limitations." *Monthly Labor Review* 96 (July 1973): 35–41. (I)

Locke, E. A. "Toward a Theory of Task Motivation and Incentives." *Organizational Behavior and Human Performance* 3 (1968): 157–189. (II)

Locke, E. A., D. B. Feren, V. M. McCaleb, K. N. Shaw, and A. T. Denney. "The Relative Effectiveness of Four Methods of Motivating Employee Performance." Paper presented at National Convention of the American Psychological Association, New York, 1979.

Maher, J. R. *New Perspectives in Job Enrichment.* New York: Van Nostrand, 1971. (I)

Miner, J. B., and J. F. Brewer. "The Management of Ineffective Performance." In M. D. Dunnette, ed. *Handbook of Industrial and Organizational Psychology.* Chicago: Rand McNally, 1976. (II)

Morgan, C. P., and R. W. Beatty. "Organizational Considerations in Applying Job Enrichment." *Colorado Business Review* 47, no. 9 (September 1974): 2–4. (I)

Reif, W., D. Ferazzi, and R. Evans. "Job Enrichment: Who Uses It and Why." *Business Horizons* 17, no. 1 (1974): 71–78. (I)

Sandler, B. E. "Eclecticism at Work—Approaches to Job Design." *American Psychologist* (October 1974): 767–773. (II)

Schappe, R. H. "Twenty-Two Arguments Against Job

Enrichment." *Personnel Journal* 53, no. 2 (1974): 116–123. (I)

"The Job Blahs: Who Wants to Work?" *Newsweek,* 26 March 1973, pp. 79–82, 84, 89. (I)

Unstot, D. D., T. R. Mitchell, and C. H. Bell, Jr. "Goal Setting and Job Enrichment: An Integrated Approach to Job Design." *Academy of Management Review* 3 (1978): 867–879. (II–R)

Walters, R. W., and Associates, Inc. *Job Enrichment for Results: Strategies for Successful Implementation.* Reading, Mass.: Addison-Wesley, 1975. (I)

White, J. K. "Individual Differences and the Job Quality—Worker Response Relationship: Review, Integration, and Comments." *Academy of Management Review* 3 (1978): 267–280. (II)

White, S. E., and T. R. Mitchell. "Job Enrichment versus Social Cues: A Comparison and Competitive Test." *Journal of Applied Psychology* 64 (1979): 1–9. (II–R)

Whitsett, D. A. "Where Are Your Unenriched Jobs?" *Harvard Business Review* 51, no. 1 (January–February 1975): 74–80. (I)

Work in America Institute. *Studies in Productivity: Highlights to the Literature* (eleven sets of abstracts). Scarsdale, New York: Work in America Institute, 1979. (I)

Name _____   Group Number _____

Date _____   Class Section _____   Hour _____   Score _____

PART A

Form 1 Considerations in Implementing Job Enrichment (JE)

Below each of the following items indicate whether it would seem to facilitate or deter the job enrichment implementation process, the effectiveness of a job enrichment program, and why. In small groups discuss what those items you decided as being facilitators have in common. What do the rest of the items have in common?

1. People in the organization seem to value hard work and involvement.

    _____
    _____

2. Initial meetings on JE are not held with top management before JE is implemented.

    _____
    _____

3. Workers generally have low skill levels.

    _____
    _____

4. There is a high degree of formality and inflexibility of organizational structure, policies, and processes.

    _____
    _____

5. There is low confidence in JE among line managers.

    _____
    _____

6. People seem presently satisfied with their jobs, based on recent surveys.

    _____
    _____

7. JE techniques used in another organization are borrowed and used "as is."

    _____
    _____

8. There is high interaction among co-workers in many departments.

    _____
    _____

9. There is a strong union which traditionally has favored and emphasized large salary increases at the bargaining table.

    _____
    _____

10. JE is introduced to managers through their regular management training programs.

    _____
    _____

11. Large sums have recently been invested for a highly automated plant and equipment.

    _____
    _____

12. Performance levels have never been measured rigorously.

    _____
    _____

Form 1 (continued)

13. Top management believes in the potential of JE, but feels that intelligent line managers learn JE on their own and implement it when (and if) they see fit, without top management input.

    _____
    _____

14. A new JE program is begun in jobs that are only marginally important to organizational success.

    _____
    _____

15. Meetings with workers and supervisors are held to come up with ideas that tend to make the relation between an employee and his or her work more meaningful.

    _____
    _____

PART B

Form 2 Job Enrichment Potential Questionnaire*

Instructions: Answer each of these questions for each of the jobs in Forms 5–9 and place the number of your answer (one through five) in the appropriate column of Form 3.

1. How much autonomy would typically be present on the job?

1	2	3	4	5
A great deal				Very little

2. Does the job involve a whole and identifiable piece of work with a beginning and an end?

1	2	3	4	5
Doing whole piece of work				Job is only tiny part of whole

3. How much variety, or the chance to do different things, is there on the job?

1	2	3	4	5
A great deal				Very little

4. In general, how significant or important is the job to the larger society; how much does it affect others' lives?

1	2	3	4	5
A great deal				Very little

5. To what extent would supervisors and/or co-workers be able and willing to let the incumbent know how well he or she is doing?

1	2	3	4	5
A great deal				Very little

6. Would the work itself, or actually doing the job, let the person in the job know how well he or she is doing?

1	2	3	4	5
A great deal				Very little

7. Does the job offer challenge?

1	2	3	4	5
A great deal				Very little

8. Does the job enable a person to be creative and imaginative, to use their own initiative?

1	2	3	4	5
A great deal				Very little

9. Does the job typically offer the chance to develop new skills and to advance in the organization and/or career?

1	2	3	4	5
A great deal				Very little

10. Does the job offer the chance to work closely with others and develop relationships with co-workers?

1	2	3	4	5
A great deal				Very little

Form 2 (continued)

11. Can a person gain recognition outside the organization from this job?

1	2	3	4	5
A great				Very
deal				little

12. Are there alternate methods to performing the job; is there flexibility in job performance?

1	2	3	4	5
A great				Very
deal				little

---

* Adapted loosely from J. R. Hackman and G. R. Oldham, "The Job Diagnostic Survey: An Instrument for the Diagnosis of Jobs and the Evaluation of Job Redesign Projects," Technical Report No. 4, Department of Administrative Sciences, Yale University, May 1974.

Name _____   Group Number _____

Date _____   Class Section _____   Hour _____   Score _____

PART B

Form 3 Job Enrichment Potential Tally Sheet

		Job Titles				
Question No.						
1						
2						
3						
4						
5						
6						
7						
8						
9						
10						
11						
12						
Job enrichment potential (Total score ÷ 12 = average)	total					
	average					

Which jobs would seem to be ready for a JE program?

PART B

Form 4 Job Description

EQUIPMENT OPERATOR I

DESCRIPTION OF WORK:

General Statement of Duties: Performs semiskilled work in the operation of light automotive or specialized equipment without final responsibility for assigned equipment.

Supervision Received: Works under supervision of technical administrator supervisor.

Supervision Exercised: None

DISTINGUISHING FEATURES: Positions assigned to Equipment Operator classes are distinguished by duties that involve utilizing mechanized equipment. Equipment Operator classes are further distinguished by having responsibility for the piece of equipment assigned. Positions assigned to City Services Worker classes are distinguished by duties that involve utilizing manual skills, although some equipment utilized by Equipment Operators may be used on an incidental basis to accomplish specific tasks.

EXAMPLES OF DUTIES: (Any one position may not include all of the duties listed, nor do the listed examples include all tasks that may be found in positions of this class.)

Operates ancillary equipment under the direction of a higher-level Equipment Operator.

Operates sewer jet equipment, locates and cleans manholes by utilizing pumps, generator, compressors, jackhammers, etc.

Operates automotive equipment such as jeeps, station wagons, passenger cars, pick-up trucks, flat beds, panel trucks and stake trucks, utility trucks, material and crew transport trucks, sign trucks, small ladder trucks, and similar equipment.

Operates farm-type tractors, including agricultural attachments.

Loads or assists in loading and unloading truck. Distributes load evenly over bed of truck. Performs general labor duties on the jobs to which equipment is assigned.

Services equipment with gas, oil, and water; reports mechanical defects.

Performs related work as required.

REQUIRED KNOWLEDGES, SKILLS, AND ABILITIES: Considerable knowledge of city and state traffic laws. Working knowledge of city street systems. Working knowledge of safety rules and regulations. Some knowledge of methods and materials used in servicing light automotive equipment. Skill in the operation of light automotive equipment. Ability to recognize and report abnormal operating functions on the equipment. Ability to perform arduous work with a full range of body movements. Ability to follow written and oral instructions. Ability to establish and maintain effective working relationships with other employees and the general public.

QUALIFICATIONS FOR APPOINTMENT:

Education: Eighth-grade completion or equivalent.

Experience: One year's experience in the operation of light automotive equipment.

    OR

Any equivalent combination of education and experience.

Necessary Special Requirements: Possession of a valid chauffeur's license issued by the state.

PART B

Form 5 Job Description

JOB TITLE:	Security trader
JOB FUNCTION:	To purchase and sell all types of securities, including, but not limited to, the following: Treasury bonds and notes, issues of governmental agencies, municipal bonds, corporate bonds, preferred and common stocks. Also would deal in certificates of deposit and commercial paper.
REPORTS TO:	Head of Investment Division
DEPARTMENT:	Trust
QUALIFICATIONS—GENERAL:	Needs college undergraduate degree or equivalent.
EXPERIENCE:	Would be helpful, but not necessary.
MACHINES AND EQUIPMENT USED:	Calculators, quote machines, telephones
RESPONSIBILITY FOR CASH AND NEGOTIABLE INSTRUMENTS:	Handles receipt and delivery of large blocks of securities at times. Deals in large amounts of negotiable securities.
PERSONAL CONTACTS:	Personal contacts are frequent with both trust customers and commercial customers as well as contacts with correspondent banks, country banks, and corporations.
JOB DETAILS:	Opens and supervises accounts for individuals, using authorization of the manager of the Investment Division. Purchases and sells securities arranging for time and place of settlement, nature of payment and other matters. Follows up on incompleted transactions. Most of this work is done by long-distance phone calls, usually to New York City, but also to Chicago, San Francisco, and other money centers. May perform other related duties within capabilities as may be requested by supervisor.

PART B

Form 6 Job Description

JOB TITLE:
Credit clerk

JOB FUNCTION:
Follow financial statements on commercial loan customers and maintenance of related index system.

REPORTS TO:
Lead credit clerk, Credit Division

DEPARTMENT:
Banking Department—Credit Division

QUALIFICATIONS—GENERAL:
High-school education or equivalent.
Skill in typing required.
Knowledge of accounting desirable.

EXPERIENCE:
Two or three months on-the-job training necessary.

MACHINES AND EQUIPMENT USED:
Typewriter
Ditto reproduction machine

RESPONSIBILITY FOR NEGOTIABLE ITEMS:
None

PERSONAL CONTACTS:
Frequent contact with lending officers in person and by telephone.

JOB DETAILS:
Assists Lead Credit Clerk in maintainence of current balance sheets and profit & loss statements on all commercial loan customers by following statements on an annual basis, by way of monthly index file and perpetual follow-up system. Responsible for transfer of all commercial loan data to diary sheets in credit files on both secured and unsecured loans. Reviews file input data sent to Credit Division from commercial loan officers to determine significance as it relates to review by others. Assists in preparation and processing of outdated file material to be transferred to record room for storage. Assists in maintainence of alphabetic index for credit files. Will serve as backup to file clerk (see file clerk—Credit Division). May perform other duties within capabilities as requested by supervisor.

PART B

Form 7 Job Description

ENGINEERING AIDE I

DESCRIPTION OF WORK:

General Statement of Duties: Performs routine subprofessional engineering work.

Supervision Received: Works under close supervision of a technical superior.

Supervision Exercised: None

EXAMPLE OF DUTIES: (Any one position may not include all of the duties listed, nor do the listed examples include all tasks that may be found in positions of this class.)

Acts as roadman, flagman, or rear chainman on a survey crew.

Uses line staff to indicate a point or places staff where directed. Uses level rod and adjusts and reads target in obtaining existing elevations, or in establishing elevations.

Drives hubs and stakes to indicate points and grades. Digs and searches for survey monuments.

Cuts and removes brush and undergrowth from instrumentman's line of sight. Cleans and cares for surveying instruments and tools.

Does routine tracing and simple drafting, such as plotting profiles and cross-sections. Makes simple mathematical computations. Performs a variety of office engineering tasks.

Performs the duties of head chainman and instrumentman as a part of in-service training.

Assists in the collection of samples and testing of construction materials.

Performs related work as required.

REQUIRED KNOWLEDGES, SKILLS, AND ABILITIES: Some knowledge of high-school mathematics, including algebra and trigonometry. Ability to make simple mathematical computations rapidly and accurately. Ability to follow oral and written instructions. Ability to do strenuous physical work. Ability to establish and maintain effective working relationships with other employees and the public.

QUALIFICATIONS FOR APPOINTMENT:

Education: High-school graduation or equivalent, including courses in algebra and trigonometry.

Experience: Six months experience in construction or related fields.

        OR

Any equivalent combination of education and experience.

PART B

Form 8 Job Description

MAINTENANCE MECHANIC I

DESCRIPTION OF WORK:

General Statement of Duties: Performs skilled and semiskilled maintenance and repair work involving a variety of trade skills.

Supervision Received: Works under supervision of a foreman.

Supervision Exercised: None.

EXAMPLE OF DUTIES: (Any one position may not include all of the duties listed, nor do the listed examples include all tasks that may be found in positions of this class.)

Performs carpentry, painting, plumbing, electrical, and other maintenance work in the repair of buildings, equipment, and related activities.

Operates equipment for snow removal and maintenance of the runways.

Assists in overhauling, cleaning, repairing and adjusting pumps, water and waste water treatment plant machinery, and related equipment.

Replaces and services equipment parts such as radiators, generators, distributors, motor mounts, engines and clutches. Rebuilds and repairs minor damage to body frames.

Performs related work as required.

REQUIRED KNOWLEDGES, SKILLS, AND ABILITIES: Considerable knowledge of the hazards and safety precautions of the construction and mechanical trades. Working knowledge of the standard practices, methods, materials, and tools of several trades. Skill in the use of tools, materials, and equipment of at least one trade, and in the use of the most common tools in several trades. Ability to learn a variety of mechanical and building maintenance skills. Ability to establish and maintain effective working relationships with employees and the public.

QUALIFICATIONS FOR APPOINTMENT:

Education: Eighth-grade completion or equivalent.

Experience: Two years experience in maintenance and repair work, including experience in equipment operation.

   OR

Any equivalent combination of education and experience.

PART C

Form 9 Implementing Job Enrichment: A Role Play*

GENERAL INSTRUCTIONS

You work in a group that does a few different tasks. J. Jaguar is the manager of several of these groups, including the one with which we are concerned. W. Heath, C. E. Adam, S. Elliott, and A. J. Andrew make up your particular group. The operation is divided into four jobs in which quality is very important. The four jobs are rather simple and each group member is familiar with all of the operations. Three of the operations involve simple physical and machinery work, but the fourth is an assembler/inspector operation. The person doing this job, because of the chance to critique others' work and assemble the entire product, has more responsibility and variety than the others. Some workers would like to exchange jobs or positions frequently, but have not done so because the methods engineers have been studying the jobs in order to find the fastest times for each. Presently, several of you will be asked to role play one of the following: the personnel director (Hooper), one of the work group members (Heath, Adam, Elliott, or Andrew), or the manager (Jaguar). In some instances, one or more observers will be present in the group. Role descriptions follow for all persons who are named above. Jaguar, Hooper, and the observers read all roles and observers complete Form 10. Work-group members should read only their own roles.

In role playing, you can begin with your written role and then expand it by making up things consistent with yourself and the role you have been asked to play.

The group's task is to decide whether or not they want a job enrichment program for the jobs they hold; if so, what their tasks would be; and, if not, why not. With the help of Jaguar, the group will arrive at a decision regarding what, if anything, they would like to change about their work.

ROLE FOR PERSONNEL ADMINISTRATOR

C. Hooper, Personnel administrator

You have asked J. Jaguar to hold a meeting with the work group to go over the jobs members perform, considering both the potential for job enrichment, as well as the results of a time and motion study. You have discussed the potential of job enrichment with J. Jaguar and administered the Job Enrichment Potential Questionnaire for the job under consideration. You strongly favor the JE approach, as you have documented recent decreases in quality and rising absenteeism and tardiness. You may sit in on the meeting and observe or serve as a resource person, but you have told Jaguar that the decision rests with her/him and the group, provided performance can be improved. However, you believe Jaguar is sold on the JE ideas you have suggested. After the group meeting, you meet separately with Jaguar and together decide what, if any, changes will be made based upon the group's decision.

ROLES FOR WORK GROUP MEMBERS

1. J. Jaguar, Supervisor (48 years old)

You are the manager who supervises the work of about twenty people. Most of the jobs are piece-rate jobs, and some of the employees work in teams and are paid on a team piece-rate basis. In one of the teams, Heath, Adam, Elliott, and Andrew work together. Each one of them does a different operation each day. W. F. Taylorly, the methods engineer, studied conditions in your section, timed each group member on each of the operations, and came up with the following timetable:

TIME PER OPERATION

	Operation 1	Operation 2	Operation 3	Operation 4 (assembler/inspector)	Total
W. Heath	16 min.	14 min.	19 min.	26 min.	75 min.
C. E. Adam	20 min.	10 min.	14 min.	36 min.	80 min.
S. Elliott	27 min.	10 min.	20 min.	29 min.	86 min.
J. Andrew	17 min.	13 min.	18 min.	20 min.	68 min.
				Average =	77.25 min.

Taylorly had observed that with the group rotating, an average time for all four operations would be a total of 77.25 minutes per complete unit. If, however, Heath worked only on the first operation, Elliott worked only on the second, Adam worked only on the third, and Andrew worked only on the fourth, the time for all four operations would

---

* Loosely adapted from N.R.F. Maier, *Psychology in Industrial Organizations*, 4th ed. (Boston: Houghton Mifflin, 1973), pp. 294–299.

Form 9 (continued)

only be 60 minutes. Thus, in an eight-hour work day, the group, by Taylorly's figures, could complete twenty-four units per day. (This is the present maximum because the fastest assembler, Andrew, can complete three units per hour.) Operations 1, 2, and 3 are pretty much the same. They involve working on one small part of a product. The fourth operation is that of assembler/inspector who inspects for defects and puts the entire subassembly together. Evaluating the others' work in this way and putting together the entire product can make the assembler/inspector feel like he or she has some autonomy and prestige, but at present this person receives no more money because the members of the group rotate and get paid on a *group* piece-rate system.

A quality problem exists as rejects have increased from 2 to 6%, and the results of administering the Job Enrichment Questionnaire (Form 2) gave the operation an average score of 4.1 for the series of four jobs. You also know absenteeism and turnover are on the rise and are concerned about this increase. Job Enrichment makes pretty good sense to you, so you have decided to take up the problem with the group. You feel they should go along with any proposed change if it will resolve the problems you face, and you will thus try to convince them of the importance of trying to change their work design. You must then convey their decision to C. Hooper, the person to whom you report. You and Hooper will make the final decisions. You are concerned that the group's decision fulfills your and Hooper's need to improve performance and try out JE, the technique you both feel has merit.

2. A. J. Andrew (23 years old)

You are the fastest of a crew that works on an assembly job. Each of you has an operation you do fastest and you are best at the assembler/inspector operation. Even though the job has some variety, it really isn't so hot; you don't earn any more money at it, yet work a little harder sometimes.

You would like to do the whole job (all four operations) instead of just parts of it, as you are bored to death and you know your quality may be slipping. In fact, you really don't care too much any more about the people on the job and are considering leaving to find a more interesting job. You have been tardy several times lately and have missed more days of work than you feel good about. But if you did the entire job yourself, you wouldn't be bored and your pay would be higher, too, because you could do the tasks faster!

3. S. Elliott (38 years old)

You work with three others on a job and get paid on a team piece-rate basis. The four of you work very well together and make a pretty good wage. The other three like to make a little more than you think is necessary, but you go along with them and work as hard as you can so as to keep the production up where they want it. They are good people, in fact, they often help you out if you fall behind, so you feel it is only fair to try to go along with the pace they set.

You like the No. 2 position the best because it is easiest, but when you get the No. 3 position, you can't keep up and you feel J. Jaguar the manager, is watching you. Sometimes the other three slow down and then Jaguar seems satisfied. You would like to get and *keep* the No. 2 job. In fact, if you don't get it, you may soon leave to find a job with less pressure.

Lately a "methods" person has been hanging around watching you and your job. You wonder what this person is up to. Can't they leave people alone who are doing all right?

4. W. Heath (26 years old)

You are one of four workers in a group and you enjoy working with them. You get paid on a team basis and you are making wages that are entirely satisfactory. Elliott isn't quite as fast as Adam and you, but when you feel Elliott is holding things up too much, each of you sneak in and help him/her out.

Except for operation No. 4, which you only get to do occasionally, the work is very monotonous. The saving thing is that you can talk when your supervisor is not watching. In this way, you get your mind off the job. You are best on the No. 1 position, so in that spot you often turn out some extra work and can sometimes make the job easier for Elliott.

You have been on this job for two years and have never run out of work. Apparently your group can make pretty good pay without running yourselves out of a job. Lately, however, the company has had some of its experts hanging around. It looks like the company is trying to work out some "speed-up" methods. If they make these jobs any simpler, you won't be able to stand the monotony. Your manager is an OK person who seldom has criticized your team's work. However, you find you have trouble making it to work on time every morning because the job is basically uneventful and routine.

5. C. E. Adam (27 years old)

You work with three others on a job that requires four separate operations. Each of you works on a different operation every day. But you have helped out others and that is satisfactory to you because you get paid on a team piece-rate basis. You could actually earn more if Elliott were a faster worker, but he/she is a swell person and you would rather have him/her in the group than someone else who might do a little bit more.

Form 9 (continued)

As you think about all four positions, you find them about equally desirable. Operation No. 4 is better as there is more variety. But they are all pretty simple and routine. The monotony doesn't bother you much because you can talk, daydream, and change your pace. By working slow for a while and then fast, you can sort of set your pace to music you hum to yourself. You like the idea of changing jobs, and even though Elliott is slow on some positions, changing has its good points; it breaks up the monotony a little.

Lately some type of expert has been hanging around some distance away with a chart in hand. The company could get more for its money if it put some of those people to work. You say to yourself, "I'd like to see one of them try to tell me how to do this job, I'd sure give them an earful."

If your manager doesn't get the "expert" out of here pretty soon, you're going to tell him/her what you think of the company dragging in spies!

Name _____   Group Number _____

Date _____   Class Section _____   Hour _____   Score _____

PART C

Form 10 Instructions for Observers of the Job Enrichment Implementation Efforts

Your job is to observe the method used by Jaguar in handling a problem with the group. Pay special attention to the following as you answer the questions below:

a) Method of presenting problems: Does Jaguar criticize, suggest a remedy, get them involved in solving the problem, request their help on a problem, or use some other approach?

b) Initial reaction of members: Do group members feel criticized or do they try to help?

c) Handling of discussion by Jaguar: Does she/he listen or argue? Try to persuade? Use threats? Or does she/he let the group decide?

d) Forms of resistance expressed by the group: Which members express fear, hostility, satisfaction with present method, etc.?

e) Pick out what you think is the best thing that Jaguar did.

Fill out the following questionnaire as you observe the group discussion.

QUESTIONNAIRE FOR OBSERVERS OF JOB ENRICHMENT IMPLEMENTATION EFFORTS

I. The group discussion

1. Observe the manager's attitude toward change during the discussion.

   a) Was he or she partial to the new method?

   | Unsupportive attitude | 0 /_/_/_/_/_/_/_/_/_/ 5   neutral   10 | Supportive attitude |

   b) Did he or she seem mainly interested in more production or in improving the job *and* its satisfaction for the group?

   | Production only | 0 /_/_/_/_/_/_/_/_/_/ 5   neutral   10 | Production and satisfaction |

   c) To what extent was the manager considerate of the objections raised by the group?

   | Inconsiderate of objections | 0 /_/_/_/_/_/_/_/_/_/ 5   neutral   10 | Considerate of objections |

   d) What effect did the manager's remarks have on the progress of the discussion?

   | Inhibited progress | 0 /_/_/_/_/_/_/_/_/_/ 5   neutral   10 | Aided progress |

2. Make notes on characteristic aspects of the discussion.

   a) Did arguments develop? If so, who was involved?

   b) Was any group member unusually stubborn and/or defensive? Who and why?

   Name   *Reason*

   1. _____   _____
   2. _____   _____
   3. _____   _____
   4. _____   _____

Form 10 (continued)

c) Were any of the group members inhibited? Who and why?

Name   *Reason*

1. _____   _____
2. _____   _____
3. _____   _____
4. _____   _____

d) Did the group members listen to each other?

Listened   0   5   10   Listened
poorly   / / / / / / / / / /   well
                         neutral

e) List below the main points of differences between group members.

1. _____
2. _____
3. _____
4. _____
5. _____

II. *Evidences of problem-resolving behavior*

a) What was agreed on, if anything?

1. _____
2. _____
3. _____
4. _____

b) In what respects was the manager willing to compromise?

Low willingness to   0   5   10   High willingness to
compromise by manager / / / / / / / / / /   compromise by manager
                                   neutral

c) What did the manager do to help or hinder a mutually acceptable work method for the benefit of the organization and its employees?

Helping behavior(s)   *Hindering behavior(s)*

1. _____   1. _____
2. _____   2. _____
3. _____   3. _____
4. _____   4. _____

III. *The discussion between the manager and the personnel administrator*

Record your overall reactions to the discussion between Jaguar and Hooper. Was Jaguar ashamed of the group's decision? Did Jaguar distort the actual conclusion reached by the group when she/he and Hooper discussed it? What was the outcome of this discussion among supervisors?

_____
_____
_____
_____
_____
_____
_____
_____

Name _____   Group Number _____

Date _____   Class Section _____   Hour _____   Score _____

ASSESSMENT OF LEARNING IN PERSONNEL ADMINISTRATION
EXERCISE 14

1. Try to state the purpose of this exercise in one concise sentence.

2. Specifically what did you learn from this exercise (i.e., skills, abilities, and knowledge)?

3. How might your learning influence your role and your duties as a personnel administrator?

4. How would you evaluate the effectiveness of a JE program?

5. How can the specialists in personnel or human-resources management interface with line managers to accomplish a JE program's objectives? (Be specific.)

6. What are the costs of a JE program likely to be? How can they be lessened?

Exercise 15
Improving performance through rewards: using positive reinforcement

PREVIEW

As a motivation tool, job enrichment (JE) operates on the premise that performance can be improved by offering workers intrinsic rewards. Intrinsic rewards come from the activity or work itself and are dispensed by oneself (e.g., a feeling of pride or autonomy as a result of enriched job content). However, there is much to suggest that performance can also be improved by offering intrinsic rewards to people. These rewards, such as money, come from external sources (the supervisor or the organization) and are gained as a result of attempting or completing a task or job. The systematic utilization of extrinsic rewards is a possible remedy for the problem of motivating workers and managers. Techniques from basic operant principles, such as the use of positive reinforcement, can point to some deficiencies in traditional organizational motivation programs. These operant techniques are the subject of this exercise. They differ from other motivational programs (e.g., JE) in that they concentrate on changing observable behavior and the environment rather than attitudes, satisfaction, or other psychological concepts which are not observable. After the basic concepts of the operant learning model are introduced, organizational practices are critiqued from an operant perspective, and a motivation program emphasizing positive reinforcement is designed.

OBJECTIVES

1. To provide feedback regarding participants' understanding of the administration of rewards in organizations through the use of behavior modification and operant concepts.

2. To begin to develop skill in assessing the effectiveness of motivation programs from an operant perspective.

3. To begin to develop skill in designing motivation programs that emphasize the use of positive reinforcement.

PREMEETING ASSIGNMENT

Read the entire exercise.

INTRODUCTION

Behavior Modification and Positive Reinforcement (PR)

Behavior modification is the general term applied to the systematic management of behavior in order to change or modify it by changing the environment. This environmental management involves the offering of rewards and punishments for desired and undesired behavior. The strategy is derived from the operant learning model, which simply posits that behavior is a function of its consequences.[1] Consequences are those

---

[1] See, e.g., B. F. Skinner, *The Technology of Teaching* (New York: Appleton-Century-Crofts, 1968); A. Bandura, *Principles of Behavior Modification* (New York: Holt, 1969); G. Dessler, *Human Behavior, Improving Performance at Work* (Reston, Virginia: Reston, 1979), Chap. 4; F. Luthans and R. Krietner, *Organization Behavior Modification* (Glenview, Ill.: Scott Foresman, 1975).

changes in the environment that elicit reward or punishment. Although B. F. Skinner is usually given credit for the development of these ideas, most of the actual applications of the operant model for humans have been through thousands of behavior modification programs and experiments in mental and correctional institutions and in schools.[2]

Recently, however, the use of operant principles to help change behaviors of working adults in organizations has received much attention. In addition to papers advocating the potential use of these ideas in work organizations, there are also reports of actual applications that have been well received by employees and management and have saved some organizations considerable amounts of money, while leading to increased productivity.[3]

What is Behavior Modification? The key to the operant approach lies in the relationship between behavior and its consequences—that is, the outcomes that are brought about by a particular behavior or inadvertently result from a behavior. The outcomes may be perceived as positive, such as monetary rewards, or negative, such as a disciplinary layoff. If these consequences increase the probability that the positive behavior producing them will occur in the future, the consequences are called positive reinforcers. For example, a positive reinforcer—a bonus for punctuality—when dispensed after the behavior it is meant to reinforce—arriving at work on time—would increase the probability that arriving on time will occur in the future. A negative reinforcer, such as a disciplinary layoff for tardiness, also may increase the probability of a future behavior, punctuality, for punctuality would remove the layoff from a worker's job environment (see Fig. 1).

These reinforcers, both positive and negative,

seem to be most effective if linked closely in time to the behaviors they are meant to control. They are thus said to be contingent on these behaviors and are not delivered unless the behavior is manifest. This contingency relationship is useful for organizations simply because if people observe through experience that the receipt of a reward, say a promotion, is contingent on their good performance, they may choose those behaviors that lead to the reward more often. If the reward (i.e., promotion) is not contingent on good performance, but on seniority, good performance will not be the only way to get the reward and employees may not perform well. Rather, they may choose simply to keep their jobs and build seniority while performing at minimally acceptable levels.

Punishment also influences behavior. Unlike reinforcement, punishment decreases the probability of the future occurrence of the behavior on which it is made contingent. For example, if tardiness is punished by layoff, tardiness may decrease in the future. But the desired behavior, punctuality, may not be increased in all cases (see Fig. 1). Not getting caught or having a coworker punch your time clock are other ways of avoiding punishment. Thus, while punishment can decrease the probability of the occurrence of one undesired behavior, there is no assurance that the desired behavior will be built in. Therefore, punishment may be most effective if it is coupled with positive reinforcement to help ensure that desired behaviors recur. Simply put, workers benefit not only from knowing what they did wrong to receive punishment, but also from knowing what they can do correctly to receive positive reinforcement.

To couple punishment with positive reinforcement, a supervisor could cut pay or lay workers off who were not at work on time. In addition, however, he or she could positively reinforce, through verbal praise or perhaps a bonus, workers who are not tardy. With this strategy, the undesirable behavior, tardiness, may decrease through punishment, *and* the desirable behavior, punctuality, may increase through positive reinforcement. The supervisor is emphasizing not only the negative aspects of an employee's behavior, but also the positive aspects.

Schedules of Reinforcement. Reinforcement and punishment can be dispensed on any one of a number of schedules. *Continuous* schedules reward or punish after every desired behavior is observed. An example would be the receipt of a compliment or a commission after each sale made by a salesperson. These schedules have the advantage of facilitating fast learning of new behavior. When a person is learning a new task, reinforcing after every correct behavior is very effective.

[2] See, e.g., Ulrich et al., *Control of Human Behavior.*

[3] See C. E. Schneier, "Behavior Modification in Management: A Review and a Critique," *Academy of Management Journal* 17 (1974): 528–548. Specific applications include W. Nord, "Improving Attendance through Rewards," *Personnel Administration* 34, no. 4 (1971): 41–47; E. Pedalino and V. Gamboa, "Behavior Modification and Absenteeism: Intervention in One Industrial Setting," *Journal of Applied Psychology* 59 (1974): 694–698; W. C. Hamner and E. P. Hamner, "Behavior Modification on the Bottom Line," *Organization Dynamics* 4, no. 4 (1976): 3–21; "Productivity Gains from a Pat on the Back," *Business Week,* January 23, 1978, 56; J. Komaki et al., "A Behavioral Approach to Occupational Safety . . . ,[4] *Journal of Applied Psychology* 63 (1978): 434–445; C. E. Schneier et al., "Improving Performance in the Public Sector Through Behavior Modification and Positive Reinforcement," *Public Personnel Management* 8 (March–April 1979): 101–110.

Strategy	Effect on probability of occurrence of contingent future behavior	Examples		
1. Positive Reinforcement	Increases	Target Behavior: Punctuality	Contingent Consequence: Add a monetary bonus	Result: Punctuality
2. Negative Reinforcement	Increases	Target Behavior: Punctuality	Contingent Consequence: Remove a cut in pay	Result: Punctuality
3. Punishment	Decreases	Target Behavior: (Decreased) Tardiness	Contingent Consequence: Add a cut in pay	Possible Results: (a) Decreased tardiness (b) Escape and avoidance of punishment through unobserved tardiness; having peers punch time clock (c) Increased punctuality

Fig. 1. Behavior modification strategies for changing behavior (From C. E. Schneier et al., "Improving Performance in the Public Sector Through Behavior Modification and Positive Reinforcement," *Public Personnel Management* 8 (March–April 1979): 104)

A problem with these schedules is that when they are removed, the behavior decreases rapidly.

A second type of schedule of dispensing rewards or punishment is an *interval* schedule. There are two types of interval schedules, fixed and ratio. A fixed-interval schedule requires reinforcement to be dispensed after a certain, fixed period of time. The first correct response elicited after the time interval has passed is reinforced (or punished). In a sense, paychecks given biweekly or monthly in an organization are examples of fixed-interval schedules, but these paychecks are seldom made contingent on specific behaviors. They are received whether an employee does very well that week or poorly.

Fixed-ratio schedules allow for reinforcement after a certain, fixed number of behaviors is observed. In this case, a worker would be docked a day's pay after three unexcused absences or given a bonus after signing up ten new customers. Rather than operate on a fixed period of time, like the fixed interval schedules, these schedules operate on a fixed number of behaviors.

Intermittent or variable-ratio schedules also dispense reinforcement or punishment after a number of behaviors, but the number changes, is unknown to the person being reinforced, and is not fixed as in fixed-ratio schedules. For example, a supervisor may give you an afternoon off (perhaps this would be a positive reinforcer for you) after one excellent report is turned in, then not again until after three reports are turned in, then after two, etc. The number of behaviors (i.e., com-

pletion of good reports) required to receive the reward varies over time. Since you do not know which behavior will bring the reward, you may be motivated to continue the desired behaviors, as the next one may be the one that brings the reward. A slot machine and other gambling devices work on the same principle of variable-ratio schedules. Because the next "play" may be a winner, we are highly motivated to insert the money and pull the arm "one more time." In some, but not all, studies, variable-ratio schedules have been found to sustain required behavior over longer periods of time than other schedules.[4]

Suppose we had one group of workers being reinforced under a fixed-interval schedule, let's say receiving verbal praise from their supervisors once every two hours. Another group would receive verbal praise,

---

[4] See G. Yukl et al., "Effectiveness of Pay Incentives Under Variable Ratio and Continuous Reinforcement Schedules," *Journal of Applied Psychology* 56 (1972): 19–23. An interesting analysis of the issue of schedules of reinforcement is offered by C. J. Berger, L. L. Cummings, and H. G. Heneman, "Expectany Theory and Operant Conditioning Predictions of Performance Under Variable Ratio and Continuous Schedules of Reinforcement," *Organizational Behavior and Human Performance* 14 (1975): 227–243. A study that found continuous schedules as effective as variable-ratio schedules is G. A. Yukl et al., "The Effectiveness of Performance Incentives Under Continuous and Variable Ratio Schedules of Reinforcement," *Personnel Psychology* 29 (1976): 221–231.

according to a variable-ratio schedule, after three correct behaviors, then after six, then after one, then after
nine, etc., averaging out over time to every six behaviors. The second group of workers would sustain the
desired behaviors over a longer period of time. The
first group might anticipate the praise, only exhibiting
desired behaviors right before each two-hour interval.
The second group would not know when the reinforcement is coming and would sustain the correct behaviors so as not to miss it. We are, of course, making the
assumption that verbal praise does in fact act as a reinforcer for these workers (i.e., it actually produces
changes in the frequency of observed behaviors it
follows).

Positive Reinforcement as a Motivation Strategy. For
organizations, the operant learning model and various
behavior modification concepts explained above may
offer a different approach to motivation problems.
Punishment and threat of punishment often have deleterious side effects, such as the building of negative
emotional feelings toward the punishing agent. When
used alone, punishment may fail to build in or shape
desired behaviors, even if it distinguishes undesired
ones. Therefore, positive reinforcement (PR) may be
a more effective way to change behavior at work. Some
consequences of behavior, such as monetary rewards,
verbal praise, promotion, or recognition, may be positive reinforcers and should be relied on heavily (see
Fig. 2). Further, as noted above, variable-ratio schedules of reinforcement may be quite useful in sustaining
desired behavior as opposed to the more-often-used
interval schedules.

Reinforcement can be useful to workers if it is
given in specific behavioral terms; this enables feedback to focus on behavioral deficiencies that can be
amended. Feedback given in general terms, such as,
"You have been doing poorly lately," does not tell the
recipient exactly which behaviors he or she is exhibiting are desirable and which are undesirable. Telling
people that their report writing needs improvement,
particularly a tighter organization of sections and a
more concise writing style, and offering examples of a
well-organized report and concise language, would be
far more beneficial. A behaviorally-based performance
appraisal system, such as BARS (Behaviorally
Anchored Rating Scales, see Exercise 4), would facilitate this type of feedback. There are specific behavioral
examples of each performance level on each of the
major aspects of a job in this type of system. A supervisor, therefore, would be able to tell subordinates
what behaviors they exhibited that were indicative of
excellent or poor performance, and what needed to be

**Fig. 2. Potentially useful positive reinforcers available in the
public organization work environment** (From C. E.
Schneier et al., "Improving Performance in the Public
Sector Through Behavior Modification and Positive
Reinforcement," *Public Personnel Management* 8
(March–April 1979): 109. Some potential reinforcers
would be more useful and practical in certain organizational settings and with certain groups of people
than others.

Feedback on performance
Verbal praise from superiors
Assignment of preferred work activities
Assignment of special projects typically performed by
    supervisors
Publicity in organization newsletters
Opportunity to attend training
Opportunities to train others
Additional or upgraded equipment (e.g., typewriters)
Awards ceremonies (cash and certificates)
Opportunity to supervise others
Opportunity to design feedback forms, reporting systems,
    schedules, charts, graphs, or other work aids
Letter of recommendation
Preferred work-space assignment
Office social events
Desk accessories
Redecoration of work environment
Solicitation of suggestions from supervisors
Solicitation of advice from supervisors
Verbal praise from customers, clients, other employees
Promotion
Job rotation

exhibited to receive better ratings. People can act on
this type of specific feedback.

In general, motivation, incentive, and pay systems in many organizations would be judged deficient
from an operant perspective simply because they do
not allow for a contingent relationship between performance and reinforcement. In many cases, rewards
are received for undesired behavior (such as performing poorly and not getting caught), or positive reinforcement and punishment may be the consequence of
the same behavior. For example, high performance is
rewarded by the supervisor, but punished by the work
group as peers intimidate the "rate-buster."

In addition, the operant perspective does note differences between people, as well as the consequences
of behavior. These differences concern the individual
reinforcement history (i.e., what reinforcers have been
used in the past) and experience of each worker. The
operant model would predict, for example, that a
given consequence of behavior may be perceived as
positive by some and negative by others. That is, some
people might, due to their backgrounds, feel that a
lottery at work for good attendance is a form of gambling and thus be opposed to it. For others, the oppor-

tunity to win a prize would be an effective reinforcer. The use of certain consequences would need to be individually determined in some instances to help ensure that the consequences are perceived in the way intended by the organization.

One of the best ways to determine what consequences of behavior may be effective as reinforcers is to experiment with a few. Those that increase (or decrease) the frequency of behavior on which they are made contingent would, given practical and cost considerations, be most effective. Workers could be given the option of one or another (e.g., a preferred work assignment or a chance to train others; time off or a bonus). Another method is to use a questionnaire listing various potential reinforcers and ask workers to rank order them.[5]

Implementing PR in Work Organizations. Although some obvious potential gains can be derived from a PR program in organizations, implementation requires careful planning and often poses problems. First, desired behavior must be identified in a very specific manner in order to know what to make the consequences contingent on. However, in higher-level positions, desired performance is difficult to pin down. What exactly does the executive do? Certainly a comprehensive job analysis (see Exercise 3) may help to identify broad categories of duties and responsibilities, but it often stops short of identifying specific behaviors that are desirable or undesirable.

We would certainly reinforce (or punish) for outcomes on the job, such as profit, sales volumes, absenteeism rates, or number of projects completed. Here, a Management by Objectives (MBO, see Exercise 5) system could be useful as it helps identify results or outputs. If we want to pinpoint specific behaviors and follow them with reinforcement (or punishment), a BARS system of performance appraisal noted above (see Exercise 4) could be helpful. Through it, various desirable and undesirable behaviors are identified.

A second important step in implementing a positive reinforcement program in an organization is to develop a pool of potential reinforcers. Money is a reinforcer for many people, but perhaps not for all. Verbal praise, participation in decision making, fringe benefits, promotion, the chance to do unusual and exciting tasks, time off, bigger offices, organization-wide recognition, and bonuses are all possible reinforcers (see Fig. 2). Discretion must be given to supervisors so they can offer reinforcers for desired performance, and these reinforcers must be shown to be ef-

fective in changing the behavior of the particular worker involved. Assessment of a worker's reinforcement preferences is often difficult; therefore, general reinforcers such as money are frequently used. When money cannot be made contingent on desired behavior as a practical matter, certain other consequences probably can. These might include verbal praise or a host of reinforcers related to the work itself (e.g., more responsibility, job rotation).

Third, the receipt of rewards in a positive reinforcement program must be made contingent on evidence of desired performance—those behaviors identified in the first step above—rather than on seniority or merely attending work. Behavior must be observed and recorded. Simple checklists can be kept by the workers themselves or supervisors that note desired behaviors and their frequency of occurrence. These have been shown to be effective ways to measure behavior in an organizational setting.[6]

Provisions must be made through organizational policy to reward desired behavior with bonuses, promotions, verbal praise, etc. Above all, workers must see the relationship between rewards (or punishment) and performance. Their beliefs are shaped by the organization's actual policies and actions that back up these policies. If seniority, attitude, appearance, or nepotism lead to rewards (i.e., are reinforced by organization) and not performance, workers will strive for these instead of performance. Thus, the contingent relationship between rewards and performance is destroyed.

Finally, rewards are most useful if they are linked closely in time to the performance they are meant to reinforce. If employees receive a compliment six weeks after they exceeded the sales quota, the compliment's effect as a reinforcer is weakened considerably according to the operant model.

Practical and Philosophical Issues. While PR has been extremely successful in some organizations,[7] few systematic PR programs have been attempted in work organizations. There are practical problems deterring such programs. Among these are:

1. The difficulty in pinpointing specific behaviors to reinforce or punish, particularly at higher-level, professional positions.

[5] See M. R. Blood, "Intergroup Comparisons of Intraperson Differences: Rewards from the Job," *Personnel Psychology* 26 (1973): 1-9.

[6] See Schneier et al., "Improving Performance"; Komaki et al., "A Behavioral Approach"; Luthans and Krietner, *Organizational Behavior Modification*.

[7] See, e.g., "At Emery Air Freight: Positive Reinforcement Boosts Performance," *Organizational Dynamics* 1 (Winter 1973): 41-50; Hamner and Hamner, "Behavior Modification"; "Productivity Gains," *Business Week*.

2. The time required to observe and record behavior frequency of workers in order to dispense contingent rewards.

3. The paperwork involved in recording worker behavior.

4. The difficulty in tying some rewards, such as money, directly to performance in some organizations and in some job types.

5. The time and resources required to train supervisors in PR principles and build their skill in implementing them.

6. Overcoming resistance to changes in pay policies, work assignments, and supervisors' responsibilities that often must accompany a PR program.

Philosophical-issues arguments against behavior modification and problems with the utility of the operant principles themselves in applied work settings have received considerable attention.[8] A few of the more common criticisms follow:[9]

1. Ignores the individuality of people by developing the same reinforcement system for all workers.

2. Restricts freedom of choice by attempting to control people's behavior.

3. Ignores that people may be motivated by the work itself, not merely by external rewards (e.g., money or praise from superiors) given for desired behavior.

Individual preferences for reinforcers can be taken into account, however, and reinforcers other than money, such as pride and esteem from a challenging job, can and are used in organizations.

As long as organizations are controlling workers' environments and offering rewards and punishments to workers, they are controlling their behavior, or certainly attempting to do so. Many "reward" systems, however, rely more on punishment than on rewards. In many organizations, improper behavior is punished much more often than proper behavior is rewarded. Many supervisors "manage by exception" by interacting with subordinates only when they are in error—an exception to what is expected. Management by exception is often really management by punishment.[10] Further, workers may not know exactly what the desired behaviors are or what it takes to receive rewards because the criteria for success are not well articulated by management, communicated to workers, or applied consistently.

PR programs may be beneficial because they open up the rewards process by identifying what is desired from workers. They then tie these behaviors to rewards and people know where they stand. The probability for favoritism and non–performance-related factors (e.g., age, race, or sex) to enter into reward decisions may be lessened.

PROCEDURE

Overview. In this exercise, you will review your understanding of PR concepts by completing Part A, a quiz on behavior modification. Then two types of motivational programs are assessed from an operant viewpoint. Finally, you are required to design a motivation program for traveling salespersons, using PR.

PART A

STEP 1: Two questionnaires (Form 1) are presented to enable you to check your understanding of operant concepts and PR. Answer the questions and review any errors you have made after the implementor notes correct responses. Be sure you have operant concepts clearly in mind before you continue with the exercise.

TIME: About 35 minutes.

PART B

STEP 2: Form groups of four to six persons and read the descriptions of two motivational programs presented in Forms 2, 3, and 4. Assess these programs from an operant standpoint by answering all of the questions on Form 2, completely filling in Form 3, and answering the questions in Form 4. Discuss the questions at the end of the descriptive material for each program, in your small groups. Reach consensus on the answers.

TIME: About one hour.

---

[8] Criticisms of the operant approach applied to management and work organizations, and its research base, are found in F. Fry, "Operant Conditioning and O. B. Mod: Of Mice and Men," *Personnel* 51 (July–August 1974): 17–24; T. C. Mawhinney, "Operant Terms and Concepts in the Description of Individual Work Behavior: Some Problems of Interpretation, Application, and Evaluation," *Journal of Applied Psychology* 60 (1975): 704–712; W. F. Whyte, "Skinnerian Theory in Organizations," *Psychology Today* 5, no. 11 (1972): 66–68+; E. A. Locke, "The Myths of Behavior Modification in Organizations," *Academy of Management Review* 2 (1977): 543–553; W. C. Hamner and D. W. Organ, *Organizational Behavior* (Dallas: BPI, 1978), pp. 60–67.

[9] Hamner and Organ, *Organizational Behavior,* pp. 60–67.

---

[10] R. W. Beatty and C. E. Schneier, "A Case for Positive Reinforcement," *Business Horizons* 18 (April 1975): 57–66.

PART C

STEP 3: Design a PR motivation program for traveling salespersons. Pertinent facts are given in Form 5. The program should be practical and use operant concepts correctly. Sketch out the program orally and have someone in the group outline it in writing, briefly noting and describing all major steps in sequence.

TIME: About one to three hours.

FOR FURTHER READING

Aldis, O. "Of Pigeons and Men." *Harvard Business Review* 39, no. 4 (1961): 59–63. (I)

Arvey, R. D., and J. M. Ivancevich. "Punishment in Organizations: A Review, Propositions, and Research Suggestions." *Academy of Management Review* 5 (1980): 123–132. (II)

"At Emery Air Freight: Positive Reinforcement Boosts Performance." *Organizational Dynamics* 1 (Winter 1973): 41–59. (I)

Bandura, A. *Principles of Behavior Modification.* New York: Holt, 1969. (II)

Beatty, R. W., and C. E. Schneier. "A Case for Positive Reinforcement." *Business Horizons* 18, no. 2 (April 1975): 57–66. (I)

Beatty, R. W., and C. E. Schneier. "Training the Hard-Core Unemployed through Positive Reinforcement." *Human Resources Management* 4 (Winter 1972): 10–17. (I)

Berger, C. J., L. L. Cummings, and H. G. Heneman. "Expectancy Theory and Operant Conditioning Predictions of Performance Under Variable Ratio and Continuous Schedules of Reinforcement." *Organizational Behavior and Human Performance* 14 (1975): 227–243. (II–R)

Blood, M. R. "Intergroup Comparisons of Intraperson Differences: Rewards from the Job." *Personnel Psychology* 26 (1976): 1–9. (II–R)

Brethower, D. M. *Behavior Analysis in Business and Industry: A Total Performance System.* Kalamazoo, Mich.: Behaviordelia, 1972. (I)

Cherrington, D. J., and J. O. Cherrington. "Participation, Performance, and Appraisal." *Business Horizons* 17, no. 6 (1974): 35–44. (I)

Connellan, T. K. *How to Improve Human Performance, Behaviorism in Business and Industry.* New York: Harper & Row, 1978. (I)

Deci, E. L. "The Hidden Costs of Rewards." *Organizational Dynamics* 3 (1975): 2–15. (I)

Deci, E. L. "The Effects of Contingent and Noncontingent Rewards and Controls on Intrinsic Motivation." *Organizational Behavior and Human Performance* 8 (1972): 217–229. (II–R)

Farris, G. F. "Chickens, Eggs, and Productivity in Organizations." *Organizational Dynamics* 3 (1975): 2–15. (I)

Goldstein, A. P., and M. Sorcher. *Changing Supervisor Behavior.* New York: Pergamon, 1974. (I)

Hamner, W. C., and E. P. Hamner. "Behavior Modification on the Bottom Line." *Organizational Dynamics* 4, no. 4 (1976): 3–21. (I)

Jablonsky, S. F., and D. C. DeVries. "Operant Conditioning Principles Extrapolated to the Theory of Management." *Organizational Behavior and Human Performance* 7 (1972): 340–358. (II)

Kerr, S. "On the Folly of Rewarding A, While Hoping for B." *Academy of Management Journal* 6 (1975): 768–783. (I)

Kim, J. S., and W. C. Hammer. "Effect of Performance Feedback and Goal Setting on Productivity and Satisfaction in an Organizational Setting." *Journal of Applied Psychology* 61 (1976): 48–57. (II–R)

Komaki, J. "Alternative Evaluation Strategies in Work Settings: Reversal and Multiple-Baseline Designs." *Journal of Organizational Behavior Management* 1 (1977): 53–77. (II)

Komaki, J., K. D. Barwick, and L. R. Scott. "A Behavioral Approach to Occupational Safety: Pinpointing and Reinforcing Safe Performance in a Food Manufacturing Plant." *Journal of Applied Psychology* 63 (1978): 434–445. (II–R)

Komaki, J., R. L. Collins, and T. J. F. Theome. "Behavioral Measurement in Business, Industry, and Government." *Behavioral Assessment* 2 (1980): 103–123. (II)

Kraut, A. I. "Behavior Modeling Symposium." *Personnel Psychology* 29 (1976): 325–370. (II)

Latham, G. P. "The Effect of Various Schedules of Reinforcement on the Productivity of Tree Planters." Paper delivered at the Annual Convention of the American Psychological Association, New Orleans, 1974. (II–R)

Lawler, E. E. *Pay and Organizational Effectiveness.* New York: McGraw-Hill, 1971. (II)

Locke, E. A. "The Myths of Behavior in Organizations." *Academy of Management Review* 2 (1977): 543–553. (II) See also J. L. Gray, *Academy of Management Review* 4 (1979): 121–129 and E. A. Locke, *Academy of Management Review* 4 (1979): 131–136. (II)

Luthans, F., and R. Krietner. *Organizational Behavior Modification.* Glenview, Ill.: Scott Foresman, 1975. (I)

Markin, R. J., and C. M. Lillis. "Sales Managers Get What They Expect." *Business Horizons* 17, no. 3 (June 1975): 51–58. (I)

Mawhinney, T. C. "Operant Terms and Concepts in the Description of Individual Work Behavior: Some Problems of Interpretation, Application, and Evaluation." *Journal of Applied Psychology* 60 (1975): 704–712. (II)

McClelland, D. C. "Money as a Motivator: Some Research Highlights." In T. T. Herbert, ed., *Organizational Behavior: Readings and Cases.* New York: Macmillan, 1976. (I)

Meichenbaum, O. *Cognitive Behavior Modification.* New York: Plenum, 1977. (II)

Meyer, H. H. "The Pay for Performance Dilemma." *Organizational Dynamics* 3 (Winter 1975): 39–50. (I)

Miller, L. M. *Behavior Management.* New York: Wiley, 1978. (I)

Nord, W. "Improving Attendance through Rewards." *Personnel Administration* 33, no. 6 (1970): 37–41. (I)

Nord, W. "Beyond the Teaching Machine: The Neglected Area of Operant Conditioning in the Theory and Practice of Management." *Organizational Behavior and Human Performance* 4 (1969): 375–401. (II)

Notz, W. W. "Work Motivation and the Negative Effects of Extrinsic Rewards." *American Psychologist* 30 (1975): 884–891. (II)

Organ, D. W. "A Reappraisal and Reinterpretation of the Satisfaction-Causes-Performance Controversy." *Academy of Management Review* 2 (1977): 46–53. (II)

Parsons, H. M. "What Happened at Hawthorne?" *Science* 183 (1974): 922–932. (I)

Pedalino, E., and V. Gamboa. "Behavior Modification and Absenteeism: Intervention in One Industrial Setting." *Journal of Applied Psychology* 59 (1974): 694–698. (II-R)

Porter, L. W. "Turning Work into Nonwork: The Rewarding Environment." In M. D. Dunnette, ed., *Work and Nonwork in the Year 2001.* Monterey, Cal.: Brooks/Cole, 1973. (I)

"Productivity Gains from a Pat on the Back." *Business Week* (23 January 1978): 56. (I)

Reynolds, G. S. *A Primer of Operant Conditioning.* Glenview, Ill.: Scott Foresman, 1968. (I)

Rotundi, T. "Behavior Modification on the Job." *Supervisory Management* 21, no. 2 (February 1976): 22–28. (I)

Schneier, C. E. "Behavior Modification in Management: A Review and Critique. *Academy of Management Journal* 17 (1974): 528–548. (I)

Schneier, C. E. "Behavior Modification: Training the Hard-Core Unemployed." *Personnel* 50, no. 3 (1973): 65–69. (I)

Schneier, C. E., and R. Pernick. "Increasing Public Sector Productivity through Organization Behavior Modification: A Successful Application." Paper delivered at National Meeting of the Academy of Management, Atlanta, 1979.

Schneier, C. E., R. Pernick, and D. E. Bryant. "Improving Performance in the Public Sector Through Behavior Modification and Positive Reinforcement." *Public Personnel Management* 8 (March–April 1979): 101–110. (I-R)

Sims, H. P. "Further Thoughts on Punishment in Organizations." *Academy of Management Review* 5 (1980): 135–138. (II)

Skinner, B. F. *Beyond Freedom and Dignity.* New York: Knopf, 1971. (I)

Ulrich, R., T. Stachnik, and J. Mawbry, eds. *Control of Human Behavior,* vols. 1, 2. Glenview, Ill.: Scott Foresman, 1970. (II-R)

Whyte, W. F. "Skinnerian Theory in Orgnaizations." *Psychology Today* 5, no.11 (1972): 66, 68+. (I)

Yukl, G. A., and G. P. Latham. "Consequences of Reinforcement Schedules and Incentive Magnitudes of Employee Performance: Problems Encountered in an Industrial Setting." *Journal of Applied Psychology* 60 (1975): 294–298. (II-R)

Yukl, G. A., G. P. Latham, and E. D. Purcell. "The Effectiveness of Performance Incentives Under Continuous and Variable Ratio Schedules of Reinforcement." *Personnel Psychology* 29 (1976): 221–232. (II-R)

Yukl, G., K. Wexley, and J. E. Seymour. "Effectiveness of Pay Incentives Under Variable Ratio and Continuous Reinforcement Schedules." *Journal of Applied Psychology* 56, no. 1 (1972): 19–23. (II-R)

Name _____ Group Number _____

Date _____ Class Section _____ Hour _____ Score _____

PART A

Form 1 Receiving Feedback on Your Understanding of PR

A. Please check the following discussion statements True or False. State any assumptions you make in deciding your response and provide any explanation you feel necessary.

	TRUE	FALSE
1. Behavior modification methods have been derived from thousands of experiments in educational organizations and institutions.	_____	_____
2. Behavior modification applications in industrial organizations afford managers quantitative data about behavior they are required to observe and record.	_____	_____
3. It is worthwhile to reward even small improvements in performance because the reward often encourages more improvement.	_____	_____
4. Behavior modification requires great financial expenditure. It is impossible to demonstrate behavior change in a small, inexpensive program.	_____	_____
5. Operant conditioning does attempt to change behavior of people, but we are constantly, often unconsciously, changing others, especially in organizations. Using operant conditioning can make desired behavior more explicit in organizations and therefore allow workers to know where they stand.	_____	_____
6. Behavior modification differs from other techniques of performance improvement in that it doesn't rely solely on the analysis of the employees' attitudes.	_____	_____
7. Reinforcers are defined as the consequences of behavior that strengthen or weaken behavior when they follow a behavior.	_____	_____
8. Without specific measurements, it is impossible to determine the success or failure of any performance-improvement program.	_____	_____
9. Managers should be aware of the basic principles of behavior modification if they are given authority to present or withdraw reinforcers.	_____	_____
10. Offering positive reinforcers for certain behaviors is a means of encouraging desired behavior.	_____	_____
11. Feedback from an operant perspective is information that quickly and accurately gives an employee a quantitative record of his or her performance.	_____	_____
12. Most managers are very aware of the effects of contingencies of reinforcement and apply them properly.	_____	_____
13. The use of reinforcement systems assumes that some employees may want more from their jobs than intrinsic satisfaction or rewards alone.	_____	_____
14. Both positive and negative reinforcement can strengthen desired work behaviors.	_____	_____
15. Compensation systems can reinforce undesirable as well as desirable employee behavior.	_____	_____
16. The frequency of scheduling reinforcement has little impact on the frequency of desired behavior demonstrated on the job.	_____	_____
17. Training courses are always good solutions to performance problems.	_____	_____
18. Performance deficiencies should be defined in terms of actual behavior observed or not observed, not the behavior the employee *may* demonstrate.	_____	_____

Form 1 (continued)

	TRUE	FALSE
19. If an employee's work output was accomplished correctly yesterday but incorrectly today, it is clear evidence that the employee lacks knowledge of the job and a training program is necessary.	_____	_____
20. Punishment alone will typically increase the occurrence of desired work behavior and decrease the occurrence of undesired behavior.	_____	_____
21. With positive reinforcement, only desired work behavior should be reinforced.	_____	_____
22. Punishment can be efficient in eliminating undesired behavior.	_____	_____
23. Desired behavior tends to remain longer after the use of fixed reinforcement schedules than variable reinforcement schedules.	_____	_____

B. For this set of statements, please indicate those that would be desirable and those that would be undesirable for the effective use of operant-conditioning/positive-reinforcement programs in work organizations. Provide any explanation you feel is required for your responses.

	DESIRABLE	UNDESIRABLE
1. Employees can guage their own progress relative to set, quantifiable standards.	_____	_____
2. The organization makes explicit to the worker the consequences for doing or not doing the job correctly.	_____	_____
3. The organization focuses on the process of how desired results are achieved, or on the behaviors used to attain desired results.	_____	_____
4. The organization does not determine the cost of performance deficiencies in dollar terms.	_____	_____
5. The organization trains supervisors to analyze performance problems and measure their frequency.	_____	_____
6. Supervisors, or a third party, alone make the measurement of a subordinate's behavior.	_____	_____
7. The organization evaluates programs based on change in on-the-job behavior.	_____	_____
8. No feedback is given the employee about performance; or feedback goes only to the manager or supervisor.	_____	_____
9. Measuring effectiveness of training programs to improve performance is based on attitudes of trainees, numbers of people asking to attend future sessions, classes, or pencil-and-paper tests given in the classroom setting.	_____	_____
10. PR programs are undertaken with no beforehand quantitative measurement of performance levels.	_____	_____
11. Feedback is given to people as the work progresses, leading to self-correction.	_____	_____
12. Feedback on performance is very specific, such as, "Here is what you did well in relation to a goal...."	_____	_____
13. Feedback on performance is obtained by the worker long after the work is completed, delayed by days or weeks.	_____	_____
14. Performance goals are not established, or they are not communicated to the workers.	_____	_____
15. Performance feedback is given to the worker, to supervisors, to managers, and to top executives (in some cases).	_____	_____
16. The organization does not estimate the total probable cost of PR solutions or compare this cost with the cost of the performance deficiency, or it works only on relatively small problems.	_____	_____

Name _____ Group Number _____

Date _____ Class Section _____ Hour _____ Score _____

PART B

Form 2 Behavior Modification Case Study I

Read over the following case study carefully.

Analyze changes in the work situation due to the change in reward structure and determine why the changes occurred. After calculating the costs of the changes on Form 3, fill in the blanks in the two columns of figures below.

Situation

A large discount retail chain store was having considerable difficulty with its salaried salespeople. Absenteeism as well as tardiness continued to increase. After using several disciplinary methods that were ineffective, the company decided to try two types of positive reinforcement procedures in an attempt to lower the cost of absenteeism and tardiness. The first program was for employees in the stores in the western region of the organization. All employees who were neither absent nor late for one month received $5.00 worth of coupons which could be used in exchange for merchandise in the store. In the stores in the eastern region, it was decided that all employees who were on time and did not miss a day of work for a month would have their names included in a drawing. Three winners of the drawing were selected at random each month and each received a portable color television (if they were previous winners they could receive merchandise comparable in value, i.e., $400). The results of the program are listed below. After reviewing the results, complete Forms 3 and 4.

	Western Region	Eastern Region
Number of employees	415	382
Total annual absenteeism (percentage of days per year for all employees before the program)	12%	11.5%
Annual paid* absenteeism before the program (as a percentage of total number of days absent)	33.3%	32.6%
Annual absenteeism percentage after program	4.5%	2%
Annual paid* absenteeism after the program (as a percentage of total number of days absent)	77.8%	75%
Annual cost of absenteeism before the program* (see Form 3)	_____	_____
Annual cost of absenteeism after the program* (see Form 3)	_____	_____
Approximate direct costs of the program**	$24,000	$14,400
Net saving from PR programs (absenteeism cost reduction less direct program cost)	_____	_____

* The cost figures make the following assumptions:
1. Employees receive fringe benefits (medical and life insurance, etc.) and taxes are withheld, equaling 30% of total wages, which must typically be paid if absent due to union contractual agreements.
2. Absent employees must be replaced with part-time workers to staff the departments and the checkouts in the discount operation (which already attempts to keep the number of employees to a minimum). The part-time workers can be procured easily and do not receive benefits.
3. The cost figures are exclusive of any drop in sales due to late employees or due to using replacement, as opposed to experienced salespersons.

** Direct costs are approximated as follows:
Western region—$5.00/month times 12 months = $60.00 times approximately 400 workers of the 415 not being absent = $24,000.
Eastern region—$400.00/month times 3 winners each month = $1,200 times 12 months = $14,400.

Name _____ Group Number _____

Date _____ Class Section _____ Hour _____ Score _____

PART B

Form 3 A Cost/Benefit Analysis of Positive Reinforcement Motivation Programs

Instructions: Using the information on Form 2, as well as the hints provided in the first row of this table, complete the table and enter the appropriate figures on Form 2. Then answer the discussion questions which follow.

	Before programs		After programs	
	Western Division	*Eastern Division*	*Western Division*	*Eastern Division*
Annual days of absenteeism	(415 employees × 240 work days/yr. × 12% absenteeism) =	(382 employees × 240 work days/yr. × 11.5% absenteeism) =	(415 × 240 × 4.5%) =	382 × 240 × 2% =
Annual days of paid absenteeism				
Annual days of unpaid absenteeism				
Annual cost of paid absences @ $63/day ($30 = salary, $9 = fringes, $24 = substitute employees)				
Annual cost of unpaid absences @ $33/day ($24 = substitutes' salary, $9 = fringes for regular employees)				
Total annual cost of absenteeism (paid and unpaid)				

DISCUSSION QUESTIONS (to be answered after Form 3 is completed)

1. What type(s) of scheduling is (are) being used for each region?

2. Which schedule is more effective for controlling behavior? Why?

3. What problems, if any, might you anticipate from the implementation of these procedures? What could be done to resolve any problems you anticipate?

4. Why is one region's program more costly than the other's and also has a higher absenteeism rate? Explain this using behavior modification concepts and principles.

Name _____   Group Number _____

Date _____   Class Section _____   Hour _____   Score _____

PART B

Form 4 Behavior Modification Case Study II

The following is a discussion* of one attempt to increase productivity (i.e., make more interesting or to offer more challenge and autonomy; see Exercise 13) in a job for which Job Enrichment was not practical. Read the paragraph below and answer the questions.

    In a recent study involving people who plant trees for a large tree-harvesting organization, bonuses were given to planters for planting bags of seedlings. Most of the planters were older women from southern and rural areas with strong moral and religious backgrounds and norms. The first crew of planters was told that, in addition to their regular base pay, they would receive a $2.00 bonus contingent on planting each entire bag of trees. The second crew was told that they would receive their base pay and a $4.00 bonus contingent on planting each bag of trees and correctly guessing the outcome of a coin toss. The third crew was told they would receive their base pay and an $8.00 bonus contingent on planting each bag of trees and correctly guessing the outcome of two coin tosses. A fourth crew, isolated geographically from the first three, was used as a control group and was paid only hourly base wages.

DISCUSSION QUESTIONS

1. What type of scheduling of reinforcement was used with each of the four crews?

2. Based only on information about behavior modification and the scheduling of reinforcement, what do you predict as the outcome of relative productivity of tree-planting crews?

3. What individual characteristics, problems, or obstacles might influence the outcomes of these crews such that they might not meet the expectations predicted in question 2?

4. Over the long run, would you expect the salaries of the crew members to differ? If so, how?

_____

*Adapted (roughly) from G. A. Yukl and G. P. Latham, "Consequences of Reinforcement Schedules and Incentive Magnitudes for Employee Performance: Problems Encountered in an Industrial Setting," *Journal of Applied Psychology* 60 (1975): 294-298.

PART C

Form 5 Designing a PR Motivation Program

Using the facts given below, design a PR motivation program for the traveling salespersons of Leon and Sons Company. Specify reinforcers, punishment, schedules of reinforcement, performance-reward contingencies, etc., and outline your procedure for implementing the program. That is, list the steps required, in sequence, to actually implement the program. Be sure to state any assumptions you have made about the company, the policies, the workers, etc.

1. The program is to be designed for a group of thirty salespersons who sell housewares to retail outlets. They work for Leon and Sons, a medium-sized midwestern housewares wholesaler. The housewares consist of glassware, kitchen gadgets, home-improvement products, etc. In fact, Leon and Sons sells so many different products, its catalogue must be carried into stores in several sections by its salespeople.

2. Each salesperson has a territory consisting of about 850 square miles, often crossing state lines. The salespersons sell to large retail and discount chain stores, as well as to small independent stores. Stores are located in cities, suburbs of large cities, and small towns.

3. The territories for each salesperson are unequal regarding sales volume, which ranges from $30,000 to $50,000 per month for each. Territories were either originally assigned on the basis of seniority and past performance or were "built up" into high-producing areas by a salesperson's own efforts and growth in the area.

4. There is fairly high turnover among the salespersons of the twelve territories that have been averaging between only $15,000 and $25,000 volume per month. Management feels these twelve territories are currently undersold and that a $25,000 to $30,000 volume per month is possible, adjusting for seasonal sales, current levels of unemployment, etc.

5. Salespersons all receive commissions at the rate of 7% on gross sales, plus a set amount for monthly expenses. Neither commission rate nor allowance for expenses vary for salespersons.

6. No bonuses or other monies are currently available (i.e., overtime, etc.), but a pension fund, life-insurance program, credit union, and health-insurance plan are all offered to salespersons. The pension and life-insurance benefits depend on the size of earnings, however.

7. One week vacation with pay is given after one year of service, two weeks after three years, three weeks after six years, and one additional week after each additional ten years of service. The average length of service for the salespersons in territories with sales volume of $30,000 to $50,000 is 10.8 years and for the remaining salessalespersons is 1.4 years.

8. The newer salespersons have complained that their territories contain few large discount chain stores, which limits their sales volume and causes them to spend much time driving to service the many small stores. They state that they sometimes must drive for four hours to write an order of $500 (a commission of only $35.00), while some territories have central buying offices for a chain of stores. In four to six hours, a salesperson can write an order for $20,000 for these stores (at a commission of $1400).

9. The companies whose lines are carried often offer trips, merchandise, and cash to salespersons who break certain sales quotas set by these manufacturers, but these seem to go only to salespersons in certain territories with the big stores.

10. There is considerable competition in the housewares wholesaling industry in the area, and each retail outlet is often serviced by three or four other housewares wholesalers in addition to Leon and Sons. Further, because many of the products are not necessities, economic slumps and high unemployment in the industrialized midwest affect sales.

11. Leon and Sons has grown considerably in the last decade. It has added nine salespersons to make the current total of thirty. It has added two new warehouses and a computerized inventory-control system, and has been able to keep many prices below those of competitors due to volume buying and the lower warehouse costs stemming from automation. The company office and its warehouses are located outside a small city where land is relatively inexpensive. However, the city is centrally located, so shipping costs to most customers are minimized. Being a family-owned business, Leon and Sons typically maintains a policy of returning profits to the organization for capital improvements. Further, because Mr. Leon, the owner, has developed an excellent reputation for honesty with manufacturers for excellent salesmanship with many customers, he has been able to acquire many of the most popular brands of merchandise for his salespersons to carry. In addition, Leon and Sons' new salespersons are typically trained and introduced to new accounts by Mr. Leon himself, which adds a personal touch many customers, especially the smaller ones, appreciate.

Form 5 (continued)

12.   At present, there is one sales manager, Roger "Smiley" O'Malley. He is a long-time employee of Leon and Sons and was the second salesperson hired many years ago. He has been sales manager for three years and gives considerable latitude to the sales force regarding the number of calls they make, how they spend their time, etc. His primary duties are to hire and fire salespersons, to assign territories, and to settle disputes or complaints arising from salespersons' interaction with clients. He feels that selling is an art: "You either have it or you don't!" he is often heard to say. He does not, therefore, feel training programs or seminars are useful.

Smiley O'Malley has periodic sales meetings to introduce new products and is openly quite friendly at these meetings with a few of the more senior salespersons, whom he also sees socially. In fact, the decision to design a motivation program was made by Mr. Leon in light of the high turnover among younger salespersons. Obviously, neither Smiley O'Malley nor several of the more senior salespersons feel it is necessary.

Name _____   Group Number _____

Date _____ Class Section _____ Hour _____ Score _____

ASSESSMENT OF LEARNING IN PERSONNEL ADMINISTRATION
EXERCISE 15

1. Try to state the purpose of this exercise in one concise sentence.

2. Specifically what did you learn from this exercise (i.e., skills, abilities, and knowledge)?

3. How might your learning influence your role and your duties as a personnel administrator?

4. What potential problems might you expect when attempting to implement a positive reinforcement motivation program in an organization?

5. What has been the nature of the criticism of PR in organizations?

6. How could an organization's motivation programs be evaluated as to their ability to improve performance or productivity?

7. Do organizations actually control workers' behavior? If so, how? Should they?

8. Would intrinsic-rewards motivation programs (e.g., job enrichment) be compatible with those that emphasize extrinsic rewards (e.g., money)? What organizational and job characteristics might determine whether these programs could be implemented simultaneously?

Exercise 16
Job evaluation and wage and salary administration

PREVIEW

This exercise concerns the allocation of financial resources to members or organizations. The purpose is to demonstrate how money can be used effectively to attract, retain, and motivate productive employees and to outline the characteristics of the type of system that would be required to effectively (as well as equitably) administer wages and salaries. For example, in order to make money an effective reinforcer or reward for desired performance, certain determinations must be made. First, desired job behavior must be defined and different methods of allocating financial rewards considered in light of organization and individual objectives. Vital data (e.g., wage and salary surveys and individual performance levels) must be gathered, and important decisions regarding the relative worth of jobs (i.e., a job evaluation) also need to be made before the level of financial rewards can be tied to each job and each organizational member. This exercise builds skill in data gathering and decision-making tasks required for the development of a rational and equitable wage and salary system. A point system of

job evaluation is designed and implemented using data from a municipality. A wage structure for several job classes and individual salary levels are determined in the exercise. A model of the wage and salary determination process is presented in Fig. 1.

OBJECTIVES

1. To build understanding of the role of money as a reward and motivator of job behavior.
2. To build skill in designing job-evaluation systems and in salary-structure determination.
3. To design an equitable merit pay system (and also meet equal pay provisions).
4. To appreciate the various factors influencing implementation of an effective, equitable salary system in an organization.

PREMEETING ASSIGNMENT

Read the entire exercise.

INTRODUCTION*
Considerations in Evaluating Jobs and Attaching Wage or Salary Levels to Them

Many obvious considerations influence an organization's allocation of pay to its members. These include

the importance of pay for the organization (as it may comprise a major proportion of total cash outflow), the organization's pay philosophy (e.g., training and

*Several of the figures in this exercise have been adapted from R. W. Beatty, N. Crandall, R. Mathis, G. T. Milkovich, and M. J. Wallace, Jr., "How to Administer Wage/

Salary Programs and Perform Job Evaluations," © 1979. The case is gratefully acknowledged.

Fig. 1. Model of the wage and salary determination process

Organization and environmental constraints	Organizational techniques	Outcomes
Labor Market Availability Labor Market Prices Legal Requirements (e.g., minimum wage, equal pay, etc.) Ability to Pay Industry Practices Organizational Philosophy (e.g., Train and Develop Skills *vs.* Buy Skills in Labor Market, etc.) Extent of Unionization	Job Analysis Job Evaluation Job Worth/Job Structure Job Grades Wage and Salary Survey	Job Pricing/Wage Structure Internal Equity External Equity Individual Equity

developing versus hiring fully proficient employees), the financial consequences of employee withdrawal (e.g., turnover, absenteeism, and tardiness) due to dissatisfaction with pay, and government regulations regarding pay systems. Another important consideration is the motivational aspect of pay—that is, the use of pay to induce people to perform at certain levels and to retain their commitment to the organization and to desired performance.

Over the last half century the field of management has developed many theories of what makes organizations effective.[1] Most deal with pay administration, but tend to assign pay relatively different degrees of importance and functions. Scientific management, for example, uses pay as the most important reward for employees. More modern management theory, however, sees money as only one of many influences on behavior. The degree to which management regards pay as an important influence on behavior and employee satisfaction often determines, to a great extent, the organization's wage and salary programs.

Compensation Packaging. There are many ways in which employees received compensation. Fig. 2 shows the various ways organizations may compensate their employees to meet employee needs (living wages, loss protection, meeting major expenses and improving their standard of living). Compensation can be very expensive, as shown in Fig. 3. In fact, most estimates

---

[1] See, e.g., H. L. Tosi and S. J. Carroll, *Management: Contingencies, Structure, and Process* (Chicago: St. Clair, 1976), Chap. 2; M. J. Gannon, *Dimensions of Management: An Integrated Perspective* (Boston: Little Brown, 1977), Chap. 2; A. N. Nash and S. J. Carroll, *The Management of Compensation* (Belmont, Cal.: Wadsworth, 1975), Chap. 3.

of the costs of fringe pay to employees average about 35% above employee wages and salaries.

Executive compensation packages have involved granting executives a "piece of the action" with stock options as the most common form of incentive and probably the most cost-effective form of compensation.

The three major types of long-term incentives used today are:

1. Nonqualified stock options permit executives to purchase stock in the future at a fixed price, usually the market price on the date of the grant.

2. Stock appreciation rights, when executives are granted the right to receive cash and/or stock for the value represented by the difference between purchase price and later market price of their stock options.

3. Performance improvement plans when cash and/or stock is awarded to executives in proportion to performance goals.

Employee Decisions Influenced by Pay. As previously noted, organizations should be concerned about the level of pay satisfaction as it can cause applicants to join an organization and employees to stay and perform effectively. On the other hand, pay dissatisfaction can lead to strikes, grievances, absenteeism, turnover, and the ineffective use of human assets. Certainly strikes cost organizations money, but grievances, absenteeism, and turnover are also expensive. Organizations are often not aware of how expensive the costs of various factors are and underestimate their importance. As discussed in Exercise 19, many of these costs are hidden. An example is the cost of having an inexperienced worker doing a job because someone has left the organization. The inexperienced worker's quality

Fig. 2. Methods of compensation for meeting employee needs (Source: R. Farrell, "Compensation & Benefits," *Personnel Journal,* November 1976. Reprinted with permission of *Personnel Journal,* Costa Mesa, CA. Copyright November 1976.)

	Basic living wage	Protect against loss	Meet major expenses	Improve standard of living
Salary	X			
Wages	X			
Commissions	X			
Life Insurance		X	X	
Survivor Benefits		X	X	
Accidental Death		X	X	
Social Security		X	X	
Salary Continuance		X	X	
Sick Pay		X	X	
Long-Term Disability		X	X	
Medical Insurance		X	X	
Workmen's Compensation		X	X	
Unemployment Benefits		X	X	
Severance Pay		X	X	
Pensions, Profit Sharing		X	X	
Credit Union			X	
Tuition Refund Program			X	
Scholarship Program			X	
Low Interest Company Loans			X	
Automobile Lease Plan			X	
Relocation Expense Plan			X	
Equity Advance Plan			X	
Bonuses			X	X
Financial Counseling		X	X	X
Prerequisites		X	X	X
Capital Accrual:				
Stock Options			X	X
Stock Purchase Plans			X	X
Thrift Incentive Plans			X	X
Savings Plans			X	X
Deferred Compensation			X	X

and/or quantity of work is likely to be low. Other costs, such as training, recruitment, and clerical requirements, are not always tied to turnover, absenteeism, tardiness, and grievances, but are often a result of these situations.

The consequences of pay dissatisfaction[2] can be more clearly seen in Fig. 4, which shows that pay dissatisfaction may eventually lead to psychological withdrawal, poor physical and mental health, etc. Certainly dissatisfaction with pay can also lead to desired outcomes, such as improved performance and lower absenteeism to earn more money. The preponderance of research evidence, however, indicates that building pay satisfaction is an effective way of managing organizations.

What then determines pay satisfaction? An experienced researcher in this area, Edward Lawler, pro-

vides several determinants of pay satisfaction in organizations. Many of these reasons for a person's dissatisfaction with pay are obvious, such as lack of skill or ability to land a higher-paying job. However, people are also dissatisfied with their pay if they *perceive* they are being paid too little for their effort or if they perceive that others with similar or lower efforts (or job importance) are receiving more than they are. Thus, much of the feeling of satisfaction or dissatisfaction with pay results from people thinking that the pay system is not equitable. Here, perceptions—how people subjectively judge a situation—are most important.[3]

Based on the above discussion, we would assume that having workers satisfied with pay would be an important organizational goal. How, then, is pay satisfaction to be achieved? This difficult and complex task may involve determining rates of pay according to per-

[2] Much of the work cited here is adapted from E. E. Lawler, III, *Pay and Organizational Effectiveness: A Psychological View* (New York: McGraw-Hill, 1971).

[3] For a fuller discussion of "equity" theory, see Lawler, *Pay and Organizational Effectiveness: A Psychological View.*

Fig. 3. Total compensation of private sector employees (Source: U.S. Department of Labor, U.S. Office of Management and Budget.)

Pay

Pay for time worked	$11,092
Vacation Pay	635
Holiday Pay	405
Other Leave	48

Retirement

Social Security	$708
Pension Plans	759

Unemployment

Unemployment compensation	$193
Severance Pay	16

Miscellaneous

Bonuses not based on output	$50
Discounts	16
Profit Sharing	141
Employee thrift plans	47
Other benefits	503

TOTAL COMPENSATION	$15,769

NOTE: Averages for 1977 for private workers in nonfarm jobs. Pay includes overtime, other premium pay and bonuses based on production. Severance pay in business is estimated.

formance level and having pay perceived as equitable, relative to job accomplishment, other organizational pay levels, and other workers in the same jobs in other organizations within the community. Reducing pay secrecy may also be an important factor helpful in raising pay satisfaction. More openness concerning actual pay rates could prevent erroneous perceptions.

Another idea organizations are using more and more often to improve satisfaction with pay, as well as to give workers more discretion over their work situations, is called a "cafeteria-style"[4] benefit plan. Here, as in a cafeteria, workers can choose among several types of benefits, merit increases, etc. Table 1 is an example of such a set of pay and fringe-benefit alternatives.

Internal Wage Structure and Job Evaluation. An internal wage structure is the determination of the "worth" or "value" of each job relative to other jobs within an organization. There are numerous methods for this determination. The objective is to provide equal pay for jobs of equal worth or importance, and

---

[4] See, e.g., L. M. Baytos, "The Employee Benefit Smorgasbord: Its Potential and Limitations," *Compensation Review* 2 (1970): 16–28.

Table 1. An Example of a "Cafeteria-Style" Benefit System in which Employees Would Be Given a Certain Number of Choices

1. Pension increase of $50.00 *Or* two extra weeks paid vacation.
2. Dental insurance *Or* three percent pay raise.
3. Ten Fridays off per year with pay *Or* four-day weeks with 9.5 hours per day.
4. Two weeks extra paid vacation *Or* dental insurance
5. Five days retirement credit each year *Or* one week extra paid vacation.
6. Merchandise at 20 percent off *Or* two-percent pay raise.
7. Three-percent pay raise *Or* eight Fridays off per year with pay.
8. Five-day week with 7.5 hours per day *Or* pension increase of $100 per year.
9. Two-percent pay raise *Or* one week extra paid vacation.
10. Free lunches in company lunchroom *Or* merchandise at 5 percent off.

an acceptable rational set of differentials between jobs not of equal worth. Thus, the rationale is that jobs are not all equally valuable to an organization and therefore are not compensated the same. For example, some jobs are in high demand and others are in low demand, some have high status and others low, some call for large amounts of responsibility and others little, some are boring and others interesting, some are risky and others safe, some demand a high degree of specialized training or education and others do not.

Labor-market information concerning demand and supply of workers or job openings collected by individual firms is not usually sufficiently detailed to use in deciding a wage structure. Further, the organization's employees may differ in their perceptions of the worth of jobs and in their own preferences as to the kinds of compensation available. Thus, other information is often necessary. This information consists of job and performance evaluations.

Job Evaluation Methods. There are various job evaluation methods in use (Fig. 5). The four methods of job evaluation (development of internal equity) to be discussed here are: the factor-comparison method, the classification method, the ranking method, and the point method.[5] While these four methods are similar in many respects, a few differences are noted below.

Although the *factor-comparison method* is quite complex, it can be a useful system. Essentially, certain "key" jobs are compared to other jobs on the basis of several factors. The key jobs are assumed to have the

---

[5] See A. Nash and S. Carroll, *The Management of Compensation,* for a more detailed discussion of job evaluation methods.

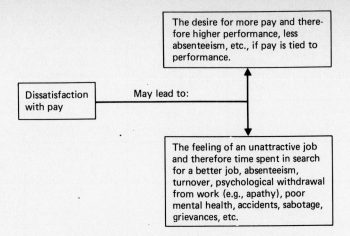

Fig. 4. Some possible consequences of pay dissatisfaction
(Adapted from E. E. Lawler, III, *Pay and Organizational Effectiveness: A Psychological View,* New York, McGraw-Hill, 1971.)

correct salary attached to them and thus represent a standard, provided there is agreement that the salaries for these jobs are correct. Indeed, identifying the key jobs is the first step in the system. The key jobs are usually compared to other jobs on the basis of mental demands, skill, working conditions, responsibility, and physical demands. Jobs are ranked from highest to lowest on these factors by evaluators. Then, the existing salary for each key job is divided up into these factors according to their relative importance in the key

job. That is, the total amount of money offered is divided into that amount offered for factor A, B, etc., based on their importance. The key jobs are placed on a scale indicating the importance of each factor; other jobs may fall above or below the key job on each factor. Then, additional jobs each are placed on the scale at the proper location. After all of the jobs appear on the scale, salaries are determined by looking at the amount of money (or points convertible to money) beside each of the factors for each job (Fig. 6). These amounts are

Fig. 5. The use of job evaluation methods (American Compensation Association Survey, 1976.)

Type of method used	Hourly			Nonexempt salaried			Exempt salaried		
1. Whole Job Methods		27.9%			30.7%			38.5%	
Ranking	21.1%			22.6%			24.1%		
Benchmark Comparison	6.7			5.3			10.1		
Grade Standards	.1			2.8			4.3		
2. Factor Methods		68.2			42.3			35.1	
3. Combinations or type not reported		3.9			27.0			26.4	

Opinion rating of plans	Good	Fair	Poor	Good	Fair	Poor	Good	Fair	Poor
1. Whole Job Methods									
Ranking	60%	39%	1%	66%	33%	1%	73%	25%	2%
Benchmark Comparison	70	30	0	66	33	1	46	54	0
Grade Standards	24	76	0	77	23	0	50	50	0
2. Whole Job Methods (weighted averages)	62	37	1	66	33	1	66	32	2
3. Factor Methods	85	9	6	84	14	2	96	4	0

Coverage: 275 larger U.S. corporations employing nearly 3,000,000 employees in 35 different business fields, including manufacturing, finance, food, insurance, transportation, utilities, and health care.

Fig. 6. Horizontal ranking (Beatty, Crandall, Mathis, Milkovich, Wallace, "How To Administer Wage/Salary Programs and Perform Job Evaluations," 1979.)

	Accountability responsibility Factor A	Physical effort Factor B	Working conditions Factor C	Mental complexity Factor D	Supervision exercised Factor E	Rate
Job A	(5) 2.00	(1) .20	(1) .20	(5) 2.00	(5) 2.00	6.40
Job B	(2) .50	(4) 1.60	(2) .50	(2) .50	(4) 1.60	4.70
Job C	(3) 1.00	(2) .50	(3) 1.00	(3) 1.00	(3) 1.00	4.50
Job D	(1) .20	(3) 1.00	(4) 1.60	(4) 1.60	(2) .50	4.90
Job E	(4) 1.60	(5) 2.00	(5) 2.00	(1) .20	(1) .20	6.00
					Total	26.50

summed to arrive at the salary (or wage) level for each job.

The *classification method* of job evaluation, often used for grading civil service jobs (i.e., GS ratings), begins with a certain number of predetermined job grades. Jobs are categorized according to their characteristics. For example, ten grades may be established, each defined as to certain characteristics the jobs in it would have. Grade three might include those jobs in which people perform tasks without direct supervision; grade one might contain those jobs in which people perform tasks under constant supervision, etc. Evaluators do not define each factor and then compare jobs on a factor-by-factor basis, as in the factor-comparison method, but define whole grades of jobs. The higher the grade, the more education, skill, etc., is required (Fig. 7).

Expert judgment is relied on very heavily here and the chances of bias or inconsistency are reasonably high, but the system is relatively easy to implement.

The *ranking methods* of job evaluation are probably the simplest. Often, job descriptions are ranked from highest to lowest in terms of worth (straight ranking). Entire jobs can be compared or they can be compared on a factor-by-factor basis—the former is usually the case (Fig. 8).

Fig. 7. Classification method (Beatty, Crandall, Mathis, Milkovich, Wallace, "How To Administer Wage/Salary Programs and Perform Job Evaluations," 1979.)

Class	Production	Administration
I Simple, routine work; no exercise of judgment; under supervisor	Laborer I	Clerk I
II Difficult, routine work; no exercise of judgment; under supervisor	Semiskilled Laborer	Secretary I
III Difficult, routine work; exercise of judgment; under supervisor	Parts Handler	Secretary II

Fig. 8. Ranking method (forced ranking) (Beatty, Crandall, Mathis, Milkovich, Wallace, "How to Administer Wage/Salary Programs and Perform Job Evaluations," 1979.)

| | One Individual's Ranking of Jobs: | | | | |
	1st	2nd	3rd	Average	Final
Job A	1	1	2	1.3	1
Job B	3	2	1	2.0	2
Job C	2	3	3	2.7	3
Job D	4	5	5	4.7	5
Job E	5	4	4	4.3	4

| | Ranking Among 3 People in a Committee: | | | |
	#1	#2	#3	Final
Job A	1	2	1	1
Job B	2	1	2	2
Job C	3	3	3	3
Job D	5	4	5	5
Job E	4	5	4	4

Without factor-by-factor ranking, the subjective judgments of evaluators may be problematic and disagreement among them is likely to increase. Although the ranking method is quick and therefore inexpensive, it is quite subjective and easily outmoded by changes in jobs.

By far the most popular method of the four major methods for determining the worth of a job is the *point method*. The point method requires evaluators to rate jobs on a factor-by-factor basis, weighting each factor (e.g., use of machinery, complexity of tasks, education, risk, etc.) in terms of its contribution to overall job worth. A scale is used to determine the extent to which each job possesses each factor. Job descriptions are studied to determine the degree to which the factor is required in performing the job. After a set of degrees on each factor has been defined and allocated a number of points, points are allocated to each job depending on the degree to which factors are required and the weight of the factors. Then, a total point score can be assigned to each job in order to compare their relative worth and eventually assign salary levels to them.

This method probably has the best chance of attaining job-evaluation objectives in most organizations. Jobs can be reliably differentiated, and the system is simple enough to be explained convincingly to employees. Table 2 demonstrates the use of factors, weights, degrees, and points, while Fig. 9 provides an example. This method is explained more fully in the activities that follow this *Introduction*.

Grades or job classes are also used in a job evaluation. Types of jobs that are similar in content, such as clerical or maintenance jobs, are considered to be within one class, or jobs are grouped by equal point ranges (e.g., 50 to 100 points, 100 to 150 points, etc.). There would typically be different grades or levels within each class also (e.g., clerical worker, I, II, III).[6] For further examples of family groupings see Figs. 10 and 11.

---

[6] A more thorough discussion can be found in Nash and Carroll, *The Management of Compensation*.

Fig. 9. An example of the point method of job evaluation

| | Job evaluation rank | | Points | | Total points | Competitive position value (benchmark) |
	Skill	Effort	Skill	Effort		
Typist	A	1	40	40	80	$13,500
Administrative	D	1	55	40	95	16,500
Salesperson	C	5	50	80	130	21,400
Controller	G	4	70	70	140	28,900
Vice-president, Personnel	H	6	75	90	165	36,000

Fig. 10. Criteria for determining jobs and job families (Beatty, Crandall, Mathis, Milkovich, Wallace, "How to Administer Wage/Salary Programs and Perform Job Evaluations," 1979.)

1. Common Skills
2. Common Occupational Qualifications
3. Common Licensing
4. Common Union Jurisdictional Demands
5. Common Career Paths
6. Common Function
7. Common Work Place or Unit
8. Common Technology
9. Tradition

Table 2. An example of the meaning of factors, weights, degrees, and points used in the point method of job evaluation. The points alloted to each factor are summed to arrive at one point total for each job.

FACTOR: A broad category of job content, qualifications, etc., which can be used to group jobs (e.g., education, training, physical demands). Each broad factor may have several subfactors.

WEIGHT: The relative worth of factors to each other, usually on a scale of 1 to 100 (e.g., education—weight 35; physical demand—weight 55, etc.). The weights do not always sum to 100.

DEGREE: The relative amount of each factor a job possesses. For example, there may be four "degrees" of the factor, education. Degree 4 could be possession of a doctoral degree; degree 3, possession of a master's degree, and so on.

POINTS: The relative worth of each degree is designated in points, with the highest number of points given to the highest degree. For example, degree 4 of education may be worth 40 points, while degree 3 is only worth 20 points, as a doctoral degree is significantly more difficult to attain than a master's degree.

Federal Legislation Concerning Wage and Salary Administration. Wages and salaries are governed quite closely by numerous federal, state, and municipal laws and regulations. As with many of the federal laws affecting organizations, the laws regulating wage and salary administration reflect the mood or climate of the nation at the time of their passage. Such factors as war, depression, and minority-group relations could have a substantial effect on the passage of certain laws. The more important of these federal laws are noted below,[7] along with a few of their key provisions.

1. *Davis-Bacon Act of 1931.* Covers federal construction and repair work for contracts in excess of $2,000. Holders of such contracts must pay laborers the prevailing wages of the applicable locality.

2. *Walsh-Healey Public Contracts Act of 1936.* Extends provisions of Davis-Bacon Act beyond federal construction contracts to nonconstruction work exceeding $10,000. Prescribed wages are industry minimums, rather than prevailing wages in localities. Overtime must be paid at one-and-one-half regular rate, with exceptions. Employers must publicly display minimum wages. Violators are often prohibited from federal contracts for three years.

3. *Fair Labor Standards Act of 1930.* Sets minimum wages, maximum hours, overtime rates, and child-labor standards. Has been updated through several amendments. (The 1980 minimum wage for covered workers was $3.25 per hour.) Farm

---

[7] This and all other laws have several additional provisions, exceptions, etc.; see, e.g., Nash and Carroll, *The Management of Compensation.*

Fig. 11. Typical composition of job families (Beatty, Crandall, Mathis, Milkovich, Wallace, "How to Administer Wage/Salary Programs and Perform Job Evaluations," 1979.)

Clerical	Production	Supervisory	Technical	Managerial
Administrative Assistant	Maintenance Technician	Plant	Project	Vice-President
Executive Secretary	Quality Controller	Superintendent	Leader	Manager
Secretary	Senior Production Worker	Shift Supervisor	Senior Engineer	Director
General Clerk	Production Worker	Group Supervisor	Engineer	Analyst
Mail Clerk	Labor Pool	1st-Level Supervisor	Engineer Trainee	Staff Assistant

workers are presently excluded, as are retail establishments with less than $250,000 in annual sales.

4. *Discrimination laws of the 1960s.* The Equal Pay Act of 1963 (amending the Fair Labor Standards Act) prohibits employers from discriminating in pay rates on the basis of sex. The Age Discrimina-

tion in Employment Act of 1967 prohibits discrimination in pay rates on the basis of age (for workers between 40 and 65 in certain types and sizes of organizations). (See also Exercise 18.) A summary of these pieces of legislation is provided below:

Federal Acts, Executive Orders, Rules and Regulations, Guidelines Pertaining to Compensation Discrimination Equal Pay Act of 1963

Section 3:   No discrimination between sexes or races by paying different wages for equal work requiring equal skill, and so on, except for seniority, merit, or quality/quantity systems or differential based on factor other than sex or race.

Civil Rights Act of 1964, Title VII, as amended by the Equal Employment Opportunity Act of 1972

Section 703(a)(1):   Unlawful to discriminate with respect to compensation because of race, color, religion, sex, or national origin.

Section 703(h):   Not unlawful to apply standards of compensation pursuant to bona fide seniority, merit, or quality/quantity systems or to employees in different work locations or to differentiate between sexes on wages if differential authorized by Fair Labor Standards Act.

Executive Order 11246, Public Policy Against Discrimination on Basis of Race, Creed, Color, or National Origin, Title 3 CFR 339, Part II

Section 202.1(1):   Unlawful for government contractor to discriminate in compensation because of race, creed, color, or national origin.

Executive Order 11375 (Amending Executive Order 11246 Relating to Equal Employment Opportunity)

Section 202.(1):   Amended to read . . . "race, color, religion, sex, or national origin."

OFCC, Sex Discrimination Guidelines, Title 41, CFR, Chapter 60, Part 60-20

Section 60-20.3(a):   Written personnel policies must expressly indicate no discrimination on account of sex.

Section 60-20.3(c):   Unlawful to discriminate on basis of sex in terms of wages.

Section 60-20.5(a):   Wage schedules must not be related to or based on sex.

OFCC, Religious and National Origin Discrimination, Title 41, CFR, Chapter 60, Part 60-50

Section 60-50.1:   Purpose and scope—including definition of religious and ethnic groups.

Section 60-50.2(a):   AA required to ensure employees treated in terms of compensation without regard to religion or national origin.

Section 60-50.5:   Provisions not intended to discriminate against employee because of race, color, religion, sex, or national origin.

EEOC Sex Discrimination Guidelines, Title 29, CFR, Chapter XIV, Part 1604

Section 1604.2(b)(3)(i)(ii):   Unlawful to adversely affect opportunities for female employees with respect to minimum wages/overtime or not to provide same benefits for male employees.

Secretary of Labor, Apprenticeship and Training Equal Opportunity, Title 29, CFR, Part 30

Section 30.3(a)(2):   Obligation to uniformly apply rules pertaining to wages.

EEOC Records and Reports, Title 29, CFR, Part 1602

Section 1602.12:   No requirement established for specific or particular order of records.

Section 1602.14(a):   Retention schedule of records related to compensation—6 months.

Secretary of Labor, Apprenticeship and Training Equal Opportunity, Title 29, CFR, Part 30

Section 30.8:   Requirement to compile and maintain adequate records related to apprenticeship rates.

ERDA Appendix 0230, Annex C-1, Cost Type Contractor Records and Retention Schedule 1

Item 26c: Retention schedule, records involving dispute on any matter of compensation alleging discrimination—3 years after settlement.

Pricing Jobs. Once jobs are put into some structure of job worth, they must be priced. The pricing of jobs (development of external equity) depends upon how an organization perceives itself in the labor market (its pay philosophy), the job groupings and key jobs it selects, and the rate ranges for each job group. Each of these factors is considered when an organization tabs its job structure to a labor market survey for pricing its jobs.

Most employers find survey data useful in several ways, for determining comparability of job rates, developing or modifying guidelines for the wage/salary structure, comparing starting salaries, developing wage/salary increase guidelines, setting policy objectives, eliminating internal pay inequities, obtaining information for equal employment opportunity and affirmative action programs, and preparing for union negotiations and labor arbitration.

Merit Pay. The final use of pay is for individual equity purposes, or merit pay determination, usually defined as "above average" performance. Thus despite the building of wage and salary structures, there must be some room for rewarding individual performance in each job class. The total pay determination can be viewed in Fig. 12, where the proportions of pay accounted for by various compensation variables are shown. Notice that individual equity (merit) is usually a small portion of total pay; however, it is a very important part of the motivation of a person within an organization. Persons are usually motivated to join organizations, attend, and perform. Performance obviously is very important, and organizations who wish to optimize individual performance must not lose sight of it. Merit is often referred to as individual equity because of the following model:

$$\frac{\text{Rewards A}}{\text{Performance A}} = \frac{\text{Rewards B}}{\text{Performance B}}$$

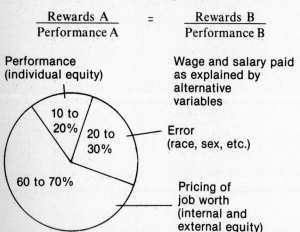

Fig. 12. Hypothetical example of the explanation of pay determination

This formula indicates that there should be a proportionate relationship between the rewards for the investments (performance) of person A compared to the rewards to the investments of person B. When there is a proportionate relationship performance equity exists. Many organizations today are attempting to develop merit programs to both encourage increased productivity and reward that productivity equitably.

Pay Discrimination. The Equal Employment Opportunity Commission (EEOC) has contracted with the National Academy of Sciences to investigate sex (pay) discrimination and perhaps to design a "universal" system of job evaluation for assessing inherent equity across diverse job groupings. The results of this study are anxiously awaited. Further, EEOC has stated that one of the major aspects is affected class analysis with focus on pay and pay progression. Methods of viewing pay discrimination are shown in Figs. 13 and 14.

PROCEDURE

Overview. A brief case study is presented in which you are able to identify various wage and salary problems occurring in an organizational setting and suggest solutions. Then an activity is included to familiarize you with the terms and essentials of the point method of job evaluation. A job evaluation is conducted for six sample jobs in an organization; salary levels and a salary structure are developed, and individual salary levels are determined based on performance data.

PART A

STEP 1: Read the case in Form 1 and then form into small groups. In your groups, you are to discuss the case and responses to the questions below.
  a) What would you recommend to Mr. Buster in this situation?
  b) How would you go about implementing your recommendations? Be specific in outlining your recommendations and/or action steps. Specifically, you should give attention to (a) the current problems concerning pay for the company, (b) solutions to the problems, and (c) the criteria that might be used to aid the organization in designing a compensation plan.

TIME: About 30 minutes.

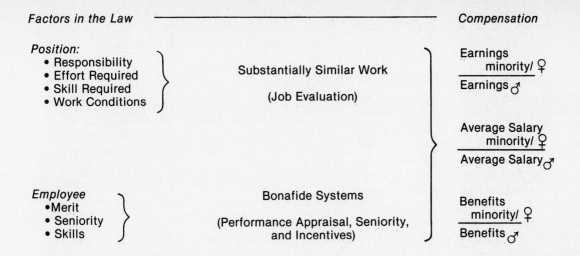

Fig. 13. A model for diagnosing equal pay discrimination

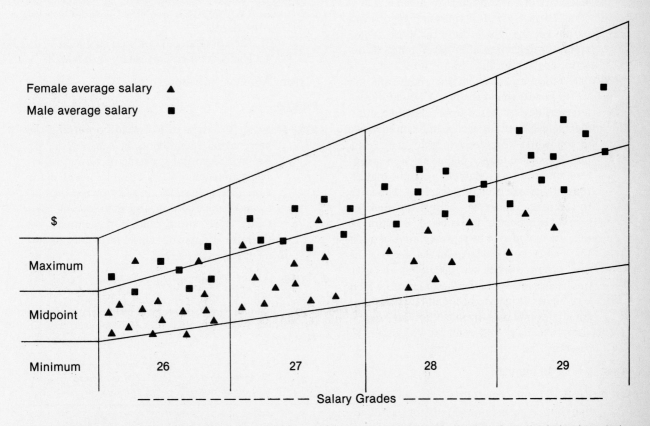

Fig. 14. Sample pay patterns within salary ranges which may be used as a preliminary indication of sex discrimination relative to pay

PART B

STEP 2: In Part B, you are to use Form 2 to determine the relative importance of each subfactor for successful performance in the three job types listed. Place a 1, 2, or 3 in each job-type column for each subfactor on the left in the form, that is, rank each subfactor separately. If you are in a small group, discuss any disagreements with other group members.

TIME: About 20 minutes.

PART C

STEP 3: Form into groups and assume you are the compensation committee of the City of Eastern Shore chosen to represent *all* employees in terms of job level and department function. One of you is from the custodial service, another is a librarian, and another is the assistant city manager. Others represent public works (streets and sanitation), city planning, personnel, and the Parks and Recreation Department. You are to assign these roles to members of your group.

Read the information provided about the small city of Eastern Shore in Form 3. Then, using Form 4, use the point system of job evaluation for the jobs in Eastern Shore. These factors were chosen after developing job descriptions for Eastern Shore jobs and were determined to represent the significant job worth factors found therein. A weighting system was devised based upon narrative statements developed for each significant increase in job worth (degree) for each factor. The points assigned to each degree are seen as representing the best judgment as to the magnitude of increase from one degree of job worth to the next. Whenever possible for each degree a "benchmark" job is listed. Benchmark jobs are intended to be representative of a job that possesses that degree on that factor. The total system is based on 1000 points and uses traditional job evaluation assumptions which give higher weights to accountability/responsibility, complexity/problem solving, supervision exercised, and contacts with others to ascertain the worth of the job.

TIME: About 20 minutes.

STEP 4: Read and study carefully the six job descriptions appearing in Forms 5 to 10 for six municipal jobs of Eastern Shore. Then, using Form 11, rate each of the six jobs with the point system in Form 4. Indicate the relative ranking of the six jobs based on their total points. Does your ranking seem logical? If not, you may want to reanalyze the jobs or change the point system. After completion of Form 11, you

should have a total number of points allocated for each of the six jobs and can simply order them relative to "worth" from lowest to highest number of points.

TIME: About 40 minutes.

STEP 5: Read and study carefully the Salary Survey (Form 12) for six municipalities in the Northeast United States. Based on this survey, your point-system evaluation and any other information in the case (Form 3), attach a yearly salary range to each of the six jobs (see Form 13). Plot the yearly salary rates against the point ranges to obtain a salary rate curve and answer the questions in Part II of Form 13.

In pricing the jobs you are to consider:
1. Your pay philosophy (e.g., make vs. buy employees, merit vs. Cost of Living Allowance, etc.)
2. Your pay ranges above the minimum for each job.*
3. The effective date of your pay plan.
4. The current rate of salary inflation.

TIME: About 35 minutes.

PART D

STEP 6: Using the data in Form 14 concerning the present job incumbents in each of the six Eastern Shore jobs, decide on an individual salary for each of the six people. Use all of the data generated so far, in addition to Form 14, to make the decision. Put the recommended salary levels, in an exact dollar amount, on Form 15, along with a brief rationale or comment for each level.

TIME: About 30 minutes.

---

* Pay minimums can be determined by applying a conversion formula to the midpoint (if it is the statistic chosen). That is,

Range minimum to maximum	Plus or minus midpoint
10%	4.8%
15	6.9
20	9.1
25	11.1
30	13.0
35	14.9
40	16.7
45	18.4
50	20.0

Formula

$$\frac{(1 + X) - (1 - X)}{1 - X} = 10\% \text{ (range minimum to maximum)}$$

$$2.10X = .10$$

$$X = \pm 4.8\% \text{ (range around midpoint)}$$

Using Midpoint Statistics

An example:

Assume the following professional job has a 35% range above minimum, with a midpoint of \$300/week; the 35% range above midpoint can be calculated by finding the range around the midpoint as calculated by:

(1) $\dfrac{\text{range}}{\text{minimum}} = 35\%$

(2) $\dfrac{(300 + 300X) - (300 - 300X)}{300 - 300X} = .35$

(3) $600X = 105 + 105X$

(4) $705X = 105$

(5) $X = 14.89\%$ (i.e. the range around the midpoint is 14.89%, where there is a 35% range above minimum)

or by:

(1) $\dfrac{\text{midpoint}}{1 + 1/2 \times \text{range}} = \text{minimum}$

(2) $\dfrac{300}{1 + .5(.35)} = 255$ (the minimum)

(3) $1.35 \times 255 = \text{maximum}$

(4) $344 = \text{maximum}$

(5) $\dfrac{344 - 255}{255} = 35\%$

FOR FURTHER READING

Adams, J. S. "Toward an Understanding of Inequity." *Journal of Abnormal and Social Psychology* 56 (1972): 75–94. (II–R)

Adams, J. S. "Inequity in Social Exchange." In L. Berkowitz, ed., *Advances in Experimental Social Psychology,* Vol. 2. New York: Academic Press, 1965, pp. 267–299. (II)

Andrews, I. R., and M. M. Henry. "Management Attitudes Toward Pay." *Industrial Relations* 3 (1963): 29–39. (I–R)

Ash, P. "The Reliability of Job Evaluation Rankings." *Journal of Applied Psychology* 32 (1948): 313–20. (II)

Baytos, L. M. "The Employee Benefit Smorgasbord: Its Potential and Limitations." *Compensation Review* 2 (1970): 16–28. (I)

Belcher, D. W. *Wage and Salary Administration.* Englewood Cliffs, N. J.: Prentice-Hall, 1962. (I)

Belcher, D. W. "Wage and Salary Administration," in D. Yoder and H. G. Heneman, Jr., *ASPA Handbook of Personnel and Industrial Relations.* Washington, D.C.: The Bureau of National Affairs, Inc., 1977. (I)

Bergmann, B. R. "Occupational Segregation, Wages, and Profits When Employers Discriminate by Race or Sex." *Eastern Economic Journal* (1974): 103–10. (II)

Bittner, R. H., and E. Rundquist. "The Rank Comparison Rating Method." *Journal of Applied Psycology* 34 (1950): 171–77. (II–R)

Blinder, A. S. "Wage Discrimination: Reduced Form and Structural Estimates." *Journal of Human Resources* 8, no. 4 (1973): 436–55. (II)

Brennan, C. W. *Wage Administration.* Homewood, Ill.: Irwin, 1963. (I)

Brown, H. P. *The Inequality of Pay.* Berkeley: University of California Press, 1972. (II)

Charles, A. W. "Installing Single-Factor Job Evaluation." *The Compensation Review* 3 (1971): 9–21. (I)

Chazen, C. "Compensation Plans: Bottom Line Results." *Management Review* 64 (November 1975): 19–25. (I)

Chesler, D. J. "Reliability and Comparability of Different Job Evaluation Systems." *Journal of Applied Psychology* 32 (1948): 465–75. (II)

Cook, A. H. "Equal Pay: Where Is It?" *Industrial Relations* 14 (1975): 158–177. (I)

Crandell, N. F. "Wage and Salary Administrative Practices and Decision Processes." *Journal of Management* (Spring 1979): 71–90. (I)

Doeringer, P., and M. Piore. *Internal Labor Markets and Manpower Analysis.* Lexington, Mass.: Heath, 1975. (II)

Dunn, J. D., and F. M. Rachel. *Wage and Salary Administration: Total Compensation Systems.* New York: McGraw-Hill, 1971. (II)

Eckstein, O., and T. W. Wilson. "The Determination of Money Wages in American Industry." *Quarterly Journal of Economics* 26 (1962): 379–414. (II–R)

Epperson, L. L. "The Dynamics of Factor Comparison/Point Evaluation." *Public Personnel Management* 4, no. 1 (1975): 38–48. (I)

Farrell, R. "Compensation and Benefits." *Personnel Journal* 55, no. 11 (November 1976): 557–563, 567. (II)

Feldstein, M. S. "Unemployment Insurance: Time for Reform." *Harvard Business Review* 53 (March–April 1975): 51–61. (I)

Foegen, J. H. "Is It Time to Clip the Fringes?" *Personnel* 49 (1972): 36–42. (I)

Foegen, J. H. "Far Out Fringe Benefits." *Personnel* 44 (1967): 65–71. (I)

Fox, W. M. "Purpose and Validity in Job Evaluation." *Personnel Journal* 41 (1962): 432–37. (I)

Giles, B. A., and G. V. Barrett. "The Utility of Merit Increases." *Journal of Applied Psychology* 55 (1971): 103–109. (II–R)

Goodman, P. J. "The Effect of Perceived Inequity on Salary Allocation Decisions." *Journal of Applied Psychology* 60 (1975): 372–375. (II–R)

Gordon, T. J., and R. E. LeBlew. "Employee Benefits, 1970–1985." *Harvard Business Review* 48 (1970): 94. (I)

Henderson, R. I. *Compensation Management.* Reston, Va.: Reston, 1979. (I)

Heneman, H. G., III. "Impact of Performance on Managerial Pay Levels and Pay Changes." *Journal of Applied Psychology* 58 (1973): 128–130. (II–R)

Henrichs, J. R. "Correlates of Employee Evaluations of Pay Increases." *Journal of Applied Psychology* 53 (1969): 481–489. (II–R)

Hulme, R. D., and R. J. Bevan. "The Blue Collar Worker Goes on Salary." *Harvard Business Review* 53 (March–April 1975): 104–112. (I)

Jacques, E. *Equitable Payment.* New York: Wiley, 1961. (I)

Jones, H. D. "Union Views on Job Evaluation: 1971 vs. 1978." *Personnel Journal* 58 (1974): 80–89. (I)

Kahne and Kohen. "Economic Perspective on the Role of Women in the American Economy." *Journal of Economic Literature* 13 (1975): 1249–74. (II)

Kline, S. M., and J. R. Maher. "Education Level and Satisfaction with Pay." *Personnel Psychology* 19 (1966): 195–208. (II–R)

Krefting, L. A., and T. A. Mahoney. "Determining the Size of a Meaningful Pay Increase." *Industrial Relations* (1977): 83–93. (II)

Lanham, E. *Administration of Wages.* New York: Harper & Row, 1963. (I)

Lanham, E. *Job Evaluation.* New York: McGraw-Hill, 1955. (I)

Lawler, E. E., III. "Compensating the New-Life-Style Worker." *Personnel* 48 (1971): 19–25. (I)

Lawler, E. E. III, and J. R. Hackman. "Corporate Profits and Employee Satisfaction: Must They be in Conflict?" *California Management Review* 14 (1971): 46–55. (I)

Lawler, E. E. III. *Pay and Organizational Effectiveness.* New York: McGraw-Hill, 1971. (II)

Lawler, E. E., III, and E. Levin. "Union Officers' Perceptions of Members' Pay Preferences." *Industrial and Labor Relations Review* 21 (1968): 509–517. (II–R)

Lawler, E. E., III. "How Much Money Do Executives Want?" *Transaction* 4 (1967): 23–29. (I)

Lawler, E. E., III. "Secrecy about Management Compensation: Are There Hidden Costs?" *Organizational Behavior and Human Performance* 2 (1967): 182–189. (II–R)

Lawler, E. E., III. "The Mythology of Management Compensation." *California Management Review* 9 (1966): 11–22. (I)

Lesieur, F. G., ed. *The Scanlon Plan: A Frontier in Labor Management Cooperation.* New York: Wiley, 1958. (I)

Lester, R. A. "Pay Differentials by Size of Establishment." *Industrial Relations* 7 (1967): 57–67. (I)

Livernash, E. R. *Wages and Benefits. A Review of Industrial Relations Research* 1 (1970): 79–144. (I)

Livernash, E. R. "The Internal Labor Market," in G. W. Taylor and F. C. Pierson (eds.) *New Concepts in Wage Determination.* New York: McGraw-Hill. 1957. Pp. 141–172. (II)

Livernash, E. R. "The Internal Wage Structure." in G. W. Taylor and F. C. Pierson (eds.) *New Concepts in Wage Determination.* New York: McGraw-Hill, 1957. pp. 141–172. (II)

Livernash, E. R. *Concepts in Wage Determination.* New York: McGraw Hill, 1957. (I)

Livis, B. *Job Evaluation: A Critical Review.* New York: Wiley, 1975. (I)

Locke, E. A. "What Is Job Satisfaction?" *Organizational Behavior and Human Performance* 4 (1969): 309–336. (II)

Louden, J. K., and J. W. Deegan. *Wage Incentives.* New York: Wiley, 1959. (I)

Lytle, C. W. *Job Evaluation Methods.* New York: Ronald Press, 1954. (I)

Madden, J. M. "The Effect of Varying the Degree of Rater Familiarity in Job Evaluation." *Personnel Administrator* 25 (1962): 42–45. (I)

Mahoney, T. A., and G. T. Milkovich. "The Internal Labor Market as a Stochastic Process," in D. Bartholomew and A. Smith, *Manpower and Management Sciences.* Lexington, Mass.: Heath, 1971. (II)

Marriott, R. *Incentive Wage Systems.* London: Staples Press, 1968. (I)

Milkovich, G. T. *Wage Differentials and Comparable Worth: The Emerging Debate.* School of Management, State University of New York, Buffalo, December, 1979. (II)

Miller, L. K., and R. L. Hamblin. "Interdependence, Differential Rewarding, and Productivity."

American Sociological Review 28 (1963): 768–777. (II–R)

Miner, M. G. "Pay Policies: Secret or Open? And Why?" *Personnel Journal* 54 (1974): 110–115. (I)

Munson, F. "Four Fallacies for Wage and Salary Administration." *Personnel* 40 (1963): 57–64. (I)

Nash, A. N., and S. J. Carroll. *The Management of Compensation.* Belmont, Calif.: Wadsworth, 1975. (II)

Nealey, S. M., and J. G. Goodale. "Worker Preferences among Time-Off Benefits and Pay." *Journal of Applied Psychology* 51 (1967): 357–361. (II–R)

Norrgard, D. L. "The Public Pay Plan: Some New Approaches." *Public Personnel Review* 32 (1971): 91–95. (II–R)

Oaxaca, R. L., "Sex Discrimination in Wages," in A. Ashenfelter and A. Rees (eds.) *Discrimination in Labor Markets.* Princeton, N. J.: Princeton University Press, 1973. (II)

Otis, J. L., and R. H. Leukart, *Job Evaluation.* 2d ed. Englewood Cliffs, N.J.: Prentice-Hall, 1954. (I)

Ozame, R. *Wages in Practice and Theory.* Madison, Wisc.: The University of Wisconsin Press, 1968. (II)

Patchen, M. *The Choice of Wage Comparisons.* Englewood Cliffs, N. J.: Prentice-Hall, 1969. (I)

Penzer, W. M. "Educational Level and Satisfaction with Pay: An Attempted Replication." *Personnel Psychology* 22 (1969): 185–199. (II–R)

Pritchard, R. D., M. D. Dunnette, and D. O. Jorgenson. "Effects of Perceptions of Equity and Inequity on Worker Performance and Satisfaction." *Journal of Applied Psychology* 56 (1972): 75–94. (II–R)

Remick, H. "Strategies for Creating Sound, Bias Free Job Evaluation Plans." *Job Evaluation and EEO: The Emerging Issues.* New York: Industrial Relations Counselors, Inc., 1978, p. 91. (II)

Robinson, D. D., and O. W. Wahlstrom. "Comparison of Job Evaluation Methods: A 'Policy-Capturing' Approach Using the Position Analysis Questionnaire." *Journal of Applied Psychology* 59, no. 5 (October 1974): 633–637. (II)

Sawhill, I. V., "The Economics of Discrimination Against Women: Some New Findings." *Journal of Human Resources* 8 (1973): 383–395. (II)

Schuster, J. R. "Executive Compensation—in the Eyes of the Beholder." *Business Horizons* 17 (1974): 79–86. (I)

Schuster, J. R., and J. A. Colletti. "Pay Secrecy: Who Is For and Against It?" *Academy of Management Journal* 16 (1973): 35–40. (I–R)

Schuster, J. R. "Another Look at Compensation Preferences." *Industrial Management Review* 10 (1969): 1–18. (I)

Schwab, D. P. *Intra-Organizational Pay Setting and Comparable Worth.* Wisconsin Working Paper No. 12–79–26, Graduate School of Business, University of Wisconsin-Madison, December, 1979. (II)

Schwab, D. P. "Conflicting Impacts of Pay on Employee Motivation and Satisfaction." *Personnel Journal* 53 (1974): 196–200. (I)

Sheifer, V. J. "Cost-of-Living Adjustment: Keeping Up with Inflation." *Monthly Labor Review* 102, no. 6 (1979): 14–17. (I)

Sibson, R. E. *Wages and Salaries—A Handbook for Line Managers.* New York: American Management Association, Inc. 1967. (I)

Smith, L. "The EEOC's Bold Foray into Job Evaluation." *Fortune* 78, no. 5 (1978): 58–60+. (I)

Thomsen, D. J. "Eliminating Pay Discrimination Caused by Job Evaluation." *Personnel* 55, no. 5 (1978): 11–22. (I)

Treiman, D. J. "Job Evaluation: An Analytical Review" Interim Report to the Equal Employment Opportunity Commission, Washington, D.C.: National Academy of Sciences, 1979. (II)

Wallace, M. J., Jr. and R. E. Steuer. "Multiple Objective Linear Programming in the Design of Internal Wage Structures." Proceedings of the 39th Annual Meeting of the Academy of Management, Atlanta, August, 1979. (II)

Wernimont, P. F., and S. Fitzpatrick. "The Meaning of Money." *Journal of Applied Psychology* 56 (1972): 218–226. (I)

Whyte, W. F. et al. *Money and Motivation.* New York: Harper, 1955. (I)

Winton, D. C., and C. R. Sutherland. "A Performance-Based Approach to Determining Executive Incentive Bonus Awards." *Compensation Review* 18 (1976): 14–26. (I)

Women's Bureau, Employment Standards Administration. "The Earnings Gap Between Women and Men." Washington, D.C.: U.S. Department of Labor, 1975. (II)

Yukl, G., K. N. Wexley, and J. D. Seymore. "Effectiveness of Pay Incentives under Variable Ratio and Continuous Reinforcement Schedules." *Journal of Applied Psychology* 56 (1972): 19–23. (II–R)

Zedek, S., and P. C. Smith. "A Psycho-Physical Determination of Equitable Payment: A Methodological Study." *Journal of Applied Psychology* 52 (1968): 343–347. (II–R)

Zollitsch, H. G., and A. Langsner. *Wage and Salary Administration.* 2d ed. Cincinnati: South-Western, 1970. (I)

PART A

Form 1 Farmhelper Manufacturing Corporation

In 1948, Steven Buster began manufacturing farm equipment. During the following years his business prospered and he added additional products and employees to the business. In the early sixties, the business moved out of the family farm and into a small factory. As the business continued to grow, it was incorporated as the Farmhelper Corporation with Steven Buster as its president. By 1980 the firm had grown to include more than 110 employees located in five modern buildings in the East Arapahoe Industrial Park, located on the edge of a major midwestern city of over one million people. As Mr. Buster saw his firm continue to grow, he began to give some thought to the employees within his organization and their current pay rates. He felt it might be time for a change.

The Organization

Farmhelper is a privately owned corporation with Mr. Buster holding most of the outstanding stock. Of the 110 employees, 60 are blue-collar workers who do piecework; the remaining are supervisors, salesmen, or others in staff roles (e.g., clerks, clerical workers, etc.). Farmhelper is unionized. Most of the blue-collar workers are skilled machinists. A variety of machinery is used in the many processes involved in producing the products (e.g., stamping, drilling, etc.). Most workers are capable of running all of the machines. The average age of the work force is thirty-three. Physical working conditions are excellent, and care is taken to maintain a safe, pleasant working environment. The organization is also very concerned with the employees' safety, Occupational Safety and Health Administration (OSHA) standards are rigidly followed.

Pay System

The pay scale throughout the organization is generally on the low side of industry averages. Most of the blue-collar workers earn between $4.80 and $7.79 an hour. The rates of the managerial workers average 9 percent below the average pay rates for similar jobs in the greater metropolitan area, and those of the unionized workers are average. There also appear to be inequities in pay rates both within and between the organization's six different departments. No formal performance-evaluation system exists, and apparently no direct relationship between performance and compensation can be argued in many cases. (The union has seniority provisions in the current contract.) Fringe benefits are few and salary levels are secret. Individuals do not seem to talk about pay or tell each other what they make. This is particularly true of the workers not covered by the union, which has recently been hit by antidiscrimination suits and publicity concerning internal mismanagement and corruption regarding its pension fund. The union is therefore seen by Farmhelper as docile at this time.

Employees appear to have mixed feelings about working at Farmhelper. Mr. Buster is very well liked and some workers seem to have a friendly and informal relationship with him. Many people seem to be highly involved in their jobs and also concerned about the success of the company, but mostly at higher levels in the organization. Satisfaction with pay, however, is generally low, and employees are extremely dissatisfied with the way pay is administered in the company. Young workers complain that they earn too much less than older workers with less-important jobs. While workers seem to trust each other and cooperate with each other in the course of their work, trust of the company seems to be low. Turnover is extremely high, about 23 percent a year. Absenteeism is also high, although the situation is not as bad as turnover. This puzzles Mr. Buster because of the relatively high unemployment rate in the city.

Summary

The organization appears to be doing well; growth in sales has continued, and financial performance has been excellent during the past few years. In the most recent fiscal year, return on investment before taxes increased 7 percent over last year and was highest in Farmhelper's history. Steven Buster is concerned about the future and has become interested in "human relations" in his organization. He has asked you to come in and work with him regarding wage and salary administration, job evaluation, and motivation of workers using pay schemes. He is concerned with both the workers covered by the union contract and those who are not. The union contract expires in four months.

Name _____ Group Number _____

Date _____ Class Section _____ Hour _____ Score _____

PART B

Form 2 The Relative Importance of Common Job Factors to Different Types of Jobs

Rank the importance for job success of each subfactor for each of the three job types. For example, if mental effort is most important for clerical jobs, you would put a 1 in the clerical column, if it is second most important for administrative/professional jobs, you put a 2 in that column, and so on. Rank all three types of jobs separately for each subfactor.

Job Factors	Job Types		
	Trades and Crafts	Administrative/Professional	Clerical
1. Job skills			
a) Knowledge			
b) Experience			
c) Special training			
2. Effort			
a) Physical			
b) Mental			
3. Responsibility			
a) Latitude/scope			
b) For product output			
c) Control exercised over others			
d) For safety of others			
4. Relationships			
a) With peers			
b) With superiors and subordinates			
5. Other Factors			
a) Working conditions			
b) Hazards and risks			
c) Complexity of work			
d) Security requirements			

PART C

Form 3 The City of Eastern Shore

Eastern Shore is a small (population 60,000) city in the central Atlantic Coast region. It is located about 75 miles from a major metropolitan area of several million people and 20 miles from a city of 125,000. Eastern Shore is basically an industrial city containing several metalworking and precision-equipment manufacturers, only one of which is a large national corporation. There are also several small foundries, a few shoe factories, and a few small electronics companies. Despite its name, Eastern Shore is about 100 miles from the ocean and is not a tourist attraction; however, it is a county seat and the center of a vegetable farming area. There is one small private liberal arts college with an enrollment of 2,500 in the city.

The municipal government of Eastern Shore, like that of so many other very small towns that grew rapidly during the 1950s and 1960s, has suddenly found itself quite large and diversified. Thirty years ago a mayor and a few part-time employees ran the city, but today there are 200 city employees. The city council consists of seven members who, six years ago, hired a city manager to run the day-to-day operations of the city. But, in the last ten years, the population has increased by 35 percent and many additional services had to be provided to the citizenry, which called for skilled workers such as the head librarian, the city engineer, the detectives in the police department, the city auditor, and the fire chief.

The city is divided into several departments, each with a director who reports to the city manager. These directors include recreation, public works, police, fire, library, finance, legal, personnel, and auditing and records. Public works, which includes water and sewer, streets, garbage, etc., is the largest department, with 76 employees. The police department has 20 workers and the fire department has 14. Recreation and the auditing and records departments each have about 30 workers. All full-time city jobs are salaried. The jobs are quite varied and include road crews, garbage collectors, machinery operators, groundskeepers, engineers, policemen, clerks, secretaries, lawyers, administrative assistants, a city planner, etc.

The city manager is forceful and successful in dealing with the city council and over the years has been able to collect taxes and float bond issues to improve municipal services and equipment. Now Eastern Shore has a new and modern library, a new high school (as well as an older one), a new city hall-jail-justice building, and has given its downtown a facelift by widening streets and adding a park and fountains. The city manager has also been able to attract and keep some excellent city employees because of his power over the budget and his innovative, growth-oriented ideas.

The city's employees have, in the past, received fewer and smaller pay increases than industrial workers in the city. The latter are almost all unionized. Their average pay increase per year has been about 7 percent over the last five years, while Eastern Shore employees have averaged only about 4 percent. There seems to be no serious talk of organizing the city workers into a union, however. The city does have pension plans, health insurance, small merit raises, and other benefits for its employees, including paid sick leave. The cost of living is rising very rapidly in the area. The entire 4 percent average salary increase noted above does not match the cost-of-living increase. At present, there is no automatic cost-of-living escalator in the salary system and merit raises have been extremely small when given.

PART C

Form 4 Job Evaluation Factors

Weight, %			Points
20	I.	Responsibility/Accountability	200
15	II.	Supervision Exercised	150
15	III.	Contacts with Others	150
10	IV.	Confidentiality	100
20	V.	Complexity/Problem Solving	200
5	VI.	Working Conditions	50
5	VII.	Physical Effort	50
10	VIII.	Preparation and Training	100
100			1000

Form 4 (continued)

I. Responsibility/Accountability

The dimension Responsibility/Accountability indicates the impact that an error with a reasonable probability of occurrence may have in the exercise of required job responsibilities. Errors may have financial or human impact.

Level	Point value	Description of characteristics and measures
0	0	Routine work performed under close supervision or in accordance with specific detailed instructions. *Benchmark:* File Clerk.
1	40	Error may result in minor confusion or damage resulting in minor expense for correction or repair. *Benchmark:* Billing Clerk, General Secretary.
2	80	Error generally confined to a single department or phase of activities and may result in moderate expense for correction or unfavorable public relationship. *Benchmark:* Administrative Secretary, Statistical Clerk, Purchasing Clerk.
3	120	Error may be serious, involving loss of time, money, damage to property, waste of materials, and/or unfavorable public relationship. *Benchmark:* Staff Social Worker, Nurses, Intake Technician, School Therapist.
4	160	Error may be difficult to detect initially and may result in serious consequences, such as significant property damage, loss of money or time and materials, or physical injury to the incumbent. *Benchmark:* Team Leaders, Coordinators, Psychologists, Clinical Manager.
5	200	Error may have extreme consequences, and can be potentially dangerous to public safety, in addition to significant property damage, loss of money, or time and materials. *Benchmark:* Executive Director.

Form 4 (continued)

II. Supervision Exercised

The supervision factor indicates the degree of bona fide supervisory responsibility assigned to the job, to what degree the job requires the employee to 1) assign tasks to others, 2) outline the methods others are to follow, 3) outline the work others are to accomplish, 4) check the progress and production of other employees, 5) handle exceptional cases referred to supervisor by others, and 6) correct the errors others have made.

Level	Point value	Description of characteristics and measures
0	0	No supervisory responsibilities. *Benchmark:* Nurses, Statistical Clerk, General Secretary.
1	30	Closely supervises routine operations. Supervises standardized procedures occasionally. First line supervisor constantly checking employees' work. *Benchmark:* Client Billing Supervisor.
2	60	Supervises but does not closely check specific details of employees' work. Advises and directs out-of-ordinary phases of work. Supervises employees who work independently but are doing routine work involving no discretion. *Benchmark:* Personnel Coordinator.
3	90	Supervises employees who are held accountable for their own work. Supervises an administrative unit or workers who work independently with a moderate degree of discretion. *Benchmark:* Business Manager, Team Manager.
4	120	Plans and directs the work of employees performing a number of diverse functions that are not directly related. May require the supervision of more than one unit. *Benchmark:* Associate Director.
5	150	Supervises an entire organizational unit. *Benchmark:* Executive Director.

Form 4 (continued)

III.   Contacts with Others

This factor appraises the responsibility required for meeting, dealing with, or influencing other persons. In rating this factor, consider how the contacts are made, how often, whether contacts involve furnishing or obtaining information only, or whether they involve influencing others.

Level	Point value	Description of characteristics and measures
0	0	Little or no contacts except with immediate associates and own supervision. *Benchmark:* Keypunch/Bookkeeper.
1	30	Contacts with other persons within the department on routine matters or occasional outside contacts, furnishing or obtaining information only; occasionally the general public. *Benchmark:* Statistical Clerk.
2	60	Regular contacts with other departments, furnishing or obtaining information or reports, requiring tact to avoid friction. Contacts with regular, predictable client load. Outside contacts where improper handling may affect results but where the primary responsibility rests with the next higher level of supervision or the general public much of the time. Must exchange information on factual matters. *Benchmark:* Billing Clerk, Mental Health Worker, Executive Secretary.
3	90	Outside or inside contacts involving carrying out center policy and programs and the influencing of others, where improper handling will affect operating results or the general public almost continuously. Or contacts involving dealing with persons of substantially higher rank on matters requiring explanation, discussion, and obtaining approvals. *Benchmark:* Team Managers, Business Manager.
4	120	Outside and inside requiring a high degree of tact, judgment, and the ability to deal with and influence persons in all types of positions. Social sensitivity and the ability to communicate are definitely required. For instance, may instruct or comfort patients and families, training and counsel other employees. *Benchmark:* Coordinator, Social Worker.
5	150	Continuous outside and inside contacts, frequently involving difficult negotiations which require a well-developed sense of strategy and timing. Incumbent provides social or psychological counseling to clients and families, makes formal instructional/persuasive presentations to groups, and/or engages in other activities that require a high level of interpersonal skills. *Benchmark:* Executive Director.

Form 4 (continued)

IV. Confidentiality

This factor appraises the integrity and discretion required in safeguarding confidential data. In rating the job, consider the character of the data, the degree to which the full import of the data is apparent on the job in question, and whether disclosure would effect internal relationships only or external, competitive relationships.

Level	Point value	Description of characteristics and measures
0	0	Little or no confidential data involved. *Benchmark:* General Secretary.
1	20	Occasionally works with confidential data, but the full import is not apparent and the effect of any disclosure would be negligible. *Benchmark:* Statistical Clerk, Billing Clerk, Keypunch/Bookkeeper.
2	40	Regularly works with some confidential data or client data which, if disclosed, might have adverse internal effect, such as budgets. *Benchmark:* Records Clerk, Technician.
3	60	Regularly works with some confidential data of major importance which, if disclosed, may be detrimental to center interests, such as payroll, personnel files, overall statistics, etc. *Benchmark:* Personnel Coordinator, Business Manager.
4	80	Complete access to client names and treatment files and to some confidential center data such as unit payroll. *Benchmark:* Team Manager, Nurse, Associate Director.
5	100	Full and complete access to reports, records, plans, programs, where utmost judgment is required to safeguard the center's interests and integrity. *Benchmark:* Executive Director.

Form 4 (continued)

V.   Complexity/Problem Solving

The mental capacity required to perform the given job as expressed in resourcefulness in dealing with unfamiliar problems, interpretation of data, initiation of new ideas, complex data analysis, creative or developmental work.

Level	Point value	Description of characteristics and measures
0	0	Seldom confronts problems not covered by job routine or organizational policy; analysis of data is negligible. *Benchmark:* General Secretary, Switchboard/Receptionist.
1	40	Follows clearly prescribed standard practice and involves straightforward application of readily understood rules and procedures. Analyzes noncomplicated data by established routine. *Benchmark:* Statistical Clerk, Billing Clerk.
2	80	Frequently confronts problems not covered by job routine. Independent judgment exercised in making minor decisions where alternatives are limited and standard policies established. Analysis of standardized data for information of or use by others. *Benchmark:* Social Worker, Executive Secretary.
3	120	Exercises independent judgment in making decisions involving nonroutine problems with general guidance only from higher supervision. Analyzes and evaluates data pertaining to nonroutine problems for solution in conjunction with others. *Benchmark:* Nurse, Accountant, Team Leader.
4	160	Uses independent judgment in making decisions that are subject to review in the final stages only. Analyzes and solves nonroutine problems involving evaluation of a wide variety of data as a regular part of job duties. Makes decisions involving procedures. *Benchmark:* Associate Director, Business Manager, Park Services Director.
5	200	Uses independent judgment in making decisions that are not subject to review. Regularly exercises developmental or creative abilities in policy development. *Benchmark:* Executive Director.

Form 4 (continued)

VI. Working Conditions

This dimension indicates the degree to which the job is located in difficult, uncomfortable, or hazardous work areas.

Level	Point value	Description of characteristics and measures
0	0	Working conditions are confined to an office or similar area. No unusual degrees of discomfort or hazards are evidenced. No client contact. *Benchmark:* General Secretary.
1	10	While the majority of duties are performed under usual working conditions, some more difficult working conditions may be present on occasion. *Benchmark:* Intake Worker.
2	20	The job requires performance of duties under somewhat difficult or hazardous conditions. Safety equipment may be required. *Benchmark:* Public Health Worker.
3	30	The job may be performed in a wide range of environmental conditions, a large portion of which may be difficult, hazardous, or uncomfortable, i.e., noise, dirt, dust, materials handled, extreme temperature, ventilation, or stress. Safety equipment may be required. *Benchmark:* Ore Preparation Worker.
4	40	The work consists almost entirely of duties that must be performed under difficult conditions. *Benchmark:* Silo Operator.
5	50	The job is continually performed under uncomfortable or hazardous conditions, i.e., noise, dirt, dust, materials handled, extreme temperature, ventilation, or stress. Safety equipment is required. *Benchmark:* Miner.

Form 4 (continued)

VII.   Physical Effort

This factor accounts for significant physical exertion required by the job and physical fatigue due to intensity and continuousness of the work.

Level	Point value	Description of characteristics and measures
0	0	No significant physical efforts required for the job beyond ordinary movement and exertion. *Benchmark:* Associate Director.
1	10	Extra physical effort, due to standing on feet or walking considerable amount of time. Above-average manual dexterity may be required. *Benchmark:* Nurse, Billing Clerk.
2	20	Almost constant or repetitive work operating machines or equipment (e.g., typing or keypunch). Very frequent standing or walking. Occasionally difficult working position. Small amounts of heavy lifting or carrying. *Benchmark:* Statistical Clerk, Keypunch/ Bookkeeper.
3	30	Heavy lifting, or extremely strenuous work is required. May require above-average physical strength to perform the duties of the position. *Benchmark:* Yard Laborer.
4	40	Sustained physical effort required in working with average materials and supplies continuously. Continuous standing or walking. Continuous operation of machines or equipment resulting in considerable fatigue. *Benchmark:* Wine Mill Operator.
5	50	Continuous standing and working in difficult positions. Lifting and carrying average to heavy weight loads. Continuous pushing and pulling of loaded carts or gurneys. Operating heavy machinery or equipment. *Benchmark:* Roller Repair Technician.

Form 4 (continued)

VIII. Preparation and Training

This measures the minimum level of knowledge and skills required in order to qualify for the job and those normally acquired through formal schooling.

Level	Point value	Description of characteristics and measures
0	0	Requires grammar school education or equivalent knowledge in order to understand and perform the work assigned. Examples: reading instructions and notes, writing simple comments and entering information on forms, performing basic arithmetic computations involving whole numbers, using simple gauges and instructions, etc. *Benchmark:* Billing Clerk, Receptionist/Switchboard.
1	20	Work requires a high-school level of knowledge of several subjects in order to prepare reports, perform calculations, keep records, and/or deal effectively with other people, specialized or technical training which may be obtained in high school or by a very brief (six months or less) period of intensive preparation outside of school (e.g., correspondence typing). *Benchmark:* Bookkeeper, Statistical Clerk.
2	40	Work requires, in addition to the skills normally acquired through a general high school education, specialized or technical training which may be obtained in high school or by a relatively brief period (more than six months but less than one year) or intensive preparation outside of school. Work may require elementary technical training such as that which would be acquired in the first year of college, technical school, or business school. *Benchmark:* Personnel Coordinator.
3	60	Work requires a professional level of knowledge in a specialized field such as that which would be acquired by completing a four-year college program. *Benchmark:* Technician, Accountant, Mental Health Worker.
4	80	Work requires a professional level of knowledge in a specialized field such as that which would be acquired by completing a four-year college program. *Benchmark:* Nurse, Business Manager.
5	100	Work requires a professional level of knowledge in a specialized field equivalent to that which is acquired through the completion of three or more years of study beyond a four-year college degree. *Benchmark:* Clinical Services Manager.

Form 4 (continued)

	Degrees					
Factors/Level	0	1	2	3	4	5
1. Responsibility/Accountability	0	40	80	120	160	200
2. Supervision Exercised	0	30	60	90	120	150
3. Contacts with Others	0	30	60	90	120	150
4. Confidentiality	0	20	40	60	80	100
5. Complexity/Problem Solving	0	40	80	120	160	200
6. Working Conditions	0	10	20	30	40	50
7. Physical Effort	0	10	20	30	40	50
8. Preparation and Training	0	20	40	60	80	100
						1000

PART C

Form 5 City of Eastern Shore—Job No. 1

SECRETARY III

DESCRIPTION OF WORK:

General Statement of Duties: Performs complete secretarial duties and administrative detail work for the chief elected official or head of a major unit of city government, requiring extensive exercise of independent judgment in the role of "Personal Assistant."

Supervision Received: Works under broad policy guidance or direction of a chief elected official or head of major unit of city government. Would rarely receive supervision by any other party and can be considered to perform duties on a "one-to-one" basis.

Supervision Exercised: Exercises supervision over personnel as assigned, or full supervision incidental to other duties.

EXAMPLES OF DUTIES: (Any one position may not include all of the duties listed, nor do the listed examples include all tasks that may be found in positions of this class.)

Performs complete secretarial duties for the chief elected official or head of a major unit of city government; handles confidential matters concerning major city policy; keeps advised of the current status of the work of the executive; collects information for the use of the executive; determines action necessary in situations arising during absence of superior.

Handles a variety of administrative details, which involves contact with various officials in the public service and in private industry; relieves the department head of administrative detail; relays departmental policies and instructions; arranges meetings; briefs correspondence and miscellaneous data.

Furnishes the public with advice and assistance requiring good knowledge of city departments, rules and regulations, and policies.

Takes complex dictation; takes notes of meetings; keeps official records and reports; prepares correspondence. Makes travel arrangements; maintains appointment calendar. Uses dictaphone, typewriter, copier, and other office equipment.

Performs related work as required.

REQUIRED KNOWLEDGES, SKILLS, AND ABILITIES: Extensive knowledge of modern office practices and procedures. Extensive knowledge of grammar, spelling, and punctuation. Thoroughly skilled in the taking and transcribing of dictation and in the operation of a typewriter. Ability to exercise initiative and sound judgment and to react resourcefully under varying conditions. Ability to establish and maintain effective relationships with the public, other agencies, and employees.

QUALIFICATIONS FOR APPOINTMENT:

Education: High-school graduation or equivalent.

Experience: Four years experience in progressively responsible general office work, including one year in a position comparable to Secretary II.

    OR

Any equivalent combination of education and experience.

PART C

Form 6 City of Eastern Shore—Job No. 2

POLICE CHIEF

DESCRIPTION OF WORK:

General Statement of Duties: Performs administrative work in planning, coordinating, and directing the activities of the city police department.

Supervision Received: Works under broad policy guidance and direction of the city manager.

Supervision Exercised: Exercises supervision over all department personnel directly or through subordinate officers.

EXAMPLES OF DUTIES: (The listed examples may not include all duties found in this class.)

In conformance with applicable laws and in accordance with the rules and regulations of the department, develops or revises department operating policies and procedures; has final authority, within given laws, rules, and regulations, on all aspects of the department's activity.

Establishes department organization, including channels of authority, responsibility, and communication; revises department organization as appropriate to maximize efficiency.

Assigns to commanding officers the authority to direct operations and supervise subordinate officers and civilian personnel within their assigned responsibility.

Has overall responsibility for the maintenance of departmental discipline and the conduct and general behavior of officers and civilian employees.

Meets with elected or appointed officials, other law-enforcement agencies, community and business representatives, and the public on all aspects of the department's activities.

Prepares, presents, and controls the departmental budget.

Organizes and participates in programs on police and safety subjects for the public; meets with associations, civic organizations, and related groups.

Researches and prepares new and revised ordinances pertaining to traffic and safety.

Performs related work, as required.

REQUIRED KNOWLEDGES, SKILLS, AND ABILITIES: Extensive knowledge of modern law-enforcement practices, procedures, techniques, and equipment. Thorough knowledge of federal, state, and local laws and ordinances governing departmental activities. Thorough knowledge of the policies, organization, rules, regulations, and procedures common to police department operations. Considerable knowledge of the principles and practices of administration. Ability to organize and coordinate department activities. Ability to communicate effectively—verbally and in writing. Ability to supervise personnel directly or through subordinate officers. Ability to establish and maintain effective working relationships with elected and appointed officials, other law-enforcement agencies, and the public. Ability to meet necessary special requirements.

QUALIFICATIONS FOR APPOINTMENT:

Education: Graduation from a college or university with an associate degree in police science.

Experience: Two years of law-enforcement experience in the rank of captain.

   OR

Any equivalent combination of education and experience.

PART C

Form 7 City of Eastern Shore—Job No. 3

DIRECTOR OF PUBLIC WORKS

DESCRIPTION OF WORK:

General Statement of Duties: Plans, organizes, and supervises the public-works program of the city.

Supervision Received: Works under broad policy guidance and direction of the city manager.

Supervision Exercised: Exercises supervision over public-works personnel directly or through subordinate supervisors.

EXAMPLES OF DUTIES: (The listed examples may not include all duties found in this class.)

Plans, coordinates, and provides overall direction for the various program activities of the department, including engineering, street construction, maintenance and repair; design and construction of public-works structures and facilities; waste-water and water and sewage plant operations.

Develops and revises the department's operating policies and procedures in accordance with applicable laws and the department's rules and regulations; has final authority, within given laws, rules, and regulations, over all aspects of the department's activity.

Establishes department organization, including channels of authority, responsibility, and communication; revises department organization to maximize efficiency.

Assigns to subordinate supervisors the authority to direct operations and supervises personnel within their assigned responsibility.

Meets with city officials, private contractors, and the public on all aspects of the department's work.

Prepares and submits department budget requests and controls the programs from viewpoint of costs.

Prepares and presents operating and special reports as necessary.

Performs related work as required.

REQUIRED KNOWLEDGES, SKILLS, AND ABILITIES: Thorough knowledge of the principles and methods of public-works administration. Thorough knowledge of the principles, methods, materials, and equipment common to public-works and utilities operations. Ability to organize and direct the activities of personnel and equipment. Ability to communicate effectively—both verbally and in writing. Ability to establish and maintain effective working relationships with employees, other agencies, and the public.

QUALIFICATIONS FOR APPOINTMENT:

Education: Graduation from a college or university with a bachelor's degree in civil engineering or a related field.

Experience: Six years of progressively responsible public-works experience, including four years in an administrative or supervisory capacity.

   OR

Any equivalent combination of education and experience.

Necessary Special Requirements: Possession of, or eligibility for within six months after employment, a state professional engineer's license.

PART C

Form 8 City of Eastern Shore—Job No. 4

CLERICAL WORKER II (Accounts Receivable)

DESCRIPTION OF WORK:

General Statement of Duties: Performs a variety of general clerical work requiring some exercise of independent judgment.

Supervision Received: Works under general supervision of a clerical, technical, or administrative superior.

Supervision Exercised: Exercises supervision of clerical personnel as assigned.

EXAMPLES OF DUTIES: (Any one position may not include all of the duties listed, nor do the listed examples include all duties that may be found in positions of this class.)

Processes reports, forms, payments, billings, or other materials; examines for accuracy and completeness; makes additions or resolves discrepancies, consulting with supervisor or other employees as appropriate.

Maintains records, files, and books according to established methods and procedures; compiles and tabulates data for records and reports; keeps books requiring ledger entries.

Accepts fees or payments, issues receipts and notices, and keeps simple records of transactions; makes simple mathematical computations.

Receives telephone and personal callers, handling any questions or matters of a nontechnical or routine nature and directing others to the appropriate staff members.

Operates simple office equipment.

Performs related work as required.

REQUIRED KNOWLEDGES, SKILLS, AND ABILITIES: Working knowledge of modern office practices and procedures. Ability to perform a variety of clerical work requiring some exercise of independent judgment. Ability to follow written and oral instructions. Ability to make simple mathematical computations. Ability to establish and maintain effective working relationships with employees, other agencies, and the public.

MINIMUM QUALIFICATIONS:

Education: High-school graduation or equivalent.

Experience: One year of experience in general clerical work.

   OR

Any equivalent combination of education and experience.

PART C

Form 9 City of Eastern Shore—Job No. 5

ASSISTANT LIBRARIAN

DESCRIPTION OF WORK:

General Statement of Duties: Performs supervisory duties relating to coordination of library activities.

Supervision Received: Works under general supervision of an administrative superior.

Supervision Exercised: Exercises supervision over personnel as assigned.

EXAMPLES OF DUTIES: (Any one position may not include all of the duties listed nor do the listed examples include all duties that may be found in positions of this class.)

Acts as assistant to the Library Director; types letters, records, and order forms; supervises library activities in absence of director.

Maintains shelf list file and count; types catalog cards, registration, and I.D. cards; assists library patrons in checking in and out library materials; reserves library materials.

Reserves 16 mm films and insures delivery to library patrons.

Instructs other staff members in proper methods of processing after cataloging; locates reading sources and other library materials, shelving and circulation desk responsibilities.

Operates a variety of office equipment, including the Regiscope and 3-M Reader Printer.

Performs related work as required.

REQUIRED KNOWLEDGES, SKILLS, AND ABILITIES: Considerable knowledge of library principles, methods, materials, and practices. Considerable knowledge of reader interest levels. Ability to assign, supervise, and inspect the work of others. Ability to exercise sound judgment in making decisions. Ability to communicate effectively verbally and in writing. Ability to establish and maintain effective working relationships with other employees and library patrons.

MINIMUM QUALIFICATIONS:

Education: Graduation from a college or university with a Master's degree in library science or a related field.

Experience: Two years of progressively responsible experience in library work.

　　　OR

Any equivalent combination of education and experience.

PART C

Form 10 City of Eastern Shore—Job No. 6

PUBLIC UTILITIES PLANT OPERATOR II

DESCRIPTION OF WORK:

General Statement of Duties: Performs skilled work in the operation, servicing, and minor maintenance of equipment in a water or waste-water plant on an assigned shift.

Supervision Received: Works under general supervision of technical superior.

Supervision Exercised: Orientation on the job of operator-in-training personnel.

EXAMPLE OF DUTIES: (Any one position may not include all of the duties listed, nor do the listed examples include all tasks that may be found in positions of this class.

Operates plant equipment to control the water flow and maintains proper conditions for treatment of water.

Performs a variety of tasks, such as inspecting and oiling pumps, monitoring chemical feeders, motors, gauges, and valves.

Operates filters, takes water samples to determine that units of the plant are functioning efficiently and the treatment process is maintained.

Makes periodic rounds of plant and pumping stations to check equipment operation and flow meter records.

Assists in orienting and instructing operator-in-training personnel in the duties and responsibilities of plant operations.

Records meter readings and reports plant operations.

May operate truck to carry solid wastes to landfill.

Performs related work as required.

REQUIRED KNOWLEDGES, SKILLS, AND ABILITIES: Considerable knowledge of the operation of motors, pumps, meters, and related equipment of a water or waste water plant. Skill in the operation of mechanical equipment. Ability to make accurate readings, keep records, and make reports. Ability to communicate effectively orally and in writing. General mechanical ability to work effectively and react quickly to situations that develop. Ability to work independently. Ability to instruct and orient other employees. Ability to establish and maintain effective working relationships with other employees and the general public.

QUALIFICATIONS FOR APPOINTMENT:

Education: High-school graduation or equivalent.

Experience: Two years experience in mechanical maintenance or repair work, including one year's experience in a water or waste-water plant.

OR

Any equivalent combination of education and experience.

Necessary Special Requirements: Must possess a Class I Water and Waste Water Plant Operator's Certificate from the state.

Name _____ Group Number _____

Date _____ Class Section _____ Hour _____ Score _____

PART C

Form 11 Job Evaluation Computation Worksheet for Six Eastern Shore Jobs

Indicate the number of points allocated to each job by entering the proper amount of points (copied from the master point system of Form 4) in each block that applies to each job. Then, total all the points allocated for each job in order to arrive at the relative ranking of the six jobs. (Note: Each job can only be at one degree level—therefore blank blocks will appear for each job.)

JOB EVALUATION

Point Recording Sheet

Job title	1. Responsibility/ accountability	2. Supervision exercised	3. Contacts with others	4. Confidentiality	5. Complexity/ problem solving	6. Working conditions	7. Physical effort	8. Preparation and training	Total
1.									
2.									
3.									
4.									
5.									
6.									

PART C

Form 12 Salary Survey Data for Six Small Municipalities in the Northeast United States*

Job Title	Municipality	Salary Range (per year)		Actual Paid Range (per year)		
		Maximum	Minimum	Maximum	Minimum	Median
Secretary to city manager	A	16,750	14,500	16,750	14,500	16,000
	B	15,900	13,750	15,000	13,750	14,400
	C	17,000	14,400	16,750	14,900	15,750
	D	15,500	14,000	15,250	14,500	14,750
	E	16,200	13,750	16,200	14,000	14,500
	F	17,250	14,750	17,000	15,000	15,500
Police chief**	A	29,250	24,500	N/A	N/A	29,250
	B	27,500	22,500	N/A	N/A	27,000
	C	29,750	24,500	N/A	N/A	29,000
	D	28,000	25,000	N/A	N/A	28,250
	E	27,000	22,500	N/A	N/A	26,500
	F	28,500	23,500	N/A	N/A	25,500
Director of public works**	A	30,300	25,250	N/A	N/A	27,400
	B	29,250	24,500	N/A	N/A	25,750
	C	29,500	23,500	N/A	N/A	27,500
	D	28,500	23,500	N/A	N/A	26,500
	E	27,000	22,750	N/A	N/A	24,750
	F	28,000	23,000	N/A	N/A	25,000
Accounts-receivable clerks	A	15,500	13,250	15,000	13,500	14,250
	B	15,000	13,500	14,750	13,500	13,750
	C	16,000	13,000	16,000	13,400	14,000
	D	14,750	13,500	14,500	13,750	14,000
	E	14,500	13,750	14,000	13,750	13,750
	F	15,750	13,250	15,500	14,500	15,250
Assistant librarian	A	18,500	15,000	17,000	15,000	16,000
	B	16,750	14,000	15,750	14,000	15,000
	C	16,500	14,000	16,000	14,750	15,250
	D	17,000	15,000	17,000	15,500	16,250
	E	17,500	14,750	17,000	14,750	15,250
	F	18,000	15,750	16,500	15,750	16,250
Public utility plant operators	A	16,750	15,250	16,500	15,250	15,250
	B	17,000	15,000	16,000	15,000	15,500
	C	16,500	15,500	16,500	16,000	16,500
	D	16,750	15,000	15,750	15,000	15,250
	E	16,000	14,500	15,500	14,750	15,000
	F	16,750	14,750	16,000	14,750	15,500

* *Illustrative data.*

** Since only one person occupies these positions in each municipality, there are no actual paid maximums and minimums. Salary range data was developed historically.

Note 1: Municipalities are all in the same geographical area (Northeastern United States) and all have between 30,000 and 65,000 populations. Municipality B received a 12 percent across-the-board pay raise last year, while all others received increases of between 5.5 percent and 9 percent, with the exception of E, which got no increase. Unions exist in C and F. In C, a new contract negotiated last year calls for about an 8.5 percent salary increase over each of the next three years for all workers, while in jurisdiction F, a new contract will be negotiated next year. The salary figure for F indicates a 7 percent raise over last year. All figures represent salary only, not fringe benefits, such as health insurance, etc.

Note 2: Data was collected as of January, 1981 and published on September 30, 1981.

Name _____   Group Number _____

Date _____   Class Section _____   Hour _____   Score _____

PART C
Form 13

Part I. Salary Structure for Six Eastern Shore Jobs

Instructions: Enter the required data for the six Eastern Shore jobs based on your analysis of the salary survey, your point system, and any other relevant data.

Job title	Appropriate point total or range for each job (min. to max.)	Appropriate yearly salary range			Range %
		maximum	midpoint	minimum	

Part II: The Relationship of Points to Salary for Six Eastern Shore Jobs

Instructions: Draw a salary rate structure here by plotting the yearly salary against points you have allocated to each of the six jobs, using midpoints of the ranges you indicated in Part I above. There should be six points in the graph which, when connected, form a line or curve that explains the relationship between job salaries and their allocated points from your point system of job evaluation. What type of relationship is indicated? Is it logical? What, if anything, needs to be changed and why? (Place your answers on reverse.)

Yearly salary rate
(midpoint of salary range above,
in thousands of dollars)

0

Points allocated to each of the six jobs (midpoint of point range)

PART D

Form 14 Data from Personnel Records of Eastern Shore Workers Currently Holding the Six Selected Jobs

Job title	Age	Sex	Formal education	Years worked for city	Years at present position	Years of previous experience		Amount of last merit raise (per month)	Overall performance rating (10 point scale)		Supervisor's current assessment of promotability
						General work experience	Specific to current job		Last period	This period	
1. Secretary to city manager	34	F	High school; secretarial school	6	6	10	4	$30	8	9	Promotable now, perhaps in highest applicable position
2. Police chief	55	M	College; police academy	14	8	21	21	$50	10	10	Promotable now, but in highest applicable position
3. Director of public works	37	M	College; master's degree	5	3	12	3	$45	9	10	Promotable now
4. Accounts-receivable clerk	43	F	High school	2	2	8	1	$8	8	7	May be promotable at future date
5. Assistant librarian	24	M	College	1	1	2	0	0	5	6	Definitely not promotable
6. Public works plant operator	27	F	Some college	2	1	3	0	0	7	8	May be promotable at future date

Name _____   Group Number _____

Date _____   Class Section _____   Hour _____   Score _____

PART D

Form 15 Recommended Salary Levels for Six Current Eastern Shore Workers

	Job title	Recommended yearly salary	Amount of Increase/Decrease	Rationale or comments
1.				
2.				
3.				
4.				
5.				
6.				

Name _____   Group Number _____

Date _____   Class Section _____   Hour _____   Score _____

ASSESSMENT OF LEARNING IN PERSONNEL ADMINISTRATION
EXERCISE 16

1. Try to state the purpose of this exercise in one concise sentence.

2. Specifically what did you learn from this exercise (i.e., skills, abilities, and knowledge)?

3. How might your learning influence your role and your duties as a personnel administrator?

4. How could a wage and salary program be evaluated as to its effectiveness?

5. What problems might you encounter from line managers as you implement a new salary system?

6. Do you feel organizations rely too heavily on money as rewards?   Why?

Section 7

PERSONNEL ADMINISTRATION AND HUMAN-RESOURCE MANAGEMENT IN THE CONTEMPORARY ENVIRONMENT

Exercise 1 emphasized the rapidly changing environment in which people in personnel jobs must operate. This external environment affects their work, just as it affects the work of others in organizations, and is one reason why personnel jobs command ever-higher prestige and salaries. The changing nature of the environment also places more demands on those in personnel; thus, complex technical and administrative skills, as well as interpersonal skills, are now required in order to meet these new challenges.

While several aspects of the contemporary environment have been discussed throughout these exercises, two have been mentioned repeatedly: equal-employment-opportunity laws and guidelines, and labor unions. Their impact on the tasks and roles of those in personnel is significant and pervades each specific personnel program discussed in previous exercises. Thus, the final exercises consider these important issues separately. Also, two relatively new issues to the personnel scene are considered here. These are research in human resources and costing the human resources function.

Exercise 17 outlines the basic legal issues regarding equal employment opportunity. It contains activities designed to illustrate and simulate the process of determining whether a personnel program violates an EEO law or federal guideline and enables you to build skill in designing and implementing affirmative action plans to increase the participation of women and minorities in an organization.

Exercise 18 considers the impact of unions on personnel programs. Rather than discuss union organizing or labor laws, the exercise attempts to illustrate the actual impact of unionization on personnel and human resource programs. Most importantly, Exercise 18 points out that unions place certain constraints on personnel programs, as well as afford certain opportunities for improving these programs. The most successful people in personnel seem to be those who recognize and plan for the former and capitalize on and seize the latter.

Exercise 19 attempts to deal with an age-old question in the human resource area—how can we cost-justify our efforts? Methods of measuring the costs of basic human resource issues such as turnover, absenteeism, etc., are shown.

Exercise 20 is intended to aid in evaluating the impact of human resource interventions. That is, how do we know (in specific terms) if the changes we introduce in organizations really make a difference. This exercise demonstrates how to measure the effect of such changes.

Exercise 17

Issues in equal employment opportunity and affirmative action

PREVIEW

If you have completed the exercise on testing (Exercise 9), you should be familiar with basic employee selection procedures which facilitate the selection of the best person to do a specific job. However, another aspect of selection must be addressed—job discrimination. Two important points should be noted at the outset: first, the personnel administrator is typically responsible for identifying any "adverse impact" an organization's selection procedures may have on protected classes (i.e., minorities and women); and second, even if the selection procedures demonstrate adverse impact, they may not be considered discriminatory *provided* they are shown to be job related. Of course, the exact definition of terms such as job related must be specified, as in the exercise, in order to fully understand the issue of discrimination in employment. Further, Congress has decided that not only must the past practices causing adverse impact be eliminated, but in many cases organizations and government contractors must actually initiate practices and programs to compensate for past discrimination. These programs are commonly called affirmative-action programs. These two topics, job discrimination and affirmative action, and their impact on the human resource function of an organization, are the focus of this exercise.

OBJECTIVES

1. To gain an understanding of the many laws that define and propose to remedy employment discrimination.

2. To build skill in identifying discriminatory personnel practices.

3. To build skills in avoiding discriminatory practices, as well as in planning for specific remedies through affirmative-action programs.

PREMEETING PREPARATION

Read the entire exercise carefully, especially the *Introduction*. (You may also find Exercise 9 a useful review.)

INTRODUCTION

Discrimination in Employment: Definition, Legal Regulation, and the Design and Implementation of Remedies at the Organizational Level*

In 1964 no one knew precisely the extent of racial discrimination in employment practices. But Congress, in creating the Equal Employment Opportunity Commission (EEOC), assumed such practices were widespread. The Commission, composed of five members appointed by the president for five-year terms, confirmed the assumption. It found that in 1966 blacks

*The terms and concepts discussed in this *Introduction* are defined in a glossary of EEO and related legal terms which is appended to this exercise.

made up only 2.6 percent of the "white-collar" head-quarters staffs of the hundred major New York City-based corporations that accounted for nearly 16 percent of the gross national product.[1]

Thus, Title VII of the Civil Rights Act of 1964 (which did not apply to government) barred discrimination in the selection of employees and contained the following passage:

> Nor shall it be unlawful employment practice for an employer to give and act upon the results of any professionally developed ability test provided that such test, its administration, or action upon the results is not designed, intended, or used to discriminate because of race, color, religion, sex, or national ancestry.[2]

The above statement is the essence of the so-called Tower Amendment, which, although it initially appears to be a simple statement, has caused much confusion in the application of selection strategies. The EEOC issued its first *Guidelines on Employment Testing Procedures* in 1966. These were revised in 1970, and reissued as the *EEOC Guidelines on Employee Selection Procedures*. These *Guidelines* applied only to the private sector when issued. They elaborated the EEOC's interpretation of the words "professionally developed test" by referencing the *Standards for Educational and Psychological Tests and Manuals,* published by the American Psychological Association in 1966 for principal use in education and research. The *EEOC Guidelines* of 1970 also define the meaning of the word "test" very broadly (effectively including any nonrandom personnel selection procedure, including interviews and application blanks). The *Guidelines* released in 1970 help define and interpret broad statements in the laws, but confusion and controversy have marked these laws from their inception and the EEOC's history has in turn been influenced by these controversies, as noted below.

The EEOC's Work Record. The passage of the Civil Rights Act of 1964 and the creation of the EEOC have had the effect of putting pressure on companies and unions to cease overt discrimination, identify covert discrimination, and open additional job opportunities for all groups where counts have revealed discrimination. In its first four years, the Commission's investigations of alleged illegal discrimination resulted in the filing of a mere handful—fewer than two dozen—federal suits to stop discrimination by employers or by unions. Most of the suits were against small companies or union locals. It was not until mid-1968 that a suit was brought against the nationwide operations of a large employer.

There are several reasons for the EEOC's slow initial performance. Congress first appropriated about $2 million for the Commission in 1964, but President Johnson did not name the commissioners until well into 1965. The chairman was James Roosevelt, But Roosevelt resigned after a few months to run for political office. So, roughly two years passed before the Commission began. When it did, it found the administrative machinery provided by Congress slow and cumbersome. Initially it could only investigate complaints against private employers, employment agencies, unions, or labor-management apprenticeship programs. Upon finding illegalities, it could only try conciliation and had to recommend to the Justice Department that suits be brought. The EEOC had no authority to hold administrative hearings on its complaints or to ban illegal union or employer discriminatory practices. Authority to hold such proceedings is a basic part of the powers of other regulatory agencies and accounts for the tremendous volume of their work. The EEOC has asked repeatedly for such authority and Congress has refused to grant it, perhaps in part because of the Commission's strong advocacy position compared to other regulatory agencies.

A change came in 1972 when the Act was expanded to include state and local governments and educational institutions. This provided coverage for 11 million and 4.3 million employees, respectively. There was also a change in procedure in that the EEOC no longer viewed discrimination as a single, isolated act, but viewed systematic discrimination that had disparate effects on "protected groups." The major charge to the EEOC was then to eliminate discrimination due to race, color, religion, sex, and national origin in hiring and to upgrade all employee conditions. It was also given the power to sue discriminatory organizations.

Of the first 175,000 EEOC cases, 63 percent were found in favor of the complainant, and at least 250 suits have been brought against employers. In 1974 alone over 6,000 cases involving women were filed, and many traditional hiring requirements, such as height, weight, working hours, childbearing, etc., have been ruled against. Millions of dollars have been paid by organizations for their discriminatory behavior. The most famous of these is probably the AT&T case, in which the company paid an estimated one-quarter of a billion dollars to various management and nonmanagement groups for discrimination. Part of

---

[1] Many of the ideas compiled here were obtained from a paper delivered by Glenn G. McClung at the IPMS-OMPO Personnel Directors' Seminar, Vail, Colorado, August 28-29, 1975. Reprinted in *Personnel Letter* No. 280, November 1975, pp. 6-8.

[2] Civil Rights Act of 1964, 42 U.S.C., 20008 *et seq,* Title VII.

these payments were in the form of back pay, wage adjustments, and promotion payments. In another case, nine steel companies (representing 73 percent of the industry's output) and unions paid $31 million in back pay (ranging from $250 to $3000 per person) to members of minority groups and to women. The organizations also established goals and timetables concerning seniority, transfer, earnings, promotions, and test validity to eliminate discrimination in the future.

Government Guidelines. The old *EEOC Guidelines* received little criticism from industry from 1966 to 1970; however, the now famous 1971 *Griggs* v. *Duke Power Co.*[3] case changed all that. In this case the United States Supreme Court said, "The administrative interpretation of the Act by the enforcing authority is entitled to great deference." Another case *(Albemarle Paper Co.* v. *Moody)*[4] seems to have affirmed that the *1970 EEOC Guidelines on Employee Selection Procedures* is "entitled to great deference" as the procedures to be used in selection design, but not "wooden application" as noted by Chief Justice Burger in his dissent in the *Moody* decision. More recent cases have continued to support the newer guidelines as they have been developed except where they conflict with well-grounded expert opinion.[5]

The *Griggs* case also established that any selection standard found to have an "adverse impact" (defined below) on protected groups must be shown to be demonstrably job related. As people interested in the field of personnel administration, we recognize that selection procedures should be job related. There is, however, controversy over the meaning of the term and how it can be demonstrated. Many feel that the *EEOC Guidelines* are so strict that compliance is impossible. Even the chief psychologist for the EEOC was forced to admit that he had never seen a study that would meet the literal requirements of the *Guidelines.* In fact, the American Psychological Association has replaced its 1966 *Standards* with a comprehensive 1974 publication. The older APA *Standards,* meant to be professional ideals, were often misinterpreted and misused as legalistic documents and therefore were radically changed. In the new *Standards* it is stated that " . . . validity is itself inferred, not measured,"[6] a considerable departure from the strictness implied in the earlier document.

Because employers were receiving conflicting signals from various federal agencies, President Nixon in 1973 established the Equal Employment Opportunity Coordinating Council.[7] The EEOCC, not be be confused with the EEOC, was charged with developing a "uniform set of federal guidelines" on which all federal agencies would agree. Numerous drafts of the *Uniform Guidelines* were released. The June 1975 draft was "less favorably" received than any which preceded it. There were two principal snags: (1) general intransigence on the part of some who oppose "uniform" *Guidelines;* and (2) EEOC's success in court made it not eager for change.

Many argue that the beginning of government intervention into employee selection began much earlier than the original EEOC *Guidelines.* The case of *Myart* v. *Motorola*[8] in 1963 certainly caught personnel psychologists and businesspersons flatfooted. Many businesses were shocked to learn that employment testing, a generally accepted management prerogative, was being challenged on the grounds of racial discrimination. Several psychologists involved in this case lined up on opposite sides of the issues. Test publishers were fearful that their sales would slacken.

More recently there has been an agreement among the four major enforcement agencies (EEOC, Office of Personnel Management, Department of Labor, and Department of Justice) upon a set of *Uniform Guidelines on Employee Selection Procedures* (1978). These guidelines were published after considerable public debate by all parties concerned, and some dissatisfaction on the part of employers may still exist. This dissatisfaction is especially related to guideline provisions such as whether the overall employment profile (the "bottom line") is acceptable defense against charges of discrimination, as opposed to examining every step in the selection process, searching (or "cosmic search") to demonstrate that the perfect selection procedure does not exist, and seeking alternative selection procedures which are equally valid, but with less adverse impact on protected groups. To clarify these as well as other statements in the guidelines, the agencies (joined by the Department of the Treasury) have published *Adoption of Questions and Answers to Clarify and Provide a Common Interpretation of the Uniform Guidelines on Employee Selection*

---

[3] *Griggs v. Duke Power Co.,* 401 U.S. 424 (1971).

[4] *Albemarle Paper Co. v. Moody,* 95 S. Ct. 2362, 2379 (1975).

[5] *United States v. State of South Carolina,* 15 FEP Cases at 1196 (1977).

[6] *Standards for Educational and Psychological Tests and Manuals* (Washington, D.C.: American Psychological Association, 1974).

[7] The Council consists of the U.S. Civil Service Commission, the EEOC, the OFCC, the U.S. Justice Department, the U.S. Department of Labor, and the U.S. Civil Rights Commission.

[8] See H.C. Lockwood, "Testing Minority Applicants for Employment," *Personnel Journal* 44 (1965): 356–360+ and W. L. French, *The Personnel Management Process,* 3d ed. (Boston: Houghton Mifflin, 1974), p. 287.

Procedures (1979). Interestingly, these were published without public debate and thus may be challenged as violating the Government Procedures Act.

During the late 1950s and the early 1960s employment testing had achieved a fashionable stature and many were adopting this latest fad in selection techniques. Unfortunately, employment tests were sold or recommended to many employers who had not a single person trained in psychological measurement or test use. Even worse, some sellers of tests rarely followed up to determine the utility of tests in selecting a work force. Concern for equal-employment-opportunity issues in the application of personnel selection procedures was virtually nonexistent at that time. The forces of the civil rights movement were also becoming evident and, after the Civil Rights Act of 1964, few employers, unions, or employment agencies were prepared to cope with the idea that tests had a discriminatory effect on minorities. In fact, there was typically no evidence of their validity in determining job success. Perhaps even more discomforting was the development of evidence that different racial groups performed equally well on a job even though they performed poorly on a test presumed to predict performance on the job in question. This set of complex environmental situations set the stage for the bulk of the EEO legislation; its major laws are reviewed below.

Major Equal Employment Opportunity (EEO) Legislation and Executive Orders. Four major federal laws are now available for seeking redress for discrimination in employment: The Civil Rights Act of 1866; Title VII of the Civil Rights Act of 1964, as amended in 1972; the Age Discrimination in Employment Act of 1967; and the Equal Pay Act of 1963. The Civil Rights Act of 1866 was seen as parallel to the 1964 act. Basically, the 1866 Act states that "All persons shall have the same right in every state and territory... as is enjoyed by White citizens..." It has purview over private as well as public acts of discrimination by race. Title VII of the 1964 law generally forbids employment discrimination on the basis of race, color, religion, sex, and national origin, as stated above. The Age Discrimination in Employment Act bans discrimination in employment on the basis of age against persons who are 40 to 70 years of age. The Equal Pay Act requires that individuals must receive equal pay, regardless of sex, if they perform equal work.

Executive Orders 11246 and 11141 (issued by the executive branch of the government) prohibit employment discrimination by contractors and subcontractors doing business with the federal government. Executive Order 11246 prohibits employment discrimination on the basis of race, color, religion, national origin;

eventually sex was included in Order No. 4. Executive Order 11141 forbids discrimination on the basis of age. The Executive Orders form the terms under which the federal government will award a contract or subcontract. Contractors who want to deal with the government accept the terms voluntarily; if they do not wish to accept the terms, they need not bid on a government contract. Executive Order 11478 prohibits discrimination against federal employees on the basis of race, color, religion, sex, or national origin. Executive Order 11345 specifically prohibits sex as a basis of discrimination. The Executive Orders operate in addition to, not instead of, the federal laws on employment discrimination.

The 1964 Civil Rights Act created the Equal Employment Opportunity Commission (EEOC) to enforce the provisions of its Title VII. The 1972 amendments to Title VII strengthened the authority of the EEOC to eliminate discrimination in employment as discussed above. In addition, the 1964 Civil Rights Act provides that the U.S. Attorney General may intervene to enforce Title VII by bringing civil suit in a federal court. In fact, an attorney who wins a case for the complainant may even receive the legal fees for the government if the complainant cannot pay. However, there have also been rulings that if EEOC loses a case it must pay the attorney's fees for the defendants.

Title VII contains several exceptions. The law does not apply to private membership clubs exempt from taxation. It does not protect members of the Communist Party of the United States or members of communist-action or communist-front groups required to register by the Subversive Activities Control Board. It does not prohibit businesses located on or near Indian reservations from giving employment preference to Indians living on or near the reservations. It does not affect federal or state laws creating special employment rights or preferences for United States veterans. The law does not apply to workers outside the United States. Aliens, like anyone else, are protected from race, sex, religious, and national-origin discrimination. National-origin bias (not hiring a person because of his or her nationality) and alienage bias (not hiring for lack of United States citizenship) are different concepts. The law also does not prohibit employment discrimination if the discriminatory action is in the interest of national security.

Title VII allows exceptions from its bans on discrimination on the basis of religion, sex, or national origin (though not on the basis of race or color) if religion, sex, or national origin is a bona fide occupational qualification (BFOQ). The BFOQ exception is interpreted narrowly by the EEOC. In order to qualify as a BFOQ exception, a particular religion, sex, or

Table 1. Reorganization of Equal Employment Authorities

Previously dispersed responsibility				Agency consolidation	
Agency	Enforcement responsibility	Discrimination covered	Employers covered	Agency	Timing
EEOC	Title VII	Race, Color, Religion, Sex, National Origin	Private and Public Nonfederal Employers and Unions	EEOC	. . .
Labor (Wage and Hour)	Equal Pay Act, Age Discrimination Act	Sex, Age	Private and Public Nonfederal Employers and Unions	EEOC	July 1979
Office of Personnel Management	Title VII, Executive Order 11478, Equal Pay Act, Age Discrimination Act, Rehabilitation Act	Race, Color, Religion, Sex, National Origin, Age, Handicapped	Federal Government	EEOC	October 1978
EEOCC*	Coordination of All Federal Equal Employment Programs	. . .	. . .	EEOC	July 1979
Labor (OFCCP)	Vietnam Veterans Readjustment Act, Rehabilitation Act	Veterans Race Handicapped	Federal Contractors	Labor (OFCCP)	
Commerce Defense Energy EPA GSA HEW HUD Interior SBA DOT Treasury	Executive Orders 11246, 11375	Race, Color, Religion, Sex, National Origin	Federal Contractors	Labor (OFCCP)	October 1978
Justice	Title VII, Executive Order 11246, Selected Federal Grant Programs	Race, Color, Religion, Sex, National Origin Varied	Public Nonfederal Employers Federal Contractors and Grantees	Justice	No Change

* A number of Federal grant statutes include a provision barring employment discrimination by recipients based on a variety of grounds including race, color, sex, and national origin. Under the reorganization plan, the activities of these agencies will be coordinated by the EEOC.

national origin must be a requirement for occupation of a job and the requirement must be necessary to the normal operation of a business (e.g., an actress's job can be given to females over males).

The 1972 amendments to Title VII eliminated the exception for educational institutions which was available under the original 1964 Civil Rights Act. Educational institutions, both public and private, are now subject to the Title VII bans on employment discrimination as to the employment of persons to perform work connected with the institutions' educational facilities. However, an exception is still made in the case of educational institutions maintained by a religous corporation or society. This exception applies only to the ban on religious discrimination (not to bans on discrimination on the basis of race, color, sex, or national

Table 2. A Review of Employment Discrimination Legislation and Federal Agencies with Enforcement Authority

Federal agency responsible for enforcement	Laws/orders granting authority to the agency	Agency's scope of authority
Equal Employment Opportunity Commission (EEOC)	1964 Civil Rights Act (78 Stat 241), as amended by 1972 EEO Act (86 Stat 103)	Can bring suits against private employers and labor unions with more than 15 employees. Suits must be preceded by efforts at conciliation and must originate in individual complaints although they may be expanded to pattern and practice suits. All Justice Department authority to bring EEO suits goes to EEOC.
Office of Personnel Management (OPM), formerly Civil Service Commission	1972 EEO Act, ExecOrder 11478 1970 Intergovernmental Personnel Act (84 Stat 1909)	Reviews and approves EEO policies of all federal agencies. Consults with state and local governments to establish and improve merit hiring systems and conducts compliance reviews.
Labor Department, Office of Federal Contract Compliance (OFCC)	ExecOrder 11246, as amended (ExecOrder 11375); Labor Department Revised Order No. 4	Requires all federal contractors with more than $50,000 in contracts to take affirmative action to bring about EEO. Authority delegated by OECC to review contract compliance. Each agency also is responsible for internal EEO, consistent with Civil Service guidelines.
Justice Department, Civil Rights Division	1964 Civil Rights Act, as amended by 1972 EEO Act	Can bring suit where there exists a *prima facie* case of a private employer or labor union with more than 15 employees engaging in a pattern or practice of discrimination. May complete individual complaint suits begun before 1972 Act. Can bring individual as well as pattern and practice suits against agencies of state and local government. (After March 1974, all of this authority was transferred to EEOC.)

origin). Before the 1972 amendments, the exception was restricted to the employment of persons working at religious activities. The amendments broadened the exception to cover all secular, as well as religious, activities of the corporation or society.

Title VII of the Civil Rights Act of 1964 and the Equal Employment Opportunity Act of 1972 thus cover the following types of organizations:

1. All private employers of fifteen or more persons.
2. All educational institutions, both public and private.
3. State and local governments.
4. Public and private employment agencies.
5. Labor unions with fifteen or more members.
6. Joint labor-management committees for apprenticeship and training.

The Age Discrimination in Employment Act of 1967 also allows exceptions from its provisions if the exceptions are based on BFOQs. In order to qualify as a BFOQ exception, a particular age limitation must be required for a job and the requirement must be necessary to the normal operation of a business. The act also provides that the Secretary of Labor, acting in the public interest, may make specific exceptions from the provisions of the act. Retirement, pension, or insurance plans and seniority systems may qualify for exception under the act if they are established in good faith with no intent to evade the law. Such plans will not excuse the failure to hire any worker because of age.

The Equal Pay Act also contains many exceptions. However, these exceptions hold up only when the Equal Pay Act is the basis used for attacking an employment practice. Equal Pay Act exceptions will not necessarily ward off an attack under Title VII. When both Title VII and the Equal Pay Act apply to an employment situation, Title VII provides that its provisions will be harmonized with the Equal Pay Act to avoid conflicting inaterpretations of the law.[9] However, Title VII also applies in cases of sex discrimination not covered by the Equal Pay Act.

In addition to the federal laws described above, state and other federal laws may be used as a basis for attacking employment practices. Minorities may bring suit against employers under:

---

[9]However, a recent ruling by the Ninth Circuit Court of Appeals in *Gunther* v. *County of Washington* may question this issue as well as a case involving Westinghouse Electric.

1. The Fourteenth Amendment to the United States Constitution, which forbids the denial of equal protection of the laws.

2. The Civil Rights Act of 1870, which proscribes racial discrimination under the cover of state law.

3. The Civil Rights Act of 1871, which addresses the right of persons deprived of rights to sue for redress.

In addition, the states have passed laws dealing with employment discrimination. Title VII invalidates state laws that are inconsistent with any of the purposes or provisions of the federal law. However, Title VII will not provide relief from a duty or liability imposed by state law if the state law does not tolerate what would be unlawful under Title VII. Neither will Title VII invalidate a state law provision that is not inconsistent with the federal law, even though employers are thereby subject to more than one set of laws. The provisions of the Equal Pay Act do not excuse noncompliance with any state law establishing higher equal-pay standards than those provided by the federal law. Correspondingly, compliance with a state law will not excuse noncompliance with the Equal Pay Act.

Federal Agencies: Their Enforcement Responsibilities and Powers. The federal agencies involved with Equal Employment Opportunity and their functions have recently been reorganized as summarized in Table 1. The legislation or executive order that grants each agency its enforcement power is shown in Table 2.

Essentially, under the reorganization the Equal Employment Opportunity Coordinating Council was abolished, the EEOC became responsible for coordinating entire federal EEO enforcement effort. Its priority tasks are:

1. Development of consistent EEO standards for entire federal government.

2. Standardization of federal data collecting procedures.

3. Development of standardized government-wide complaint and compliance review methods.

Further, former President Carter issued an executive order consolidating federal contract compliance under the Department of Labor, OFCCP, thus eliminating the eleven separate contract agencies now responsible for enforcement. OFCCP avoided being folded into EEOC as a result of its aggressive enforcement posture in 1977 when it debarred 20 companies from future federal contracts, more than the combined total for the prior 12-year period. EEOC and OFCCP performance will be reviewed in 1981. EEOC has authority to enforce EEO rights for federal employees, previously enforced somewhat loosely by the Civil Service Commission. EEOC has no direct impact on federal contractors. As of July 1, 1979, EEOC has enforcement authority for Equal Pay Act and Age Discrimination in Employment Act. This centralizes federal enforcement of sex discrimination and strengthens EEOC's investigative powers. EEOC will be able to initiate sex discrimination investigations of employers *without prior* complaints or prolonged negotiations.

The impact of reorganization is that employers should benefit from more consistent compliance standards and decreased paperwork. Employers may expect more pattern and practice discrimination suits, more sophisticated investigation procedures, and tougher enforcement.

The standards announced by EEOC for identifying target companies for pattern and practice suits include:

1. Polices resulting in low utilization of available females and minorities.

2. Female and minority work force lower than other companies in same labor market using workers with same skill levels.

3. Large female and minority total work force, but low utilization in higher-paid jobs.

4. Policies not justified by business necessity that result in adverse impact on females and minorities.

5. Restricting employment opportunities for females and minorities (those who have influence over other employers because of size, impact on local economy, or competitive position in their industry.)

6. High turnover and/or expansion companies who are not providing females and minorities with fair access to resulting job opportunities.

The EEOC was established to receive and, on its own initiative, to investigate job-discrimination complaints. Where the Commission finds the charge to be justified, against individuals or against groups, it attempts through conciliation to reach an agreement. Should it fail in its efforts, however, the Commission has the power to go directly into federal court to enforce the law. In addition, interested organizations may also file suits on behalf of individuals or groups who feel that they have been discriminated against by their employers and, in this connection, can claim back pay, damages, and legal fees. Furthermore, an aggrieved individual can also go to court directly to sue an employer for alleged discriminatory practices. The EEOC issues appropriate periodic guidelines to assist companies in making sure that their employment systems are in compliance with the law.

Enforcement powers under the Age Discrimination Act, the Equal Pay Act, and Executive Order 11246 are vested in the Department of Labor. The Wage and Hour Division of the Labor Department is charged with administration of the Equal Pay Act. The Secretary of Labor is charged with administration and enforcement of the Age Act and Executive Order 11246. Under orders from the secretary, the authority and responsibility for administration and enforcement of the Age Act belong to the Wage and Hour Administrator. The Office of Federal Contract Compliance (OFCC) was created to administer and enforce Executive Order 11246. The director of the OFCC has the authority to carry out the Executive Order and the responsibility for coordinating matters relating to Title VII with the EEOC and the Department of Justice.

Executive Orders 11141 and 11478 direct the heads of government departments and agencies to take appropriate action to publicize the government policy against age discrimination. Acting upon the directive, the General Services Administration (GSA) has issued regulations to implement Executive Order 11141. With the reorganization the Department of Labor (DOL) will enforce compliance with Executive Order 11141. Also, although the Civil Service Commission (now the Office of Personnel Management) was charged by the president with the responsibility of providing leadership and guidance in fulfilling the terms of Executive Order 11478, EEOC will now handle this responsibility. The 1972 amendments to Title VII also give the EEOC the authority to investigate alleged violations of the nondiscrimination provisions of Title VII as they apply to federal employees.

To help employers, labor unions, employment agencies, and joint labor-management committees to interpret and complement the law and the executive orders on employee discrimination, the previously mentioned *Guidelines* were issued. In addition, EEOC has issued guidelines on sex discrimination, religious discrimination, national-origin discrimination, and, of course, on testing and selecting employees, as well as recent Affirmative Action Guidelines (January 19, 1979).

The EEOC has also issued a release on prehire inquiries and has issued regulations on reporting and record keeping. The Wage and Hour Division of the Department of Labor has issued regulations on record keeping and interpretative bulletins on equal pay for equal work and on age discrimination. The Secretary of Labor has issued regulations on equal employment opportunity in apprenticeship and training and on the ratio of apprentices to journeymen on federal construction work. The OFCC has issued regulations on the duties of contractors under Executive Order 11246,

on affirmative-action programs by government contractors, and on testing and selecting of employees by government contractors. It has also issued sex-discrimination guidelines. The GSA has issued regulations on equal employment opportunity in several areas, including nondefense procurement contracts and nondiscrimination because of age on such contracts. The Office of Personnel Management has issued regulations on equal federal employment opportunity (see *For Further Reading*).

Executive Orders Number 11246 and 11375 (and Office of Federal Contract Compliance Revised Orders Number 4 and 14) affect all organizations that hold federal contracts. Adherence to these Executive Orders is administered by the Office of Federal Contract Compliance of the United States Department of Labor. These orders apply specifically to contractors and subcontractors with federal contracts in excess of $50,000, or who employ fifty or more people. The orders, once again, prohibit discrimination in employment, but in addition, *also* require that each organization develop and implement affirmative-action programs (discussed in detail below), regularly audited by an assigned federal compliance agency, to remedy the effects of past discriminatory practices.

Specifically, under these presidential orders, a government contractor is required to furnish a results-oriented written commitment for an affirmative-action program together with specific goals and timetables for their attainment. Most significantly, an organization found not to be in compliance with Revised Order Number 4 (which calls for concrete affirmative-action programs) faces the possibility of cancellation of its government contracts.

Avoiding Job Discrimination and Complying with the Laws. Due to the complexity, ambiguity, and number of laws, guidelines and Executive Orders regarding discrimination, compliance is not always a simple matter. Further, laws continue to be changed and interpreted by court decisions, often making earlier decisions and practices of questionable legality. Obviously, the best way to comply with EEO laws would be to develop a rational, systematic set of personnel programs that are job- and performance-based. Translated into actual personnel practice, however, such a system would vary widely across organizations. It would also require considerable and diverse knowledge, skills, and abilities, as previous exercises in this book have pointed out. Many organizations, often due to their small size or their lack of awareness of the laws, simply do not have the expertise to comply in *every* technical sense at this time. However, a considerable amount can be done to help assure compliance; this actually constitutes nothing more than sound personnel practice.

The EEOC specifically advocates the following principles to help avoid discrimination.

1. *A total personnel assessment system.* EEDC advocates systems that are nondiscriminatory within the spirit of the law and places special emphasis on the following:
    a) Careful job analysis to define skill requirements.
    b) Special efforts in recruiting minorities.
    c) Screening and interviewing related to job requirements.
    d) Tests selected on the basis of specific job-related criteria.
    e) Comparison of test performance versus job performance.
    f) Retesting.
    g) Tests which are validated for minorities.

2. *Objective administration of tests.* It is essential that tests be administered by personnel who are skilled not only in technical details, but also in establishing proper conditions for test taking. Members of disadvantaged groups tend to be particularly sensitive in test situations and those giving tests should be aware of this and be able to alleviate a certain amount of anxiety.[10]

What Is "Adverse Impact"? Rather than trying to determine if an employer's practices were designed or intended to be discriminatory, the courts have looked first at the apparent results of discrimination and, secondly, at the procedures and practices that led to these apparent results.[11] The result of apparent discrimination is generally referred to as "adverse impact" and it can be established in several ways. Adverse impact would be concluded, for example, when there are disproportionate representations of minority and nonminority or sex groups among present employees in different types of jobs. Adverse impact would also be concluded upon finding differential rates of selection or corresponding rejection rates for the various minority and nonminority or sex groups applying for different jobs. The selection rate is defined as the number hired compared to the number of applicants for any class covered by Title VII. If the selection rate of applicants from a class covered by Title VII is less than four-fifths (although some judges are using two-thirds), the rate for the remaining applicants, adverse impact is concluded. For instance, if 90 percent of male applicants are selected and 30 percent of female applicants (a covered class) are selected, adverse impact would be concluded because 30 percent is less than four-fifths of 90 percent. However, if 85 percent of the male applicants are selected and 75 percent of the female applicants are selected, adverse impact would not be concluded. Seventy-five percent is more than four-fifths of 85 percent and thus "test bias" is not assumed. According to Hunter and Schmidt most attempts to define bias are based exclusively on use of statistical techniques, a basis that is independent of the content of the test and criterion and makes no *explicit* assumptions about the causal explanations of statistical findings.[12] This approach is without explicit regard to substantive and causal analysis and is "doomed to failure."

Regardless of the use or nonuse of statistical techniques, there are three ethical positions relative to discrimination. The first is *unqualified individualism* which is to give the job to the person best qualified to serve. The second is *quotas,* giving fair shares of jobs based on population percentages. The third is *qualified individualism* which does not predict separately lines for minorities and nonminorities, and instead ignores race (i.e., uses one overall regression line). Each of the three ethical positions uses a different definition of the term discrimination:

> *Unqualified individualism*—"discriminate" means to treat unfairly. If there is a valid difference between races (e.g., not accounted for by available ability tests), then to refuse to recognize this difference is unfair because it penalizes those persons in the higher performing groups.

> *Quota*—"discriminate" means to select a higher proportion of persons from one group than from the other group.

---

[10] As previously noted, the Commission will not recommend any particular test, but adopts the 1966 *Standards for Educational and Psychological Tests and Manuals* (Washington, D.C.: American Psychological Association, 1966), prepared by a joint committee on the American Psychological Association, American Educational Research Association, and National Council on Measurement in Education. The revised (1974) edition of this publication, endorsed by the panel of psychologists consulted by the Commission, was prepared by recognized spokesmen for the profession and establishes standards and technical merits of evaluation procedures.

[11] This approach may be somewhat in debate, given recent rulings in *Washington* v. *Davis* and *Furnco* v. *Waters* over the intent as opposed to results issue.

[12] F. L. Schmidt and J. E. Hunter. Adapted from H. G. Heneman, "Research Roundup," *The Personnel Administrator* (May 1977): 58–59. Readings in this area should also include: T. A. Cleary, "Test bias: Prediction of Grades of Negro and White Students in Integrated Colleges," *Journal of Educational Measurement* (1968): 115–124; R. B. Darlington, "Another Look at 'Cultural Fairness,'" *Journal of Educational Measurement* 8 (1971): 71–82; R. L. Thorndike, "Concepts of Culture-Fairness," *Journal of Educational Measurement* 8 (1971): 63–70.

Qualified individualism—"discriminate" means means to treat differentially. Blacks and whites are treated differently even if it is statistically warranted that they not be.

Thus it can be seen that with different definitions, each of the three ethical types would suggest different practices.

Hunter and Schmidt also offer several types of statistical definitions of *test fairness:*

1. *Cleary's definition:* A test is unbiased only if the regression lines for minorities and nonminorities are identical (see Fig. 1).

2. *Thorndike's definition:* This begins with assumption that the slopes of the two regression lines are equal. If the regression line for minorities is higher than for nonminorities, the test is unfair to the minority group. If the regression line for nonminorities is higher, the test is not labeled as unfair to nonminorities. (All of which causes operational problems, so Thorndike's operational results are very much like a quota system).

3. *Darlington's definition:* This is an esoteric way of setting quotas by "doctoring" criterion scores (*not* predictor scores). The remedy is to subtract a constant from nonminority test scores (to provide a culturally optimum test result).

Each ethical and statistical approach has advantages and disadvantages, and Hunter and Schmidt discuss these in detail. They conclude:

1. The several different ethical approaches are irreconcilable.

2. The scientific principles used to justify the statistical procedures vary considerably in their plausibility among varying real life situations.

3. Any purely statistical approach to the problem of test bias is doomed to rather immediate failure.

4. There may be no way to resolve the above problems objectively. Each person must make his or her own explicit choice depending on his or her

values and beliefs. (However, the legislative history of EEO does offer some hope. For example, see the *Griggs* decision.)

Adverse impact can also be demonstrated by statistically significant differences in selection rates: For large numbers of applicants, it can be more sensitive than the four-fifths rule of thumb. There are statistical tools available for assessing the statistical significance of differences in proportions of percentages.[13] Employers would be well advised to perform these statistical analyses to see if, in fact, the tests (and "nontest" standards such as interviews) being used are disqualifying a statistically significant greater percentage of minorities. If not, the government guidelines do not require submission of evidence of validity.

Finally, it has been attempted to demonstrate adverse impact by merely comparing an organization's employment profile with Standard Metropolitan Statistical Area (SMSA) population or external labor market availability data. Obviously, these data could be treated statistically, but judges may not find the need to do so, as has been the case in recent decisions.[14]

The legal conclusion of unfair discrimination is based on two conditions being established, one by the charging party and one by the respondent in Title VII cases. If a charging party can establish that an employer's hiring, transfer, promotion, membership, training, referral, or retention practices result in adverse impact on an individual or a class protected by Title VII, the court then places the burden of proof on the respondent employer for evidence that the selection procedure having adverse impact is job related or is predictive of performance on the job. This is, of course, the demonstration of evidence for validity. A validation study of job relatedness of any selection procedure found to have adverse impact is the first rebuttal by a Title VII respondent employer to a charge of discrimination. If a respondent cannot convince the court that the selection procedure resulting in adverse impact is job related, then the court may conclude that unfair discrimination has been established. If, on the other hand, the respondent can convince the court that a selection procedure resulting in adverse impact is based on related considerations of competence not equally possessed by all groups covered by Title VII, the fact

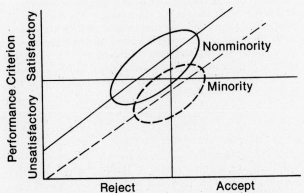

Fig. 1. An example of Cleary's unequal regression lines

---

[13] See any introductory statistics text and/or relevant references listed in *For Further Reading,* Exercise 9.

[14] See, for example, *International Brotherhood of Teamsters* v. *United States,* 431 U.S. 324, 14 FEP Cases at 1521 (1977); *Furnco Construction Corp.* v. *Waters,* 438 U.S. 567, 17 FEP Cases 1062, 1063 (June 29, 1978); *Hazelwood School District* v. *United States,* 15 FEP Cases 1, 10 (1977); and EEOC v. *Radiator Specialty Company,* 78-1291 (4th Cir. 1979).

that adverse impact is found may be moot, provided the employer can demonstrate that selection procedures having a lesser adverse impact are unavailable for use. One of the ways an employer can demonstrate that such alternative procedures (e.g., different types of tests) having lesser adverse impact are unavailable is to show that when a choice was made between several alternative procedures, all having validity, the final choice was based on that procedure having the least adverse impact on protected or covered groups.

The legal conclusion of disallowed or illegal discrimination thus is based on a showing of adverse impact by a charging party and lack of unacceptable evidence of job relatedness on the part of the respondent employer. Table 3 presents some examples of lawful and unlawful inquiries made in selection. As you can see, many "standard" inquiries *can* be unlawful.

Testing and Discrimination. In defining the scope of practices covered, "the term 'test' is defined as any pencil-and-paper or performance measure used as a basis for any promotion decision." Also included in the definition of tests are "formal scored quantified or standardized techniques of assessing job suitability including specific qualifying or disqualifying personal history or background requirements, specific educational or work history requirements and scored interviews." Unscored interviews are also covered if the interview is part of an employer's selection procedure that results in adverse impact on a class of applicants covered by Title VII. Thus, the chance of violating the law can come from any number of practices, such as performance appraisals or interviews, in addition to pencil-and-paper tests themselves. As stressed throughout these exercises, each personnel activity must therefore be designed properly and be job related.

Establishing valid selection practices, as discussed in detail in Exercise 9, is a difficult and often time-consuming activity. It is, however, a necessary one and can be facilitated by the other personnel programs. The two types of criterion-related validity, predictive and concurrent validities (see Exercise 9), would be the type of evidence accepted from an employer by a court if discriminatory practices were charged. In conducting such validation studies, several important guidelines must be followed, such as the use of a large enough sample size and the proper administration of any tests.[15]

Five primary considerations in conducting a criterion-related validation are noted in the *Guidelines.*

1. The sample of subjects must be representative of the normal or typical candidate group for the job or jobs in question in the local labor market.

2. Tests must be administered and scored under controlled and standardized conditions, with proper

safeguards to protect the security of test scores and to insure the scores do not enter into any judgments of employee adequacy that are to be used as criterion measures.

3. The work behaviors or other criteria of employee adequacy which the test is intended to predict or identify must be fully described. Such criteria may include measures other than actual work proficiency—such as training time, supervisory ratings, regularity of attendance, and tenure. Whatever criteria are used, they must represent major or critical work behaviors as revealed by careful job analysis. With respect to using standards for higher jobs than the one the person is being selected for, if job progression structures and seniority provisions are so established that new employees will probably, within a reasonable period of time and in a great majority of cases, progress to a higher level, it may be considered that candidates are being evaluated for jobs at that higher level. However, where job progression is not nearly automatic or the time spent is such that higher-level jobs or employees' potential may be

---

[15] See American Psychological Association *Standards,* and relevant references in *For Further Reading.* Also it should be noted that the common assumptions about sample size (i.e., from 30 to 100) may be gross underestimates as shown from the following calculation:

Assuming an equal number in each group, the sample size required in each group is given by

$$N = \frac{2(Z_2 - Z_1)^2}{E(d_{fz})^2} + 3$$

where

N = the number required in each group,

Z_1 = the Z score corresponding to the desired level of power ($Z_1 = -1.28$ for power of .90),

Z_2 = the Z score corresponding to the alpha level ($Z_2 = 1.96$ when alpha = .05, two-tailed), and

$E(d_{fz})$ = the expected value of the difference between the two correlations is Fisher's Z formula.

For illustration, consider the case in which the desired statistical power is .90 and the test is two-tailed. The reliability of both measures is .70 and the first true r is .30 while the second is .50. The expected computed value of the first correlation is $.30\sqrt{.70}\sqrt{.70} = .21$. In Fisher's Z this is .213. The expected computed value for the second correlation r is $.50\sqrt{.70}\sqrt{.70} = .35$. In Fisher's Z form, this is .365. Therefore, $E(d_{fz}) = .365 - .213 = .152$. We then obtain

$$N = \frac{2[1.96 - (-1.28)]^2}{(.152)^2} + 3 = 912$$

Obviously, there are very few instances where sample sizes reach one thousand.

Source: F. L. Schmidt and J. E. Hunter, "Moderator Research and the Law of Small Numbers," *Personnel Psychology* 31 (1978): 215–232.

expected to change in significant ways, it shall be considered that candidates are being evaluated for a job at or near the entry level.

4. Supervisory rating techniques should be carefully developed and the ratings should be closely examined for evidence of bias.

5. Differential validity data must be generated and results separately reported for minority and non-minority groups whenever technically feasible.

Evidence of content or construct validity as defined in the *APA Standards* may be utilized. In effect, the *Guidelines* have explicitly recognized parity among validity strategies. However, evidence for content or construct validity should be accompanied by sufficient information from a job analysis to demonstrate the relevance of the content in the case of job knowledge or proficiency, or the relevance of the construct in the case of measures of personality traits or characteristics.[16] According to the *Guidelines* evidence of content validity alone may be acceptable for well-developed tests that consist of suitable samples of the essential knowledge, skills, or behaviors composing the job in question. It must be cautioned that the types of knowledge, skills, or behaviors contemplated here do not include those that can be acquired in a brief orientation to the job.

A final note on discriminatory practices: If an organization's selection procedures show no "adverse impact" (i.e., this organization is not discriminatory), there is no legal requirement that they validate selection procedures. It should also be noted that previously it was assumed that any method could be used to discriminate against white males, but recent cases involving the fourteenth amendment may have changed this.

Affirmative Action. Federal equal-employment opportunity laws now require federal contractors to take positive steps to assure that current practices are nondiscriminatory and that any continuing effects of past discrimination be erased. Affirmative action, as called for by Executive Orders No. 11246 and 11375, is the method by which the employer, contractor, or party administering an apprenticeship program insures that those positive steps have been, are being, or will be taken to achieve equal employment opportunity.

Affirmative action was ambiguously defined in Presidential Executive Orders No. 11246 and 11375 in

that it "required companies contracting with the federal government to take affirmative action to recruit and promote minorities and females," but the order did not spell out what affirmative action meant or what obligations such contractors would have. Revised Order No. 4, issued under President Nixon, defined contractors' obligations and established how an affirmative-action program should be developed. Affirmative-action programs are now being used by the EEOC as a remedy where a complaint has been filed and a pattern or practice of discrimination has taken place. As previously noted, new affirmative action guidelines were issued by EEOC in 1979.

Many companies have had an explicit or implicit nondiscrimination policy; so an affirmative-action program can be viewed not as a new policy, but rather as a continuation of an existing one with a new and stronger emphasis. A company has four avenues open in developing a nondiscriminatory policy. The first is *passive nondiscrimination,* or a willingness in all decisions regarding hiring, promotion, and pay to treat the sexes and races alike. Second, *pure affirmative action* involves a concerted effort to expand the pool of applicants, so no one is excluded because of past or present discrimination. Third is *affirmative action with preferential hiring,* which means the company has a large labor pool and systematically favors women and minority-group members.[17] The final alternative, *hard quotas,* implies that a specific number or proportion of minority-group members must be hired. Quotas, unless imposed by a court, have been found to be illegal.[18]

The government's objective in establishing affirmative action is based on the second alternative, but the real issue involved probably concerns the affirmative-action programs stated in the third alternative. In other words, perhaps the best way to ensure that *everything* possible is being done to eliminate discrimination

---

[16] For a discussion of the different types of validity, see Exercises 9 and 17; *For Further Reading;* and C. E. Schneier, "Content Validity: The Necessity of a Behavioral Job Description," *The Personnel Administrator* 21, no. 2 (1976): 38–44.

[17] Recently, federal courts found that certain types of preferential treatment in promotion or selection when done under policies of an affirmative-action program, may be legal. Thus, "reverse discrimination" has been held to be illegal. However, these decisions will no doubt be appealed by the organizations involved, and a Supreme Court ruling may be necessary. The potential illegality of reverse discrimination leaves organizations in an ambiguous position regarding EEO and stresses the tentative nature of EEO guidelines and laws and their continually emerging status. The necessity of both a completely job-related personnel system, as well as requiring personnel professionals to keep abreast of latest developments in EEO, cannot be overstated.

[18] This was determined in a March 23, 1973 agreement among the Department of Justice, United States Civil Service Commission, Equal Employment Opportunity Commission, and the Office of Federal Contract Compliances.

Table 3. General Guidelines to Lawful and Unlawful Employment Practices*

Types of inquiries of job applicants typically made by employers in selection	Lawful practice(s) related to inquiry	Possibly unlawful practice(s) related to inquiry
1. Name	Inquiry as to full name. "Have you worked for this organization under a different name? Is any additional information relative to change of name or nickname necessary to enable a check on your work and educational record? If yes, explain."	Inquiry into any title that indicates race, color, religion, sex, national origin, or ancestry.
2. Address	Inquiry into place and length of current and previous addresses.	Specific inquiry into foreign addresses that would indicate national origin.
3. Sex	Inquiry to establish BFOQ	Any inquiry that would indicate sex.
4. Religion/creed	Inquiry to establish BFOQ	a) Any inquiry to indicate or identify denation or customs. b) May not be told this is a Protestant, Catholic, or Jewish organization. c) Request of a recommendation or reference from someone in clergy.
5. Birthplace or national origin	Inquiry to establish BFOQ	a) Any inquiry into place of birth. b) Any inquiry into place of birth of parents, grandparents, or spouse. c) Any other inquiry into national origin.
6. Race or color	Inquiry to establish BFOQ	Any inquiry that would indicate race or color.
7. Citizenship	a) Whether or not a U.S. citizen. b) If not, whether intends to become one. c) If U.S. residence is legal. d) If spouse is citizen. e) Require proof of citizenship after being hired.	a) If native-born or naturalized. b) Proof of citizenship before hiring. c) Whether parents or spouse are native-born or naturalized.
8. Age	a) Request proof of age in form of work permit issued by school authorities. b) Require proof of age by birth certificate after hiring.	Require birth certificate or baptismal record before hiring.
9. Photographs	May be required *after* hiring for identification purposes.	Require photograph *before* hiring.
10. Education	a) Inquiry into what academic, professional, or vocational schools attended. b) Inquiry into language skills, such as reading and writing of foreign languages.	a) Any inquiry asking specifically the nationality, racial, or religious affiliation of a school. b) Inquiry as to what is mother tongue or how foreign-language ability was acquired, unless necessary for job.
11. Relatives	Inquiry into name, relationship, and address of person to be notified in case of emergency.	Any inquiry about a relative that is unlawful (e.g., race or religion inquiries).

12. Organization	a) Inquiry into organization memberships, excluding any organization the name or character of which indicates the race, color, religion, sex, national origin, or ancestry of its members. b) What offices are held, if any.	Inquiry into all clubs and organizations where membership is held.
13. Military service	a) Inquiry into service in U.S. Armed Forces. b) Rank attained. c) Which branch of service. d) Require military discharge certificate after being hired.	a) Inquiry into military service in armed service of any country but United States. b) Request military service records.
14. Work schedule	Inquiry into willingness to work required work schedule.	Any inquiry into willingness to work any any particular religious holiday.
15. Other qualifications	Any question that has a direct reflection (i.e., can be shown to be job related) on the job to be applied for.	Any non-job-related inquiry that may present information permitting unlawful discrimination.
16. References	General personal and work references not relating to race, color, religion, sex, national origin, or ancestry.	Request references specifically from clergymen or any other persons who might reflect race, color, religion, sex, national origin, or ancestry of applicant.
17. Experience	Applicant's work experience. Other countries visited.	
18. Notice in case of emergency	Names of persons to be notified.	Name and address of relative to be notified in case of accident or emergency.
19. Credit rating	None.	Any questions concerning credit rating, charge accounts, etc.
20. Miscellaneous	Notice to applicants that any misstatement or omissions of material facts in the application may be cause for dismissal.	
21. Marital and family status	Whether applicant can meet specified work schedules or has activities, commitments, or responsibilities that may hinder the meeting of work attendance requirements. Inquiries as to a duration to stay on job or as to anticipated absences that are made to males and and females alike.	Any inquiries indicating whether an applicant is married, single, divorced, engaged, etc. Number and age of children. Any questions concerning pregnancy. Any such question that directly or indirectly results in limitation of job opportunity in any way.
22. Handicaps	Whether applicant has any handicaps or health problems either sensory, mental, or physical that may affect work performance or that the employer should consider in determining job placement.	General inquiries (i.e., "Do you have any any handicaps?") that would tend to divulge handicaps or health conditions that do not relate reasonably to fitness to perform the job.

* This table was developed after the general guidelines used by a state government as taken from the *Guidelines*.

is to develop and vigorously implement an affirmative-action plan (in addition to a job-related personnel system for all employees). Such a plan can be a valuable management tool, as well as a means to comply with the law. Even the process of developing a plan can be an extraordinarily useful diagnostic management activity. Such diagnoses include the following: a review to determine if the organization is employing blacks, Spanish-speaking Americans, American Indians, women, and members of other minority groups in quantities that make sense in terms of the availability of qualified members of these groups (see *Hazelwood* case cited on page 524) in the labor supply; an examination to discover if minority-group members and women are clustered in lower-level jobs with little opportunity to advance to better-paying positions; and a close scrutiny of policies, procedures, and practices that may tend to favor one group over another. All of these analyses can be helpful to management in improving the organization's ability to get the best qualified people to serve its clients or customers.

Goals, Timetables, and Quotas. Once the affirmative-action plan is developed, it can serve as the basic management guide to action, providing it has enough specificity to be meaningful. Managers and supervisors at all levels can use it to guide their actions and measure their progress. The plan should provide for the establishment of reasonable employment goals for certain groups (i.e., to increase minority employment by actively seeking minority members and perhaps changing recruiting practices), as distinguished from mandatory *quotas* (i.e., to have 14 percent black managers within one year).[19] It can call for deadlines by which certain programs (such as special recruiting programs of training programs) can be initiated or completed. These goals and timetables are appropriate for problem areas, for they will encourage progress. Areas for affirmative action might be those organizations, localities, occupations, and grade levels where minority and female employment does not come up to reasonable expectations in view of the supply of qualified minority-group members or women in the recruiting areas and the availability of job opportunities.

In large organizations, numerical goals (to be distinguished from hard quotas) should be developed at the divisional, departmental, and organizational level—rather than on a broader level—in order to take into account special circumstances. In this way, detailed statistics on minority groups and women will aid in identifying areas where additional affirmative action is required and can be translated into specific action plans for the level or component concerned. To be valid, goals and timetables must be closely aligned with estimated turnover data and anticipated hiring, as well as estimated changes in the total number of positions by job classification for the period covered by the timetable.

Goals can be qualitative as well as quantitative. For example, an organization that has lost a substantial proportion of minority employees through turnover or layoff due to union seniority provisions may find that its climate for employment of minorities is poor. In such a case, new goals might include attempts to improve the attitude of other employees and supervisors toward acceptance of a minority group; to provide more effective orientation and motivation of new employees; to evaluate and improve training operations; or to strengthen grievance and discrimination appeal processes. An affirmative-action plan should establish specific steps leading toward achievement of these goals.

As with other management programs, an affirmative-action program needs periodic evaluation. Evaluation of operations may result in the conclusion that a greater number of minority-group employees should be employed throughout the organization or one of its components. In other situations, the component may have acceptable program results overall, but improvements may be needed in certain locations, divisions, grades, or occupations. Evaluations should lead to new updated goals and target progress dates based on the needs of the program.

Affirmative Action: Illustrative Court Cases. Some important recent EEO cases include the Supreme Court Decision in *Albemarle Paper Co.* v. *Moody*[20] that back pay can be awarded in an employment testing case, even though no bad faith is established on the part of the employer. Albemarle had failed to meet EEOC's standards for adequate empirical validations which reaffixed the use of the 1970 *EEOC Guidelines* (although a reading of the opinions would seem to indicate that the Court is less than totally enamored of the earlier *Guidelines*).

A second case is that of *Douglas* v. *Hampton*,[21] which involved the U.S. Civil Service Commission (now the Office of Personnel Management). The issue was whether employers must show that *predictive*

---

[19] Often the goals and timetables are set relative to the population. Obviously, local SMSAs are also considered.

[20] *Albemarle Paper Co.,* v. *Moody,* 95 S. Ct. 2362, 2379 (1975).

[21] *Douglas* v. *Hampton,* D.C. Circuit Court of Appeals, 512 F. 2nd. 976, 1975.

validation studies (see Exercise 9) are infeasible before they can defend the validity of the test on other grounds. At least for the moment, the *Guidelines* have received another nod from the courts.

Finally, a less well-known case with enormous implications is that of *Brito* v. *Zia*,[22] which was decided in the Tenth Circuit Court of Appeals. In this case, the court held that the Zia Company's employee performance evaluations, used for lay-off, were, in fact, *tests* under the meaning of *EEOC Guidelines* and were thus subject to empirical validation as required by EEOC. This decision, of course, brings performance appraisal practices under the impact of EEO laws, as discussed in Exercise 4.

Two recent EEOC cases are worth noting. Although women lost in the United States Supreme Court on the treatment of pregnancy-related disabilities like other sickness and accident disabilities under disability income insurance plans, Congress took up the women's position and passed legislation defining pregnancy as a disability.[23] The Davis case involved both the use of aptitude testing in employment as a tool for making decisions purely on merit, and the extent, if any, to which training success can be a criterion of test "job relatedness." The courts held that training criterion was adequate wholly aside from showing relationship of training performance to job performance.[24]

Thus, EEO laws are having an increasingly large impact on personnel programs. These programs include not only selection, but also training, wage and salary administration, and performance appraisal, to name a few. The modern personnel administrator and his or her staff must be knowledgeable both in the laws themselves and in the design and implementation of programs to facilitate compliance.

PROCEDURE

Overview. First, you will become familiar with EEO issues through a self-quiz and a method of determining "adverse impact." You will then be given completed information on an organization's affirmative-action program. You are to evaluate the program and present your evaluation to the organization's managing com-

mittee. Finally, you construct affirmative-action programs in increasing levels of sophistication.

PART A

STEP 1: Form 1 provides a series of questions about EEO and affirmative action. You are to place a check in the column you believe is appropriate. Discuss your answers in a small group and then listen to the correct answers given by your implementor.

STEP 2: Form 2 asks you to determine if "adverse impact" has been witnessed for persons who are members of protected groups under current guidelines. Assume that the minimum selection ratio is 4/5 for each stage in the selection process. You are to determine if "adverse impact" was observed. If so, what must now be done, given that the first of two steps in demonstrating that job discrimination exists has been completed? (Refer to *Introduction.*)

TIME: About 55 minutes.

PART B

STEP 3: In Form 3 you are to assess the data and discuss how you believe the organization stands in terms of its affirmative action status. Specifically what actions would you recommend?

STEP 4: In Form 4 you are to review the transition matrix provided for females from 1976 to 1981. What success and problems do you observe and what actions would you recommend the organization take to avoid any adverse consequences?

TIME: About one to one and one-half hours.

PART C

STEP 5: Littleco is an assembly plant in a southern metropolitan area. Small groups, each representing the personnel department, are to construct the company's affirmative-action proposal (Form 11) and make oral and written reports to the managing committee of this small organization. Your group is to use Form 5 to assess the current job levels of the minority and women employees of Littleco and show how the affirmative-action program should be advanced. Include recommended changes for job levels in the analysis on Form 11 by using the Littleco employment profiles (Forms 6, 7, 8, and 9). Form 10 pro-

---

[22] *Brito* v. *Zia Company,* 478 F. 2d 1200 (1973).

[23] *General Electric Co.* v. *Gilbert,* Docket No. 74–1589. This same issue is also presented in *Liberty Mutual Insurance Co.* v. *Wetzel.* Docket No. 74–1245. The Court will decide the two cases together.

[24] *Washington* v. *Davis,* Docket No. 74–1492.

vides information on labor market availability of each job category.

TIME: About one and one-half hours for analysis and to 50 minutes for presentation.

FOR FURTHER READING*

American Psychological Association, Taskforce on Employment and Testing of Minority Groups. "Job Testing and the Disadvantaged." *American Psychologist* 24 (1969): 637–650. (II)

Baughman, E. E. *Black Americans: A Psychological Analysis.* New York: Macmillan, 1971. (II)

Beatty, R. W. "A Two-Year Study of the Effect of Basic Education, Job Skill, and Self-Esteem with the Job Success of the Hard-Core Unemployed." *Personnel Psychology* (1975): 165–174. (II–R)

Beatty, R. W. "Supervisory Behavior Related to Hard-Core Unemployed Job Success over a Two-Year Period." *Journal of Applied Psychology* 57 (1974): 38– 42. (II–R)

Beatty, R. W. "Blacks as Supervisors: A Study of Training, Job Performance, and Employers' Expectations." *Academy of Management Journal* 16 (1973): 196–206. (II–R)

Beatty, R. W. "First and Second Level Supervision and the Job Performance of the Hard-Core Unemployed." *Proceedings of the American Psychological Association Annual Meetings,* Washington, D.C., 1971. (II–R)

Beatty, R. W., M. W. Holloway, and C. E. Schneier. "Making Organizations Humane and Productive for Minorities." In *Handbook on Making Organizations Humane and Productive.* W. Nord and H. Meltzer, eds. New York: John Wiley & Sons, in press.

Beatty, R. W., and C. E. Schneier. "Reducing Welfare Roles through Employment: The Changes Required in Society, Organizations, and Individuals." *The Forensic Quarterly* 41, no. 3 (1973): 380–390. (I)

Bell, D. "Bonuses, Quotas, and the Employment of Black Workers." *Journal of Human Resources* 6 (1971): 304–320. (II)

Bem, S. L., and D. J. Bem. "Does Sex-Biased Job Advertising 'Aid and Abet' Sex Discrimination?" *Journal of Applied Psychology* 5 (1973): 6–18. (II–R)

Bloch, H. R., and R. L. Pennington. "Measuring Discrimination; What Is the Relevant Labor Market." *Personnel* 57 (1980): 21–29. (I)

Bloom, L. Z., K. Cobunn, and J. Pearlman. *The New Assertive Woman.* New York: Delacorte, 1975. (I)

Boyle, M. B. "Equal Opportunity for Women is Smart Business." *Harvard Business Review* 51 (May–June 1973): 85–95. (I)

Brummet, R. L., W. C. Pyle, and E. G. Flamholtz. "Human Resource Accounting in Industry." *Personnel Administration* (July–August 1969). (I)

Business Week. "Up the Ladder, Finally." 24 November 1975, pp. 58–68. (I)

Connolly, W. B. *A Practical Guide to Equal Employment Opportunity: Laws, Principles, and Practices.* Vols. 1 and 2. New York: Law Journal Press, 1975. (I)

Doeringer, P., ed. *Programs to Employ the Disadvantaged.* Englewood Cliffs, N.J.: Prentice-Hall, 1969. (I)

Dowey, L. M. "Women in Labor Unions." *Monthly Labor Review* 94 (1971): 42–48. (I)

Equal Employment Opportunity Commission. *Personnel Testing and Equal Employment Opportunity.* Washington, D.C.: U.S. Government Printing Office, 1970. (I)

Equal Employment Opportunity Court Cases. U.S. Civil Service Commission Bureau of Intergovernmental Personnel Programs. Washington, D.C.: U.S. Government Printing Office, March 1974. (I)

Erickson, J. R., and K. S. McGovern. *Equal Employment Practice Guide.* Committee on Equal Employment Opportunity of the Council on Labor Law and Labor Relations, Federal Bar Association, March, 1979. (I)

Falk, C. "Backtracking on Job Bias?" *Wall Street Journal,* February 9, 1978. (I)

Farr, J. L., B. S. O'Leary, and C. J. Bartlett. "Ethnic Group Membership as a Moderator of Job Performance." *Personnel Psychology* 24 (1971): 604–636. (II–R)

Federal Register. "Part 60–3—Employee Testing and Other Selection Procedures." January 17, 1974. Vol. 39, no. 12. (II)

Federal Register. "Adoption of Questions and Answers to Clarify and Provide a Common Interpretation of the Uniform Guidelines on Employee Selection Procedures." March 2, 1979. Vol. 44, No. 43. (II)

Federal Register. "Affirmative Action Guidelines—Technical Amendments to the Procedural Regulations." January 19, 1979, Part XI, Vol. 44, no. 14. (II)

Goldberg, P. "Are Women Prejudiced against Women?" *Transaction* 5 (1968): 28–31. (I)

Goodman, P., and P. Salipante. "Organizational Rewards and Retention of the Hard-Core Unemployed." *Journal of Applied Psychology* 61 (1976): 12–21. (II–R)

---

* See also *For Further Reading,* Exercise 9.

Goodman, P., P. Salipante, and H. Paransky. "Hiring, Training, and Retaining the Hard-Core Unemployed: A Selected Review." *Journal of Applied Psychology* 58 (1973): 23–33. (II)

Greenman, R. L., and E. J. Schmertz. *Personnel Administration and the Law.* Washington, D.C.: Bureau of National Affairs, Inc., 1972. (I)

Guion, R. M. "Content Validity in Moderation." *Personnel Psychology* 31, no. 2 (Summer 1978): 205–213.

Guion, R. M. "Content Validity—The Source of My Discontent." *Applied Psychological Measurement* 1 (1977): 1–10. (II–R)

Hall, F. S., and M. H. Albrecht. *The Management of Affirmative Action.* Santa Monica, Cal.: Goodyear, 1979. (I)

Heinen, J. S. et al. "Developing the Woman Manager." *Personnel Journal* 54 (1975): 282–286.

Higgins, J. M. "The Complicated Process of Establishing Goals for Equal Employment." *Personnel Journal* 54 (December 1975): 631–637. (I)

Hodgson, J. D. "Title 41—Public Contracts and Property Management: Part 60–3—Employee Testing and Other Selection Procedures." *Federal Register* (36F.R. 7532), 1971. (I)

Horgan, N. J. "Upgrading Underqualified Minority Workers." *Personnel* 49 (January–February 1972): 59–64. (I)

Hunter, J. E., and F. L. Schmidt. "Critical Analysis of the Statistical and Ethical Implications of Various Definitions of Test Bias." *Psychological Bulletin* 33, no. 6 (1976): 1053–1071. (II–R)

Hunter, J. E., F. L. Schmidt, and J. M. Rauschenberger. "Fairness of Psychological Tests: Implications of Four Definitions for Selection Utility and Minority Hiring." *Journal of Applied Psychology* 62, no. 3 (1977): 245–260. (II–R)

Janger, A. *Employing the Disadvantaged: A Company Perspective.* New York: Conference Board, 1972. (I)

Job Discrimination Handbook. Waterford, Conn.: Bureau of Business Practice, 1974. (I)

Jones, E. H. *Blacks in Business.* New York: Grosset, 1971. (I)

Karp, W. "Steer Clear of Job Discrimination Suits." *Management Digest* (July 1979): 25–28. (I)

Kilberg, W. J. "Progress and Problems in Equal Employment Opportunity." *Labor Law Journal* 24, no. 10 (October 1973): 651–661. (I)

Levine, M. J. *The Untapped Human Resource: The Urban Negroes and Employment Reality.* Morristown, N.J.: General Learning Press, 1972.

Loring, R., and T. Wells, *Breakthrough: Women in Management.* New York: Van Nostrand, 1972. (I)

McBee, M. L., and K. A. Blake, eds. *The American Woman: Who Will She Be?* Beverly Hills, Cal.: Glencoe, 1974. (I)

McGovern, K., ed. *Equal Employment Practice Guide.* Committee on Equal Employment and Collective Bargaining of the Council on Labor Law and Labor Relations, Federal Bar Association, October, 1978. (I)

Mennerick, L. A. "Organizational Structuring of Sex Roles in a Nonstereotyped Industry." *Administrative Science Quarterly* 20 (1975): 570–586. (II–R)

Montagu, A. *The Natural Superiority of Women.* Rev. ed. New York: Macmillan, 1970. (I)

Nasen, R. W. "The Dilemma of Black Mobility in Management." *Business Horizons* 15, no. 4 (1972): 57–68. (I)

O'Leary, V. E. *Toward Understanding Women.* Monteray, Cal.: Brooks/Cole, 1979. (I)

Ornati, O. A., and E. Giblin. "The High Cost of Discrimination." *Business Horizons* 17 (February 1975): 35–40. (I)

Ornati, O. A., and A. Pisano. "Affirmative Action: Why Isn't It Working?" *The Personnel Administrator* 17 (September–October 1972): 50–52. (I)

Osipow, S. H., ed. *Emerging Woman: Career Analysis and Outlooks.* Columbus: Merrill, 1975. (I)

Padfield, H. *Stay Where You Are: A Study of Unemployables in Industry.* Philadelphia: Lippincott, 1973. (I)

Pati, G. C., and P. E. Fahey. "Affirmative Action Programs: Its Realities and Challenges." *Law Labor Journal* 24, no. 6 (June 1973). (I)

Pearson, D. W. "OFCC and EEOC Demands—Guidelines to Frustration." *The Personnel Administrator* 18 (November–December 1973): 21–25. (I)

Pendergrass, V. E. et al. "Sex Discrimination Counseling." *American Psychologist* 31 (1976): 36–46. (I)

Perry, L. W. "The Mandate and Impact of Title VII." *Labor Law Journal* 26 (December 1975): 743–749. (I)

Purcell, T. V., and G. F. Cavanagh. "Blacks in the Industrial World: Issues for the Manager." New York: Free Press, 1972. (I)

Rosen, B., and T. H. Jerdee. "Influences of Sex Role Stereotypes on Personnel Decisions." *Journal of Applied Psychology* 59 (1974): 9–14. (II–R)

Rosen, B., and T. H. Jerdee. "Sex Stereotyping in the Executive Suite." *Harvard Business Review* 52 (1974): 45–58. (I)

Salipante, P., and P. Goodman. "Training, Counseling, and Retention of the Hard-Core Unemployed." *Journal of Applied Psychology* 61 (1976): 1–11. (II–R)

Sargent, A. G. *The Androgynous Manager,* New York: AMACOM, 1981. (I)

Schein, V. E. "Relationships between Sex Role Stereotypes and Requisite Management Characteristics among Female Managers." *Journal of Applied Psychology* 60 (1975): 340–344. (II–R)

Schmidt, F. L., and J. E. Hunter. "Moderator Research and the Law of Small Numbers." *Personnel Psycyhology* 31 (1978): 215–232. (II–R)

Schmidt, F. L., and J. E. Hunter. "The Future of Criterion-Related Validity Studies in Title VII Employment Discrimination Cases." *The Personnel Administrator* 22, no. 9 (1977): 39–42. (I)

Schneier, C. E. "Content Validity: The Necessity of a Behavioral Job Description." *The Personnel Administrator* 21, no. 2 (1976): 38–44. (I)

Schneier, C. E. "Behavior Modification: Training the Hard-Core Unemployed." *Personnel* 50, no. 3 (1973): 65–69. (I)

Seligman, D. "How Equal Opportunity Turned into Employment Quotas." *Fortune* 87, no. 3 (March 1973): 160–168. (I)

Sharf, J. "Facing Reverse Discrimination." *American Psychologist* 32 (March 1977): 6, 21. (I)

Smith, L. " 'Equal Opportunity' Rules Are Getting Tougher." *Fortune* 97, no. 12 (June 1978): 152–156. (I)

Smith, L. "What's It Like for Women Executives?" *Dun's Review* 106 (December 1975): 58–61. (I)

Sowell, T. "Affirmative Action Reconsidered." *Public Interest* 42 (Winter 1976): 47–65. (I)

Swanson, S. G. "The Effect of the Supreme Court's Seniority Decisions." *Personnel Journal* 56, no. 12 (December 1977): 625–627. (I)

Sweet, J. A. *Women in the Labor Force.* New York: Seminar, 1973. (I)

U.S. Civil Service Commission. *Equal Employment Opportunity Counseling: A Guidebook.* Rev. ed. (Prepared by office of Federal Equal Employment Opportunity.) Washington, D.C.: U.S. Government Printing Office, 1975. (I)

U.S. Civil Service Commission. *Guidelines for the Development of an Affirmative Action Plan.* (Prepared by Bureau of Intergovernmental Personnel Programs.) Washington, D.C.: U.S. Government Printing Office, 1975. (I)

U.S. Equal Employment Opportunity Commission. *A Directory of Resources for Affirmative Recruitment.* Washington, D.C.: U.S. Government Printing Office, 1975. (I)

U.S. News and World Report. "The American Woman." 8 December 1975, pp. 54–64+. (I)

Van Dusen, R. A., and E. B. Sheldon. "The Changing Status of American Women." *American Psychologist* 31 (1976): 106–116. (I)

Vetter, L. "Career Counseling for Women." *The Counseling Psychologist* 4 (1973): 54–67. (I)

Waldman, E., and B. J. McEddy. "Where Women Work—An Analysis by Industry and Occupation." *Monthly Labor Review* 97, no. 5 (1974): 3–13. (I–R)

Young, R. A. *Recruiting and Hiring Minority Employees.* New York: AMACOM, 1969. (I)

Zimpel, L., ed. *The Disadvantaged Worker: Readings in Developing Minority Manpower.* Reading, Mass.: Addison-Wesley, 1971. (I)

Relevant Court Cases:

Albemarle Paper Co. v. *Moody,* 95 S. Ct. 2362, 2379 (1975).

Brito v. *Zia Company,* 478 F.2d 1200 (1973).

Douglas v. *Hampton,* D.C. Circuit Court of Appeals, 512 F.2d 976 (1975).

EEOC v. *Radiator Specialty Company,* 78–1291 (4th Cir. 1979).

General Electric Co. v. *Gilbert,* Docket no. 74–1589.

Griggs v. *Duke Power Co.,* 401 U.S. 424 (1971).

Hazelwood School District v. *United States,* 15 FEP Cases 1, 10 (1977).

International Brotherhood of Teamsters v. *United States,* 14 FEP Cases at 1521 (1977).

Washington v. *Davis,* Docket No. 74–1492.

Waters v. *Furnco Construction Corp.,* 551 F.2d 1085 (7th Cir. 1977).

United States v. *State of South Carolina,* 15 FEP Cases at 1196 (1977).

APPENDIX

Glossary of EEO and Legal Terms*

Affected Class

Those groups of minorities, females, the elderly, and the disabled who, by virtue of past discrimination, continue to suffer the effects of such discrimination. Affected-class status must be determined by statistical analysis and/or court decision.

Affidavit

A written declaration of facts made voluntarily under oath. This is made without notice to the opposing party and without the opportunity for cross-examination.

---

* A few of the more common legal terms are listed here as an aid to understanding the *Introduction* and activities of the exercise. For more complete coverage, see H. C. Black, *Black's Law Dictionary* (St. Paul: West, 1968).

Affirmative Action

Any activity initiated by an employer that contributes toward the greater utilization of minorities, females, the elderly, and the disabled, including goals established by units and timetables for completion.

Affirmative Action Groups

Those persons identified by the federal and state laws and the County Board of Commissioners to be specificially protected from employment discrimination; includes minorities, females, the elderly, and the disabled.

Affirmative-Action Plan

A document required of government contractors under regulations of the OFCC. The employer is obliged to compare the internal distribution of minorities and females to their incidence in the external labor market and to determine whether or not the employer is at parity with the external labor market. The affirmative action plan is a statement of goals, timetables, and programs indicating how the employer plans to move from his current status of parity.

Amicus Curiae

A party not involved in a lawsuit but who has an interest in its outcome and who submits arguments to the court to aid it in making its judgment.

Answer

A response by the person who is sued.

Bench Trial

Follows discovery by both parties and is always before a judge in Title VII proceedings and never before a jury.

BFOQ or BOQ

"Bona fide occupational qualification," or a minimum qualification requirement needed as a prerequisite to be hired and succeed on that job. BFOQs, if challenged, must be demonstrated to be valid by the employer. The courts have interpreted BFOQ very narrowly, especially with regard to sex. Each applicant must be treated as an individual in comparing his or her skills to the skills required to perform the job.

Brief

In American practice, a paper written by a lawyer to serve as a basis for his or her later oral argument to the court. Its use is largely to inform the court of the lawyer's argument, authorities on questions of law, and desired interpretation of the case.

Burden of Proof

The responsibility for demonstrating to the requisite degree the truth of one's claim; the affirmative duty of proving or disproving the claim at issue.

Business Necessity

Criteria placed on applicants that are valid and necessary for the effective conduct of the organization objectives and the particular job if based on safe and efficient operation of the business (from *Griggs*). The courts have consistently struck down overly stringent criteria that have been shown to have a disparate effect on affirmative-action-category groups.

Career Ladder

Composed of jobs requiring related and increasingly more responsible duties, through which employees advance by experience and in-service training. Career ladders should be equal in quantitative opportunity and salary range for those jobs having high affirmative-action-group utilization compared with those having primarily white male incumbents.

Charging Party

Person alleging that he or she is aggrieved as the result of an unlawful employment practice.

Compliance Agencies

Organizations established under the OFCC as internal subunits of major government departments or agencies, including, for example, the Atomic Energy Commission; Department of Health, Education and Welfare; or the Department of Labor. They are charged with the administration of Executive Order 11246, Revised Orders No. 4 and No. 14, and with the collection and analysis of EEO Reports and affirmative action plans. Their powers of enforcement include the ability to deny government business to contractors found in violation.

Complaint

The first paper filed by a plaintiff.

Compliance

Developing legal practices, within the limits of the nondiscrimination laws and their interpretations by the courts. While organizations, through self-analysis and official changes, can remove their exposure to class-action suits through complying with all civil-rights legislation, individual cases of discrimination can be avoided through training, sessions with managers, supervisors, and other employees in the personnel process.

Conciliation

A settlement through administrative processes, such as those initiated by EEOC; a means by which a case is settled by resolution of charges without a trial.

Consent Decree

By comparison, the judicial counterpart to conciliation; a formal court document approved by a judge.

Decision

Result of legal action which generally goes one of two directions—dismissal of charges or injunction.

Defendant

The person(s) or organization(s) being sued.

Deposition

A written declaration of facts made voluntarily out of court but under oath in the presence of the opposing party, who may conduct cross-examination in front of a court reporter.

Discrimination

A conclusion of the courts that plaintiffs have shown adverse impact and employers have failed to demonstrate business necessity. Thus, a conclusion of law based on a demonstration of adverse impact by the plaintiff and failure by a defendant to demonstrate that the practice was job related to the court's satisfaction.

Discovery

The legal term for the investigation phase after a complaint is filed and the defendant has answered.

Disparate Effect or Disparate Impact

The result of an employment policy, practice, or procedure that, in practical application, has less favorable consequences for an affirmative-action group than for the dominant group.

Distribution Rate

(1) The degree (percentages) to which a given protected class is employed in the various job titles, job classes, and other units within the employing organization; and (2) the degree (percentages) to which individuals of a given protected class are involved in various employment transactions (for example, applications for employment, hiring, placement, promotion, separation, etc.).

EEOC

A federal Equal Employment Opportunity Commission which has the power to bring suits, subpoena witnesses, issue guidelines that have the force of law, render decisions, provide technical assistance to employers, provide legal assistance to complainants, etc.

Employment Parity

When the proportion of affirmative-action groups in the external labor market is equivalent to their proportion in the company work force without reference to classification.

Employment Process

Under Title VII, the employment process includes recruitment, applicant flow, hiring job placement, compensation, promotion, transfer, termination, shift assignments, geographical and departmental assignments, and all other such activities.

Expert Witness

An individual qualified by credentials to give opinion testimony. Although this term has to be limited to a specific application, generally, in test validation at least, a master's degree in psychology and experience in the field is required.

External Labor Area

The geographic area from which an employer may reasonably be expected to recruit new workers. In a compliance sense, this total labor market has submarkets within it, comprised of persons with the requisite skills, experience, etc., to fill given jobs.

External Labor Market

The civilian work force within a labor area.

Findings of Fact

Where the judge serves as an umpire and "calls them as he or she sees them" or understands the facts to be.

GED

General Educational Department—The GED certificate is the high-school equivalency certificate, generally recognized as equal to a high-school diploma for all practical purposes.

Goals

Good faith quantitative objectives an employer voluntarily sets as the minimum progress that can be achieved within a certain time period through all-out efforts at outreach recruitment, validating selection criteria, creation of trainee positions, career ladders, etc. Setting goals and objectives are considered proper and legal responses to underutilization of minority groups by various federal agencies.

Human-Relations Training

Interpersonal skill development, especially with respect to affirmative-action-group awareness, communication, and compatible attitude development. Techniques may include T-groups, seminars, workshops, role reversal, attitude assessment, etc.

Incidence Rate

A measurement of the degree to which a specific protected class is involved in any of the various steps of the employment process. If, out of a group of eighty black males, twenty are promoted, the incidence rate is 25 percent. As a measure of compliance, the incidence rate is compared with the degree to which the specific protected class is represented in the external labor market.

Injunction

May either require that a certain practice be stopped or that something be done in the future; orders other actions, such as relief, to affected class members.

Interrogatories

Written questions drawn up and served on an opposing party with a prescribed time period to answer. The party must then serve answers to the questions under oath. Sometimes used in the deposition procedure.

Jury Trial

More formal than a bench trial; a jury hears the case.

Litigation

A judicial controversy; lawsuits.

Making Whole

Award of back pay employees would have received but for the effects of the unlawful practice.

Mandamus

An order issued by a court to a private or municipal corporation; an executive, judicial, or administrative officer; or to an inferior court commanding the performance of a particular act with the responsibility of the latter party.

Objectives

Similar to goals, a good-faith effort to meet numerical goals through modifications in employment procedures and practice. Goals and objectives are set after careful external and internal labor analysis.

Occupational Parity

When the proportion of affirmative-action-group employees in all occupational levels is equivalent to their respective availability in the qualified external labor market. Eventually, with the goal of equal educational and training opportunities, employment parity and occupational parity may be equal.

OFCC

Office of Federal Contract Compliance—has set guidelines for all federal contractors with respect to nondiscrimination and affirmative action.

Parity

The long-term goal of affirmative action, reached when employment and occupational parity are identical.

Participation Rate

(1) The percentage of incumbents of a job title, class, department, or other organization unit (including the whole organization) who belong to a given protected class; and (2) the percentage of individuals involved in an employment-process transaction (for example, application for employment, hiring, placement, promotion, separation) who belong to a given protected class.

Per se

A violation for which there is no defense.

Plaintiff

The person who initiates litigation.

Present Effects of Past Patterns of Discrimination

The EEOC and the courts have consistently held that employers are liable for correcting situations in which employees continue to suffer the "present effects of past patterns of discrimination." Simply stated, this can mean that an employee (or group of employees) who should (in the eyes of the Commission and/or the courts) have been promoted three years ago (whether a complaint had been lodged or not) are still entitled to be "made whole," accomplished through retroactive pay or other means.

Prima Facie

Violation where evidence is shown that an employment practice has an adverse impact affecting an individual as a member of a similarly affected class covered by Title VII. It shifts the burden to the defendant. The elements necessary to support the claim have been presented and unless evidence can be presented to rebut the previous arguments, the claim will be supported. In the EEO area, statistics of underutilization can be sufficient to make a *prima facie* case for discrimination. It is then the responsibility of the employer to justify those statistics through "business necessity," BFOQs, etc.

Protected Class

Legally identified groups (by race, color, religion, sex, and national origin) that are specifically protected by statute against employment discrimination.

Probable Cause

Reasonable on the basis of the evidence but not certain or proved. Before initiating court action, the EEOC makes a determination of *no cause, probable cause,* or *cause.* In incidents of probable cause or cause, pretrial negotiations and conciliation generally resolve the issues before the case can get into court.

Quotas

Fixed hiring and promotion rates based on race, sex, etc., which must be met at all costs and do not take into consideration the availability, education, or training of the external labor force, of protected class members, or the employer's internal labor situation with respect to projected manpower requirements. Quotas are considered to be last-resort measures available only for the courts to impose when good faith efforts do not exist. Court cases are currently being decided as to their advisability and legality.

Rebut

An answer to an argument, a *prima facie* case, or a presumption.

Relevant Labor Pool

The total number of incumbent employees who are in position for a specific promotion, or all candidates who could conceivably be considered for a promotion.

Remand

To send back. For example, if a court of appeals finds further action is necessary in a case or if further testimony is needed to decide the case, it will remand the case to the lower court.

Respondent

That person against whom an administrative charge of discrimination is filed.

SMSA

Standard Metropolitan Statistical Area—the area of employee recruitment against which parity and utilization levels are compared. The SMSA may vary depending on level of job class, availability of applicants, location of work station, etc.

Stipulation

An agreement between the opposing parties, somewhat akin to a contract, identifying which facts or issues are not disputed. Used as a time-serving device to narrow a case down to the essential matters.

Subpoena

An order of the court commanding individuals (or documents) to appear and give testimony. Derived from the Latin *sub* (under) and *poena* (penalty) because failure to appear may be considered contempt of court.

Summary Judgment

Could be issued by the court at the point where there is *no* dispute of material facts.

Systemic Discrimination

Equal employment opportunity may be denied as the inevitable consequence of some established business practice, persisting over a period of time, rather than of a specific overt action against an aggrieved party. Such a result of the "system" is systemic discrimination and has been at the root of most Title VII settlements to date. Inadvertent and usually unintentional, the disparate effect produced by systemic discrimination constitutes a prime area of vulnerability for most businesses.

Timetables

Consecutive time (generally an affirmative action, a timetable covers one year) during which the specific quantitative goals and objectives for that period are to be met and evaluations of progress made before beginning the subsequent timetable with its own specific goals and objectives.

Title VII of the Civil Rights Act of 1964
(as amended by the Equal Employment
Opportunity Act of 1972)

The first legislation to make it an unlawful employment practice to discriminate on the basis of race, color, religion, sex, or national origin. All other federal and state EEO legislation is patterned after or supportive of Title VII.

Underutilization

Term used to describe a lower number of affirmative action-group employees than parity would predict. Once underutilization is quantitatively established, the burden of proof rests on the employer to demonstrate that the underutilization is the legitimate effect of BFOQ and valid criteria of business necessity (also called underrepresentation).

Utilization Analysis

As audit of the current distribution, participation, compensation, and movements of an organization's employees. The analysis is made by job grade, title, and lines of progression for all sex and race groups, across all units of the organization, for each step of the employment process. Current distribution must be analyzed in terms of relevant external labor markets, and such comparisons must be made at each step of the employment process. A utilization analysis establishes a legal and accurate basis for realistic goal setting.

Validity

The extent to which a test, criterion, or qualification measures the trait (some job performance ability) for which it is being used, rather than some other trait. "Business necessity" considerations are addressed to the usefulness of the test in predicting job performance and the minimum cut-off scores.

Name _____ Group Number _____

Date _____ Class Section _____ Hour _____ Score _____

PART A

Form 1 EEO and Affirmative Action Review Questionnaire

	True	False	Undecided
1. It would be inappropriate for courts to impose goals and timetables on employers engaged in discriminatory practices.			
2. Unions may be held liable for labor contracts that are overtly or covertly discriminatory.			
3. State and local governments were subject to the Civil Rights Act of 1964 before 1972.			
4. If an employer can show an employee profile which demonstrates that the organization does not discriminate, there is no legal requirement that the organization validate its selection procedures.			
5. Goals are determined by analyzing the job classifications within a unit or organization.			
6. Some lawyers may now receive their fee from the government if they win an EEOC case.			
7. A voluntarily developed affirmative-action plan is a management guideline and is not a legal document.			
8. Failure to impose quotas means failure of commitment to EEO.			
9. EEOC is an affirmative-action agency.			
10. Affirmative-action plans are not required of every organization by law, they are only recommended by guidelines.			
11. Criteria for determining job requirements for minorities and women for the same positions should be the same as for white males.			
12. The EEO Act gave the Civil Service Commission enforcement responsibilities for eliminating discrimination in state and local governments.			
13. EEOC is responsible for nondiscrimination and affirmative action among government contractors.			
14. The responsibility for remedying unintentional or covert discrimination practices remains with the employer.			
15. The new EEO Act (1972) prohibits discrimination based on age, race, religion, and sex, and national origin.			
16. Complaints of race or sex discrimination may be filed on the basis of a specific practice or on the basis of systematic discrimination.			
17. Affirmative-action programs are designed to achieve equal employment opportunity only for minorities.			

Form 1 (continued)

18. An important distinction can be made between quotas and goals.			
19. It is wise to involve a representative group of employees in the development of affirmative-action programs.			
20. Numerical goals, as well as quotas, are incompatible with merit principles for promotions, etc.			
21. The development of voluntary affirmative-action programs is a protection for employers if a complaint of race or sex discrimination is filed.			
22. Attaining an affirmative-action goal may sometimes require hiring less-qualified persons over better-qualified ones.			

Name _____ Group Number _____

Date _____ Class Section _____ Hour _____ Score _____

PART B

Form 2 Calculations of Adverse Impact

In the data below, show the following:

1. The selection ratio for *each* step in the hiring process.
2. Where adverse impact exists.
3. What could be done to either:
   a. avoid adverse impact, or
   b. provide sufficient defense arguments for the validity of the "test" where adverse impact is shown.

	Pass applications	*Pass interview*	*Pass work sample*	*Jobs offered/ hired*
Non-minority 400	100	80	40	30
Minority 100	25	10	10	10

Number of Openings = 40

1) _____

_____

_____

_____

2) _____

_____

_____

_____

3) _____

_____

_____

_____

PART B

Form 3 Employment Patterns for a Series of Job Titles within an Organization

		1977	1978	1979	1980	1981
Manager	M	0.00%	.50%	2.22%	2.23%	1.83%
	♀	0.00%	0.00%	0.00%	.43%	.46%
Sales Agent I	M	2.90%	1.82%	2.48%	2.48%	1.72%
	♀	0.00%	0.00%	0.00%	0.00%	0.00%
Sales Agent II	M	6.06%	5.72%	4.51%	3.66%	4.76%
	♀	.11%	0.00%	0.00%	0.00%	.25%
Supv. & Asst. Supv.	M	7.84%	12.20%	8.93%	11.11%	10.53%
	♀	54.32%	51.00%	46.43%	48.21%	47.36%
Cook	M	0.00%	0.00%	0.00%	.44%	.44%
	♀	100.00%	100.00%	100.00%	99.00%	99.00%
Admin. Assistant	M	8.77%	8.70%	14.32%	14.77%	15.20%
	♀	100.00%	100.00%	99.72%	98.96%	98.66%
Agent III	M	6.16%	5.56%	4.78%	6.70%	5.63%
	♀	96.35%	99.13%	84.21%	83.48%	85.45%
Agent IV	M	3.77%	4.05%	10.92%	9.38%	9.45%
	♀	83.81%	82.43%	61.34%	57.81%	57.84%
Technician I	M	3.77%	4.05%	10.92%	9.38%	9.45%
	♀	83.81%	82.43%	61.34%	57.81%	57.84%
Technician II	M	2.66%	2.37%	2.15%	3.63%	23.53%
	♀	0.00%	0.00%	0.00%	0.00%	34.12%
Maintenance Worker	M	78.27%	22.89%	21.57%	27.91%	1.09%
	♀	0.00%	1.20%	15.69%	34.88%	14.13%
Secretary	M	0.00%	0.00%	0.00%	0.00%	17.78%
	♀	98.42%	96.97%	99.40%	92.77%	90.00%
Accounting Clerk	M	3.42%	6.47%	7.94%	16.12%	8.43%
	♀	78.43%	81.47%	87.93%	89.24%	92.45%

M [Minority
♀ [Women

Action Recommended _____

_____

_____

_____

(Continue on separate sheet.)

PART B

Form 4 Employee Transition Chart for Females 1976–1981

1981

		TM	D	M	S	TA	TB	TC	IV	III	II	I	OUT	Total
Top Management	TM	3 / .50											3 / .50	6
Director	D		5 / 1.00										0 / 0	5
Manager	M			41 / .82									9 / .18	50
Supervisor	S			6 / .33	12 / .67								0 / 0	18
Technician A	TA			8 / .20	4 / .10	20 / .50							8 / .20	40
Technician B	TB					56 / .56	22 / .22						22 / .22	100
Technician C	TC			14 / .07		12 / .06	26 / .13	54 / .27				14 / .07	80 / .40	200
Clerical IV	IV												0 / 0	0
Clerical III	III							13 / .50					13 / .50	26
Clerical II	II			9 / .09		9 / .09					27 / .27		55 / .55	100
Clerical I	I			6 / .03				6 / .03	6 / .03	6 / .03	16 / .08	44 / .22	116 / .58	200

Numbers above diagonal line are actual number of employees. Numbers below are percentages.

Actions Recomended _____

PART C

Form 5 Littleco Employment Status Worksheet

Littleco
Work Force Analysis

Salary Range/Wage Grade or Code	EEO Category	All Employees			Minorities											Total Minorities
					Male					Female					
		Total	Male	Female	Black	Hispanic	Asian American	American Indian	Black	Hispanic	Asian American	American Indian			
Total															
Grand Total															

PART C

Form 6 Employee Codes for Littleco Personnel Records

RACE CODE

    B = Black (Negro)
    O = Oriental (Asian American)
    AI = American Indian
SSA = Spanish Surname American (Mexican, Cuban, Spanish, Puerto Rican, Latin)
    W = Caucasian

SALARY LEVEL

    1 = 30,000 +
    2 = 20–25,000
    3 = 18–20,000
    4 = 16–18,000
    5 = 14–16,000
    6 = 12–14,000
    7 = 10–12,000
    8 = 6–10,000

EDUCATION

    D = Doctorate
    M = Masters
    B = Bachelor
    H = High school
    G = Grade school

DEPARTMENT CODE

    A = General administration
    M = Marketing
    P = Production
    E = Engineering
    PS = Personnel
    MT = Maintenance
    F = Finance

EEO CATEGORIES

    1 = Officials and managers
    2 = Professionals
    3 = Technicians
    4 = Sales representatives
    5 = Office and clerical
    6 = Skilled craft workers/craftspersons
    7 = Paraprofessionals
    8 = Security guards
    9 = Operatives
    10 = Laborers (unskilled)
    11 = Service/maintenance workers

PART C

Form 7 Littleco Employment by Sex Category

Employee number	Job category	Salary	Department	Seniority (in years)	Education	Sex	Race	Age
1	1	1	A	10	M	M	W	60
84	1	2	A	2	M	M	W	32
98	1	2	PS	11	D	M	W	41
24	2	5	A	1	M	M	B	27
46	2	4	M	20	M	M	W	40
90	2	3	PS	16	M	M	O	37
4	4	2	M	20	M	M	W	45
6	4	2	P	20	B	M	W	40
36	4	4	PS	15	B	M	W	35
39	4	7	A	2	H	M	W	45
78	4	5	M	1	B	M	W	21
14	5	8	P	5	H	M	W	19
37	5	8	M	4	H	M	W	26
45	5	6	MT	11	B	M	W	31
53	5	6	F	5	H	M	W	37
60	5	6	A	3	B	M	W	27
85	5	4	F	29	H	M	W	65
20	3	3	E	15	B	M	W	55
35	3	6	P	7	H	M	W	41
50	3	6	P	5	H	M	W	33
51	3	5	M	8	B	M	W	28
57	3	5	E	2	B	M	W	28
74	3	4	P	20	H	M	W	40
79	3	3	E	15	M	M	W	45
7	6	3	F	15	B	M	W	41
8	6	3	E	16	B	M	W	36
10	6	4	P	15	B	M	W	55
12	6	5	P	15	H	M	W	57
18	6	5	P	11	B	M	W	32
22	6	7	E	19	H	M	W	37
25	6	3	F	16	B	M	W	41
31	6	4	A	19	B	M	W	41
32	6	6	E	27	H	M	W	61
48	6	6	F	19	B	M	W	49
55	6	8	F	1	H	M	W	27
62	6	6	M	9	H	M	W	32
64	6	8	F	1	H	M	W	22
68	6	7	E	16	H	M	W	32
72	6	5	P	7	B	Sex	W	35
77	6	5	PS	8	B	M	W	48
99	6	7	MT	9	H	M	W	28
2	7	4	F	15	M	M	W	35
34	7	4	P	3	B	M	W	33
44	7	8	E	1	H	M	W	21
49	7	7	P	9	H	M	SSA	26
54	7	4	PS	19	H	M	W	49
59	7	5	PS	11	B	M	W	31
71	7	4	M	11	B	M	W	47
91	7	7	M	1	H	M	W	26
96	7	5	A	2	B	M	W	29

Form 7 (continued)

Employee number	Job category	Salary	Department	Seniority (in years)	Education	Sex	Race	Age
16	8	5	A	22	B	M	W	41
26	8	6	PA	21	H	M	W	38
40	8	4	E	3	B	M	W	58
43	8	6	E	6	B	M	W	26
65	8	8	PS	16	H	M	W	46
67	8	6	E	21	H	M	W	51
75	8	6	PA	21	H	M	W	37
81	8	6	PS	16	H	M	W	51
88	8	5	E	20	B	M	W	40
19	9	4	P	26	B	M	W	46
29	9	7	M	5	H	M	W	29
41	9	7	F	9	H	M	W	29
47	9	7	P	7	H	M	AI	27
61	9	8	MT	7	H	M	SSA	37
63	9	6	P	23	B	M	W	43
69	9	8	A	5	H	M	SSA	29
70	9	8	P	8	H	M	W	27
83	9	6	P	13	H	M	W	43
87	9	6	PS	7	B	M	W	27
92	9	5	E	20	H	M	W	41
11	11	6	F	5	G	M	W	63
15	11	8	MT	10	H	M	B	30
58	11	8	P	9	H	M	SSA	29
89	11	7	F	15	H	M	SSA	35
94	11	6	M	9	H	M	W	53
95	11	7	P	5	H	M	O	37
97	11	6	E	9	B	M	W	60
3	10	7	E	10	H	M	B	35
23	10	8	MT	16	H	M	SSA	37
30	10	8	E	15	H	M	B	35
52	10	7	P	10	H	M	O	45
100	10	7	F	8	H	M	SSA	31
5	1	1	A	15	D	F	W	53
33	5	6	MT	6	H	F	SSA	60
42	5	8	A	8	H	F	W	18
73	5	7	MT	5	H	F	W	42
86	5	8	MT	4	H	F	SSA	63
56	6	7	MT	5	H	F	W	55
13	9	7	MT	10	H	F	W	27
80	9	6	MT	3	B	F	B	41
21	11	7	P	8	G	F	W	44
38	11	8	A	8	H	F	B	47
9	10	8	P	1	G	F	W	35
17	10	6	MT	9	H	F	W	43
27	10	7	MT	7	G	F	SSA	29
28	10	8	MT	7	H	F	W	24
66	10	7	MT	3	H	F	W	43
76	10	7	MT	3	G	F	W	39
82	10	8	MT	2	H	F	O	37
93	10	8	MT	3	H	F	W	23

FORM C

Form 8 Littleco Employment by Race Category

Employee number	Job category	Salary	Department	Seniority (in years)	Education	Sex	Race	Age
1	1	1	A	10	M	M	W	60
5	1	1	A	15	D	F	W	53
84	1	2	A	2	M	M	W	32
98	1	2	PS	11	D	M	W	41
46	2	4	M	20	M	M	W	40
4	4	2	M	20	M	M	W	45
6	4	2	P	20	B	M	W	40
36	4	4	PS	15	B	M	W	35
39	4	7	A	2	H	M	W	45
78	4	5	M	1	B	M	W	21
42	5	8	A	8	H	F	W	18
85	5	4	F	29	H	M	W	65
37	5	8	M	4	H	M	W	26
53	5	6	F	5	H	M	W	37
60	5	6	A	3	B	M	W	27
73	5	7	MT	5	H	F	W	42
45	5	6	MT	11	B	M	W	31
14	5	8	P	5	H	M	W	19
74	3	4	P	20	H	M	W	40
51	3	5	M	8	B	M	W	28
57	3	5	E	2	B	M	W	28
20	3	3	E	15	B	M	W	55
35	3	6	P	7	H	M	W	41
50	3	6	P	5	H	M	W	33
79	3	3	E	15	M	M	W	45
62	6	6	M	9	H	M	W	32
7	6	3	F	15	B	M	W	41
18	6	5	M	11	B	M	W	32
22	6	7	E	19	H	M	W	37
64	6	8	F	1	H	M	W	22
68	6	7	E	16	H	M	W	32
8	6	3	E	16	B	M	W	36
12	6	5	P	15	H	M	W	57
72	6	5	P	7	B	M	W	35
77	6	5	PS	8	B	M	W	48
10	6	4	P	15	B	Sex	W	55
32	6	6	E	27	H	M	W	61
55	6	8	F	1	H	M	W	27
25	6	3	F	16	B	M	W	41
48	6	6	F	19	B	M	W	49
31	6	4	A	19	B	M	W	55
56	6	7	MT	5	H	F	W	55
99	6	7	MT	9	H	M	W	28
44	7	8	E	1	H	M	W	21
54	7	4	PS	19	H	M	W	49
59	7	5	PS	11	B	M	W	31
71	7	4	M	11	B	M	W	47
96	7	5	A	2	B	M	W	29
2	7	4	F	15	M	M	W	35

Form 8 (continued)

Employee number	Job category	Salary	Department	Seniority (in years)	Education	Sex	Race	Age
34	7	4	P	3	B	M	W	33
91	7	7	M	1	H	M	W	26
26	8	6	PA	21	H	M	W	38
40	8	4	E	3	B	M	W	58
65	8	8	PS	16	H	M	W	46
81	8	6	PS	16	H	M	W	51
43	8	6	E	6	B	M	W	26
16	8	5	A	22	B	M	W	41
88	8	5	E	20	B	M	W	40
67	8	6	E	21	H	M	W	51
75	8	6	PA	21	H	M	W	37
29	9	7	M	5	H	M	W	29
41	9	7	F	9	H	M	W	29
19	9	4	P	26	B	M	W	46
13	9	7	MT	10	H	F	W	27
63	9	6	P	23	B	M	W	43
83	9	6	P	13	H	M	W	43
70	9	8	P	8	H	M	W	27
87	9	6	PS	7	B	M	W	27
92	9	5	E	20	H	M	W	41
97	11	6	E	9	B	M	W	60
11	11	6	F	5	G	M	W	63
21	11	7	P	8	G	F	W	44
94	11	6	M	9	H	M	W	53
9	10	8	P	1	G	F	W	35
93	10	8	MT	3	H	F	W	23
66	10	7	MT	3	H	F	W	43
76	10	7	MT	3	G	F	W	39
17	10	6	MT	9	H	F	W	43
28	10	8	MT	7	H	F	W	24
24	2	5	A	1	M	M	B	27
80	9	6	MT	3	B	F	B	41
15	11	8	MT	10	H	M	B	30
38	11	8	A	8	H	F	B	47
3	10	7	E	10	H	M	B	35
30	10	8	F	15	H	M	B	35
33	5	6	MT	6	H	F	SSA	60
86	5	8	MT	4	H	F	SSA	63
49	7	7	P	9	H	M	SSA	26
61	9	8	MT	7	H	M	SSA	37
69	9	8	A	5	H	M	SSA	29
58	11	8	P	9	H	M	SSA	29
89	11	7	F	15	H	M	SSA	35
27	10	7	MT	7	G	F	SSA	29
23	10	8	MT	16	H	M	SSA	37
100	10	7	F	8	H	M	SSA	31
47	9	7	P	7	H	M	AI	27
90	2	3	PS	16	M	M	O	37
95	11	7	P	5	H	M	O	37
52	10	7	P	10	H	M	O	45
82	10	8	MT	2	H	F	O	37

PART C

Form 9 Littleco Employment by Age

Employee number	Job category	Salary	Department	Seniority (in years)	Education	Sex	Race	Age
42	5	8	A	8	H	F	W	18
14	5	8	P	5	H	M	W	19
78	4	5	M	1	B	M	W	21
44	7	8	E	1	H	M	W	21
64	6	8	F	1	H	M	W	22
93	10	8	MT	3	H	F	W	23
28	10	8	MT	7	H	F	W	24
37	5	8	M	4	H	M	W	26
49	7	7	P	9	H	M	SSA	26
91	7	7	M	1	H	M	W	26
43	8	6	E	6	B	M	W	26
24	2	5	A	1	M	M	B	27
60	5	6	A	3	B	M	W	27
55	6	8	F	1	H	M	W	27
13	9	7	MT	10	H	F	W	27
47	9	7	P	7	H	M	AI	27
70	9	8	P	8	H	M	W	27
87	9	6	PS	7	B	M	W	27
51	3	5	M	8	B	M	W	28
57	3	5	E	2	B	M	W	28
99	6	7	MT	9	H	M	W	28
96	7	5	A	2	B	M	W	29
29	9	7	M	5	H	M	W	29
41	9	7	F	9	H	M	W	29
69	9	8	A	5	H	M	SSA	29
58	11	8	P	9	H	M	SSA	29
27	10	7	MT	7	G	F	SSA	29
15	11	8	MT	10	H	M	B	30
45	5	6	MT	11	B	M	W	31
59	7	5	PS	11	B	M	W	31
100	10	7	F	8	H	M	SSA	31
84	1	2	A	2	M	M	W	32
18	6	5	P	11	B	M	W	32
62	6	6	M	9	H	M	W	32
68	6	7	E	16	H	M	W	32
50	3	6	P	5	H	M	W	33
34	7	4	P	3	B	M	W	33
36	4	4	PS	15	B	M	W	35
72	6	5	P	7	B	M	W	35
2	7	4	F	15	M	M	W	35
89	11	7	F	15	H	M	SSA	35
3	10	7	E	10	H	M	B	35
9	10	8	P	1	G	F	W	35
30	10	8	F	15	H	M	B	35
8	6	3	E	16	B	M	W	36
90	2	3	PS	16	M	M	O	37
53	5	6	F	5	H	M	W	37
22	6	7	E	19	H	M	W	37
75	8	6	PA	21	H	M	W	37
61	9	8	MT	7	H	M	SSA	37

Form 9 (continued)

Employee number	Job category	Salary	Department	Seniority (in years)	Education	Sex	Race	Age
95	11	7	P	5	H	M	O	37
23	10	8	MT	16	H	M	SSA	37
82	10	8	MT	2	H	F	O	37
26	8	6	PA	21	H	M	W	38
76	10	7	MT	3	G	F	W	39
46	2	4	M	20	M	M	W	40
6	4	2	P	20	B	M	W	40
74	3	4	P	20	H	M	W	40
88	8	5	E	20	B	M	W	40
98	1	2	PS	11	D	M	W	41
35	3	6	P	7	H	M	W	41
7	6	3	F	15	B	M	W	41
25	6	3	F	16	B	M	W	41
31	6	4	A	19	B	M	W	41
16	8	5	A	22	B	M	W	41
80	9	6	MT	3	B	F	B	41
92	9	5	E	20	H	M	W	41
73	5	7	MT	5	H	F	W	42
63	9	6	P	23	B	M	W	43
83	9	6	P	13	H	M	W	43
17	10	6	MT	9	H	F	W	43
66	10	7	MT	3	H	F	W	43
21	11	7	P	8	G	F	W	44
4	4	2	M	20	M	M	W	45
39	4	7	A	2	H	M	W	45
79	3	3	E	15	M	M	W	45
52	10	7	P	10	H	M	O	45
65	8	8	PS	16	H	M	W	46
19	9	4	P	26	B	M	W	46
71	7	4	M	11	B	M	W	47
38	11	8	A	8	H	F	B	47
77	6	5	PS	8	B	M	W	48
48	6	6	F	19	B	M	W	49
54	7	4	PS	19	H	M	W	49
67	8	6	E	21	H	M	W	51
81	8	6	PS	16	H	M	W	51
5	1	1	A	15	D	F	W	53
94	11	6	M	9	H	M	W	53
20	3	3	E	15	B	M	W	55
10	6	4	P	15	B	M	W	55
56	6	7	MT	5	H	F	W	55
12	6	5	P	15	H	M	W	57
40	8	4	E	3	B	M	W	58
1	1	1	A	10	M	M	W	60
33	5	6	MT	6	H	F	SSA	60
97	11	6	E	9	B	M	W	60
32	6	6	E	27	H	M	W	61
86	5	8	MT	4	H	F	SSA	63
11	11	6	F	5	G	M	W	63
85	5	4	F	29	H	M	W	65

PART C

Form 10 Littleco SMSA Population — Data by Job Category

1980 Census Last Occupation of the Experienced Unemployed
Standard Metropolitan Statistical Area (SMSA)

	TOTAL ALL RACES			WHITE			NEGRO			SPANISH HERITAGE[1]			ALL OTHER RACES			TOTAL MINORITY	
	Total	Male	Female	Total	Male	Female	Total	Male	Female	Total	Male	Female	Total	Male	Female	Total	Male
TOTAL ALL OCCUPATIONS	17,908	10,758	7,150	16,547	9,970	6,577	1,035	593	442	2,459	1,624	835	326	195	131	3,820	2,412
Professional, Technical & Kindred workers	1,720	942	778	1,644	899	745	61	33	28	112	72	40	15	10	5	183	115
Accountants	92	63	29	87	58	29	5	5	0	0	0	0	0	0	0	5	5
Architects	5	5	0	5	5	0	0	0	0	0	0	0	0	0	0	0	0
Computer specialists	32	15	17	32	15	17	0	0	0	0	0	0	0	0	0	NA	0
Engineers — Total	NA	152	NA	NA	152	NA	NA	0	NA	NA	0	NA	0	0	0	0	0
Aeronautical & astronautical	15	15	0	15	15	0	0	0	0	0	0	0	0	0	0	0	0
Civil	NA	21	NA	NA	21	NA	NA	0	NA	NA	0	NA	0	0	0	NA	0
Electrical & electronic	35	35	0	35	35	0	0	0	0	0	0	0	0	0	0	0	0
Mechanical	19	19	0	19	19	0	0	0	0	0	0	0	0	0	0	0	0
Other engineers	62	62	0	62	62	0	0	0	0	0	0	0	0	0	0	NA	0
Lawyers & judges	NA	11	NA	NA	11	NA	NA	0	NA	NA	0	NA	0	0	0	NA	0
Librarians	NA	NA	5	NA	NA	5	0	0	0	NA	NA	0	NA	NA	0	NA	NA
Mathematical specialists	NA	NA	0	NA	NA	0	0	0	0	NA	NA	0	NA	NA	0	NA	NA
Life & physical scientists	64	41	23	64	41	23	0	0	0	0	0	0	0	0	0	0	0
Chemists	NA	12	NA	NA	12	NA	0	0	0	0	0	0	0	0	0	0	0
Other life & physical scientists	NA	29	NA	NA	29	NA	0	0	0	0	0	0	0	0	0	0	0
Physicians, dentists, & related practitioners	NA	8	NA	NA	8	NA	NA	0	NA	NA	0	NA	0	0	0	NA	0
Dentists	0	0	0	0	0	0	0	0	0	0	0	0	0	0	0	0	0
Pharmacists	NA	4	NA	NA	4	NA	NA	0	NA	NA	0	NA	0	0	0	NA	0
Physicians, medical & osteopathic	4	4	0	4	4	0	0	0	0	0	0	0	0	0	0	0	0
Other related practitioners	0	0	0	0	0	0	0	0	0	0	0	0	0	0	0	0	0
Registered nurses, dieticians, & therapists	NA	NA	111	NA	NA	105	6	0	6	NA	NA	7	NA	NA	0	NA	NA
Dieticians	15	0	15	9	0	9	6	0	6	7	0	7	0	0	0	13	0
Registered nurses	NA	NA	85	NA	NA	85	0	0	0	NA	NA	0	NA	NA	0	NA	NA
Therapists	NA	NA	11	NA	NA	11	0	0	0	NA	NA	0	NA	NA	0	NA	NA
Health technologists & technicians	56	25	31	56	25	31	0	0	0	0	0	0	0	0	0	0	0
Religious workers	0	0	0	0	0	0	0	0	0	0	0	0	0	0	0	0	0
Social scientists	48	21	27	48	21	27	0	0	0	0	0	0	0	0	0	26	21
Social & recreation workers	73	34	39	64	30	34	9	4	5	17	17	0	5	0	5	52	16
Teachers — Total	336	84	252	318	84	234	13	0	13	34	16	18	5	0	5	16	16
College & university	51	29	22	51	29	22	0	0	0	16	16	0	5	0	5	21	0
Elementary & prekindergarten	160	6	154	146	6	140	9	0	9	7	0	7	0	0	0	4	0
Secondary	79	33	46	75	33	42	4	0	4	0	0	0	0	0	0	0	0
Other teachers	46	16	30	46	16	30	0	0	0	0	0	0	0	0	0	29	29
Engineering & science technicians	162	143	19	145	126	19	17	17	0	12	12	0	0	0	0	6	6
Draftsmen & surveyors	NA	68	NA	NA	62	NA	6	6	0	0	0	0	0	0	0	0	0
Electrical & electronic engineering technicians	NA	31	NA	NA	20	NA	11	11	0	0	0	0	0	0	0	11	11
Other engineering & science technicians	NA	44	NA	NA	44	NA	0	0	0	12	12	0	0	0	0	12	12
Technicians, except health, & engineering science	48	48	0	48	48	0	0	0	0	8	8	0	0	0	0	8	8
Airline pilots	25	25	0	25	25	0	0	0	0	0	0	0	0	0	0	0	0
Writers, artists, & entertainers	259	147	112	246	134	112	7	7	0	17	11	6	6	6	0	30	24
Actors & dancers	24	0	24	24	0	24	0	0	0	0	0	0	0	0	0	0	0
Authors, editors, & reporters	NA	NA	11	NA	NA	11	NA	NA	0	NA	NA	6	NA	NA	0	NA	NA
Other professional, technical, & kindred workers	258	145	113	250	141	109	4	0	4	17	8	9	4	4	0	25	12
Managers & administrators, except form buyers, purchasing agents, & sales managers	772	609	163	755	597	158	17	12	5	28	28	0	0	0	0	45	40
Restaurant, cafeteria, & bar managers	100	75	25	100	75	25	0	0	0	0	0	0	0	0	0	0	0
School administrators	NA	NA	20	NA	NA	20	0	0	0	NA	NA	0	0	0	0	NA	NA
Specified managers & administrators, public administration	10	5	5	10	5	5	0	0	0	7	7	0	0	0	0	7	7
Managers & administrators, n.e.c.[2] — salaried	NA	38	NA	NA	32	NA	6	6	0	0	0	0	0	0	0	5	6
Manufacturing	346	284	62	335	278	57	11	6	5	5	5	0	0	0	0	16	11
Wholesale & retail trade	NA	48	NA	NA	48	NA	NA	0	NA	0	0	0	0	0	0	NA	0
Transportation, communications, & other public utilities	105	80	25	99	74	25	6	6	0	0	0	0	0	0	0	6	6
All other industries	NA	14	NA	NA	14	NA	NA	0	NA	0	0	0	0	0	0	NA	0
Managers & administrators, n.e.c.[2] self-employed	179	142	37	174	142	32	5	0	5	5	5	0	0	0	0	10	5
Construction	89	78	11	89	78	11	0	0	0	0	0	0	0	0	0	0	0
Manufacturing	20	20	0	20	20	0	0	0	0	0	0	0	0	0	0	0	0
Wholesale & retail trade	4	4	0	4	4	0	0	0	0	0	0	0	0	0	0	0	0
All other industries	35	30	5	35	30	5	0	0	0	0	0	0	0	0	0	0	0
Sales Workers	30	24	6	30	24	6	0	0	0	0	0	0	0	0	0	0	0
Demonstrators, hucksters, & peddlers	1,259	653	606	1,194	612	582	53	35	18	90	39	51	12	6	6	155	80
Insurance agents, brokers & underwriters	NA	NA	31	NA	NA	31	NA	NA	0	NA	NA	4	0	0	0	NA	NA
Insurance, real estate agents & brokers	NA	34	NA	NA	30	NA	4	4	0	NA	0	NA	NA	0	NA	NA	4
Real estate agents & brokers	NA	NA	25	NA	NA	25	NA	NA	0	NA	NA	0	0	0	0	NA	NA
	NA	20	NA	NA	20	NA	0	0	0	NA	0	NA	NA	0	NA	NA	0

Form 10 (continued)

	TOTAL ALL RACES			WHITE			NEGRO			SPANISH HERITAGE[1]			ALL OTHER RACES			TOTAL MINORITY	
	Total	Male	Female	Total	Male	Female	Total	Male	Female	Total	Male	Female	Total	Male	Female	Total	Male
Sales representatives, manufacturing industries	NA	31	NA	NA	25	NA	0	0	0	NA	8	NA	NA	6	NA	NA	14
Sales representatives, wholesale trade	NA	106	NA	NA	101	NA	5	5	0	NA	0	NA	NA	0	NA	NA	5
Sales clerks, retail trade	569	186	383	541	176	365	28	10	18	34	17	17	0	0	0	62	27
Salesmen & women, retail trade	95	84	11	89	78	11	6	6	0	0	0	0	0	0	0	6	6
Salesmen of services & construction	NA	40	NA	NA	40	NA	0	0	0	NA	8	NA	NA	0	NA	NA	8
Other sales workers	308	152	156	292	142	150	10	10	0	36	6	30	6	0	6	52	16
Clerical & kindred workers	2,827	576	2,251	2,657	550	2,107	92	5	87	275	52	223	78	21	57	445	78
Bank tellers & cashiers	276	28	248	254	23	231	17	0	17	33	5	28	5	5	0	55	10
Bookkeepers & billing clerks	NA	54	NA	NA	43	NA	NA	0	NA	NA	0	NA	NA	11	NA	NA	11
Bookkeepers	NA	NA	201	NA	NA	201	NA	NA	0	NA	NA	11	NA	NA	0	NA	NA
Cashiers	NA	NA	223	NA	NA	206	NA	NA	17	NA	NA	28	NA	NA	0	NA	NA
Counter clerks, except food	NA	NA	77	NA	NA	65	NA	NA	3	NA	NA	7	NA	NA	9	NA	NA
Enumerators & interviewers	NA	NA	27	NA	NA	27	NA	NA	0	NA	NA	0	NA	NA	0	NA	NA
File clerks	NA	NA	101	NA	NA	85	NA	NA	16	NA	NA	27	NA	NA	0	NA	NA
Mail handlers & clerks	NA	43	NA	NA	43	NA	NA	0	NA	NA	0	NA	NA	0	NA	NA	0
Office machine operators	NA	NA	93	NA	NA	93	NA	NA	0	NA	NA	31	NA	NA	0	NA	NA
Bookkeeping & billing machine oprs.	15	0	15	15	0	15	0	0	0	4	0	4	0	0	0	4	0
Keypunch operators	NA	NA	41	NA	NA	41	NA	NA	0	NA	NA	4	NA	NA	0	4	0
Other office machine operators	NA	NA	37	NA	NA	37	NA	NA	0	NA	NA	12	NA	NA	0	NA	NA
Payroll & timekeeping clerks	5	0	5	5	0	5	0	0	0	0	0	0	0	0	0	0	0
Receptionists	NA	NA	91	NA	NA	88	NA	NA	3	NA	NA	7	NA	NA	0	0	0
Secretaries	NA	NA	433	NA	NA	407	NA	NA	7	NA	NA	45	NA	NA	19	NA	NA
Stenographers	5	0	5	5	0	5	0	0	0	0	0	0	0	0	0	0	0
Telephone operators	53	0	53	53	0	53	0	0	0	0	0	0	0	0	0	0	0
Typists	NA	NA	314	NA	NA	299	NA	NA	6	NA	NA	24	NA	NA	9	NA	NA
Other clerical & kindred workers	1,054	451	603	989	441	548	40	5	35	90	47	43	25	5	20	155	57
Craftsmen & kindred workers	2,709	2,540	169	2,565	2,418	147	114	92	22	413	389	24	30	30	0	557	511
Apparel craftsmen & upholsterers	NA	18	NA	NA	18	NA	NA	0	NA	NA	0	NA	0	0	0	NA	0
Bakers	NA	15	NA	NA	15	NA	NA	0	NA	NA	12	NA	0	0	0	NA	12
Cabinetmakers	13	13	0	13	13	0	0	0	0	5	5	0	0	0	0	5	5
Construction craftsmen	NA	1,263	NA	NA	1,200	NA	NA	49	NA	NA	197	NA	14	14	0	NA	260
Carpenters	NA	571	NA	NA	543	NA	NA	17	NA	NA	57	NA	11	11	0	NA	85
Excavating, grading, & road machine operators	113	113	0	110	110	0	0	0	0	12	12	0	3	3	0	15	15
Electricians	38	38	0	38	38	0	0	0	0	0	0	0	0	0	0	0	0
Masons & tile setters	117	117	0	113	113	0	4	0	0	47	47	0	0	0	0	51	51
Painters & paperhangers	NA	202	NA	NA	179	NA	NA	23	NA	NA	16	NA	0	0	0	NA	39
Plasterers & cement finishers	NA	92	NA	NA	92	NA	NA	0	NA	NA	43	NA	0	0	0	NA	43
Plumbers & pipe fitters	56	56	0	56	56	0	0	0	0	6	6	0	0	0	0	6	6
Other construction craftsmen	NA	74	NA	NA	69	NA	NA	5	NA	NA	16	NA	0	0	0	NA	21
Foremen, n.e.c.[2]	132	105	27	132	105	27	0	0	0	17	17	0	0	0	0	17	17
Manufacturing	NA	49	NA	NA	49	NA	0	0	0	17	17	0	0	0	0	8	8
Nonmanufacturing industries	NA	56	NA	NA	56	NA	NA	0	NA	9	9	0	0	0	0	9	9
Linemen & servicemen, tel. & power	22	22	0	22	22	0	0	0	0	9	9	0	0	0	0	9	9
Locomotive engineers & firemen	6	6	0	6	6	0	0	0	0	0	0	0	0	0	0	0	0
Mechanics & repairmen	NA	305	NA	NA	290	NA	NA	5	NA	NA	38	NA	10	10	0	NA	53
Air conditioning, heating, & refrigeration	13	13	0	13	13	0	0	0	0	0	0	0	0	0	0	0	0
Aircraft	0	0	0	0	0	0	0	0	0	0	0	0	0	0	0	0	0
Automobile, including body	135	135	0	131	131	0	0	0	0	18	18	0	4	4	0	22	22
Radio & television	NA	35	NA	NA	30	NA	NA	5	NA	NA	0	NA	0	0	0	NA	5
Other mechanics & repairmen	NA	122	NA	NA	116	NA	NA	0	NA	NA	20	NA	6	6	0	NA	26
Metal craftsmen, except mechanics	NA	184	NA	NA	169	NA	NA	9	NA	NA	35	NA	6	6	0	NA	50
Machinists & job and die setters	NA	51	NA	NA	45	NA	NA	0	NA	NA	9	NA	6	6	0	NA	15
Sheetmetal workers & tinsmiths	NA	88	NA	NA	79	NA	NA	9	NA	NA	18	NA	6	6	0	NA	27
Tool and die makers	13	13	0	13	13	0	0	0	0	0	0	0	0	0	0	0	0
Other metal craftsmen	32	32	0	32	32	0	0	0	0	8	8	0	0	0	0	8	8
Printing craftsmen	NA	35	NA	NA	35	NA	NA	0	NA	NA	13	NA	0	0	0	NA	13
Compositors & typesetters	NA	4	NA	NA	4	NA	NA	0	NA	NA	6	NA	0	0	0	NA	6
Pressmen & plate printers, printing	26	26	0	26	26	0	0	0	0	0	0	0	0	0	0	0	0
Other printing craftsmen	NA	5	NA	NA	5	NA	NA	0	NA	NA	7	NA	0	0	0	NA	7
Stationary engineers & power station operators	16	16	0	16	16	0	0	0	0	0	0	0	0	0	0	0	0
Other craftsmen & kindred workers	700	558	142	649	529	120	51	29	22	87	63	24	0	0	0	138	92
Operatives, except transportation	2,368	1,359	1,009	2,135	1,228	907	176	100	76	497	238	259	57	31	26	730	369
Assemblers	260	116	144	249	111	138	11	5	6	59	38	21	0	0	0	70	43
Bottling & canning operatives	NA	NA	3	NA	NA	0	NA	NA	3	NA	NA	0	NA	NA	0	NA	NA
Checkers, examiners, & inspectors; manufacturing	73	23	50	73	23	50	0	0	0	12	6	6	0	0	0	12	6
Dressmakers & seamstresses, except factory	23	0	23	23	0	23	0	0	0	11	0	11	0	0	0	11	0
Garage workers & station attend'ts	NA	180	NA	NA	170	NA	NA	6	NA	NA	12	NA	NA	4	NA	NA	22
Graders & sorters, manufacturing	4	0	4	4	0	4	0	0	0	0	0	0	0	0	0	0	0
Laundry & dry cleaning operatives, n.e.c.[2]	99	40	59	67	30	37	21	10	11	61	20	41	11	0	11	93	30
Meat cutters & butchers	NA	15	NA	NA	15	NA	NA	0	NA	NA	6	NA	NA	0	NA	NA	6
Mine operatives, n.e.c.[2]	35	35	0	35	35	0	0	0	0	0	0	0	0	0	0	0	0

Form 10 (continued)

	TOTAL ALL RACES			WHITE			NEGRO			SPANISH HERITAGE[1]			ALL OTHER RACES			TOTAL MINORITY	
	Total	Male	Female	Total	Male	Female	Total	Male	Female	Total	Male	Female	Total	Male	Female	Total	Male
Packers & wrappers, except produce	215	42	173	191	42	149	20	0	20	55	7	48	4	0	4	79	7
Painters, manufactured articles	NA	36	NA	NA	36	NA	NA	0	NA	NA	0	NA	NA	0	NA	NA	0
Precision machine operatives	NA	45	NA	NA	45	NA	NA	0	NA	NA	0	NA	NA	0	NA	NA	0
Sawyers	6	6	0	6	6	0	0	0	0	0	0	0	0	0	0	0	0
Sewers & stitchers	NA	NA	102	NA	NA	91	NA	NA	5	NA	NA	23	NA	NA	6	NA	NA
Stationary firemen	0	0	0	0	0	0	0	0	0	0	0	0	0	0	0	0	0
Textile operatives	5	5	0	5	5	0	0	0	0	0	0	0	0	0	0	0	0
Welders & flamecutters	NA	60	NA	NA	60	NA	NA	0	NA	NA	5	NA	NA	0	NA	NA	5
Other metalworking operatives	NA	56	NA	NA	56	NA	NA	0	NA	NA	5	NA	NA	0	NA	NA	5
Other specified operatives	532	339	193	475	292	183	30	25	5	103	54	49	27	22	5	160	101
Misc. & nonspecified operatives	619	361	258	534	302	232	80	54	26	145	85	60	5	5	0	230	144
Occupation:																	
Machine operatives, misc. specified	NA	123	NA	NA	119	NA	NA	4	NA	NA	65	NA	0	0	0	NA	69
Machine operatives, nonspecified	NA	77	NA	NA	61	NA	NA	16	NA	NA	14	NA	0	0	0	NA	30
Miscellaneous operatives	NA	90	NA	NA	77	NA	NA	8	NA	NA	6	NA	5	5	0	NA	19
Nonspecified operatives	NA	71	NA	NA	45	NA	NA	26	NA	NA	0	NA	0	0	0	NA	26
Industry:																	
Manufacturing	515	289	226	443	243	200	67	41	26	119	72	47	5	5	0	191	118
Durable goods	158	113	45	134	89	45	19	19	0	37	23	14	5	5	0	61	47
Wood products, including furniture	18	18	0	18	18	0	0	0	0	0	0	0	0	0	0	0	0
Primary metal industries	0	0	0	0	0	0	0	0	0	0	0	0	0	0	0	0	0
Fabricated metal industries	NA	0	NA	NA	0	NA	0	0	0	NA	0	NA	0	0	0	NA	0
Machinery, including electrical	35	31	4	35	31	4	0	0	0	23	23	0	0	0	0	23	23
Motor vehicles & equipment	NA	4	NA	NA	4	NA	0	0	0	NA	0	NA	0	0	0	NA	0
Transportation equipment, except motor vehicles	13	13	0	13	13	0	0	0	0	0	0	0	0	0	0	0	0
Other durable goods	88	47	41	64	23	41	19	19	0	14	0	14	5	5	0	38	24
Nondurable goods	357	176	181	309	154	155	48	22	26	82	49	33	0	0	0	130	71
Food & kindred products	122	59	63	103	52	51	19	7	12	36	24	12	0	0	0	55	31
Apparel & other fabricated textile products	4	0	4	4	0	4	0	0	0	0	0	0	0	0	0	0	0
Paper & allied products	9	9	0	9	9	0	0	0	0	0	0	0	0	0	0	0	0
Chemicals & allied products	16	16	0	11	11	0	5	5	0	0	0	0	0	0	0	5	5
Other nondurable goods	206	92	114	182	82	100	24	10	14	46	25	21	0	0	0	70	35
Nonspecified manufacturing industries	0	0	0	0	0	0	0	0	0	0	0	0	0	0	0	0	0
Nonmanufacturing industries	104	72	32	91	59	32	13	13	0	26	13	13	0	0	0	39	26
Transportation, communication, & other public utilities	NA	15	NA	NA	11	NA	4	4	0	NA	0	NA	0	0	0	NA	4
Wholesale & retail trade	NA	30	NA	NA	25	NA	5	5	0	NA	13	NA	0	0	0	NA	18
All other industries	NA	27	NA	NA	23	NA	4	4	0	NA	0	NA	0	0	0	NA	4
Transportation equipment operatives	753	742	11	701	690	11	32	32	0	89	89	0	20	20	0	141	141
Bus drivers	NA	11	NA	NA	5	NA	6	6	0	0	0	0	0	0	0	6	6
Taxicab drivers & chauffeurs	NA	27	NA	NA	27	NA	0	0	0	0	0	0	0	0	0	0	0
Truck drivers & deliverymen	NA	531	NA	NA	496	NA	15	15	0	64	64	0	20	20	0	99	99
Other transportation equip. operatives	NA	173	NA	NA	162	NA	11	11	0	25	25	0	0	0	0	36	36
Laborers, except farm	1,723	1,592	131	1,523	1,405	118	154	148	6	469	436	33	46	39	7	669	623
Construction laborers	NA	503	NA	NA	460	NA	NA	43	NA	NA	216	NA	NA	0	NA	NA	259
Freight, stock, & material handlers	NA	400	NA	NA	378	NA	NA	18	NA	NA	62	NA	NA	4	NA	NA	84
Other specified laborers	NA	411	NA	NA	323	NA	NA	65	NA	NA	88	NA	NA	23	NA	NA	176
Miscellaneous & nonspecified laborers	NA	278	NA	NA	244	NA	NA	22	NA	NA	70	NA	NA	12	NA	NA	104
Industry:																	
Manufacturing	NA	97	NA	NA	90	NA	NA	7	NA	NA	21	NA	NA	0	NA	NA	28
Durable goods	57	57	0	50	50	0	7	7	0	14	14	0	0	0	0	21	21
Wood products, including furniture	11	11	0	11	11	0	0	0	0	0	0	0	0	0	0	0	0
Metal industries	15	15	0	8	8	0	7	7	0	0	0	0	0	0	0	7	7
Metal Industries	15	15	0	8	8	0	0	0	0	0	0	0	0	0	0	9	9
Machinery, including electrical	10	10	0	10	10	0	0	0	0	9	9	0	0	0	0	5	5
Transportation equipment	12	12	0	12	12	0	0	0	0	5	5	0	0	0	0	5	5
Other durable goods	9	9	0	9	9	0	0	0	0	NA	7	NA	NA	0	NA	NA	7
Nondurable goods	NA	40	NA	NA	40	NA	NA	0	NA	NA	0	NA	NA	0	NA	NA	0
Food & kindred products	NA	22	NA	NA	22	NA	NA	0	NA	NA	0	NA	NA	0	NA	NA	0
Nonspecified manufacturing indust's	0	0	0	0	0	0	0	0	0	0	0	0	0	0	0	0	0
Manufacturing Industries	NA	181	NA	NA	154	NA	NA	15	NA	NA	49	NA	NA	12	NA	NA	76
Railroads & railway express service	NA	12	NA	NA	6	NA	NA	0	NA	NA	0	NA	NA	6	NA	NA	6
Transportation, except railroads	NA	5	NA	NA	5	NA	NA	0	NA	NA	0	NA	NA	0	NA	NA	0
Communications, utilities & sanitary services	NA	15	NA	NA	15	NA	NA	0	NA	NA	0	NA	NA	0	NA	NA	0
Wholesale & retail trade	NA	55	NA	NA	55	NA	NA	0	NA	NA	21	NA	NA	0	NA	NA	21
All other nonmanufacturing indust's	NA	94	NA	NA	73	NA	NA	15	NA	NA	28	NA	NA	6	NA	NA	49
Farmers & farm managers	36	36	0	36	36	0	0	0	0	0	0	0	0	0	0	0	0
Farm laborers & farm foremen	257	222	35	246	211	35	0	0	0	63	54	9	11	11	0	74	65
Paid farm laborers & farm foremen	248	217	31	237	206	31	0	0	0	59	54	5	11	11	0	70	65
Unpaid family workers	9	5	4	9	5	4	0	0	0	4	0	4	0	0	0	4	0
Service workers, except private household	2,923	1,380	1,543	2,595	1,233	1,362	271	120	151	382	227	155	57	27	30	710	374
Cleaning service workers	676	450	226	580	396	184	91	54	37	119	101	18	5	0	5	215	155
Chambermaids & maids	NA	NA	101	NA	NA	86	NA	NA	15	NA	NA	0	0	0	0	NA	NA
Other cleaning service workers	NA	NA	125	NA	NA	98	NA	NA	22	NA	NA	18	5	0	5	NA	NA

Form 10 (continued)

Denver Standard Metropolitan Statistical Area

	TOTAL ALL RACES			WHITE			NEGRO			SPANISH HERITAGE[1]			ALL OTHER RACES			TOTAL MINORITY	
	Total	Male	Female	Total	Male	Female	Total	Male	Female	Total	Male	Female	Total	Male	Female	Total	Male
Food service workers	1,435	618	817	1,250	534	716	138	57	81	142	70	72	47	27	20	327	154
Cooks, except private household	214	140	74	177	126	51	17	4	13	25	16	9	20	10	10	62	30
Busboys & dishwashers	NA	275	NA	NA	229	NA	NA	34	NA	NA	35	NA	NA	12	NA	NA	81
Waitresses & food counter workers	NA	NA	542	NA	NA	499	NA	NA	33	NA	NA	44	NA	NA	10	NA	NA
Other food service workers	404	203	201	345	179	166	54	19	35	38	19	19	5	5	0	97	43
Health service workers	218	18	200	199	18	181	14	0	14	21	9	12	5	0	5	40	9
Nursing aides, orderlies, & attendants	NA	NA	131	NA	NA	117	14	0	14	NA	NA	12	0	0	0	NA	NA
Practical nurses	33	0	33	28	0	28	0	0	0	0	0	0	5	0	5	5	0
Personal services workers	273	118	155	260	109	151	13	9	4	40	20	20	0	0	0	53	29
Hairdressers & cosmetologists	NA	58	NA	NA	58	NA	NA	0	NA	NA	13	NA	0	0	0	NA	13
Protective service workers	NA	64	NA	NA	64	NA	NA	0	NA	NA	8	NA	0	0	0	NA	8
Firemen, fire protection	14	14	0	14	14	0	0	0	0	0	0	0	0	0	0	0	0
Guards & watchmen	27	27	0	27	27	0	0	0	0	8	8	0	0	0	0	8	8
Policemen & detectives	NA	17	NA	NA	17	NA	NA	0	NA	8	8	0	0	0	0	8	8
Other protective service workers	6	6	0	6	6	0	0	0	0	0	0	0	0	0	0	0	0
Private household workers	183	15	168	150	5	145	33	10	23	26	0	26	0	0	0	59	10
Private household workers, living in	9	0	9	9	0	9	0	0	0	0	0	0	0	0	0	0	0
Private household workers, living out	174	15	159	141	5	136	33	10	23	26	0	26	0	0	0	59	10
Unemployed persons, last worked in 1959 or earlier	378	92	286	346	86	260	32	6	26	15	0	15	0	0	0	47	6

1   Spanish heritage persons are included in the White data and Total Minority data.

2   Not elsewhere classified.

NA   Not available.

PART C

Form 11 EEO Goal Report Sheet

EEO Category	All			Minorities											% of Total		Availability, %		Under-utilization (yes) or (no)		Ultimate Goals				12-Month Goals														
	Total	Male	Female	Male					Female							Min.	Fem.	Min.	Fem.	Min.	Fem.	Minority		Female		Job Openings							Goals						Backup Goals	
				Black	Hispanic	Asian-Amer. Pac. Isl.	Amer. Ind./ Alas. Nat.		Black	Hispanic	Asian-Amer. Pac. Isl.	Amer. Ind./ Alas. Nat.										No. %	Date	No. %	Date	Projection			How Filled			Minority			Female			H/G %	FEM. %
																										Attr.	Expan.	Total	From Within	New Hire	Total	Prom.	New Hire	Date	Prom.	New Hire	Date		

Name _____   Group Number _____

Date _____   Class Section _____   Hour _____   Score _____

ASSESSMENT OF LEARNING IN PERSONNEL ADMINISTRATION
EXERCISE 17

1. Try to state the purpose of this exercise in one concise sentence.

2. Specifically what did you learn from this exercise (i.e., skills, abilities, and knowledge)?

3. How might your learning influence your role and your duties as a personnel administrator?

4. What would be the potential benefits for an organization if it successfully developed an affirmative-action program? What would be the potential costs?

5. How could an affirmative-action program be evaluated as to its effectiveness?

6. At what stage(s) should the personnel staff charged with developing an affirmative-action program or complying with EEOC guidelines coordinate its efforts with line managers? How could such coordination be achieved?

7. Precisely what is "adverse impact"?

8. What would be the areas of interdependence between affirmative-action programs and the following human-resource programs: interviewing, testing, assessing training needs, designing training and development programs, human-resource planning, wage and salary administration, motivation programs, and union contractual administration? (Use additional sheets.)

Exercise 18

The impact of unions on personnel administration and human resource management: constraints and opportunities

PREVIEW

Labor unions are a very visible and powerful element in the workings of a postindustrial society such as exists in the United States. They are no longer limited to craft or industrial workers, but now include virtually all types of occupations, including white-collar and professional ones. The internal operations of an organization that has a labor union are often quite different from those of one without a union; virtually every phase of human resource management is affected directly or indirectly.

Developing human resource programs when unions are present, as well as direct negotiation with the union as to working conditions, wages, and other aspects of employment, are tasks typically given to the personnel department or the industrial- or employee-relations department of an organization. As illustrated in previous exercises, the personnel administrator and his or her staff are constrained and influenced by the concerns and objectives of different groups, notably government and management. Labor unions must now be added to the list. As was noted in Exercise 1, personnel administrators are often required to walk a fine line in attempting to please each of these three groups simultaneously.

The constraints unions place on human resource management are often quite obvious, such as promotion and wage and salary decisions that must be made within contract provisions. But a union also can present potential opportunities for cooperation between labor and management which can benefit individuals, organizations, and the personnel department. For example, a union's affirmative-action program can be coordinated with an organization's such that recruitment, selection, training, and placement costs are shared. This exercise explores the constraints and opportunities unions present to personnel administration.

OBJECTIVES

1. To provide an overview of the impact of labor unions on personnel and human resource program design and implementation.

2. To provide information about major labor laws, labor-relations terminology, and labor concepts—all prerequisites to establishing an effective labor-relations program.

3. To build skill in interpreting union agreement (contract) language and provisions, and in computing the economic cost of certain contractual provisions.

4. To begin to build skills in contract administration by analyzing several grievance situations, and in contract negotiation and bargaining by negotiating several issues of a contract.

PREMEETING PREPARATION

Read the *Introduction, Procedure, Appendixes,* and all forms in Parts A, B, and C. Read only Forms 6–9 and 13 of Part D. Do not read Forms 10, 11, or 12 until you are assigned a role by your *implementor.* For Form 4 of Part B, you will need a copy of a union contract. Read Form 4 well in advance of the time you plan to fill it out in order to allow sufficient time to obtain a contract from a local or national union office,

a library, an acquaintance who is a union member, or other source.

INTRODUCTION

Labor Relations: An Introduction to Policy, Practice, and Contract Negotiation and Administration*

When a union represents employees of an organization, personnel-administration decisions and programs are subject to the terms specified in the labor contract. Because of this potential constraint, personnel administration becomes more complex in a unionized company. As part of management, personnel cannot act unilaterally when unions exist. It must consult the contract and perhaps union officials first. For example, if a vacancy occurs in a supervisory position, rather than interviewing all existing workers in a department in order to find the most qualified applicant, the personnel staff must consult the contract. It may specify who the promotion must be given to through its seniority provisions. In addition, if workers are not unionized, various personnel practices affect the potential attraction a union may have for employees. The employees' desire to unionize or not would, of course, depend in part on the type of personnel or human-resource management decisions currently being made, their scope, and their fairness. Thus, knowledge about unions and skill in dealing with them is essential for all managers, but particularly for those in personnel, as they typically have primary responsibility for direct relations with the union.

The impact of unions on personnel is significant and complex, and stems from the union's impact on an employer in general. Managerial control over personnel programs and policy is restricted, as is managerial authority. However, as will be later pointed out, the union may present opportunities for more effective human resource management along with these constraints. In their efforts to deal with the demands of unions, management, and government simultaneously, wise personnel staffs look for these opportunities. This *Introduction* touches upon the union's appeal to workers, the development of labor unions in this country, labor legislation, and labor-contract negotiation and administration. The final section of this review notes how some specific personnel programs are typically affected by labor unions, as well as the positive consequences of

unionism for personnel administration. Given the size and importance of this area and our space limitations, this review must be brief and selective.[1]

Why Workers Join Unions. Unions are formal groups of workers founded to represent workers' interests to management. Given differences in status and resources, as well as other reasons, workers acting individually cannot be expected to have major influence over managerial decisions, unless, of course, management actively seeks their participation. However, there is strength in numbers. Collectively, workers can have considerable power and influence. When this influence is channeled through labor unions with large memberships, financial resources, technical expertise, and professional leadership it becomes impossible to ignore.

Unions offer self-protection to their members from real and perceived exploitation and mistreatment by employers. Through collective action workers can improve wages, working conditions, hours, and other aspects of the work environment. Vast gains have been realized in these areas over the years.

Unions also offer workers self-expression.[2] Strikes, grievances, meetings, and other activities offer a relief from the monotony of many jobs. The union brings with it opportunities for action, for developing personal abilities and skills, for recognition, for interpersonal relationships, and for excitement. Anyone who has been involved in a strike or a union organizing campaign may attest to the last item.

The promise of solidarity or togetherness is also a motivation to join unions. A "we-feeling" or cohesion is fostered among people who share the same problems, frustrations, and life circumstances. Besides providing a vent for frustration and an outlet for action, unions pull together people who are in similar positions. These shared problems and experiences—the feeling that one is not alone—is important to many.

---

* The legislation and terminology mentioned here are detailed in *Appendixes A* and *B,* respectively, of this exercise.

---

[1] Refer to *For Further Reading* for sources containing more information about the issues covered here.

[2] M. S. Myers, *Managing without Unions* (Reading, Mass.: Addison-Wesley, 1976), Chap. 5.

Of course, people join unions for reasons other than self-protection, self-expression, and solidarity. Many join through real or perceived coercion by others; others have little choice due to the control unions have over entry into certain trades; and some join primarily for economic benefits, others to become active leaders, and others to gain personal power and position.

The Development of Labor Unions. Unions in one form or another have existed in this country since it was formed over 200 years ago. In the early days of unionism, unions were largely fraternal organizations. After the country became industrialized, unions sought to influence employers, but initially they had little impact. Employers could discharge union members at will, and uneven financial situations in the late 1800s and early 1900s often forced persons to accept whatever jobs and conditions they were offered. Legally, too, employers had the upper hand, for they could require employees to sign (yellow dog) contracts indicating they would not join unions.

Under the Sherman Anti-Trust Act of 1890 (see *Appendix A*) union efforts to exert pressure on employers were considered illegal conspiracies. This conspiracy doctrine limited union activity severely. Unions during the late 1800s were primarily concerned with social reform and better working conditions. They were, in a minority of cases, led by people with deep philosophical differences from the free-enterprise, capitalistic business values that prevailed as this country moved rapidly toward industrialization.

The Civil War brought a somewhat relaxed stance toward unions, and after the war several nation-wide associations of various sorts were attempted. The National Labor Union was the first of these, established in Baltimore in 1866, but it had a very brief life. In 1869 the Knights of Labor, including members of craft unions as well as skilled and unskilled labor, was formed in Philadelphia. The Knights were successful at centralizing unionizing efforts for some years and had over 700,000 members at one time. In 1886 the American Federation of Labor (AFL) was formed; it has since merged (in 1955) with the Congress of Industrial Organizations (CIO). The AFL-CIO is the largest organization of its type and is extremely powerful and visible today in general political and economic spheres.

In the 1930s, a deep split occurred between craft unions, composed of members of such occupations as typographers, and industrial unions, made up of plumbers, brick layers, carpenters, semiskilled and unskilled workers in selected industries. A faction of those in the AFL decided unskilled workers should also be unionized, as industrialization made craft workers increasingly less important. After facing stiff initial opposition from within the AFL, since craft unions felt the inclusion of unskilled labor would dilute their earnings and power, this minority group favoring unskilled unionization broke off to form the CIO. Eventually, as craft unions did decline and industrial unionization became increasingly prevalent during the 1940s and 1950s, the AFL and CIO merged.

Today, about one in four non-agricultural workers belongs to a union[3], and the composition of unions is changing to include white-collar workers. Office and professional workers in government, insurance, finance, trades and services, and educational organizations have organized. Service professionals, such as law enforcement workers and fire fighters, have also joined unions.

Unions are concerned with many issues in addition to economic ones—they provide recreational, educational, financial, health, and other services to their members. Unions, in a way, are now big business. They are often very well off financially and, due to pension funds and other assets, control huge sums of money—consequently, their investment decisions affect the entire United States economy. Some are extremely active politically. They work for various candidates at all levels, and public endorsement from a large national union's president is a highly prized benefit to politicians. Unions have research branches, sponsor grants and fellowships, and hold various types of meetings, conventions, and workshops. They hire professionals of almost every type, including accountants, economists, lawyers, personnel specialists, librarians, communications experts, psychologists, and others. However, a brief look at United States labor laws and the chronological emergence of unions indicates that the modern-day national union, housed in a high-rise downtown headquarters building staffed by highly trained professionals, is a rather recent phenomenon.

United States Labor Legislation.[4] Employers initially responded to unions in this country with strong opposition. They felt that unions posed a threat to the authority and freedom of management. While there were no early laws that specifically protected employers and few viable employer associations or groups to counteract unions' power, courts were used to challenge unions quite successfully. The balance of

---

[3] D. Yoder, *Personnel Management and Industrial Relations,* 6th ed. (Englewood Cliffs, N.J.: Prentice-Hall, 1976), Chap. 16.

[4] See also *Appendix A.*

power was clearly in the employer's favor. Unions were considered conspiracies, and injunctions were issued by the courts which prohibited unions and their members from certain activities, such as strikes or picketing. The courts felt such activities damaged employers' private properties and infringed on their rights to operate their businesses.

Employers' associations eventually developed to counteract unions—some to unify employers' positions and hence their power, others to destroy unions and prevent bargaining. They maintained "blacklists" of union organizers, members, and sympathizers, and employed strike breakers and armed guards to crush strikes and picket lines. Currently, both employers' and unions' tactics are strictly limited and controlled by various "unfair labor practices" issued through legislation (discussed below).

Some employers now bargain together with other organizations in an industry to form "master" agreements with a union. They have formed numerous trade and other types of associations, such as the National Association of Manufacturers, which lobby for favorable legislation and conduct advertising and educational campaigns to convey employers' points of view. Employers have, for the most part, recognized the role of unions. They have developed effective bargaining techniques and other strategies, but their posture toward unions still rums from cooperation to open conflict.

No matter what the general posture of any particular employer or union may be toward the other, as a group, both have been very active in influencing United States public policy and legislation relevant to unions. This legislation's development has generally reflected the prevailing attitude in the country toward unions, an attitude that has shifted back and forth from antiunion to prounion to neutrality.[5]

The conspiracy doctrine noted above marks the antiunion period. Under the Sherman Anti-Trust Act of 1890, courts interpreted union activity as conspiracies to restrain trade and, therefore, outlawed them. Until various court cases stemming from the Clayton Act of 1914 were decided, union activity was basically illegal. The legal doctrine severely constrained union activities.

The Clayton Act, also meant to curb monopolies and restraint of trade, did severely limit the use of injunctions against labor practices and asserted the right to strike. Court rulings, however, nullified the intention of the Clayton Act, and unions continued to face a hostile legal environment.

---

[5] See Yoder, *Personnel Management and Industrial Relations,* for a more detailed account of labor-legislation trends.

The Railway Labor Act of 1926 was the first law to specifically state a favorable United States stand toward collective bargaining. This act granted employees the legal right to engage in collective bargaining. The prounion period, spurred by depression and characteristics of the political climate, had begun.

The Norris-LaGuardia Act of 1932 helped unions further by restricting injunctions and stating that collective-bargaining attempts must be made before disputes can be brought to court. But the National Labor Relations Act (Wagner Act) of 1935 was the key piece of legislation favoring unions. Its impact was monumental: it stated that the policy of the United States was to encourage collective bargaining, defined several employer unfair labor practices that were prohibited, and established the National Labor Relations Board (NLRB) to administrate the act.

From 1935 to 1947 unions grew very rapidly. Strikes, political activity, and the charges by employers that the 1935 act was too biased in favor of unions, among other factors, led to the passage of the Taft-Hartley Act in 1947. This act represented a shift back to the employer side of the continuum representing United States policy regarding unions. The Taft-Hartley Act specified several union excesses. Reporting and disclosure rules were also established for unions to allow public scrutiny of their internal operations.

In 1959, passage of the Landrum-Griffin Act signalled a return to neutrality in United States labor legislation. Both unions and management were given more stringent reporting and disclosure rules. Unions were prohibited from exploiting their members financially and in other respects, and provisions prohibiting secondary boycotts and hot-cargo agreements, as well as provisions to assure union democracy, were written.

While other legislation since 1959 has certainly influenced labor relations, the laws noted above were fundamental. They established the framework of United States labor relations and mirrored the prevailing attitudes toward organized labor as unions were developing. Recent legislation, with the exceptation of the 1964 and 1972 Equal Employment Opportunity Laws (see Exercise 18), is narrow in scope. Laws deal with specific aspects of human-resource management, such as wages (see Exercise 16), not with overall labor relations.

Collective Bargaining and Labor Contract Negotiations. In the early days of collective bargaining, little real negotiation or discussion took place. Depending on the relative strength of the union and management, one notified the other of wage rates and other conditions. If there was a dispute, a strike or lockout often resulted. Today, collective bargaining—the process of negotiation, administration, and interpretation of collective agreements, as well as dispute settlements—is still emerging and changing.

Collective bargaining is actually a form of industrial democracy. Management and union representatives sit down at a table and deliberate, argue, discuss, bargain, haggle, and try to influence each other regarding various aspects of the employment situation. Their eventual agreement is written up as a contract which becomes "industrial law," enforceable in court, governing the parties. They must bargain in good faith; that is, they must agree to meet, to continue to meet, to offer proposals and counterproposals, and to try to reach agreement.

In this country, most contracts are negotiated by a single company and a single union, called single-employer bargaining. This bargaining can be for one plant or location of an organization, or for several. Recently, however, multiple-employer bargaining has become more common. Organizations come together to bargain with one or more unions simultaneously. Such bargaining can be set up by labor market (e.g., a city), by geographical region (e.g., the Southwest), or by industry. Single-employer bargaining is common in manufacturing, but if a large organization has several plants organized by the same national union (e.g., GM and United Auto Workers), each local union at each plant will send representatives to a national board which will formulate the major contract proposals. Then, a master agreement will be negotiated with the company and each local may bargain with each individual plant for supplemental provisions.

Multiemployer bargaining is common in construction, lumbering, mining, trucking, textiles, and steel. It has the advantage for the employer of reducing competition from other organizations by limiting advantages they might achieve in separate negotiations—for example, lower wages that would permit them to sell their competing products cheaper. For smaller unions, it is efficient and sometimes beneficial to bargain with several employers at once. However, the consumer may suffer, as multiemployer bargaining may result in higher wages (and therefore prices). When a strike occurs, the whole industry may be shut down and product availability shrinks.

Contract Negotiation. In the early days of contract negotiation, unions demanded certain provisions and management's first response was a simple "no"—since they had no idea what the union would propose, they were not prepared to respond with counterproposals. Now, months are often spent preparing for negotiations. Research is conducted on both sides to gather information about industry agreements, trends, how well the current contract is working, financial situations, etc. The costs of possible demands are estimated. Often, unions poll their members to ascertain their desires. Priority issues are decided on and overall strategy is discussed. Besides background data, both sides need to know the laws and procedures established by the National Labor Relations Board and legislation regarding unfair labor practices to assure compliance.

The negotiating teams typically consist of the local union president, a few additional local union officials, perhaps an official from the international union, the labor relations or personnel administrator from the organization, and one or more of his or her staff, and sometimes other experts (e.g., lawyers, financial experts, line managers, or executives). The initial meeting is important because a climate is established that usually continues throughout the negotiations. It varies from belligerence and conflict to cooperation. Rules and procedures are agreed on for subsequent sessions; initial proposals may be exchanged; and each side may ask the other to explain the proposals in order to ascertain how important they might be to the proposing side or how well thought out and defensible they might be.

Negotiations are not unlike a good poker game: bluffing tactics, feinted anger, appeals to the press or observers, and very careful divulging of one's "hand" are common strategies. Total candor is seldom seen. Neither side wants the other to know how it will ultimately go or how important each item may really be. Some proposals must be attained, others are desirable but not critical, and others are merely for trading purposes.

As negotiations continue, proposals may be accepted, amended, or withdrawn; counterproposals may be made; and/or compromises may be settled on. The most important issues usually come last. If one party proposes a solution definitely outside of the "bargaining zone," or tolerance limit, of the other and the first party does not change the proposal, a deadlock may result.[6] Of course, acceptance, rejection, deadlock, or compromise on any issue is determined by the many characteristics of each individual situation.

Negotiators realize they must secure the approval of their superiors, as well as the rank-and-file members in the case of the union for any agreements made. Union members will seldom, however, fail to ratify a contract

---

[6] For a very interesting discussion of the psychology of negotiations and strategy in bargaining, see R. Stagner and H. Rosen, *The Psychology of Union-Management Relations* (Belmont, Cal.: Wadsworth, 1965).

and it must be renegotiated. Union leaders try to prevent this, as it speaks poorly for their ability to represent their constituents. Therefore, there is little to gain in negotiations by trying to push something through that is unrealistic, unreasonable, will not work, or will not be ratified.

Each side uses several types of pressure to help gain acceptance of their demands. The most powerful weapon for the union is usually the strike, a cessation of work which can force the employer to cease operations. The seriousness of strikes often makes them a last-resort tactic.[7] Picketing involves parading in front of the organization and other locations with banners or posters which signify a dispute is in progress; the objective is to enlist support, publicize the strike, and often to prevent other employees from entering the building. Boycotts prevent union members (and other parties in a secondary boycott) from buying employer products or services. Grievances are also a dispute tactic. They are formal complaints filed with an organization arising out of a dispute over the contract. The contract typically has provisions for handling these grievances which must be followed.

One of the employer's most effective responses to a union dispute is the lockout, or a refusal to employ the workers during the dispute. Lockouts are sometimes used if violence or damage to property has occurred. However, employers are typically reluctant to use a lockout due to lost revenue and unfavorable public opinion. They usually attempt to continue operations while a dispute or strike is in progress. This keeps their organization earning revenues, sometimes lowers prestige of union leaders, and can gain more favorable provisions as the power of the strike is lessened.

On the other hand, deep-seated bitterness may develop if an organization continues to operate during a strike, and this can lead to problems in future negotiations. Negotiations occur for each contract and some victories may be "hollow" ones if the "losing" side enters the next set of negotiations seeking to make up for lost ground or to "teach the other side a lesson." Retaliation and revenge, which can result from bitter relations, unreasonable demands, violence, destruction of property, or inflexibility on the part of either side, color subsequent negotiations and block cooperation.

If a strike or lockout occurs, sooner or later both sides feel its effects. Unions have only so much money in their "strike funds" and employers can suspend operations only so long before they lose customers or are unable to pay their expenses. When disputes arise

---

[7] Several types of strikes are defined in *Appendix B*.

that cannot be settled by negotiations, outside third parties are often called in. A conciliator may be used to reestablish communication between the parties and set a climate more favorable to negotiation. A mediator may be used to offer suggestions and proposals. An arbitrator or an umpire may also be called in to actually decide the dispute after hearing both sides. Usually arbitration becomes necessary as contracts are administered and grievances occur, rather than as they are negotiated. Finally, the government may intervene to settle a dispute, strike, and/or lockout if there is a threat to national security or public welfare.

The Labor Agreement. Several substantive issues or provisions are typically contained in most labor agreements, as well as additional ones particular to the two parties involved. Union security is usually the first substantial area dealt with in the contract, for it concerns the union's right to exist and continue to exist. A contract provision may specify the union has security by stating that all employees must join the union (i.e., a union shop), or must pay a fee to the union but do not have to join (i.e., an agency shop). Unions, of course, are opposed to employees who do not join the union but benefit from the gains it obtains. Most employer groups resent compulsory unionism, however, and feel a union shop grants a union too much power.

A second area covered in the agreement is management rights. Management seeks to obtain agreement that certain areas (e.g., product pricing, accounting methods, directing employees, job content, etc.) are exclusive management rights. Although unions typically concede that the above areas are rightfully in management's domain, the two parties sharply disagree over certain others. Among these latter issues are work standards, discipline, work scheduling, work assignment, and promotions. Unions often do have a say in many of these now.

Wages, the third major area in contracts, includes many specific items, such as wage adjustment, job evaluation and classification, premium pay, call-in pay, time study, cost-of-living increases, and any number of fringe benefits. This area is of crucial economic importance to both sides, and the skill of negotiators is often evaluated on the basis of these quantifiable items. Obviously, too many considerations enter into wage and benefit determination to enumerate; financial position of the organization, general economic conditions, precedents, historic trends, and labor demand and supply are but a few.

Job rights are another key contract area. Unions attempt to provide security for their members by controlling transfer, promotion, demotion, termination, and layoff decisions. Seniority is usually the criterion unions seek to use for such decisions, but employers often feel strict seniority rules restrict their freedom to make decisions based on merit. Usually layoffs are made on the basis of seniority, while promotions are based on seniority and merit.

Grievance handling is the final important substantive area of contracts. Grievances can arise over any number of issues, such as disciplinary actions, promotions, pay, or work rules. The contract specifies a procedure used to resolve such grievances and thereby gives the aggrieved parties recourse. Typically, the grievance moves from the supervisor and shop steward or union committee person (where most are settled) to a shop committee consisting of members of labor and management, to an appeal committee consisting of higher-level officials of both sides, and finally perhaps to arbitration, where a third party decides the grievance. The filing of a grievance signifies that the aggrieved party feels the organization has not administered the contract faithfully, and the grievance procedure provides a means to decide how the contract should be interpreted.

Contract Administration. After a contract is ratified or accepted, both sides must conduct their affairs according to its provisions. However, no written contract can predict all of the problems that may be encountered as it is used. In order to administer the contract effectively, each side has certain responsibilities.

One such responsibility is communication and interpretation. The contract provisions must be communicated to all parties concerned and interpreted for them in everyday language to facilitate compliance. Next, consistency in interpretation and administration over time and across departments is vital to assure fairness. New interpretations should be publicized. Flexibility and adaptability are required—the contract must be somewhat pliable as it is applied. When novel situations arise for which there is no specific guideline, labor and management must cooperate to interpret the contract in a reasonable manner. Sometimes contracts contain reopening clauses which specify that during the term of the contract certain clauses may be renegotiated as situations warrant. Provisions and amendments are often necessary to allow the contract to realistically reflect the dynamic nature of the work setting.

Administration of a union contract is a difficult process for management and labor. Further, it is a day-to-day process, not a periodic one, as is contract negotiation. A spirit of cooperation is essential, but administration is certainly aided by negotiating a reasonable and thorough contract initially, and by making certain all parties, particularly union stewards and first-line supervisors, are very familiar with the contract.

The Impact of Labor Unions on Personnel Programs and Decisions: Some Examples. The union contract and the existence of the union itself influence the personnel function in many ways. They affect decisions personnel staffs and line managers are able to make, as well as basic personnel-program design and implementation. In regard to decision making, a union contract specifies precedent and standard procedure, and it is therefore difficult, for example, to overlook an infraction of a rule made by a longstanding employee with an excellent record or to administer a less-severe punishment to an employee who had an exceptionally valid reason for violating a contract provision. The personnel administrator's staff must advise managers to look at the rule, not the person. In practice, this is difficult and distasteful to some.

Union contracts typically rely heavily on seniority. Seniority provisions can be beneficial in that they do reward loyalty. But the personnel administrator's staff must take seniority into account, often ignoring ability altogether, as it makes decisions. Accordingly, it may be impossible to give a promotion to a young, very able worker, or due to contract provisions regarding wage differentials, it may be impossible to give that same person a merit raise as a reward for performance. Such raises may only be possible with a certain seniority level. Finally, due to contract provisions, a supervisor may lose discretion in administering other bonuses, such as allowing someone to leave work early for a special occasion or as a reward. Hence, altruism must give way to due process or the rules and procedures specified in the contract.

Besides influencing various specific decisions made in regard to human resources, union contracts affect basic personnel programs. Seniority provisions influence performance-appraisal programs and bonus or motivation programs, such that the criteria for these programs becomes job tenure instead of merit. Selection procedures are also affected—for example, the contract may specify that vacancies be posted and filled from within whenever possible. Thus, selection procedures must be directed toward internal, rather than external, sources. Recruiting would also be affected, of course, as would human resource plans and forecasts which attempt to predict future human resource needs and their sources.

The union's existence and specific contract provisions do not necessarily make personnel programs less efficient or more difficult, but they must be taken into account as these programs are designed and implemented. In addition, since the various major personnel programs are so interdependent, a union's effect on one has an effect on others. Viable programs are possible if the union's impact is taken into account as the programs are designed and planned, not after implementation has begun, only to find a contractual provision that prohibits a specific practice.

Using the Union to Positive Advantage. The title of this exercise suggests that unions present constraints *and* opportunities for personnel administration. Such opportunities are often overlooked, especially if managers stereotype the union in a negative way. Opportunites are available in several areas. First, the union can share some of the record-keeping function of personnel, as it, too, keeps various records on its members which can serve as a check on company records. Second, the union's existence may help to bring some problems that otherwise would have been overlooked to the attention of proper officials. Real inequity between job types and their pay scales is an example. The union representative in the organization, the steward, can assist line managers by spotting problems. Third, the contract shifts some of the discipline burden to the union itself. Discipline takes considerable time and resources, as well as judgment, which can easily be attacked as capricious, subjective, or biased. With detailed grievance procedures and other rules, management can save the time and effort normally spent devising various disciplinary actions.

The union can also serve as an effectual communication link to employers, particularly through the steward, and the contract can facilitate the acceptance of certain management decisions that may be difficult for workers to understand and agree with. For example, the contract may specify holiday provisions or overtime rules—decisions management would otherwise have to justify to workers.

Although these advantages are possible, they are by no means assured or perhaps even typical. Many in personnel look upon unions as creating enormous problems, additional work, and expense. The degree to which a union presents constraints or opportunities to personnel depends on the individual situation and the posture of union-management relations in that situation. There are, however, potential advantages in almost every situation and these benefits should be fully explored.

Summary. The *Introduction* was intended to introduce the topic of labor unions and their relation to

personnel administration. As can be seen, the impacts are many and complex. Unions are now a fixed part of human-resource management. They remain viable in manufacturing, but are becoming increasingly large and powerful in the white-collar and professional jobs, both because the relative numbers of these jobs are increasing and because job holders have seen the effective results of collective action and power.

Organized labor in this country is still very much an emerging and changing movement, influenced heavily by general economic conditions, the political climate, public sentiment, and past precedent. Recent controversies, such as the right of public employees to strike, compulsory (forced) arbitration, and bargaining for such noneconomic issues as quality of working life, reflect these influences. The typical union member has also changed to reflect the demographic and value shifts in the country. Younger workers who are more mobile, more independent, better educated, and perhaps concerned with more than just economic gains, are now union members. Their job expectations are high and are channeled into areas not typically considered important in unions.

These trends may change, but the importance of organized labor and collective bargaining will no doubt remain and unions will continue to be a variable for personnel staffs to consider as they perform their duties. While some obvious impacts, both positive and negative, on personnel administration were discussed here, generalizations are tenuous in that their truth necessarily depends on each specific situation. However, a union's presence shifts some human resource-program priorities, specifies the design and implementation procedures of others, amends others significantly, and necessitates and/or precludes others entirely. Personnel or human resource decisions and programs are seldom effective if the presence of a labor union is not given its appropriate weight in personnel planning.

PROCEDURE

Overview. In this exercise, a set of review questions is given to assess your understanding of labor laws and terminology. Then, an example of the economic cost of a change in fringe benefits is presented. A questionnaire is designed to help you become familiar with actual labor-contract language and its possible effects on personnel programs. Next, several case studies of grievance situations are given. You are to analyze these cases and act as arbitrator. A simulated contract negotiation is also included in the exercise.

PART A

STEP 1: Review the *Introduction* and the *Appendixes* in this exercise and then answer the questions on Form 1. Discuss your answers in a small group and/or compare your answers with those your implementor reads.

TIME: About 55 minutes.

PART B

STEP 2: Read Form 2 carefully. Some background information and current contract provisions regarding benefits for an organization are given. Then, fill out Form 3 in order to compute the actual dollar costs of various changes in benefits written into a union contract. State any assumptions you made in computing the costs and decide whether or not it is feasible for the organization to proceed with a new project it has planned, based on its total anticipated labor costs.

TIME: About 50 minutes.

STEP 3: Form 4 requires the use of a union contract. Obtain a current contract from a local or national union office, a union member you may know, the contract used where you work, a library. One may be supplied by your implementor. Then, find the relevant articles in the contract that are noted on Form 4 and paraphase these where indicated on the form to familiarize yourself with the language used. Answer the questions posed after each contract article in order to become acquainted with the impact contract provisions might have on other personnel programs.

TIME: About one and one-half hours.

PART C

STEP 4: Form 5 contains brief descriptions of two grievances. Read each one carefully and note that each grievance has gone to arbitration— that is, it could *not* be settled through the contract's normal grievance procedure. You are the arbitrator who must decide each case. Note the issue posed on the form. Decide whether the action taken by the organization was proper and justified. Decide whether or not you will allow the action to stand as is or will amend it in some way. Include your

rationale in the space provided and state any assumptions about contract provisions or language you have made.

TIME: About one hour.

PART D

STEP 5: Form 6 contains general instructions for participants in a simulated contract-renegotiation activity. Forms 7 and 8 contain background information pertinent to the activity. Form 9 contains a statement of current contract provisions for the newspaper around which the simulation is developed. Read these forms carefully.

TIME: About 45 minutes.

STEP 6: Divide into groups of five or seven persons. Designate either two or three persons to be negotiators for the *union* and two or three to be negotiators for *management*. Remaining person(s) is (are) observer/arbitrator(s). Once the roles have been assigned, management-negotiating-team members should read *only* Form 10, which contains a statement of their initial position and their roles. Union-negotiating-team members should read *only* Form 11, containing the same information for the union team. Observer(s) should read Forms 10, 11, and 12. Negotiating-team members should be prepared to conduct a renegotiation of the union contract for the *Daily Post*. They should concentrate on the issues given to each on Forms 10 and 11 and use their role descriptions as a jumping-off place for their behavior. Both sides, as well as the observer/arbitrator(s), should read Form 13, which contains some guidelines for negotiations, and should also be very familiar with the background data presented in earlier forms of Part D. The ultimate objective is to renegotiate the contract (see Step 7). Members of each team may want to meet to discuss their strategy and to formulate their initial proposal, which can be in writing.

TIME: About 35 minutes to two hours, depending on whether strategy meetings are held and their length.

STEP 7: The actual renegotiation should now begin, using the issues noted on Forms 10 and 11 as the primary agenda. Plan to negotiate for about one to two hours. The teams may want to break once or twice to confer or caucus among themselves as proposals are brought up and/or preliminary agreements are or are not made. Team members should attempt to bargain effectively in relation to the particular organization they represent (i.e., union or management) and to bargain in good faith (e.g., do not storm out of the room and refuse to bargain). Observers should note the answers to questions on Part I of Form 12 as they carefully observe the negotiation process. If the agreement is reached through bargaining, the observer should fill out Part III of Form 12 fully in the presence of negotiators.

The teams should then discuss the process and the fairness and appropriateness of their contract. The observer can provide feedback on their behavior during negotiations.

TIME: About one-and-one-half to two-and-one-half hours.

STEP 8: If the bargaining results in a deadlock over one or more issues, binding arbitration will be used to resolve the deadlock. The observer(s) then becomes the arbitrator(s) and listens to both sides, weighs information, and arguments, perhaps consulting other sources (see *For Further Reading*) for precedent and background information, and makes a final decision. The proposals of either side could be accepted, a compromise struck, or a new alternative developed and used. The arbitrator then fills out Part II of Form 12 and the discussion noted in the second paragraph of Step 7 above is conducted.

TIME: About 45 minutes (not including the discussion counted in the same estimate given in Step 7).

FOR FURTHER READING

Aaron, B., J. R. Gorodin, and J. L. Stern, eds. *Public Sector Bargaining.* Washington, D.C.: The Bureau of National Affairs, 1979. (I)

Acuff, F. L., and M. Villere, "Games Negotiators Play." *Business Horizons* 19, no. 1 (February 1976): 70–76. (I)

Atwood, J. F. "Collective Bargaining's Challenge: Five Imperatives for Public Managers." *Public Personnel Management* 5 (January–February 1976): 24–32. (I)

Barbash, J. *American Unions: Structure, Government, and Politics.* New York: Random House, 1967. (I)

Beal, E. F., E. D. Wickersham, and P. Kienest. *The Practice of Collective Bargaining.* 3d ed. Homewood, Ill.: Irwin, 1973. (I)

Black, J. M. *Positive Discipline.* New York: AMACOM, 1970. (I)

Blake, R. R., H. A. Shepard, and J. S. Mouton. *Managing Intergroup Conflict in Industry.* Houston: Gulf, 1964. (I)

Bloch, R. I. "Race Discrimination in Industry and the Grievance Process." *Labor Law Journal* 21 (1970): 627–644. (I)

Block, R. N. "Legal and Traditional Criteria in the Arbitration of Set Discrimination Grievances." *Arbitration Journal* 32 (1977): 241–255. (II)

Bowers, M. H. *Labor Relations in the Public Safety Services.* Chicago: International Personnel Management Association, 1974. (I)

Brown, M. A. "Collective Bargaining on the Campus: Professors, Associations, and Unions." *Labor Law Journal* 21 (March 1970): 167–181. (II)

Bureau of National Affairs. *Grievance Guide,* 4th ed. Washington, D.C.: BNA, 1972. (I)

Chamberlain, N. W. *Collective Bargaining.* New York: McGraw-Hill, 1956. (I)

Cohen, S. "Does Public Employee Unionism Diminish Democracy?" *Industrial and Labor Relations Review* 32 (1979): 189–195. (II)

Davis, P. A. "Before the NLRB Election: What You Can and Can't Do." *Personnel* 44 (July–August 1967): 8–18. (I)

Derber, M., W. E. Chalmers, and R. Stagner. "The Labor Contract: Provisions and Practice." *Personnel* 54 (1958): 19–30. (I)

Dubin, R. "Attachment to Work and Union Militancy." *Industrial Relations* 12 (1973): 57–64. (II–R)

Dubin, R. "Power and Union–Management Relations." *Administrative Science Quarterly* 2 (1957): 60–81. (II)

Dunlop, J. T. *Industrial Relations Systems.* New York: Holt, 1958. (II)

Dunlop, J. T., and N. W. Chamberlain, eds. *Frontiers of Collective Bargaining.* New York: Harper, 1967. (II)

Ellis, D. S., L. Jacobs, and G. Mills. "A Union Authorization Election: The Key to Winning." *Personnel Journal* 51 (1972): 246–254. (I)

England, G. W., N. C. Agarwal, and R. E. Trerise. "Union Leaders and Managers: A Comparison of Value Systems." *Industrial Relations* 10 (1971):

211–226. (II–R)

Feller, D. E., "A General Theory of the Collective Bargaining Agreement." *California Law Review,* 61, no. 3 (1973): 663–856. (I)

Fielly, A. C. *Interpersonal Conflict Resolution.* Glenview, Ill.: Scott Foresman, 1974. (I)

Frey, R. L., and J. S. Adams. "The Negotiator's Dilemma: Simultaneous In-Group and Out-Group Conflict." *Journal of Experimental Social Psychology* (1972): 331–346. (II–R)

Gilroy, T. P., and A. C. Russo. *Bargaining Unit Issues: Problems, Criteria, Tactics.* Chicago: International Personnel Management Association, 1975. (I)

Goldoff, A. C., and D. C. Tatge. "Union–Management Cooperation in New York." *Public Productivity Review* 3 (Summer 1978): 35–47. (I)

Hagberg, E. C., and M. J. Levine. *Labor Relations.* St. Paul: West, 1978. (I)

Healy, J. J., ed. *Creative Collective Bargaining.* Englewood Cliffs, New Jersey: Prentice-Hall, 1965. (I)

Heneman, H. G., and D. Yoder. *Labor Economics,* 2d ed. Cincinnati: South-Western, 1965. (I)

Imberman, W., and M. Taracena. "Is There an Alternative to a Strike?" *S.A.M. Advanced Management Journal* 43 (Winter 1978): 4–13. (I)

Industrial Relations Research Association. *Proceedings of Annual Meetings.* Madison, Wisconsin (annually). (II–R)

Klimoski, R. J., and R. A. Ash. "Accountability and Negotiator Behavior." *Organizational Behavior and Human Performance* 11 (1974): 409–425. (II–R)

Le Grande, L. H. "Women in Labor Organizations: Their Ranks Are Increasing." *Monthly Labor Review* 101 (August 1978): 8–14. (I–R)

Lewin, D. "Public Sector Labor Relations: A Review Essay." *Labor History* 18 (Winter 1977): 133–145. (II)

Lewin, D., P. Feuille, and T. A. Kochan, eds. *Public Sector Labor Relations.* Glen Ridge, New Jersey: Horton, 1977. (I)

McKelvey, J. T. "Sex and the Single Arbitrator." *Industrial and Labor Relations Review* 24 (1971): 335–353. (I)

Mitchell, M. S. "Public Sector Union Security: The Impact of *Abood.*" *Labor Law Journal* 29 (1978): 697–711. (II)

Muench, G. A. "A Clinical Psychologist's Treatment of Labor–Management Conflicts." *Personnel Psychology* 13 (1960): 165–172. (I)

Myers, A. H., and D. P. Twomey. *Labor Law and Legislation.* 5th ed. Cincinnati: South-Western, 1975. (I)

Myers, M. S. *Managing with Unions.* Reading, Mass.: Addison-Wesley, 1976. (I)

Nash, A. N., and J. B. Miner, eds. *Personnel and Labor Relations: An Evolutionary Approach.* New York: Macmillan, 1973. (I)

National Industrial Conference Board. *White Collar Unionization.* New York: Conference Board, 1970. (I)

Paterson, L. T., and J. Liebert. *Management Strike Handbook.* Chicago: International Personnel Management Association, 1975. (I)

Pattefer, J. C. "Effective Grievance Arbitration." *California Management Review* 13, no. 2 (1970): 12–18. (I)

Peterson, R. and L. Tracy. "Testing a Behavioral Theory Model of Labor Negotiations." *Industrial Relations* 16, 1 (1977): 35–50. (II–R)

"Public Sector Arbitration: Symposium." *Industrial Relations* 14 (October 1975): 302–326. (II)

Robbins, S. R. *Managing Organizational Conflict.* Englewood Cliffs, New Jersey: Prentice-Hall, 1975. (I)

Rubin, J. Z. and B. R. Brown. *The Social Psychology of Bargaining and Negotiation.* New York: Academic, 1975. (I)

Sayles, L. R., and G. Strauss. *The Local Union.* Rev. ed. New York: Harcourt Brace, 1967.

Schreisheim, C. A. "Job Satisfaction, Attitudes Toward Unions, and Voting in a Union Representation Election." *Journal of Applied Psychology* 63 (1978): 548–552. (II–R)

Selekman, B. M. *Labor Relations and Human Relations.* New York: McGraw-Hill, 1947. (I)

Skibbins, G. J., and C. S. Weymur. "The 'Right to Work' Controversy." *Harvard Business Review* 44, no. 4 (July–August 1966): 6–19. (I)

Sloan, A. A., and F. Whitney. *Labor Relations,* 2d ed. Englewood Cliffs, New Jersey: Prentice-Hall, 1972. (I)

Solmick, L. M. "Unionism and Fringe Benefit Expenditures." *Industrial Relations* 17 (1978): 102–107. (II–R)

Stagner, R., and H. Rosen. *Psychology of Union–Management a Relations.* Belmont, Cal.: Wadsworth, 1965. (I)

Staudohar, P. D. "Results of Final-Offer Arbitration of Bargaining Disputes." *California Management Review* 18 (Fall 1975): 57–61. (I)

Strauss, G., and P. Feuille. "Industrial Relations Research: A Critical Analysis." *Industrial Relations* 17 (1978): 259–277. (II)

Strauss, G. "Union Government in the U.S.: Research Past and Future." *Industrial Relations* 16 (May 1977): 215–242. (II)

Thomas, K. "Conflict and Conflict Management." In M. D. Dunnette, ed., *Handbook of Industrial and Organizational Psychology.* Chicago: Rand McNally, 1976. (II)

Vidmar, N. "Effects of Representational Rules and Mediators on Negotiation Effectiveness." *Journal of Personality and Social Psychology* 17 (1971): 48–58. (II–R)

Walton, R. E., and R. B. McKersie. *A Behavioral Theory of Labor Negotiations.* New York: McGraw-Hill, 1965. (II)

Weitzman, J. P. *The Scope of Bargaining in Public Employment.* New York: Praeger, 1975. (II)

Wirtz, W. W. *Labor and the Public Interest.* New York: Harper, 1964. (I)

Wortman, M. S., and C. W. Randle. *Collective Bargaining: Principles and Practices.* 2d ed. Boston: Houghton Mifflin, 1966. (I)

APPENDIX A

Important Federal Labor Laws and Their Provisions (most terms used here are defined in Appendix B).

Title and date	Major provisions
A. Sherman "Anti-Trust" Act 1980	As applied to labor organizations through court interpretation, the act was used to show that certain union practices, such as the boycott, were illegal, as they restrained interstate trade.
B. Clayton Act 1914	Noted that the labor of humans was not a commodity or article of commerce. Therefore, unions were not illegal *per se*. No injunctions against unions could be made, unless necessary in order to prevent irreparable injury to property. The right to strike was also stated. Courts interpreted the law somewhat unfavorably as far as unions were concerned, limiting the use of boycotts and allowing unions to be sued even though they were not incorporated organizations.
C. Railway Labor Act 1926 (amended 1934, 1951)	Declared that employees have the right to bargain collectively through their own representatives. Yellow-dog contracts and closed shops were outlawed; union shops, checkoff, elections of representatives were permitted. Extended to cover air carriers and subsidiary activities of railroads (e.g., deliveries, terminals).
D. Norris-LaGuardia Act 1932	Prohibits use of injunctions in labor disputes. (Injunctions, after the Clayton Act, had become very popular to prohibit picketing, etc.). Federal courts could still use injunctions if unlawful acts were threatened, occurred, or were likely and there was no adequate remedy for damages. Injunctions could not be used to restrain employees from refusing to work or from being members of unions. Parties seeking relief must have made reasonable efforts to settle disputes by negotiation.
E. National Industrial Recovery Act 1933	A foundation for the 1935 Wagner Act; states employees have the right to bargain collectively. Created National Labor Board as a temporary agency to deal with labor problems.
F. National Labor Relations Act (Wagner Act) 1935	Declared that public policy of United States was to encourage and facilitate collective bargaining. Employees had the right to join and form labor organizations and elect representatives. Prohibited "unfair labor practices" of employers, including the following: interfering in employees' rights noted above, dominating labor unions, discriminating against employees on the basis of union membership, refusing to bargain collectively, and discriminating against employees for filing charges under the Act. Created the National Labor Relations Board (NLRB) to administer the Act. The Board was to prevent unfair labor practices, certify unions as bargaining agents, and determine bargaining units.
G. Taft-Hartley Labor Management Relations Act 1947 (amended 1951)	Specified and changed Wagner Act Provisions and NLRB. NLRB increased to five members. Provisions for judicial review of Board decisions was made. Specified the following union unfair labor practices: restraining or coercing employees in exercise of their rights under the Act, causing or attempting to cause employer to discriminate against employee on basis of union membership, refusing to bargain in good faith, inducing or encouraging workers to stop working in order to force employer to bargain with a union when another union has been certified as bargaining agent, charging excessive or discriminatory fee for union membership, causing or attempting to cause an employer to pay for work not performed. Established the Federal Mediation and Conciliation Service (FMCS) as a separate agency to mediate disputes. Attempted to remove communists from positions of influence in unions; required financial statements of unions to be filed, including expense receipts and officers' salaries; forbade strikes against federal government.

Appendix A (continued)

Title and date	Major provisions
H. Labor Management Reporting and Disclosure Act (Landrum-Griffin Act) 1959	Allowed states to act in situations where NLRB refused to act, in organizations NLRB did not cover, etc.; unions cannot coerce or boycott against a secondary employer; retailers of products of manufacturers with whom a union has a dispute cannot picket on this account; no group may be forced to agree not to handle products of a struck employer (hot-cargo agreements); closed shops were permitted in the construction industry. Periodic public reports are demanded covering employers, unions, consultants, employees. Title I, a "Bill of Rights" for union members, included provisions assuring members equal rights in nominating candidates, voting, and attending and participating in meetings. Procedures for dues, fees, and assessments are specified and disciplinary measures taken by unions against their members are limited by rules. Copies of the union agreement must be given to all members. Union elections are controlled in order to help assure democracy. Union internal affairs, such as financial affairs, use of trusteeships, and domination by racketeers, are controlled.
Other laws	Several other laws have direct or indirect impact on labor relations, but all were not specifically designed to apply to labor unions. They include the Davis-Bacon Act of 1931 (amended 1950), the Walsh-Healey Public Contracts Act of 1936, the Byrnes Anti-Strike-Breaking Act of 1938, the Hobbs Anti-Racketeering Act of 1946, the Lea Act of 1946, the Welfare and Pension Act of 1964 (amended 1972), The Fair Labor Standards Act of 1938 (amended 1955, 1961, 1963, 1966, 1967, 1969, 1972), the Service Contracts Act of 1965, and the Occupational Safety and Health Act of 1970. These laws, as well as others, affect labor practices and thus personnel policies. Several are explained in previous exercises [see also S. M. Myers, *Managing without Unions* (Reading, Mass.: Addison-Wesley, 1976), for a more detailed discussion].

APPENDIX B

A Glossary of Common Terms in the Areas of Labor Unions/Collective Bargaining

Affiliated Unions

A large federation of well over 100 national unions which was formed in 1955 from the Congress of Industrial Organizations (CIO) and the American Federation of Labor (AFL). The CIO was formed in 1938 to organize unskilled and semiskilled workers in mass-production industries and was the outgrowth of a minority faction of the AFL (founded in 1886). The AFL was primarily craft oriented.

Agency Shop

All employees in the bargaining unit pay a service fee to the union, but do not have to join it.

Appeal

The recourse available to a party when a decision is made against it; rules establish the appeal procedure for grievances, often resulting in arbitration.

Arbitrator

An impartial umpire both parties agree to use to resolve disputes by making an award or decision after weighting positions and facts; a judge.

Authorization Cards

Cards signed by workers and accepted by NLRB, indicating their intention to authorize the union to be their bargaining representative.

Automatic Extension

A clause in a union contract which allows the contract to remain in effect after its expiration date as long as negotiations are in progress regarding its renewal.

Award

The decision rendered by an arbitrator; typically must be written.

Bargaining Agent

The union certified by the NLRB to represent a group of workers, jobs, etc., in negotiations with management.

Bargaining Unit

Those jobs, occupations, industries, locales, crafts, or organizations represented by the union.

Bilateral

Negotiated jointly by union and management.

Business Agent

The local union official who represents the members in matters of economic and political concern.

Business Union

A union that emphasizes economic gains by collective action.

Appendix B (continued)

Certification

State or federal labor relations boards' sanctioning, after a vote is taken according to various procedures, that a bargaining agent exists.

Checkoff

Procedure whereby union dues are automatically deducted from workers' pay checks and forwarded to the union by the employer.

Closed Shop

Only union members can be employed. The union agrees to supply workers.

Closed (Antiunion) Shop

An organization that refuses employment to union members; typically illegal.

Collective Bargaining

The process by which conditions of employment are determined by representatives of unions and management. The representatives are authorized to act as agents for the groups and the method of reaching agreement consists of each side offering proposals and counterproposals.

Company Unions

A labor organization consisting of workers of only one company, frequently "dominated" by the company.

Compulsory Arbitration

Two parties are forced by law to submit their disagreements to an arbitrator who will decide them.

Conciliator

A third party who attempts to establish communications between union and management and help facilitate an agreement.

Consent Election

An election to recognize a bargaining agent (union), held when the petition to hold a representation election is not contested; the election is held by secret ballot without a preelection hearing.

Contract Administration

Interpreting and applying the terms of the union contract on a day-to-day basis; operating an organization under a union contract.

Craft Union

A union consisting of members who all perform a single craft for their livelihood (e.g., typographers).

Decertification

The process by which a bargaining agent is declared to no longer represent the employees within a bargaining unit.

Discharge

Terminating an employee's association with an organization.

Appendix B (continued)

Due Process

The right given to someone to use the entire existing grievance procedure or other procedures established to resolve disputes before an action stands; typically used in reference to public-sector labor relations.

Economic Strike

Union members stop working in order to enforce their demands for higher wages or other benefits.

Escalator Clauses

Contract articles that provide for automatic increases in a specified area if the index used to evaluate the area rises (e.g., escalator clauses for cost-of-living index changes are reflected in increased wages).

Featherbedding

Restriction of work output to maintain earnings and protected jobs.

Good Faith

In bargaining, the tacit agreement that parties must communicate and negotiate, match proposals with counterproposals if they are not accepted, and agree to meet with the other party.

Grievance

A formal complaint filed by a worker against an organization due to any one of a number of actions it or a particular person has taken in regard to the worker.

Grievance Procedure

The formal, agreed-on procedure for handling a grievance; usually consists of three or more sequential steps, beginning with a supervisor and a steward and perhaps ending in arbitration or mediation.

Independent Unions

Unions without any larger, national or international affiliation.

Industrial Union

A union consisting of members with a variety of skills (unskilled, semiskilled, and craft members) who are employed in a single industry (e.g., automobile industry).

Injunction

Legally precluding a union (or management) from certain acts or activities (e.g., picketing).

Just Cause

The circumstances under which an organization's action (e.g., discharge) is considered permissible, according to the terms of an agreement and other considerations involving the particular situation.

Knights of Labor

An organization of craft, skilled, and semiskilled labor formed in Philadelphia in 1869. It had over 700,000 members by 1886, but declined very rapidly in power and size due to unsuccessful strikes and the diverse interests of its members.

Labor Contract

A written statement of provisions and terms of employment which represents the outcome of the collective-bargaining process.

Appendix B (continued)

Labor Movement

The development and rise to power of labor unions which has accompanied the long-term process of industrialization or partial industrialization.

Lockout

The shutting down of an organization by its management or their refusal to permit union members to work in order to force a union to cease certain tactics or to preclude the acceptance of certain demands made by a union.

Management Rights

Those conditions management initially sets either unilaterally or bilaterally (i.e., with the union) as the status quo; these areas are precluded from negotiation and are reserved exclusively for management control.

Mass Picketing

Large groups of people attempting to block the way of those wishing to enter a building; a protest tactic.

Master Contract

A union agreement negotiated with several employers and an employer's association within an industry and/or area.

Mediator

A third party who attempts to resolve conflict and impasse between union and management by actively suggesting compromises (overlaps with conciliation in practice).

Negotiation

The process of making proposals and counterproposals, bargaining, and arriving at an eventual agreement, if possible.

No-Strike Clause

A contract clause forbidding work stoppages for the duration of the contract.

Open Shop

Employees are not required to join the union or pay a service fee.

Organized Labor

Labor unions and their members; formal groups of workers.

Picketing

Placing persons with signs noting a strike is in progress at locations around an organization and at entrances; the picketers publicize the strike and hope to prevent workers (and others) from entering the building(s).

Political Action (Union)

Union's degree of participation and initiative in the political process; includes support of candidates and issues with human resources and financial assistance, educational material, endorsements, etc.

Posting

Notifying workers of new job openings, transfer and promotion opportunities, etc., by placing written notice in a conspicuous place (e.g., bulletin boards); place and duration of posting are typically fixed by contract provisions.

Appendix B (continued)

Preferential Shop

Organization in which management gives first chance or opportunity for employment to union members.

Primary Boycott

The refusal of a union to allow its members to purchase goods or services of an organization involved in a labor dispute.

Public Sector

Organizations belonging to federal, state, or municipal governments, agencies, administrative boards, etc., which are essentially "public" organizations and are nonprofit.

Rank and File

Union membership.

Reopening Clause

An article in a union contract that permits one or more opportunities to renegotiate specified terms throughout the duration of the contract.

Secondary Boycott

Unions' attempts to influence various third parties, such as suppliers, customers, and the public at large, to cease purchasing products or services from an organization involved in a labor dispute; generally illegal.

Seniority System

The procedure for deciding preferences in the assignment of jobs, vacation selection, transfer, promotion, shifts, etc., based on job tenure; longer tenure indicates higher seniority.

Sit-Down Strike

Union members cease working but do not leave their work stations; generally illegal.

Slow-Down Strike

Union members limit or restrict output while at work.

Sweetheart Clause

A general policy statement, typically included at the beginning of an agreement, that indicates the spirit with which each side enters into the contract; specific responsibilities are spelled out and each side may promise to cooperate.

Sympathy Strike

Union members stop working to support other union members on strike in the same or another organization.

Voluntary Checkoff

Procedure whereby employer deducts union dues (and often other fees) from paychecks and forwards these amounts to the union, only if the worker gives his or her approval to do so.

Unfair Labor Practices

Practices relating to labor management relations, contract negotiation and administration, and the relationships management and unions each have with their employees and members, respectively, which are strictly prohibited by various labor laws.

Appendix B (continued)

Unilateral Decision

Decided independently by either the union or by management.

Union

A continuing, long-term formal association of workers formed to advance their interests.

Union Security

A union's degree of strength and/or susceptibility to undermining and weakening; provisions in a contract designed to help assure the continuation and power of a union; right of a union to speak for its members; the assurance the employer will recognize the union.

Union Shop

An organization in which all employees in the bargaining unit must become union members within a certain period of time after they are hired, usually 30 days.

Union Steward

The counterpart of an organization's supervisor or foreman; he or she works on the job with union members and represents them in disputes or grievances with the organization.

Wildcat (Outlaw) Strike

A cessation of work by union members undertaken without proper authorization from union officials; often occurs quickly, without warning.

Work Rules

Those rules specifying the pace of work and the amount of human resources to be assigned to various tasks.

Yellow-Dog Contract

A contract workers sign as they begin employment, stating they will not join a union; typically illegal.

Name _____ Group Number _____

Date _____ Class Section _____ Hour _____ Score _____

PART A

Form 1 A Review of Your Understanding of Labor Laws and Terminology

As a review of labor laws and terminology, answer the questions below briefly.

A. Labor Laws

1. List each of the laws discussed in *Appendix A* of the *Introduction* by its identifying letter and tell whether each was favorable, unfavorable, or neutral from the unions' point of view. Indicate very briefly why you answered as you did.

2. Regarding their application to labor unions, what were the differences between the Sherman and Clayton Acts?

3. List employer and union unfair labor practices.

4. What types of disclosures did unions and management have to make under the Landrum-Griffin Act? Why do you feel these disclosures and provisions had to be legislated?

Form 1 (continued)

B. Terminology

1. Distinguish between wildcat, sit-down, sympathetic, and slow-down strikes.

2. Distinguish between conciliation, mediation, arbitration, negotiation, and bargaining.

3. Distinguish between business, craft, industrial, company, affiliated, and unaffiliated unions.

4. Distinguish between the AFL-CIO and the Knights of Labor.

5. Distinguish between closed, open, union, agency, preferential, and closed (antiunion) shops.

6. What does the term "bargain in good faith" actually mean in practice?

7. Why do you suppose primary boycotts are typically legal and secondary boycotts are typically illegal?

PART B

Form 2 Computation of Benefits Costs Due to Changes Anticipated in Union Contract:
The Built Fast to Last Corporation

The Built Fast to Last Construction, Development, and Real Estate Corporation, a large company in the Northwest, employs several types of workers, including skilled and craft laborers, clerical workers, professionals (e.g., such as accountants and architects), salespersons, etc. It is deciding whether or not to purchase and develop an 850-acre plot of land in an ideal suburban location. Condominiums and some single-family detached houses are planned for the land.

Built Fast to Last must consider several factors as they make their decision. Among these are the current local supply and demand for housing, the location, interest rates on construction loans, zoning and sewer permits, future plans for building a shopping area, and attracting light industry to the area. One significant consideration, of course, is labor cost. Because so many different types of workers are required over the two-year period of development, wage, salary, and fringe-benefit costs are difficult to project. However, since the vast majority of the potential workers will be unionized, current union contracts, coupled with historical company accounting data, are quite helpful.

Of all the types of workers needed, Built Fast to Last is most concerned with plumbers and pipefitters. Very shortly after the project is scheduled to begin, the current labor contract with the plumbers expires. (The company is large enough to maintain its own permanent force of plumbers who work on whatever project is ongoing.) After the new contract is negotiated, Built Fast to Last will certainly have increased labor costs, for the plumbers have been publicizing their need for substantially improved benefits. They argue their real income has declined considerably due to inflation over the last three years, but perhaps more important, their demand for a significant pay increase three years ago was fulfilled at the expense, they feel, of fringe benefits. They make it very clear that they are going to "catch up" on benefits this time!

Built Fast to Last will operate on a small profit margin in the proposed project due to projected increases in materials and labor costs during the two years of the project. The plumber's new contract could add enough to the company's fixed labor costs to make the project only marginally profitable. Since no other major group of unionized workers required for the project will need to renegotiate their contract during the term of the project and since Built Fast to Last needs to use ninety of its plumbers for two years, any additional costs resulting from the new contract could be very large and could therefore affect the decision to proceed with the project. To make matters worse, these costs can only be estimated—the contract expires three months after the project is to begin and thus exact costs are unknown.

Built Fast to Last has reliable information concerning what the plumbers will ask for in the new contract in the way of wage and benefit increases. It also knows its current benefit cost per plumber, based on figures from a project just completed. The relevant figures for current benefit costs and anticipated changes being sought by the unions are given below. Built Fast to Last has decided that if the anticipated benefit costs for plumbers are estimated at lower than $2,500,000 for all of the plumbers over the two years of the project (one-and-three-fourths years after the new contract would take effect), it would go ahead with the project if the figure is higher than $2,500,000, it must reconsider and perhaps attempt to look over its estimates of overtime, other salary costs, material costs, interest payments, etc., to be sure they are accurate before it makes a final decision.

Look over the figure and data below, compute the benefits costs for the plumbers asked for on Form 3, and tell whether the additional benefit costs are within the guidelines given above.

Current Benefits Costs for Plumbers Hired by Built Fast to Last*

Specific benefit	Dollar amount	Proposed contract change anticipated by Built Fast to Last (increases over present dollar amounts, in percent)
Employee Security and Health		
Life, health, and accident insurance	575.00	Increase an average of 5%
Workman's compensation	304.00	Increase an average of 4%
Sick leave	635.00	Increase an average of 8%
Pension plan	840.00	Increase an average of 3%
Social security	1027.00	No effect
Unemployment insurance	84.00	Increase an average of 4%
Supplemental unemployment benefits	568.00	Increase an average of 4%
Severance pay	187.00	No effect

---

* These are average costs per worker per year. Built Fast to Last employs plumbers year-round. The costs are based on $22,475, the average yearly wage of the plumbers employed on a current project. The wage does not include overtime. The contract changes will go into effect three months after the two-year construction project begins. The plumbers work seven-hour days, five days a week. Two-week vacations are average, as are ten paid holidays.

Form 2 (continued)

Specific benefit	Dollar amount	Proposed contract change anticipated by Built Fast to Last (increases over present dollar amounts, in percent)
Time Not Worked		
Vacations	936.00	Increase an average of 10%
Holidays	936.00	Increase an average of 10%
Personal excused absences	100.00	Increase an average of 10%
Grievances and negotiations	117.00	No effect
Reporting time	150.00	No effect
Employee Services		
Christmas bonuses	475.00	No effect
Social and recreational opportunities	45.00	No effect
Educational opportunities and subsidies	70.00	Increase an average of 11%
Total	*2,829.00*	
Basic wage per hour	12.84	Increase 6% first year Increase 8% second year
Average overtime hours/worker/year (overtime rate = $1\frac{1}{2}$ regular rate)	72	No effect
TOTAL		

Name _____ _____   Group Number _____

Date _____   Class Section _____   Hour _____   Score _____

PART B

Form 3 Computation of Anticipated Change in Cost of Benefits for Built Fast to Last Plumbers*

Anticipated New Cost of Benefits and Wage Increase Per Plumber:

Employee Security and Health

   Life, health, and accident insurance   _____

   Workman's compensation   _____

   Sick leave   _____

   Pension plan   _____

   Social security   _____

   Unemployment compensation   _____

   Supplemental unemployment benefits   _____

   Severance pay   _____

Time Not Worked

   Vacations   _____

   Holidays   _____

   Personal excused absences   _____

   Grievance and negotiations   _____

   Reporting time   _____

Employee Services

   Christmas bonus   _____

   Social and recreational opportunities   _____

   Educational opportunities and subsidies   _____

TOTAL   _____

Total per plumber over two-year period of project   _____

Total for ninety plumbers over project period   _____

Should Built Fast to Last reconsider the project based on its anticipated benefit and wage cost? Why or why not?

_____
* Not accounting for inflation

Name _____   Group Number _____

Date _____   Class Section _____   Hour _____   Score _____

PART B

Form 4 Contractual Language of Union Agreements and Its Impact on Other Personnel Programs

In order to familiarize yourself with the language of union contracts, secure one or more actual agreements from local unions. (These can be easily obtained by calling the union and explaining the reason for the request). Once a few contracts are obtained, or some sample contract language is given to you by your implementor, find the articles or specific paragraphs dealing with each of the issues listed below and copy or paraphrase the articles in the spaces provided. Then, answer each of the questions posed about each issue in order to consider how such issues would impact various management decisions.

Article 1: Seniority

Copy or paraphrase contract articles/paragraphs here:

Questions:
1. What impact might the seniority article have on layoff and promotion decisions?

2. What impact might the seniority article have on job evaluation and classification?

3. What impact might the seniority article have on scheduling vacations?

4. What impact might the seniority article have on performance appraisal?

Form 4 (continued)

Article 2:   Rates and Wages

Copy or paraphrase contract article/paragraphs here:

Questions:

1. What impact would the rates-and-wages article have on wage and salary administration?

2. What impact would the rates-and-wages article have on piece-rate and bonus-plan administration?

Article 3:   Hours of Work

Copy or paraphrase contract article/paragraphs here:

Questions:

1. What impact might the hours-of-work article have on wage and salary administration?

2. What impact might the hours-of-work article have on training programs?

Name _____   Group Number _____

Date _____   Class Section _____   Hour _____   Score _____

PART C

Form 5 Grievance Issues and Analyses

Read each of the following sets of facts pertaining to a situation in which a grievance was filed. Then, read the issue of the grievance—it is stated as a question. Assume each grievance has progressed through the entire normal grievance procedure and, according to contract provisions, must be settled by an arbitrator. Assume the role of the arbitrator and write out your decision and a rationale for it. If you assume there are specific contractual agreements that would have a direct bearing on your decision, state these assumptions.

Grievance Situation 1:

Facts: A seven-day suspension was imposed on a grievant for failing to return to his assigned duties at the request of his supervisor. Due to various previous disputes, the grievant would not assume his regular duties until he was able to meet with the assistant plant manager. When called in for a meeting with his supervisor, the grievant allegedly made offensive remarks and was subsequently discharged. The discharge came one month after the suspension. The supervisor reported harassment and threats by the grievant. Insubordination justifies suspension according to the contract. The supervisor, during the month between the initiation of the suspension and the discharge, did not act on continued derogatory remarks, threats, and failure to assume assigned duties on the part of the grievant. These were ignored. The grievance was filed after the discharge. According to the contract, discharge is considered a last-resort action after "every reasonable effort is made" to restore proper attitudes.

Issue: Was there just cause for the suspension?

Was there just cause for the discharge?

Decision and Rationale:

Grievance Situation 2:

Facts: While working at his desk, a general foreman observed the grievant operating a nearby transactor. (This machine is used to record workers' attendance. Each worker has a badge that is to be inserted into the transactor at the end of each day. The worker's number, as well as the time of insertion, is recorded electronically by the machine). He heard two distinct operations of the transactor. The grievant had his back to the foreman and thus the foreman did not actually see the grievant record two badges, although his motions and the machine's noises indicated he had. The computer printout subsequently obtained indicated that the grievant had rung out another worker's badge, as well as his own. This was concluded because two ring-outs were shown at exactly the same time and the foreman observed no one use the machine for several minutes before and after the grievant had. Ringing out two badges was prohibited by the contract and up to a one-month suspension was indicated as a punishment. The foreman prepared a written signed statement of his observations and conclusions, which he turned over to the grievant's immediate supervisor. The grievant was not questioned or notified by the foreman at the time of the alleged offense or at any time subsequent to it. The supervisor did not question the grievant

Form 5 (continued)

or conduct an investigation, a procedure he is obligated to perform under the contract. The statement showed that the foreman suspended the grievant for one month and the supervisor initiated the punishment. It was put into effect immediately and when the grievant was notified, the grievance was filed. During the course of the normal grievance procedure initiated after the grievance was filed, two workers testified that they had been with the grievant at the time and that he had not committed the offense. However, on several other significant matters, when questioned alone, their testimony conflicted both with each other and with the grievant. The union argued that the suspension was not warranted, based on the fact that the foreman did not see the grievant commit the alleged offense. The foreman agreed, upon questioning, that alternative explanations for what he saw and heard the grievant do did exist and that the evidence was circumstantial.

Issue: Was the grievant suspended for just cause?

Decision and Rationale:

PART D

Form 6 Labor Contract Renegotiation: A Skill-Building Session

General Instructions: This activity requires groups of from five to seven persons. A management and a union negotiating team of two or three persons each are formed, and one to three observers/arbitrators are also required. Roles for all participants follow this introduction. Choose one of the following five craft unions whose contract with the *Daily Post* will expire in one month: typographical, pressmen, stereotypes, photoengravers, mailers (see Forms 7 and 8). You will renegotiate this union's contract. Once you have chosen one of the five unions and have been given a role as either a member of the management or union negotiating team or an observer/arbitrator, read *only* your appropriate role information (and the role information for the other member(s) of your team). (Observers/arbitrators can read all role descriptions.) Also carefully read the background information about the *Daily Post* (Form 7), the current agreement information, the newspaper-craft-union facts, the guidelines for negotiators, and the bargaining strategy and roles for your side *only*. This information follows as Forms 7–13.

Once you have looked over the information, you are to prepare for a contract-renegotiation session. Formulate your strategy, your proposals, etc. Then, conduct the session for a period of one to two hours. Each side will use its strategy or position (Form 10 or 11) as a jumping-off point in this bargaining activity. The objective is to renegotiate with the *Daily Post* the contract of the craft union you chose above. You may meet and exchange initial proposals, dismiss to study them, and meet again to negotiate or conduct the entire renegotiation in one meeting. Assume that both sides are interested in the issues contained on the list of Current Agreement Provisions (Form 9) and that the union members will ratify the contract negotiated. The observer watches the negotiations carefully and fills out everything applicable on Form 12. Also see the *Procedure* to this exercise for instructions.

If, after a few hours, certain issues cannot be resolved, the observer(s) becomes an arbitrator (or arbitration panel). The arbitrator(s) listens to the arguments, views, and positions of each side; weighs all factors he, she, or they feel relevant, including how other issues were decided; and makes decisions that are binding—that is, each side must accept them. The arbitrator could adopt a win-lose strategy and accept the demands of either side on any issue in arbitration, or could compromise.

Members of both negotiating teams, as well as the observer/arbitrator or panel, may want to gather additional background data on union contracts in the newspaper industry or on the craft union they select. This information can be obtained by asking for a copy of the current contract from a local union, by visiting a newspaper and interviewing various industrial-relations staff members, by interviewing local union officials, and/or by looking up information about the newspaper industry's labor relations and the craft unions in the library. *For Further Reading* contains relevant general references. As much of contract administration relies on past precedent, having such precedents in mind, in addition to that data given in the exercise, would improve the effectiveness of the negotiating activity. Further, certain characteristics of your own local newspaper and craft unions and their contract negotiations can be obtained via the fact-finding methods noted above (e.g., a history of strikes, etc.) and can be incorporated into your negotiations to add realism. Remember to read all of the material carefully and to formulate your strategy and an initial position before negotiations begin.

PART D

Form 7 Background Information for the Daily Post

The *Daily Post* is a daily newspaper with a current circulation of 460,000. It is located in a large metropolitan area in the Great Plains region of the country. The *Post* is a morning paper and, except for a few weekly papers and suburban papers, it has no major competition at this time in the area. The *Post* is also one of twelve papers owned by a very large communications holding company. Like most newspapers in this country, it began many years ago as a family business. The paper was bought by the holding company about seven years ago.

The *Post* has a conservative editorial policy. Some have accused it of favoring big business; its editors, however, deny such charges. The paper has backed the incumbent governor of its state, a Republican, and has generally opposed Democratic political candidates. Syndicated columnists include very well-known "moderates" based in New York and Chicago. The paper has won a few Pulitzer prizes for reporting and its Sunday editions are considered excellent in the industry.

The *Post* has had a somewhat stormy relationship with its various craft unions over the years. The founders of the paper were very antiunion. Unions only made a significant incursion into the work force about fifteen or twenty years ago. Now, virtually all employees are unionized. However, the contract negotiations, particularly with the craft unions (e.g., pressmen, stereotypers), have been very bitter and several strikes have resulted. On a few occasions in the early 1960s, some violence accompanied these strikes—for example, presses were destroyed and several fights occurred. Since the holding company purchased the paper, the negotiations have been somewhat more peaceful, although the *Post* certainly still has a reputation for antiunionism, which it feels is undeserved. It locked out the pressmen three years ago for eleven weeks and threatened to replace its photoengravers with nonunionized persons a few years ago when they struck, but could not locate enough nonunion skilled labor to do so.

The management of the *Post* has gone on record as saying that while the unionized workers are competent and individually are good workers, the unions' leaders are threatening to ruin the country financially by demanding exorbitant wage increases, costly benefits, and inefficient work rules. A few of the descendants of the founding family, who still hold high positions in the paper, were recently forbidden by the paper's parent company from taking any direct part in contract negotiations due to their past behavior at the bargaining table. The unions were able to capitalize on such lack of control and emotional involvement in the past, according to the parent company.

Financially, the *Post* is only in fair shape. Inflation has hurt it in the past few years. In addition, high cost overruns on the estimates for its newly completed printing facilities and expanded office facilities forced it to add additional short- and long-term debts it had not anticipated. With high interest rates, these debt repayments are causing somewhat of a strain on cash flow. Advertising revenue is holding steady, but the large retail establishments and chains are putting more and more of their advertising in a few small suburban papers, most of which are printed once or twice weekly. As more and more people move to the suburbs, the *Post* fears this trend may grow.

The stock of the *Post*, the majority of which is held by its parent company, is doing reasonably well, considering the current volatile market. New presses and other equipment, a good year for the parent company, and some favorable publicity from excellent investigative reporting and an exposé of corrupt Democratic state political officials have all helped the stock price.

There is pressure on the *Post's* management from the parent company to go to a smaller, tabloid-size paper, to soften editorial rhetoric somewhat, to hire a few nationally known reporters, and generally to modernize the look and image of the paper. As yet, these changes have been resisted, but with circulation only holding steady for the past two years, no rise in advertising revenue, and the talk of another (evening) newspaper looking for a new location in the area, these changes may be pushed through by the parent company soon.

The management of the *Post* feels that the residents of the area are not ready for a "slick Eastern" paper. The current round of union negotiations may be crucial to the paper's financial stability, and its management is already indicating that pay raises demanded by unions could ruin it. The financial statements, however, show that profit has held steady in the past three years and is the highest in the history of the paper, adjusting for inflation. In addition, dividends to shareholders are above the average declared for newspapers of the *Post's* size.

PART D
Form 8 Newspaper Craft Unions Supplemental Data

Table 1. Duration of Union Contracts (percentage comparisons)

Craft	Less than 1 year	1 year	18 mos.	2 years	30 mos.	3 years	More than 3 years
Typographical	0.0	10.8	2.2	42.0	8.0	35.7	1.3
Pressmen	0.3	9.2	2.6	35.8	4.2	37.6	10.3
Stereotypers	0.0	10.2	4.1	29.7	8.4	38.0	9.6
Photoengravers	0.0	7.2	0.4	34.5	9.8	40.9	7.2
Mailers	1.0	8.0	4.0	26.6	10.2	44.2	6.0

Table 2. Hours Constituting a Work Week (by number of contracts reviewed)

Craft	30	31	32	33	34	35	36	37	38	39	40	41
Typographical	0	0	5	4	6	70	41	250	18	2	22	0
Pressmen	3	0	4	5	6	73	31	216	14	1	31	2
Stereotypers	7	4	4	0	2	42	24	121	2	5	4	1
Photoengravers	0	0	0	0	0	27	12	47	0	0	0	0
Mailers	1	1	3	0	1	1	32	19	79	1	8	0

Table 3. Average Hourly Wage Scales since 1965 (in dollars per hour)

Craft	1967	1968	1969	1970	1971	1972	1973	1974	1975	1976	1977	1978	1979	1980
Typographical	3.99	4.16	4.20	4.69	4.99	5.37	5.62	5.84	6.01	6.22	6.43	6.61	6.93	7.31
Pressmen	4.03	4.20	4.45	4.70	5.05	5.37	5.68	5.87	6.13	6.31	6.42	6.69	7.24	7.64
Stereotypers	4.23	4.44	4.71	4.99	5.40	5.80	6.17	6.32	6.71	6.83	6.91	7.04	7.62	8.04
Photoengravers	4.57	4.75	5.04	5.32	5.65	6.13	6.37	6.41	6.62	6.84	6.97	7.21	7.47	7.86
Mailers	3.91	3.99	4.26	4.57	4.99	5.38	5.61	5.80	5.96	6.17	6.21	6.41	6.84	7.32

Table 4. Holiday Provisions Paid when not Worked—Holidays, Birthdays, Floating Days, etc. (percentage comparisons)

Craft	0 day	1 day	2 days	3 days	4 days	5 days	6 days	7 days	8 days	9 days	10 days	11 days	12 days
Typographical	2.3	0.7	0.0	0.0	0.5	1.6	29.2	42.1	15.0	4.2	4.0	0.4	0.0
Pressmen	6.7	0.8	0.0	0.0	0.0	1.5	24.3	41.0	16.7	4.4	4.0	0.0	0.6
Stereotypers	4.5	1.0	0.0	0.0	0.0	3.4	20.7	41.5	17.0	5.0	5.9	1.0	0
Photoengravers	8.8	0.8	1.0	1.0	0.0	5.0	16.7	44.3	14.7	6.3	1.4	0	0.0
Mailers	0.0	0.0	0.0	0.0	1.2	2.4	20.4	47.4	12.1	9.3	5.0	1.2	1.0

Form 8 (continued)

Table 5. Vacation Maximums (by number of contracts reviewed)

Crafts	Max. vacation less than 3 wks.	Max. vacation equals 3 wks.	Max. vacation equals 4 wks.	Max. vacation equals 6 wks.	Max. vacation greater than 6 wks.
Typographical	4	61	309	44	4
Pressmen	1	58	259	47	4
Stereotypers	0	19	160	26	2
Photoengravers	1	3	70	18	0
Mailers	0	17	105	15	1

Table 6. Analysis of Contracts' Provisions for Pension—Employer's Contribution (by number of contracts surveyed)

Crafts	No provision	3% of wage	4% of wage	5% of wage	$8.00/shift	$20.00/week
Typographical	50	42	21	3	74	11
Pressmen	32	18	24	7	83	21
Stereotypers	11	97	12	6	142	81
Photoengravers	21	37	27	8	110	42
Mailers	67	7	·10	14	131	11

Table 7. Average Amount of Wage Scale Differential for Night vs. Day Shifts (in dollars per hour; craft averages)

Craft	
Typographical	0.183
Pressmen	0.192
Stereotypes	0.203
Photoengravers	0.179
Mailers	0.194

Table 8. Strike Activity (per 100 contracts)

Craft	
Typographical	1.22
Pressmen	1.53
Stereotypers	0.21
Photoengravers	3.92
Mailers	1.31

PART D

Form 9 Current Agreement Provisions and Other Relevant Facts for Contract Renegotiation

			Craft		
	Typographical	Pressmen	Stereotypers	Photoengravers	Mailers
Duration of present (expiring) contract	1 yr.	2 yrs.	2 yrs.	30 mos.	18 mos.
Hours constituting a workweek	36.5 hrs.	37 hrs.	37 hrs.	36 hrs.	38 hrs.
Average hourly wage scale	$7.24	$7.59	$8.32	$7.58	$7.04
Holiday provisions paid	6 days	8 days	9 days	7 days	6 days
Vacations maximum	4 wks.	4 wks.	3 wks.	4 wks.	3 wks.
Provision for pension	5% wage	none	3% wage	$7.00/shift	$20.00/wk.
Average wage scale differential for night shift	$.162/hr.	$.190	$.167	$.166	$.183

Discharge Appeal Procedure (all crafts):

All discharge cases shall be disposed of under the following procedure: A discharged employee may first appeal his or her case to the manager of the office from which discharged. Both the foreman and the discharged employee shall appear at the manager meeting, and failure to do so shall constitute forfeiture of the case by the party failing to appear. If the appeal is sustained, the President of the Union at the direction of the Union's Executive Committee and the Publisher of the newspaper, or their authorized representatives, shall constitute an Appeal Board. This Board shall consider the case and make all reasonable efforts to decide it. In the event of failure to agree, a third member shall be added to the Appeal Board, and the decision arrived at by the three (3) person Board shall be final. The third member shall be a qualified person, who must be agreed upon by both union and management, and who is not affiliated in any way with either group or related groups. Fees charged by such a person will be shared equally by union and management. The time factor in cases before this Board shall be as follows: The manager meeting shall be held within five (5) days. The time for consideration by the two (2) person Board shall be within five (5) days, and the time allowed for the three (3) person Board decision shall be twenty (20) days. The time limits established in the foregoing may be extended by mutual agreement. It is the intent of both parties to this agreement that the entire procedure specified herein shall be consummated within thirty (30) days from the date of discharge. The Appeal Board, either two (2) or three (3) persons, may provide compensation to the discharged greivant for time lost. In no case shall reimbursement be in a sum greater than the working time actually lost, multiplied by straight-time rates.

Transfer Policy (all crafts):

All employees have the right to file for a transfer if a vacancy or new job occurs. All employees with satisfactory performance ratings, providing they have been on the job at least one year prior to the transfer request, may be considered for the transfer. The final decision tests with the immediate superiors of the two positions in question. All vacancies or new job openings are to be posted for at least five (5) working days on a centralized bulletin board. Only bids made during the time of posting shall be considered.

PART D

Form 10 Information for Management Negotiating Team

Initial Management Position*—to Be Read by Management Negotiating Team Only

The management of the *Post* has instructed the negotiators to remain firm on all issues, particularly those regarding the wage increase, the benefits demands, and the workweek. While it realizes it must give up some things and move off its first position, it has yet to draft a specific set of initial proposals, or answers to the union's initial position. The management of the *Post* is always geared up to give the unions a battle on "principle," but this time the paper's precarious financial position must be considered in planning a negotiation strategy.

Roles for Contract Renegotiation—to Be Read by Management Negotiating Team Only

Management Negotiator No. 1: Robert Deals, personnel administrator, *Daily Post*

Robert Deals is a very well-respected and experienced personnel administrator who has been with the *Post* for fifteen years. He almost single-handedly managed the personnel changes required after the takeover of the *Post* by its current parent company, and was able to staff the *Post* with the parent company's management without disrupting operations or hurting feelings. He is tactful and very knowledgeable in the area of personnel. Despite its alleged antiunion stance, the *Post* has been a leader in affirmative-action programs and has never had an EEOC complaint filed against it, largely due to Deals' efforts. The union regards him as an honest, skillful, and tough negotiator; it respects him.

Management Negotiator No. 2: Perry White, managing editor, *Daily Post*

Perry White is an "old-school" editor and a very close friend of one of the sons of the founder of the *Post*. He began his fifty-two-year career in journalism with the *Post* as an office boy. He is a firm believer in free enterprise and freedom of the press and a conservative Republican of considerable power in the state. He makes no attempt to hide his contempt for unions; according to him, they are restricting management's right to manage and leading us toward socialism. His knowledge of contract negotiations is very limited, but his knowledge of the newspaper business and what is best for the *Post* is extensive. He is not an extremely able negotiator, but is reserved and thoughtful. He never loses his temper and respects Robert Deals.

Management Negotiator No. 3: Lois Lain (use only if there are three negotiators on each team)

Lois Lain is the assistant personnel administrator. She has been at this position for three years, but has been with the *Post* for ten years. Deals considers her his successor and an able one. She has had an enormous impact on the *Post*'s affirmative-action programs and has dealt with grievances and other union matters skillfully. Lain is a very popular speaker at women's groups in the state and has done much to enhance the image of the *Post*. She is working on a doctorate in industrial relations and is very interested in contract negotiations, although she has little experience in that area. The management of the paper considers her to be an extremely valuable employee for many reasons. However, Perry White and she have one large point of disagreement. Her husband is a newscaster and commentator for a local TV station and has in the past criticized the editorial stance the *Post* has taken on various political and community issues.

---

* Also see Form 13.

PART D

Form 11 Information for Union Negotiating Team

Initial Union Demands (all crafts) in order of Priority*—to Be Read by Union Negotiating Team Only

1. An across-the-board wage increase of 9.3 percent the first year of the contract, 8.2 percent the second year, and 7.6 percent the third year.
2. A three-year contract.
3. A change in the following benefits:
   a) Maximum vacation should be five weeks.
   b) Holidays paid should be ten.
   c) Pension contribution should be 5 percent of wage.
4. Workweek should be 36 hours.
5. Discharge cases should go directly to an arbitrator if they are appealed.
6. Transfers should be made completely according to seniority, providing the applicant meets the job specifications of the new job.
7. Job vacancies must be posted for ten working days and applications or bids for jobs must be accepted for an additional ten days.
8. Bids for transfer can also be accepted up to ten days after the posting period.

The local unions (of all five crafts) are prepared to bargain in good faith; however, realizing the reputation of the *Post*, they are determined to make up for what they consider to be less-than-adequate contract benefit provisions in the past.

Roles for Contract Renegotiation—to Be Read by Union Negotiating Team Only

Union Negotiator No. 1:   Samuel Stompers, president, local union (whichever craft union is chosen)

Samuel Stompers is forty years old and has been president of the local for one year. He is considered a reform and liberal president, having recently defeated the president of long-standing in a very rough election. The newer and younger workers identify with him. He is interested in economic gains, of course, but also talks a great deal about the "quality of work life." He is an able administrator and has won the respect of the national union leaders through his ability to run the local efficiently (and profitably) and by his knowledge and skill in negotiations and membership drives. He had been on the local negotiating team for three years prior to his election. Stompers is a very liberal Democrat and a local school-board member. He is quite ambitious and seriously considering running for city council; most agree he would win easily.

Union Negotiator No. 2:   Susan B. Abel, representative of national union (use whichever union is chosen)

Susan B. Abel is a very experienced union negotiator and high-level officer in the national union. She is typically sent to help in local negotiations with especially tough managements. Abel, an appointed union official, is a former administrator in the United States Department of Labor under two different Democratic administrations. She is a woman who literally grew up with unionism, as her father was for many years the national president of a very large union during the stormy period of the 1920s and 1930s. She feels that economic gains are vital in helping to reduce the differences between socioeconomic classes in the United States. Abel knows Stompers only by reputation. As this is one of the first local contracts in the national union to be renegotiated, she is hoping to set a precedent for sizable gains.

Union Negotiator No. 3:   Louis D. Lewis, executive vice president, local union (use only if there are three negotiators on each team)

Louis Lewis is a very experienced negotiator and has been in various union positions for several years. He has been employed at the *Daily Post* for over twenty years. In fact, many consider him to be the key worker at the *Post* responsible for the success of the union's early organizing efforts. Lewis, of course, has never been a favorite of the *Post*'s management, but no one doubts his skill at his job, his loyalty to the union, or his integrity. Several years ago, Lewis and one of the sons-in-law of the founder of the *Post* appeared on a local TV show and ended up losing their tempers, verbally attacking one another, and generally creating a scene on live local television which the station, the paper, and the union have yet to forget.

---

* Also see Form 13.

Name _____ Group Number _____

Date _____ Class Section _____ Hour _____ Score _____

PART D

Form 12 Worksheet for Observer(s)/Arbitrator(s)

Observer(s)/Arbitrator(s) Roles:

As observer and possibly arbitrator, you need to prepare carefully for the renegotiation by studying the facts of the case and all other material presented here. As observer, your objective will be to analyze and evaluate the renegotiation by answering the questions below in Part I. This information should then be fed back to the team members and discussed after the renegotiation is settled (see also the *Procedure*). If an arbitrator is needed due to the inability of the parties to reach agreement on one or more issues, you will hear and decide these issues alone, or as a member of a panel. Remember: you are an outside, "objective" third party. As an arbitrator, fill out Part II below. After the renegotiation is completed, write down the final new contract provisions and language, with the assistance of both teams, in Part III. Be sure all issues are settled before you fill out Part III.

PART I: Observation of Renegotiation

1. Summarize each side's initial position briefly.

2. Comment on the "reasonableness" of these initial positions. Were they simply set up as bargaining positions from which to move to compromises?

3. Comment on the cohesiveness and singularity of purpose within each team. Did intrateam conflicts deter efficient negotiation?

4. Did the negotiators work from a basis of logic, reason, and fact, or from emotion and ideology?

5. Were the teams flexible? Did they "move off their first position" in the spirit of good-faith bargaining?

Form 12 (continued)

6. Which team was the most skillful? Why?

7. Was there a "winner" in the renegotiation? If so, who was it and why?

PART II: Arbitration

1. State each issue that could not be settled in negotiation and each side's final position on the issue.

2. For each issue, indicate your decision as arbitrator and the rationale used for your decisions.

3. Why was binding arbitration necessary in this situation? What could or should each team have done to eliminate the need for binding arbitration?

PART III: Final Contract Provisions

Write each provision that will be in the new contract below.

PART D

Form 13 Some General Guidelines for Negotiators*

1. Carefully prepare for the negotiations. Study all relevant data and have it at your fingertips.
2. Formulate an initial position on each issue; develop a rationale and gather facts to support your positions.
3. Consider objectives of your organization, past practices, trends, etc. as you develop a strategy.
4. What management "rights" does management feel cannot be surrendered?
5. What principles and gains must be maintained according to the union?
6. What are the real desires of the employees?
7. Use clear and concise language.
8. Do not allow emotions and anger to interfere with your negotiating effectiveness.
9. Clear up any misunderstandings or conflicts within your negotiating team before the negotiations begin.
10. Prepare a three-way comparison: management proposal, union proposal, and present contract. Bargain weighing all three.
11. Present evidence for your positions clearly and have copies for all concerned. Evidence in writing is perhaps more persuasive than evidence given verbally.
12. Do not make demands that have no real advantage for your organization, as you may have to concede something valuable in order to get them.
13. Prioritize your demands. Decide what you will probably not give up, what you will give up if pressed, and what you will demand which you are actually using as a bargaining point or "stalking horse" for trading purposes.
14. Retain flexibility; be ready to change your course if it becomes necessary; try not to "burn bridges" behind you.
15. When agreement is reached on an item, make sure the exact language is developed and the item is initialed by the other team before you proceed.
16. Do not violate a confidence by using "off-the-record" conversations held away from the bargaining setting to undercut the position of another (opposing) negotiator.
17. Do not mislead the opposition by promising what you cannot or will not deliver, or by hinting you will reciprocate when you will not. Your credibility is important and cannot be destroyed.
18. Do not leave the bargaining table after an agreement is reached until you have gone over the entire agreement and reviewed its language, etc. It may be late and you may be tired, but a quick review just to make sure is wise.
19. Negotiating is an art and a science. Further, experience is valuable, as is knowledge of the opposing team members personalities, positions, and views, as well as relevant information about your own and the other organization. However, despite the importance of facts, objectives, precedents, financial reports, etc., much of what happens at the bargaining table gets down to personalities and interpersonal relations. Drama also plays a part—feigning anger, bluffing, putting on a show for the press or rank-and-file, and hedging are all used, sometimes very effectively. The important point to remember with regard to your behavior at the bargaining table is that the behavior should be instrumental to attaining the objectives you seek, as well as consonant with your own and the organization's personal philosophy, values, and position.
20. Negotiating does not necessarily involve "defeating" the other side. When negotiations are put in a win-lose context, neither side may be successful and the "winner" may gain a very hollow victory. The dictionary definition of negotiate is "confer with" or "parley," not "do battle with."

_____

* Can apply to union and management negotiators.

Name _____   Group Number _____

Date _____   Class Section _____   Hour _____   Score _____

ASSESSMENT OF LEARNING IN PERSONNEL ADMINISTRATION
EXERCISE 18

1. Try to state the purpose of this exercise in one concise sentence.

2. Specifically what did you learn from this exercise (i.e., skills, abilities, and knowledge)?

3. How might your learning influence your role and your duties as a personnel administrator?

4. How might you evaluate the effectiveness or performance of a negotiator (for unions or management)?

5. Given the current economic conditions in this country and the political environment, what trends do you foresee regarding labor relations and unionism? Will unionism grow in the next decade? Why or why not? What types of employees and jobs are "ripe" for unionization? Why?

6. What positive effects would the existence of a union in an organization have on the operation of the personnel or human-resource-management functions of the organization?

Exercise 19
Costing human resources

PREVIEW

In this exercise you will learn how to determine the costs of some basic human-resource functions such as the costs of recruitment, selection, turnover, absenteeism, overtime, etc.

OBJECTIVES

1. To demonstrate that the costs of human resources can be measured.
2. To provide information on the methods which may be used in costing human resources.
3. To build skills in application of human resource costing methodology and demonstrate the costs v. benefits of personnel systems components.

PREMEETING PREPARATION

Read *Introduction, Procedure,* and all forms in Parts A, B, and C as well as Forms 1, 2, and 3. You may begin to do the calculations required as soon as it is assigned by your implementor.

INTRODUCTION
Using Costs to Determine the Contribution of Human Resources

There is much discussion about the value of human resources to organizations. In fact, there have been a few attempts to place a value on human resources through human-resource accounting. However, outside of a few published pieces on actually costing human resources, organizations seldom determine the costs incurred with respect to human resources.

This is surprising, especially because human resources are usually the largest single cost for organizations, often about 60 to 65% of an organization's total annual expenditures. This is true not only at the organizational level, but also for each manager since the organizational unit under a manager's supervision often reveals human resources to be its largest expenditure. Organizations usually hold managers accountable for how efficiently and effectively they use the other resources under their jurisdiction, such as material and financial resources, but seldom do organizations hold managers accountable in rigorous terms for human resources. Perhaps this is because organizations have not attempted to use cost measures to account for managerial effectiveness or ineffectiveness, efficiency or inefficiency in the use of human resources.

For example, if we were to try to determine the efficiency of the personnel function in gross terms, we might consider measures such as the ratio of sales dollars to employee, earnings per employee, payroll compared to earnings, costs per hire, etc. But these measures have not traditionally been used and it is doubtful if they will be used in the very near future.

Table 1. Areas of Human Resource Costing

Attracting	Hiring	Developing	Keeping	Losing
Advertising	Application	On-the-job training	Wages	Turnover
Recruiting	blanks	Orientation	Merit pay	Absenteeism
visits	Application	Upgrade	Error rates	Exit interviews
Agency fees	processing	training	Bonuses and	Severance pay
Literature	Interviewing	Safety training	awards	Sick leave pay
Public	Medical exams	Initial employee	Performance	Unemployment
relations	Testing	costs in:	appraisals	compensation
	Reference	production,	Performance	Retirement
	checks	maintenance,	appraisal	Tardiness
	Applicant	supervision,	reviews	Work stoppages
	travel	accidents,	Benefits	
	expenses	waste	Social Security	
	Overhead		Ineffective	
			performance	
			Accidents	
			Grievances	
			Downtime	

However, there is a lot occurring in the human-resource costing area today, as we shall discuss.

AREAS OF COSTING

When considering the costing of human resources, there are some obvious areas on which to focus. These are the basic human-resource functions of attracting, hiring, developing, helping, and losing human resources. With each of these issues there are several costs involved, as can be seen in Table 1.

Obviously, some of these costs are controllable (e.g., hiring, wages and benefits costs) while some are less controllable (e.g., turnover, absenteeism, social security). Thus, the objective in human resource costing, is not only to measure the costs of human resources, but also to develop means of reducing the costs of human resources by making prudent decisions related to the more "controllable" cost factors.

For example, in the turnover of human resources there are several contributing factors, or reasons, for leaving, like "another job," "returning to school," "better salary." These are much more controllable than causes of turnover such as death, poor health, and family reasons. Thus, an organization must determine which of its human-resource costs are somewhat controllable and devote resources to reducing these costs. By focusing on the controllable costs of turnover, an organization might reduce turnover of its best employees by offering promotions or job design changes,

increases in salary, better working conditions, educational benefits, etc. The important concept is that an organization must recognize which human-resource costs are controllable and work to reduce these.

Often the many costs of human resources are "hidden" or indirect costs such as the costs of benefits as shown in Table 2. The many hidden costs include insurance, pensions, taxes, vacations, rest periods, holidays, unemployment compensation, sick leave, profit sharing, bonuses, thrift plans, meals, company discounts, education expenditures, etc. Clearly, there are *many* costs incurred when bringing an applicant into an organization. In fact, many other essential costs are incurred in having a *human* resource at work (such as parking lots, water fountains, restrooms, etc.), but these are never found in costing methods.

Benefits costs are incurred upon hiring an employee. However, there are also the entire costs of the personnel department, for if we were not hiring human resources there would be no need for the personnel (or human-resources) unit in organizations. An example of the many personnel costs and how the burden is distributed is shown in Table 3. Certainly the personnel unit within an organization is itself a large cost; how this function is costed is of critical importance not only to the organization, but also to the personnel profession.

There are also concerns about identifying other areas of human-resource costing which could aid the organization in human-resource planning (see Exercise 2). That is, if we were to model what would happen to the organization in terms of human-resource costs

Table 2. Weekly Costs of Benefits per Employee by Industry in 1979

	Per employee Per week
ALL INDUSTRIES	$ 106.92
MANUFACTURING:	
Petroleum industry	175.48
Chemicals and allied industries	135.79
Transportation equipment	128.17
Primary metals industries	126.44
Machinery (excluding electrical)	113.83
Electrical machinery, equipment and supplies	106.81
Fabricated metal products (excluding machinery and transportation equipment)	102.38
Instruments and miscellaneous products	101.00
Stone, clay and glass products	100.94
Food, beverages and tobacco	99.87
Printing and publishing	98.35
Pulp, paper, lumber and furniture	97.35
Rubber, leather and plastic products	88.67
Textile products and apparel	59.58
NONMANUFACTURING:	
Public utilities	143.58
Miscellaneous nonmanufacturing industries (research, engineering, education, government agencies, mining, construction, etc.)	111.06
Banks, finance and trust companies	101.48
Insurance companies	101.31
Wholesale and retail trade	74.17
Hospitals	64.60
Department stores	58.35

Source: "Employee Benefits 1979," *Nation's Business,* Washington, D.C., 1979. Reprinted by permission.

if it were to expand (or retrench), certain indices such as proportion of pretax earnings, sales, or value added (as shown in Table 4) would be critical.

In planning for growth, organizations could attempt to influence the "controllable" human resource costs. One way of viewing this is to calculate the costs per hire for each new human resource added by the organization. Hiring costs for the job of a sales representative are shown in Table 5. The costs are divided into several areas such as the costs of terminating an employee, direct hiring costs, training costs, and indirect impacts on sales. All of these costs then comprise the costs incurred for hiring additional sales representatives (or replacing those leaving).

HOW TO COST HUMAN RESOURCES

In attempting to cost human resources, the first step is to define clearly the construct to be measured. This sounds obvious, but consider the problems of absenteeism. When is an absence, an absence? In other words, when should an organization begin counting someone as absent? When does an absence end and sick leave (or long-term disability) or turnover begin? This sounds ridiculous, but precise definition of each of these concepts is essential if each is to be treated as a unique human-resource cost and measured in the same way by all units of an organization. Mirvis and Macy (1976b) have been leaders in the human resource costing field and have provided basic definitions of some of the concepts to cost (see Table 6). Thus, when starting to cost any human resource variable a precise definition of the construct must be determined initially.

Once the concept has been defined with precision the formulas and the various components which enter the formulas must be determined. Table 7 shows the formulas used by Mirvis and Macy in their costing of several critical human-resource variables.

The procedures used by Mirvis and Macy to measure absenteeism are shown in Fig. 1. Here are presented a series of decision rules to guide those involved in computing the costs of absenteeism. This "tree diagram" could then be used readily by various persons within an organization, and a relatively standardized measure of absenteeism cost used to evaluate a unit of managerial efficiency.

Table 3. Cost Allocations of Personnel Programs

Activity	% of all organizations			
	Entire cost allocated to Personnel dept. budget	Entire cost allocated to other depts.	Costs shared between Personnel and other depts.	N/A (no such activity budgeted)
Hiring				
Recruiting rank and file	68	8	20	4
College recruiting	58	6	14	22
Executive recruiting	50	15	24	11
Testing	64	4	6	26
Preemployment physical exams	63	14	6	17
Training				
Orientation for new employees	61	11	24	24
Rank and file OJT	9	65	18	8
Skill training for upgrading	18	45	26	11
Supervisory training	45	17	33	5
Management development	38	13	40	9
Educational of scholarship program	54	28	6	12
Appraisal and compensation				
Management performance appraisal	48	16	16	20
Nonmanagement appraisal	46	18	16	20
Wage and salary administration	80	3	12	5
Job evaluation	81	3	9	7
Promotion, transfer & separation procedures	62	15	15	8
Benefits and Services				
Vacation and leave procedures	35	46	17	2
Administration of health & other insurance plans	72	13	15	. . .
Administration of pension or profit sharing programs	67	12	15	6
Administration of savings or stock plans	36	9	15	40
Health & medical services	60	15	15	10
Counseling programs	61	5	10	24
Recreation and social programs	55	10	17	18
Housing or moving services	33	42	15	10
Legal or financial services (credit union)	20	25	12	43
Other Activities				
Employee relations-discipline and/or grievance handling	56	6	24	14
Employee communications & publications	60	21	17	2
Safety programs	50	17	28	5
EEO/Affirmative Action programs	83	1	14	2
Personnel research	83	. . .	5	12
Union relations (no union-55 firms)	28	4	13	55

Source: *Bulletin to Management,* June 6, 1974, Bureau of National Affairs, Washington, D.C.

Measures of turnover costs are also difficult to measure. The problem is often in separating turnover costs from regular hiring costs. Thus, total turnover cost should include the costs of replacement, but not all costs of hiring because many hiring costs may be for additional hires required for an organization's growth. These are not replacement costs.

The actual cost of turnover includes many variables in the areas of recruiting, selecting, training and developing, and exiting. Some of these items involved are shown in Table 8. Clearly, these are but a few of the many costs involved in replacing employees. Some items are obviously much easier to measure than others (e.g., unemployment insurance costs per employee), while others are much more difficult to measure precisely (e.g., lost productivity), and thus estimates (or "guesstimates") must be obtained.

It should again be noted that the objective of cost-

Table 4. Organizational Performance and Human Resource Costs

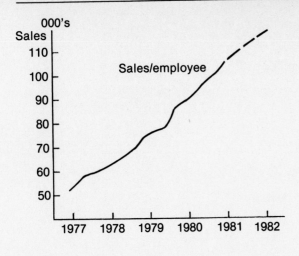

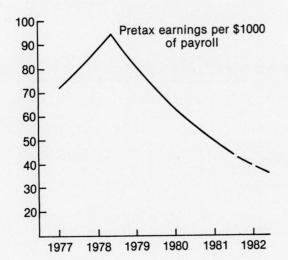

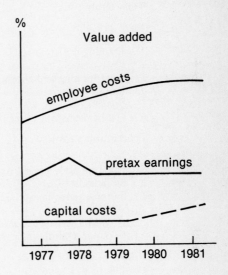

ing both absenteeism and turnover is *not* to eliminate them, but to control these costs at an optimal level of organizational efficiency and effectiveness. We do not wish to eliminate absenteeism completely, for if we have everyone coming to work regardless of illness we may incur a far greater risk of organizationwide illness which could soon severely hamper effectiveness. Likewise, we do not wish to eliminate turnover. What we would like to do is to lose our hiring mistakes (or selection "misses" and keep our successful employees (selection "hits"). Obviously, if our selection system

"hits" every time, we may have no need for turnover, but this is unrealistic, for it is very difficult to measure an individual's motives and career changes which may lead to turnover irrespective of the appropriateness of other skills for the job. Thus, costing employee withdrawal (absenteeism and turnover) is not done with the intent of eliminating these costs. Rather, we want to be able to measure these aspects of running an organization, so that we can use them in evaluating organizational units and managers (e.g., cost-benefit analysis of turnover).

Table 5. An Example of Costing Sales Representative Additions/Replacement Costs

A. Termination costs*
1. Severance pay
2. Auto/storage
3. Sample/equipment storage
4. Vacant territory coverage/mailings
5. Unemployment compensation

Total termination costs $_____

B. Hiring costs
1. Agency fees
2. Advertising expenses
3. Testing and interviewing time
    (for all involved)
4. Travel costs (applicant, interviewers)
5. Relocation expenses
6. Extra social security taxes
7. Medical examinations

Total hiring costs $_____

C. Training costs
1. Training center costs
2. Field training by trainer
3. Field training and coaching by manager
4. Training materials
5. Travel associated with training
6. Field trainers out of territory

Total training costs $_____

D. Estimated monthly impact on territory
1. Business lost (or)
2. Business potential not realized
    Subtotal
    x vacant territory months
    =   Total monthly impact on territory** $_____

Total average cost per hire
(total of A, B, C, and D)

    x Number of terminations/resignations
    =   Annual turnover cost $_____
    x% of turnover considered "controllable"
       (usually 30 to 50%)
    =   Annual controllable turnover cost $_____

* Use average cost per representative hired or terminated for all calculations.

** There is also adverse impact on territories staffed by unsuccessful salespeople who will eventually terminate.

Table 6. Behavioral Definitions and Recording Categories

Definition	*Recording category*
Absenteeism: Each absence or illness over four hours.	Voluntary: Short-term illness (less than three consecutive days), personal business, personal leave day, family illness.
	Involuntary: Long-term illness (more than three consecutive days), short-term leave of absence (jury duty, maternity, military), funerals, out-of-plant accidents, lack of work (temporary lay off), presanctioned days off.
Tardiness: Each absence or illness under four hours.	Voluntary: Same as absenteeism.
	Involuntary: Same as absenteeism.
Turnover: Each departure beyond organizational boundary.	Voluntary: Resignation.
	Involuntary: Termination, disqualification, requested resignation, long-term leave of absence, permanent layoff, retirement, death.
Strikes and work stoppages: Each day lost due to work strike or stoppage.	Sanctioned: Union-authorized strike, company-authorized lockout.
	Unsanctioned: Work slowdown, walkout, sitdown.
Accidents and work-related illnesses: Each recordable injury, illness, or death from a work-related accident or from exposure to the work environment.	Major: Occupational Safety and Health (OSHA) accident, illness, or death which results in medical treatment by a physician or registered professional person understanding orders from a physician.
	Minor: Non-OSHA accident or illness which results in one-time treatment and subsequent observation not requiring professional care.
Grievance: Written grievance in accordance with labor-management contract.	Stage: Recorded by step (first step—arbitration).
Productivity*: Resources used in production of acceptable outputs (comparison of inputs with outputs).	Output: Product or service quality (units or $).
	Input: Direct and/or Indirect (Labor in hours or $).
Production quality: Resources used in production of unacceptable output.	Resource utilized: Scrap (Unacceptable in-plant products in units or $). Customer returns (unacceptable out-of-plant products in units or $). Recoveries (salvageable products in units or $). Rework (additional direct and/or indirect labor in hours or $).
Downtime: Unscheduled breakdown of machinery.	Downtime: Duration of breakdown (hours or $).
	Machine repair: Nonpreventative maintenance ($).
Inventory, material, and supply variance: Unscheduled resource utilization.	Variance: Over-or-under utilization of supplies, materials, inventory (due to theft, inefficiency, and so on).

* Reports only labor inputs

Source: B. A. Mirvis and P. H. Macy, "A Methodology for Assessment of Quality of Work Life and Organizational Effectiveness in Behavioral-Economic Terms," *Administrative Science Quarterly* 21 (1976): 212-226.

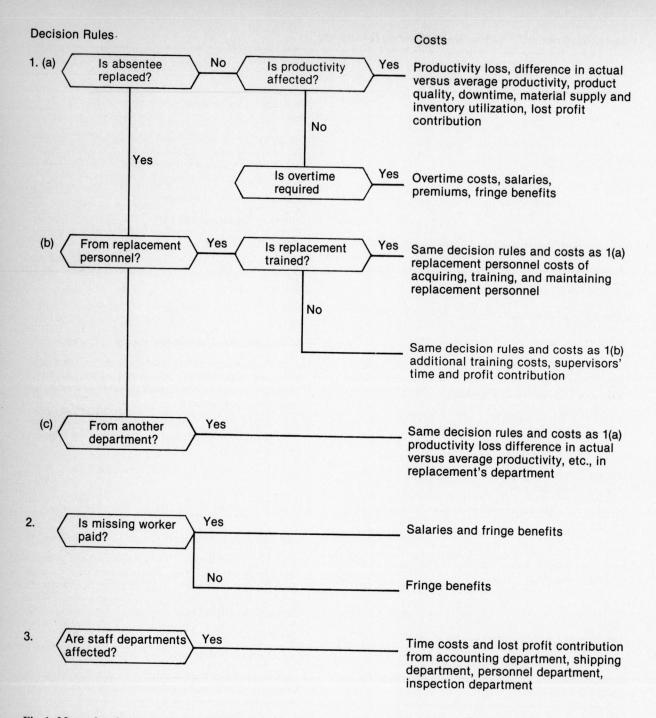

Fig. 1. Measuring the costs of absenteeism (Source: P. H. Mirvis and B. A. Macy, "A Methodology for Assessment of Quality of Work Life and Organizational Effectiveness in Behavioral-Economic Terms," *Administrative Science Quarterly* 21 (1976): 221–226)

Table 7. Behavioral Measures and Computational Formulas

Absenteeism rate*	Σ Absence days $\div$ [Average work-force size $\times$ working days]
Tardiness rate*	Σ Tardiness incidents $\div$ [Average work-force size $\times$ working days]
Turnover rate (monthly)	Σ Turnover incidents $\div$ Average work-force size
Strike rate (yearly)	[Σ Striking workers $\times$ strike days] $\div$ [Average work-force size $\times$ working days]
Accident rate (yearly)	Σ Accidents, illnesses $\div$ Total yearly hours worked $\times$ 200,000†
Grievance rate (yearly)	Plant: Σ Grievance incidents $\div$ Average work-force size Individual: Σ Aggrieved individuals $\div$ Average work-force size
Productivity total	Output of goods or services (units or \$) $\div$ Direct and/or indirect labor (hours or \$)
Production below standard	Productivity (actual versus engineered standard)
Product quality total	Scrap + customer returns + rework − recoveries (\$)
Product quality below standard	Product quality (actual versus engineered standard)
Downtime	Labor (\$) + repair costs or dollar value of replaced equipment (\$)
Inventory, supply, and material usage‡	Variance (actual versus standard utilization) (\$)

* Sometimes combined as Σ hours missing $\div$ [average work-force size $\times$ working hours].

† Base for 100 full-time equivalent workers (40 hours $\times$ 50 weeks).

‡ Often subsumed under total productivity below standard figure.

Source: P. H. Mirvis and B. A. Macy, "A Methodology for Assessment of Quality of Work Life and Organizational Effectiveness in Behavioral-Economic Terms," *Administrative Science Quarterly* 21 (1976): 212–226. Reprinted by permission.

Table 8. Employee Replacement Cost Components

Recruiting	Selecting	Training and development	Exiting

1) Advertising
2) College recruiting
3) Employment agency fees
 	
4) Literature
  Brochures
  Pamphlets
 	
5) Public relations activities
	1) Application blanks
	2) Evaluating applications
	3) Interviewing time
	  Personnel department
	  Line managers
	4) Medical examinations
	5) Test construction
	6) Test validation
	7) Candidate evaluation
	8) Reference checking
	9) Travel expenses
	  Actual travel
	  Reservations
	  Conducted tours
	10) Personnel department (overhead) allocation of burden
		1) Employment processing
		2) Orientation
		
		3) Indoctrination and on-the-job training
		
		4) Break-in
		  Decreased production
		  Increased supervision
		  Increased maintenance
		  Increased accidents
		5) Formal training programs
		  Waste of materials
		  Lost productivity
			1) Exit interview
			2) Severance pay
			
			3) Extra Social Security
			
			4) Extra UIC (unemployment insurance costs)
			5) Reduced productivity
			  Increased waste of materials
			  Increased maintenance
			  Loss in productivity of exiting employee
			  Loss or productivity of colleagues
			  Increased accidents

EXAMPLES OF HUMAN RESOURCE COSTING

As noted in Table 8, there are many areas to be costed in human resources. However, below we will demonstrate costing only in the areas of turnover, absenteeism, selection, and attitudes.

Turnover.[1] Although turnover costs have been noted earlier for the sales jobs, turnover formulas noted in Table 7, and alternative items to cost turnover noted in Table 8, we feel there is enough information available on turnover costing to provide a more detailed analysis. This analysis includes three major turnover costing areas: separation costs, replacement costs, and training costs.

Separation costs include exit interviews, separation pay, unemployment tax, and the burden of the administrative functions related to terminations. These items can be costed by the following formulas:

Separation costs				*Formula*			
Exit interview (S_1)	=	Cost of interviewers' time	$\times$	Time required prior to interview	+	Time required for interview	$\times$
				Interviewer's pay rate during period	$\times$	Number of turnovers during period	+
				Terminated employee's time required for the interview	$\times$	Weighted average pay* rate for terminated employees	$\times$
				Number of turnovers during period			
Administrative functions related to terminations (S_2)	=	Time required by Personnel dept. for administrative functions related to terminations	$\times$	Average Personnel dept. employee's pay rate	$\times$	Number of turnovers during period	
Separation pay (S_3)	=	Amount of separation pay per employee terminated	$\times$	Number of turnovers during period			
Unemployment tax (S_4)	=	(Unemployment tax rate for following year	$-$	base rate) $\times$ budgeted taxable wages			

* The weighted average pay rate for terminated employees is calculated as follows:

$$\text{Weighted average pay rate per terminated employee} = \frac{\Sigma \text{ (Pay rate} \times \text{number of employees terminated at this rate)}}{\text{Number of employees terminated during this period}}$$

Thus the total separation costs (Σ_5) would be $S_1 + S_2 + S_3 + S_4$.

---

[1] Many ideas for this turnover costing model come from Howard L. Smith and Larry E. Watkins, "Managing Manpower Turnover Costs," *The Personnel Administrator* 23, 46–50.

The basic costs of replacing an employee can be calculated by the following set of formulas:

Costs	Formula			
Notification of job opening (R_1)	= advertising and employment agency fees per termination	+ time required for communicating job availability	$\times$ personnel dept. employee's pay rate	$\times$ number of turnovers replaced during period
Preemployment administrative functions (R_2)	= time required by Personnel dept. for preemployment administrative functions	$\times$ average Personnel dept. employee's pay rate	$\times$ number of turnovers replaced during period	
Entrance interview (R_3)	= time required for interview	$\times$ interviewer's rate	$\times$ number of interviews during period	
Staff meeting (R_4)	= time required for meeting	$\times$ Personnel dept. employee's pay rate	+ dept. rep. pay rate	$\times$ number of meetings during period
Postemployment acquisition & dissemination of information (R_5)	= time required for acquiring & disseminating information	$\times$ average Personnel dept. employee's pay rate	$\times$ number of turnovers replaced during period	
In-house medical examinations (R_6)	= time required for examination	$\times$ examiner's pay rate	+ cost of supplies used	$\times$ number of turnovers replaced during period
or				
Contracted medical examinations (R_7)	= Rate per examination $\times$ number of turnovers replaced during period			

Thus the total costs of replacing employees who leave (Σ) is represented by $R_1 + R_2 + R_3 + R_4 + R_5 + R_6$ (or R_7).

Training employees to become successful replacements for terminated employees, a most difficult area to cost, is demonstrated by the following formulas:

Cost	Formula
Training materials (T_1)	= unit cost of informational package $\times$ number of instructions during period
Formal instruction (T_2)	= hours of instruction $\times$ average pay rates for all trainers and instructors
Instruction job title (T_3)	= number of hours required for instruction $\times$ new employee's pay rate $\times$ number of training sessions

The total costs for replacing employees could then be calculated for each job title (or for the entire organization) by summing the costs incurred for each of the turnover areas costed (i.e., $S + R + T$).[2] For each managerial unit, a chart could be kept to record turnover costs for use as a cost control measure for the unit. An example of such a control chart is presented in Table 9.

---

[2] This has been done by Cascio and Phillips in "Performance Testing: A Rose Among Thorns?" *Personnel Psychology* (1979): 751–766, esp. 764.

Table 9. Monthly Labor Turnover Control Form

Department-Wire Mill	Job Classification-Wire drawers	

L.L. Treece	Costs	
Average Work Force 108	(1) Separation	$ 120
Current T.O. Rate 3.2/mo., 38.4/yr.	(2) Hiring	642
Current T.O. Cost 8496/mo.; 101,952	(3) Training	1,893
	(including lost production and lost productivity)	
	Total	$2,655

Month	Next Year's Projected Turnover		Budgeted Turnover		Actual Turnover					Actual Cost		Comments
	No.	Cost	No.	Cost	Quits	Dismiss	Layoff	Other	Total	Amt.	% Budget	
Jan.	6	15,930	5	13,275	7	3			10	26,550	+ 200%	
Feb.	3	7,965	2	5,310	1	1			2	5,310	0	
Mar.	1	2,655	1	2,655	3	1			4	10,620	+ 400%	
Apr.	3	7,965	2	5,310	2	1		1	4	10,620	+ 200%	
May	5	13,275	3	7,965	3	3	8*		14	16,890	+ 212%	Includes
Jun.	3	7,965	1	2,655	3	1			4	10,620	+ 400%	$960 un-
Jul.	3	7,965	1	2,655	2			2	4	10,620	+ 400%	controllable
Aug.	5	13,275	2	5,310	5	1			6	15,930	+ 300%	costs of
Sept.	7	18,585	5	13,275	3	1		4	8	21,240	+ 160%	separation
Oct.	2	5,310	0	0						0	0	
Nov.	9	23,893	3	7,915	1	1			2	5,310	− 67%	
Dec.	3	7,965	1	2,655	1	1			2	5,310	+ 200%	
TOTAL	50	132,748	26	68,980	31	14	8	7	60	139,020	+ 202%	

* Only separation costs occur for the 8 layoffs.

The performance of a supervisor in the management of human resources could then be evaluated, at least in part, by these costs of turnover.

Absenteeism. Costs in the area of absenteeism are somewhat easier to calculate than are those of turnover costs. You may remember that Fig. 1 illustrated a model for making decisions relative to absenteeism costs. Essentially, the costs of absenteeism were broken into three categories: employee replacement, paying the absentee, and staff costs. For example, if a retail clerk is absent and a replacement clerk is "called in," but only two hours after starting time, the situation requires overtime of a worker from the previous shift (who makes $10 per hour). Also assume the employee has taken a sick day at full pay. The costs of this one incident are calculated as follows:

Replacement Costs:	
Productivity Loss	0
Overtime Costs (2 hours @ time and one half)	30
Replacement Costs(6 hours @ $10)	60
Orientation Costs (½ hour of supv. time @ $16/hr)	8
Absentee Costs:	
Absentee Salary (8 hours @ $10)	80
Absentee Benefits (35% of Salary)	28
Staff Costs:	
Personnel and Processing Costs (½ hour @ $30)	22
	$228

Table 10. Factors Influencing Selection Utility

Validity of selection procedure
Selection ratio
Cost of selection

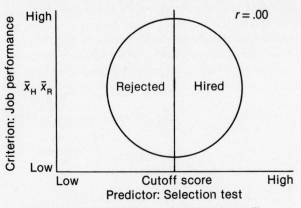

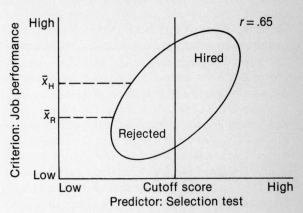

$\bar{x}_R$ mean job performance of those "rejected"

Fig. 2. Differences in statistical test validity

$\bar{x}_H$ mean job performance of those "hired"

Thus, the cost of one absence was $228, compared to the $108 cost incurred had the employee reported to work. The absence then cost the organization an additional $120. If this can be considered a typical absence and the absenteeism rate for the organization is 5% of a labor force of 800, this represents an average absenteeism rate of 40 persons per day at $228 or $9120 per day! If we compute this for an annual working period of 340 working days per year (which is not unrealistic in the retail business), the cost could be a staggering $3,100,800. This cost is incurred without accounting for productivity losses or perhaps overstaffing with additional *permanent* employees used as a ready supply to cover absenteeism. In some industries (e.g., automobile manufacturing), it has been estimated that there is an overhiring of 15% to cover the high rate of absenteeism.[3]

Selection. The costing of a selection method to demonstrate its benefit to the organization is a more complex procedure than absenteeism and turnover costing. As noted in Exercise 9, there are several concepts important to the effectiveness and cost of the selection process. The first is utility, which is merely the overall worth (of one selection method over another) to the organization. Selection utility is then influenced by the validity of the selection procedure, the selection ratio, and the percent of successful incumbents. This is illustrated in

---

[3] It should be noted that the total cost of absenteeism cited above ($3,100,800) includes $1,632,000 of additional costs that would not be incurred if the absence did not occur.

Table 10. Essentially, the higher the validity of a test, the higher its utility.

Therefore, if a new selection procedure has higher validity than the present methods, it has greater utility for the organization, assuming the costs of the two procedures are equivalent. Figure 2 shows this relationship graphically by demonstrating that the only difference between the illustrations is the correlation coefficient about $r = .00$ on the left and about $r = .65$ on the right. The different scatter plots show differences in test validity.

The left chart shows no relationship between test score and job performance, whereas in the right chart there is clearly a positive relationship. In the left chart the average job performance of those "hired" is equal to that of those "rejected." In test validation, it is assumed that all job candidates are hired. This is necessary to measure the true relationship between predictor and criterion measures. Otherwise, restriction of range may occur and spuriously depress the "true" correlation coefficient. Therefore, "rejected" candidates represent what selection decisions would be for future job candidates after validating the predictor.

In the right chart of Figure 2, there is a clear difference between the mean performance scores of the two groups. Thus, the higher validity of the test means higher utility to the organization, since on the average better job performers would be hired. The selection ratio is the percentage of job applicants who are actually hired, so a low selection ratio means few persons are hired from those who apply. As the selection ratio goes down, the utility of a selection procedure goes up.

Figure 3 shows that if the organization hires all who apply (a situation more common than many realize), the average job performance of those hired ($\bar{X}_H$) is moderate. If 80 percent of those applying are hired, the average level of job performance goes up. However, if only the top 20 percent are hired, the average job performance of this group is still higher (when test validity remains constant). Also, it should be noted that selection procedures can also be thought of as *rejection* procedures. Thus, an organization must decide whether it's worthwhile to use a selection procedure to reject applicants. For some jobs, this could be a waste of time and money if most people hired can perform the job successfully. Therefore, the percent of presently successful employees (base rate) is relevant for selection utility. If the percentage is high, there is serious doubt about the need for a selection procedure to reject those few candidates unable to do the job. Thus, the organization must compare the percentages of successful employees using present methods with the percentage of successful employees using the new selection method. If the new method yields a higher percentage, it increases the utility of the selection procedure. This is most likely when the percentage of presently successful employees is low because it's easier to make an improvement.

Thus, the utility of a selection procedure may depend upon the validity of a test, the previous selection ratio, and the base rate of success of previous employees. The situation in which it would be most favorable to explore the development of an alternative selection procedure would, therefore, be one in which there was previously a high selection ratio and a low base rate of success. If a selection procedure with a high validity could be developed, the utility of the procedure in terms of increasing value of those selected would most likely be favorable.

The basic utility formula for calculating the gain in financial terms is as follows:

$$\triangle U = N\, o_e\, r_{ye}\, \xi\, (Y') - NC_y$$

where

$\triangle U$ = gain in utility,

N = number of applicants,

o_e = standard deviation of criterion (in dollars),

r_{ye} = validity coefficient (correlation between selection procedure and dollar scale evaluated outcomes),

$\xi\, (Y')$ = the ordinate at the cutting score, and

C_y = cost of putting one person through the selection procedure.

Cascio and Silbey have demonstrated the utility of an assessment center using the above formula with the results depicted in Table 11.

Schmidt, Hunter, McKenzie and Muldrow (see *For Further Reading*) demonstrate the impact of using improved testing procedures for computer programmers. Although they make some questionable assumptions about the growth of the economy and the need for computer programmers, they effectively make the case for the financial impact of improved testing, as shown in Table 12.

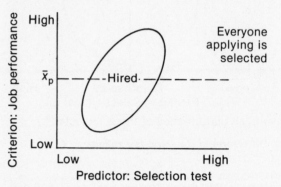

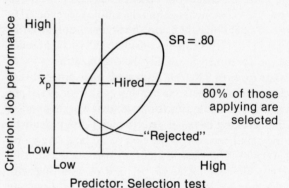

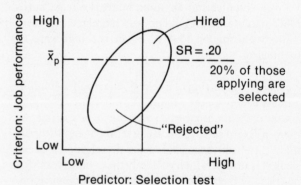

$\bar{x}_p$ mean job performance of those "hired"

Fig. 3. Impacts of differing selection ratios on average performance when test validity remains constant (Source: W. F. Cascio and V. Silbey, "Utility of the Assessment Center as a Selection Device," *Journal of Applied Psychology* 64, no. 2 (1979): 11)

Table 11. Sample Utility Analysis Output

Type of cost	Per candidate	Total
Recruitment	$101.00	$10,100.00
Processing & induction	$10.00	$1,000.00
Ordinary selection	$290.00	$29,000.00
Assessment center	$403.28	$40,238.00
Training	$450.00	$22,500.00
	1st year	*5-year total*
Criterion *SD*	$9,500.00	$41,409.54

Ordinary selection

Validity	Incremental	Total cost	Gain in utility
.25	$412,956.62	$62,600.00	$350,356.62

Assessment center[a]

Validity	Incremental gain	Gain in utility	Per selectee A.C. payoff[b]	Total A.C. payoff[b]
.05	$82,591.33	$8,663.33	$-6,833.87	$-341,693.30
.10	$165,182.65	$91,254.65	$-5,182.04	$-259,101.98
.15	$247,773.97	$173,845.97	$-3,530.21	$-176,510.65
.20	$330,365.30	$256,437.30	$-1,878.39	$-93,919.32
.25	$412,956.62	$339,028.62	$-226.56	$-11,328.00
.30	$495,547.95	$421,619.95	$1,425.27	$71,263.32
.35	$578,139.27	$504,211.27	$3,077.09	$153,854.65
.40	$660,730.60	$586,802.60	$4,728.92	$236,445.98
.45	$743,321.92	$669,393.92	$6,380.75	$319,037.30
.50	$825,913.25	$751,985.25	$8,032.57	$401,628.62
.55	$908,504.56	$834,576.56	$9,684.40	$484,219.94
.60	$991,095.89	$917,167.89	$11,336.23	$566,811.27
.65	$1,073,687.20	$999,759.20	$12,988.05	$649,402.58
.70	$1,156,278.55	$1,082,350.55	$14,639.88	$731,993.92
.75	$1,238,869.86	$1,164,941.86	$16,291.70	$814,585.23
.80	$1,321,461.20	$1,247,533.20	$17,943.53	$897,176.58
.85	$1,404,052.52	$1,330,124.52	$19,595.36	$979,767.89
.90	$1,486,643.84	$1,412,715.84	$21,247.18	$1,062,359.22
.95	$1,569,235.17	$1,495,307.17	$22,899.01	$1,144,950.55

Note: Quota for selection = 50. Selection ratio = .50. Ordinate at selection ratio = .399. Number recruited = 100. Number of assessment centers = 8.

[a] Total cost = $73,928.00.

[b] A.C. = assessment center.

Source: W. F. Cascio and V. Silbey. "Utility of an Assessment Center as a Selection Device," *Journal of Applied Psychology* 64 (1979): 11.

Employee Attitudes. Mirvis and Lawler[4] have attempted to demonstrate the financial impact of employee attitudes. Surveys of employee attitudes demonstrated their impact on absenteeism, turnover, and performance. Essentially, they were able to show that

the costs of absenteeism, turnover, and performance (calculated as demonstrated previously) are influenced by changes in job satisfaction. The costs of absenteeism ($66.45 per day), turnover ($2,522.03 per incident), and performance improvement ($23.62 per month) for 160 bank employees netted a saving of $17,664, with an improvement in job satisfaction of only one-half of one standard deviation.

The many examples cited above should provide

[4] P. H. Mirvis and E. E. Lawler, "Measuring the Financial Impact of Employee Attitudes," *Journal of Applied Psychology,* 62 (1977): 1-8.

Table 12.   Estimated Productivity Increase from One Year's Use of Programmer Aptitude Test to Select Computer Programmers in U.S. Economy (in millions of dollars)

Selection ratio	True validity of previous procedure				
	.00	.20	.30	.40	.50
.05	1,605	1,184	973	761	550
.10	1,367	1,008	828	648	468
.20	1,091	804	661	517	373
.30	903	666	547	428	309
.40	753	555	455	356	257
.50	622	459	376	295	218
.60	501	370	304	238	172
.70	387	285	234	183	132
.80	273	201	165	129	93

Source: F. J. Schmidt, J. E. Hunter, R. C. McKenzie, and T. W. Muldrow, "Impact of Valid Selection Procedures on Work-Force Productivity, *Journal of Applied Psychology* 64 (1979).

some idea of the numerous efforts now being undertaken in the costing of human resources. Continued efforts in this area are critical for personnel professionals hoping to demonstrate their worth within the organization by using the same measurement tools as their counterparts.

PROCEDURE

PART A

STEP 1: Select a human resource area in an organization, describe what components you would cost and what method you would use to cost the items, and provide an example of what the actual costs might be. You may wish to select an area such as absenteeism, orientation or training, benefits, selection, turnover, recruitment, etc. You should specify the type of organization, its size, job title and number of employees in the title, the salaries and benefits paid, and any other assumptions necessary for you to build your costing procedure. Your data are to be recorded on Form 1.

TIME:

STEP 2: You are to calculate the costs of hiring permanent versus temporary employees. You are to assume that you have an available labor supply of temporary employees who can report to work on notice, are nearly as proficient as the regular workers, and work 40 hours per week. The task required is estimated to take a total of 2,000 hours to complete for

permanent employees at 2,400 hours for temporary employees. Thus, permanent employees are more efficient by a factor of 58% (2,000 ÷ 3,400 hours). The project must be done in the next twenty-five weeks. You are also to calculate the breakeven costs (in hours) which make it advantageous to use permanent as compared to temporary employees. You are to use Form 2 for the costs and Form 3 to calculate the breakeven point.

TIME:

STEP 3: Using the utility formula shown on page 608 calculate the gain in utility where:

$$N = 600$$
$$o_e = \$4,600$$
$$r_{ye} = \$.75$$
$$\xi(Y') = 46$$
$$C_y = \$236$$

TIME:

FOR FURTHER READING

Baran, H. A. *USAF Military Personnel Costing: Problems and Approaches.* Brooks Air Force Base, Texas; U.S. Air Force Technical Report 77–39, August, 1977. (I)

Brogden, H. E. "When Testing Pays Off." *Personnel Psychology* 2 (1949): 171–183. (II)

Brogden, H. E. "On the Interpretation of the Correlation Coefficient as a Measure of Predictive Efficiency." *Journal of Educational Psychology* 37 (1946): 65–76. (II–R)

Brogden, H. and E. Taylor. "The Dollar Criterion—Applying the Cost Accounting Concept to Criterion Construction." *Personnel Psychology* 3 (1950): 133–154. (II–R)

Brummet, R., E. Flamholtz, and W. Pyle. "Human Resource Accounting—A Challenge for Accountants." *The Accounting Review* 43 (1968): 217–224. (II)

Bureau of National Affairs, *Bulletin to Management,* June 6, 1974, Washington, D.C. (I)

Cascio, L. F. "Responding to the Demand for Accountability: A Critical Analysis of Three Utility Models." *Organizational Behavior and Human Performance* 25 (1980): 32–45. (II–R)

Cascio, L. F., and L. Phillips. "Performance Testing: A Rose Among Thorns?" *Personnel Psychology* (1979): 751–766.

Cascio, W. F. and V. Silbey. "Utility of the Assessment Center as a Selection Device." *Journal of Applied Psychology* 64, no. 2 (1979): 11. (II–R)

Flamholtz, E. *Human Resource Accounting.* Encino, Cal.: Dickenson, 1974. (I)

Lawler, E. E. and J. G. Rhode. *Information and Control in Organizations.* Pacific Palisades, Cal.: Goodyear, 1976. (I)

Likert, R. and D. G. Bowers. "Improving the Accuracy of P/L Reports by Estimating the Change in Dollar Value of the Human Organization." *Michigan Business Review* 25 (1973): 15–24. (I)

Macy, B. A. and P. H. Mirvis. "Measuring Quality of Work and Organizational Effectiveness in Behavioral–Economic Terms." *Administrative Science Quarterly* 21 (1976): 212–226. (II–R)

Mirvis, P. H. and E. E. Lawler. "Measuring the Financial Impact of Employee Attitudes." *Journal of Applied Psychology* 62 (1977): 1–8. (II–R)

Mirvis, P. H. and B. A. Macy. "Accounting for the Costs and Benefits of Human Resource Development Programs: An Interdisciplinary Approach." *Accounting, Organizations and Society* 1 (1976): 179-194. (a) (II–R)

Mirvis, P. H. and B. A. Macy, "Human Resource Accounting: A Measurement Perspective." *Academy of Management Review* 1 (1976): 74–83. (b) (II)

Mirvis, P. H. and B. A. Macy, "A Methodology for Assessment of Quality of Work Life and Organizational Effectiveness in Behavioral–Economic Terms." *Administrative Science Quarterly* 21 (1976): 212–226. (II–R)

Rhode, J. and E. E. Lawler. "Auditing Change: Human Resource Accounting." In M. D. Dunnette, ed., *Work and Nonwork in the Year 2001.* Monterey, Cal.: Brooks/Cole, 1973. (I)

Roche, W. J., Jr. "A Dollar Criterion in Fixed Treatment Employee Selection." In L. J. Cronback and G. C. Gleser, eds., *Psychological Tests and Personnel Decisions.* 2d ed. Urbana: University of Illinois Press, 1965. (II)

Schmidt, F. E., J. E. Hunter, R. C. McKenzie, and T. W. Muldrow. "Impact of Valid Selection Procedures on Work-Force Productivity." *Journal of Applied Psychology* 64 (1979): 609–626. (II–R)

Smith, H. L. and L. E. Watkins. "Managing Manpower Turnover Costs." *The Personnel Administrator* 23 (1978): 46–50. (I)

Survey Research Center. *Michigan Organizational Assessment Package.* Ann Arbor, Mich.: Institute for Social Research, 1975. (I)

U.S. Chamber of Commerce. "Employee Benefits 1977." Washington, D.C.: 1978. (I)

PART A

Form 1 Human Resource Cost Model

Organization Type _____   Numbers of Employees _____

Job Title _____   Numbers of Incumbents _____

Average Monthly Salary of
Employees in This Job Title _____   Benefits as a
Percent of Salary _____ %

Benefits in
Dollars per Month $ _____

Other Assumptions: _____

_____

_____

_____

| Area Costed: _____ | | |
Cost Components	Cost Formulas	Actual Costs
1.		
2.		
3.		
4.		
5.		
6.		
7.		
8.		
9.		
10.		
11.		
12.		

PART A

Form 2 Permanent/Temporary Employee Alternative Cost Model

PERMANENT EMPLOYEE
RECURRING COSTS:

	Cost per hour per employee			
Salary	12.00			
Fringe benefits (25%)	3.00		Total	
Administration	.12	Task time	employee cost	
Supervision	.60	in hours	for the task	
Total	15.72	× ⎡2,000⎤ =	⎡____⎤	
			(A)	

NONRECURRING COSTS:

	Cost per employee		
		Number of	
Recruiting and selecting	2,008	permanent	
Training	775	employees	
Other	0	hired	
	$2,783	× ⎡____⎤ = ⎡____⎤	
		(B)	
Total cost per employee		= ⎡____⎤	
		(A + B)	

TEMPORARY EMPLOYEE
RECURRING COSTS:

	Cost per hour per employee		
Salary	10.00		
Fringe benefits	0		
Administration	1.00		Total
Supervision	1.00	Task time	employee cost
Other	0	in hours	for the task
Total	12.00	× ⎡3,400⎤ = ⎡____⎤	
		(A)	

NONRECURRING COSTS:

		Number of	
Recruiting	200	company	
Training	0	employees	
Other	375	hired	
Total	575	× ⎡____⎤ = ⎡____⎤	
		(B)	
Total cost per employee		= ⎡____⎤	
		(A + B)	

PART A

Form 3 Calculating Permanent vs. Temporary Employee Breakeven Cost

Nonrecurring
costs
Temporary

Nonrecurring
costs
Permanent

0	−	

=

A

Nonrecurring
costs
Permanent

=

0.155

B

Nonrecurring
costs
Temporary

0

=

0

C

Recurring
costs
Permanent

Recurring
costs
Temporary

	−		+	

B − C

=

D

BREAKEVEN POINT IN HOURS   =

(A/D)

ASSESSMENT OF LEARNING IN PERSONNEL ADMINISTRATION

EXERCISE 19

1. What was the purpose of this exercise?

2. What new concepts did you learn from this exercise?

3. What new skills did you learn from this exercise?

4. What would you do differently if you were a personnel administrator?

5. How would you go about convincing line managers of the value of personnel programs?

Exercise 20

Research in personnel/human resources

PREVIEW

An important issue that increasingly confronts personnel/human resource (P/HR) professionals is the reliance upon research data for the design, use, and defense of P/HR functions in organizations. In the past, the research and application aspects of P/HR have been far too separate. In this exercise you will learn about P/HR research in terms of its history, methods, and future needs.

OBJECTIVES

1. To introduce concepts will call for the evaluation of whatever interventions are made by the personnel department.
2. To develop an awareness of research design methodology.
3. To develop skills in the design of P/HR research as well as in applying statistical tools.

PREMEETING ASSIGNMENT

Read entire exercise.

INTRODUCTION

Using Research to Support Personnel Programs

P/HR research is becoming more relevant and more prevalent. Why is this change occurring? Unfortunately, it is not totally voluntary on the part of practitioners and academics to better demonstrate the value of the personnel function (see Exercise 19), but often an involuntary response to an externally imposed set of demands—equal employment opportunity and affirmative action. However, firms have also found that the need to remain competitive in international markets requires increasing the productivity of human resources. These seemingly irreconcilable demands, resolving social problems and increasing human produc-

tivity simultaneously, are the impetus for much of the new interest in research by both practitioners and academics.

P/HR RESEARCH: PAST AND PRESENT

Research in P/HR in organizations dates to the early 1900s. These early studies were done primarily by applied psychologists in selection and placement. Pioneers in scientific management were not involved in personnel research, but the scientific management movement undoubtedly influenced P/HR research as organizations began to take data-based approaches to organizational problems. An early P/HR publication was Hugo Munsterberg's 1913 text, *The Psychology of Industrial Efficiency*.[1] The *Journal of Applied Psychology* was soon established, and the *Journal of Personnel Research* followed.[2]

Research was given new importance by government programs to assist the complex P/HR problems required by World War I. These programs emphasized problems of manpower placement or classification. In Great Britain, the Industrial Fatigue Research Board was established to conduct studies on fatigue of industrial workers and hours and conditions of work. After World War I, psychologists who participated in military research programs were employed by organizations to introduce similar research programs for civilians. Some work (in public utility and insurance companies) became quite well known. World War II brought such activity to the fore again.[3]

Since World War II, P/HR research has expanded to broader organizational issues. Prewar research focused on individual differences. Recent research includes studies of performance appraisal methods, training, motivation, and organizational problems such as the effects of structural arrangements, group processes, communication problems, leadership style, etc.

However, much P/HR research in organizations has not progressed beyond data collection and application (i.e., research and development). Often researchers may be conducting respectable studies which are seldom published in professional journals because, from management's point of view, research is needed not for professional contributions (i.e., journals) but for solutions to management problems. Also research publications may be discouraged because of a fear of disclosing "trade secrets" or a lack of willingness to share new ideas or findings. Further, in many organizations, P/HR research may not be accepted as an important activity. P/HR decisions are perceived to be based on more subjective data than those elsewhere in the organization. The lack of a perceived need for research data for P/HR decision making keeps P/HR a low organizational priority. Yet such attitudes appear to be changing as management becomes aware of the importance of effective human-resource utilization.[4]

If this is an accurate assessment of the state of P/HR research, what are the major research issues facing the field? The first is the accountability (or efficiency) of the P/HR function itself. As discussed in Exercise 19, it seems as if P/HR responsibilities are often on the low end of the organizational "totem pole." Obviously, *we* know the critical contributions P/HR makes to organization. But whatever data P/HR brings to organizational "pie-dividing" conferences are perceived as "soft," and we often ask other members of the organization to accept the data on faith. Such arguments are hadly persuasive when faced with organization units such as marketing, production, and finance, which demonstrate in tidy, "hard," quantitative terms the organizational value of plant expansion, advertising campaigns, investment decisions, etc. Thus in the face of such "hard" data (compared to "soft" P/HR data), other areas receive priority status as targets for organizational funds. P/HR must therefore become more empirical as should be the case when approximately 60–65 percent of all organizational expenditures are *direct* P/HR costs!

Second, P/HR practitioners must also learn more about how to measure variables such as employee physical (absenteeism, turnover) and psychological (sub-standard work) withdrawal, beyond merely measuring financial impact. This is a question of *effectiveness* as opposed to the efficiency issues mentioned earlier. There are several areas in which we must be more effective. These include macro issues such as human-resource planning (and its subset, affirmative action planning) to meet organizational goals and timetables. In addition, there are micro P/HR issues in which we must be more effective, such as the design of performance appraisal and selection systems and the development of better training and motivation systems.

How to Research P/HR?

Most P/HR decisions are made in a context of uncertainty. For example, when deciding to start a performance appraisal, compensation, job enrichment, or training program, the personnel administrator is not certain whether it will prove effective or not. Re-

[1] H. Musterberg, *The Psychology of Industrial Efficiency* (Boston: Houghton Mifflin, 1913).

[2] This journal changed its name to the *Personnel Journal* (and to some extent its character) in 1927. For the most part, studies of the kind that were published in the *Journal of Personnel Research* appear today in *Personnel Psychology*. The *Personnel Journal* publishes more to the needs and interests of the practitioners than to P/HR researchers.

[3] A review of the history of P/HR is available in C. Ling, *The Management of Personnel Relations* (Homewood, Ill.: Richard D. Irwin, 1965) pp. 460–507; and A. Nash and J. Miner, *Personnel and Labor Relations, an Evolutionary Approach* (New York: Macmillan, 1973) pp. 163–251.

[4] See W. Glueck, "Evaluation of the Personnel Function and Personnel's Future," *Personnel: A Diagnostic Approach* rev. ed. (Dallas: Business Publications, Inc., 1978), chap. 21 pp. 731–757.

grettably, most of the administrator's "research" experience has come through personal trial and error experiences or observations of others' experiences. Unfortunately, the personnel administrator may have constructed his or her own "theories" to explain the performance of different individuals and thus which individuals should be selected, etc. The problem is that these "lay" theories may or may not be correct and are not based on any empirical research.

The major shortcoming of most "armchair" theories is the methodological weakness of their supporting data. For example, the administrator may construct a theory from observing two training groups differing in both performance and age. If the differences between the two groups in both performance and age are substantial, the individual is likely to conclude that age is a cause of performance. Moreover, if several groups with the same pattern of data are observed, the administrator's confidence in the causal inferences about age is likely to increase. Unfortunately, neither of these sources of *cross-sectional* data provides a highly valid basis for causal inference. In the case of the two-group comparison, statistical instability may have accounted for the results. In the comparison of many such groups, the threat of statistical instability is lessened, but the accuracy of causal inference is not greatly increased. The problem with drawing causal inference from a static-group comparison is that any other factor may have caused age and performance to vary together, and the direction of causation may merely be reversed.

The administrator may also utilize *longitudinal* data. Rather than rely solely upon static differences, the administrator may look for covariation over time. A number of laboratory studies have shown that causal inferences are most likely to be drawn when two variables covary over time and a change in one variable closely follows a change in another.[5] Unfortunately, causal inference from observing covariation over time generally is the weakest of longitudinal designs. For example, using Campbell and Stanley's[6] notation in which X represents a change in an independent variable or treatment (e.g., training method) and O represents an observation of a dependent variable (e.g., per-

formance), many administrators have probably experienced some of these designs:

1. $O \; X_1 \; O$

2. $O \; X_1 \; X_2 \; O$

3. $O \; X_1 \; X_2 \; X_3 \; O$

4. $X_1 \; O$
       O

The personnel administrator may have changed X and then observed a change in the observation O from time 1 to time 2. Or the administrator may have attempted more than one change and observed an effect. In the third case, the administrator may have made several changes with only one posttreatment observation. In the fourth case, the administrator made a change in one group and not in another and believes that one group is now different from the other. However, in none of these instances are we entirely confident of valid causal inference, regardless of the apparent change in the dependent variable(s).

The basic designs just presented will be explained in greater detail later. But before we go further we should make certain that we understand that experimental methodology is not the only way of researching P/HR. Listed below are some other methods of research that are often used. Certainly they vary in their applicability and rigor for P/HR purposes, but each method, if used appropriately, can be useful in understanding research phenomena, or can at least contribute to other research providing more insight to the problem under study.

1. *Historical*—An accurate and objective reconstruction of the past, usually designed to accept or refute a hypothesis. Example: A study detailing the use of "scientific management" practices in organizations and their similarity to behavior modification practices during the last fifty years or the impact of the Civil Rights Act of 1964 on the employment of minorities in organizations.

2. *Descriptive*—A factual and accurate systematic description of a situation or problem. Example: A questionnaire study of employees by demographic characteristics and needs to determine the appropriate mix of benefits the organization should offer; or a quantitative job analysis procedure to describe the nature and differences in tasks and qualifications required in a job.

3. *Developmental*—An investigation of change over time. Example: A study of managerial skill change and future organizational needs for managers over time.

[5] For example, see A. Bavelas, A. H. Hastorf, A. E. Gross, and W. R. Kite, "Experiments in Alteration of Group Structure," *Journal of Experimental Social Psychology* 1 (1965): 199–218; F. Heider and M. Simmel, "An Experimental Study of Apparent Behavior," *American Journal of Psychology* 57 (1944): 243–59; A. Michotte, *The Perception of Causality* (New York: Basic Books, 1963).

[6] See, e.g., D. T. Campbell and J. E. Stanley, *Experimental and Quasi-Experimental Designs for Research.* (Chicago: Rand McNally, 1966), see also Exercise 11.

4. *Case and Field Studies*—An intensive study of an individual group or organizational unit including its background, present status, and interactions. Example: an intensive study of employees who have experienced a drug-abuse or alcohol-treatment program.

5. *Correlational*—A study that evaluates the relationships or extent of covariation between factors. Example: A study of the predictability of a specific employment test by investigating the relationship of test scores to future job performance.

6. *"Ex Post Facto"*—A study designed to explore possible causal relationships by observing a result and searching for circumstances which might provide a plausible explanation. Example: A study of employee absenteeism in an attempt to determine if work unit, supervision received, age, etc., are the "causes" of absenteeism.

7. *Quasi-experimental*—An attempt to determine causality, although without complete control over relevant variables (e.g. internal and external validity). Example: An investigation of the effects of managerial training on job performance in a field study where randomization of subjects or close control of treatments is impossible.

8. *Experimental*—A causal study where groups are randomized, and one or more receives treatments, while others serve as controls (i.e., do not receive treatments) such that the cause and effect of the treatment can be studied. Example: Randomly assigning employees to groups, some of which receive training and some of which do not, and assessing the effect of training by comparing the groups (see Exercise 12).

9. *Action Research*—Developing and evaluating on-going interventions in organizations without adequate controls or randomization in an attempt to determine the effectiveness of the intervention. Example: Attempts to evaluate the effects of a new "group problem solving" method or decision method within the organization. (In many respects, action research is similar to quasi-experimental designs.)

Examples of several types of designs using the same X and O are shown in Table 1 below with notations concerning their advantages and disadvantages. A description of the types of experimental error that are threats to internal validity (i.e., cause and effect) and external validity (i.e., generalizability) are shown in Table 2.

Table 1. Research Designs

Design	Advantages and disadvantages
1. After only without control group: $X\ O$	Errors due to history, maturation, testing, instrument decay, and selection.
2. Before and after without control group: $O_1\ X\ O_2$	Errors due to history, maturation, testing, instrument decay, and regression.
3. After only with control group comparison: $X\ O_1$ O_2	Error due to selection, regression, and mortality.
4. Randomized after only control group design: $X\ O_1$ O_2	Controls for but does not measure effects of history, maturation.
5. Before and after with control group design: $O_1\ X\ O_2$ $O_3\ \ \ O_4$	Error due to interaction of testing and treatment (X).
6. Randomized four-group design (Solomon): $O_1\ X\ O_2$ $O_3\ \ \ O_4$ $X\ O_5$ O_6	Combines features of designs 4 and 5. Controls for and also measures effects of history, maturation, and testing.
7. Randomized reversal designs: $O_1\ X_1\ O_2\ O_3\ X_2\ O_4$ $O_5\ \ \ O_6\ O_7\ \ \ O_8$	Subjects serve as own controls and intersubject variability is eliminated. Controls for history, motivation, regression,

* See also Exercise 11.

Table 2. Threats to Internal and External Validity

Threats to internal validity	*Threats to external validity*
1. *History:* events, other than the experimental treatment, occurring between pretest and posttest and thus providing alternate explanations of effects.	1. *Interaction effects of testing:* the effect of a pretest in increasing or decreasing the respondent's sensitivity or responsiveness to the experimental variable, thus making the results obtained for a pretested population unrepresentative of the effects of the experimental variable for the unpretested universe from which the experimental respondents were selected.
2. *Maturation:* processes within the respondents or observed social units producing changes as a function of the passage of time per se, such as growth, fatigue, secular trends, etc.	2. *Interaction of selection and experimental treatment:* unrepresentative responsiveness of the treated population.
3. *Instability:* unreliability of measures, fluctuations in sampling persons or components, autonomous instability of repeated or "equivalent" measures. (This is the only threat to which statistical tests of significance are relevant.)	3. *Reactive effects of experimental arrangements:* "artificially"; conditions making the experimental setting atypical of conditions of regular application of the treatment; "Hawthorne effects."
4. *Testing:* the effect of taking a test upon the scores of a second testing. The effect of publication of a social indicator upon subsequent readings of that indicator.	4. *Multiple-treatment interference:* where multiple treatments are jointly applied; effects atypical of the separate application of the treatments.
5. *Instrument decay:* in which changes in scoring on a measurement instrument or changes in the observers used may produce changes in measurements.	5. *Irrelevant responsiveness of measures:* all measures are complex, and all include it relevant components that may produce apparent effects.
6. *Regression artifacts:* pseudo-shifts occurring when persons or treatment units have been selected upon the basis of their extreme scores.	6. *Irrelevant replicability of treatments:* treatments are complex, and replications of them may fail to include those components actually responsible for the effects.
7. *Selection:* biases resulting from differential recruitment of comparison groups, producing different mean levels on the measure of effects.	
8. *Experimental mortality:* the differential loss of respondents from comparison groups.	
9. *Selection-maturation interaction:* selection biases resulting in differential rates of "maturation" or autonomous change.	

Note: Internal validity refers to the level of confidence one has in whether a change in variable X actually caused a change in variable Y.
External validity refers to the level of confidence one has in whether such a causal relationship can be generalized.
Adapted from D. T. Campbell, "Reforms as Experiments," *American Psychologist* 24 (1969): 409–429.

An overview of what we have discussed this far with respect to methodology (research designs and data collection) is shown in Table 3. This table also shows some aspects of measurement considerations and statistical methodologies which we will now explore.

Table 3. Methodology and Statistics

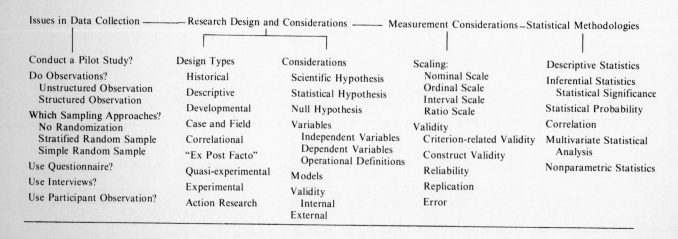

Issues in Data Collection ———	Research Design and Considerations ———		Measurement Considerations —	Statistical Methodologies
	Design Types	Considerations	Scaling:	Descriptive Statistics
Conduct a Pilot Study?	Historical	Scientific Hypothesis	Nominal Scale	Inferential Statistics
Do Observations?	Descriptive	Statistical Hypothesis	Ordinal Scale	Statistical Significance
Unstructured Observation	Developmental	Null Hypothesis	Interval Scale	Statistical Probability
Structured Observation	Case and Field	Variables	Ratio Scale	Correlation
Which Sampling Approaches?	Correlational	Independent Variables	Validity	Multivariate Statistical
No Randomization	"Ex Post Facto"	Dependent Variables	Criterion-related Validity	Analysis
Stratified Random Sample	Quasi-experimental	Operational Definitions	Construct Validity	Nonparametric Statistics
Simple Random Sample	Experimental	Models	Reliability	
Use Questionnaire?	Action Research	Validity	Replication	
Use Interviews?		Internal	Error	
Use Participant Observation?		External		

The use of statistics in P/HR research is obviously critical, for we must be able to infer conclusions from sample information. Statistics are tools that enable us to make decisions from quantitative information There are two classifications of statistics, descriptive and inferential. Descriptive statistics offer us a concise quantitative picture of a body of information. Inferential statistics offer us a way of estimating the risks we are taking in making conclusions from data collected.

In measuring information in a quantitative way, we often avoid using imprecise qualitative concepts such as "usually," "often," etc., and instead use numbers to provide precise, reliable meanings to data collected. However, to provide these more precise, quantifiable meanings, we must have operational definitions of the phenomena under study which merely means the assignment of numbers to events. Thus, we must precisely define what we wish to count and then count it. For example, the concepts of absenteeism, tardiness, and turnover all involve time away from a job and must have very clear operational definitions in order that there is no measurement overlap in our counting of these events (e.g., double counting).

Further, there are various levels of measurement to be considered. There are basic categories of measurement for us to consider in attempting to quantify P/HR

events—nominal, ordinal, interval, and ratio. Each of these methods of quantitative differentiation is described below:

1. *Nominal*—This method of differentiation merely allows us to count by categories such as numbers of managers versus nonmanagers, males versus females, job titles (e.g., executives, secretaries, assemblers, etc.). Nominal data only serves to provide clarification.

2. *Ordinal*—This method of differentiation classifies by category and order within category. For example, eight welders (a nominal differentiation) could be classified by their rank in job performance with the welders given a "1" being the best, etc. The major shortcomings of ordinal data are that they tell us a sequence but *not* the magnitude of difference between items in the sequence. For example, how much better is the welder with the highest rank than the next highest welder, etc.

3. *Interval*—This differentiation provides us with categorizations (i.e., nominal), ranks (i.e., ordinal), *and* with the magnitude of differences between the positions (i.e., ranks). Most of the data used in P/HR research (e.g., test scores) are assumed to be interval measures.

Table 4. Levels of Differentiation and Appropriate Statistics

Levels of differentiation	Relationships measured	Examples of appropriate descriptive statistics	Appropriate inferential statistical tests
Nominal	1. Equivalence	Mode Frequency Contingency coefficient	*Nonparametric statistical tests:* — Chi-Square — Sign Test — Binomial
Ordinal	1. Equivalence 2. Order	Median Percentile Spearman r_8 Kendall$_T$ Kendall *W*	
Interval	1. Equivalence 2. Order 3. Ratio of Intervals	Mean Standard deviation Pearson product-moment correlation Multiple product-moment correlation	*Nonparametric and parametric statistical tests:* — Z Test — Analysis of Variance — *t*-Test
Ratio	1. Equivalence 2. Order 3. Ratio of Intervals 4. Ratio of Values	Geometric mean Coefficient of variation	

Source: C. Anderson and A. Nash, "Statistical Methods for PAIR," in *Planning and Auditing PAIR*, Bureau of National Affairs, 1977.

4. *Ratio*—This method of differentiation is the most precise of those described here. It assumes an absolute zero point for comparison purposes; thus, precise ratios can be obtained. In reality, there are very few ratio measures. In P/HR work, ratio measures can often be used for units produced, absenteeism, turnover, and workforce staffing levels. Clearly, if one employee produces 26 coffee pots per day and another only 13, one has twice the productivity of the other.

There are two important reasons for concern about levels of measurement differentiation. The first is simply precision of measurement. The second is the choice of the statistical tool to be applied in understanding the data. In other words, there are different descriptive and inferential statistical tools to be used for different levels of measurement. Table 3 provides an analysis of the levels of differentiation and the statistics appropriate for each. It should be noted that parametric tests are preferred (when the data is either interval or ratio) because they are more accurate in estimating the risk taken in inferring from a sample to a population (i.e., external validity). A description of the statistical tools cited in Table 4 is not intended here. Many of these statistics are described in Exercise 9 or can be found in a basic statistics text.

Perhaps it should go without saying that sampling is a critical variable not only in reducing P/HR research costs, but also more importantly, for external validity inferences. Thus, samples must be representative of the population studied. To obtain greater representation, a sample may be stratified so that certain categories (e.g., women) may be included at or near a 50% rate *if* they represent 50% of the population under study. However, if a population is impossible to categorize easily (i.e., very heterogeneous), then a larger sample must be drawn to ensure representativeness.

Another factor in research which is often overlooked is the review of existing literature which may need evaluation prior to undertaking a program. It is imperative that existing literature be reviewed to ascertain what has been attempted and how it was attempted. Regrettably, it appears that many of the efforts to implement new P/HR programs are initated not only without much thought toward evaluation, but also without much attention to the readily available literature. Clearly, there is no paucity of personnel literature, with varying degrees of sophistication, that can aid immensely in gathering ideas for designing P/HR programs as well as help to formulate researchable hypotheses and designs to evaluate the project. These include *Personnel Psychology, Journal of Applied Psychology, The Personnel Journal,* and the many others available through professional associations and libraries.

Perhaps the literature review is really the key to the formulation of a researchable hypothesis for it aids considerably in helping to clarify the problem at hand. A researchable hypothesis is a statement in very specific terms detailing a relationship to be tested. The hypothesis is stated in the form of an "expected" relationship which is developed from an understanding of the project at hand as well as from available literature. Some guidelines to use in the development of a researchable hypothesis are found in Table 5.

Table 5. Basic Formulation of P/HR Research Problems: Common Mistakes in Problem Formulation

1. Defining objectives in such general or ambiguous terms that your interpretations and conclusions will be arbitrary and invalid.
2. Undertaking a research project without reviewing existing literature on the subject.
3. Failure to make explicit and clear the underlying assumptions so that they can be evaluated.
4. Collecting data without a well-defined plan or purpose, often hoping to make some sense out of them afterward.
5. Taking a "batch of data" that already exists and attempting to fit meaningful research questions to it.
6. Failure to anticipate alternative rival hypotheses which challenge the interpretations and conclusions reached.

After the hypothesis has been stated (for example, "If we train sales representatives, we will see a sales "increase"), then we must determine how the variables pertaining to data will be measured.

Progress has recently been made in the development of generally applicable, reliable, and valid instruments for measuring many common P/HR variables. Instruments are available for collecting job information and for measuring attitudes, managerial styles, achievement motivation, and many other variables (see e.g., Exercise 13).

There are some significant advantages to using existing instruments. Time and money are saved, and the instruments are developed with more expertise. The use of uniform instruments greatly enhances the extension of research findings to a more general understanding. This should be emphasized strongly, because failure to use uniform instruments has contributed to diverse findings in presumably similar research settings. Existing instruments must have satisfied necessary criteria for validity and reliability and be re-evaluated for any unique group not included in the sample used to assess validity when the instrument was developed. In many instances tailor-made instruments are required because of inapplicability of existing instruments for the study.

The last steps in a research project are the analysis, presentation, and interpretation of the data collected. In these areas, statistical techniques make their major contribution, as noted in Exercise 9. Research reports should be brief and easily understood! The basic idea is that facts should be separated from editorial interpretations. A common erroneous assumption is that the readers of reports are just as involved and interested in each detail as are the researchers. A summary of the study at the beginning should satisfy the vast majority of readers who are interested in a general idea of what the study attempted and its main results. Thus, the report should also include a results section that conveys summarized findings of the study and a section devoted to discussion, interpretation, and conclusions, that explains the results.

Guidelines to follow in the basic design of P/HR research are shown in Table 6.

Table 6. Basic Steps in Planning and Conducting P/HR Research

1. Clearly identify the problem area and write a preliminary problem statement.
2. Survey the literature relating to the problem statement.
3. Define the actual problem for investigation in definitive, specific terms.
4. Formulate testable hypotheses and define the operational variables.[1]
5. State the underlying assumptions that have impact on the interpretation of results.
6. Develop the research design to maximize internal and external validity including:[2]

    Subjects selection,

    Control and/or manipulation of relevant variables.

    Establishment of criteria to evaluate outcomes.

    Instrumentation for both independents and dependent (criterion) variables.

7. Specify the data collection procedures.
8. Select the data analysis/statistical methodology appropriate for the design and method of measurement.
9. Collect the data.
10. Evaluate the findings and draw conclusions.
11. Prepare the final report.

---

[1] Variables are usually classified into three categories:

a. *Independent* (input, manipulated, treatment, or stimulus) variables, so called because they are "independent" of the outcome itself; instead, they are presumed to cause, effect, or influence the outcome.

PROCEDURE

PART A

STEP 1: You are about to begin research for your organization on one of the following topics:

Job Satisfaction
Intrinsic Motivation
Performance Appraisal
Training Welders
Absenteeism
Career Management
Work-related Stress
Others:

1. _____
2. _____
3. _____

You are to select a topic from above and complete on Form 1 the following:

1. The relevant articles found in your literature review.
2. A list of the operational variables you plan to use and how you would measure each variable.
3. The hypothesized relationships between variables.
4. The specified procedural steps to be followed in setting up the project.
5. The general methodology to use to determine if your project will "work."
6. A statement of the specific criteria used to measure the effectiveness of your project.

TIME:

PART B

STEP 2: In this part you are to go into much greater depth in P/HR research than you did in Part

b. *Dependent* (output, outcome, or response) variables, so called because they are "dependent" on the independent variables; the outcome presumably depends on how these input variables are managed or manipulated.

c. *Control* (background, classificatory, or organismic) variables, so called because they need to be controlled, held constant, or randomized so that their effects are neutralized, cancelled out, or equaled for all conditions. Typically included are such factors as age, sex, IQ, SES (socioeconomic status), educational level, and motivational level; it is often possible to redefine these particular examples as either independent or dependent variables, according to the intent of the research.

A fourth category is often cited, having to do with conceptual states within the organism: intervening variables (higher-order constructs). These cannot be directly observed or measured and are hypothetical conceptions intended to explain processes between the stimulus and response. Such concepts as learning, intelligence, perception, motivation, need, self, personality, trait, and feeling illustrate this category.

[2] See Table 1.

A. Here you are to specifically develop a comprehensive research study. This means you are to carry the project all the way from the idea stage through the design stage *without* actually collecting the data. Then you are to do *all* of the preliminary work on a research project with the exception of data collection and analysis (which hopefully you have done in previous projects).

TIME:

FOR FURTHER READING

Argyris, C. "Problems and New Directions for Industrial Psychology." In M. D. Dunnette, ed., *Handbook of Industrial Organizational Psychology*. Chicago: Rand McNally, 1976. (I)

Banner, D. K. "The Politics of Evalution Research." *Omega* 2 (1974): 736–774. (I)

Bevelas, A., A. H. Hastorf, A. E. Gross, and W. R. Kite. "Experiments in Alteration of Group Structure." *Journal of Experimental Social Psychology* 1 (1965): 199–218. (II–R)

Bem, D. J. "Self-perception: The Dependent Variable of Human Performance." *Organizational Behavior and Human Performance* 2 (1976): 105–121. (II–R)

Bennett, C. A., and A. A. Lumsdaine. "Social Program Evaluation: Definitions and Issues." In C. A. Bennett and A. A. Lumsdaine, eds., *Evaluation and Experiment: Some Critical Issues in Assessing Social Programs*. New York: Academic Press, 1975. (II)

Berk, R. A., and P. H. Rossi. "Doint Good or Worse: Evaluation Research Politically Reexamined." *Social Problems* 23 (1976) 337–349. (II)

Bruner, J. S., and A. Taguiri. "The Perception of People." In G. Lindzey, ed., *Handbook of Social Psychology*. Reading, Mass.: Addison-Wesley, 1954. (II)

Calder, B. J., and B. M. Straw. "Self-perception of Intrinsic and Extrinsic Motivation." *Journal of Personality and Social Psychology* 31 (1975): 599–605. (II–R)

Campbell, D. T. "Reforms as Experiments." *American Psychologist* 24 (1969): 409–429. (II)

Campbell, D. T., and J. C. Stanley. *Experimental and Quasi-Experimental Designs for Research*. Chicago: Rand McNally, 1966. (II)

Cohen, A. R. "Upward Communication in Experimentally Created Hierarchies." *Human Relations* 11 (1958): 41–53. (II–R)

Cook, T. D., and D. T. Campbell. "The Design and Conduct of Quasi-Experiments and True Experiments in Field Settings." In M. D. Dunnette, ed., *Handbook of Industrial and Organizational Psychology*. Chicago: Rand McNally, 1976. (II)

Deci, E. L. "The Effects of Externally Mediated Rewards on Intrinsic Motivation." *Journal of Personality and Social Psychology* 18 (1971): 105–115. (II–R)

Glass, G. V., V. L. Willson, and J. M. Gottman. *Design and Analysis of Time-Series Experiments*. Boulder, Colorado: Colorado Associated University Press, 1975. (II)

Hackman, J. R., and G. R. Oldham. "Motivation Through the Design of Work: Test of a Theory" *Organizational Behavior and Human Performance* 16 (1976): 250–279. (II–R)

Heider, F., and M. Simmel. "An Experimental Study of Apparent Behávior." *American Journal of Psychology* 57 (1944): 243–259. (II–R)

Janis, I. L. *Victims of Groupthink: A Psychological Study of Foreign Policy Decisions and Fiascos*. Boston: Houghton Mifflin, 1972. (I)

Jones, E. E., and V. A. Harris. "The Attribution of Attitudes." *Journal of Experimental Social Psychology* 3 (1967): 1–24. (II–R)

Jones, E. E., K. E. Davis, and K. E. Gergen. "Role Playing Variations and Their Informational Value for Person Perception." *Journal of Abnormal and Social Psychology* 63 (1961): 302–310. (II–R)

Kelley, H. H. "The Processes of Causal Attribution." *American Psychologist* 28 (1973): 107–128. (II)

Kelley, H. H. "Attribution Theory in Social Psychology." In D. Levine, ed., *Nebraska Symposium on Motivation*. Lincoln: University of Nebraska Press, 1967. (II)

Kerlinger, F. N. *Foundations of Behavioral Research*, 2nd ed. New York: Holt, 1973. (II)

Kirk, R. E. *Introductory Statistics*. Belmont, Cal.: Wadsworth, 1978. (I)

Kruglanski, A. W., I. Freedman, and G. Zeevi. "The Effects of Extrinsic Incentives on Some Qualitative Aspects of Task Performance." *Journal of Personality* 39 (1971) 606–617. (II–R)

Lawler, E. E., and J. R. Hackman. "Impact of Employee Participation in the Development of Pay Incentive Plans: A Field Experiment." *Journal of Applied Psychology* 53 (1969): 467–471. (II–R)

Lepper, M. R., D. Greene, and R. E. Nisbett. "Undermining Children's Intrinsic Interest with Extrinsic Rewards: A Test of the Over-justification Hypothesis." *Journal of Personality and Social Psychology* 28 (1973): 129–137. (II–R)

Likert, R. *Human Organization: Its Management and Value.* New York: McGraw-Hill, 1967. (I)

Lindblom, C. E. "The Science of Muddling Through." *Public Administration Review* 19 (1959): 79–88. (I)

McCain, L. J., and R. McCleary. "The Statistical Analysis of Interrupted Time Series of Quasi-Experiments." In T. D. Cook and D. T. Campbell, eds., *The Design and Analysis of Quasi-Experiments in Field Settings.* Chicago: Rand McNally, 1976. (II)

Michotte, A. *The Perception of Causality.* New York: Basic Books, 1963. (II)

Mowday, R. T., and R. M. Steers (eds.). *Research in Organizations.* Santa Monica, Cal.: Goodyear, 1979. (II)

Nelson, C. R. *Applied Time Series Analysis for Managerial Forecasting.* San Francisco: Holden Day, 1973. (II)

Nord, W. R. "Beyond the Teaching Machine: The Neglected Area of Operant Conditioning in the Theory and Practice of Management." *Organizational Behavior and Human Performance* 4 (1969): 375–401. (II)

Pfeffer, J. "Power and Resource Allocation in Organizations." In B. M. Staw and G. R. Salancik, eds., *New Directions in Organizational Behavior.* Chicago: St. Clair Press, 1977. (II)

Pondy, L. R. "Two Faces of Evaluation." In H. W. Metton and D. Watson, eds., *Accounting for Social Goals and Social Organization.* Columbus, Ohio: Grid, 1977. (II)

Ridgeway, V. "Dysfunctional Consequences of Performance Measures." *Administrative Science Quarterly* 1 (1956): 240–247. (II–R)

Riecken, H. W., and R. F. Boruch, eds. *Social Experimentation: A Method for Planning and Evaluating Social Intervention Intervention.* New York: Academic Press, 1974. (II)

Rosenberg, M. J. "The Conditions and Consequences of Evaluation Apprehension." In R. Rosenthal and R. L. Rosnow, eds., *Artifacts in Behavioral Research.* New York: Academic Press, 1969. (II)

Schutte, J. E. *Everything You Always Wanted to Know about Elementary Statistics.* Englewood Cliffs, N.J.: Prentice-Hall, 1977. (I)

Scriven, M. "The Methodology of Evaluation." In R. W. Tyler, R. M. Gagne, and M. Scriven, eds., *Perspectives of Curriculum Evaluation.* Chicago: Rand McNally, 1967. (II)

Staw, B. M. (ed.). *Research in Organizational Behavior,* vol. 1. Greenwich, Conn.: JAI Press, 1979 (annually). (II)

Staw, B. M., and F. W. Fox. "Escalation: Some Determinants of Commitment to a Previously Chosen Course of Action." *Human Relations* 30 (1977): 431–450. (II–R)

Staw, B. M. "Attribution to the 'Causes' of Performance: A General Alternative Interpretation of Cross-Sectional Research on Organizations." *Organizational Behavior and Human Performance* 13 (1975): 414–432. (II–R)

Staw, B. M. "Attitudinal and Behavioral Consequences of Changing a Major Organizational Reward: A Natural Field Experiment." *Journal of Personality and Social Psychology* 29 (1974): 742–751. (II–R)

Stone, E. *Research Methods in Organizational Behavior.* Santa Monica, Cal.: Goodyear, 1978. (II)

Tesser, A., and S. Rosen. "The Reluctance to Transmit Bad News." In C. Berkowitz, ed., *Advances in Experimental Social Psychology.* New York: Academic Press, 1975. (II)

Thibault, J. W., and H. W. Riecken. "Some Determinants and Consequences of the Perception of Social Causality." *Journal of Personality* 24 (1955): 113–133. (II–R)

Webb, E. J., D. T. Campbell, R. D. Schwartz, and L. Sechrest. *Unobtrusive Measures: Non-Reactive Research in the Social Sciences.* Chicago: Rand McNally, 1966. (II)

Weiss, C. H. "Evaluation Research in the Political Contest." In E. L. Struening and M. Guttentag, eds., *Handbook of Evaluation Research.* Beverly Hills, Cal.: Sage Publications, 1975. (II)

Weiss, C. H. "Where Politics and Evaluation Research Meet." *Evaluation* 1 (1973): 37–45. (I)

Wortman, P. M. "Evaluation Research: A Psychological Perspective." *American Psychologist* 30 (1975): 562–575. (II)

PART A

Form 1 Designing a Research Study

Project Title: _____ Date: _____

Instructions: Please provide information on your research for each of the areas below.

Literature Review:

Title	*Author(s)*	*Journal*	*Date*	*Pages*

(Add sources on separate sheet.)

Variables:

Variable Name	*Variable Measure*

Hypotheses:

If . . .	*Then*

Implementation of Project (be *very* specific here):

Step 1. _____

Step 2. _____

Step 3. _____

Step 4. _____

Form 1 (continued)

Step 5. _____

Step 6. _____

Step 7. _____

Step 8. _____

Methodology for Evaluation:

Description of Design	*Statistical Tools Used*
_____	_____
_____	_____
_____	_____
_____	_____

Determination of Effectiveness of Project Initiated:

Method: _____

_____

_____

_____

_____

_____

_____

PART B

Form 2 Conducting P/HR Research

Instructions for Use of Questionnaire: Assume you are a P/HR professional. You know that there are several P/HR problems in your organization and that to solve them they must be researched. Your group is to research one of the problems listed and to provide a research design to plan and guide your study. You have laid out the following major outline categories, "A" through "F" below. Now you are going to fill in each of the blank spaces in your outline. Be brief, specific, and objective. Be prepared to report on and discuss any portion of your completed outline during the discussion period. (Use additional sheets as required.)

A. First, select your research study from one of the following situations (check one):

   1. ☐ You are constantly losing your best employees.

   2. ☐ Supervisors who take training courses get lower performance ratings than those who don't.

   3. ☐ You are using an assessment procedure that has not been validated.

   4. ☐ The number of grievances in the plant is double that of last year's.

   5. ☐ The merit pay-based performance ratings for managers are 80% A (highest); 5% B; 5% C; 0% D.

   6. ☐ Your professional personnel staff ratio is 1.5, while for our industry the ratio is 2.30.

B. Now state the problem you just selected from the list above, and write down what you plan to study in specific terms.

C. When the study is done, what question(s) do you expect to be able to answer?

D. Spell out your specific research hypotheses, stated in operational terms that will produce objective measures and evaluation (write in).

E. Specify your research design and procedures:

   1. Subjects

   2. Data Needed

   3. Variables

      Assumptions:

      Hypotheses (i.e., if . . . , then):

Form 2 (continued)

4. Research Instruments

   Standard:

   To be developed:

5. Plans for Pilot Study (Pretest)

6. Data Gathering Techniques (including sampling)

   Questionnaires:

   Dummy tables (graphs to present data):

7. Specific Methods of Analysis (e.g., historical, case, survey, statistical, field, simulation, etc.)

8. Expected Limitations of Study (and why?)

9. Cost-Benefits Expected (specify)

10. How Do You Plan to Use Results? (e.g., publication, communication, reports, cross-validation or follow-up, etc.)

Name _____   Group Number _____

Date _____ Class Section _____ Hour _____ Score _____

ASSESSMENT OF LEARNING IN PERSONNEL ADMINISTRATION
EXERCISE 20

1. What was the purpose of this exercise?

2. What did you learn from this exercise?

3. Combining Exercises 9 and 20 what statistical tools should be used for which types of data?

4. Why would you do P/HR research in an organization?

5. If we could find a way to "cost out" all human resource variables (see Exercise 19) would we still need to do P/HR research?

INDEX

8120

8120